Walt Disney's

Donald Duck

by Carl Barks

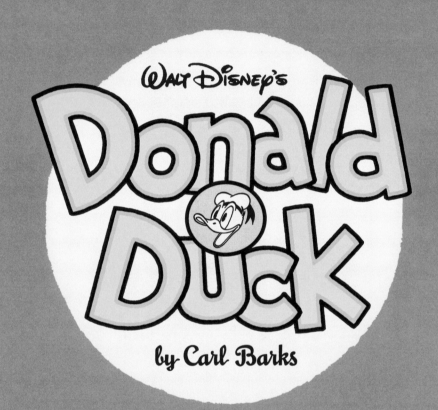

Editor: GARY GROTH
Associate Editor: J. MICHAEL CATRON
Cover Designer: JACOB COVEY
Layout Designer: TONY ONG
Colorist: RICH TOMMASO
Production: PAUL BARESH
Associate Publisher: ERIC REYNOLDS
Publisher: GARY GROTH

Walt Disney's Donald Duck: "A Christmas For Shacktown" is copyright ©2012 Disney Enterprises, Inc. All contents copyright ©2012 Disney Enterprises, Inc. unless otherwise noted. All rights reserved. This is Volume 11 of The Complete Carl Barks Disney Library. Permission to quote or reproduce material for reviews must be obtained from the publisher.

Fantagraphics Books, Inc.
7563 Lake City Way NE
Seattle WA 98115

To receive a free catalogue of more books like this, as well as an amazing variety of cutting-edge graphic novels, classic comic book and newspaper strip collections, eclectic prose novels, visually stunning art books, and uniquely insightful cultural criticism, call (800) 657-1100 or visit Fantagraphics.com. Follow us on Twitter at @fantagraphics and on Facebook at facebook.com/fantagraphics.

Special thanks to: Jason T. Miles, Thomas Jensen, Kim Thompson, and Susan Daigle-Leach.

Second Printing: October, 2013
ISBN 978-1-60699-574-7

Printed in Singapore

Also available in this series:
Walt Disney's Donald Duck: "*Lost In The Andes*"
Walt Disney's Uncle Scrooge: "*Only A Poor Old Man*"
Walt Disney's Donald Duck: "*A Christmas for Shacktown*"
Walt Disney's Donald Duck: "*The Old Castle's Secret*"
Walt Disney's Donald Duck: "*Christmas on Bear Mountain*"

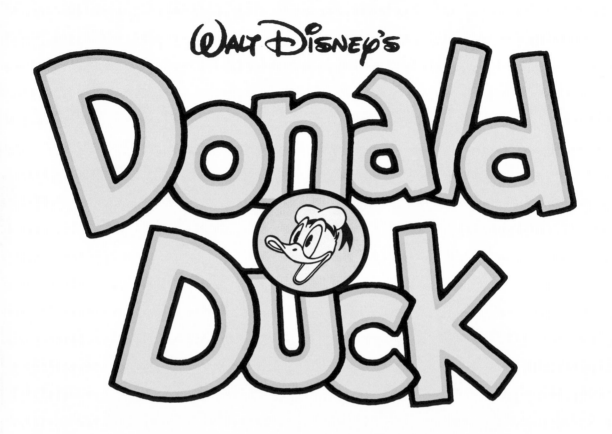

Walt Disney's

Donald Duck

"A Christmas For Shacktown"

by Carl Barks

FANTAGRAPHICS BOOKS

Contents

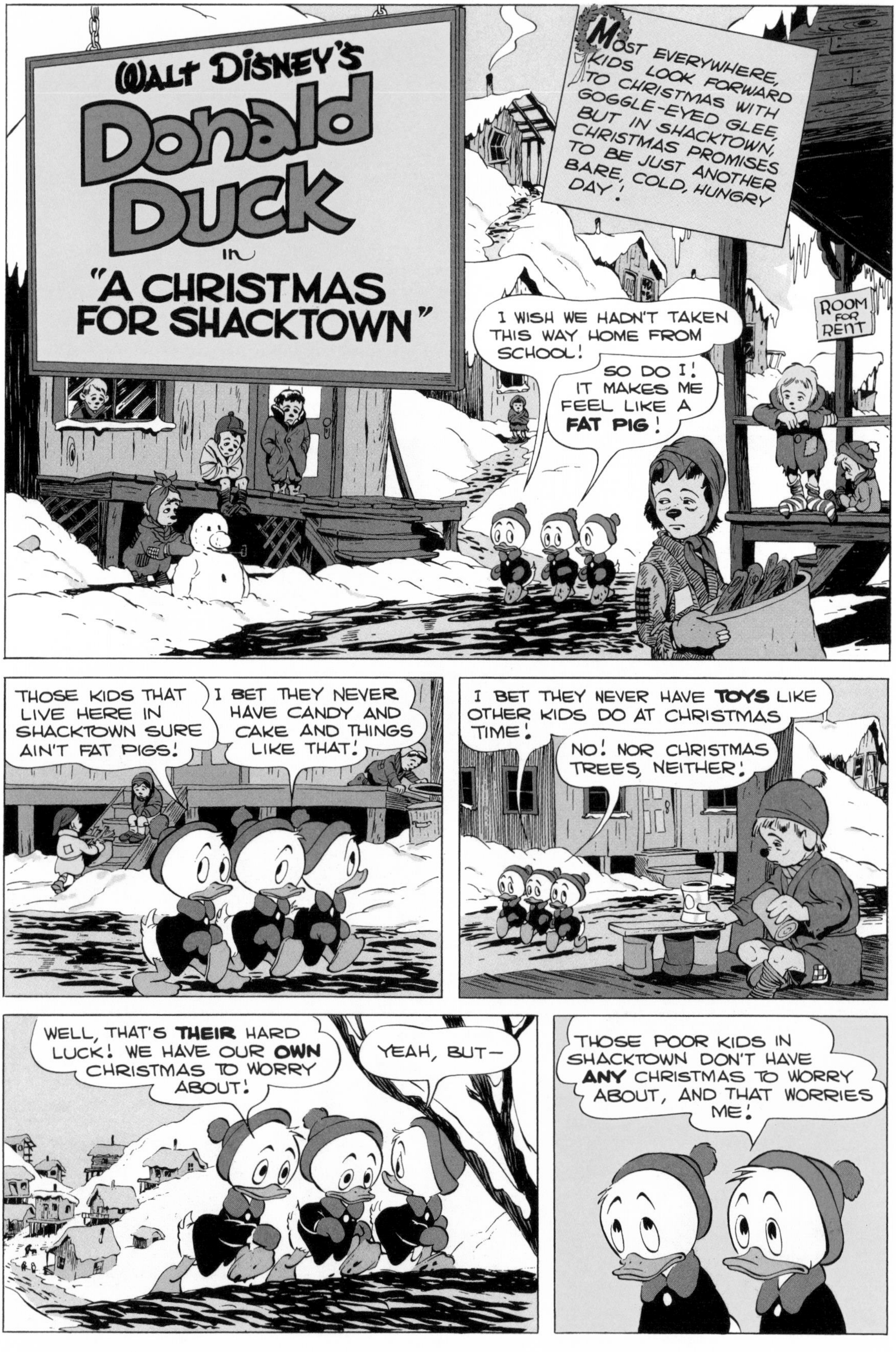
WALT DISNEY'S
Donald Duck
in
"A CHRISTMAS FOR SHACKTOWN"
MOST EVERYWHERE, KIDS LOOK FORWARD TO CHRISTMAS WITH GOGGLE-EYED GLEE, BUT IN SHACKTOWN, CHRISTMAS PROMISES TO BE JUST ANOTHER BARE, COLD, HUNGRY DAY!
ROOM FOR RENT
I WISH WE HADN'T TAKEN THIS WAY HOME FROM SCHOOL!
SO DO I! IT MAKES ME FEEL LIKE A FAT PIG!
THOSE KIDS THAT LIVE HERE IN SHACKTOWN SURE AIN'T FAT PIGS!
I BET THEY NEVER HAVE CANDY AND CAKE AND THINGS LIKE THAT!
I BET THEY NEVER HAVE TOYS LIKE OTHER KIDS DO AT CHRISTMAS TIME!
NO! NOR CHRISTMAS TREES, NEITHER!
WELL, THAT'S THEIR HARD LUCK! WE HAVE OUR OWN CHRISTMAS TO WORRY ABOUT!
YEAH, BUT—
THOSE POOR KIDS IN SHACKTOWN DON'T HAVE ANY CHRISTMAS TO WORRY ABOUT, AND THAT WORRIES ME!

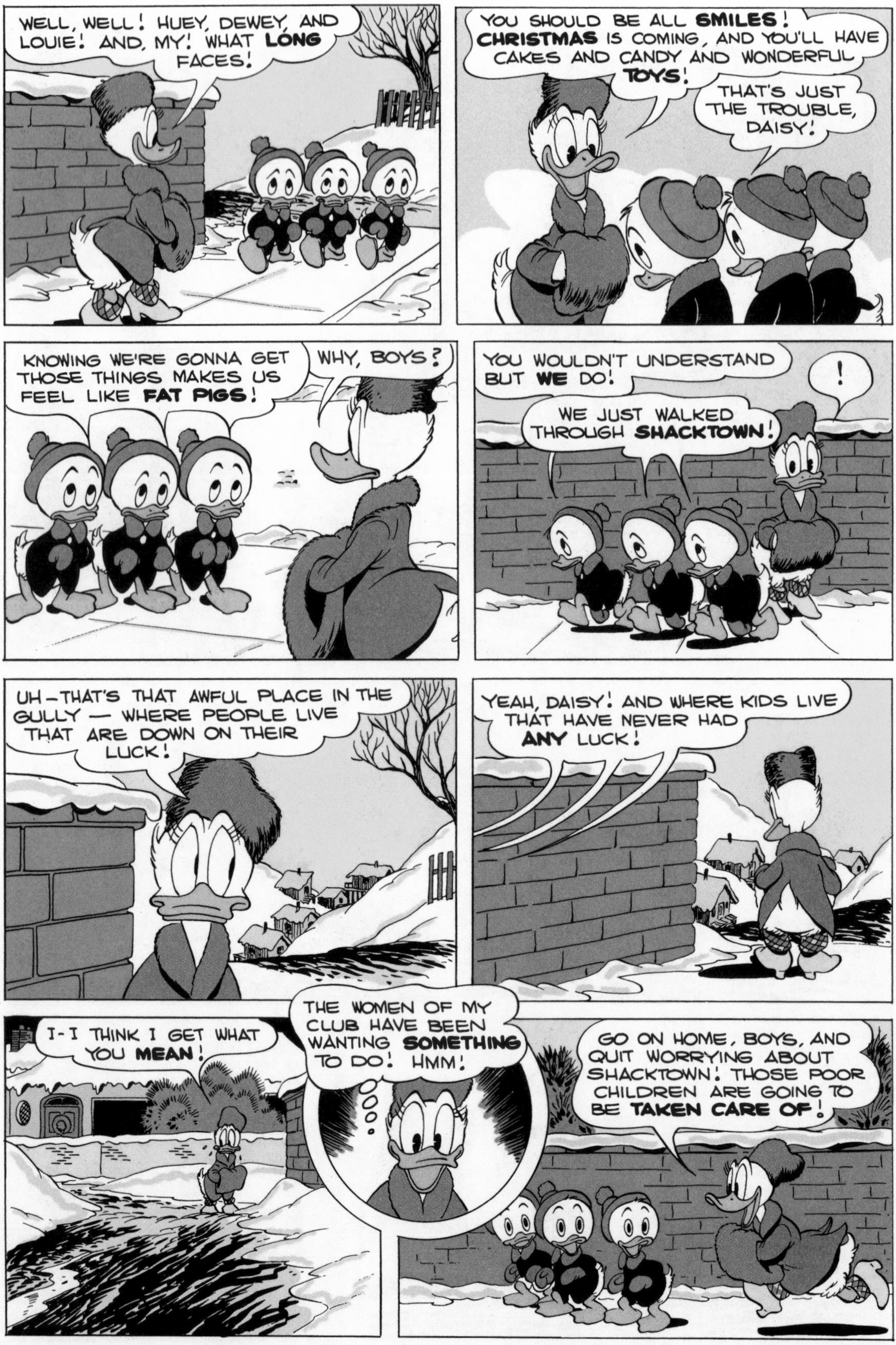

WELL, WELL! HUEY, DEWEY, AND LOUIE! AND, MY! WHAT LONG FACES!
YOU SHOULD BE ALL SMILES! CHRISTMAS IS COMING, AND YOU'LL HAVE CAKES AND CANDY AND WONDERFUL TOYS!
THAT'S JUST THE TROUBLE, DAISY!
KNOWING WE'RE GONNA GET THOSE THINGS MAKES US FEEL LIKE FAT PIGS!
WHY, BOYS?
YOU WOULDN'T UNDERSTAND BUT WE DO!
!
WE JUST WALKED THROUGH SHACKTOWN!
UH—THAT'S THAT AWFUL PLACE IN THE GULLY — WHERE PEOPLE LIVE THAT ARE DOWN ON THEIR LUCK!
YEAH, DAISY! AND WHERE KIDS LIVE THAT HAVE NEVER HAD ANY LUCK!
I-I THINK I GET WHAT YOU MEAN!
THE WOMEN OF MY CLUB HAVE BEEN WANTING SOMETHING TO DO! HMM!
GO ON HOME, BOYS, AND QUIT WORRYING ABOUT SHACKTOWN! THOSE POOR CHILDREN ARE GOING TO BE TAKEN CARE OF!

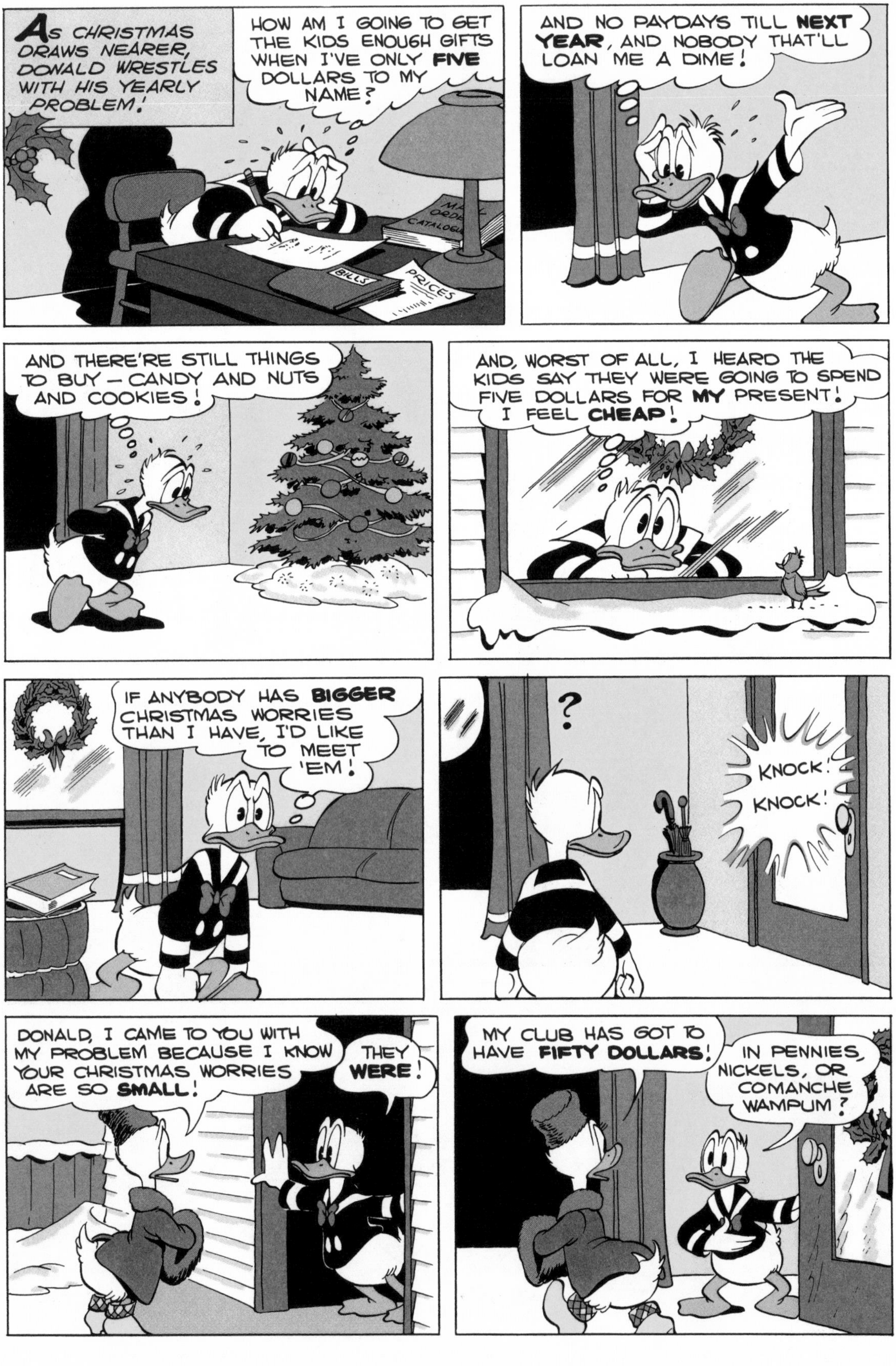
AS CHRISTMAS DRAWS NEARER, DONALD WRESTLES WITH HIS YEARLY PROBLEM!
HOW AM I GOING TO GET THE KIDS ENOUGH GIFTS WHEN I'VE ONLY FIVE DOLLARS TO MY NAME?
BILLS
PRICES
AND NO PAYDAYS TILL NEXT YEAR, AND NOBODY THAT'LL LOAN ME A DIME!
AND THERE'RE STILL THINGS TO BUY—CANDY AND NUTS AND COOKIES!
AND, WORST OF ALL, I HEARD THE KIDS SAY THEY WERE GOING TO SPEND FIVE DOLLARS FOR MY PRESENT! I FEEL CHEAP!
IF ANYBODY HAS BIGGER CHRISTMAS WORRIES THAN I HAVE, I'D LIKE TO MEET 'EM!
?
KNOCK! KNOCK!
DONALD, I CAME TO YOU WITH MY PROBLEM BECAUSE I KNOW YOUR CHRISTMAS WORRIES ARE SO SMALL!
THEY WERE!
MY CLUB HAS GOT TO HAVE FIFTY DOLLARS!
IN PENNIES, NICKELS, OR COMANCHE WAMPUM?

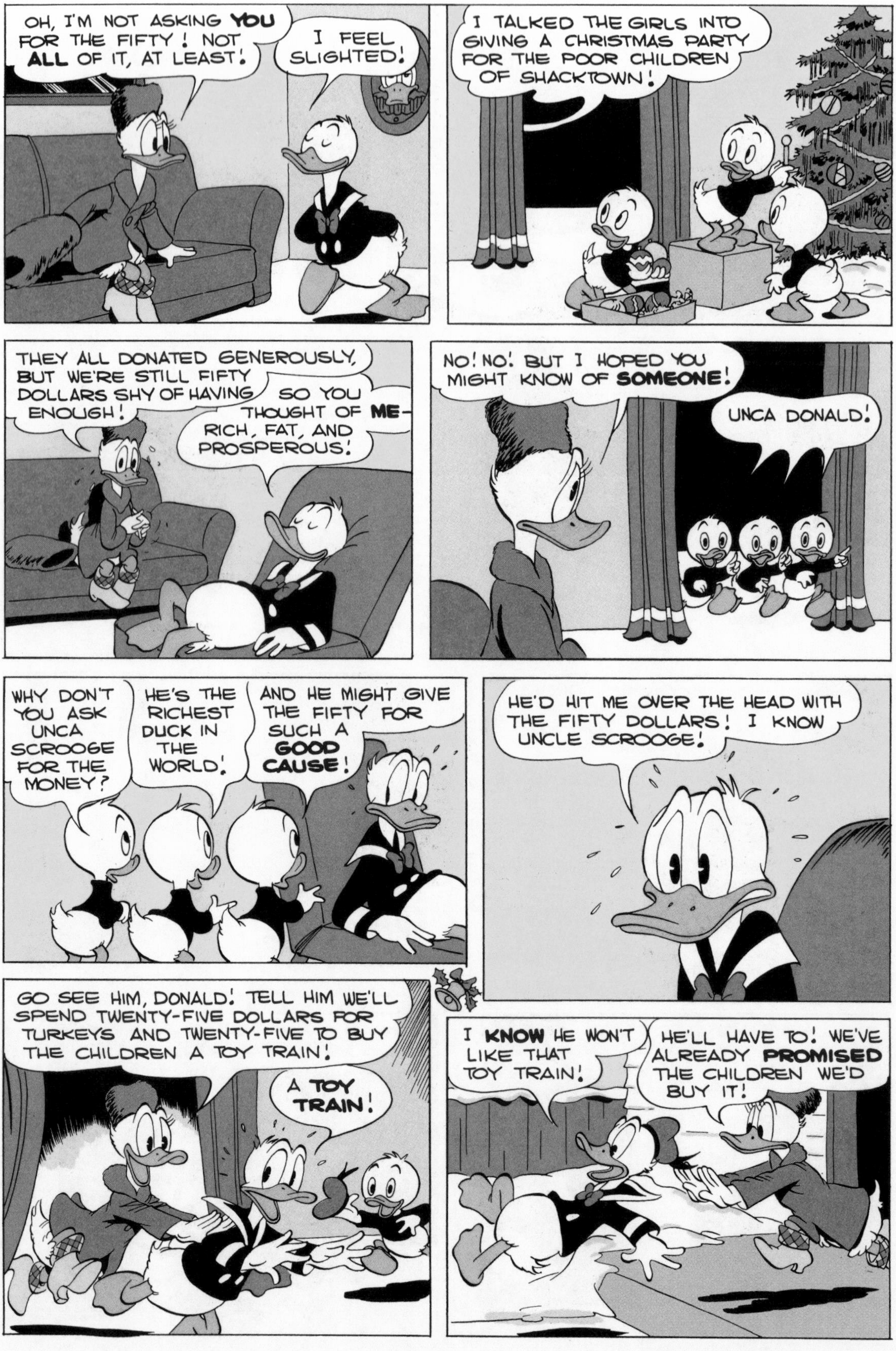
OH, I'M NOT ASKING **YOU** FOR THE FIFTY! NOT **ALL** OF IT, AT LEAST!
I FEEL SLIGHTED!
I TALKED THE GIRLS INTO GIVING A CHRISTMAS PARTY FOR THE POOR CHILDREN OF SHACKTOWN!
THEY ALL DONATED GENEROUSLY, BUT WE'RE STILL FIFTY DOLLARS SHY OF HAVING ENOUGH!
SO YOU THOUGHT OF **ME**— RICH, FAT, AND PROSPEROUS!
NO! NO! BUT I HOPED YOU MIGHT KNOW OF **SOMEONE**!
UNCA DONALD!
WHY DON'T YOU ASK UNCA SCROOGE FOR THE MONEY?
HE'S THE RICHEST DUCK IN THE WORLD!
AND HE MIGHT GIVE THE FIFTY FOR SUCH A **GOOD CAUSE**!
HE'D HIT ME OVER THE HEAD WITH THE FIFTY DOLLARS! I KNOW UNCLE SCROOGE!
GO SEE HIM, DONALD! TELL HIM WE'LL SPEND TWENTY-FIVE DOLLARS FOR TURKEYS AND TWENTY-FIVE TO BUY THE CHILDREN A TOY TRAIN!
A **TOY TRAIN**!
I **KNOW** HE WON'T LIKE THAT TOY TRAIN!
HE'LL HAVE TO! WE'VE ALREADY **PROMISED** THE CHILDREN WE'D BUY IT!

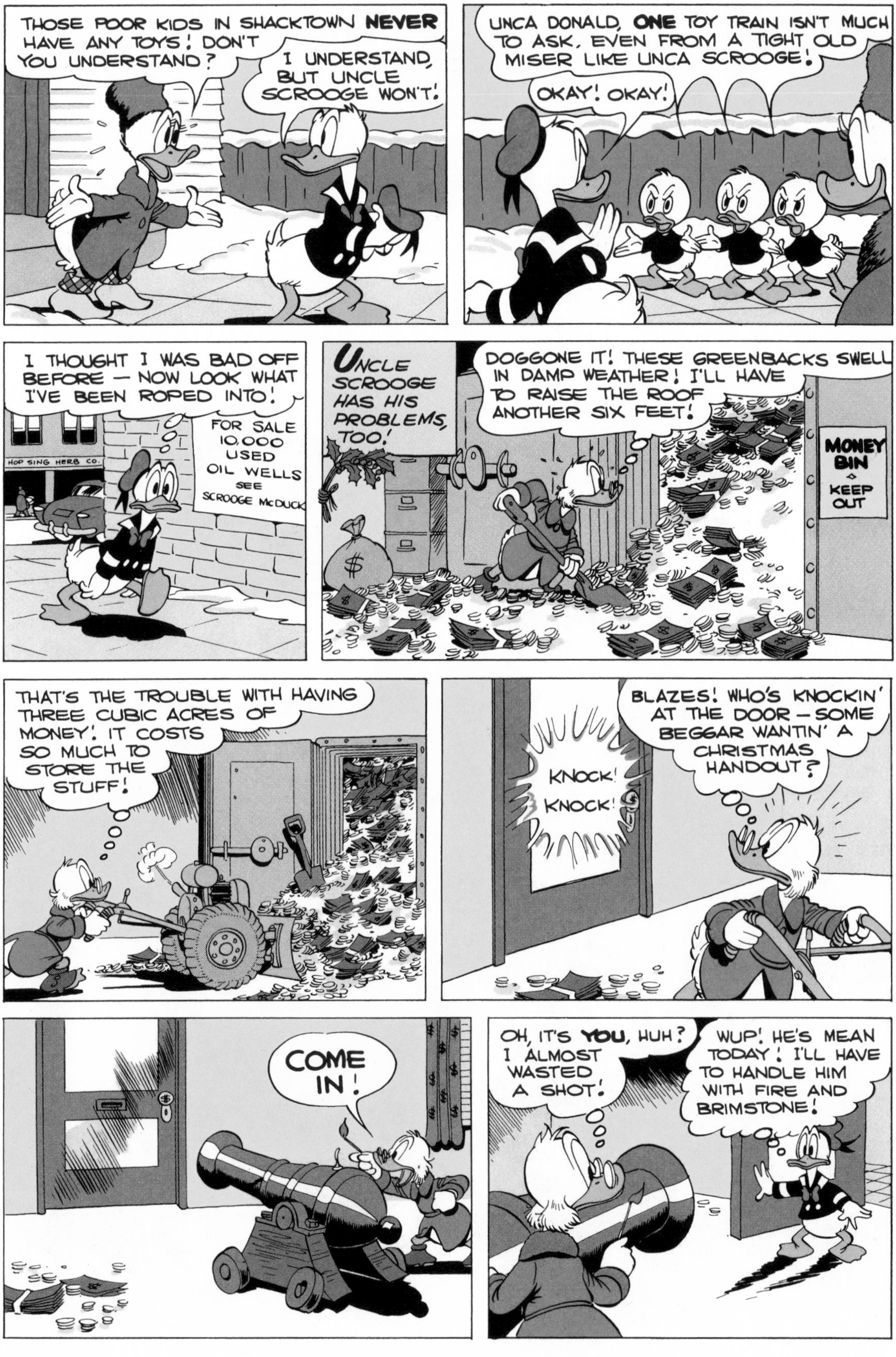

THOSE POOR KIDS IN SHACKTOWN **NEVER** HAVE ANY TOYS! DON'T YOU UNDERSTAND?
I UNDERSTAND, BUT UNCLE SCROOGE WON'T!
UNCA DONALD, **ONE** TOY TRAIN ISN'T MUCH TO ASK, EVEN FROM A TIGHT OLD MISER LIKE UNCA SCROOGE!
OKAY! OKAY!
I THOUGHT I WAS BAD OFF BEFORE — NOW LOOK WHAT I'VE BEEN ROPED INTO!
HOP SING HERB CO.
FOR SALE 10,000 USED OIL WELLS SEE SCROOGE McDUCK
UNCLE SCROOGE HAS HIS PROBLEMS, TOO!
DOGGONE IT! THESE GREENBACKS SWELL IN DAMP WEATHER! I'LL HAVE TO RAISE THE ROOF ANOTHER SIX FEET!
MONEY BIN KEEP OUT
THAT'S THE TROUBLE WITH HAVING THREE CUBIC ACRES OF MONEY! IT COSTS SO MUCH TO STORE THE STUFF!
KNOCK! KNOCK!
BLAZES! WHO'S KNOCKIN' AT THE DOOR — SOME BEGGAR WANTIN' A CHRISTMAS HANDOUT?
COME IN!
OH, IT'S **YOU**, HUH? I ALMOST WASTED A SHOT!
WUP! HE'S MEAN TODAY! I'LL HAVE TO HANDLE HIM WITH FIRE AND BRIMSTONE!

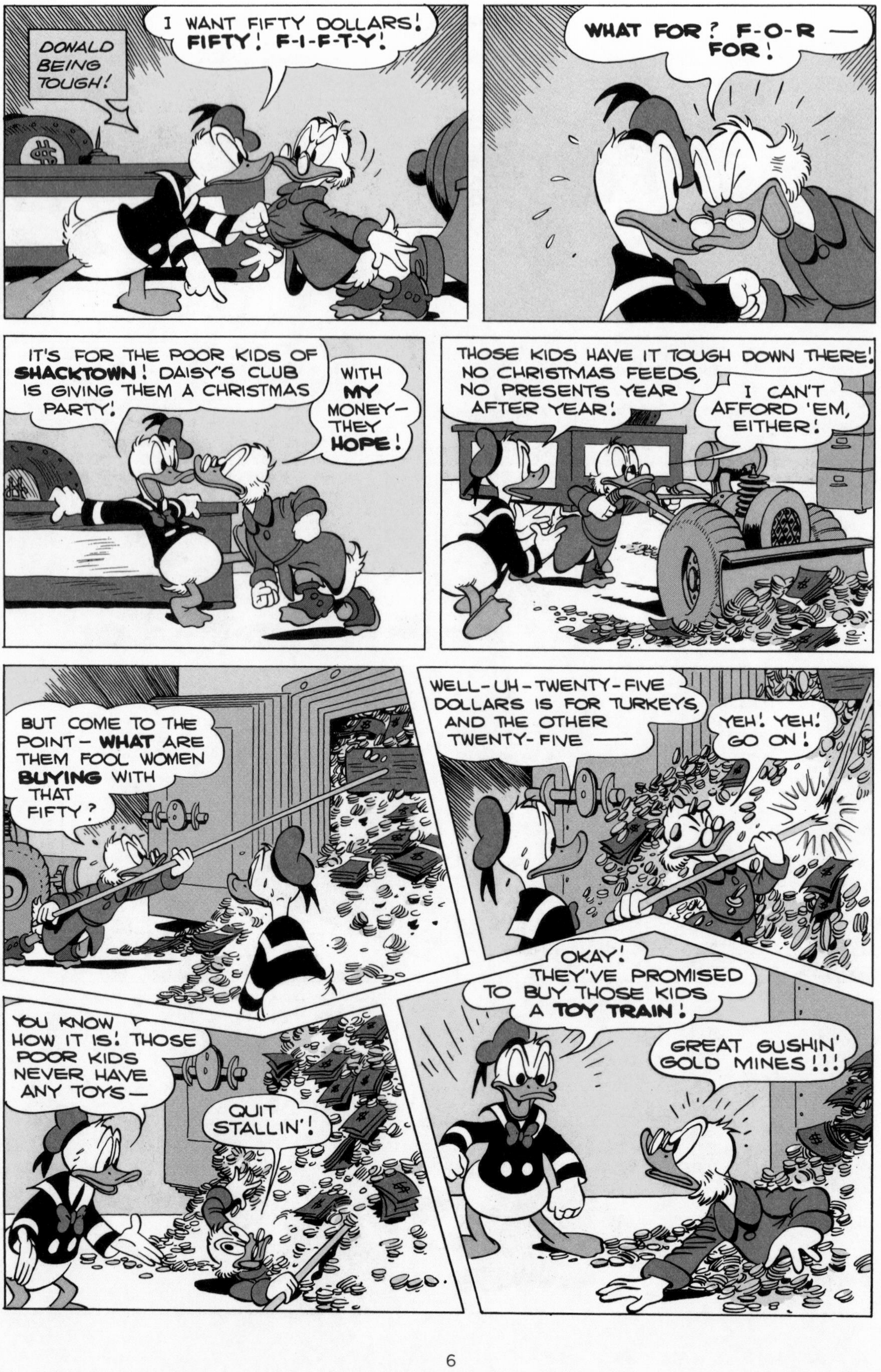
DONALD BEING TOUGH!
I WANT FIFTY DOLLARS! FIFTY! F-I-F-T-Y!
WHAT FOR? F-O-R — FOR!
IT'S FOR THE POOR KIDS OF SHACKTOWN! DAISY'S CLUB IS GIVING THEM A CHRISTMAS PARTY!
WITH MY MONEY— THEY HOPE!
THOSE KIDS HAVE IT TOUGH DOWN THERE! NO CHRISTMAS FEEDS, NO PRESENTS YEAR AFTER YEAR!
I CAN'T AFFORD 'EM, EITHER!
BUT COME TO THE POINT— WHAT ARE THEM FOOL WOMEN BUYING WITH THAT FIFTY?
WELL—UH—TWENTY-FIVE DOLLARS IS FOR TURKEYS, AND THE OTHER TWENTY-FIVE —
YEH! YEH! GO ON!
YOU KNOW HOW IT IS! THOSE POOR KIDS NEVER HAVE ANY TOYS—
QUIT STALLIN'!
OKAY! THEY'VE PROMISED TO BUY THOSE KIDS A TOY TRAIN!
GREAT GUSHIN' GOLD MINES!!!

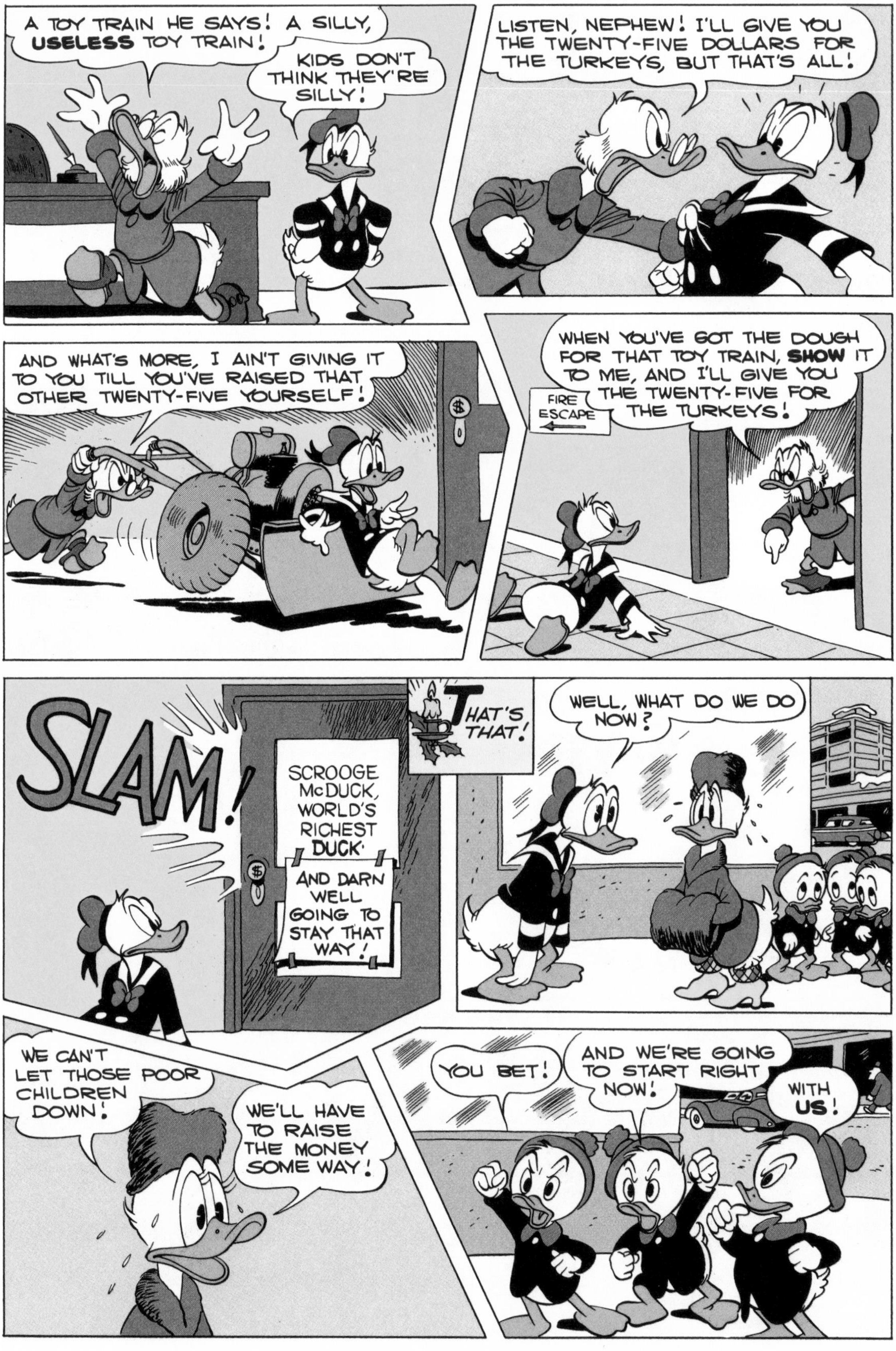
A TOY TRAIN HE SAYS! A SILLY, USELESS TOY TRAIN!
KIDS DON'T THINK THEY'RE SILLY!
LISTEN, NEPHEW! I'LL GIVE YOU THE TWENTY-FIVE DOLLARS FOR THE TURKEYS, BUT THAT'S ALL!
AND WHAT'S MORE, I AIN'T GIVING IT TO YOU TILL YOU'VE RAISED THAT OTHER TWENTY-FIVE YOURSELF!
FIRE ESCAPE
WHEN YOU'VE GOT THE DOUGH FOR THAT TOY TRAIN, SHOW IT TO ME, AND I'LL GIVE YOU THE TWENTY-FIVE FOR THE TURKEYS!
SLAM!
SCROOGE McDUCK, WORLD'S RICHEST DUCK
AND DARN WELL GOING TO STAY THAT WAY!
THAT'S THAT!
WELL, WHAT DO WE DO NOW?
WE CAN'T LET THOSE POOR CHILDREN DOWN!
WE'LL HAVE TO RAISE THE MONEY SOME WAY!
YOU BET!
AND WE'RE GOING TO START RIGHT NOW!
WITH US!

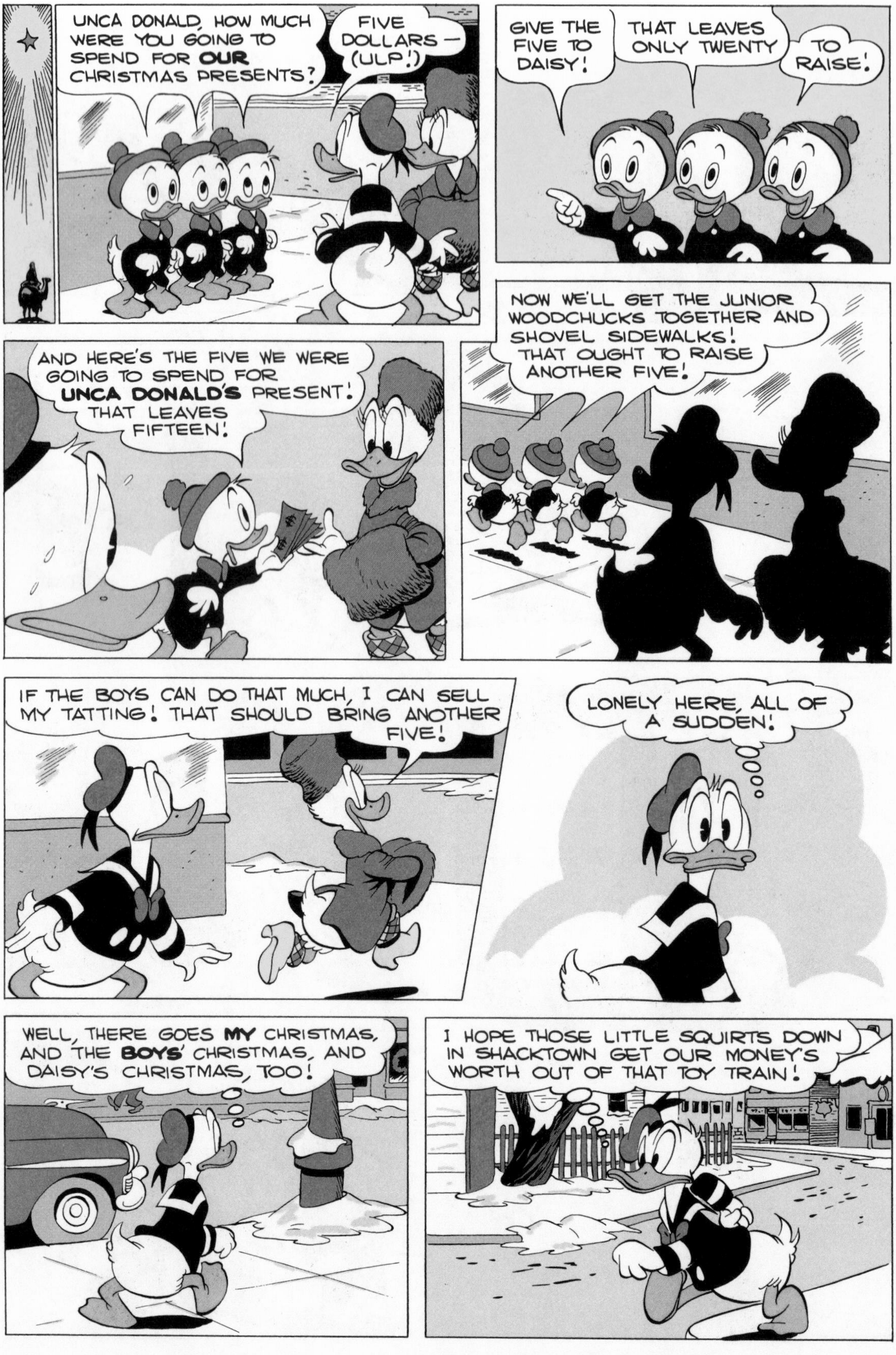
UNCA DONALD, HOW MUCH WERE YOU GOING TO SPEND FOR **OUR** CHRISTMAS PRESENTS?
FIVE DOLLARS— (ULP!)
GIVE THE FIVE TO DAISY!
THAT LEAVES ONLY TWENTY
TO RAISE!
AND HERE'S THE FIVE WE WERE GOING TO SPEND FOR **UNCA DONALD'S** PRESENT! THAT LEAVES FIFTEEN!
NOW WE'LL GET THE JUNIOR WOODCHUCKS TOGETHER AND SHOVEL SIDEWALKS! THAT OUGHT TO RAISE ANOTHER FIVE!
IF THE BOYS CAN DO THAT MUCH, I CAN SELL MY TATTING! THAT SHOULD BRING ANOTHER FIVE!
LONELY HERE, ALL OF A SUDDEN!
WELL, THERE GOES **MY** CHRISTMAS, AND THE **BOYS'** CHRISTMAS, AND DAISY'S CHRISTMAS, TOO!
I HOPE THOSE LITTLE SQUIRTS DOWN IN SHACKTOWN GET OUR MONEY'S WORTH OUT OF THAT TOY TRAIN!

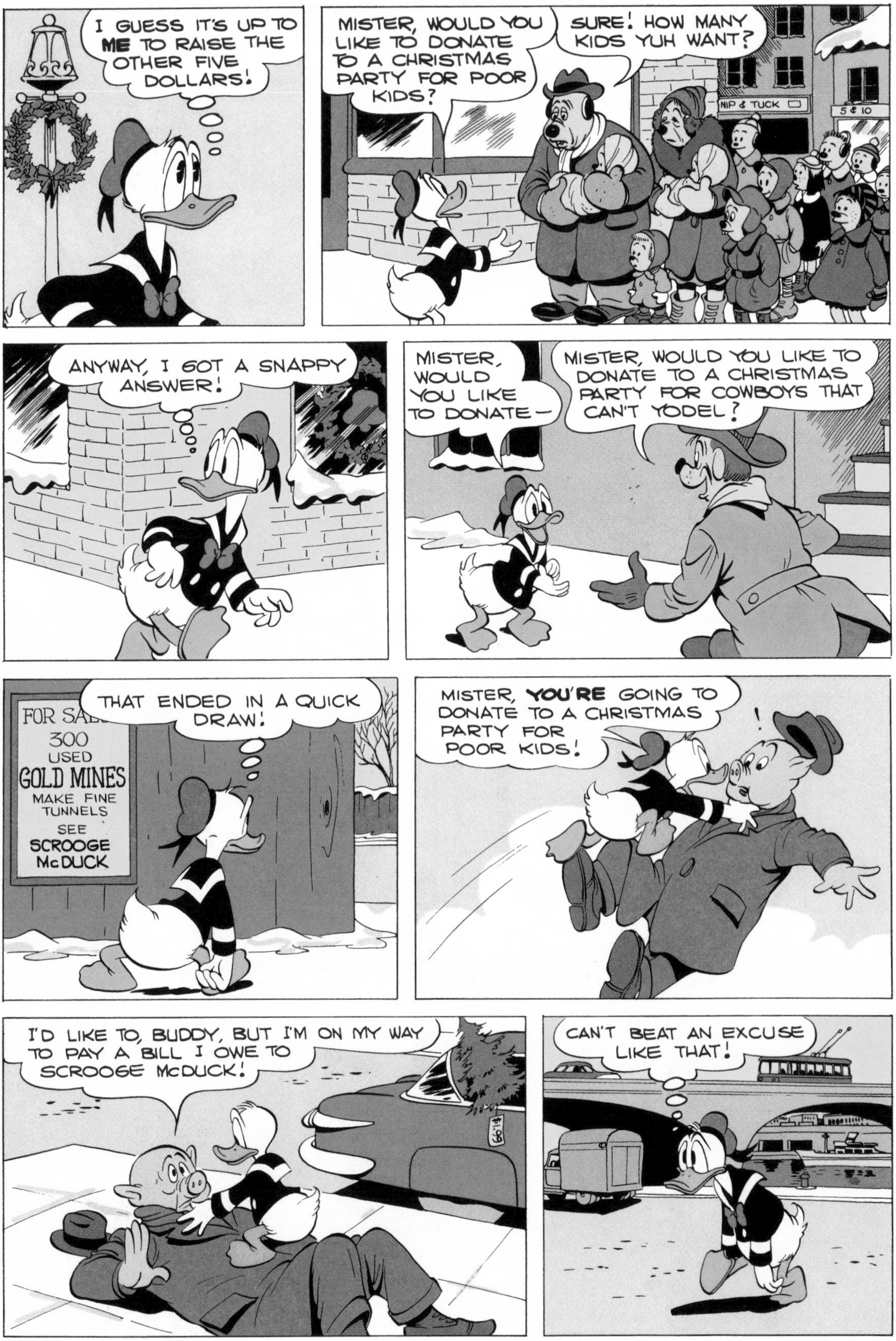
I GUESS IT'S UP TO **ME** TO RAISE THE OTHER FIVE DOLLARS!
MISTER, WOULD YOU LIKE TO DONATE TO A CHRISTMAS PARTY FOR POOR KIDS?
SURE! HOW MANY KIDS YUH WANT?
NIP & TUCK
5¢ 10
ANYWAY, I GOT A SNAPPY ANSWER!
MISTER, WOULD YOU LIKE TO DONATE—
MISTER, WOULD YOU LIKE TO DONATE TO A CHRISTMAS PARTY FOR COWBOYS THAT CAN'T YODEL?
300 USED GOLD MINES MAKE FINE TUNNELS SEE SCROOGE McDUCK
THAT ENDED IN A QUICK DRAW!
MISTER, **YOU'RE** GOING TO DONATE TO A CHRISTMAS PARTY FOR POOR KIDS!
!
I'D LIKE TO, BUDDY, BUT I'M ON MY WAY TO PAY A BILL I OWE TO SCROOGE McDUCK!
CAN'T BEAT AN EXCUSE LIKE THAT!

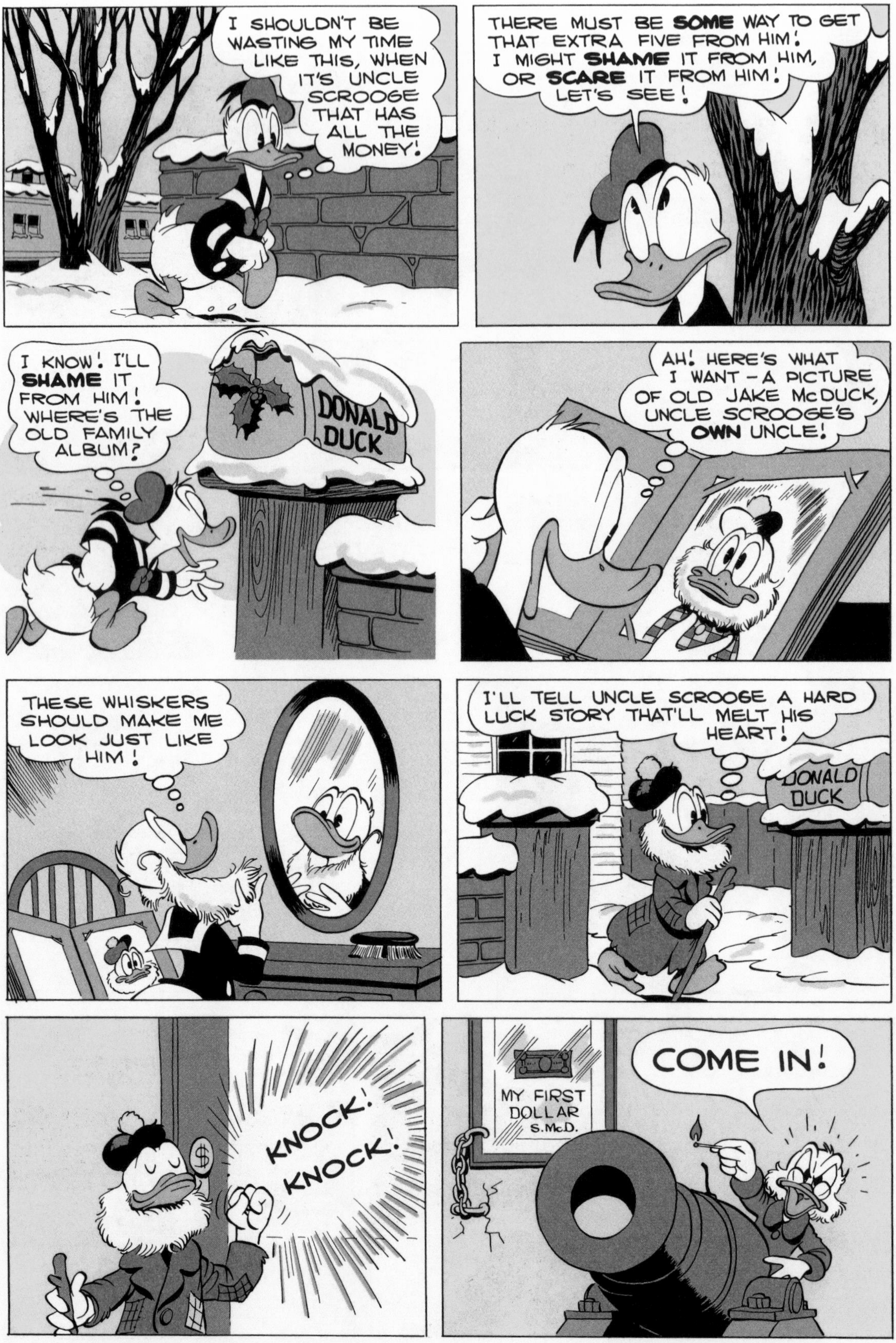
I SHOULDN'T BE WASTING MY TIME LIKE THIS, WHEN IT'S UNCLE SCROOGE THAT HAS ALL THE MONEY!
THERE MUST BE SOME WAY TO GET THAT EXTRA FIVE FROM HIM! I MIGHT SHAME IT FROM HIM, OR SCARE IT FROM HIM! LET'S SEE!
I KNOW! I'LL SHAME IT FROM HIM! WHERE'S THE OLD FAMILY ALBUM?
DONALD DUCK
AH! HERE'S WHAT I WANT – A PICTURE OF OLD JAKE McDUCK, UNCLE SCROOGE'S OWN UNCLE!
THESE WHISKERS SHOULD MAKE ME LOOK JUST LIKE HIM!
I'LL TELL UNCLE SCROOGE A HARD LUCK STORY THAT'LL MELT HIS HEART!
DONALD DUCK
KNOCK! KNOCK!
MY FIRST DOLLAR S.McD.
COME IN!

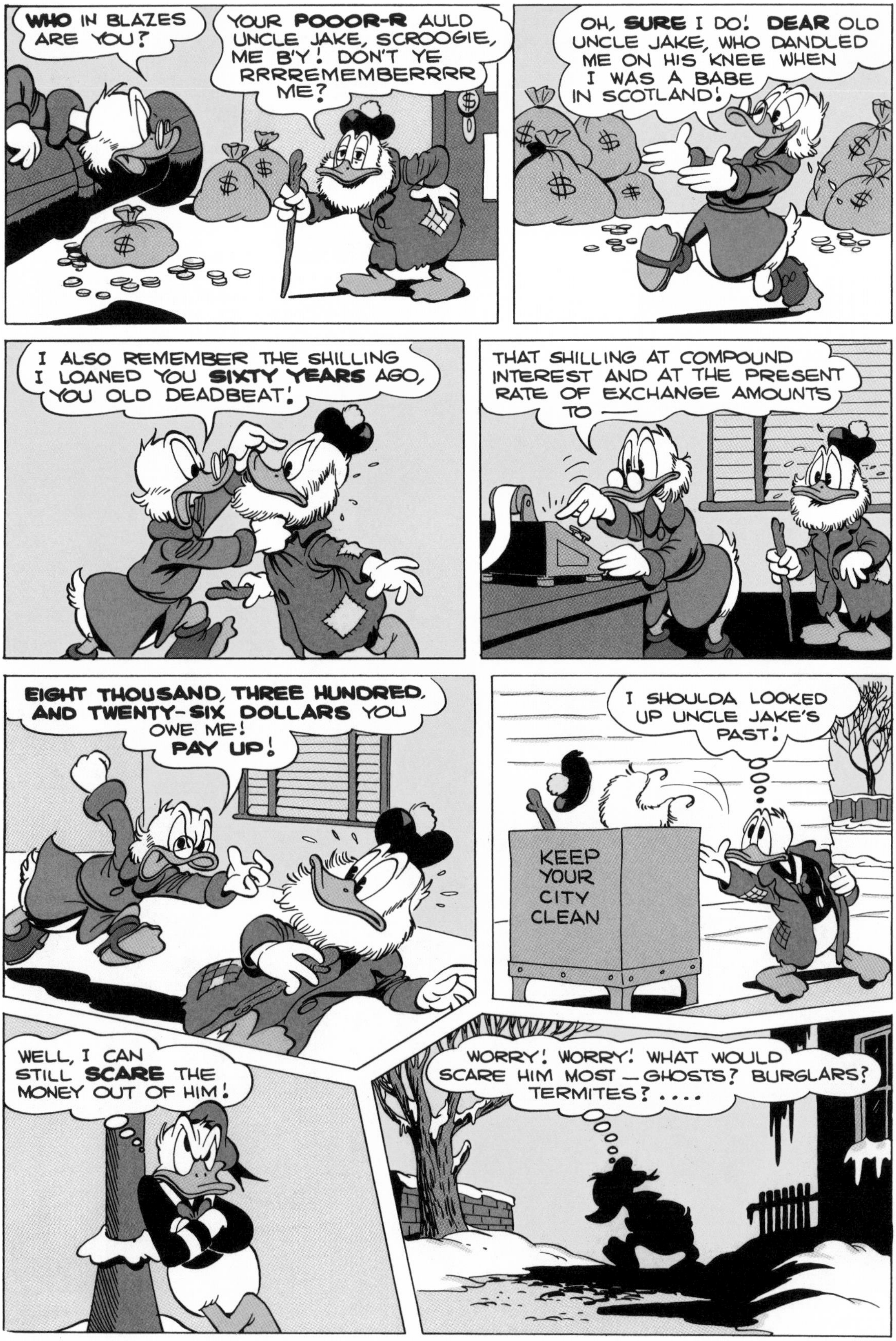
WHO IN BLAZES ARE YOU?
YOUR POOOR-R AULD UNCLE JAKE, SCROOGIE, ME B'Y! DON'T YE RRRREMEMBERRRR ME?
OH, SURE I DO! DEAR OLD UNCLE JAKE, WHO DANDLED ME ON HIS KNEE WHEN I WAS A BABE IN SCOTLAND!
I ALSO REMEMBER THE SHILLING I LOANED YOU SIXTY YEARS AGO, YOU OLD DEADBEAT!
THAT SHILLING AT COMPOUND INTEREST AND AT THE PRESENT RATE OF EXCHANGE AMOUNTS TO —
EIGHT THOUSAND, THREE HUNDRED, AND TWENTY-SIX DOLLARS YOU OWE ME! PAY UP!
I SHOULDA LOOKED UP UNCLE JAKE'S PAST!
KEEP YOUR CITY CLEAN
WELL, I CAN STILL SCARE THE MONEY OUT OF HIM!
WORRY! WORRY! WHAT WOULD SCARE HIM MOST — GHOSTS? BURGLARS? TERMITES? ....

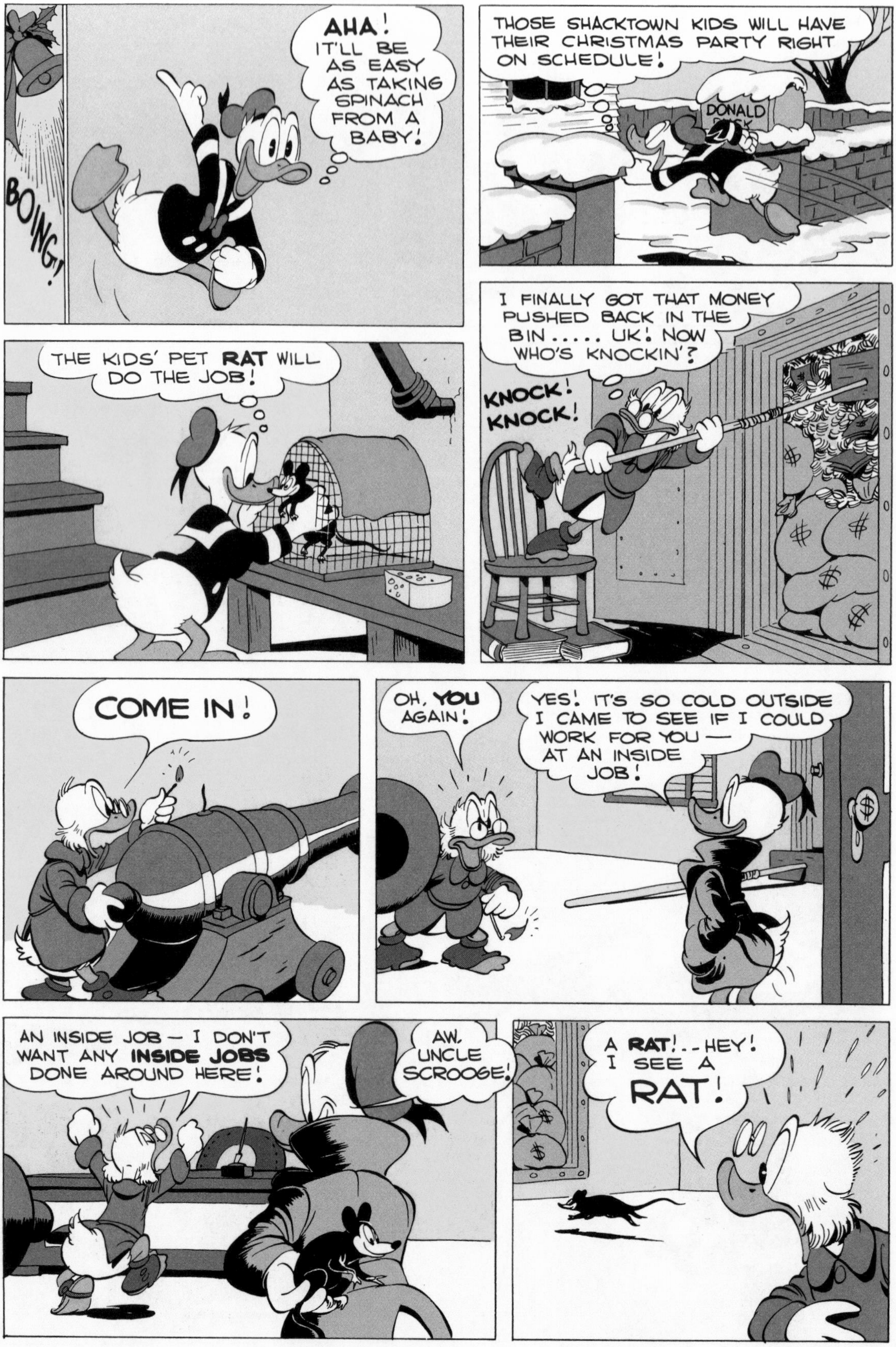
BOING!!
AHA! IT'LL BE AS EASY AS TAKING SPINACH FROM A BABY!
THOSE SHACKTOWN KIDS WILL HAVE THEIR CHRISTMAS PARTY RIGHT ON SCHEDULE!
DONALD
THE KIDS' PET RAT WILL DO THE JOB!
I FINALLY GOT THAT MONEY PUSHED BACK IN THE BIN..... UK! NOW WHO'S KNOCKIN'?
KNOCK! KNOCK!
COME IN!
OH, YOU AGAIN!
YES! IT'S SO COLD OUTSIDE I CAME TO SEE IF I COULD WORK FOR YOU — AT AN INSIDE JOB!
AN INSIDE JOB — I DON'T WANT ANY INSIDE JOBS DONE AROUND HERE!
AW, UNCLE SCROOGE!
A RAT!..HEY! I SEE A RAT!

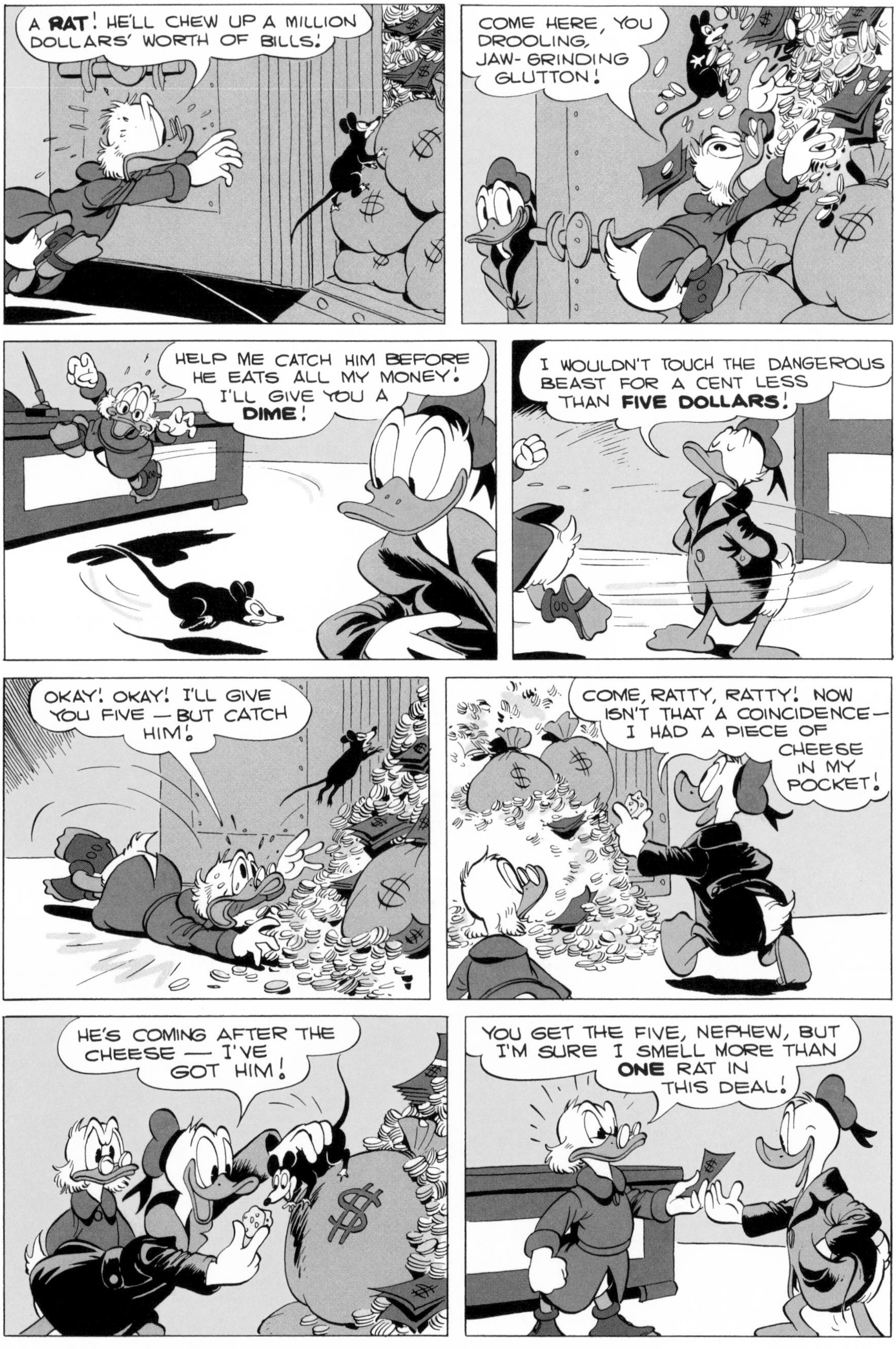
A RAT! HE'LL CHEW UP A MILLION DOLLARS' WORTH OF BILLS!
COME HERE, YOU DROOLING, JAW-GRINDING GLUTTON!
HELP ME CATCH HIM BEFORE HE EATS ALL MY MONEY! I'LL GIVE YOU A DIME!
I WOULDN'T TOUCH THE DANGEROUS BEAST FOR A CENT LESS THAN FIVE DOLLARS!
OKAY! OKAY! I'LL GIVE YOU FIVE — BUT CATCH HIM!
COME, RATTY, RATTY! NOW ISN'T THAT A COINCIDENCE— I HAD A PIECE OF CHEESE IN MY POCKET!
HE'S COMING AFTER THE CHEESE — I'VE GOT HIM!
YOU GET THE FIVE, NEPHEW, BUT I'M SURE I SMELL MORE THAN ONE RAT IN THIS DEAL!

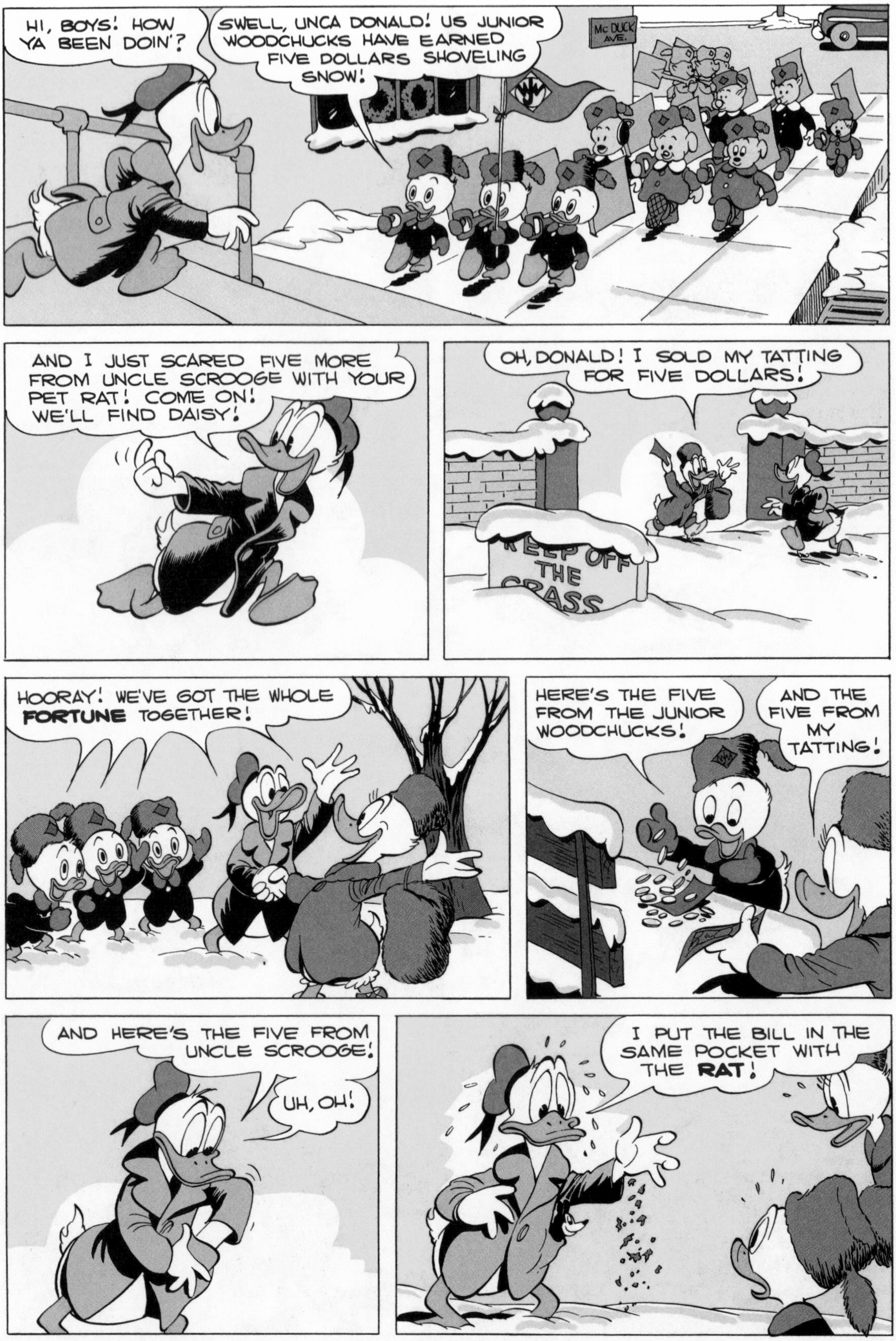
HI, BOYS! HOW YA BEEN DOIN'?
SWELL, UNCA DONALD! US JUNIOR WOODCHUCKS HAVE EARNED FIVE DOLLARS SHOVELING SNOW!
McDUCK AVE.
AND I JUST SCARED FIVE MORE FROM UNCLE SCROOGE WITH YOUR PET RAT! COME ON! WE'LL FIND DAISY!
OH, DONALD! I SOLD MY TATTING FOR FIVE DOLLARS!
KEEP OFF THE GRASS
HOORAY! WE'VE GOT THE WHOLE **FORTUNE** TOGETHER!
HERE'S THE FIVE FROM THE JUNIOR WOODCHUCKS!
AND THE FIVE FROM MY TATTING!
AND HERE'S THE FIVE FROM UNCLE SCROOGE!
UH, OH!
I PUT THE BILL IN THE SAME POCKET WITH THE **RAT**!

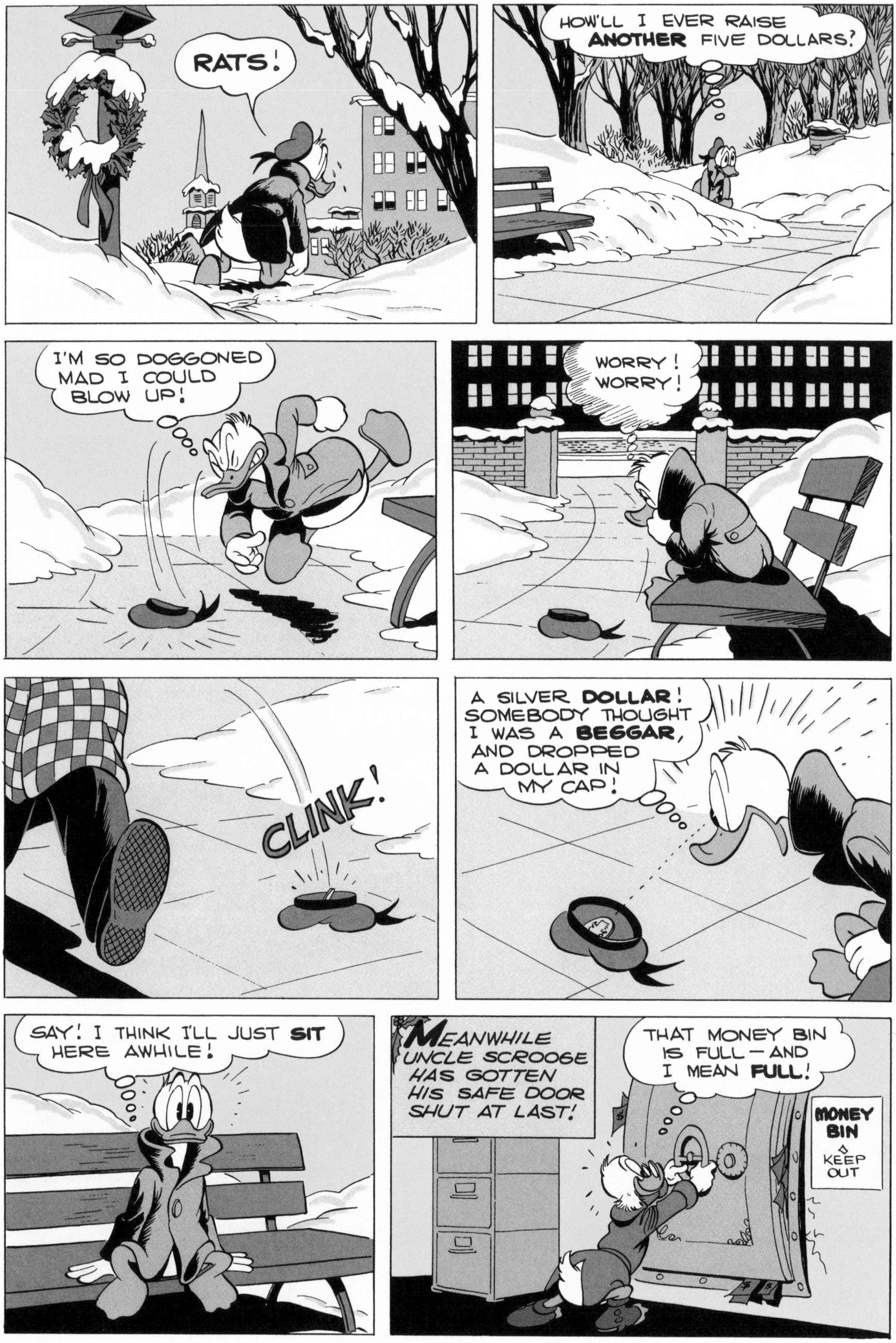
RATS!
HOW'LL I EVER RAISE ANOTHER FIVE DOLLARS?
I'M SO DOGGONED MAD I COULD BLOW UP!
WORRY! WORRY!
CLINK!
A SILVER DOLLAR! SOMEBODY THOUGHT I WAS A BEGGAR, AND DROPPED A DOLLAR IN MY CAP!
SAY! I THINK I'LL JUST SIT HERE AWHILE!
MEANWHILE UNCLE SCROOGE HAS GOTTEN HIS SAFE DOOR SHUT AT LAST!
THAT MONEY BIN IS FULL—AND I MEAN FULL!
MONEY BIN
KEEP OUT

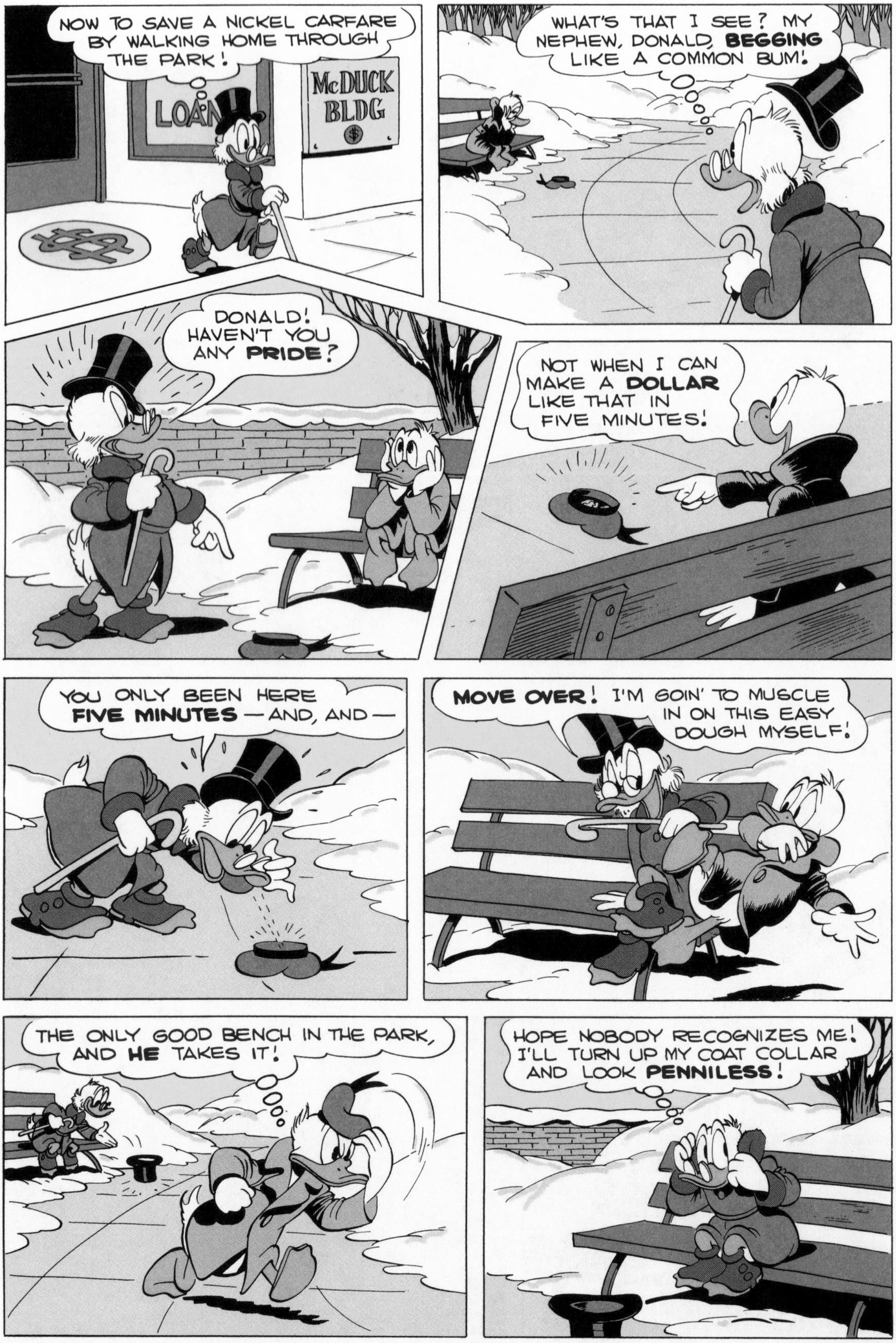
NOW TO SAVE A NICKEL CARFARE BY WALKING HOME THROUGH THE PARK!
LOAN
McDUCK BLDG
WHAT'S THAT I SEE? MY NEPHEW, DONALD, BEGGING LIKE A COMMON BUM!
DONALD! HAVEN'T YOU ANY PRIDE?
NOT WHEN I CAN MAKE A DOLLAR LIKE THAT IN FIVE MINUTES!
YOU ONLY BEEN HERE FIVE MINUTES—AND, AND—
MOVE OVER! I'M GOIN' TO MUSCLE IN ON THIS EASY DOUGH MYSELF!
THE ONLY GOOD BENCH IN THE PARK, AND HE TAKES IT!
HOPE NOBODY RECOGNIZES ME! I'LL TURN UP MY COAT COLLAR AND LOOK PENNILESS!

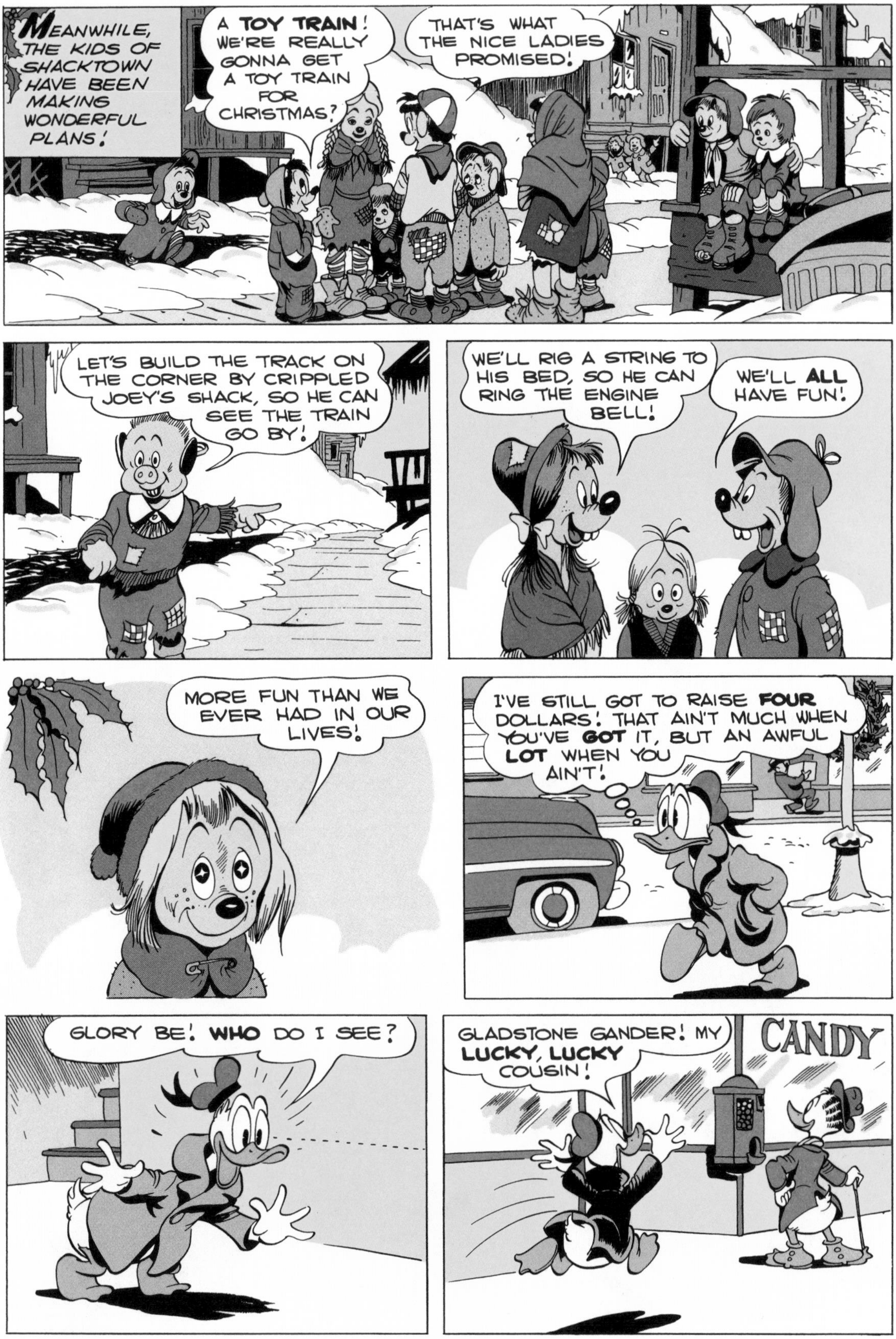
MEANWHILE, THE KIDS OF SHACKTOWN HAVE BEEN MAKING WONDERFUL PLANS!
A TOY TRAIN! WE'RE REALLY GONNA GET A TOY TRAIN FOR CHRISTMAS?
THAT'S WHAT THE NICE LADIES PROMISED!
LET'S BUILD THE TRACK ON THE CORNER BY CRIPPLED JOEY'S SHACK, SO HE CAN SEE THE TRAIN GO BY!
WE'LL RIG A STRING TO HIS BED, SO HE CAN RING THE ENGINE BELL!
WE'LL ALL HAVE FUN!
MORE FUN THAN WE EVER HAD IN OUR LIVES!
I'VE STILL GOT TO RAISE FOUR DOLLARS! THAT AIN'T MUCH WHEN YOU'VE GOT IT, BUT AN AWFUL LOT WHEN YOU AIN'T!
GLORY BE! WHO DO I SEE?
GLADSTONE GANDER! MY LUCKY, LUCKY COUSIN!
CANDY

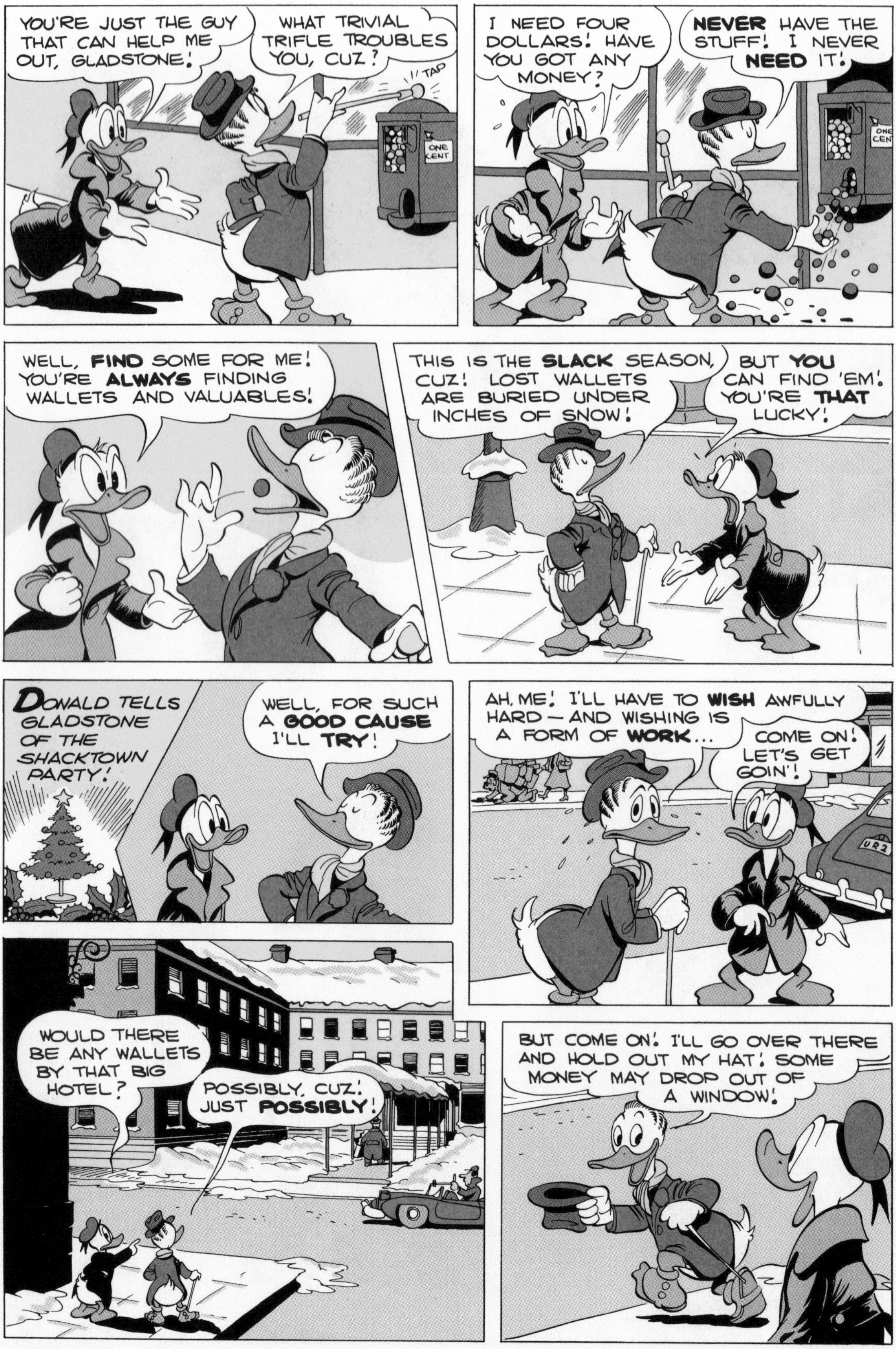
YOU'RE JUST THE GUY THAT CAN HELP ME OUT, GLADSTONE!
WHAT TRIVIAL TRIFLE TROUBLES YOU, CUZ?
TAP
ONE CENT
I NEED FOUR DOLLARS! HAVE YOU GOT ANY MONEY?
NEVER HAVE THE STUFF! I NEVER NEED IT!
ONE CENT
WELL, FIND SOME FOR ME! YOU'RE ALWAYS FINDING WALLETS AND VALUABLES!
THIS IS THE SLACK SEASON, CUZ! LOST WALLETS ARE BURIED UNDER INCHES OF SNOW!
BUT YOU CAN FIND 'EM! YOU'RE THAT LUCKY!
DONALD TELLS GLADSTONE OF THE SHACKTOWN PARTY!
WELL, FOR SUCH A GOOD CAUSE I'LL TRY!
AH, ME! I'LL HAVE TO WISH AWFULLY HARD — AND WISHING IS A FORM OF WORK...
COME ON! LET'S GET GOIN'!
UR2
WOULD THERE BE ANY WALLETS BY THAT BIG HOTEL?
POSSIBLY, CUZ! JUST POSSIBLY!
BUT COME ON! I'LL GO OVER THERE AND HOLD OUT MY HAT! SOME MONEY MAY DROP OUT OF A WINDOW!

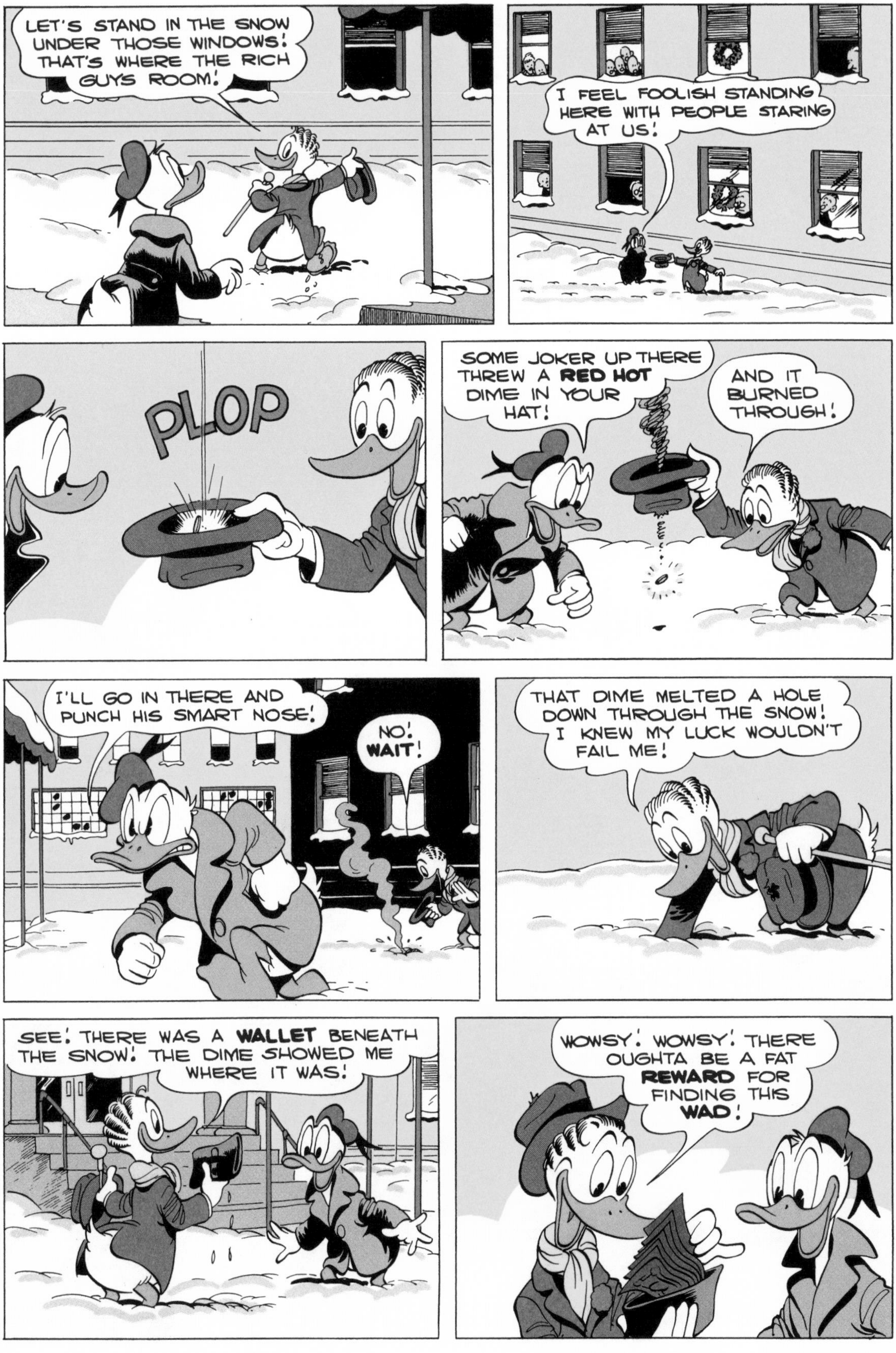
LET'S STAND IN THE SNOW UNDER THOSE WINDOWS! THAT'S WHERE THE RICH GUYS ROOM!
I FEEL FOOLISH STANDING HERE WITH PEOPLE STARING AT US!
PLOP
SOME JOKER UP THERE THREW A **RED HOT** DIME IN YOUR HAT!
AND IT BURNED THROUGH!
I'LL GO IN THERE AND PUNCH HIS SMART NOSE!
NO! **WAIT**!
THAT DIME MELTED A HOLE DOWN THROUGH THE SNOW! I KNEW MY LUCK WOULDN'T FAIL ME!
SEE! THERE WAS A **WALLET** BENEATH THE SNOW! THE DIME SHOWED ME WHERE IT WAS!
WOWSY! WOWSY! THERE OUGHTA BE A FAT **REWARD** FOR FINDING THIS **WAD**!

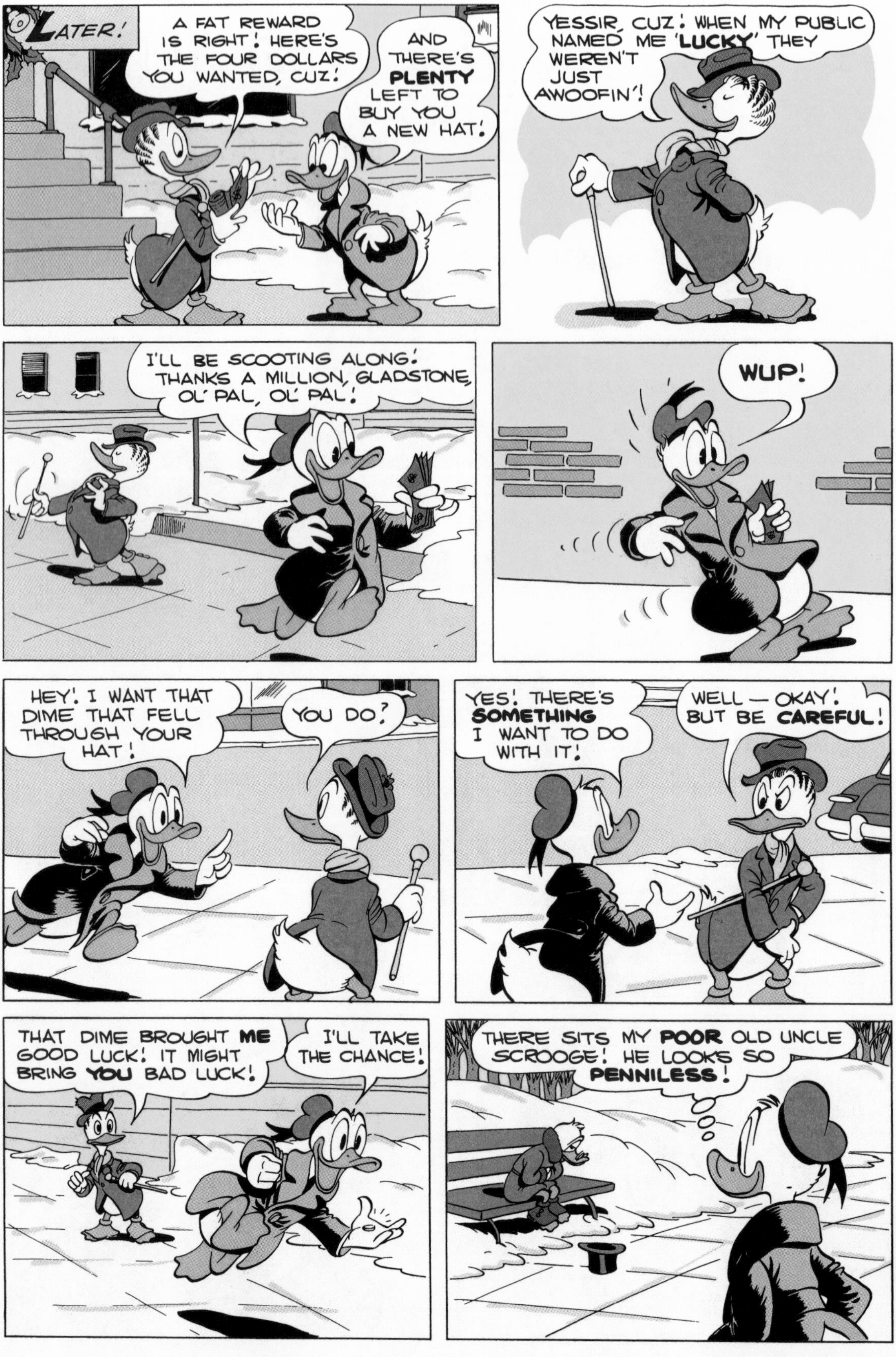
LATER!
A FAT REWARD IS RIGHT! HERE'S THE FOUR DOLLARS YOU WANTED, CUZ!
AND THERE'S PLENTY LEFT TO BUY YOU A NEW HAT!
YESSIR, CUZ! WHEN MY PUBLIC NAMED ME 'LUCKY' THEY WEREN'T JUST AWOOFIN'!
I'LL BE SCOOTING ALONG! THANKS A MILLION, GLADSTONE, OL' PAL, OL' PAL!
WUP!
HEY! I WANT THAT DIME THAT FELL THROUGH YOUR HAT!
YOU DO?
YES! THERE'S SOMETHING I WANT TO DO WITH IT!
WELL — OKAY! BUT BE CAREFUL!
THAT DIME BROUGHT ME GOOD LUCK! IT MIGHT BRING YOU BAD LUCK!
I'LL TAKE THE CHANCE!
THERE SITS MY POOR OLD UNCLE SCROOGE! HE LOOKS SO PENNILESS!

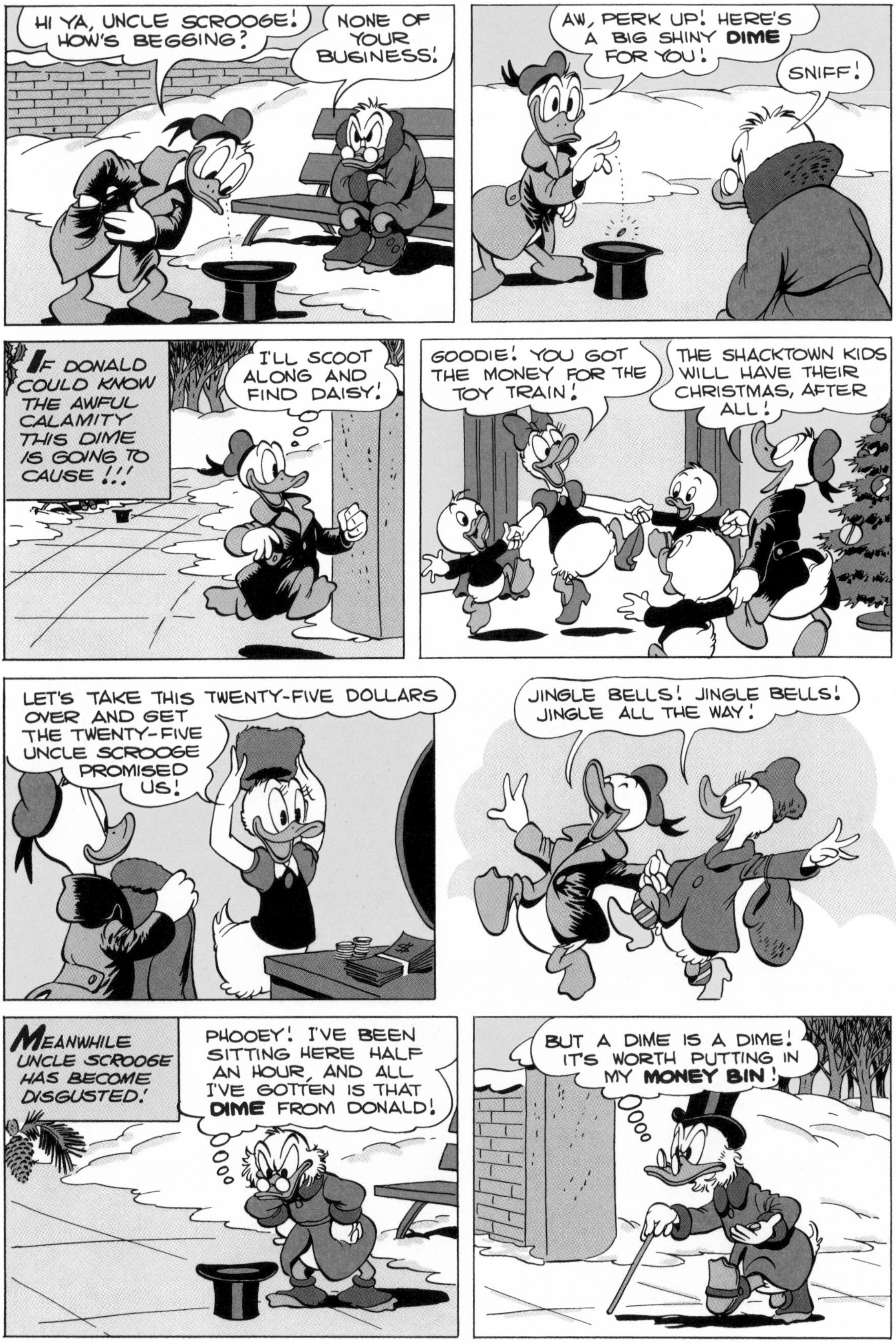

HI YA, UNCLE SCROOGE! HOW'S BEGGING?
NONE OF YOUR BUSINESS!
AW, PERK UP! HERE'S A BIG SHINY **DIME** FOR YOU!
SNIFF!
IF DONALD COULD KNOW THE AWFUL CALAMITY THIS DIME IS GOING TO CAUSE!!!
I'LL SCOOT ALONG AND FIND DAISY!
GOODIE! YOU GOT THE MONEY FOR THE TOY TRAIN!
THE SHACKTOWN KIDS WILL HAVE THEIR CHRISTMAS, AFTER ALL!
LET'S TAKE THIS TWENTY-FIVE DOLLARS OVER AND GET THE TWENTY-FIVE UNCLE SCROOGE PROMISED US!
JINGLE BELLS! JINGLE BELLS! JINGLE ALL THE WAY!
MEANWHILE UNCLE SCROOGE HAS BECOME DISGUSTED!
PHOOEY! I'VE BEEN SITTING HERE HALF AN HOUR, AND ALL I'VE GOTTEN IS THAT **DIME** FROM DONALD!
BUT A DIME IS A DIME! IT'S WORTH PUTTING IN MY **MONEY BIN**!

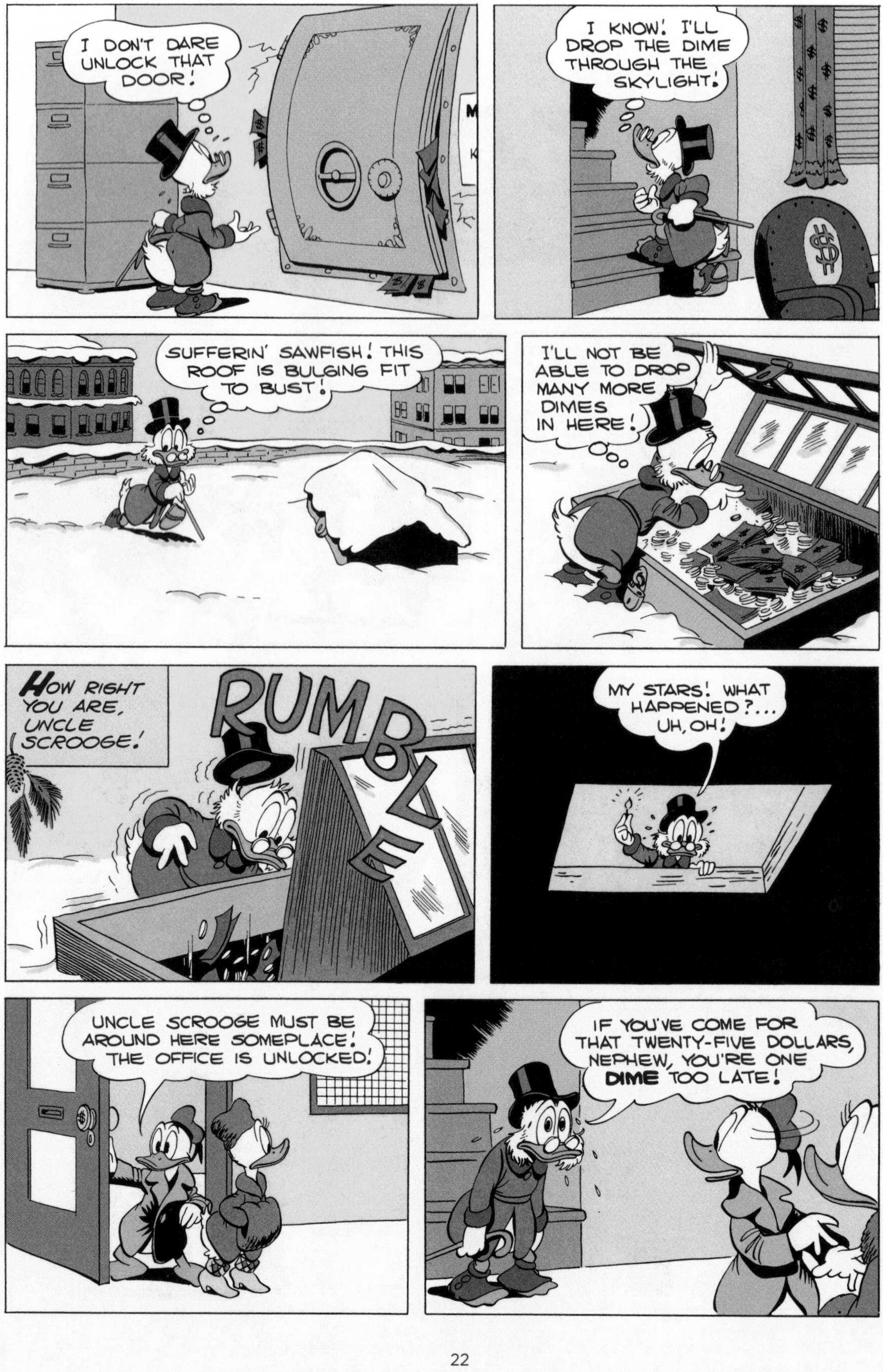
I DON'T DARE UNLOCK THAT DOOR!
I KNOW! I'LL DROP THE DIME THROUGH THE SKYLIGHT!
SUFFERIN' SAWFISH! THIS ROOF IS BULGING FIT TO BUST!
I'LL NOT BE ABLE TO DROP MANY MORE DIMES IN HERE!
HOW RIGHT YOU ARE, UNCLE SCROOGE!
RUMBLE
MY STARS! WHAT HAPPENED?... UH, OH!
UNCLE SCROOGE MUST BE AROUND HERE SOMEPLACE! THE OFFICE IS UNLOCKED!
IF YOU'VE COME FOR THAT TWENTY-FIVE DOLLARS, NEPHEW, YOU'RE ONE **DIME** TOO LATE!

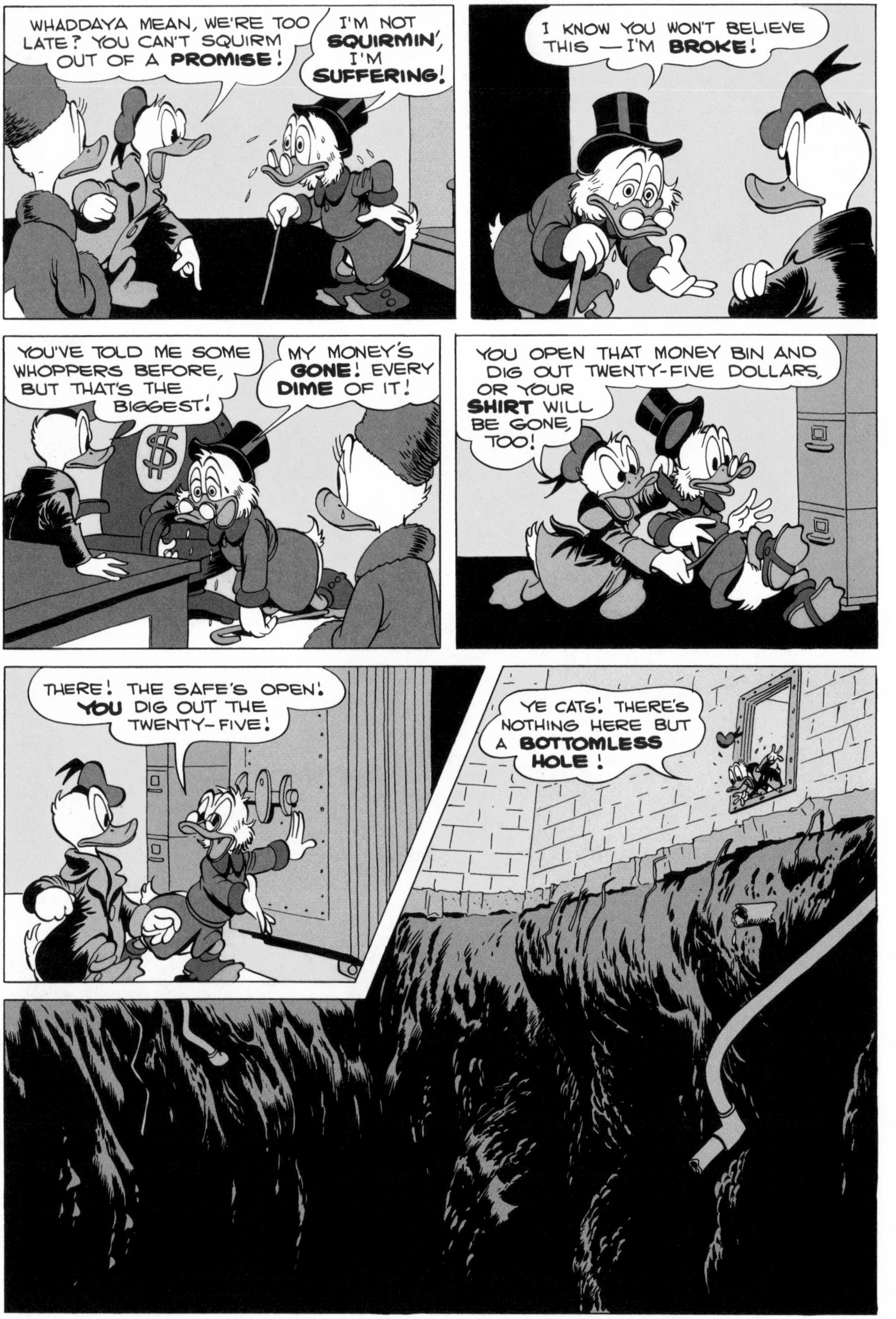
WHADDAYA MEAN, WE'RE TOO LATE? YOU CAN'T SQUIRM OUT OF A PROMISE!
I'M NOT SQUIRMIN', I'M SUFFERING!
I KNOW YOU WON'T BELIEVE THIS — I'M BROKE!
YOU'VE TOLD ME SOME WHOPPERS BEFORE, BUT THAT'S THE BIGGEST!
MY MONEY'S GONE! EVERY DIME OF IT!
YOU OPEN THAT MONEY BIN AND DIG OUT TWENTY-FIVE DOLLARS, OR YOUR SHIRT WILL BE GONE, TOO!
THERE! THE SAFE'S OPEN! YOU DIG OUT THE TWENTY-FIVE!
YE CATS! THERE'S NOTHING HERE BUT A BOTTOMLESS HOLE!

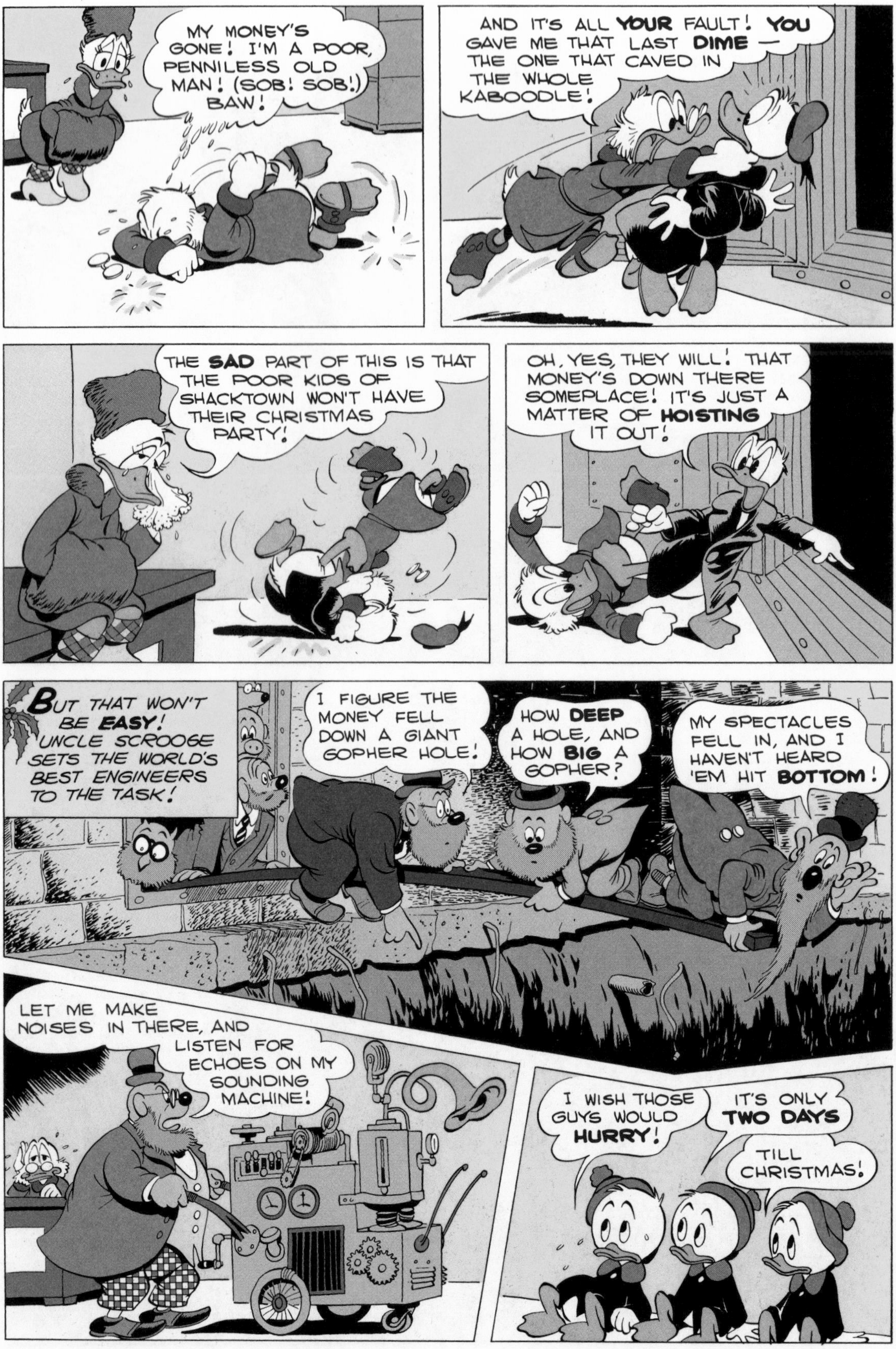
MY MONEY'S GONE! I'M A POOR, PENNILESS OLD MAN! (SOB! SOB!) BAW!
AND IT'S ALL YOUR FAULT! YOU GAVE ME THAT LAST DIME — THE ONE THAT CAVED IN THE WHOLE KABOODLE!
THE SAD PART OF THIS IS THAT THE POOR KIDS OF SHACKTOWN WON'T HAVE THEIR CHRISTMAS PARTY!
OH, YES, THEY WILL! THAT MONEY'S DOWN THERE SOMEPLACE! IT'S JUST A MATTER OF HOISTING IT OUT!
BUT THAT WON'T BE EASY! UNCLE SCROOGE SETS THE WORLD'S BEST ENGINEERS TO THE TASK!
I FIGURE THE MONEY FELL DOWN A GIANT GOPHER HOLE!
HOW DEEP A HOLE, AND HOW BIG A GOPHER?
MY SPECTACLES FELL IN, AND I HAVEN'T HEARD 'EM HIT BOTTOM!
LET ME MAKE NOISES IN THERE, AND LISTEN FOR ECHOES ON MY SOUNDING MACHINE!
I WISH THOSE GUYS WOULD HURRY!
IT'S ONLY TWO DAYS
TILL CHRISTMAS!

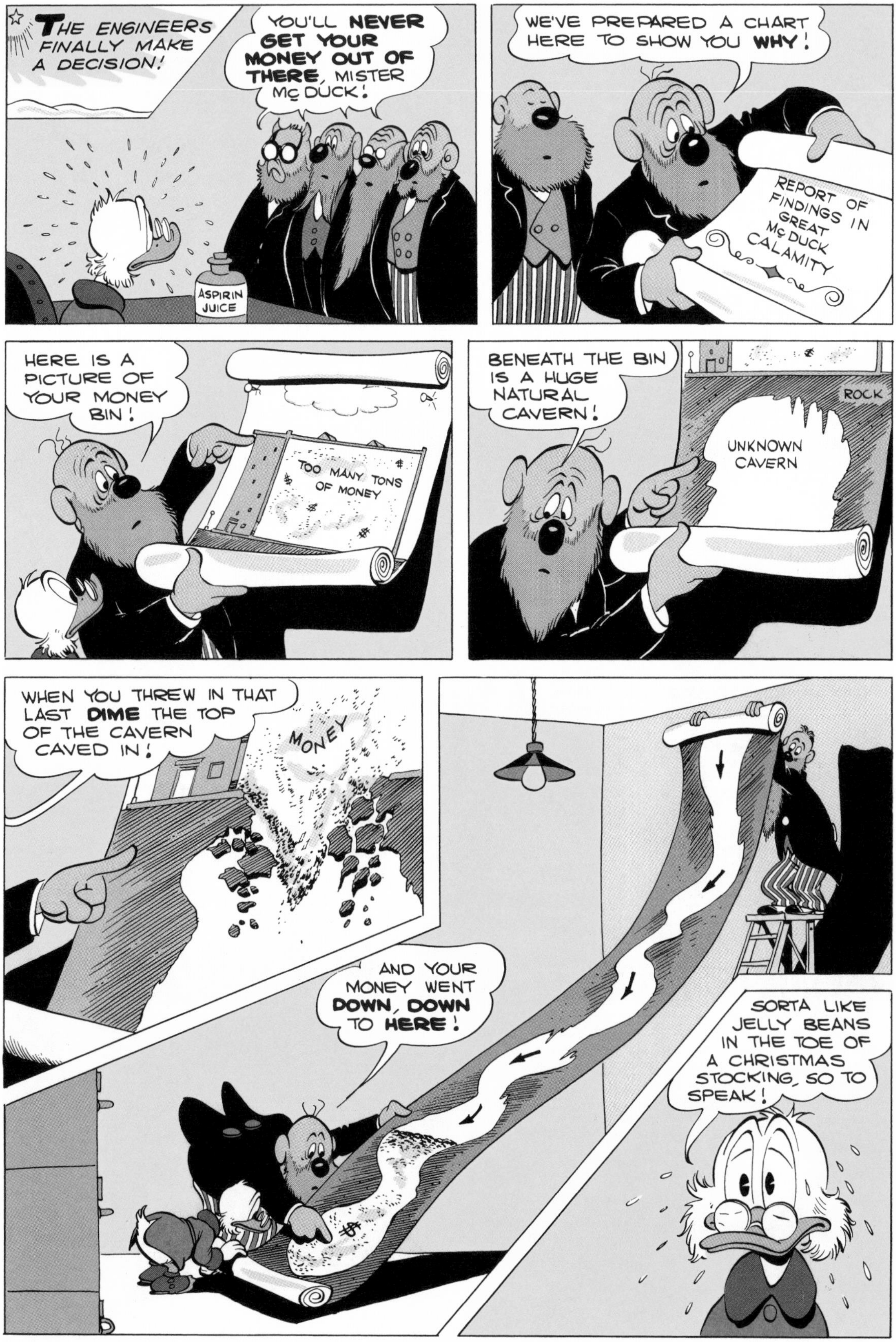
THE ENGINEERS FINALLY MAKE A DECISION!
YOU'LL NEVER GET YOUR MONEY OUT OF THERE, MISTER McDUCK!
ASPIRIN JUICE
WE'VE PREPARED A CHART HERE TO SHOW YOU WHY!
REPORT OF FINDINGS IN GREAT McDUCK CALAMITY
HERE IS A PICTURE OF YOUR MONEY BIN!
TOO MANY TONS OF MONEY
BENEATH THE BIN IS A HUGE NATURAL CAVERN!
ROCK
UNKNOWN CAVERN
WHEN YOU THREW IN THAT LAST DIME THE TOP OF THE CAVERN CAVED IN!
MONEY
AND YOUR MONEY WENT DOWN, DOWN TO HERE!
SORTA LIKE JELLY BEANS IN THE TOE OF A CHRISTMAS STOCKING, SO TO SPEAK!

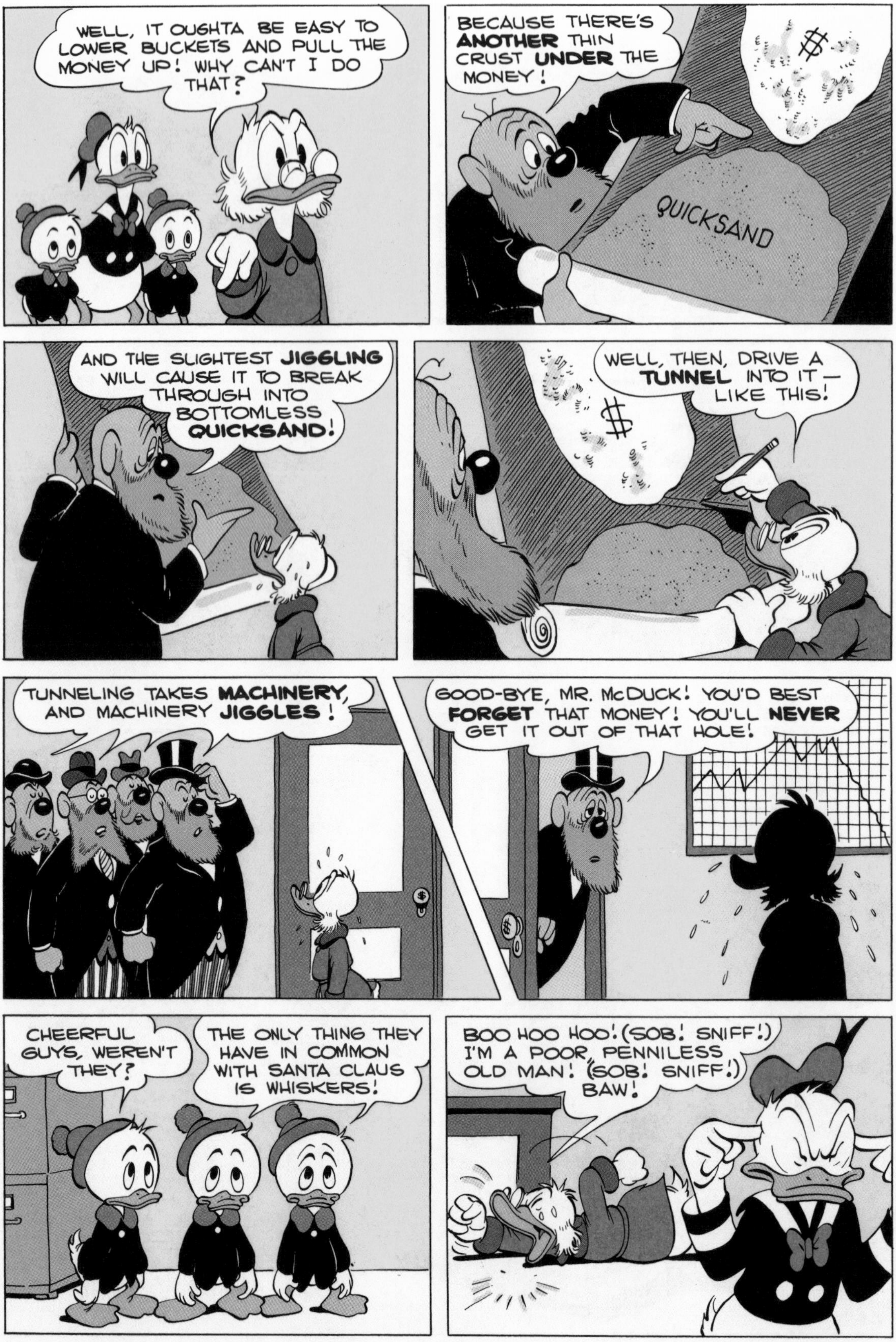
WELL, IT OUGHTA BE EASY TO LOWER BUCKETS AND PULL THE MONEY UP! WHY CAN'T I DO THAT?
BECAUSE THERE'S **ANOTHER** THIN CRUST **UNDER** THE MONEY!
QUICKSAND
AND THE SLIGHTEST **JIGGLING** WILL CAUSE IT TO BREAK THROUGH INTO BOTTOMLESS **QUICKSAND**!
WELL, THEN, DRIVE A **TUNNEL** INTO IT— LIKE THIS!
TUNNELING TAKES **MACHINERY**, AND MACHINERY **JIGGLES**!
GOOD-BYE, MR. McDUCK! YOU'D BEST **FORGET** THAT MONEY! YOU'LL **NEVER** GET IT OUT OF THAT HOLE!
CHEERFUL GUYS, WEREN'T THEY?
THE ONLY THING THEY HAVE IN COMMON WITH SANTA CLAUS IS WHISKERS!
BOO HOO HOO! (SOB! SNIFF!) I'M A POOR, PENNILESS OLD MAN! (SOB! SNIFF!) BAW!

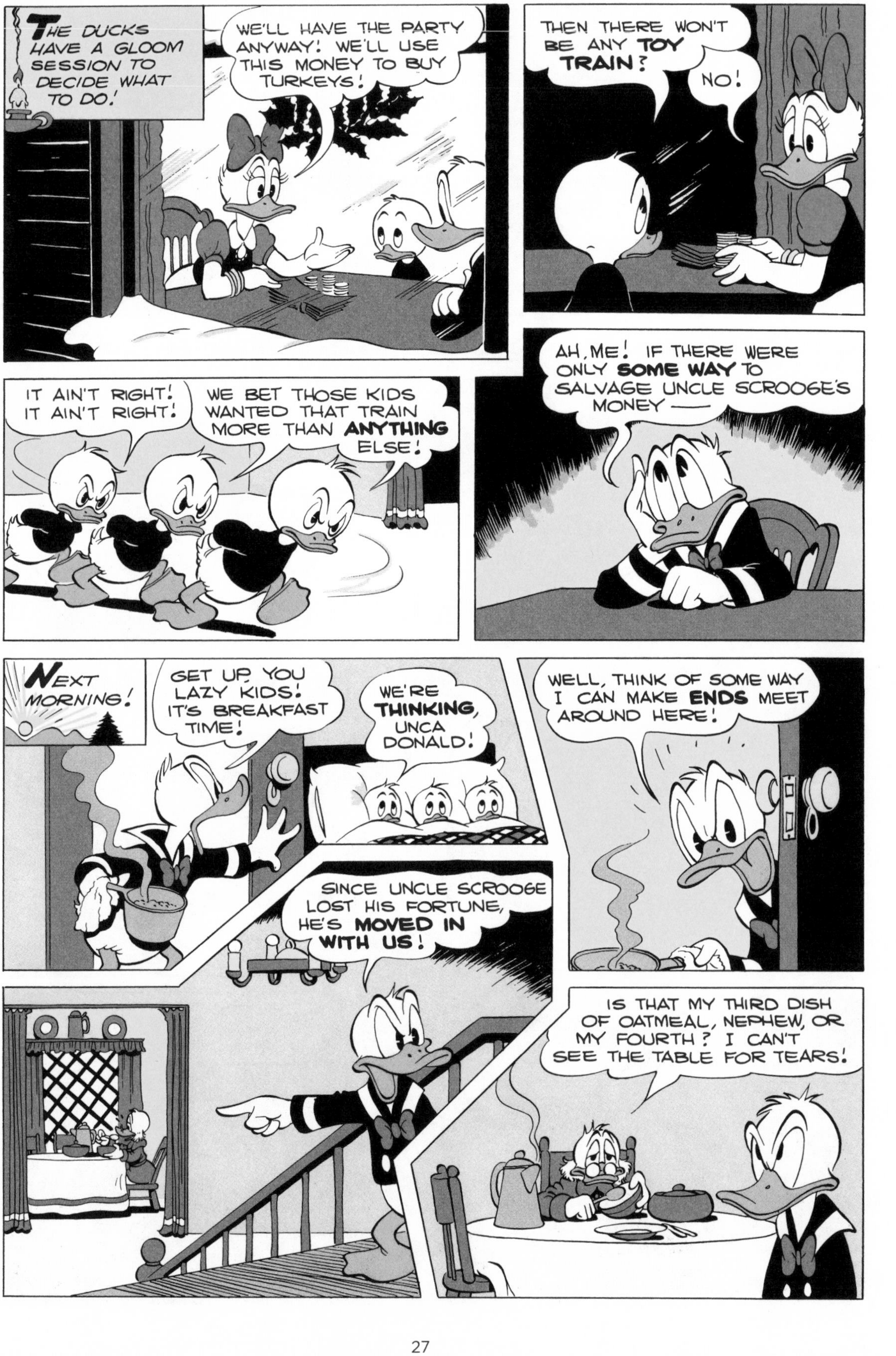
THE DUCKS HAVE A GLOOM SESSION TO DECIDE WHAT TO DO!
WE'LL HAVE THE PARTY ANYWAY! WE'LL USE THIS MONEY TO BUY TURKEYS!
THEN THERE WON'T BE ANY TOY TRAIN?
NO!
IT AIN'T RIGHT! IT AIN'T RIGHT!
WE BET THOSE KIDS WANTED THAT TRAIN MORE THAN ANYTHING ELSE!
AH, ME! IF THERE WERE ONLY SOME WAY TO SALVAGE UNCLE SCROOGE'S MONEY —
NEXT MORNING!
GET UP, YOU LAZY KIDS! IT'S BREAKFAST TIME!
WE'RE THINKING, UNCA DONALD!
WELL, THINK OF SOME WAY I CAN MAKE ENDS MEET AROUND HERE!
SINCE UNCLE SCROOGE LOST HIS FORTUNE, HE'S MOVED IN WITH US!
IS THAT MY THIRD DISH OF OATMEAL, NEPHEW, OR MY FOURTH? I CAN'T SEE THE TABLE FOR TEARS!

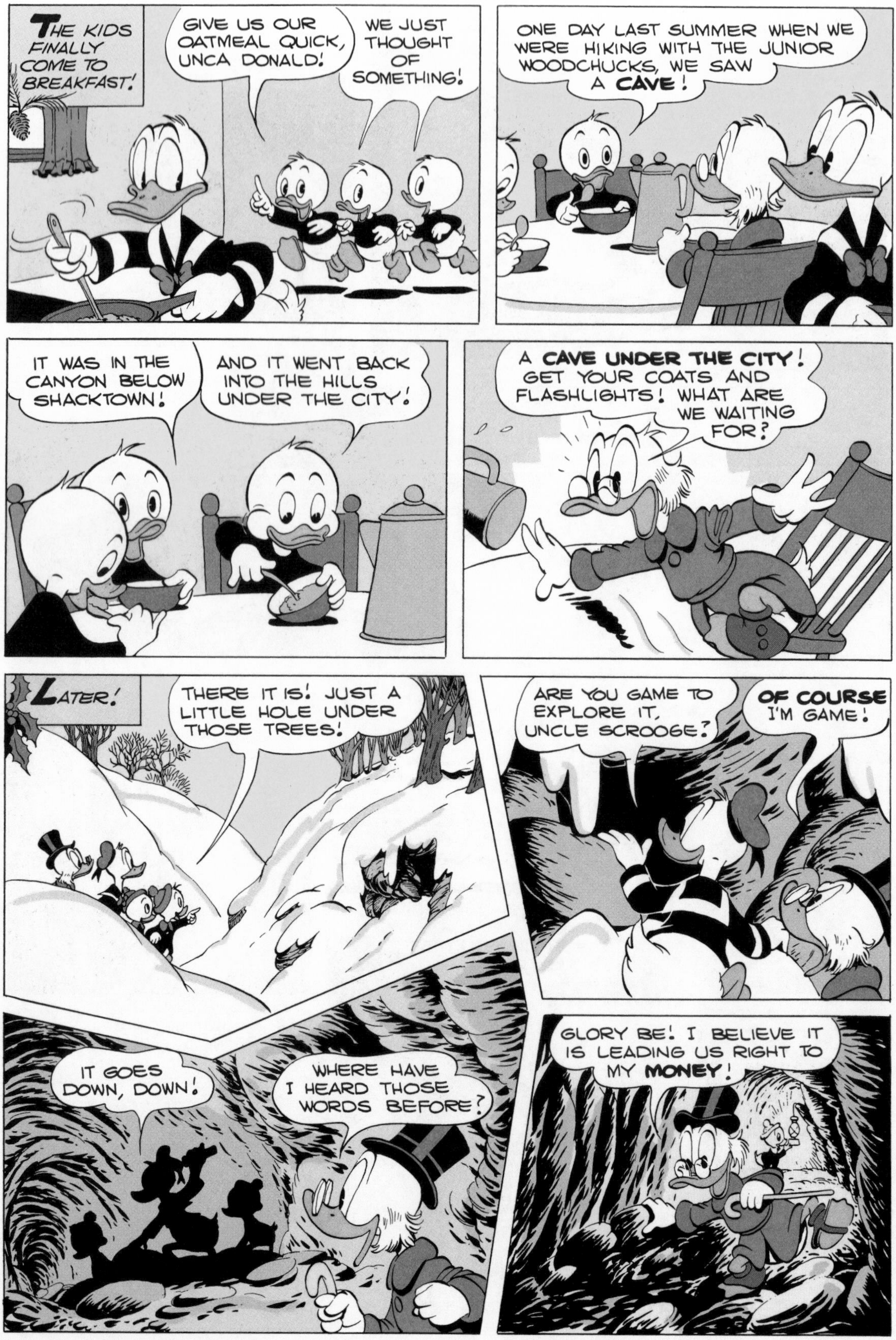
THE KIDS FINALLY COME TO BREAKFAST!
GIVE US OUR OATMEAL QUICK, UNCA DONALD!
WE JUST THOUGHT OF SOMETHING!
ONE DAY LAST SUMMER WHEN WE WERE HIKING WITH THE JUNIOR WOODCHUCKS, WE SAW A CAVE!
IT WAS IN THE CANYON BELOW SHACKTOWN!
AND IT WENT BACK INTO THE HILLS UNDER THE CITY!
A CAVE UNDER THE CITY! GET YOUR COATS AND FLASHLIGHTS! WHAT ARE WE WAITING FOR?
LATER!
THERE IT IS! JUST A LITTLE HOLE UNDER THOSE TREES!
ARE YOU GAME TO EXPLORE IT, UNCLE SCROOGE?
OF COURSE I'M GAME!
IT GOES DOWN, DOWN!
WHERE HAVE I HEARD THOSE WORDS BEFORE?
GLORY BE! I BELIEVE IT IS LEADING US RIGHT TO MY MONEY!

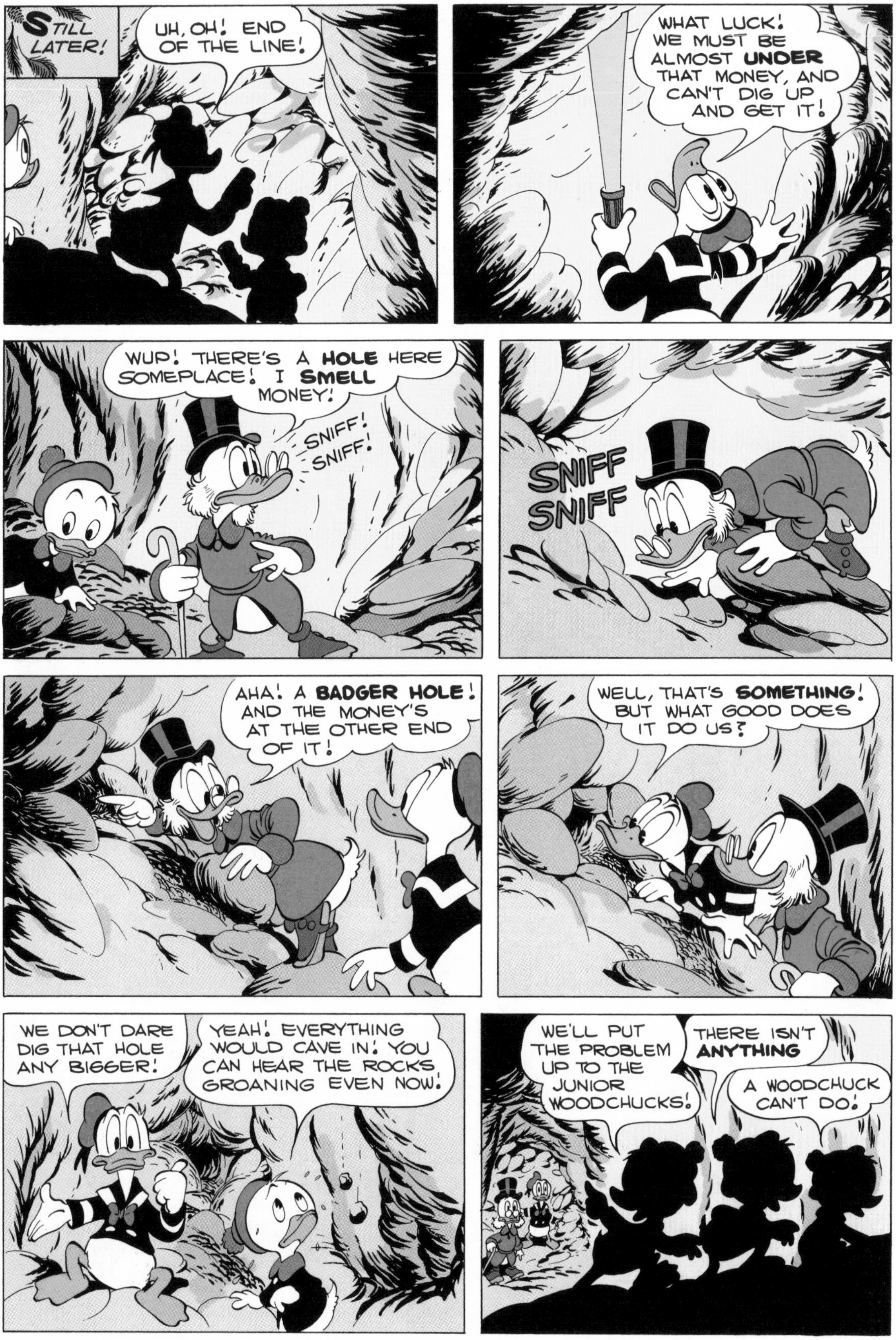
STILL LATER!
UH, OH! END OF THE LINE!
WHAT LUCK! WE MUST BE ALMOST UNDER THAT MONEY, AND CAN'T DIG UP AND GET IT!
WUP! THERE'S A HOLE HERE SOMEPLACE! I SMELL MONEY!
SNIFF! SNIFF!
SNIFF SNIFF
AHA! A BADGER HOLE! AND THE MONEY'S AT THE OTHER END OF IT!
WELL, THAT'S SOMETHING! BUT WHAT GOOD DOES IT DO US?
WE DON'T DARE DIG THAT HOLE ANY BIGGER!
YEAH! EVERYTHING WOULD CAVE IN! YOU CAN HEAR THE ROCKS GROANING EVEN NOW!
WE'LL PUT THE PROBLEM UP TO THE JUNIOR WOODCHUCKS!
THERE ISN'T ANYTHING
A WOODCHUCK CAN'T DO!

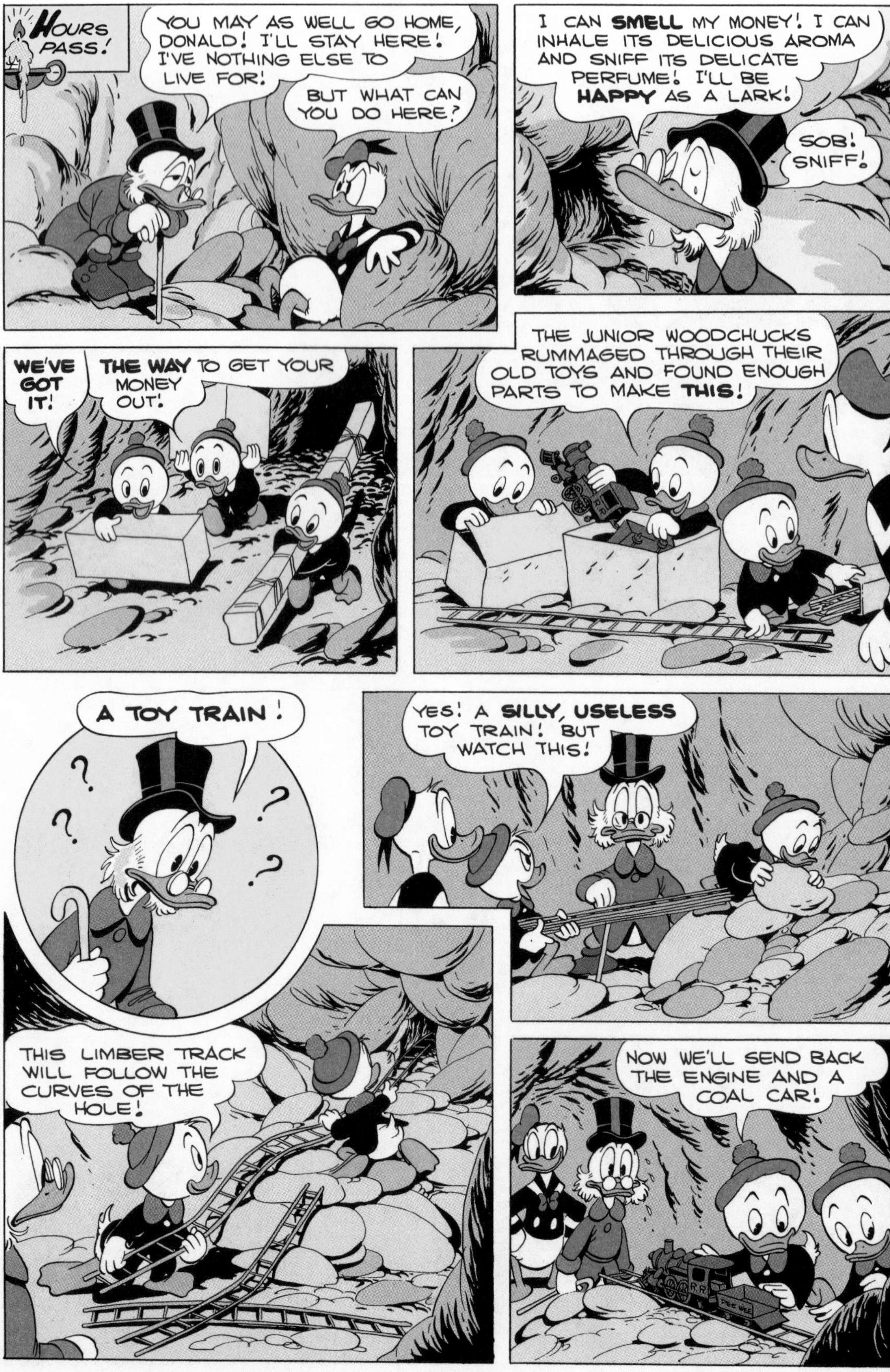
HOURS PASS!
YOU MAY AS WELL GO HOME, DONALD! I'LL STAY HERE! I'VE NOTHING ELSE TO LIVE FOR!
BUT WHAT CAN YOU DO HERE?
I CAN SMELL MY MONEY! I CAN INHALE ITS DELICIOUS AROMA AND SNIFF ITS DELICATE PERFUME! I'LL BE HAPPY AS A LARK!
SOB! SNIFF!
WE'VE GOT IT!
THE WAY TO GET YOUR MONEY OUT!
THE JUNIOR WOODCHUCKS RUMMAGED THROUGH THEIR OLD TOYS AND FOUND ENOUGH PARTS TO MAKE THIS!
A TOY TRAIN!
YES! A SILLY, USELESS TOY TRAIN! BUT WATCH THIS!
THIS LIMBER TRACK WILL FOLLOW THE CURVES OF THE HOLE!
NOW WE'LL SEND BACK THE ENGINE AND A COAL CAR!

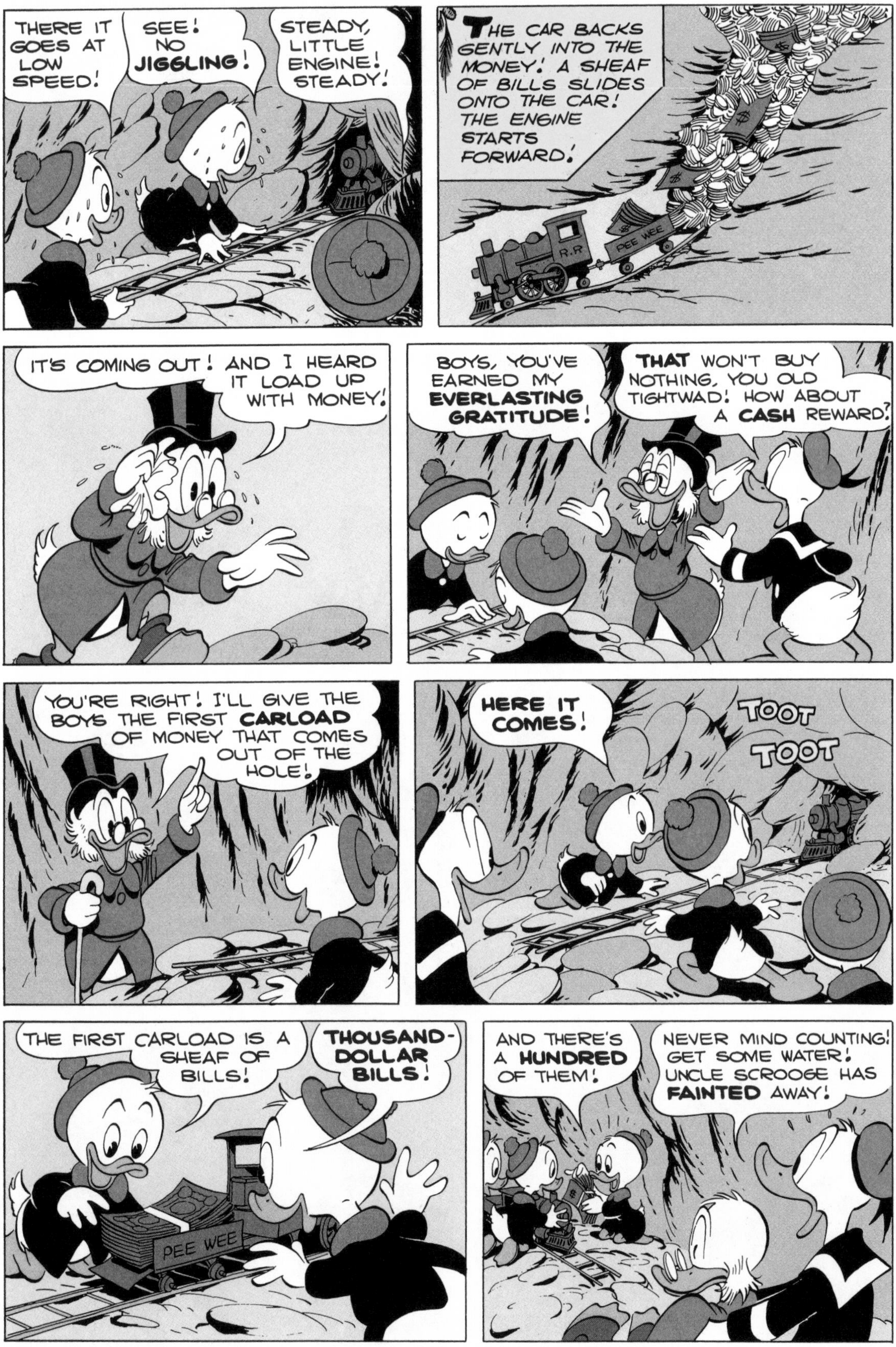
THERE IT GOES AT LOW SPEED!
SEE! NO JIGGLING!
STEADY, LITTLE ENGINE! STEADY!
THE CAR BACKS GENTLY INTO THE MONEY! A SHEAF OF BILLS SLIDES ONTO THE CAR! THE ENGINE STARTS FORWARD!
R.R
PEE WEE
IT'S COMING OUT! AND I HEARD IT LOAD UP WITH MONEY!
BOYS, YOU'VE EARNED MY EVERLASTING GRATITUDE!
THAT WON'T BUY NOTHING, YOU OLD TIGHTWAD! HOW ABOUT A CASH REWARD?
YOU'RE RIGHT! I'LL GIVE THE BOYS THE FIRST CARLOAD OF MONEY THAT COMES OUT OF THE HOLE!
HERE IT COMES!
TOOT
TOOT
THE FIRST CARLOAD IS A SHEAF OF BILLS!
THOUSAND-DOLLAR BILLS!
PEE WEE
AND THERE'S A HUNDRED OF THEM!
NEVER MIND COUNTING! GET SOME WATER! UNCLE SCROOGE HAS FAINTED AWAY!

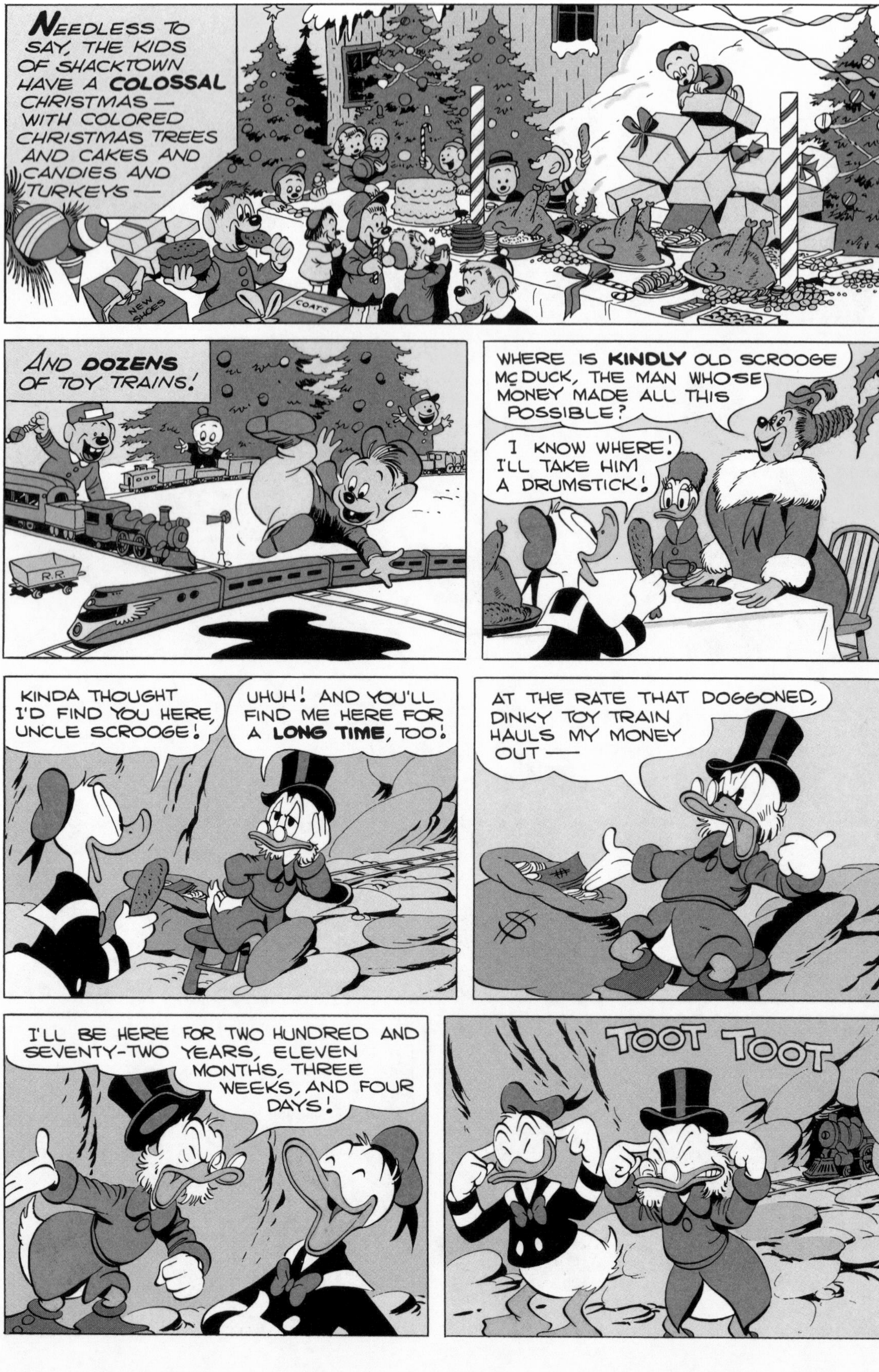
NEEDLESS TO SAY, THE KIDS OF SHACKTOWN HAVE A **COLOSSAL** CHRISTMAS — WITH COLORED CHRISTMAS TREES AND CAKES AND CANDIES AND TURKEYS —
NEW SHOES
COATS
AND **DOZENS** OF TOY TRAINS!
R.R.
WHERE IS **KINDLY** OLD SCROOGE McDUCK, THE MAN WHOSE MONEY MADE ALL THIS POSSIBLE?
I KNOW WHERE! I'LL TAKE HIM A DRUMSTICK!
KINDA THOUGHT I'D FIND YOU HERE, UNCLE SCROOGE!
UHUH! AND YOU'LL FIND ME HERE FOR A **LONG TIME**, TOO!
AT THE RATE THAT DOGGONED, DINKY TOY TRAIN HAULS MY MONEY OUT —
I'LL BE HERE FOR TWO HUNDRED AND SEVENTY-TWO YEARS, ELEVEN MONTHS, THREE WEEKS, AND FOUR DAYS!
TOOT TOOT

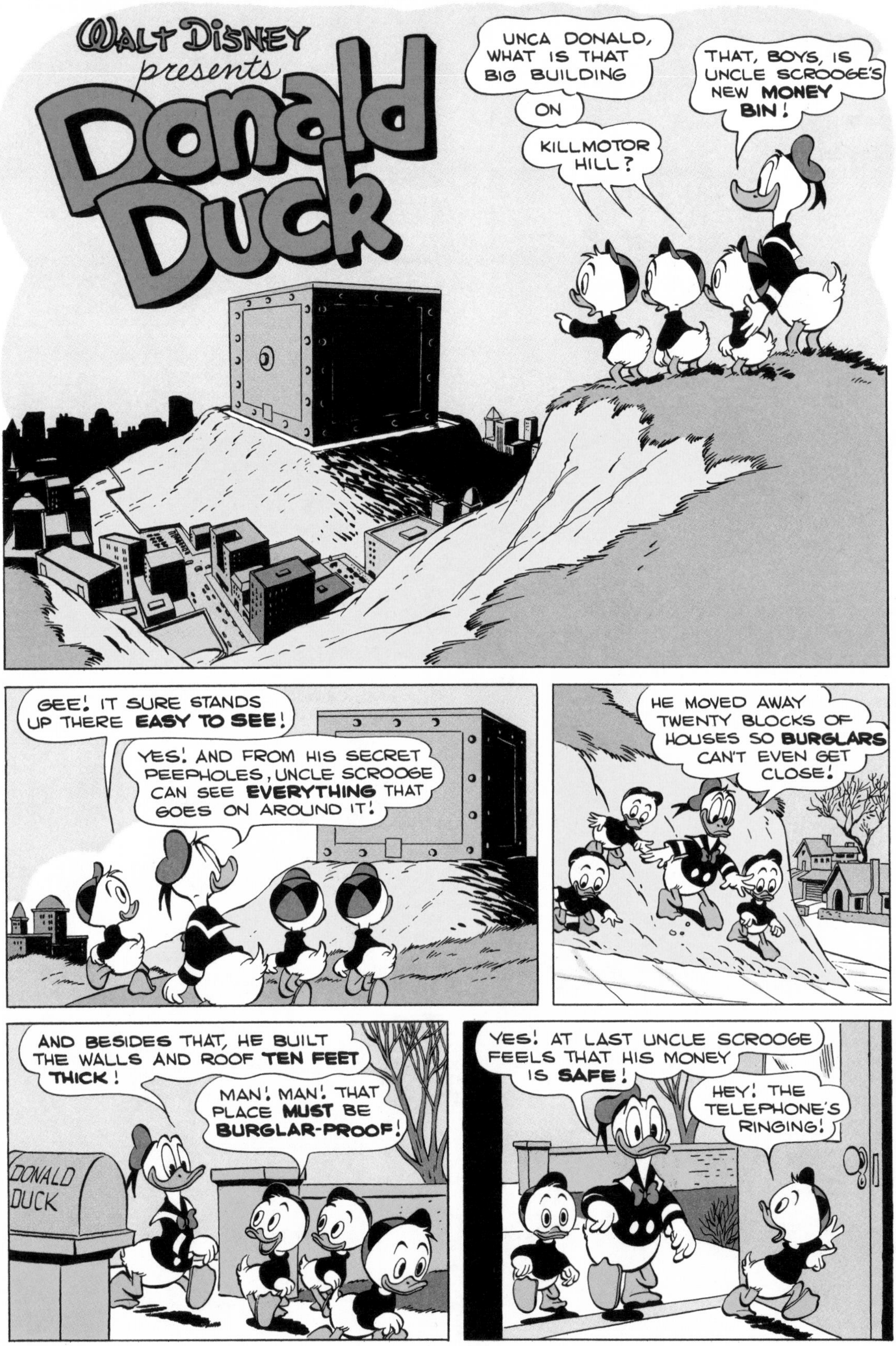
WALT DISNEY
presents
Donald Duck
UNCA DONALD, WHAT IS THAT BIG BUILDING
ON
KILLMOTOR HILL?
THAT, BOYS, IS UNCLE SCROOGE'S NEW MONEY BIN!
GEE! IT SURE STANDS UP THERE EASY TO SEE!
YES! AND FROM HIS SECRET PEEPHOLES, UNCLE SCROOGE CAN SEE EVERYTHING THAT GOES ON AROUND IT!
HE MOVED AWAY TWENTY BLOCKS OF HOUSES SO BURGLARS CAN'T EVEN GET CLOSE!
AND BESIDES THAT, HE BUILT THE WALLS AND ROOF TEN FEET THICK!
MAN! MAN! THAT PLACE MUST BE BURGLAR-PROOF!
DONALD DUCK
YES! AT LAST UNCLE SCROOGE FEELS THAT HIS MONEY IS SAFE!
HEY! THE TELEPHONE'S RINGING!

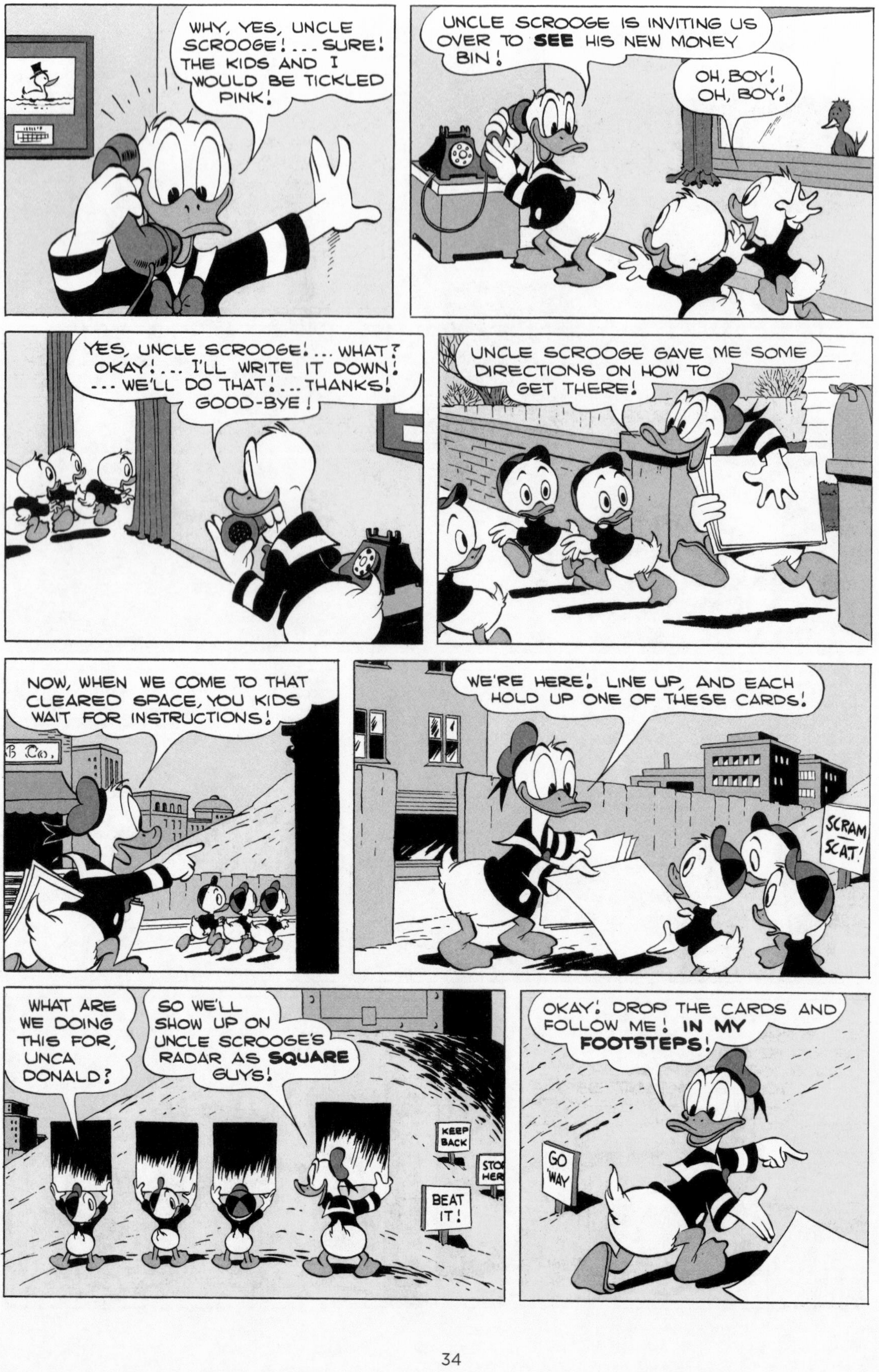
WHY, YES, UNCLE SCROOGE! ... SURE! THE KIDS AND I WOULD BE TICKLED PINK!
UNCLE SCROOGE IS INVITING US OVER TO **SEE** HIS NEW MONEY BIN!
OH, BOY! OH, BOY!
YES, UNCLE SCROOGE! ... WHAT? OKAY! ... I'LL WRITE IT DOWN! ... WE'LL DO THAT! ... THANKS! GOOD-BYE!
UNCLE SCROOGE GAVE ME SOME DIRECTIONS ON HOW TO GET THERE!
NOW, WHEN WE COME TO THAT CLEARED SPACE, YOU KIDS WAIT FOR INSTRUCTIONS!
WE'RE HERE! LINE UP, AND EACH HOLD UP ONE OF THESE CARDS!
SCRAM
SCAT!
WHAT ARE WE DOING THIS FOR, UNCA DONALD?
SO WE'LL SHOW UP ON UNCLE SCROOGE'S RADAR AS **SQUARE** GUYS!
KEEP BACK
BEAT IT!
OKAY! DROP THE CARDS AND FOLLOW ME! **IN MY FOOTSTEPS**!
GO 'WAY

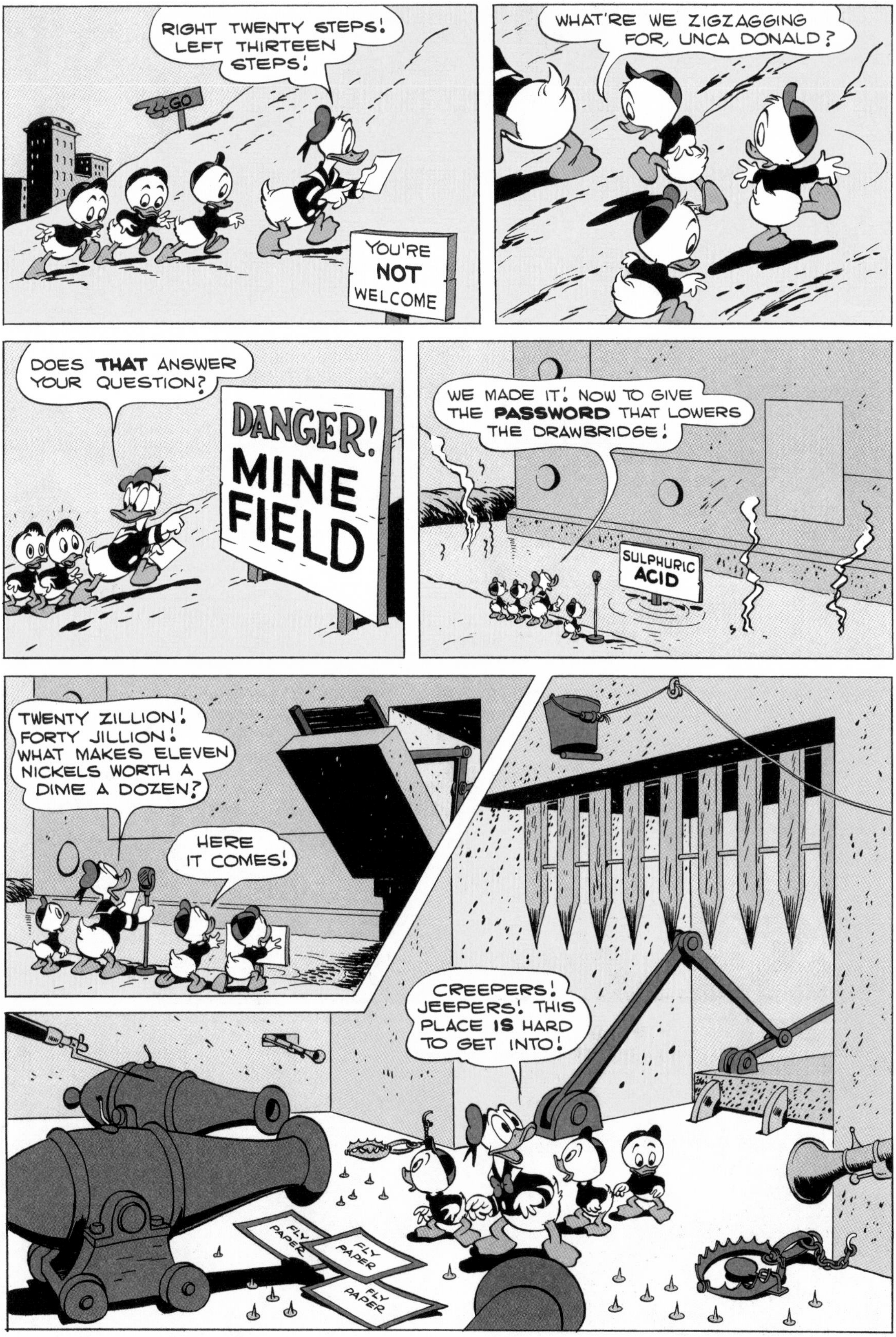
RIGHT TWENTY STEPS! LEFT THIRTEEN STEPS!
GO
YOU'RE NOT WELCOME
WHAT'RE WE ZIGZAGGING FOR, UNCA DONALD?
DOES THAT ANSWER YOUR QUESTION?
DANGER! MINE FIELD
WE MADE IT! NOW TO GIVE THE PASSWORD THAT LOWERS THE DRAWBRIDGE!
SULPHURIC ACID
TWENTY ZILLION! FORTY JILLION! WHAT MAKES ELEVEN NICKELS WORTH A DIME A DOZEN?
HERE IT COMES!
CREEPERS! JEEPERS! THIS PLACE IS HARD TO GET INTO!
FLY PAPER
FLY PAPER
FLY PAPER

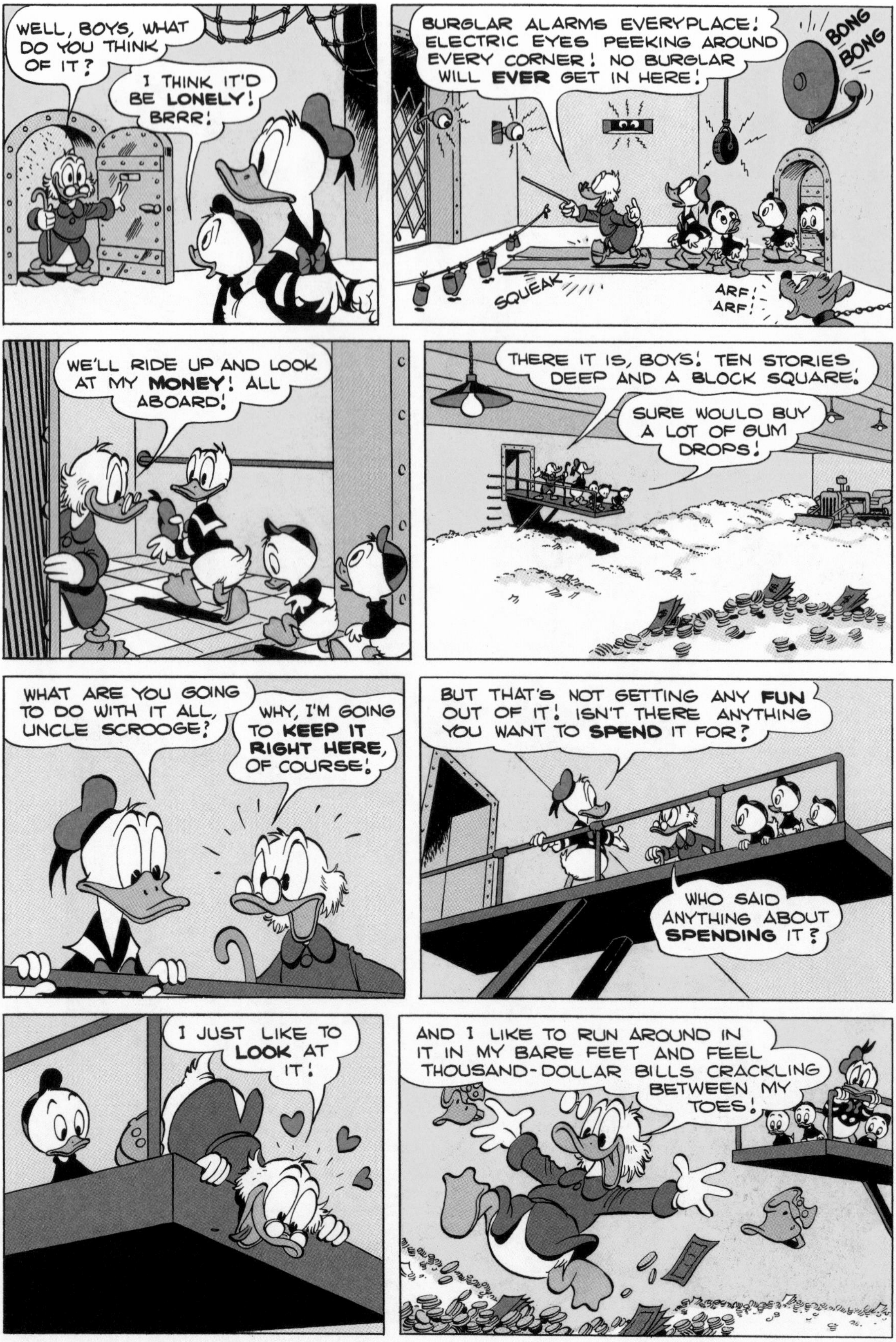
WELL, BOYS, WHAT DO YOU THINK OF IT?
I THINK IT'D BE **LONELY**! BRRR!
BURGLAR ALARMS EVERYPLACE! ELECTRIC EYES PEEKING AROUND EVERY CORNER! NO BURGLAR WILL **EVER** GET IN HERE!
BONG BONG
SQUEAK
ARF! ARF!
WE'LL RIDE UP AND LOOK AT MY **MONEY**! ALL ABOARD!
THERE IT IS, BOYS! TEN STORIES DEEP AND A BLOCK SQUARE!
SURE WOULD BUY A LOT OF GUM DROPS!
WHAT ARE YOU GOING TO DO WITH IT ALL, UNCLE SCROOGE?
WHY, I'M GOING TO **KEEP IT RIGHT HERE**, OF COURSE!
BUT THAT'S NOT GETTING ANY **FUN** OUT OF IT! ISN'T THERE ANYTHING YOU WANT TO **SPEND** IT FOR?
WHO SAID ANYTHING ABOUT **SPENDING** IT?
I JUST LIKE TO **LOOK** AT IT!
AND I LIKE TO RUN AROUND IN IT IN MY BARE FEET AND FEEL THOUSAND-DOLLAR BILLS CRACKLING BETWEEN MY TOES!

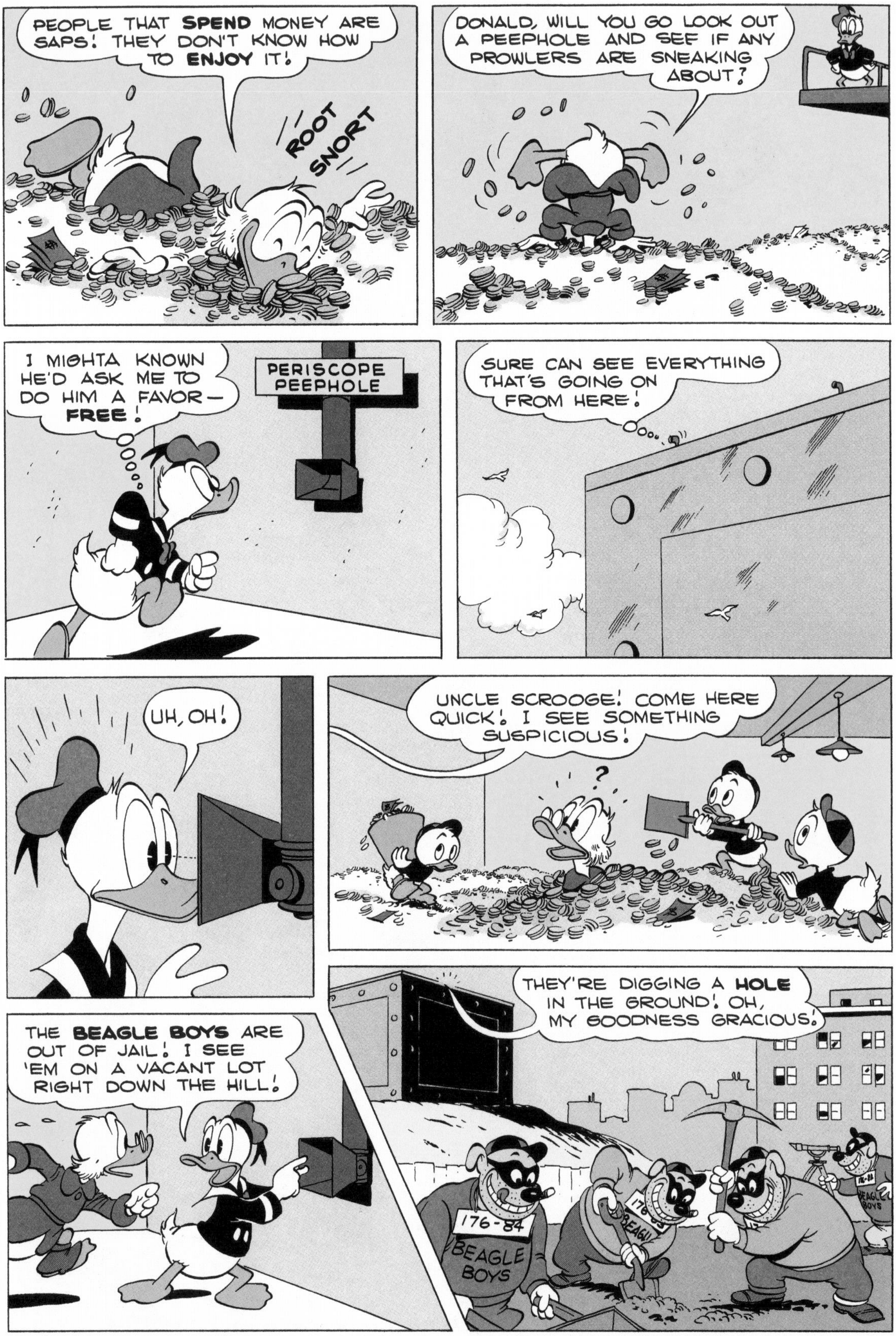
PEOPLE THAT SPEND MONEY ARE SAPS! THEY DON'T KNOW HOW TO ENJOY IT!
ROOT
SNORT
DONALD, WILL YOU GO LOOK OUT A PEEPHOLE AND SEE IF ANY PROWLERS ARE SNEAKING ABOUT?
I MIGHTA KNOWN HE'D ASK ME TO DO HIM A FAVOR— FREE!
PERISCOPE PEEPHOLE
SURE CAN SEE EVERYTHING THAT'S GOING ON FROM HERE!
UH, OH!
UNCLE SCROOGE! COME HERE QUICK! I SEE SOMETHING SUSPICIOUS!
?
THE BEAGLE BOYS ARE OUT OF JAIL! I SEE 'EM ON A VACANT LOT RIGHT DOWN THE HILL!
THEY'RE DIGGING A HOLE IN THE GROUND! OH, MY GOODNESS GRACIOUS!
176-84
BEAGLE BOYS

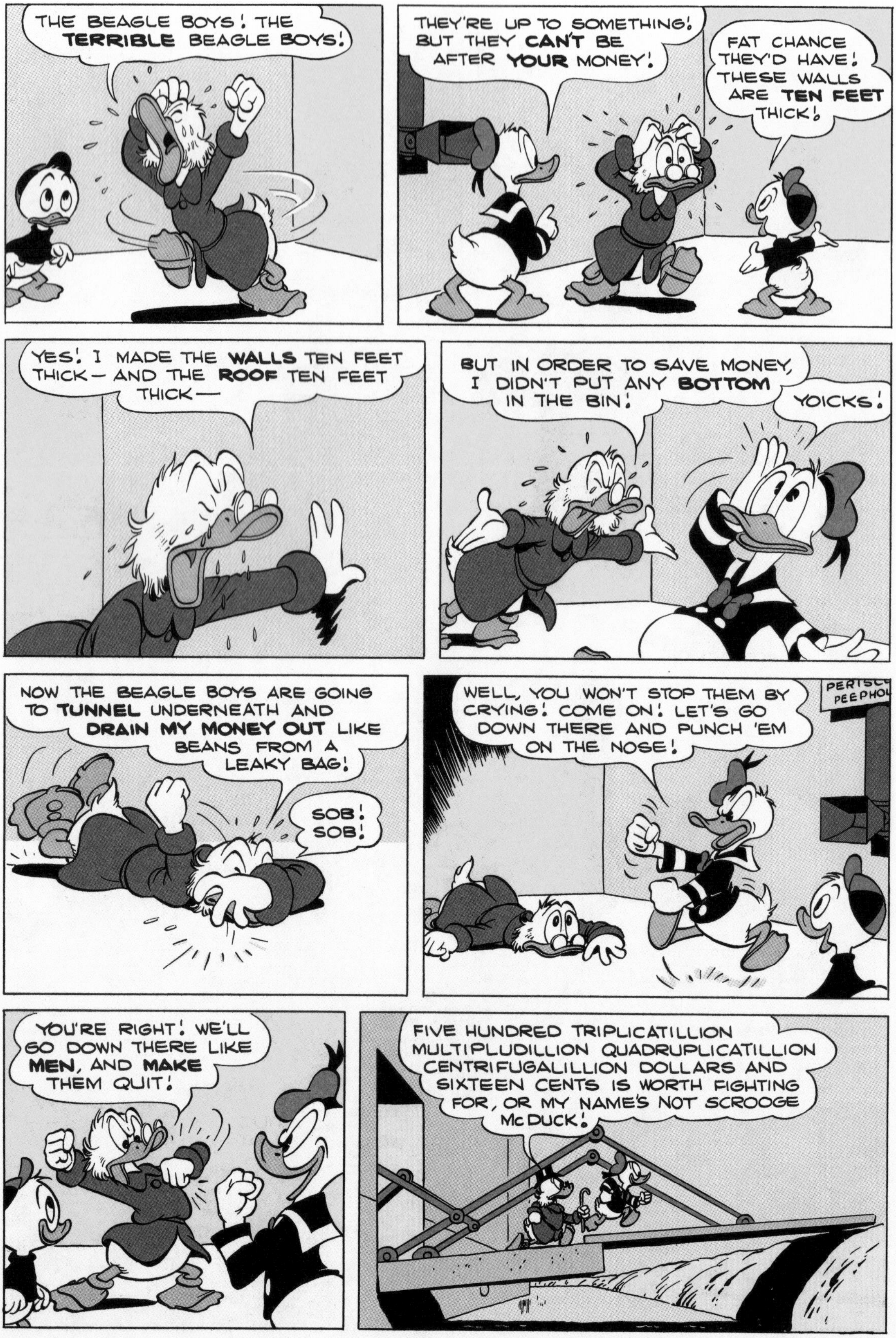
THE BEAGLE BOYS! THE TERRIBLE BEAGLE BOYS!
THEY'RE UP TO SOMETHING! BUT THEY CAN'T BE AFTER YOUR MONEY!
FAT CHANCE THEY'D HAVE! THESE WALLS ARE TEN FEET THICK!
YES! I MADE THE WALLS TEN FEET THICK— AND THE ROOF TEN FEET THICK—
BUT IN ORDER TO SAVE MONEY, I DIDN'T PUT ANY BOTTOM IN THE BIN!
YOICKS!
NOW THE BEAGLE BOYS ARE GOING TO TUNNEL UNDERNEATH AND DRAIN MY MONEY OUT LIKE BEANS FROM A LEAKY BAG!
SOB! SOB!
WELL, YOU WON'T STOP THEM BY CRYING! COME ON! LET'S GO DOWN THERE AND PUNCH 'EM ON THE NOSE!
YOU'RE RIGHT! WE'LL GO DOWN THERE LIKE MEN, AND MAKE THEM QUIT!
FIVE HUNDRED TRIPLICATILLION MULTIPLUDILLION QUADRUPLICATILLION CENTRIFUGALILLION DOLLARS AND SIXTEEN CENTS IS WORTH FIGHTING FOR, OR MY NAME'S NOT SCROOGE McDUCK!

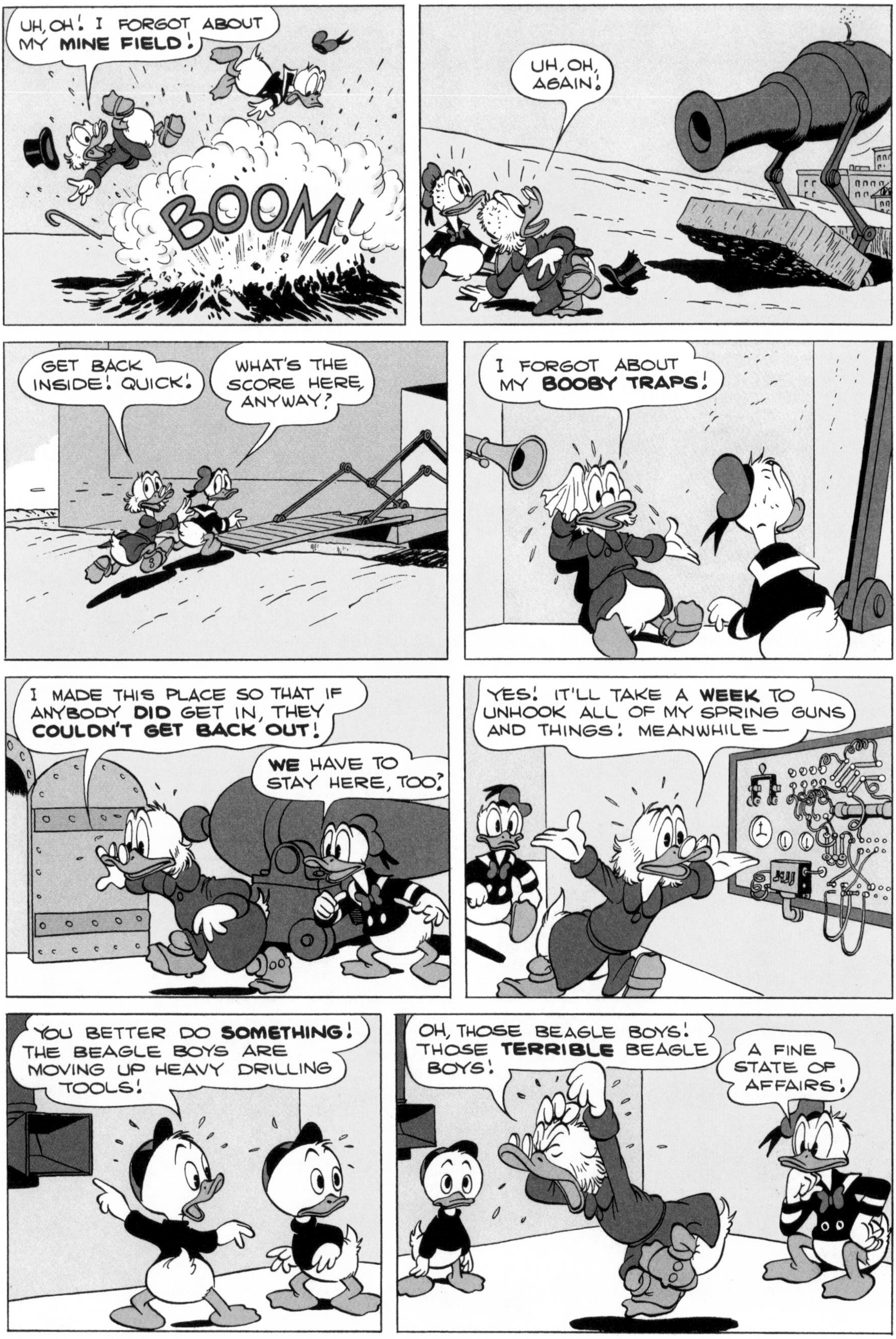
UH, OH! I FORGOT ABOUT MY **MINE FIELD**!
BOOM!
UH, OH, AGAIN!
GET BACK INSIDE! QUICK!
WHAT'S THE SCORE HERE, ANYWAY?
I FORGOT ABOUT MY **BOOBY TRAPS**!
I MADE THIS PLACE SO THAT IF ANYBODY **DID** GET IN, THEY **COULDN'T GET BACK OUT**!
WE HAVE TO STAY HERE, TOO?
YES! IT'LL TAKE A **WEEK** TO UNHOOK ALL OF MY SPRING GUNS AND THINGS! MEANWHILE—
YOU BETTER DO **SOMETHING**! THE BEAGLE BOYS ARE MOVING UP HEAVY DRILLING TOOLS!
OH, THOSE BEAGLE BOYS! THOSE **TERRIBLE** BEAGLE BOYS!
A FINE STATE OF AFFAIRS!

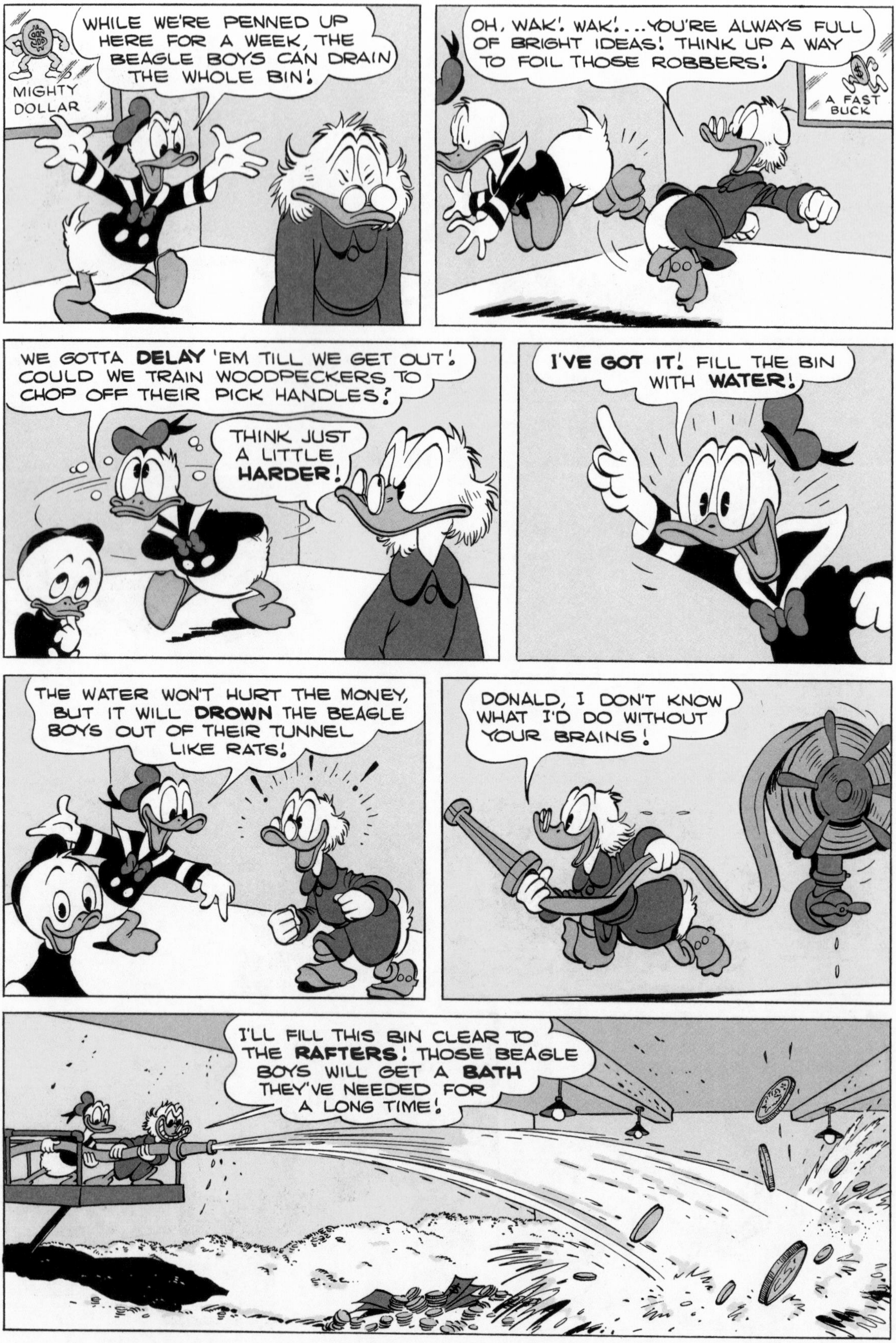
MIGHTY DOLLAR
WHILE WE'RE PENNED UP HERE FOR A WEEK, THE BEAGLE BOYS CAN DRAIN THE WHOLE BIN!
OH, WAK! WAK!...YOU'RE ALWAYS FULL OF BRIGHT IDEAS! THINK UP A WAY TO FOIL THOSE ROBBERS!
A FAST BUCK
WE GOTTA DELAY 'EM TILL WE GET OUT! COULD WE TRAIN WOODPECKERS TO CHOP OFF THEIR PICK HANDLES?
THINK JUST A LITTLE HARDER!
I'VE GOT IT! FILL THE BIN WITH WATER!
THE WATER WON'T HURT THE MONEY, BUT IT WILL DROWN THE BEAGLE BOYS OUT OF THEIR TUNNEL LIKE RATS!
DONALD, I DON'T KNOW WHAT I'D DO WITHOUT YOUR BRAINS!
I'LL FILL THIS BIN CLEAR TO THE RAFTERS! THOSE BEAGLE BOYS WILL GET A BATH THEY'VE NEEDED FOR A LONG TIME!

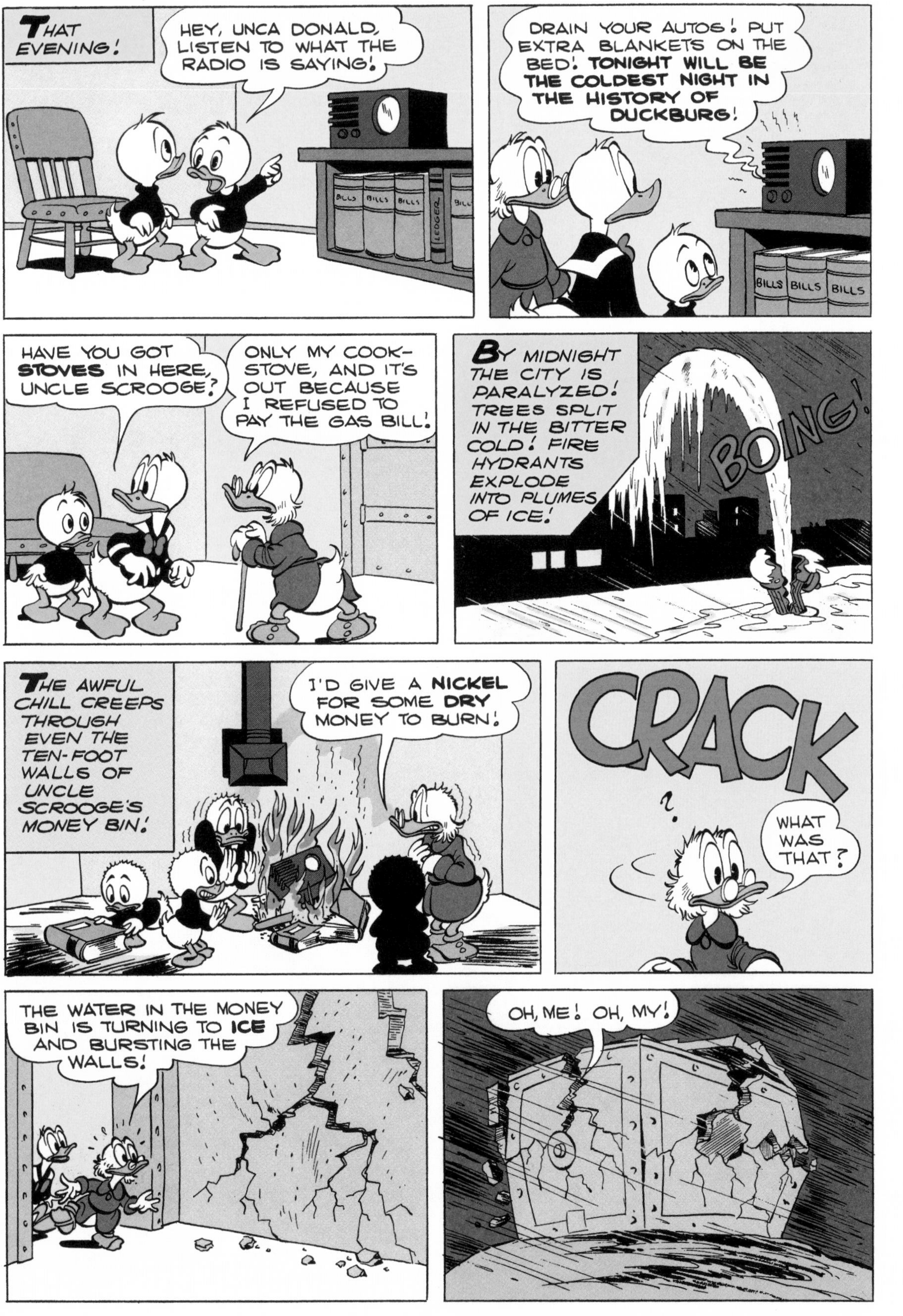

THAT EVENING!
HEY, UNCA DONALD, LISTEN TO WHAT THE RADIO IS SAYING!
BILLS BILLS BILLS LEDGER BILLS
DRAIN YOUR AUTOS! PUT EXTRA BLANKETS ON THE BED! TONIGHT WILL BE THE COLDEST NIGHT IN THE HISTORY OF DUCKBURG!
BILLS BILLS BILLS
HAVE YOU GOT STOVES IN HERE, UNCLE SCROOGE?
ONLY MY COOK-STOVE, AND IT'S OUT BECAUSE I REFUSED TO PAY THE GAS BILL!
BY MIDNIGHT THE CITY IS PARALYZED! TREES SPLIT IN THE BITTER COLD! FIRE HYDRANTS EXPLODE INTO PLUMES OF ICE!
BOING!
THE AWFUL CHILL CREEPS THROUGH EVEN THE TEN-FOOT WALLS OF UNCLE SCROOGE'S MONEY BIN!
I'D GIVE A NICKEL FOR SOME DRY MONEY TO BURN!
CRACK
WHAT WAS THAT?
THE WATER IN THE MONEY BIN IS TURNING TO ICE AND BURSTING THE WALLS!
OH, ME! OH, MY!

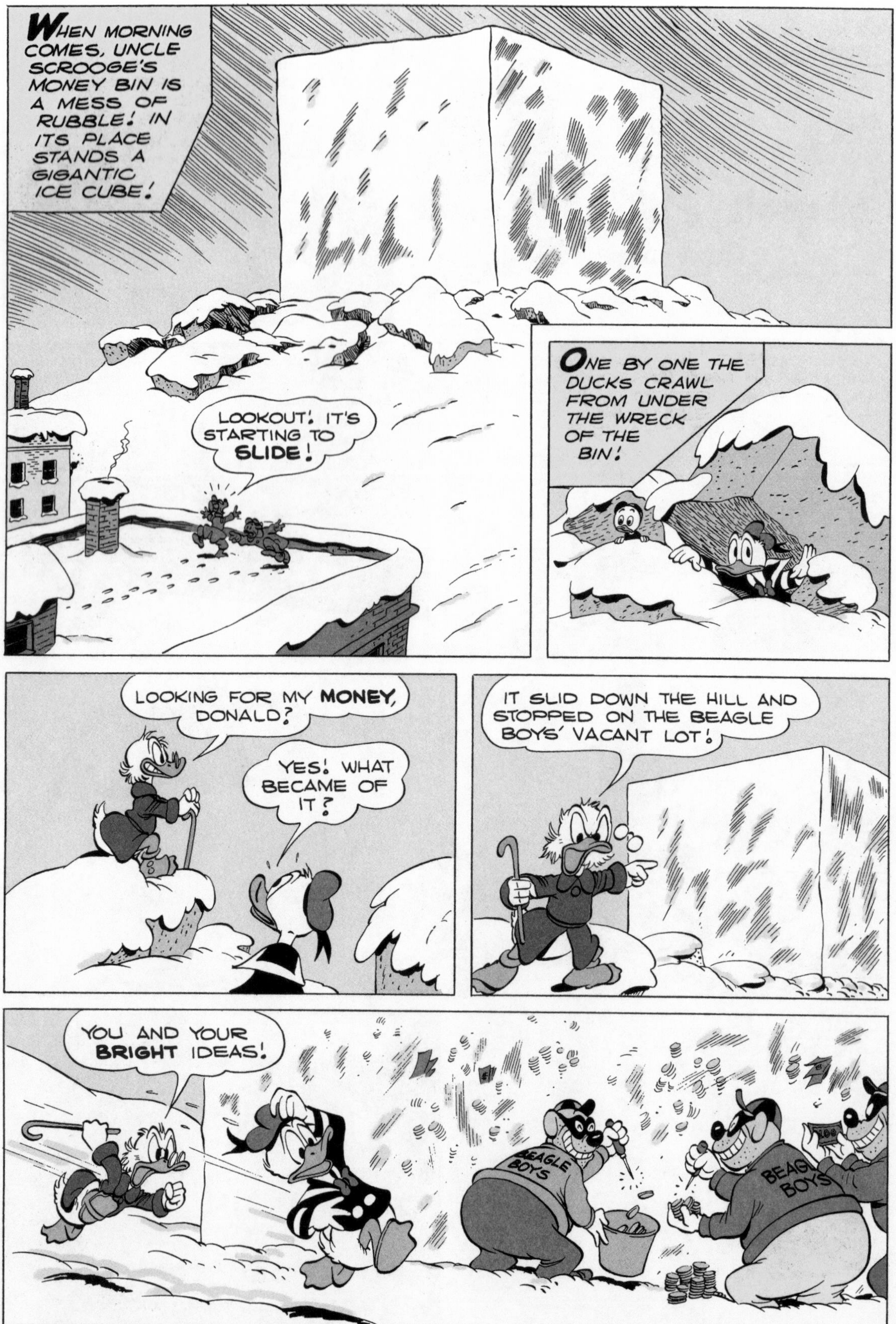
WHEN MORNING COMES, UNCLE SCROOGE'S MONEY BIN IS A MESS OF RUBBLE! IN ITS PLACE STANDS A GIGANTIC ICE CUBE!
LOOKOUT! IT'S STARTING TO SLIDE!
ONE BY ONE THE DUCKS CRAWL FROM UNDER THE WRECK OF THE BIN!
LOOKING FOR MY MONEY, DONALD?
YES! WHAT BECAME OF IT?
IT SLID DOWN THE HILL AND STOPPED ON THE BEAGLE BOYS' VACANT LOT!
YOU AND YOUR BRIGHT IDEAS!
BEAGLE BOYS
BEAG BOYS

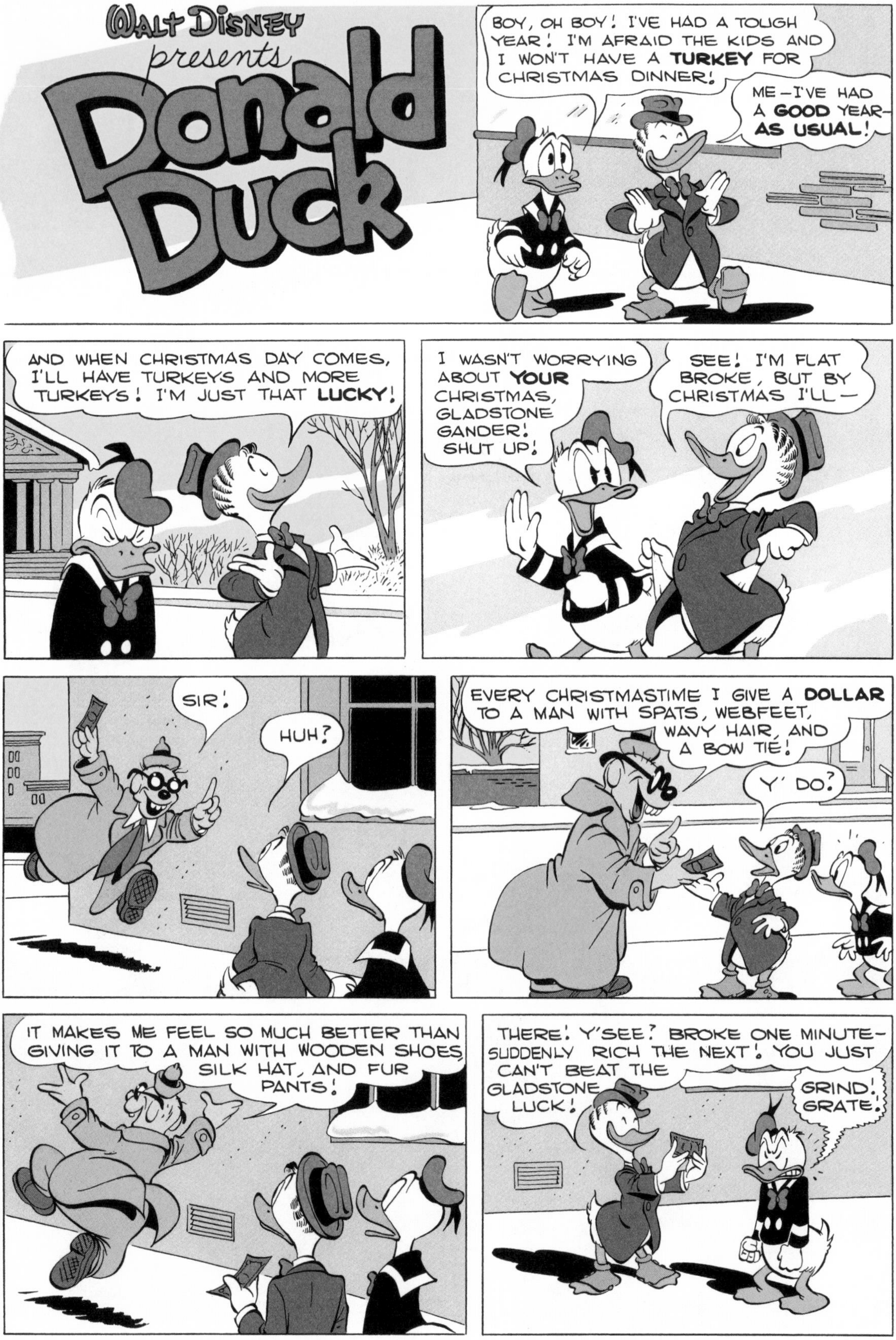
WALT DISNEY presents Donald Duck
BOY, OH BOY! I'VE HAD A TOUGH YEAR! I'M AFRAID THE KIDS AND I WON'T HAVE A TURKEY FOR CHRISTMAS DINNER!
ME—I'VE HAD A GOOD YEAR—AS USUAL!
AND WHEN CHRISTMAS DAY COMES, I'LL HAVE TURKEYS AND MORE TURKEYS! I'M JUST THAT LUCKY!
I WASN'T WORRYING ABOUT YOUR CHRISTMAS, GLADSTONE GANDER! SHUT UP!
SEE! I'M FLAT BROKE, BUT BY CHRISTMAS I'LL—
SIR!
HUH?
EVERY CHRISTMASTIME I GIVE A DOLLAR TO A MAN WITH SPATS, WEBFEET, WAVY HAIR, AND A BOW TIE!
Y' DO?
IT MAKES ME FEEL SO MUCH BETTER THAN GIVING IT TO A MAN WITH WOODEN SHOES, SILK HAT, AND FUR PANTS!
THERE! Y'SEE? BROKE ONE MINUTE—SUDDENLY RICH THE NEXT! YOU JUST CAN'T BEAT THE GLADSTONE LUCK!
GRIND! GRATE!

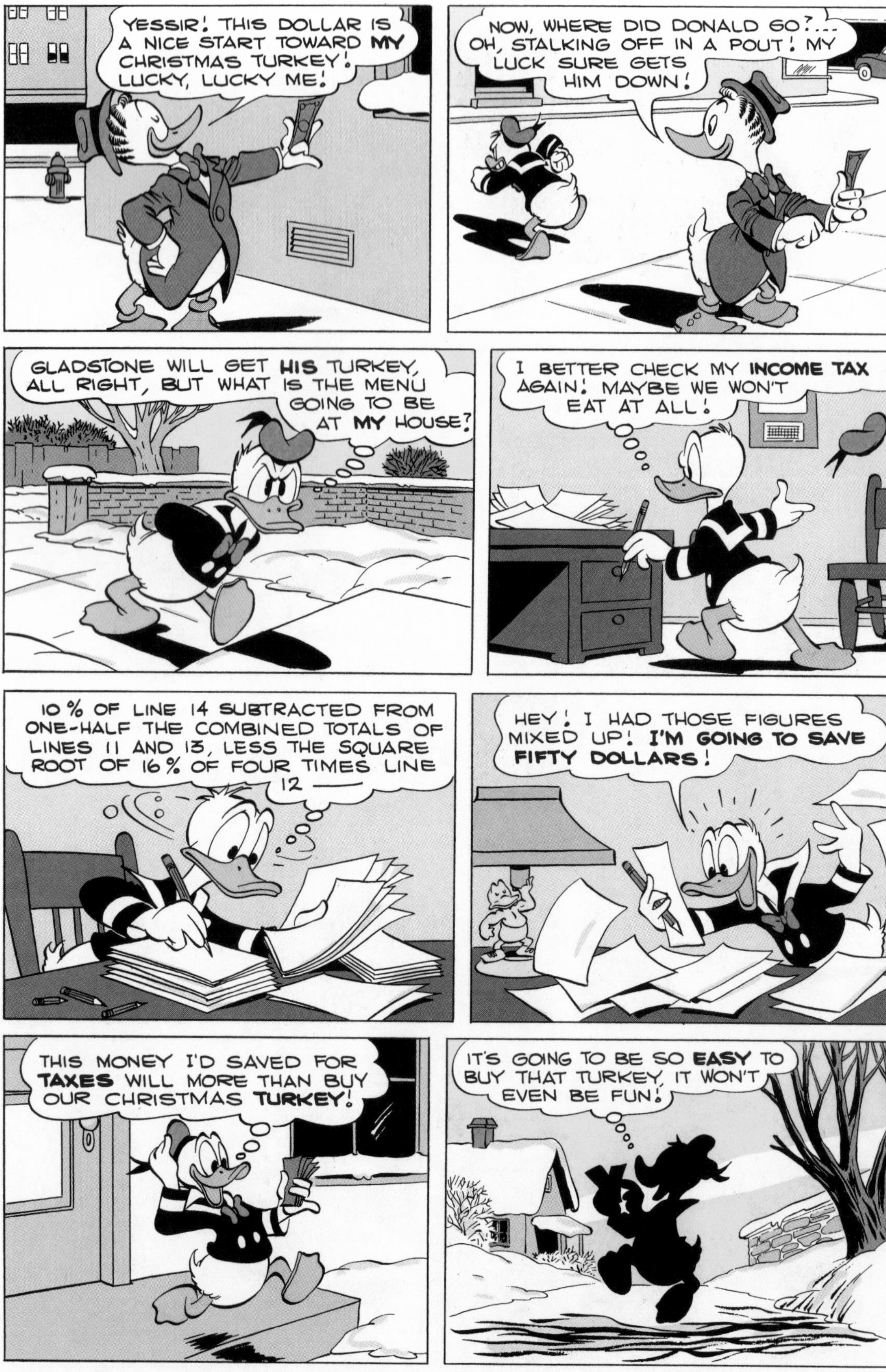

YESSIR! THIS DOLLAR IS A NICE START TOWARD MY CHRISTMAS TURKEY! LUCKY, LUCKY ME!
NOW, WHERE DID DONALD GO?... OH, STALKING OFF IN A POUT! MY LUCK SURE GETS HIM DOWN!
GLADSTONE WILL GET HIS TURKEY, ALL RIGHT, BUT WHAT IS THE MENU GOING TO BE AT MY HOUSE?
I BETTER CHECK MY INCOME TAX AGAIN! MAYBE WE WON'T EAT AT ALL!
10 % OF LINE 14 SUBTRACTED FROM ONE-HALF THE COMBINED TOTALS OF LINES 11 AND 13, LESS THE SQUARE ROOT OF 16 % OF FOUR TIMES LINE 12 ——
HEY! I HAD THOSE FIGURES MIXED UP! I'M GOING TO SAVE FIFTY DOLLARS!
THIS MONEY I'D SAVED FOR TAXES WILL MORE THAN BUY OUR CHRISTMAS TURKEY!
IT'S GOING TO BE SO EASY TO BUY THAT TURKEY, IT WON'T EVEN BE FUN!

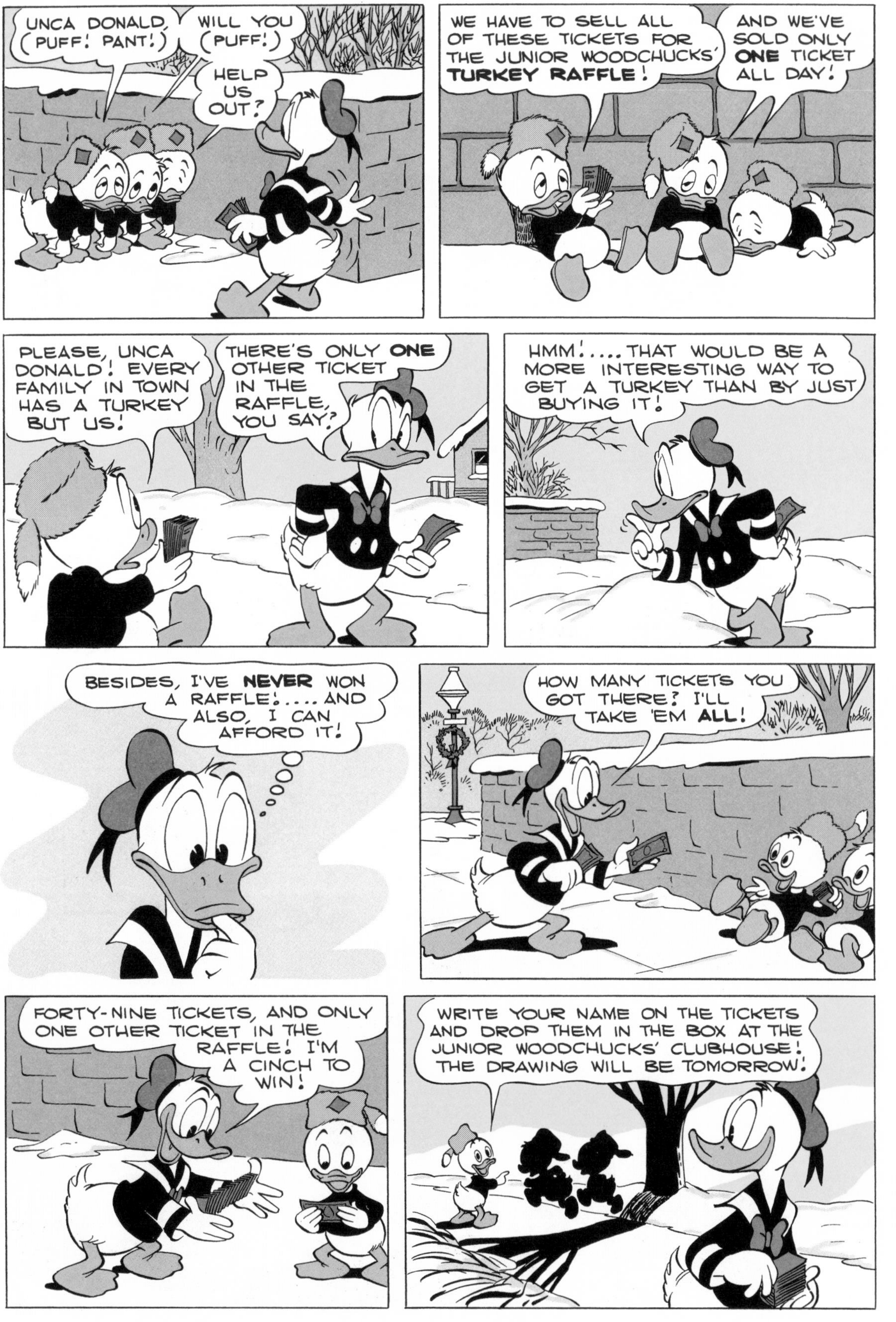
UNCA DONALD, (PUFF! PANT!)
WILL YOU (PUFF!)
HELP US OUT?
WE HAVE TO SELL ALL OF THESE TICKETS FOR THE JUNIOR WOODCHUCKS' TURKEY RAFFLE!
AND WE'VE SOLD ONLY ONE TICKET ALL DAY!
PLEASE, UNCA DONALD! EVERY FAMILY IN TOWN HAS A TURKEY BUT US!
THERE'S ONLY ONE OTHER TICKET IN THE RAFFLE, YOU SAY?
HMM!.....THAT WOULD BE A MORE INTERESTING WAY TO GET A TURKEY THAN BY JUST BUYING IT!
BESIDES, I'VE NEVER WON A RAFFLE!.....AND ALSO, I CAN AFFORD IT!
HOW MANY TICKETS YOU GOT THERE? I'LL TAKE 'EM ALL!
FORTY-NINE TICKETS, AND ONLY ONE OTHER TICKET IN THE RAFFLE! I'M A CINCH TO WIN!
WRITE YOUR NAME ON THE TICKETS AND DROP THEM IN THE BOX AT THE JUNIOR WOODCHUCKS' CLUBHOUSE! THE DRAWING WILL BE TOMORROW!

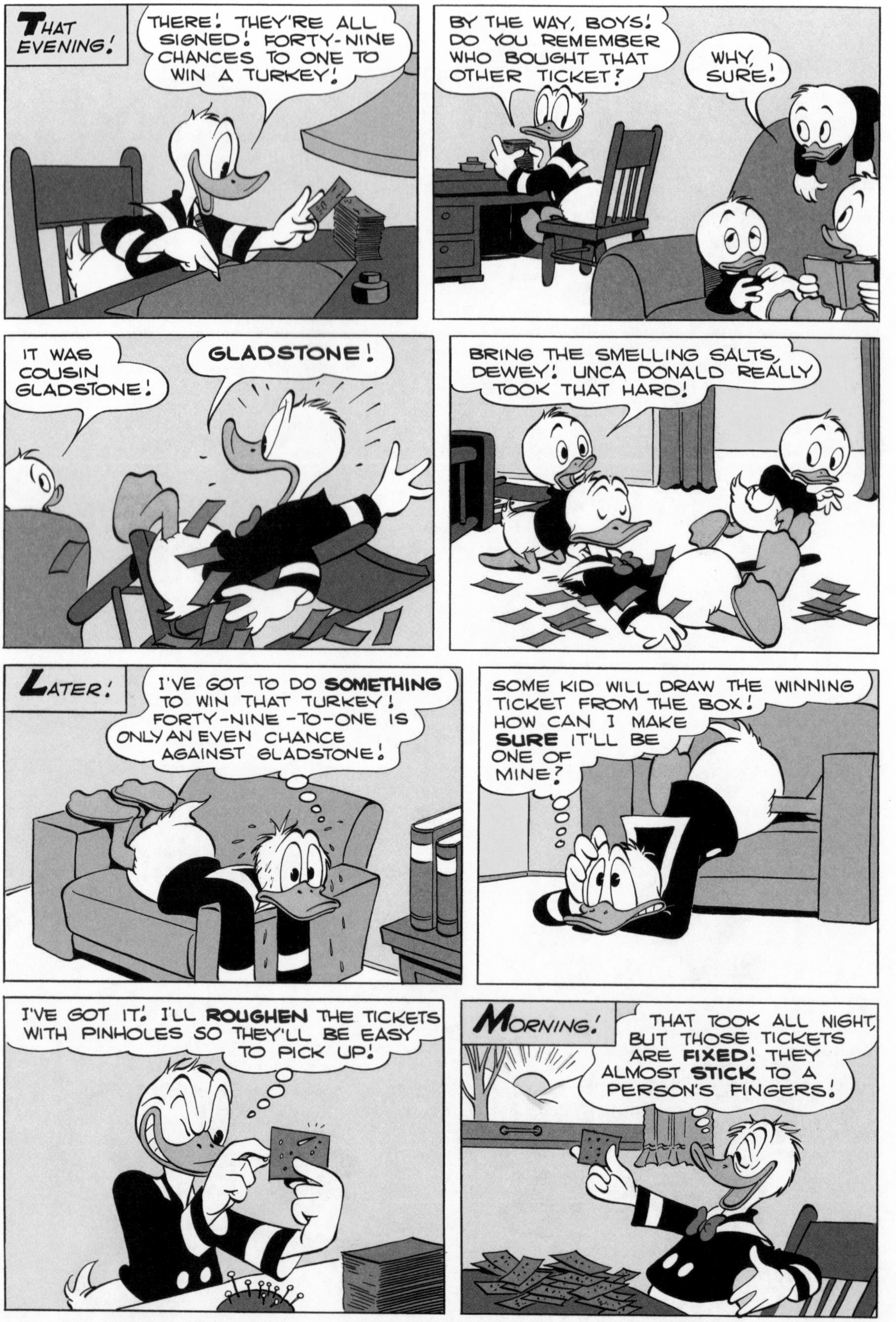
THAT EVENING!
THERE! THEY'RE ALL SIGNED! FORTY-NINE CHANCES TO ONE TO WIN A TURKEY!
BY THE WAY, BOYS! DO YOU REMEMBER WHO BOUGHT THAT OTHER TICKET?
WHY, SURE!
IT WAS COUSIN GLADSTONE!
GLADSTONE!
BRING THE SMELLING SALTS, DEWEY! UNCA DONALD REALLY TOOK THAT HARD!
LATER!
I'VE GOT TO DO SOMETHING TO WIN THAT TURKEY! FORTY-NINE-TO-ONE IS ONLY AN EVEN CHANCE AGAINST GLADSTONE!
SOME KID WILL DRAW THE WINNING TICKET FROM THE BOX! HOW CAN I MAKE SURE IT'LL BE ONE OF MINE?
I'VE GOT IT! I'LL ROUGHEN THE TICKETS WITH PINHOLES SO THEY'LL BE EASY TO PICK UP!
MORNING!
THAT TOOK ALL NIGHT, BUT THOSE TICKETS ARE FIXED! THEY ALMOST STICK TO A PERSON'S FINGERS!

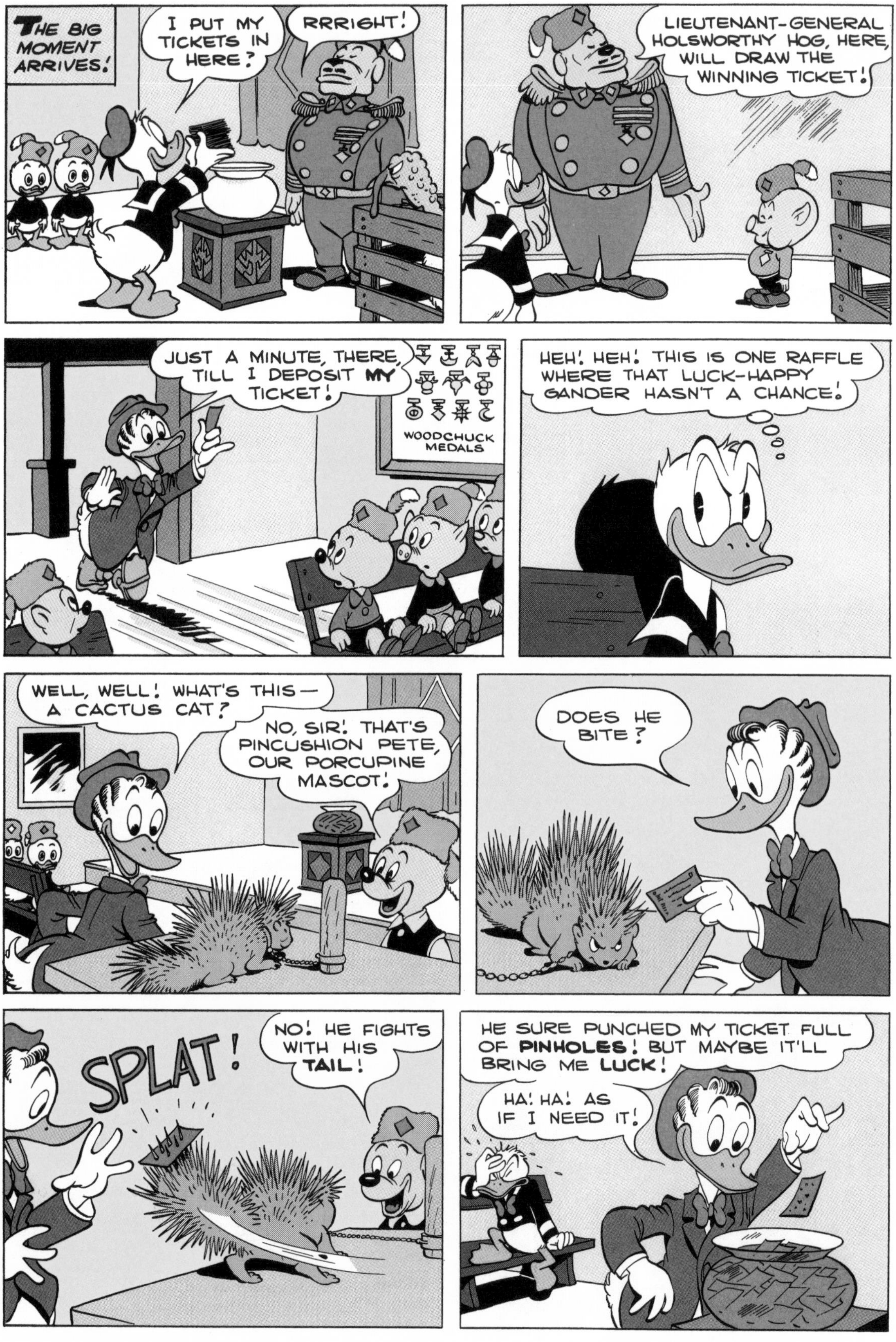
THE BIG MOMENT ARRIVES!
I PUT MY TICKETS IN HERE?
RRRIGHT!
LIEUTENANT-GENERAL HOLSWORTHY HOG, HERE, WILL DRAW THE WINNING TICKET!
JUST A MINUTE, THERE, TILL I DEPOSIT MY TICKET!
WOODCHUCK MEDALS
HEH! HEH! THIS IS ONE RAFFLE WHERE THAT LUCK-HAPPY GANDER HASN'T A CHANCE!
WELL, WELL! WHAT'S THIS— A CACTUS CAT?
NO, SIR! THAT'S PINCUSHION PETE, OUR PORCUPINE MASCOT!
DOES HE BITE?
SPLAT!
NO! HE FIGHTS WITH HIS TAIL!
HE SURE PUNCHED MY TICKET FULL OF PINHOLES! BUT MAYBE IT'LL BRING ME LUCK!
HA! HA! AS IF I NEED IT!

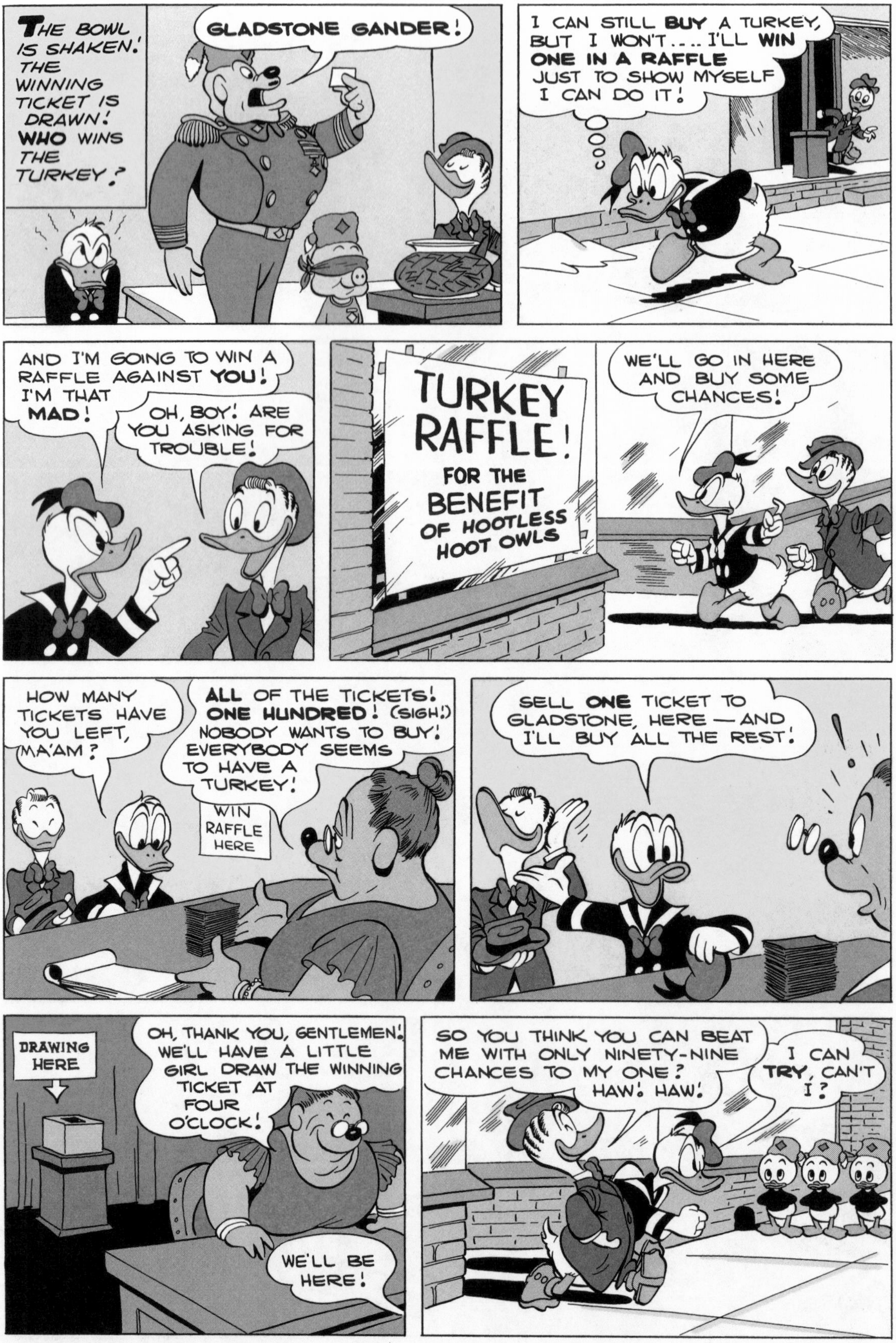
THE BOWL IS SHAKEN! THE WINNING TICKET IS DRAWN! WHO WINS THE TURKEY?
GLADSTONE GANDER!
I CAN STILL BUY A TURKEY, BUT I WON'T.... I'LL WIN ONE IN A RAFFLE JUST TO SHOW MYSELF I CAN DO IT!
AND I'M GOING TO WIN A RAFFLE AGAINST YOU! I'M THAT MAD!
OH, BOY! ARE YOU ASKING FOR TROUBLE!
TURKEY RAFFLE! FOR THE BENEFIT OF HOOTLESS HOOT OWLS
WE'LL GO IN HERE AND BUY SOME CHANCES!
HOW MANY TICKETS HAVE YOU LEFT, MA'AM?
ALL OF THE TICKETS! ONE HUNDRED! (SIGH!) NOBODY WANTS TO BUY! EVERYBODY SEEMS TO HAVE A TURKEY!
WIN RAFFLE HERE
SELL ONE TICKET TO GLADSTONE, HERE — AND I'LL BUY ALL THE REST!
!
DRAWING HERE
OH, THANK YOU, GENTLEMEN! WE'LL HAVE A LITTLE GIRL DRAW THE WINNING TICKET AT FOUR O'CLOCK!
WE'LL BE HERE!
SO YOU THINK YOU CAN BEAT ME WITH ONLY NINETY-NINE CHANCES TO MY ONE? HAW! HAW!
I CAN TRY, CAN'T I?

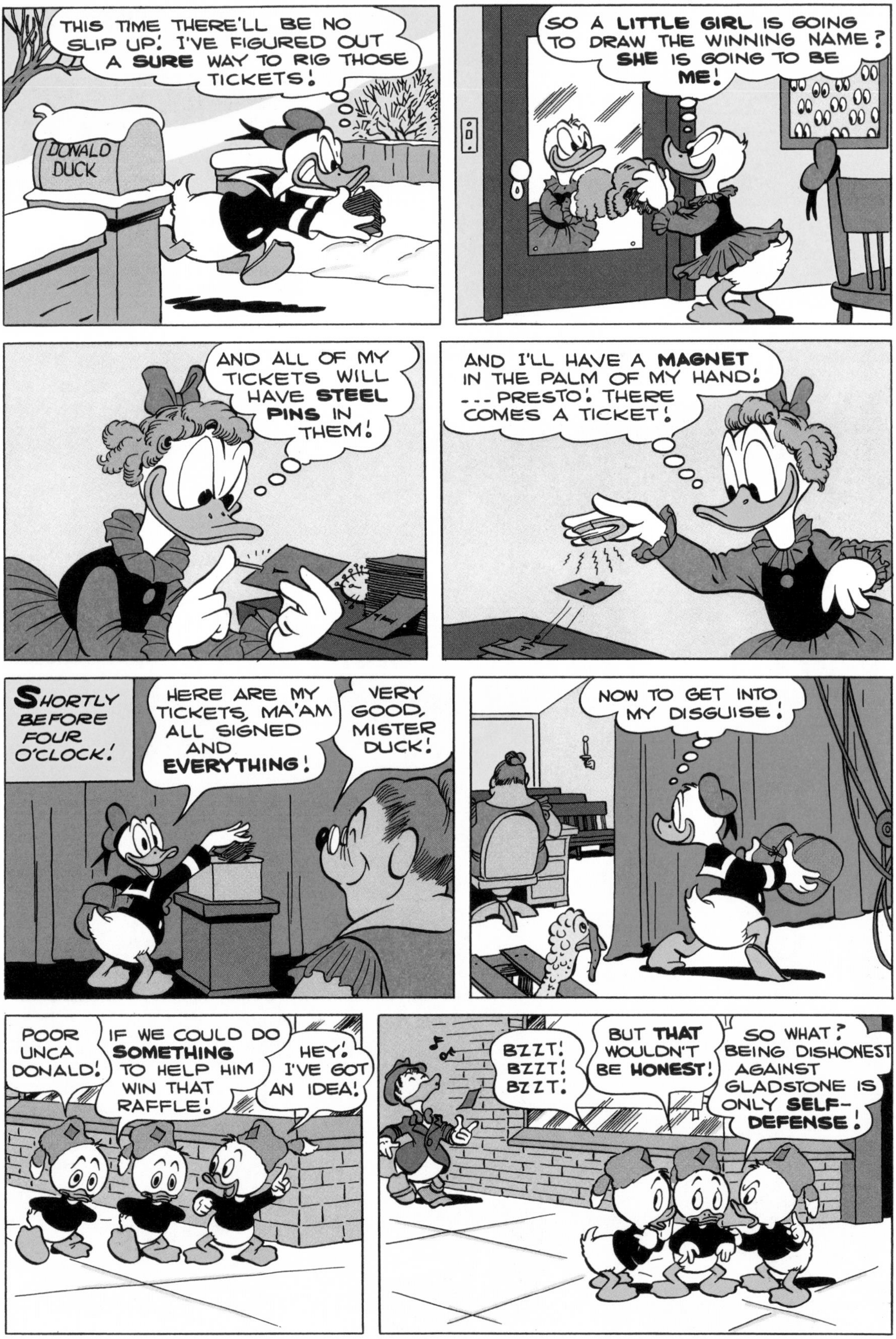
THIS TIME THERE'LL BE NO SLIP UP! I'VE FIGURED OUT A **SURE** WAY TO RIG THOSE TICKETS!
DONALD DUCK
SO A **LITTLE GIRL** IS GOING TO DRAW THE WINNING NAME? **SHE** IS GOING TO BE **ME**!
AND ALL OF MY TICKETS WILL HAVE **STEEL PINS** IN THEM!
AND I'LL HAVE A **MAGNET** IN THE PALM OF MY HAND! ---PRESTO! THERE COMES A TICKET!
SHORTLY BEFORE FOUR O'CLOCK!
HERE ARE MY TICKETS, MA'AM ALL SIGNED AND **EVERYTHING**!
VERY GOOD, MISTER DUCK!
NOW TO GET INTO MY DISGUISE!
POOR UNCA DONALD!
IF WE COULD DO **SOMETHING** TO HELP HIM WIN THAT RAFFLE!
HEY! I'VE GOT AN IDEA!
BZZT! BZZT! BZZT!
BUT **THAT** WOULDN'T BE **HONEST**!
SO WHAT? BEING DISHONEST AGAINST GLADSTONE IS ONLY **SELF-DEFENSE**!

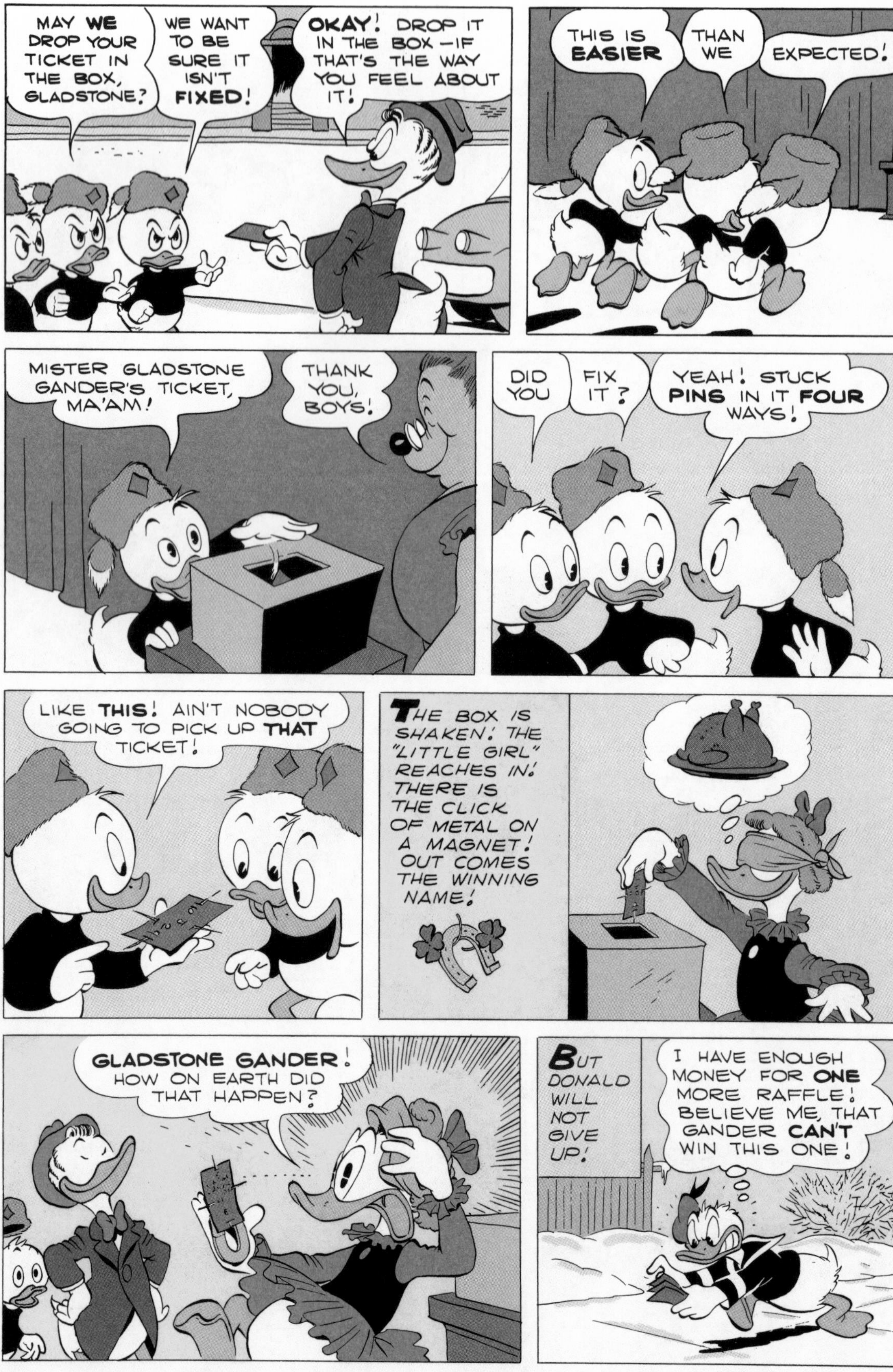
MAY WE DROP YOUR TICKET IN THE BOX, GLADSTONE?
WE WANT TO BE SURE IT ISN'T FIXED!
OKAY! DROP IT IN THE BOX — IF THAT'S THE WAY YOU FEEL ABOUT IT!
THIS IS EASIER
THAN WE
EXPECTED!
MISTER GLADSTONE GANDER'S TICKET, MA'AM!
THANK YOU, BOYS!
DID YOU
FIX IT?
YEAH! STUCK PINS IN IT FOUR WAYS!
LIKE THIS! AIN'T NOBODY GOING TO PICK UP THAT TICKET!
THE BOX IS SHAKEN! THE "LITTLE GIRL" REACHES IN! THERE IS THE CLICK OF METAL ON A MAGNET! OUT COMES THE WINNING NAME!
GLADSTONE GANDER! HOW ON EARTH DID THAT HAPPEN?
BUT DONALD WILL NOT GIVE UP!
I HAVE ENOUGH MONEY FOR ONE MORE RAFFLE! BELIEVE ME, THAT GANDER CAN'T WIN THIS ONE!

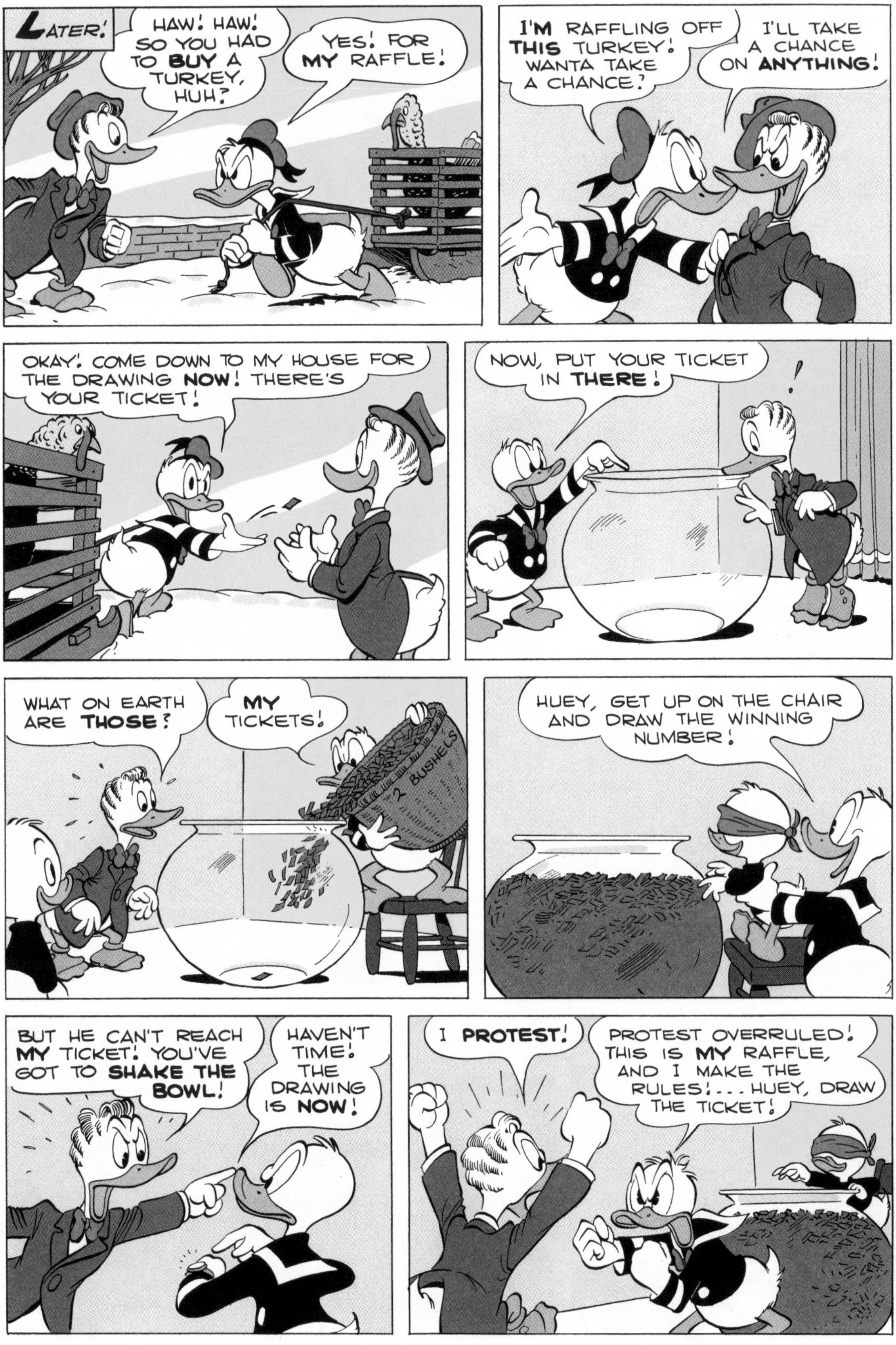
LATER!
HAW! HAW! SO YOU HAD TO BUY A TURKEY, HUH?
YES! FOR MY RAFFLE!
I'M RAFFLING OFF THIS TURKEY! WANTA TAKE A CHANCE?
I'LL TAKE A CHANCE ON ANYTHING!
OKAY! COME DOWN TO MY HOUSE FOR THE DRAWING NOW! THERE'S YOUR TICKET!
NOW, PUT YOUR TICKET IN THERE!
!
WHAT ON EARTH ARE THOSE?
MY TICKETS!
2 BUSHELS
HUEY, GET UP ON THE CHAIR AND DRAW THE WINNING NUMBER!
BUT HE CAN'T REACH MY TICKET! YOU'VE GOT TO SHAKE THE BOWL!
HAVEN'T TIME! THE DRAWING IS NOW!
I PROTEST!
PROTEST OVERRULED! THIS IS MY RAFFLE, AND I MAKE THE RULES!... HUEY, DRAW THE TICKET!

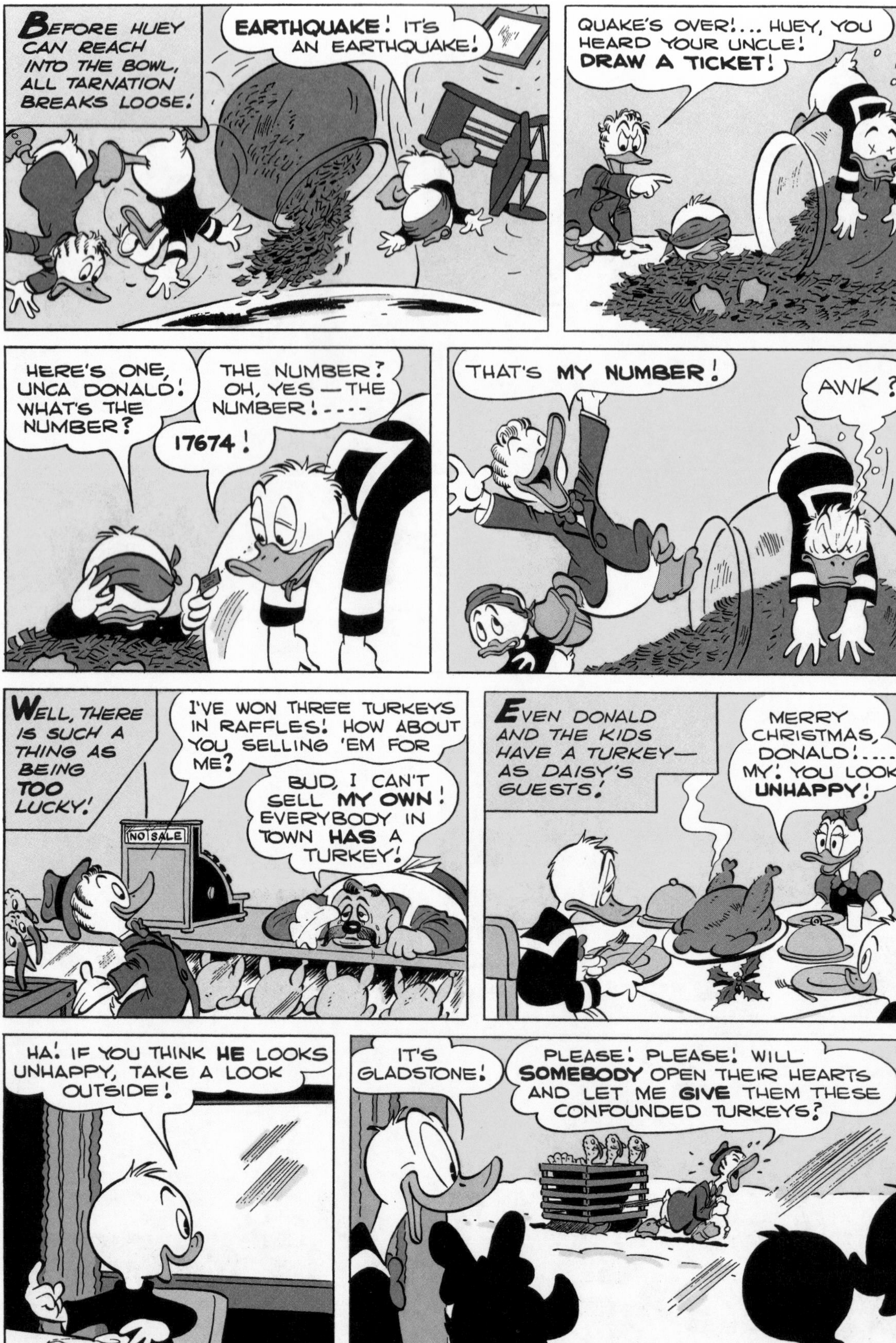
BEFORE HUEY CAN REACH INTO THE BOWL, ALL TARNATION BREAKS LOOSE!
EARTHQUAKE! IT'S AN EARTHQUAKE!
QUAKE'S OVER!... HUEY, YOU HEARD YOUR UNCLE! DRAW A TICKET!
HERE'S ONE, UNCA DONALD! WHAT'S THE NUMBER?
THE NUMBER? OH, YES—THE NUMBER!----
17674!
THAT'S MY NUMBER!
AWK?
WELL, THERE IS SUCH A THING AS BEING TOO LUCKY!
I'VE WON THREE TURKEYS IN RAFFLES! HOW ABOUT YOU SELLING 'EM FOR ME?
NO SALE
BUD, I CAN'T SELL MY OWN! EVERYBODY IN TOWN HAS A TURKEY!
EVEN DONALD AND THE KIDS HAVE A TURKEY— AS DAISY'S GUESTS!
MERRY CHRISTMAS, DONALD!.... MY! YOU LOOK UNHAPPY!
HA! IF YOU THINK HE LOOKS UNHAPPY, TAKE A LOOK OUTSIDE!
IT'S GLADSTONE!
PLEASE! PLEASE! WILL SOMEBODY OPEN THEIR HEARTS AND LET ME GIVE THEM THESE CONFOUNDED TURKEYS?

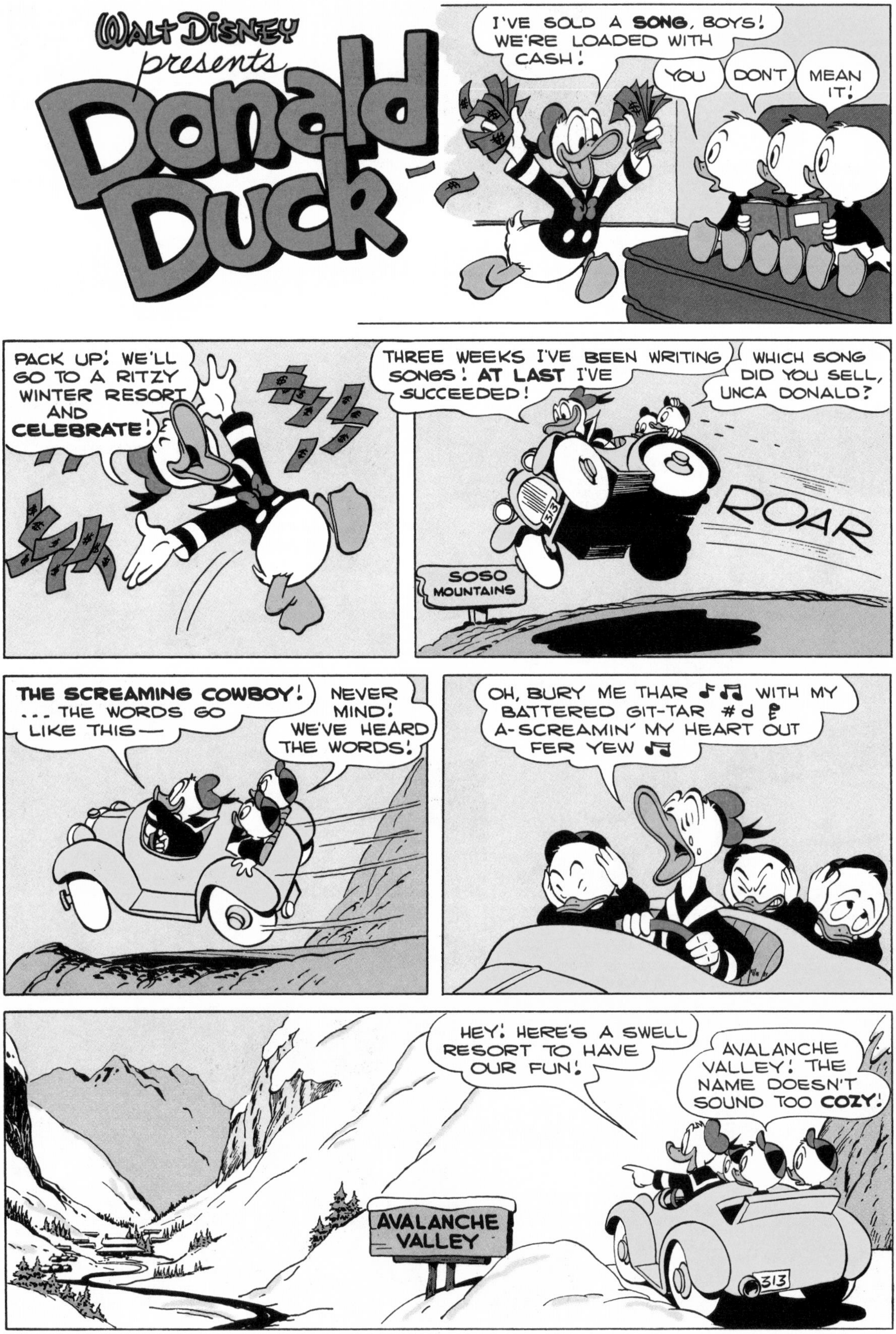
WALT DISNEY
presents
Donald Duck
I'VE SOLD A SONG, BOYS! WE'RE LOADED WITH CASH!
YOU
DON'T
MEAN IT!
PACK UP! WE'LL GO TO A RITZY WINTER RESORT AND CELEBRATE!
THREE WEEKS I'VE BEEN WRITING SONGS! AT LAST I'VE SUCCEEDED!
WHICH SONG DID YOU SELL, UNCA DONALD?
SOSO MOUNTAINS
ROAR
313
THE SCREAMING COWBOY! ... THE WORDS GO LIKE THIS—
NEVER MIND! WE'VE HEARD THE WORDS!
OH, BURY ME THAR WITH MY BATTERED GIT-TAR A-SCREAMIN' MY HEART OUT FER YEW
HEY! HERE'S A SWELL RESORT TO HAVE OUR FUN!
AVALANCHE VALLEY! THE NAME DOESN'T SOUND TOO COZY!
AVALANCHE VALLEY
313

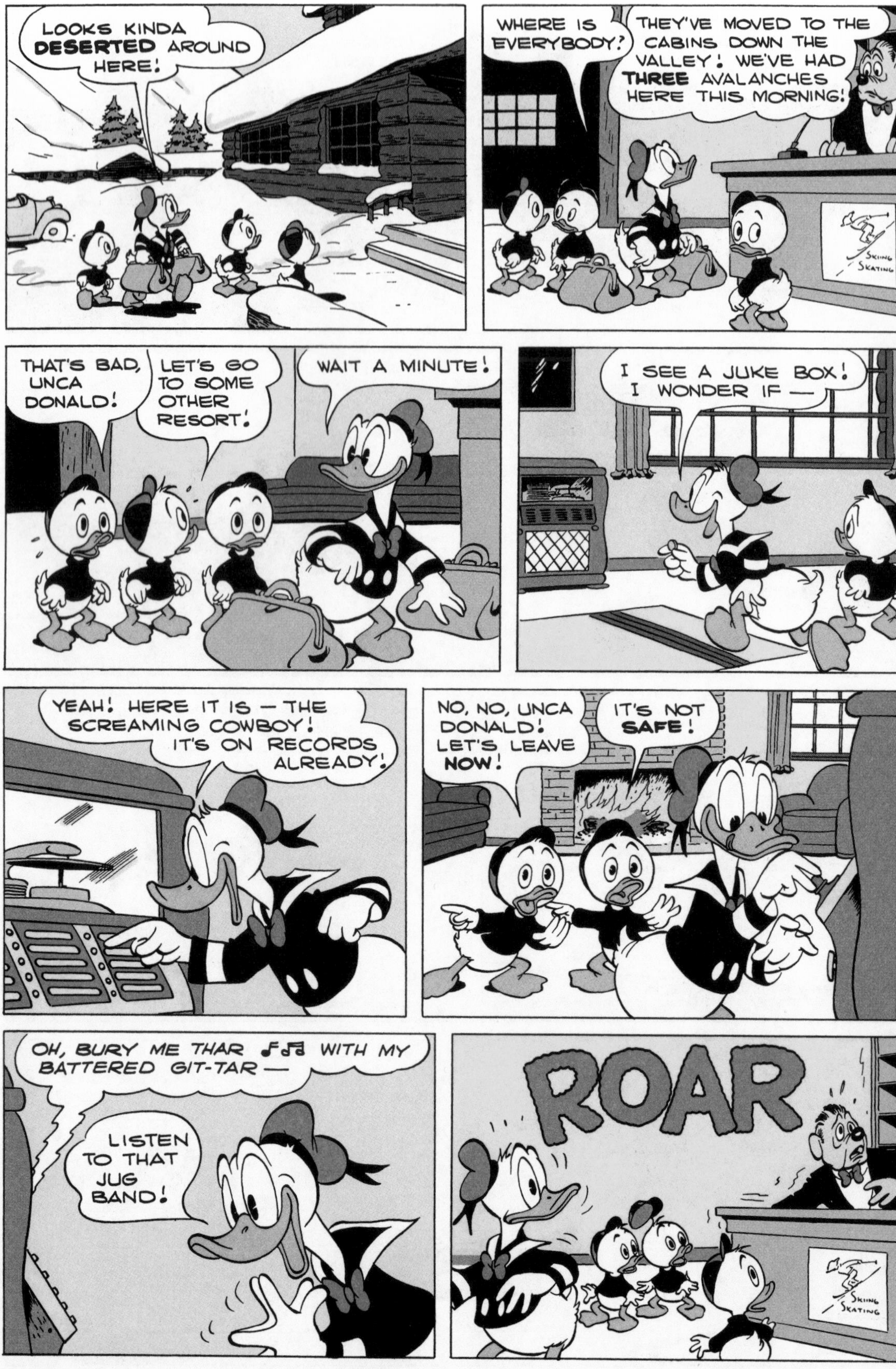
LOOKS KINDA DESERTED AROUND HERE!
WHERE IS EVERYBODY?
THEY'VE MOVED TO THE CABINS DOWN THE VALLEY! WE'VE HAD THREE AVALANCHES HERE THIS MORNING!
SKIING
SKATING
THAT'S BAD, UNCA DONALD!
LET'S GO TO SOME OTHER RESORT!
WAIT A MINUTE!
I SEE A JUKE BOX! I WONDER IF —
YEAH! HERE IT IS — THE SCREAMING COWBOY! IT'S ON RECORDS ALREADY!
NO, NO, UNCA DONALD! LET'S LEAVE NOW!
IT'S NOT SAFE!
OH, BURY ME THAR WITH MY BATTERED GIT-TAR —
LISTEN TO THAT JUG BAND!
ROAR
SKIING
SKATING

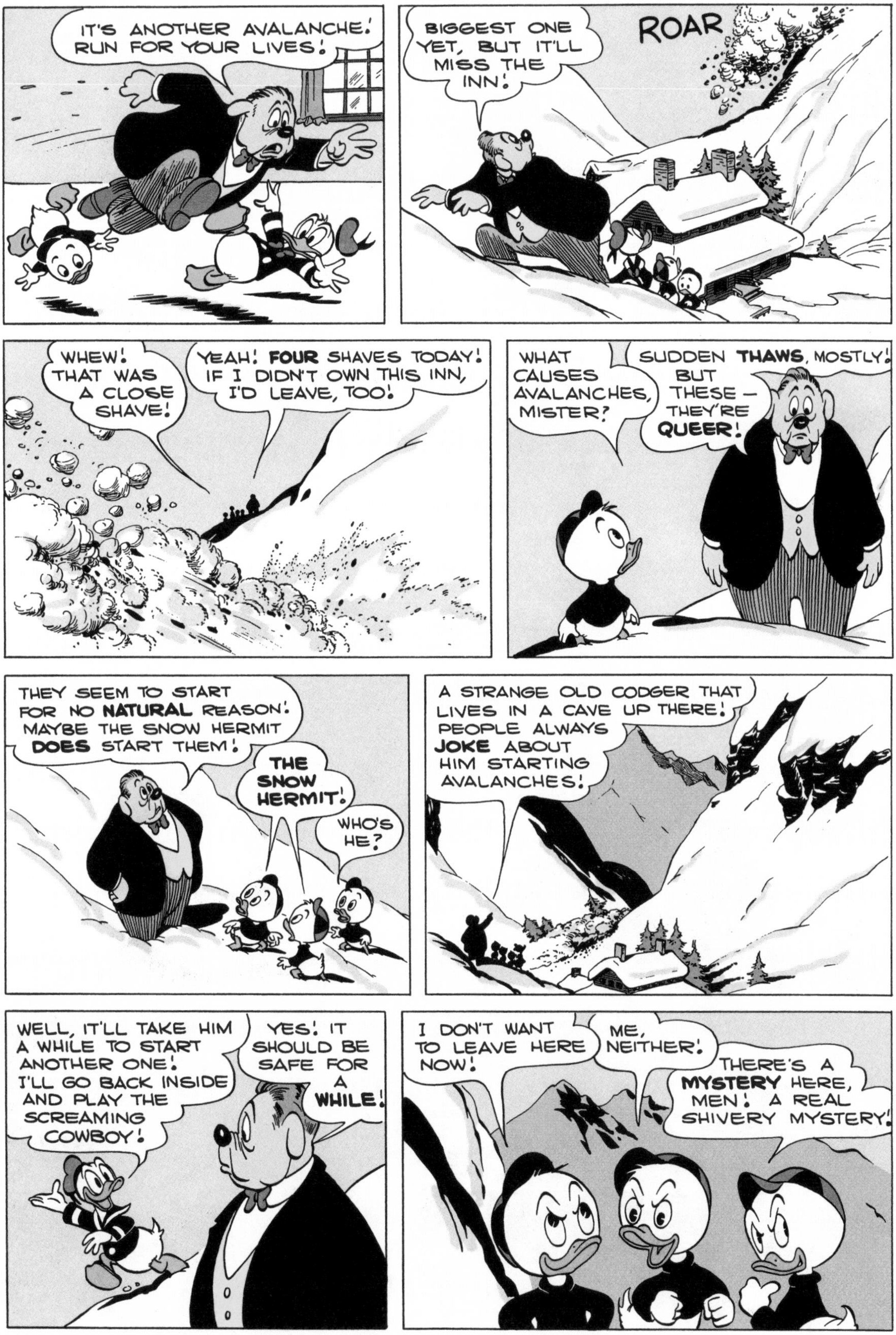
IT'S ANOTHER AVALANCHE! RUN FOR YOUR LIVES!
BIGGEST ONE YET, BUT IT'LL MISS THE INN!
ROAR
WHEW! THAT WAS A CLOSE SHAVE!
YEAH! FOUR SHAVES TODAY! IF I DIDN'T OWN THIS INN, I'D LEAVE, TOO!
WHAT CAUSES AVALANCHES, MISTER?
SUDDEN THAWS, MOSTLY! BUT THESE — THEY'RE QUEER!
THEY SEEM TO START FOR NO NATURAL REASON! MAYBE THE SNOW HERMIT DOES START THEM!
THE SNOW HERMIT!
WHO'S HE?
A STRANGE OLD CODGER THAT LIVES IN A CAVE UP THERE! PEOPLE ALWAYS JOKE ABOUT HIM STARTING AVALANCHES!
WELL, IT'LL TAKE HIM A WHILE TO START ANOTHER ONE! I'LL GO BACK INSIDE AND PLAY THE SCREAMING COWBOY!
YES! IT SHOULD BE SAFE FOR A WHILE!
I DON'T WANT TO LEAVE HERE NOW!
ME, NEITHER!
THERE'S A MYSTERY HERE, MEN! A REAL SHIVERY MYSTERY!

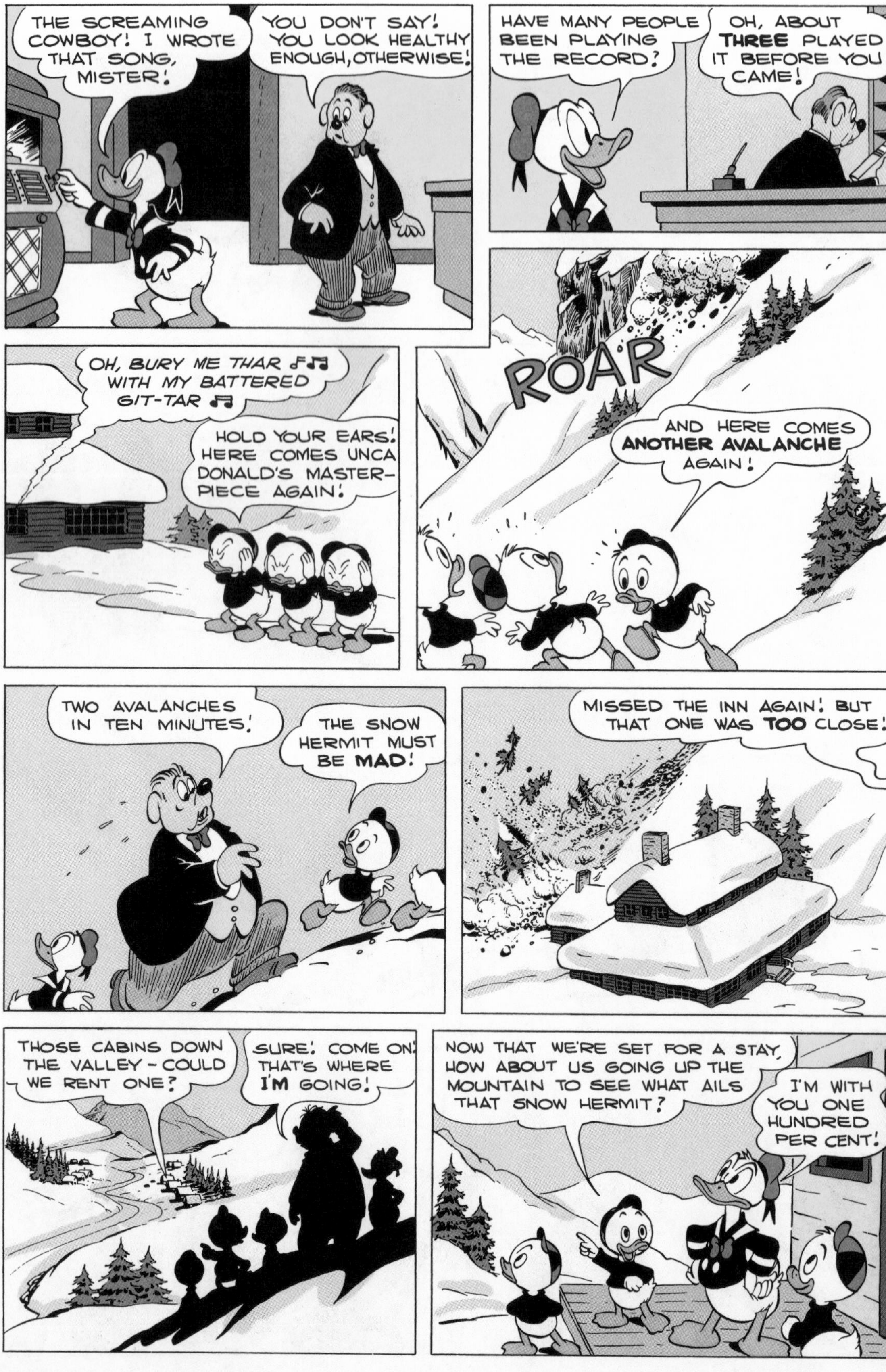
THE SCREAMING COWBOY! I WROTE THAT SONG, MISTER!
YOU DON'T SAY! YOU LOOK HEALTHY ENOUGH, OTHERWISE!
HAVE MANY PEOPLE BEEN PLAYING THE RECORD?
OH, ABOUT THREE PLAYED IT BEFORE YOU CAME!
OH, BURY ME THAR WITH MY BATTERED GIT-TAR
HOLD YOUR EARS! HERE COMES UNCA DONALD'S MASTER-PIECE AGAIN!
ROAR
AND HERE COMES ANOTHER AVALANCHE AGAIN!
TWO AVALANCHES IN TEN MINUTES!
THE SNOW HERMIT MUST BE MAD!
MISSED THE INN AGAIN! BUT THAT ONE WAS TOO CLOSE!
THOSE CABINS DOWN THE VALLEY - COULD WE RENT ONE?
SURE! COME ON! THAT'S WHERE I'M GOING!
NOW THAT WE'RE SET FOR A STAY, HOW ABOUT US GOING UP THE MOUNTAIN TO SEE WHAT AILS THAT SNOW HERMIT?
I'M WITH YOU ONE HUNDRED PER CENT!

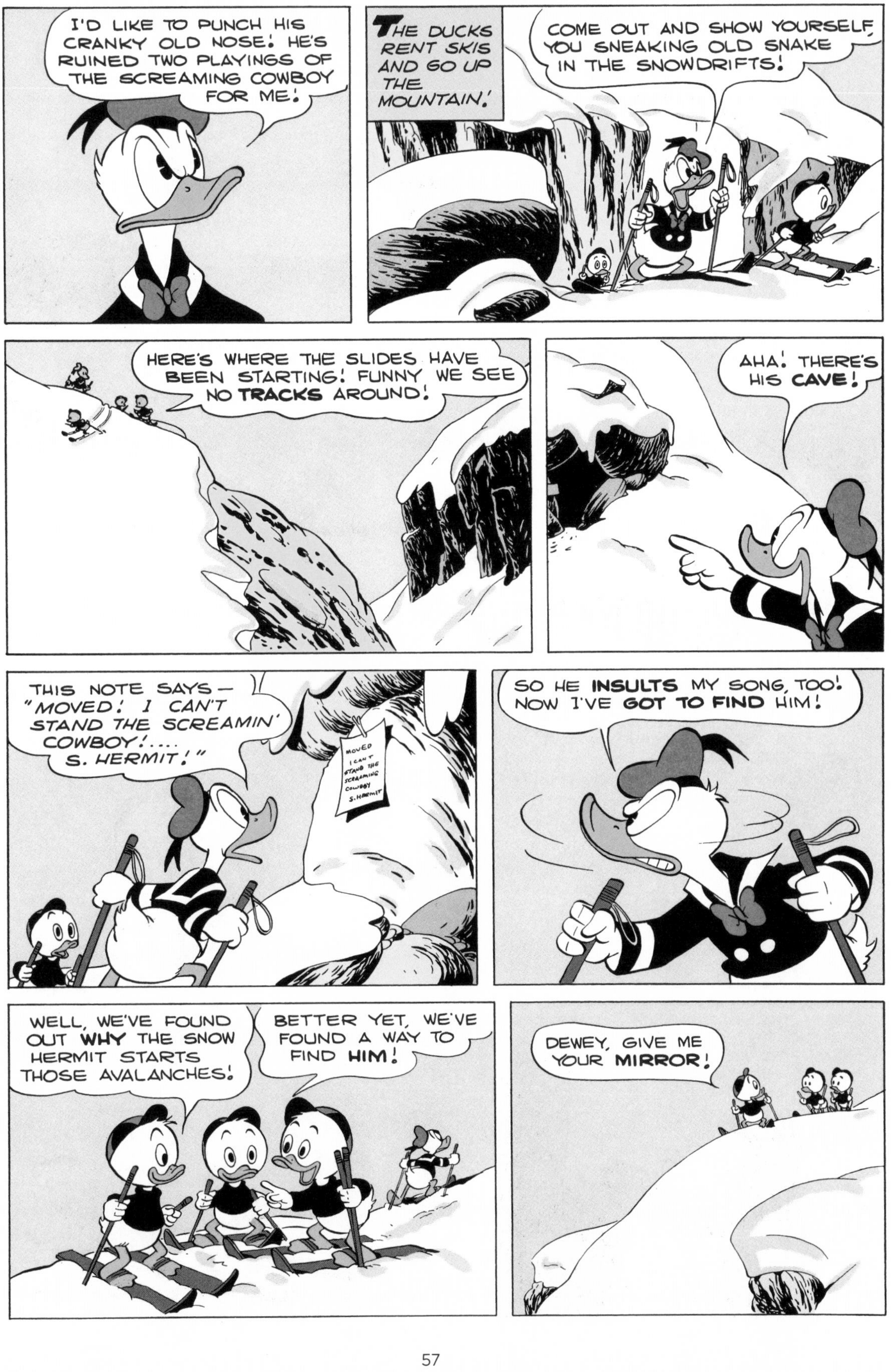
I'D LIKE TO PUNCH HIS CRANKY OLD NOSE! HE'S RUINED TWO PLAYINGS OF THE SCREAMING COWBOY FOR ME!
THE DUCKS RENT SKIS AND GO UP THE MOUNTAIN!
COME OUT AND SHOW YOURSELF, YOU SNEAKING OLD SNAKE IN THE SNOWDRIFTS!
HERE'S WHERE THE SLIDES HAVE BEEN STARTING! FUNNY WE SEE NO TRACKS AROUND!
AHA! THERE'S HIS CAVE!
THIS NOTE SAYS— "MOVED! I CAN'T STAND THE SCREAMIN' COWBOY!.... S. HERMIT!"
MOVED I CAN'T STAND THE SCREAMING COWBOY S.HERMIT
SO HE INSULTS MY SONG, TOO! NOW I'VE GOT TO FIND HIM!
WELL, WE'VE FOUND OUT WHY THE SNOW HERMIT STARTS THOSE AVALANCHES!
BETTER YET, WE'VE FOUND A WAY TO FIND HIM!
DEWEY, GIVE ME YOUR MIRROR!

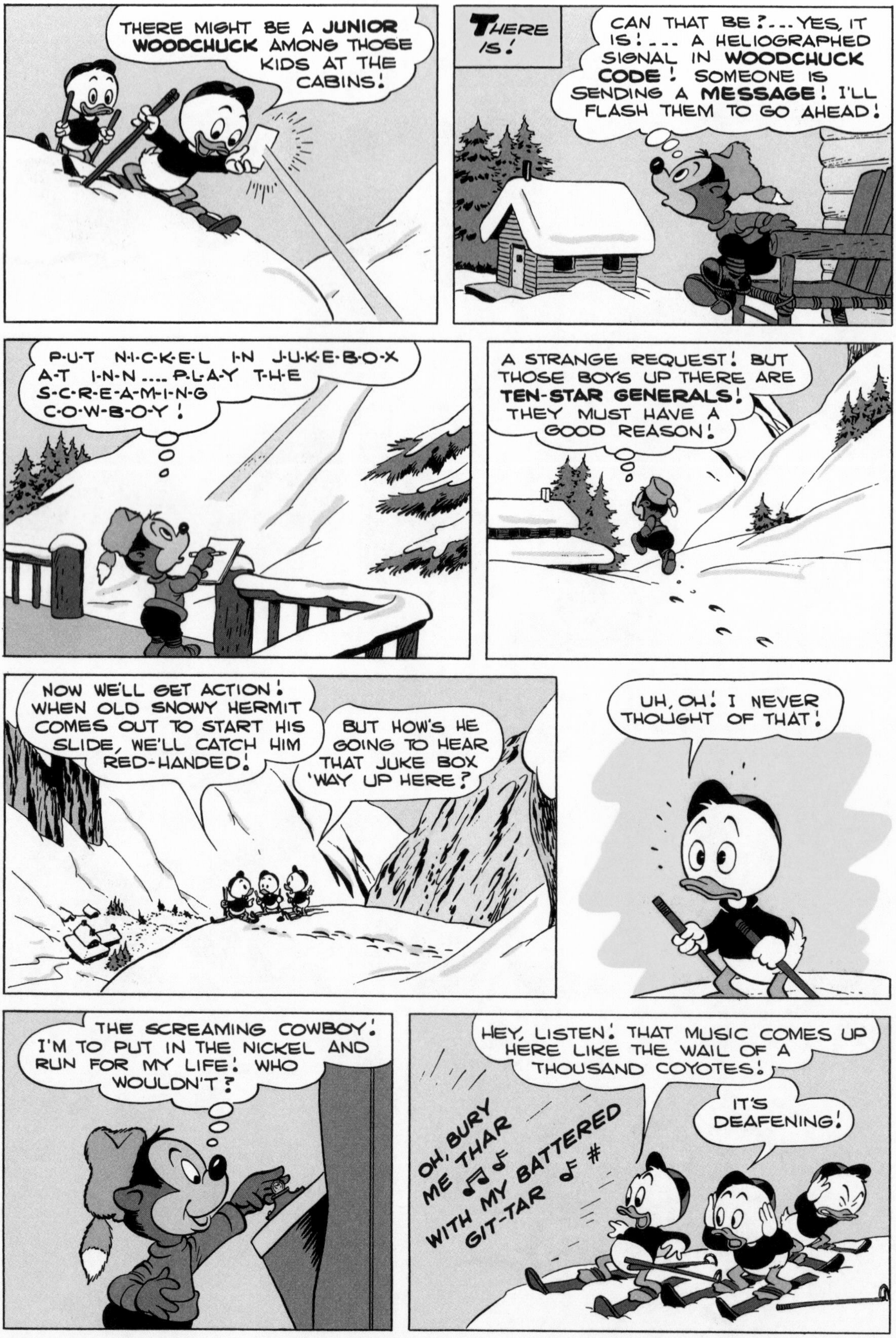

THERE MIGHT BE A **JUNIOR WOODCHUCK** AMONG THOSE KIDS AT THE CABINS!
THERE IS!
CAN THAT BE?...YES, IT IS!... A HELIOGRAPHED SIGNAL IN **WOODCHUCK CODE**! SOMEONE IS SENDING A **MESSAGE**! I'LL FLASH THEM TO GO AHEAD!
P-U-T N-I-C-K-E-L I-N J-U-K-E-B-O-X A-T I-N-N.... P-L-A-Y T-H-E S-C-R-E-A-M-I-N-G C-O-W-B-O-Y!
A STRANGE REQUEST! BUT THOSE BOYS UP THERE ARE **TEN-STAR GENERALS**! THEY MUST HAVE A GOOD REASON!
NOW WE'LL GET ACTION! WHEN OLD SNOWY HERMIT COMES OUT TO START HIS SLIDE, WE'LL CATCH HIM RED-HANDED!
BUT HOW'S HE GOING TO HEAR THAT JUKE BOX 'WAY UP HERE?
UH, OH! I NEVER THOUGHT OF THAT!
THE SCREAMING COWBOY! I'M TO PUT IN THE NICKEL AND RUN FOR MY LIFE! WHO WOULDN'T?
HEY, LISTEN! THAT MUSIC COMES UP HERE LIKE THE WAIL OF A THOUSAND COYOTES!
OH, BURY ME THAR WITH MY BATTERED GIT-TAR
IT'S DEAFENING!

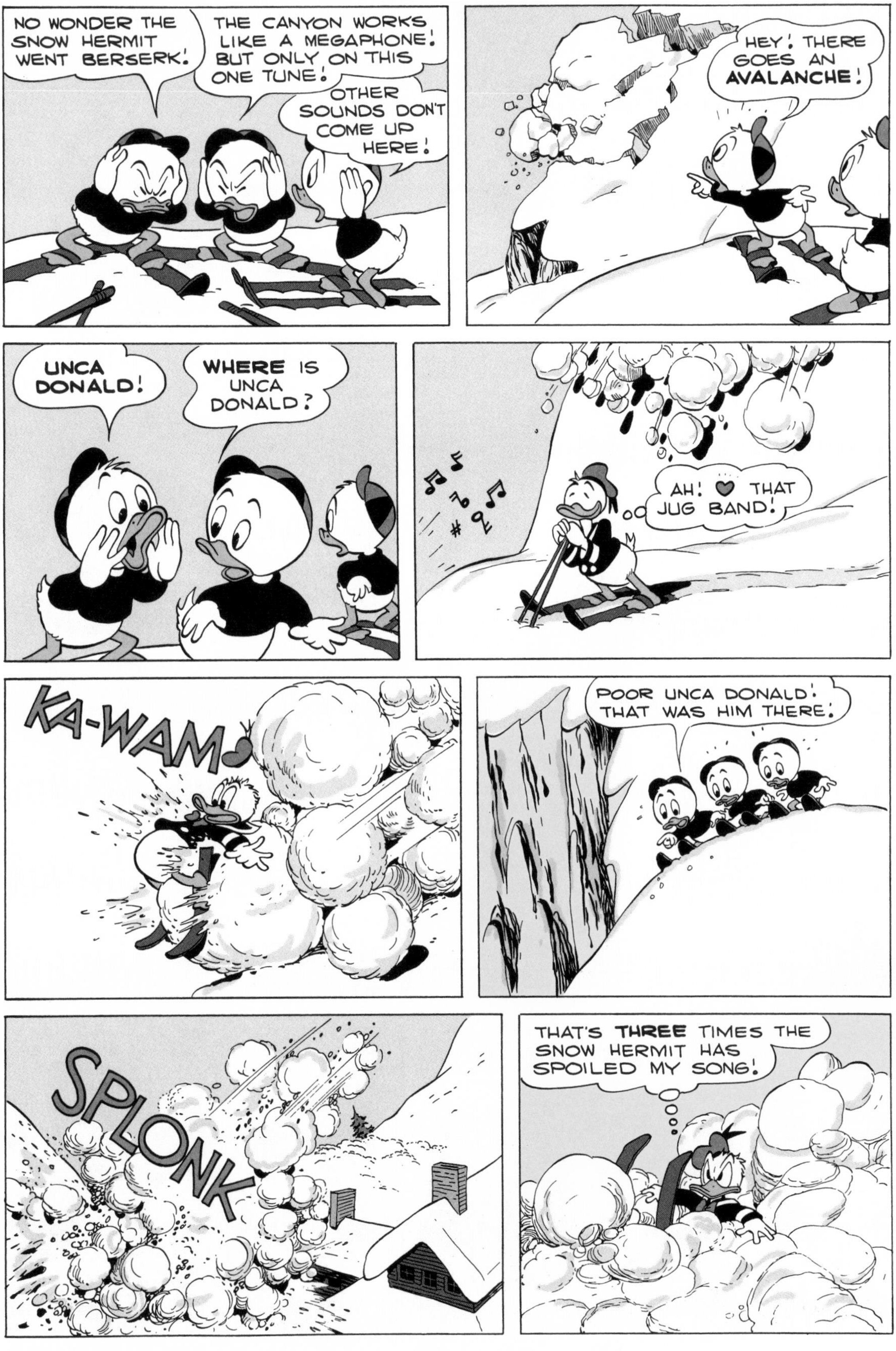
NO WONDER THE SNOW HERMIT WENT BERSERK!
THE CANYON WORKS LIKE A MEGAPHONE! BUT ONLY ON THIS ONE TUNE!
OTHER SOUNDS DON'T COME UP HERE!
HEY! THERE GOES AN AVALANCHE!
UNCA DONALD!
WHERE IS UNCA DONALD?
AH! ♥ THAT JUG BAND!
KA-WAM
POOR UNCA DONALD! THAT WAS HIM THERE!
SPLONK
THAT'S THREE TIMES THE SNOW HERMIT HAS SPOILED MY SONG!

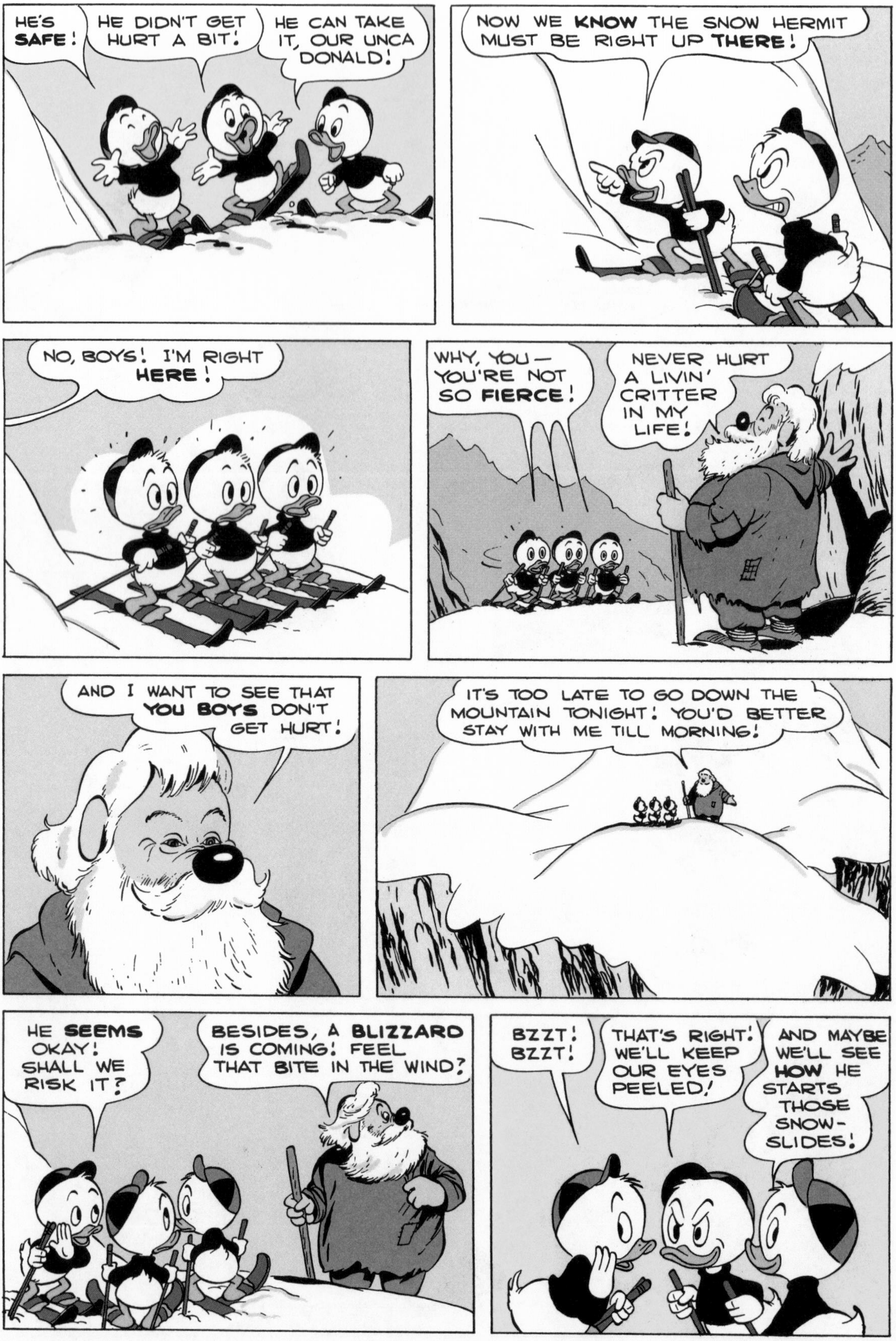
HE'S SAFE!
HE DIDN'T GET HURT A BIT!
HE CAN TAKE IT, OUR UNCA DONALD!
NOW WE KNOW THE SNOW HERMIT MUST BE RIGHT UP THERE!
NO, BOYS! I'M RIGHT HERE!
WHY, YOU— YOU'RE NOT SO FIERCE!
NEVER HURT A LIVIN' CRITTER IN MY LIFE!
AND I WANT TO SEE THAT YOU BOYS DON'T GET HURT!
IT'S TOO LATE TO GO DOWN THE MOUNTAIN TONIGHT! YOU'D BETTER STAY WITH ME TILL MORNING!
HE SEEMS OKAY! SHALL WE RISK IT?
BESIDES, A BLIZZARD IS COMING! FEEL THAT BITE IN THE WIND?
BZZT! BZZT!
THAT'S RIGHT! WE'LL KEEP OUR EYES PEELED!
AND MAYBE WE'LL SEE HOW HE STARTS THOSE SNOW-SLIDES!

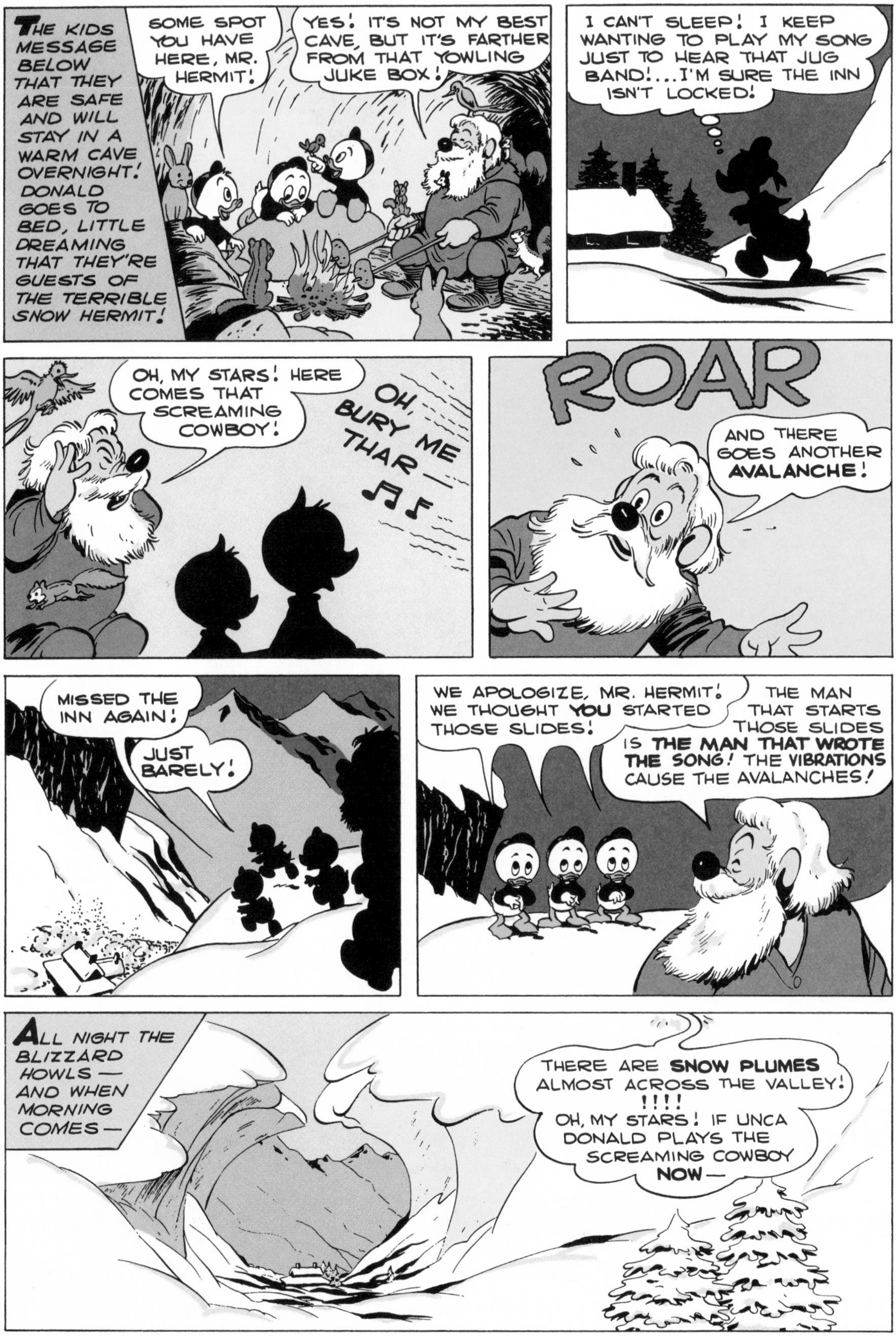
THE KIDS MESSAGE BELOW THAT THEY ARE SAFE AND WILL STAY IN A WARM CAVE OVERNIGHT! DONALD GOES TO BED, LITTLE DREAMING THAT THEY'RE GUESTS OF THE TERRIBLE SNOW HERMIT!
SOME SPOT YOU HAVE HERE, MR. HERMIT!
YES! IT'S NOT MY BEST CAVE, BUT IT'S FARTHER FROM THAT YOWLING JUKE BOX!
I CAN'T SLEEP! I KEEP WANTING TO PLAY MY SONG JUST TO HEAR THAT JUG BAND!...I'M SURE THE INN ISN'T LOCKED!
OH, MY STARS! HERE COMES THAT SCREAMING COWBOY!
OH, BURY ME THAR—
ROAR
AND THERE GOES ANOTHER AVALANCHE!
MISSED THE INN AGAIN!
JUST BARELY!
WE APOLOGIZE, MR. HERMIT! WE THOUGHT YOU STARTED THOSE SLIDES!
THE MAN THAT STARTS THOSE SLIDES IS THE MAN THAT WROTE THE SONG! THE VIBRATIONS CAUSE THE AVALANCHES!
ALL NIGHT THE BLIZZARD HOWLS — AND WHEN MORNING COMES —
THERE ARE SNOW PLUMES ALMOST ACROSS THE VALLEY!
!!!!
OH, MY STARS! IF UNCA DONALD PLAYS THE SCREAMING COWBOY NOW —

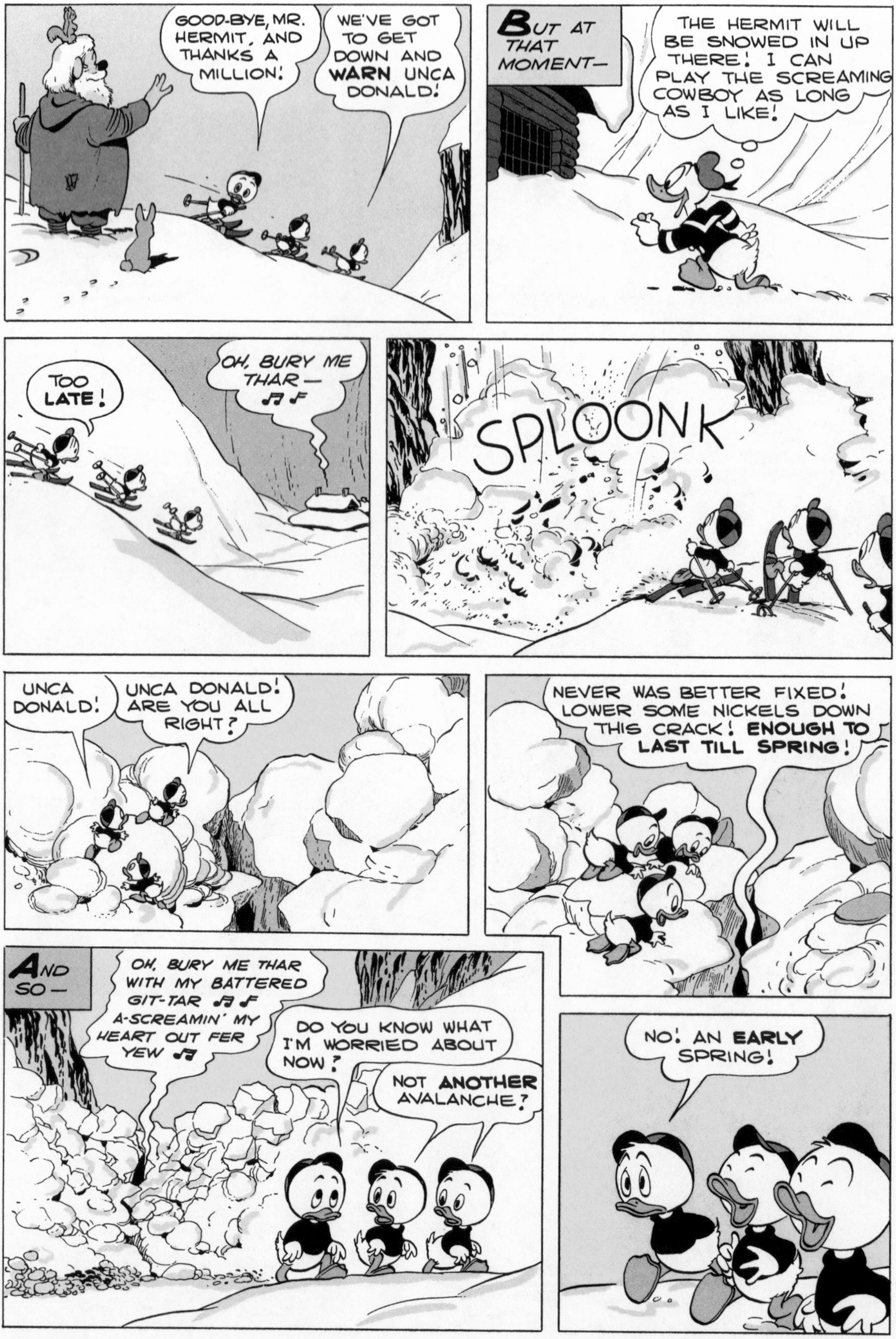
GOOD-BYE, MR. HERMIT, AND THANKS A MILLION!
WE'VE GOT TO GET DOWN AND WARN UNCA DONALD!
BUT AT THAT MOMENT—
THE HERMIT WILL BE SNOWED IN UP THERE! I CAN PLAY THE SCREAMING COWBOY AS LONG AS I LIKE!
TOO LATE!
OH, BURY ME THAR—
SPLOONK
UNCA DONALD!
UNCA DONALD! ARE YOU ALL RIGHT?
NEVER WAS BETTER FIXED! LOWER SOME NICKELS DOWN THIS CRACK! ENOUGH TO LAST TILL SPRING!
AND SO—
OH, BURY ME THAR WITH MY BATTERED GIT-TAR A-SCREAMIN' MY HEART OUT FER YEW
DO YOU KNOW WHAT I'M WORRIED ABOUT NOW?
NOT ANOTHER AVALANCHE?
NO! AN EARLY SPRING!

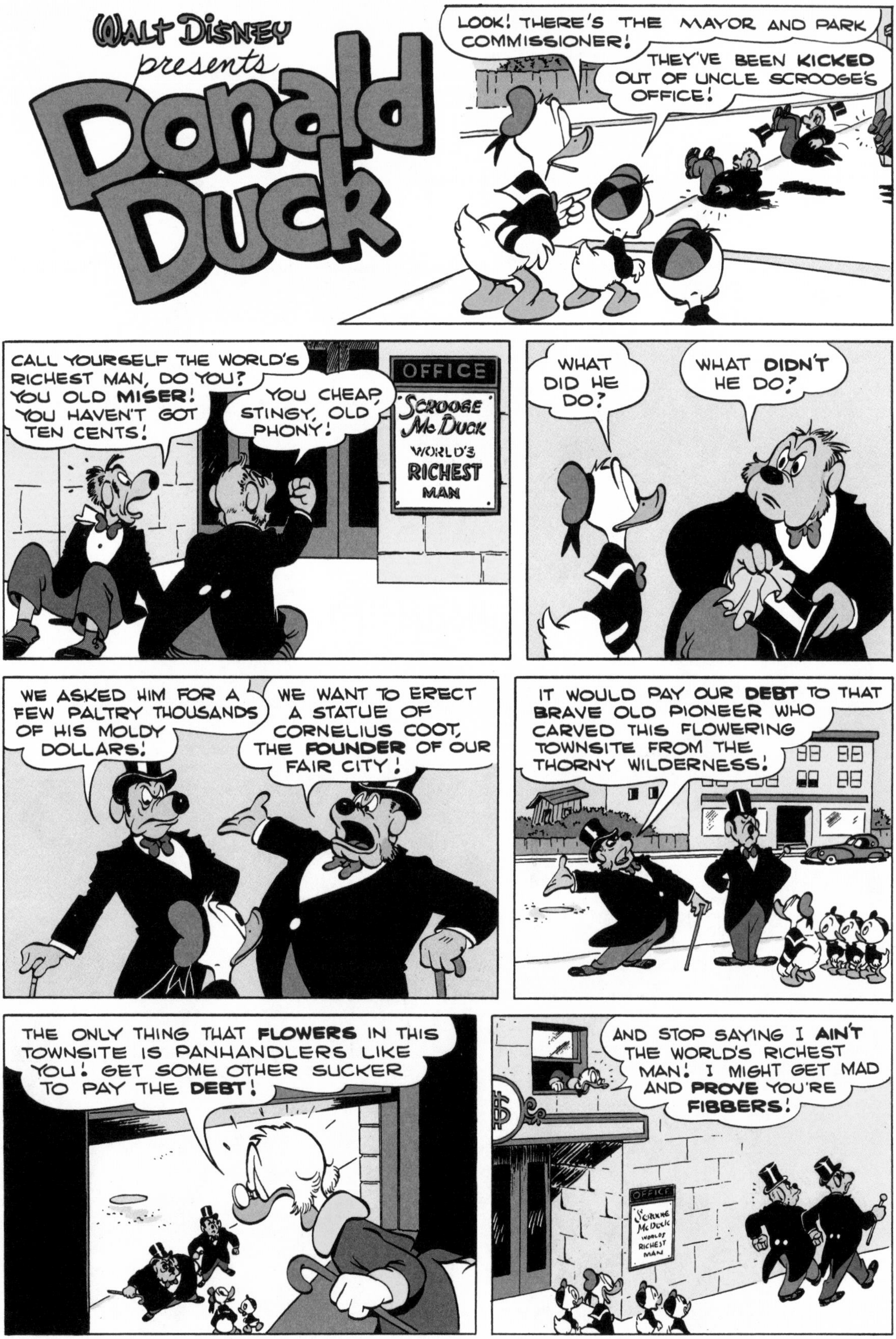
Walt Disney presents
Donald Duck
LOOK! THERE'S THE MAYOR AND PARK COMMISSIONER!
THEY'VE BEEN KICKED OUT OF UNCLE SCROOGE'S OFFICE!
CALL YOURSELF THE WORLD'S RICHEST MAN, DO YOU? YOU OLD MISER! YOU HAVEN'T GOT TEN CENTS!
YOU CHEAP STINGY, OLD PHONY!
OFFICE
SCROOGE McDUCK WORLD'S RICHEST MAN
WHAT DID HE DO?
WHAT DIDN'T HE DO?
WE ASKED HIM FOR A FEW PALTRY THOUSANDS OF HIS MOLDY DOLLARS!
WE WANT TO ERECT A STATUE OF CORNELIUS COOT, THE FOUNDER OF OUR FAIR CITY!
IT WOULD PAY OUR DEBT TO THAT BRAVE OLD PIONEER WHO CARVED THIS FLOWERING TOWNSITE FROM THE THORNY WILDERNESS!
THE ONLY THING THAT FLOWERS IN THIS TOWNSITE IS PANHANDLERS LIKE YOU! GET SOME OTHER SUCKER TO PAY THE DEBT!
AND STOP SAYING I AIN'T THE WORLD'S RICHEST MAN! I MIGHT GET MAD AND PROVE YOU'RE FIBBERS!

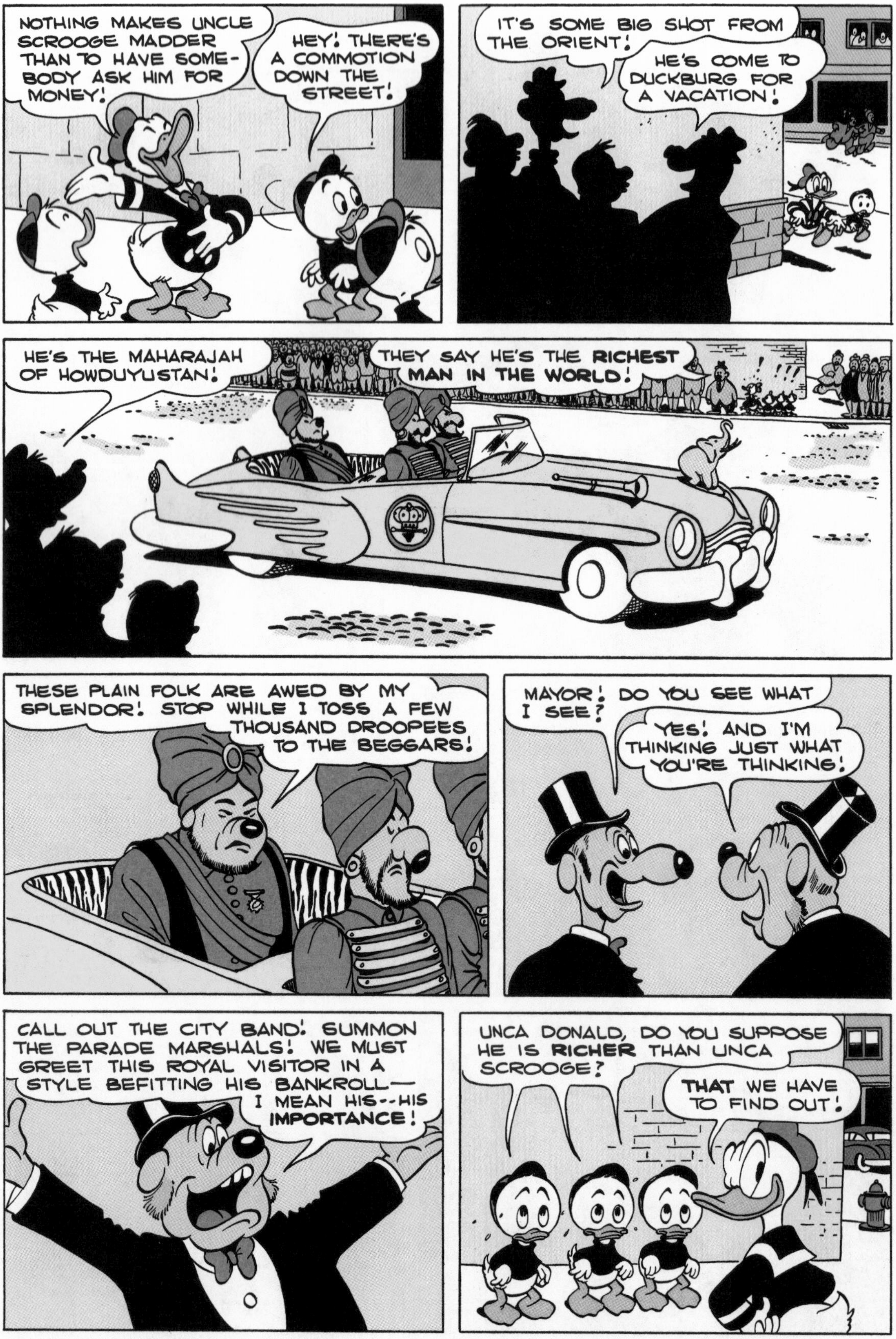
NOTHING MAKES UNCLE SCROOGE MADDER THAN TO HAVE SOMEBODY ASK HIM FOR MONEY!
HEY! THERE'S A COMMOTION DOWN THE STREET!
IT'S SOME BIG SHOT FROM THE ORIENT!
HE'S COME TO DUCKBURG FOR A VACATION!
HE'S THE MAHARAJAH OF HOWDUYUSTAN!
THEY SAY HE'S THE RICHEST MAN IN THE WORLD!
!!!!
THESE PLAIN FOLK ARE AWED BY MY SPLENDOR! STOP WHILE I TOSS A FEW THOUSAND DROOPEES TO THE BEGGARS!
MAYOR! DO YOU SEE WHAT I SEE?
YES! AND I'M THINKING JUST WHAT YOU'RE THINKING!
CALL OUT THE CITY BAND! SUMMON THE PARADE MARSHALS! WE MUST GREET THIS ROYAL VISITOR IN A STYLE BEFITTING HIS BANKROLL— I MEAN HIS--HIS IMPORTANCE!
UNCA DONALD, DO YOU SUPPOSE HE IS RICHER THAN UNCA SCROOGE?
THAT WE HAVE TO FIND OUT!

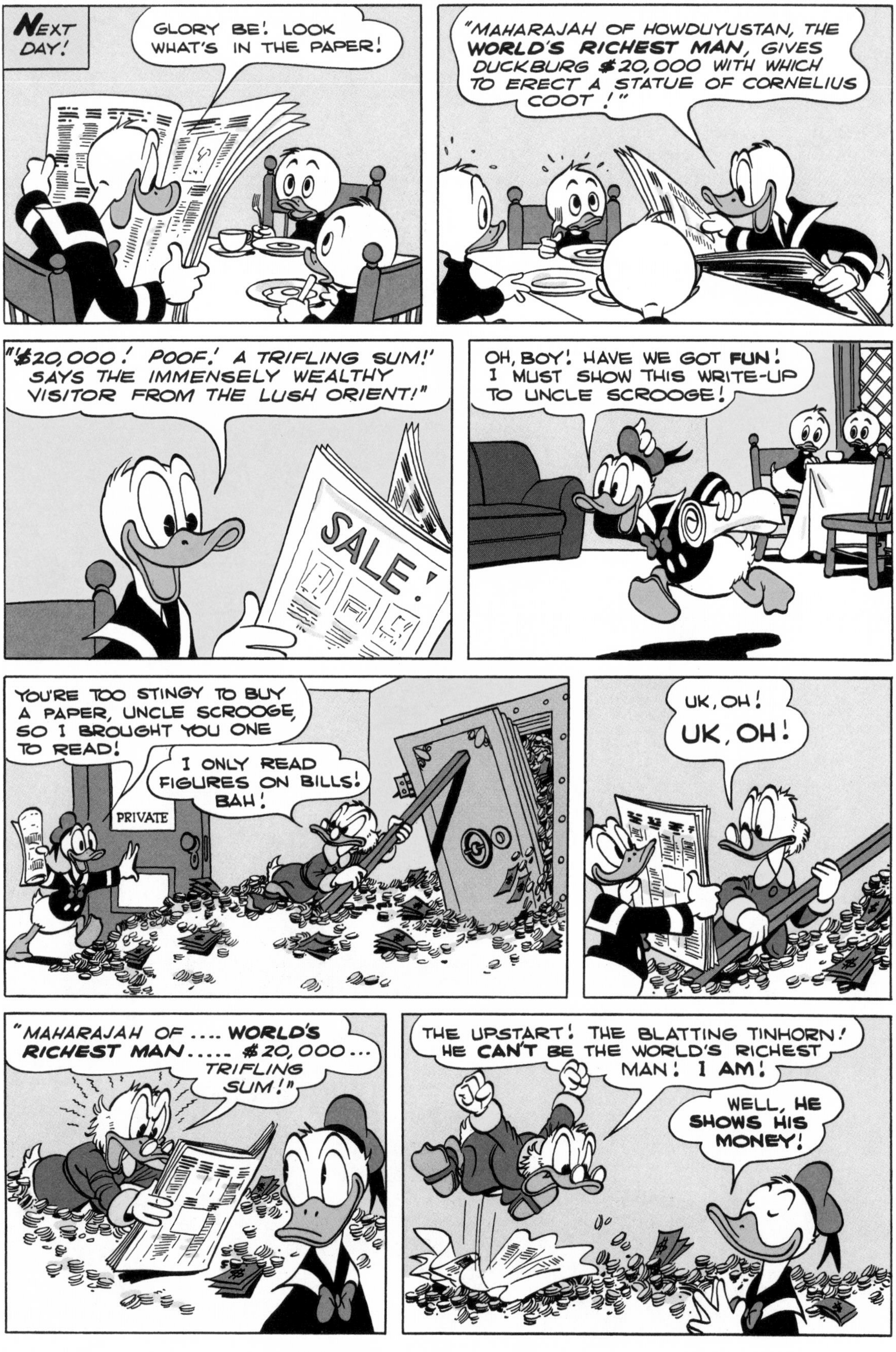
NEXT DAY!
GLORY BE! LOOK WHAT'S IN THE PAPER!
"MAHARAJAH OF HOWDUYUSTAN, THE WORLD'S RICHEST MAN, GIVES DUCKBURG $20,000 WITH WHICH TO ERECT A STATUE OF CORNELIUS COOT!"
"'$20,000! POOF! A TRIFLING SUM!' SAYS THE IMMENSELY WEALTHY VISITOR FROM THE LUSH ORIENT!"
SALE!
OH, BOY! HAVE WE GOT FUN! I MUST SHOW THIS WRITE-UP TO UNCLE SCROOGE!
YOU'RE TOO STINGY TO BUY A PAPER, UNCLE SCROOGE, SO I BROUGHT YOU ONE TO READ!
I ONLY READ FIGURES ON BILLS! BAH!
PRIVATE
UK, OH!
UK, OH!
"MAHARAJAH OF .... WORLD'S RICHEST MAN..... $20,000... TRIFLING SUM!"
THE UPSTART! THE BLATTING TINHORN! HE CAN'T BE THE WORLD'S RICHEST MAN! I AM!
WELL, HE SHOWS HIS MONEY!

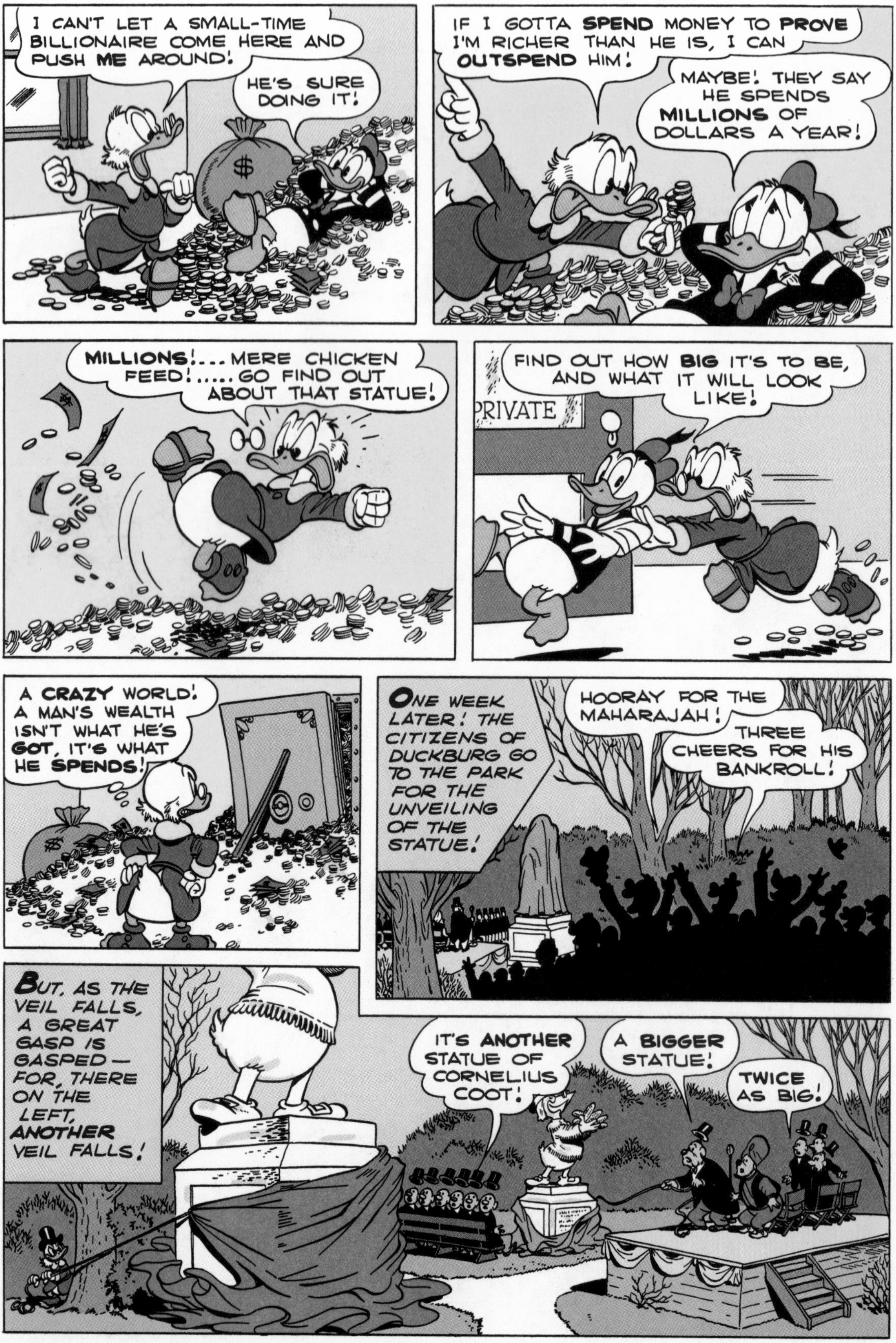
I CAN'T LET A SMALL-TIME BILLIONAIRE COME HERE AND PUSH ME AROUND!
HE'S SURE DOING IT!
IF I GOTTA SPEND MONEY TO PROVE I'M RICHER THAN HE IS, I CAN OUTSPEND HIM!
MAYBE! THEY SAY HE SPENDS MILLIONS OF DOLLARS A YEAR!
MILLIONS!... MERE CHICKEN FEED!..... GO FIND OUT ABOUT THAT STATUE!
FIND OUT HOW BIG IT'S TO BE, AND WHAT IT WILL LOOK LIKE!
PRIVATE
A CRAZY WORLD! A MAN'S WEALTH ISN'T WHAT HE'S GOT, IT'S WHAT HE SPENDS!
ONE WEEK LATER! THE CITIZENS OF DUCKBURG GO TO THE PARK FOR THE UNVEILING OF THE STATUE!
HOORAY FOR THE MAHARAJAH!
THREE CHEERS FOR HIS BANKROLL!
BUT, AS THE VEIL FALLS, A GREAT GASP IS GASPED— FOR, THERE ON THE LEFT, ANOTHER VEIL FALLS!
IT'S ANOTHER STATUE OF CORNELIUS COOT!
A BIGGER STATUE!
TWICE AS BIG!

WHO HAS SOUGHT TO **OUTDO** ME? WHO HAS **DARED** MAKE MY $20,000 LOOK LIKE TWO-BITS!

"ERECTED IN HONOR OF BRAVE, OLD CORNELIUS COOT BY SCROOGE McDUCK, WORLD'S **RICHEST** MAN!"

AND 'RICHEST' IS SPELLED WITH 22-KARAT **GOLD**!

THE UPSTART! THE BRASH **TINHORN**! NOBODY CAN OUTDO THE MAHARAJAH OF HOWDUYUSTAN!

SUMMON THE ARTISANS! CLEAR MORE TREES! I SHALL ERECT **ANOTHER** STATUE OF CORNELIUS COOT!

GET THE DOPE ON THIS NEW STATUE! HOW BIG AND HOW FANCY?

I'LL HAVE IT FOR YOU TONIGHT!

ANOTHER WEEK! ANOTHER UNVEILING!

HE HAS DONE IT AGAIN! OVERNIGHT HE BUILDS STATUES **BIGGER** THAN MINE!

CORNELIUS COOT

ERECTED BY SCROOGE McDUCK WORLD

ERECTED BY MAHARAJAH OF HOWDUYUSTAN

CORNELIUS COOT

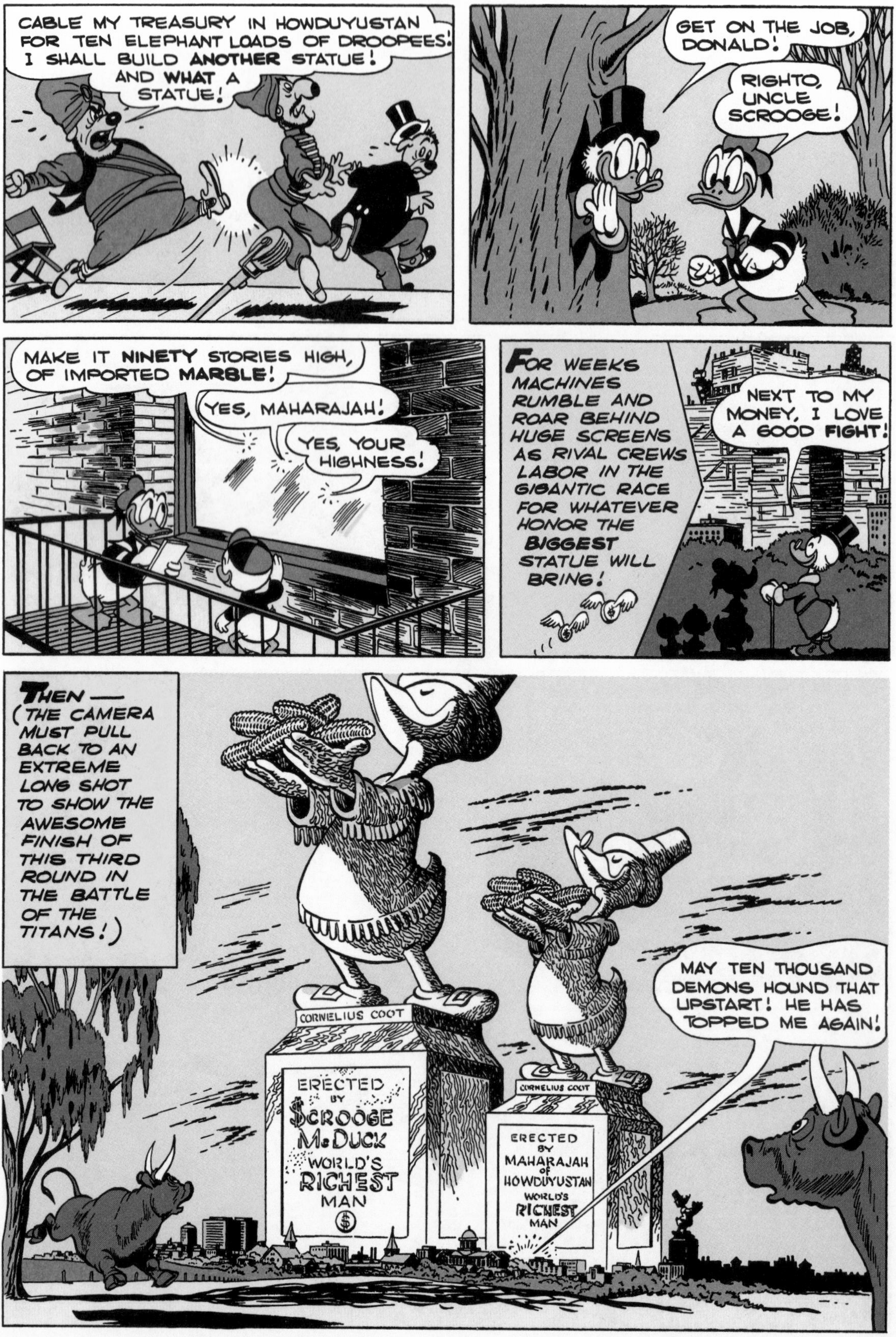

CABLE MY TREASURY IN HOWDUYUSTAN FOR TEN ELEPHANT LOADS OF DROOPEES! I SHALL BUILD ANOTHER STATUE!
AND WHAT A STATUE!
GET ON THE JOB, DONALD!
RIGHTO, UNCLE SCROOGE!
MAKE IT NINETY STORIES HIGH, OF IMPORTED MARBLE!
YES, MAHARAJAH!
YES, YOUR HIGHNESS!
FOR WEEKS MACHINES RUMBLE AND ROAR BEHIND HUGE SCREENS AS RIVAL CREWS LABOR IN THE GIGANTIC RACE FOR WHATEVER HONOR THE BIGGEST STATUE WILL BRING!
NEXT TO MY MONEY, I LOVE A GOOD FIGHT!
THEN — (THE CAMERA MUST PULL BACK TO AN EXTREME LONG SHOT TO SHOW THE AWESOME FINISH OF THIS THIRD ROUND IN THE BATTLE OF THE TITANS!)
CORNELIUS COOT
ERECTED BY $CROOGE McDUCK WORLD'S RICHEST MAN
CORNELIUS COOT
ERECTED BY MAHARAJAH OF HOWDUYUSTAN WORLD'S RICHEST MAN
MAY TEN THOUSAND DEMONS HOUND THAT UPSTART! HE HAS TOPPED ME AGAIN!

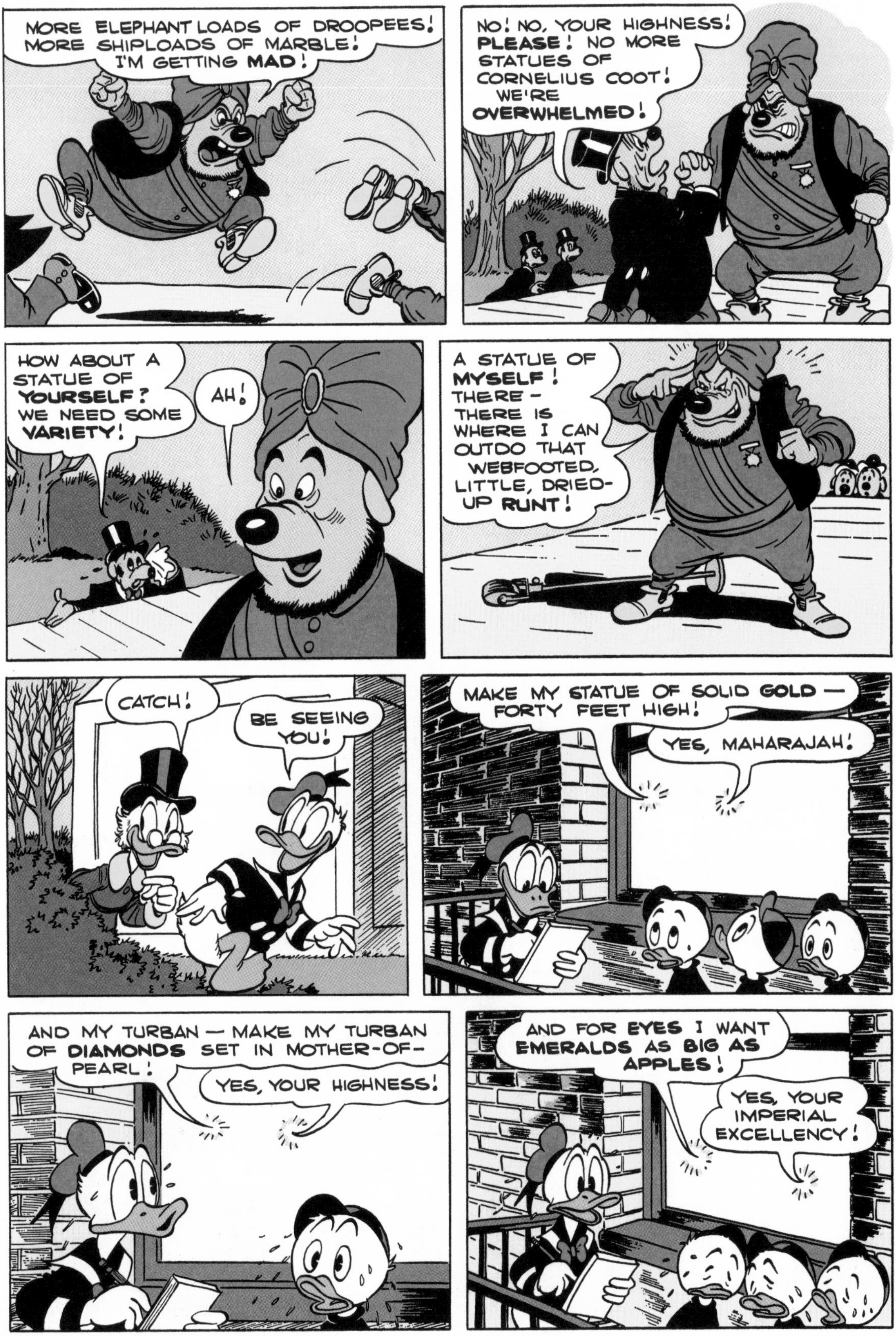
MORE ELEPHANT LOADS OF DROOPEES! MORE SHIPLOADS OF MARBLE! I'M GETTING MAD!
NO! NO, YOUR HIGHNESS! PLEASE! NO MORE STATUES OF CORNELIUS COOT! WE'RE OVERWHELMED!
HOW ABOUT A STATUE OF YOURSELF? WE NEED SOME VARIETY!
AH!
A STATUE OF MYSELF! THERE— THERE IS WHERE I CAN OUTDO THAT WEBFOOTED, LITTLE, DRIED-UP RUNT!
CATCH!
BE SEEING YOU!
MAKE MY STATUE OF SOLID GOLD— FORTY FEET HIGH!
YES, MAHARAJAH!
AND MY TURBAN—MAKE MY TURBAN OF DIAMONDS SET IN MOTHER-OF-PEARL!
YES, YOUR HIGHNESS!
AND FOR EYES I WANT EMERALDS AS BIG AS APPLES!
YES, YOUR IMPERIAL EXCELLENCY!

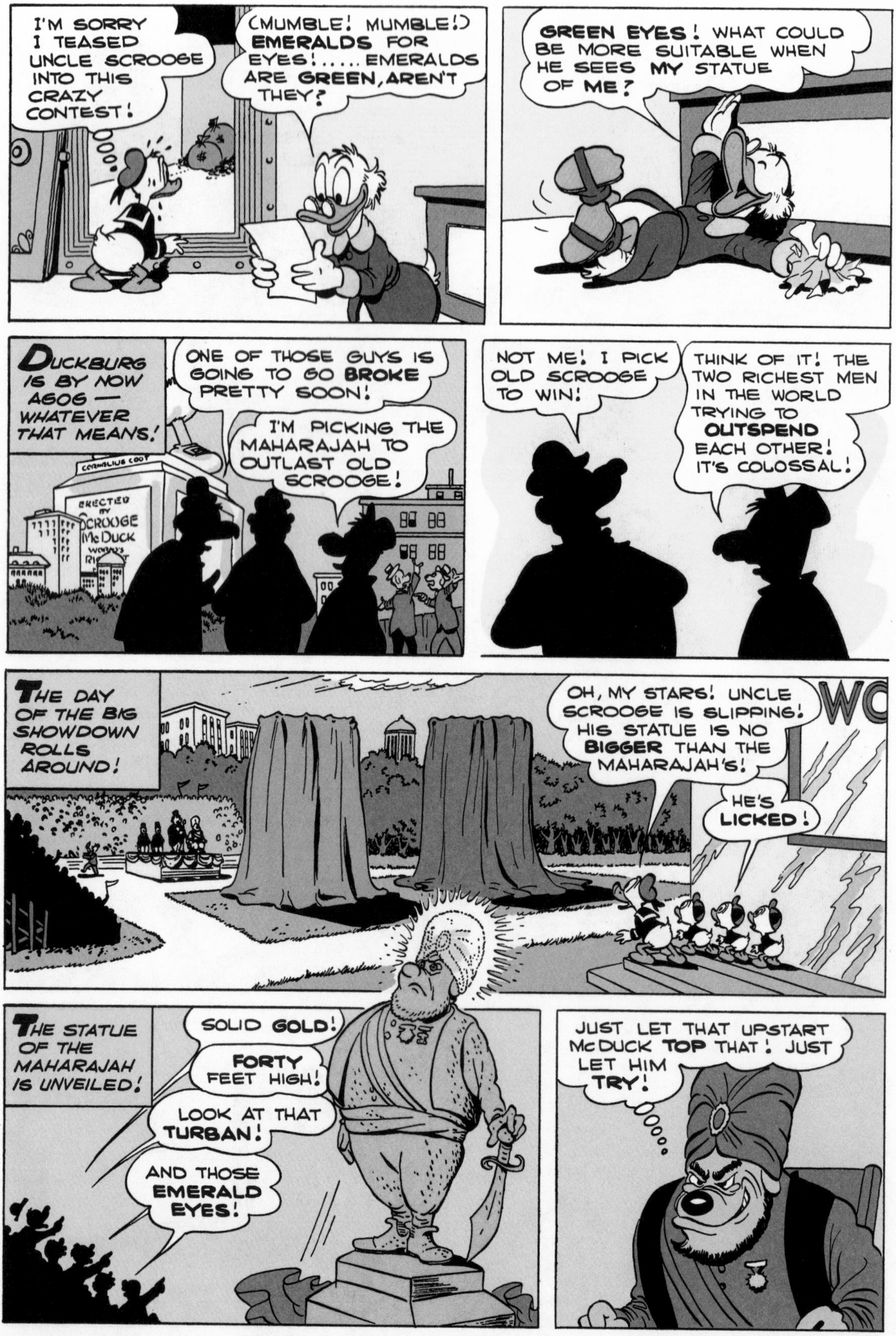
I'M SORRY I TEASED UNCLE SCROOGE INTO THIS CRAZY CONTEST!
(MUMBLE! MUMBLE!) EMERALDS FOR EYES!..... EMERALDS ARE GREEN, AREN'T THEY?
GREEN EYES! WHAT COULD BE MORE SUITABLE WHEN HE SEES MY STATUE OF ME?
DUCKBURG IS BY NOW AGOG — WHATEVER THAT MEANS!
ONE OF THOSE GUYS IS GOING TO GO BROKE PRETTY SOON!
I'M PICKING THE MAHARAJAH TO OUTLAST OLD SCROOGE!
CORNELIUS COOT
ERECTED BY SCROOGE McDUCK
NOT ME! I PICK OLD SCROOGE TO WIN!
THINK OF IT! THE TWO RICHEST MEN IN THE WORLD TRYING TO OUTSPEND EACH OTHER! IT'S COLOSSAL!
THE DAY OF THE BIG SHOWDOWN ROLLS AROUND!
OH, MY STARS! UNCLE SCROOGE IS SLIPPING! HIS STATUE IS NO BIGGER THAN THE MAHARAJAH'S!
HE'S LICKED!
WO
THE STATUE OF THE MAHARAJAH IS UNVEILED!
SOLID GOLD!
FORTY FEET HIGH!
LOOK AT THAT TURBAN!
AND THOSE EMERALD EYES!
JUST LET THAT UPSTART McDUCK TOP THAT! JUST LET HIM TRY!

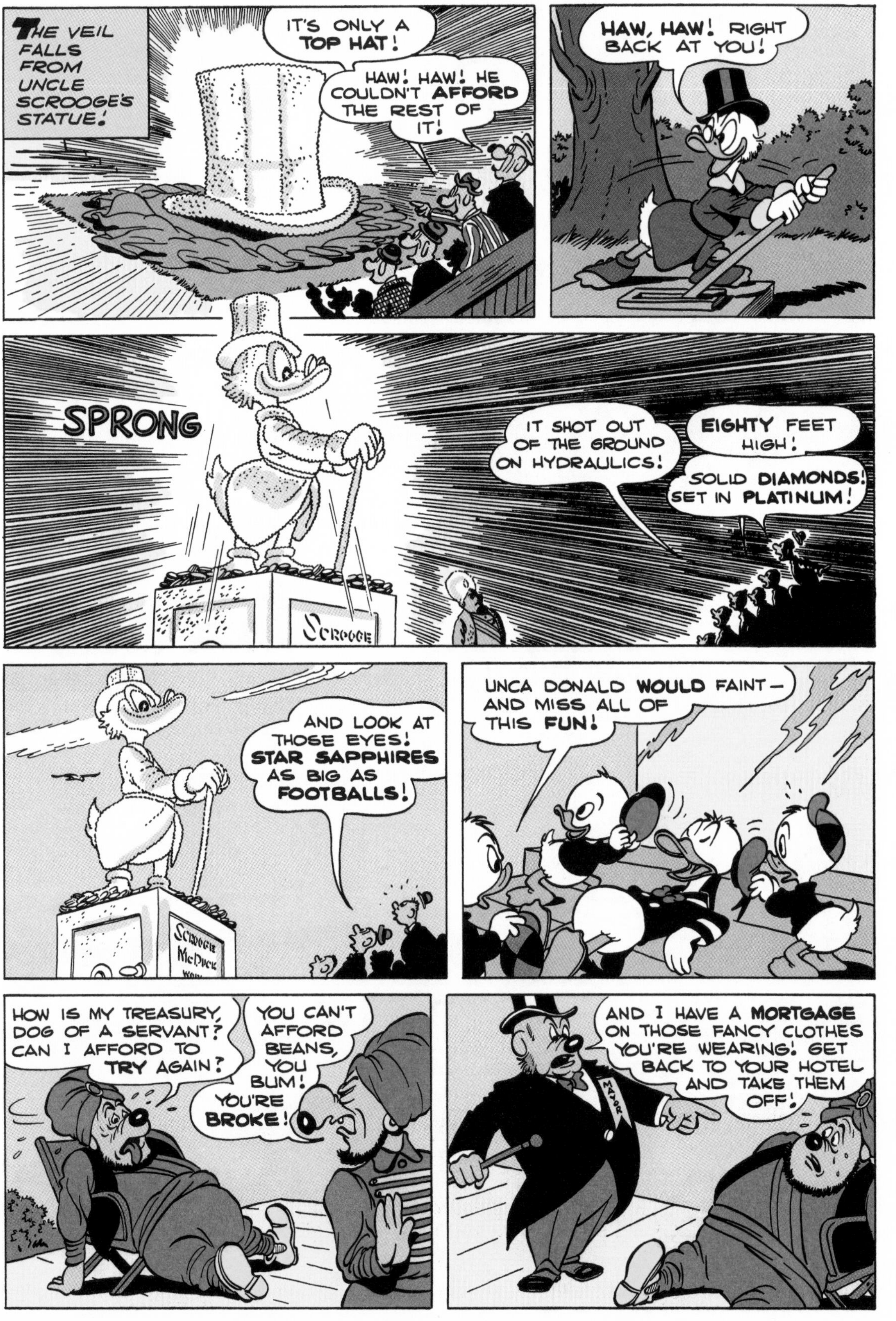
THE VEIL FALLS FROM UNCLE SCROOGE'S STATUE!
IT'S ONLY A TOP HAT!
HAW! HAW! HE COULDN'T AFFORD THE REST OF IT!
HAW, HAW! RIGHT BACK AT YOU!
SPRONG
SCROOGE
IT SHOT OUT OF THE GROUND ON HYDRAULICS!
EIGHTY FEET HIGH!
SOLID DIAMONDS! SET IN PLATINUM!
AND LOOK AT THOSE EYES! STAR SAPPHIRES AS BIG AS FOOTBALLS!
SCROOGE McDUCK
UNCA DONALD WOULD FAINT— AND MISS ALL OF THIS FUN!
HOW IS MY TREASURY, DOG OF A SERVANT? CAN I AFFORD TO TRY AGAIN?
YOU CAN'T AFFORD BEANS, YOU BUM! YOU'RE BROKE!
AND I HAVE A MORTGAGE ON THOSE FANCY CLOTHES YOU'RE WEARING! GET BACK TO YOUR HOTEL AND TAKE THEM OFF!
MAYOR

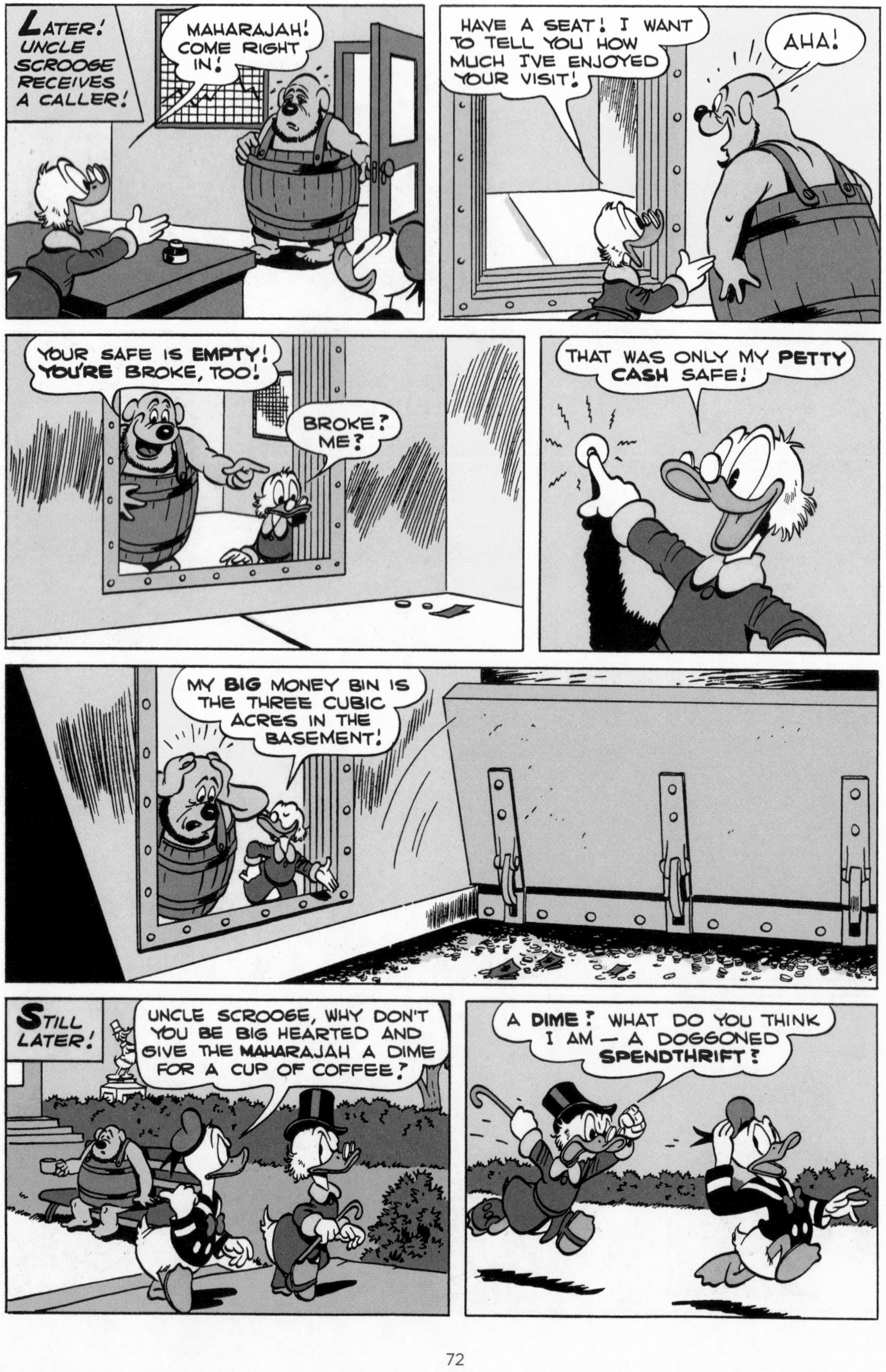
LATER! UNCLE SCROOGE RECEIVES A CALLER!
MAHARAJAH! COME RIGHT IN!
HAVE A SEAT! I WANT TO TELL YOU HOW MUCH I'VE ENJOYED YOUR VISIT!
AHA!
YOUR SAFE IS EMPTY! YOU'RE BROKE, TOO!
BROKE? ME?
THAT WAS ONLY MY PETTY CASH SAFE!
MY BIG MONEY BIN IS THE THREE CUBIC ACRES IN THE BASEMENT!
STILL LATER!
UNCLE SCROOGE, WHY DON'T YOU BE BIG HEARTED AND GIVE THE MAHARAJAH A DIME FOR A CUP OF COFFEE?
A DIME? WHAT DO YOU THINK I AM — A DOGGONED SPENDTHRIFT?

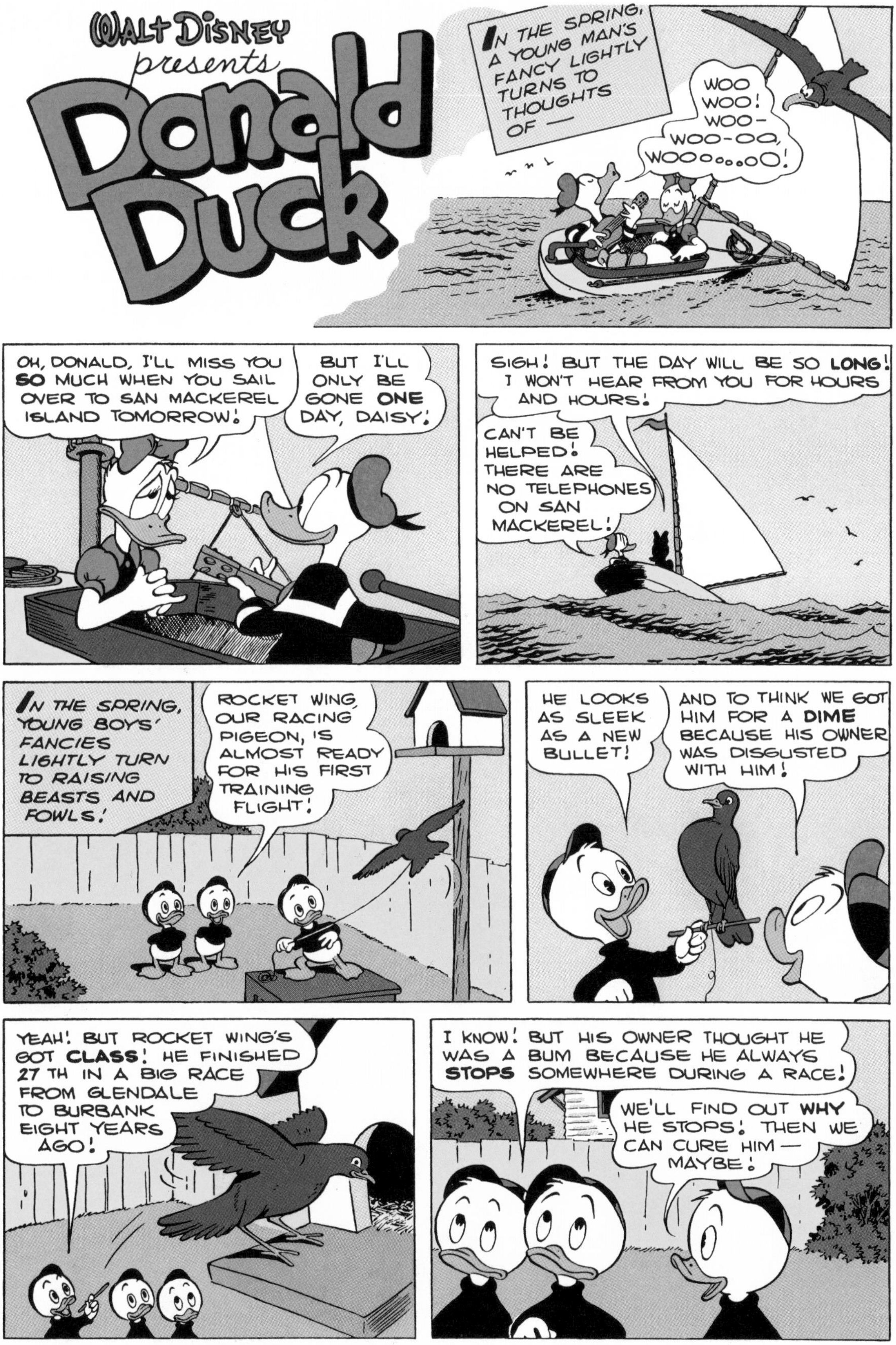
Walt Disney presents Donald Duck
IN THE SPRING, A YOUNG MAN'S FANCY LIGHTLY TURNS TO THOUGHTS OF —
WOO WOO! WOO— WOO-OO, WOOooooO!
OH, DONALD, I'LL MISS YOU SO MUCH WHEN YOU SAIL OVER TO SAN MACKEREL ISLAND TOMORROW!
BUT I'LL ONLY BE GONE ONE DAY, DAISY!
SIGH! BUT THE DAY WILL BE SO LONG! I WON'T HEAR FROM YOU FOR HOURS AND HOURS!
CAN'T BE HELPED! THERE ARE NO TELEPHONES ON SAN MACKEREL!
IN THE SPRING, YOUNG BOYS' FANCIES LIGHTLY TURN TO RAISING BEASTS AND FOWLS!
ROCKET WING, OUR RACING PIGEON, IS ALMOST READY FOR HIS FIRST TRAINING FLIGHT!
HE LOOKS AS SLEEK AS A NEW BULLET!
AND TO THINK WE GOT HIM FOR A DIME BECAUSE HIS OWNER WAS DISGUSTED WITH HIM!
YEAH! BUT ROCKET WING'S GOT CLASS! HE FINISHED 27 TH IN A BIG RACE FROM GLENDALE TO BURBANK EIGHT YEARS AGO!
I KNOW! BUT HIS OWNER THOUGHT HE WAS A BUM BECAUSE HE ALWAYS STOPS SOMEWHERE DURING A RACE!
WE'LL FIND OUT WHY HE STOPS! THEN WE CAN CURE HIM — MAYBE!

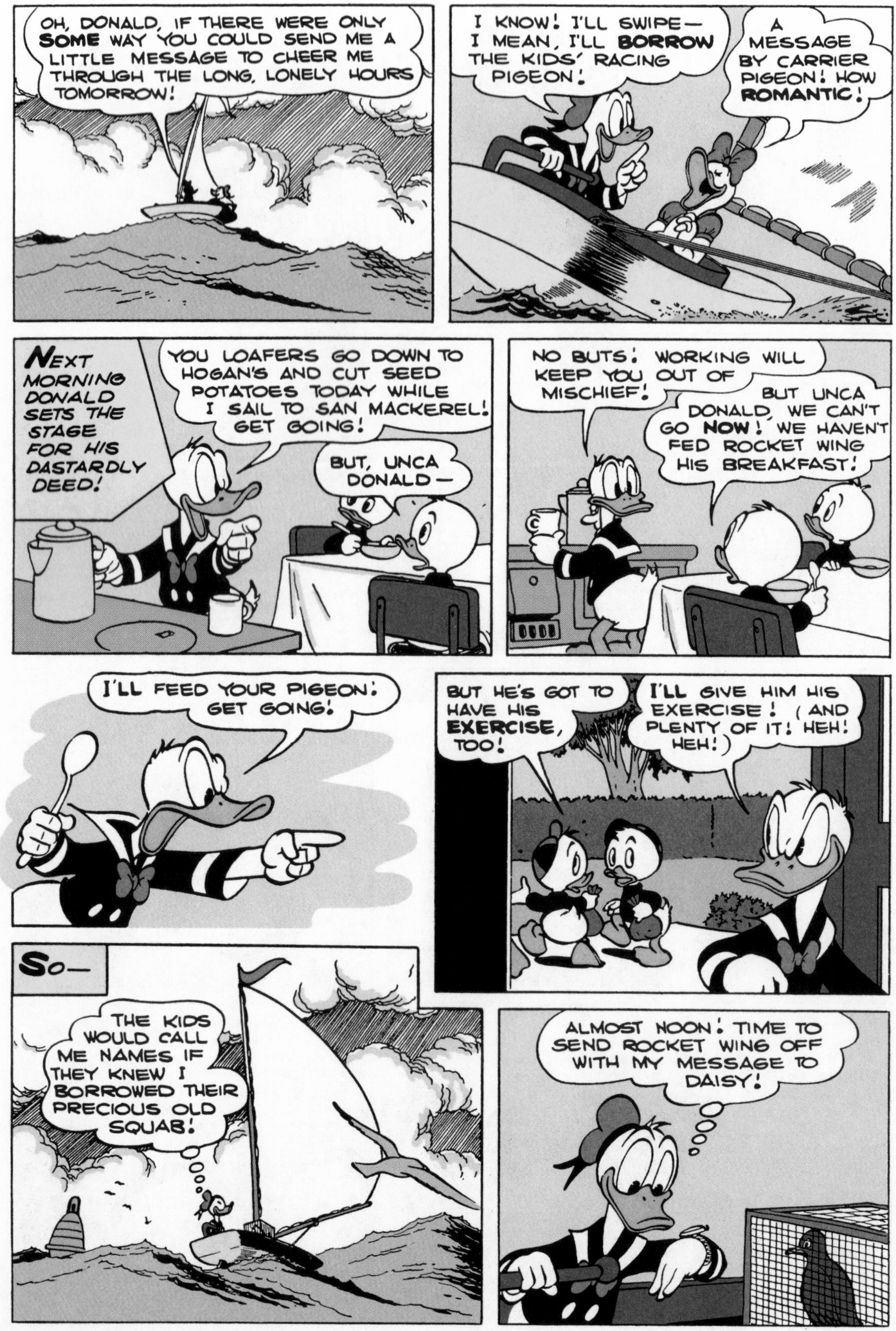
OH, DONALD, IF THERE WERE ONLY SOME WAY YOU COULD SEND ME A LITTLE MESSAGE TO CHEER ME THROUGH THE LONG, LONELY HOURS TOMORROW!
I KNOW! I'LL SWIPE— I MEAN, I'LL BORROW THE KIDS' RACING PIGEON!
A MESSAGE BY CARRIER PIGEON! HOW ROMANTIC!
NEXT MORNING DONALD SETS THE STAGE FOR HIS DASTARDLY DEED!
YOU LOAFERS GO DOWN TO HOGAN'S AND CUT SEED POTATOES TODAY WHILE I SAIL TO SAN MACKEREL! GET GOING!
BUT, UNCA DONALD—
NO BUTS! WORKING WILL KEEP YOU OUT OF MISCHIEF!
BUT UNCA DONALD, WE CAN'T GO NOW! WE HAVEN'T FED ROCKET WING HIS BREAKFAST!
I'LL FEED YOUR PIGEON! GET GOING!
BUT HE'S GOT TO HAVE HIS EXERCISE, TOO!
I'LL GIVE HIM HIS EXERCISE! (AND PLENTY OF IT! HEH! HEH!)
SO—
THE KIDS WOULD CALL ME NAMES IF THEY KNEW I BORROWED THEIR PRECIOUS OLD SQUAB!
ALMOST NOON! TIME TO SEND ROCKET WING OFF WITH MY MESSAGE TO DAISY!

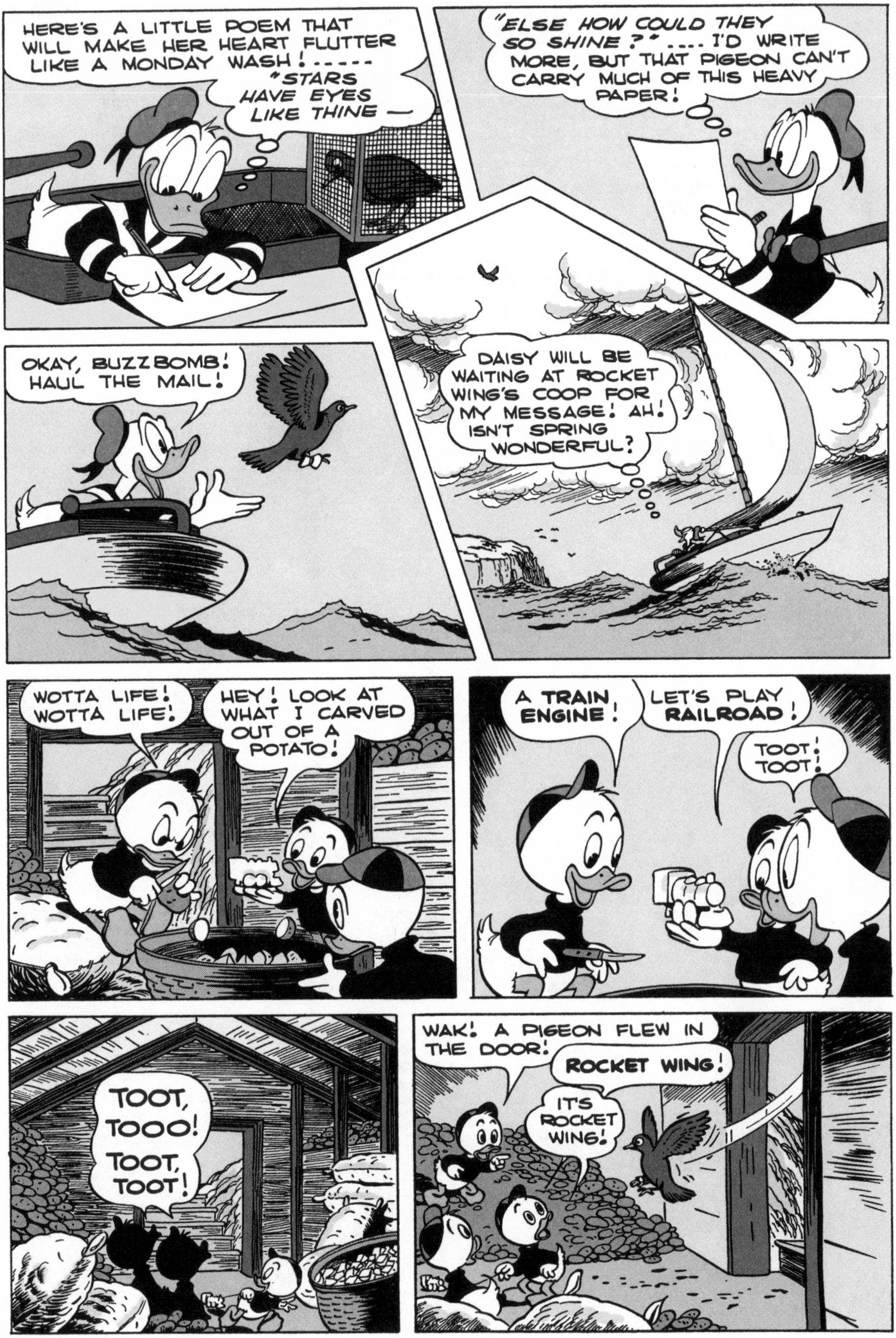

HERE'S A LITTLE POEM THAT WILL MAKE HER HEART FLUTTER LIKE A MONDAY WASH! -----
"STARS HAVE EYES LIKE THINE —
"ELSE HOW COULD THEY SO SHINE?" .... I'D WRITE MORE, BUT THAT PIGEON CAN'T CARRY MUCH OF THIS HEAVY PAPER!
OKAY, BUZZBOMB! HAUL THE MAIL!
DAISY WILL BE WAITING AT ROCKET WING'S COOP FOR MY MESSAGE! AH! ISN'T SPRING WONDERFUL?
WOTTA LIFE! WOTTA LIFE!
HEY! LOOK AT WHAT I CARVED OUT OF A POTATO!
A TRAIN ENGINE!
LET'S PLAY RAILROAD!
TOOT! TOOT!
TOOT, TOOO! TOOT, TOOT!
WAK! A PIGEON FLEW IN THE DOOR!
ROCKET WING!
IT'S ROCKET WING!

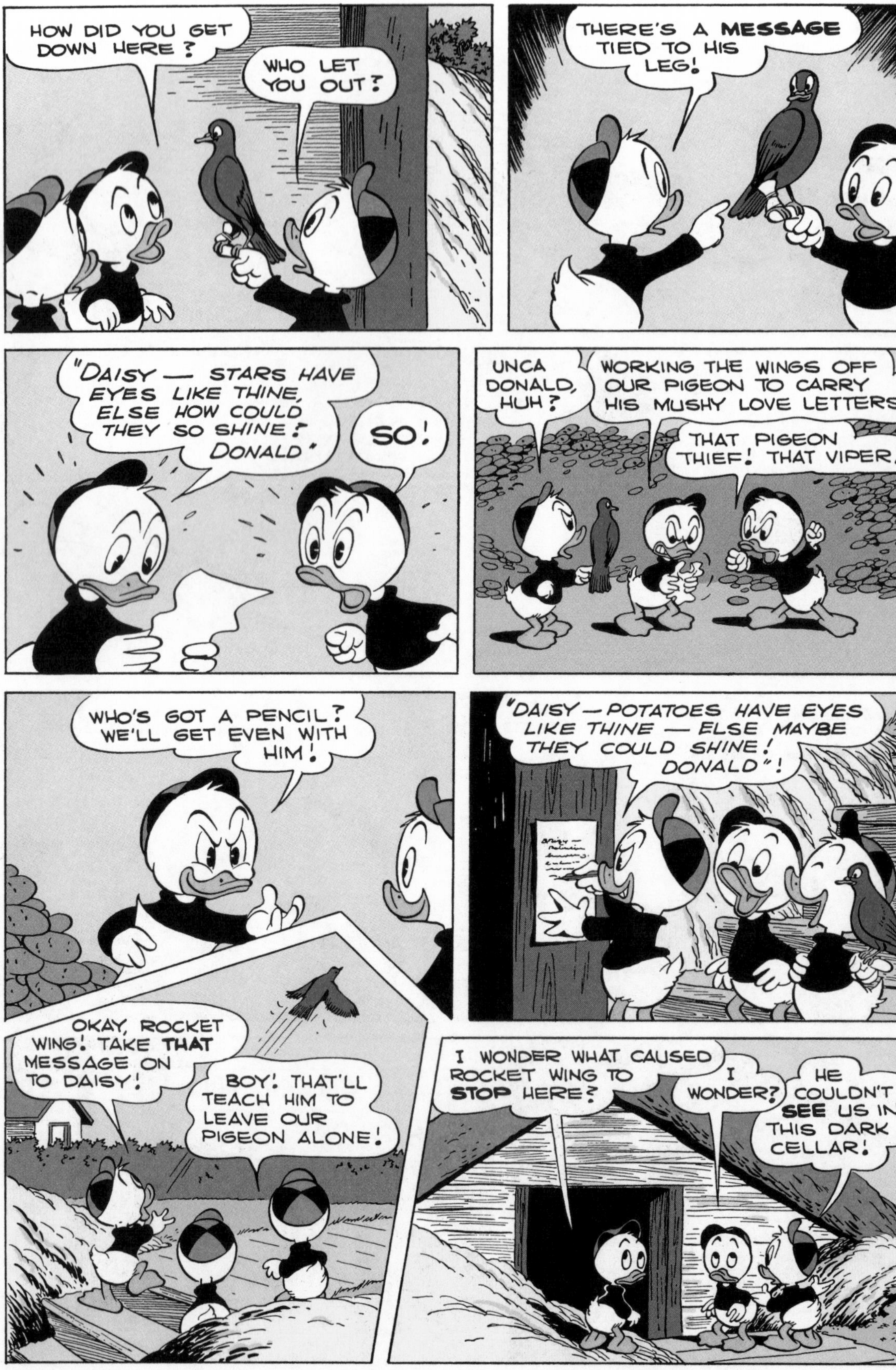
HOW DID YOU GET DOWN HERE?
WHO LET YOU OUT?
THERE'S A **MESSAGE** TIED TO HIS LEG!
"DAISY — STARS HAVE EYES LIKE THINE, ELSE HOW COULD THEY SO SHINE? DONALD"
SO!
UNCA DONALD, HUH?
WORKING THE WINGS OFF OUR PIGEON TO CARRY HIS MUSHY LOVE LETTERS!
THAT PIGEON THIEF! THAT VIPER!
WHO'S GOT A PENCIL? WE'LL GET EVEN WITH HIM!
"DAISY — POTATOES HAVE EYES LIKE THINE — ELSE MAYBE THEY COULD SHINE! DONALD"!
OKAY, ROCKET WING! TAKE **THAT** MESSAGE ON TO DAISY!
BOY! THAT'LL TEACH HIM TO LEAVE OUR PIGEON ALONE!
I WONDER WHAT CAUSED ROCKET WING TO **STOP** HERE?
I WONDER?
HE COULDN'T **SEE** US IN THIS DARK CELLAR!

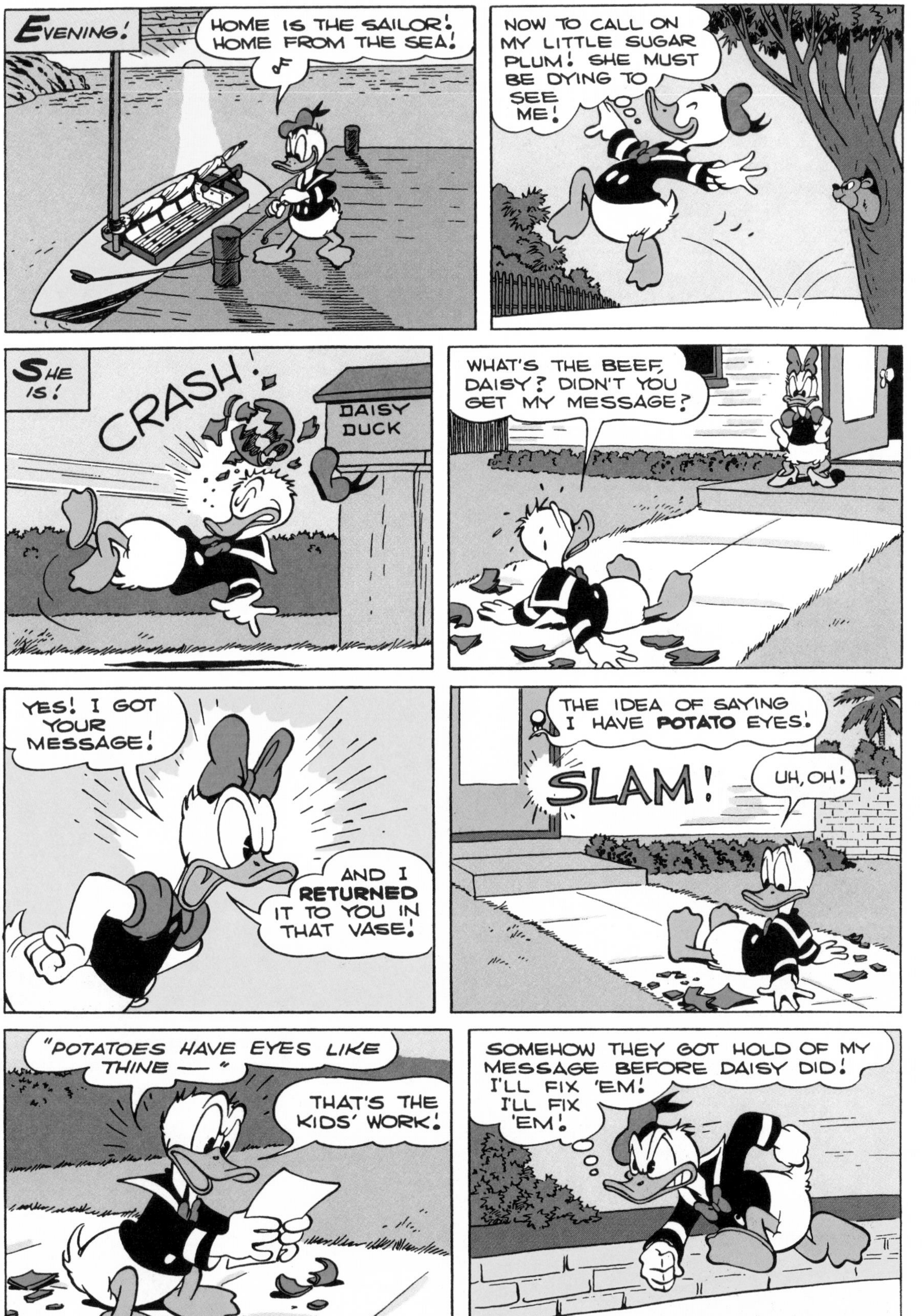
EVENING!
HOME IS THE SAILOR! HOME FROM THE SEA!
NOW TO CALL ON MY LITTLE SUGAR PLUM! SHE MUST BE DYING TO SEE ME!
SHE IS!
CRASH!
DAISY DUCK
WHAT'S THE BEEF, DAISY? DIDN'T YOU GET MY MESSAGE?
YES! I GOT YOUR MESSAGE!
AND I **RETURNED** IT TO YOU IN THAT VASE!
THE IDEA OF SAYING I HAVE **POTATO** EYES!
SLAM!
UH, OH!
"POTATOES HAVE EYES LIKE THINE —"
THAT'S THE KIDS' WORK!
SOMEHOW THEY GOT HOLD OF MY MESSAGE BEFORE DAISY DID!
I'LL FIX 'EM! I'LL FIX 'EM!

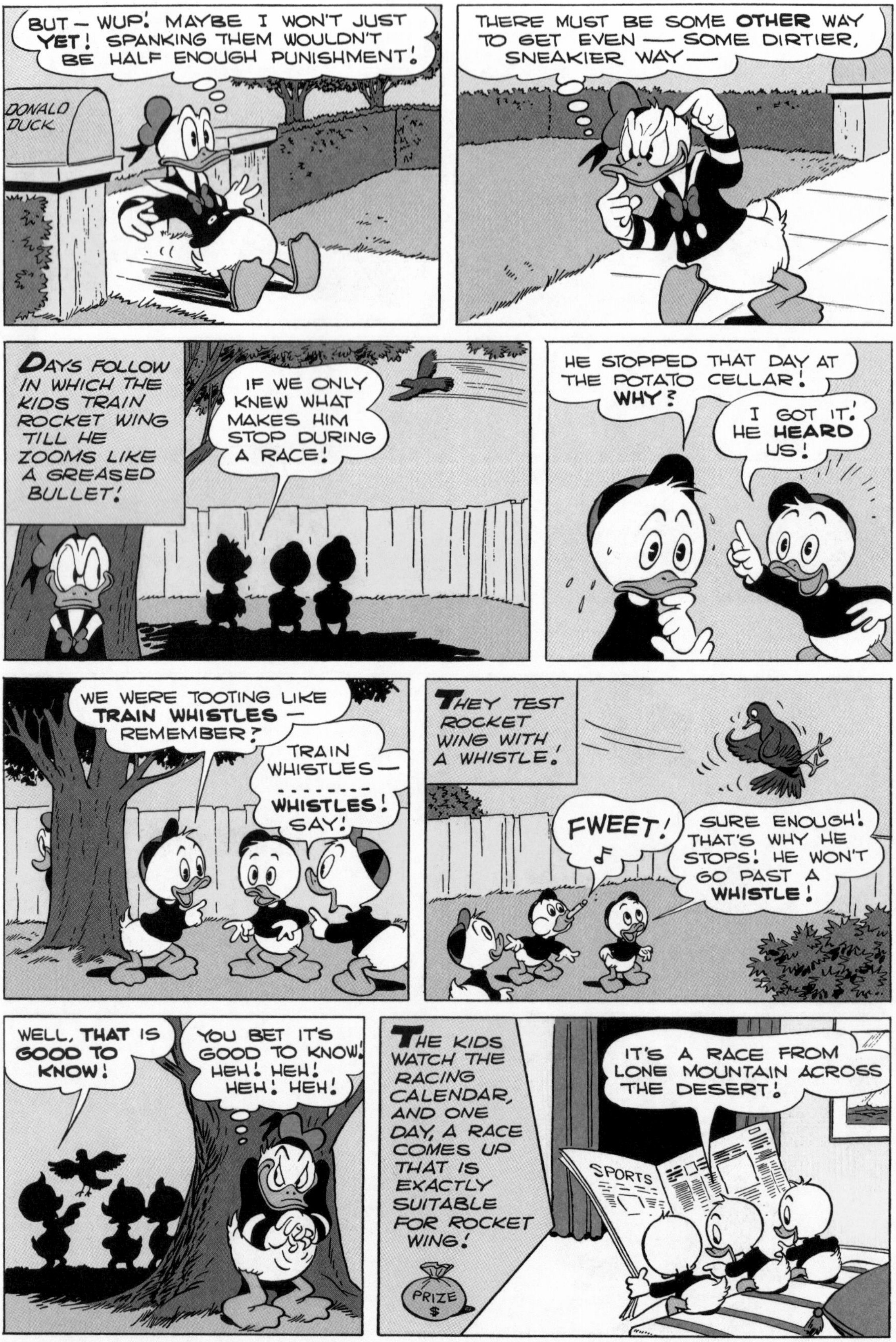

DONALD DUCK
BUT — WUP! MAYBE I WON'T JUST YET! SPANKING THEM WOULDN'T BE HALF ENOUGH PUNISHMENT!
THERE MUST BE SOME OTHER WAY TO GET EVEN — SOME DIRTIER, SNEAKIER WAY —
DAYS FOLLOW IN WHICH THE KIDS TRAIN ROCKET WING TILL HE ZOOMS LIKE A GREASED BULLET!
IF WE ONLY KNEW WHAT MAKES HIM STOP DURING A RACE!
HE STOPPED THAT DAY AT THE POTATO CELLAR! WHY?
I GOT IT! HE HEARD US!
WE WERE TOOTING LIKE TRAIN WHISTLES — REMEMBER?
TRAIN WHISTLES — -------- WHISTLES! SAY!
THEY TEST ROCKET WING WITH A WHISTLE!
FWEET!
SURE ENOUGH! THAT'S WHY HE STOPS! HE WON'T GO PAST A WHISTLE!
WELL, THAT IS GOOD TO KNOW!
YOU BET IT'S GOOD TO KNOW! HEH! HEH! HEH! HEH!
THE KIDS WATCH THE RACING CALENDAR, AND ONE DAY, A RACE COMES UP THAT IS EXACTLY SUITABLE FOR ROCKET WING!
PRIZE $
IT'S A RACE FROM LONE MOUNTAIN ACROSS THE DESERT!
SPORTS

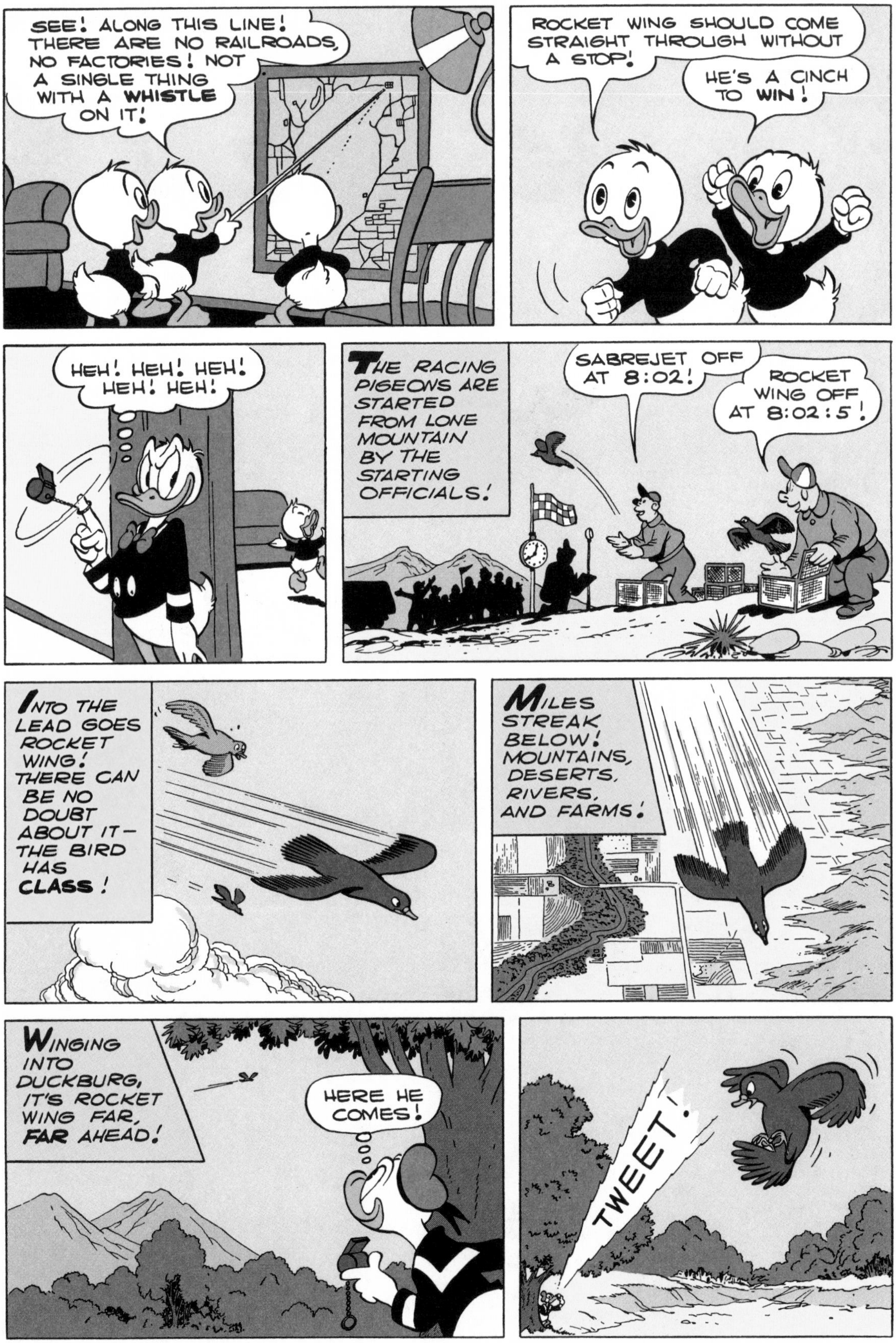

SEE! ALONG THIS LINE! THERE ARE NO RAILROADS, NO FACTORIES! NOT A SINGLE THING WITH A **WHISTLE** ON IT!
ROCKET WING SHOULD COME STRAIGHT THROUGH WITHOUT A STOP!
HE'S A CINCH TO **WIN**!
HEH! HEH! HEH! HEH! HEH!
THE RACING PIGEONS ARE STARTED FROM LONE MOUNTAIN BY THE STARTING OFFICIALS!
SABREJET OFF AT 8:02!
ROCKET WING OFF AT 8:02:5!
INTO THE LEAD GOES ROCKET WING! THERE CAN BE NO DOUBT ABOUT IT— THE BIRD HAS **CLASS**!
MILES STREAK BELOW! MOUNTAINS, DESERTS, RIVERS, AND FARMS!
WINGING INTO DUCKBURG, IT'S ROCKET WING FAR, **FAR** AHEAD!
HERE HE COMES!
TWEET!

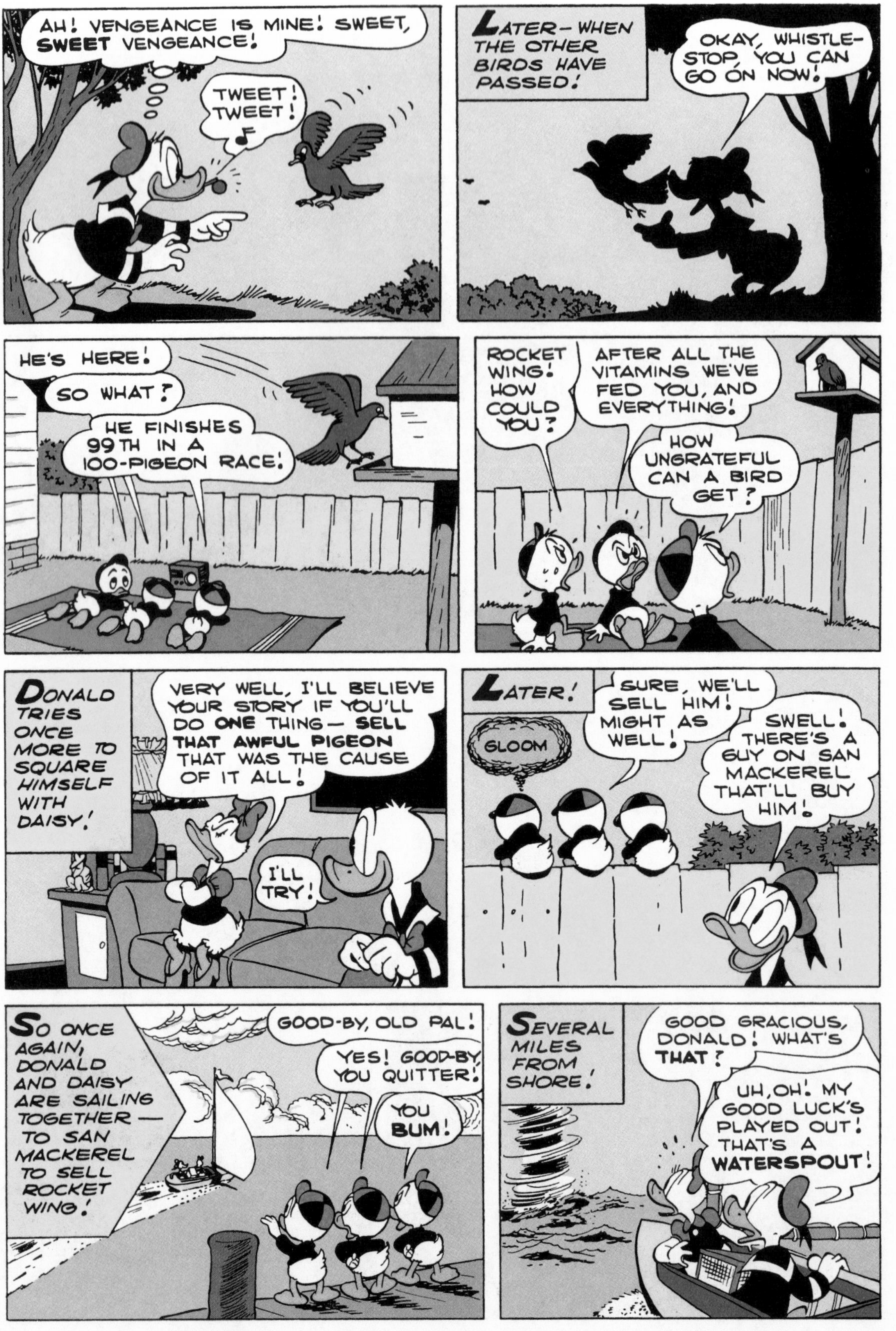
AH! VENGEANCE IS MINE! SWEET, SWEET VENGEANCE!
TWEET! TWEET!
LATER—WHEN THE OTHER BIRDS HAVE PASSED!
OKAY, WHISTLE-STOP, YOU CAN GO ON NOW!
HE'S HERE!
SO WHAT?
HE FINISHES 99TH IN A 100-PIGEON RACE!
ROCKET WING! HOW COULD YOU?
AFTER ALL THE VITAMINS WE'VE FED YOU, AND EVERYTHING!
HOW UNGRATEFUL CAN A BIRD GET?
DONALD TRIES ONCE MORE TO SQUARE HIMSELF WITH DAISY!
VERY WELL, I'LL BELIEVE YOUR STORY IF YOU'LL DO ONE THING— SELL THAT AWFUL PIGEON THAT WAS THE CAUSE OF IT ALL!
I'LL TRY!
LATER!
GLOOM
SURE, WE'LL SELL HIM! MIGHT AS WELL!
SWELL! THERE'S A GUY ON SAN MACKEREL THAT'LL BUY HIM!
SO ONCE AGAIN, DONALD AND DAISY ARE SAILING TOGETHER— TO SAN MACKEREL TO SELL ROCKET WING!
GOOD-BY, OLD PAL!
YES! GOOD-BY, YOU QUITTER!
YOU BUM!
SEVERAL MILES FROM SHORE!
GOOD GRACIOUS, DONALD! WHAT'S THAT?
UH, OH! MY GOOD LUCK'S PLAYED OUT! THAT'S A WATERSPOUT!

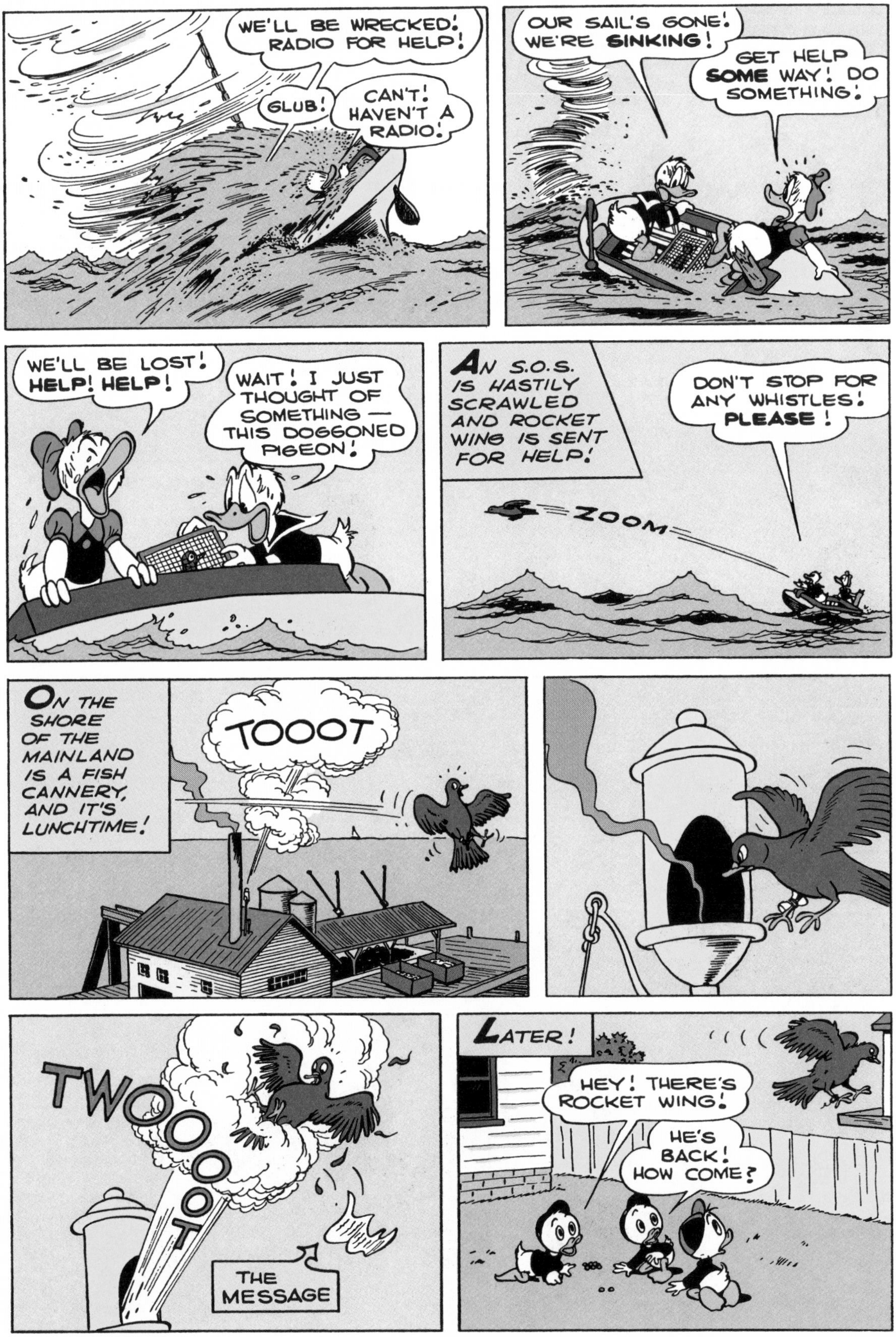
WE'LL BE WRECKED! RADIO FOR HELP!
GLUB!
CAN'T! HAVEN'T A RADIO!
OUR SAIL'S GONE! WE'RE SINKING!
GET HELP SOME WAY! DO SOMETHING!
WE'LL BE LOST! HELP! HELP!
WAIT! I JUST THOUGHT OF SOMETHING — THIS DOGGONED PIGEON!
AN S.O.S. IS HASTILY SCRAWLED AND ROCKET WING IS SENT FOR HELP!
DON'T STOP FOR ANY WHISTLES! PLEASE!
ZOOM
ON THE SHORE OF THE MAINLAND IS A FISH CANNERY, AND IT'S LUNCHTIME!
TOOOT
TWOOOOOT
THE MESSAGE
LATER!
HEY! THERE'S ROCKET WING!
HE'S BACK! HOW COME?

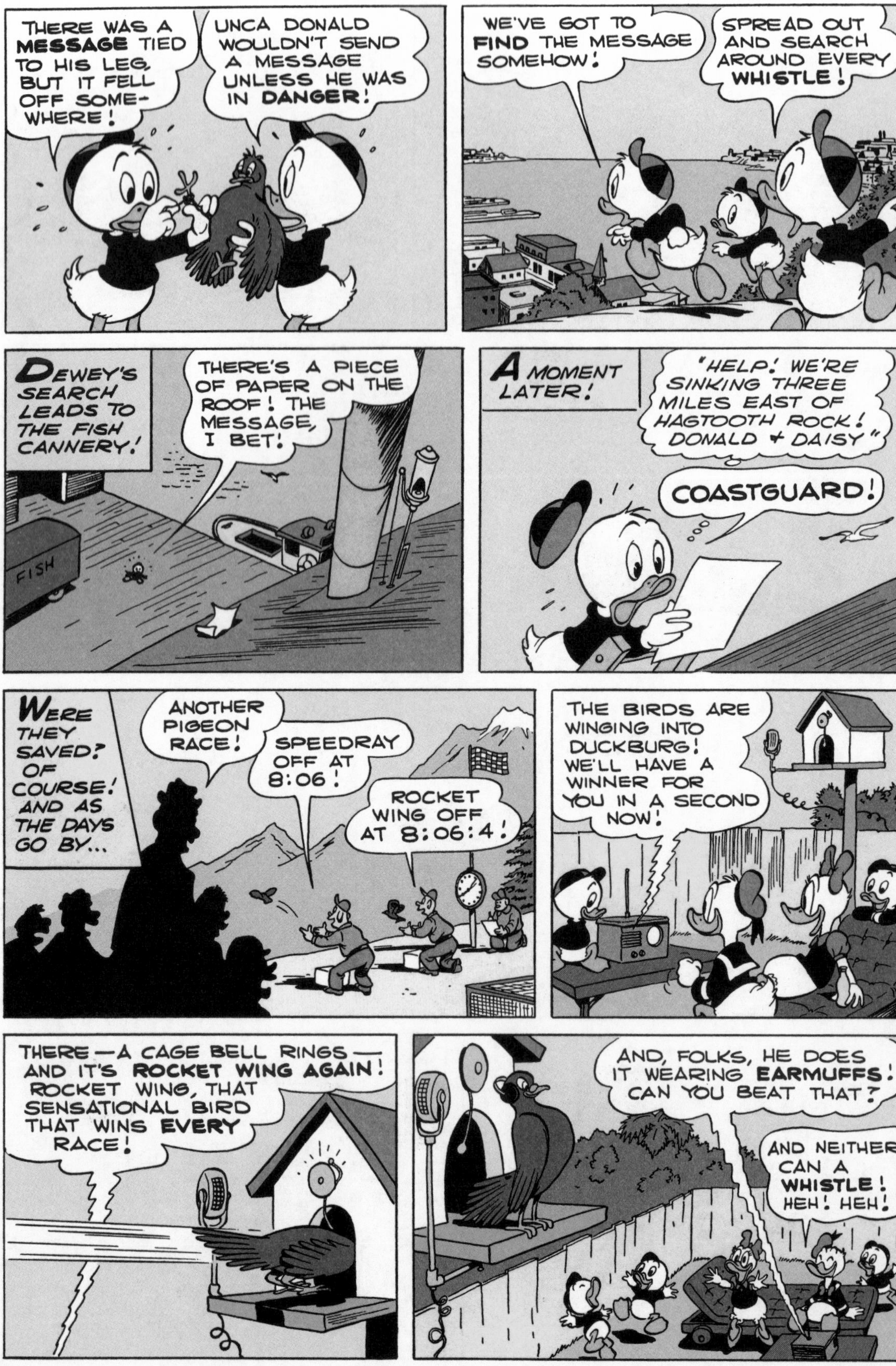

THERE WAS A MESSAGE TIED TO HIS LEG, BUT IT FELL OFF SOME-WHERE!
UNCA DONALD WOULDN'T SEND A MESSAGE UNLESS HE WAS IN DANGER!
WE'VE GOT TO FIND THE MESSAGE SOMEHOW!
SPREAD OUT AND SEARCH AROUND EVERY WHISTLE!
DEWEY'S SEARCH LEADS TO THE FISH CANNERY!
THERE'S A PIECE OF PAPER ON THE ROOF! THE MESSAGE, I BET!
FISH
A MOMENT LATER!
"HELP! WE'RE SINKING THREE MILES EAST OF HAGTOOTH ROCK! DONALD + DAISY"
COASTGUARD!
WERE THEY SAVED? OF COURSE! AND AS THE DAYS GO BY...
ANOTHER PIGEON RACE!
SPEEDRAY OFF AT 8:06!
ROCKET WING OFF AT 8:06:4!
THE BIRDS ARE WINGING INTO DUCKBURG! WE'LL HAVE A WINNER FOR YOU IN A SECOND NOW!
THERE—A CAGE BELL RINGS—AND IT'S ROCKET WING AGAIN! ROCKET WING, THAT SENSATIONAL BIRD THAT WINS EVERY RACE!
AND, FOLKS, HE DOES IT WEARING EARMUFFS! CAN YOU BEAT THAT?
AND NEITHER CAN A WHISTLE! HEH! HEH!

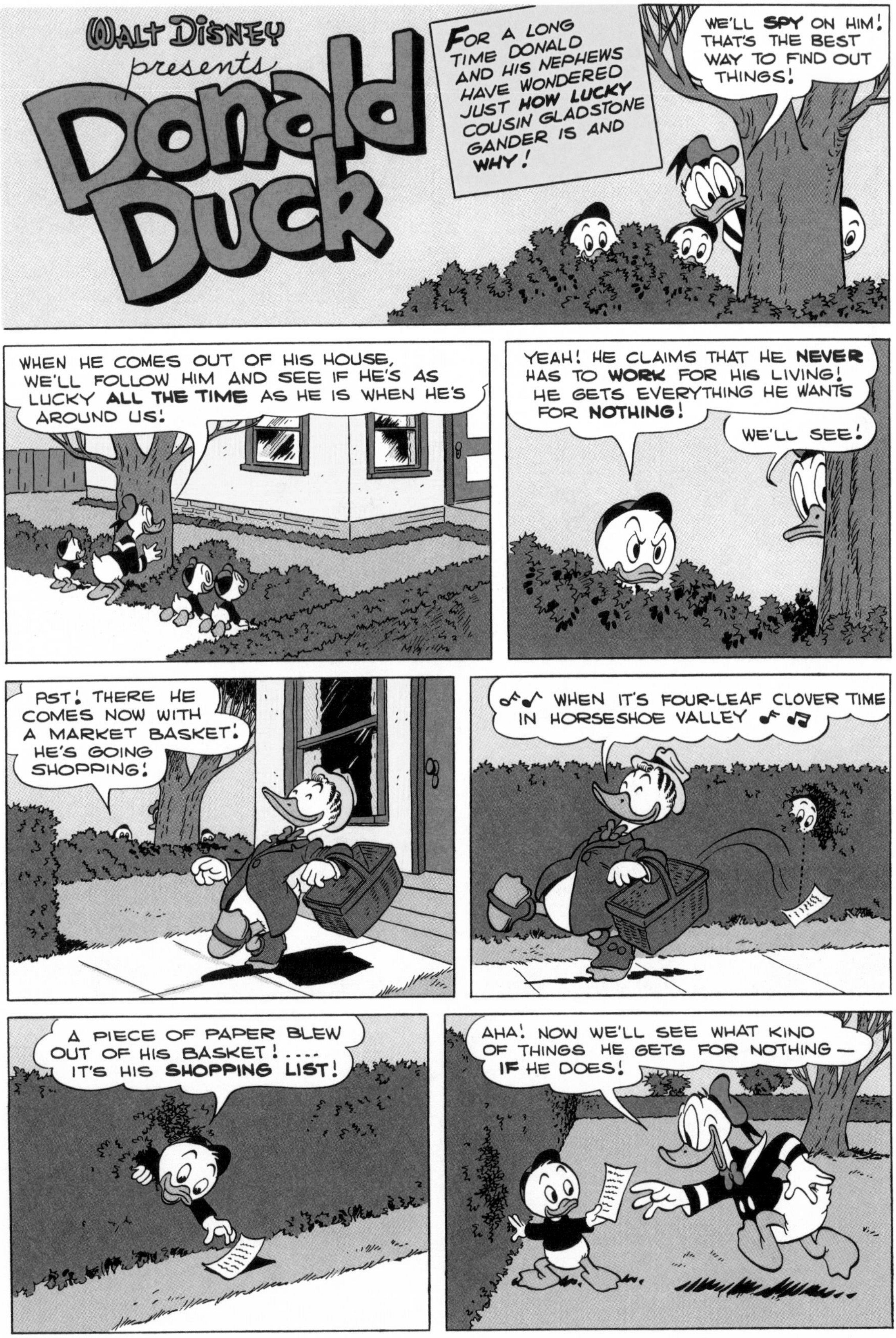
WALT DISNEY
presents
Donald Duck
FOR A LONG TIME DONALD AND HIS NEPHEWS HAVE WONDERED JUST HOW LUCKY COUSIN GLADSTONE GANDER IS AND WHY!
WE'LL SPY ON HIM! THAT'S THE BEST WAY TO FIND OUT THINGS!
WHEN HE COMES OUT OF HIS HOUSE, WE'LL FOLLOW HIM AND SEE IF HE'S AS LUCKY ALL THE TIME AS HE IS WHEN HE'S AROUND US!
YEAH! HE CLAIMS THAT HE NEVER HAS TO WORK FOR HIS LIVING! HE GETS EVERYTHING HE WANTS FOR NOTHING!
WE'LL SEE!
PST! THERE HE COMES NOW WITH A MARKET BASKET! HE'S GOING SHOPPING!
WHEN IT'S FOUR-LEAF CLOVER TIME IN HORSESHOE VALLEY
A PIECE OF PAPER BLEW OUT OF HIS BASKET! .... IT'S HIS SHOPPING LIST!
AHA! NOW WE'LL SEE WHAT KIND OF THINGS HE GETS FOR NOTHING — IF HE DOES!

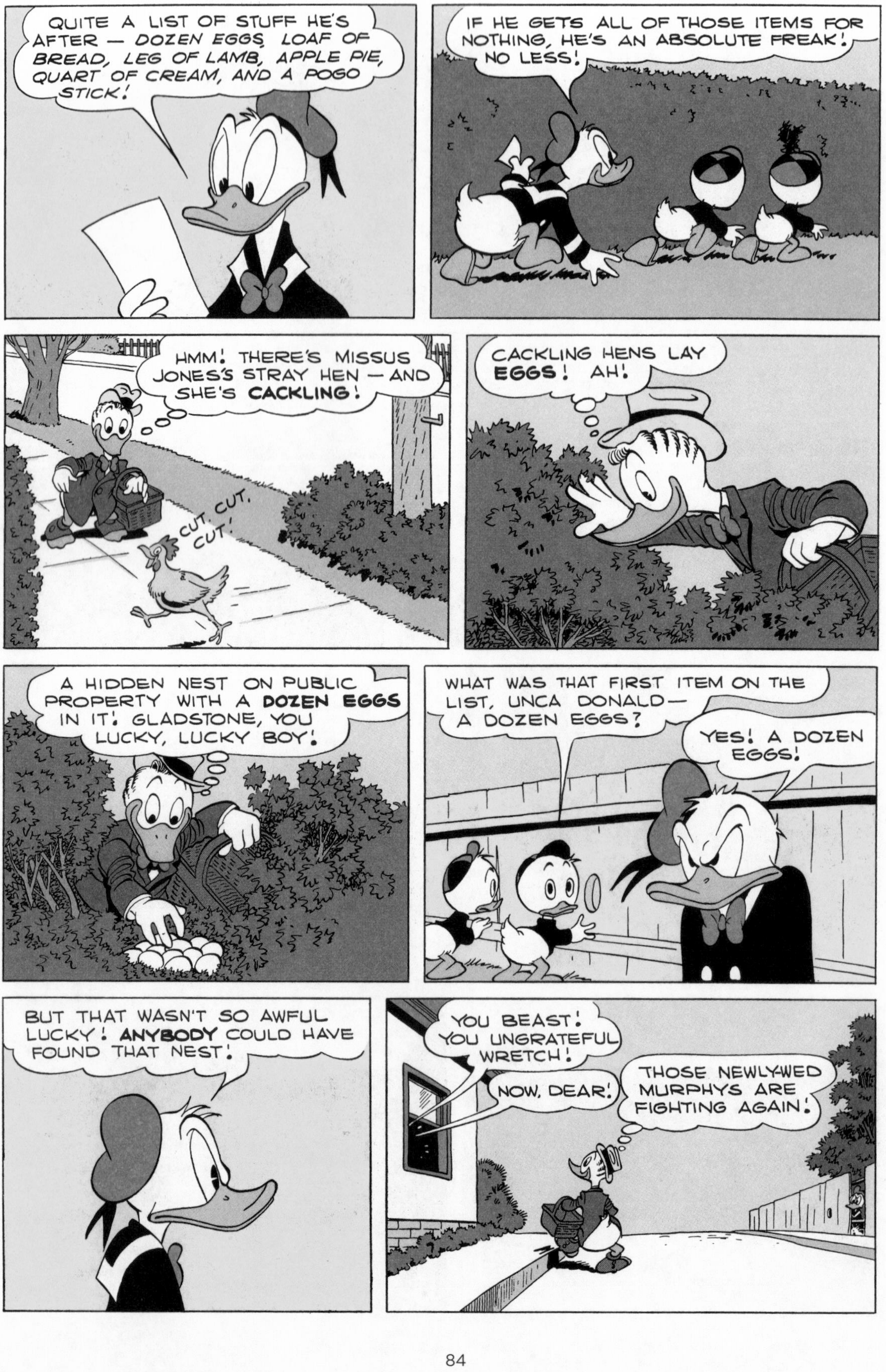
QUITE A LIST OF STUFF HE'S AFTER — DOZEN EGGS, LOAF OF BREAD, LEG OF LAMB, APPLE PIE, QUART OF CREAM, AND A POGO STICK!
IF HE GETS ALL OF THOSE ITEMS FOR NOTHING, HE'S AN ABSOLUTE FREAK! NO LESS!
HMM! THERE'S MISSUS JONES'S STRAY HEN — AND SHE'S CACKLING!
CUT CUT, CUT!
CACKLING HENS LAY EGGS! AH!
A HIDDEN NEST ON PUBLIC PROPERTY WITH A DOZEN EGGS IN IT! GLADSTONE, YOU LUCKY, LUCKY BOY!
WHAT WAS THAT FIRST ITEM ON THE LIST, UNCA DONALD — A DOZEN EGGS?
YES! A DOZEN EGGS!
BUT THAT WASN'T SO AWFUL LUCKY! ANYBODY COULD HAVE FOUND THAT NEST!
YOU BEAST! YOU UNGRATEFUL WRETCH!
NOW, DEAR!
THOSE NEWLY-WED MURPHYS ARE FIGHTING AGAIN!

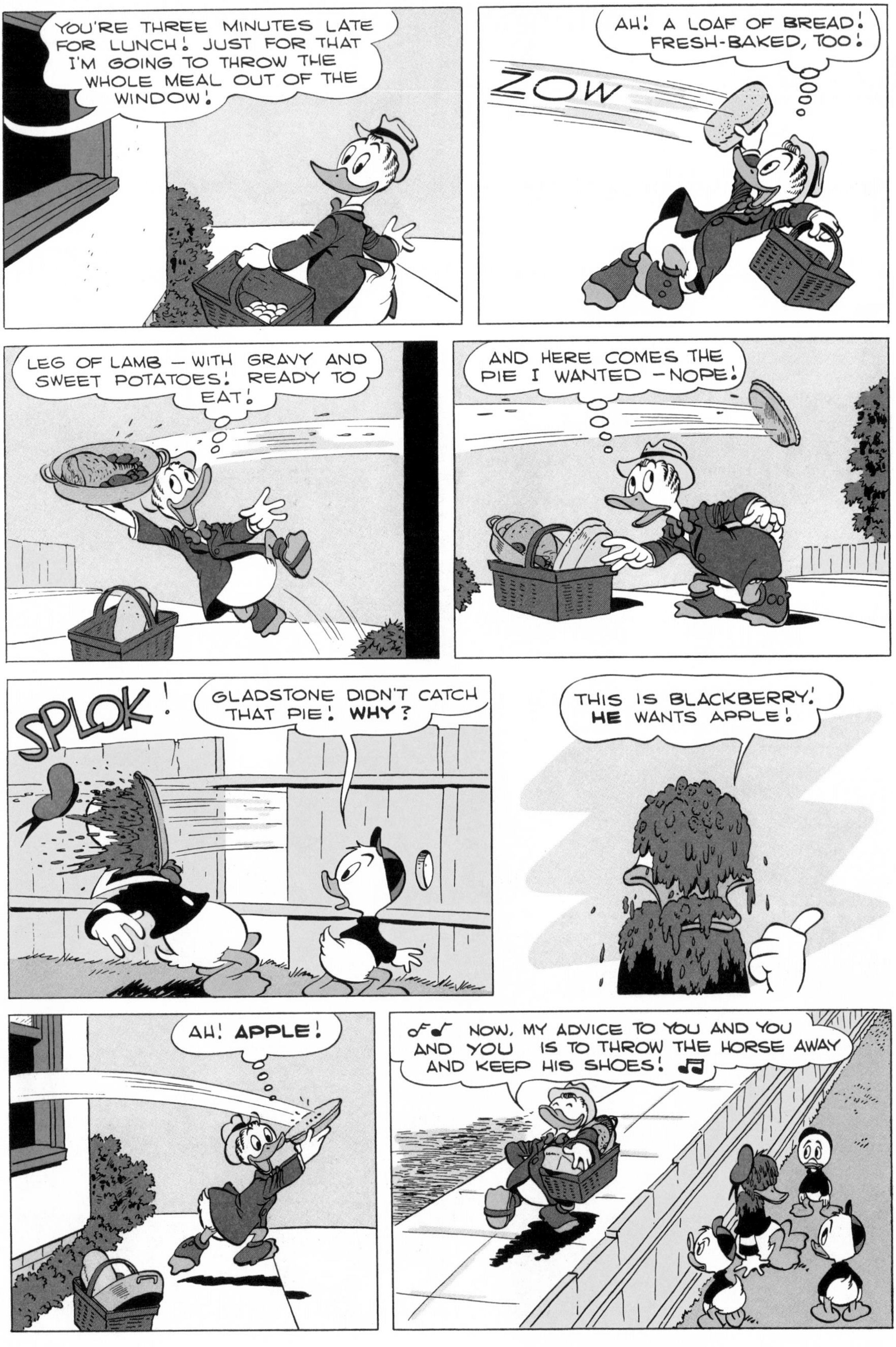
YOU'RE THREE MINUTES LATE FOR LUNCH! JUST FOR THAT I'M GOING TO THROW THE WHOLE MEAL OUT OF THE WINDOW!
AH! A LOAF OF BREAD! FRESH-BAKED, TOO!
ZOW
LEG OF LAMB — WITH GRAVY AND SWEET POTATOES! READY TO EAT!
AND HERE COMES THE PIE I WANTED — NOPE!
SPLOK!
GLADSTONE DIDN'T CATCH THAT PIE! WHY?
THIS IS BLACKBERRY! HE WANTS APPLE!
AH! APPLE!
NOW, MY ADVICE TO YOU AND YOU AND YOU IS TO THROW THE HORSE AWAY AND KEEP HIS SHOES!

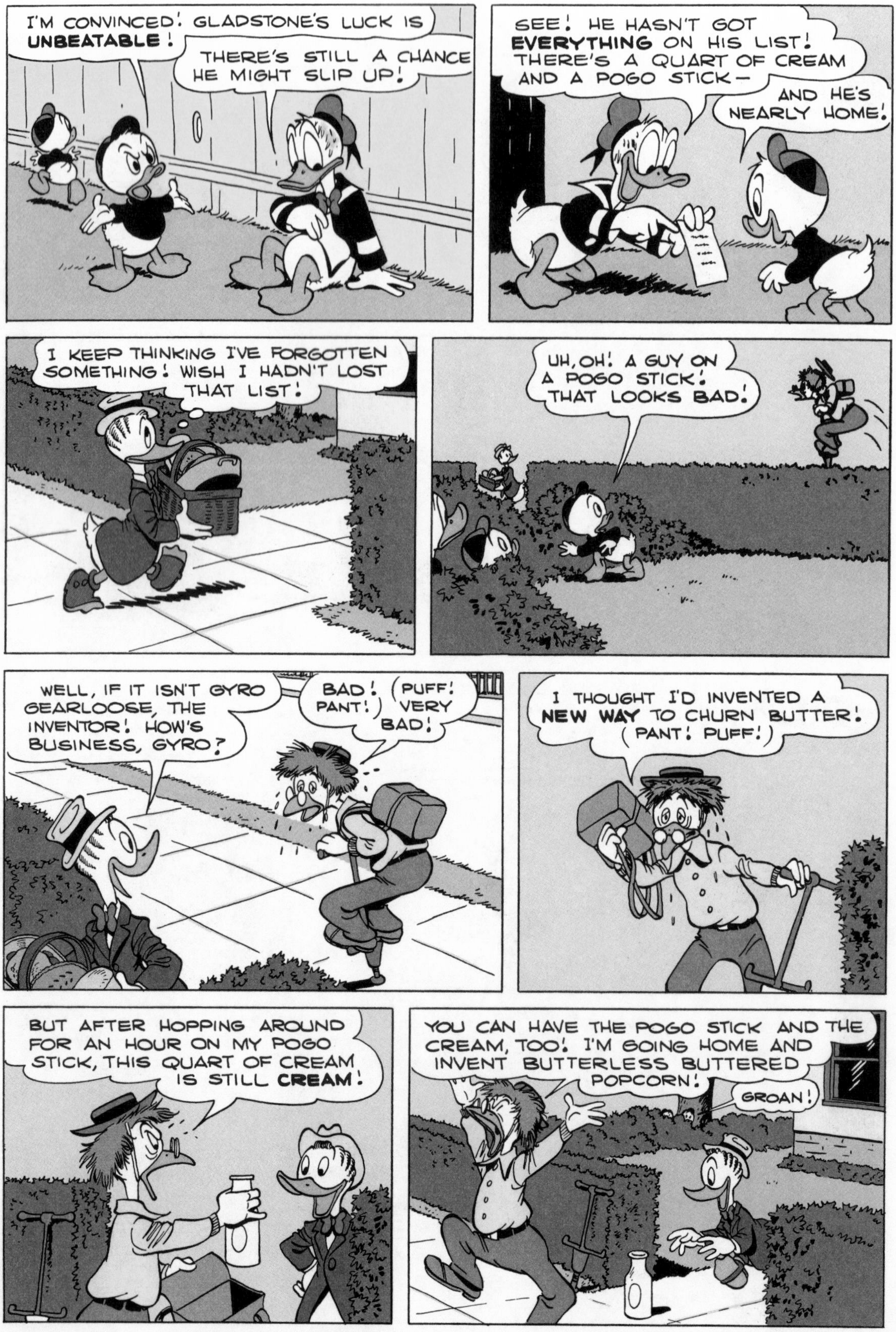
I'M CONVINCED! GLADSTONE'S LUCK IS UNBEATABLE!
THERE'S STILL A CHANCE HE MIGHT SLIP UP!
SEE! HE HASN'T GOT EVERYTHING ON HIS LIST! THERE'S A QUART OF CREAM AND A POGO STICK—
AND HE'S NEARLY HOME!
I KEEP THINKING I'VE FORGOTTEN SOMETHING! WISH I HADN'T LOST THAT LIST!
UH, OH! A GUY ON A POGO STICK! THAT LOOKS BAD!
WELL, IF IT ISN'T GYRO GEARLOOSE, THE INVENTOR! HOW'S BUSINESS, GYRO?
BAD! (PUFF! PANT!) VERY BAD!
I THOUGHT I'D INVENTED A NEW WAY TO CHURN BUTTER! (PANT! PUFF!)
BUT AFTER HOPPING AROUND FOR AN HOUR ON MY POGO STICK, THIS QUART OF CREAM IS STILL CREAM!
YOU CAN HAVE THE POGO STICK AND THE CREAM, TOO! I'M GOING HOME AND INVENT BUTTERLESS BUTTERED POPCORN!
GROAN!

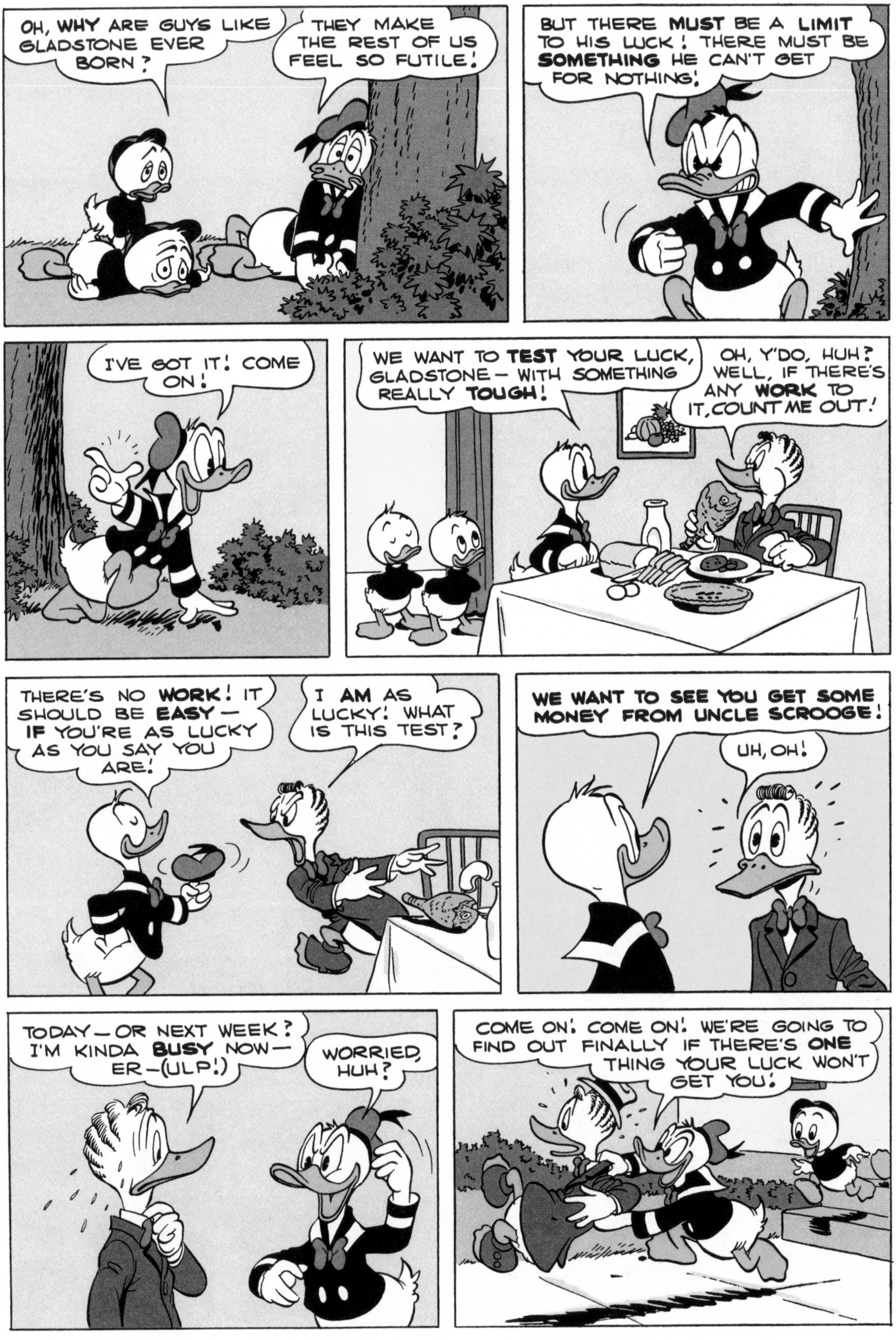
OH, WHY ARE GUYS LIKE GLADSTONE EVER BORN?
THEY MAKE THE REST OF US FEEL SO FUTILE!
BUT THERE MUST BE A LIMIT TO HIS LUCK! THERE MUST BE SOMETHING HE CAN'T GET FOR NOTHING!
I'VE GOT IT! COME ON!
WE WANT TO TEST YOUR LUCK, GLADSTONE— WITH SOMETHING REALLY TOUGH!
OH, Y'DO, HUH? WELL, IF THERE'S ANY WORK TO IT, COUNT ME OUT!
THERE'S NO WORK! IT SHOULD BE EASY— IF YOU'RE AS LUCKY AS YOU SAY YOU ARE!
I AM AS LUCKY! WHAT IS THIS TEST?
WE WANT TO SEE YOU GET SOME MONEY FROM UNCLE SCROOGE!
UH, OH!
TODAY—OR NEXT WEEK? I'M KINDA BUSY NOW— ER—(ULP!)
WORRIED, HUH?
COME ON! COME ON! WE'RE GOING TO FIND OUT FINALLY IF THERE'S ONE THING YOUR LUCK WON'T GET YOU!

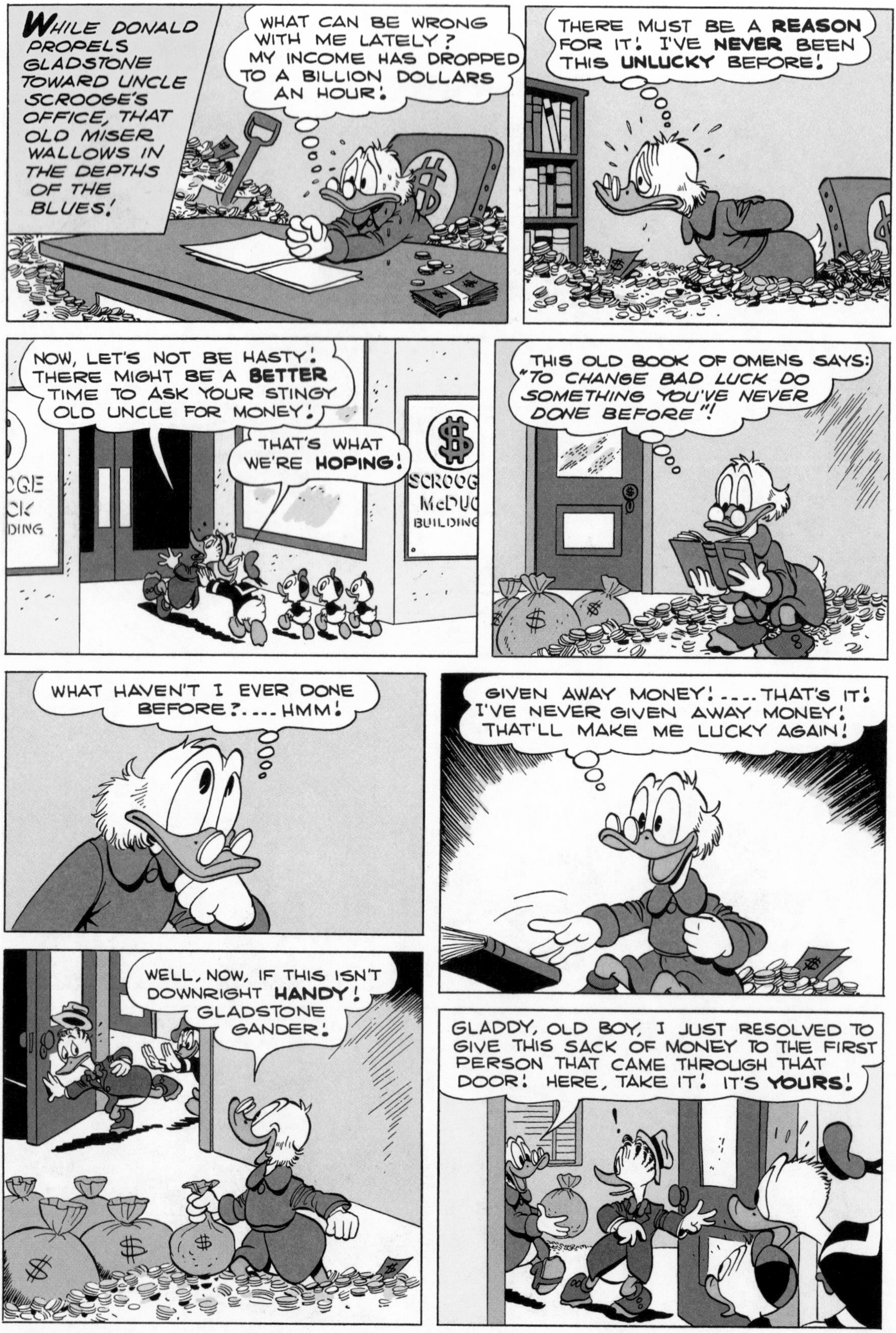
WHILE DONALD PROPELS GLADSTONE TOWARD UNCLE SCROOGE'S OFFICE, THAT OLD MISER WALLOWS IN THE DEPTHS OF THE BLUES!
WHAT CAN BE WRONG WITH ME LATELY? MY INCOME HAS DROPPED TO A BILLION DOLLARS AN HOUR!
THERE MUST BE A REASON FOR IT! I'VE NEVER BEEN THIS UNLUCKY BEFORE!
NOW, LET'S NOT BE HASTY! THERE MIGHT BE A BETTER TIME TO ASK YOUR STINGY OLD UNCLE FOR MONEY!
THAT'S WHAT WE'RE HOPING!
SCROOG McDUC BUILDING
THIS OLD BOOK OF OMENS SAYS: "TO CHANGE BAD LUCK DO SOMETHING YOU'VE NEVER DONE BEFORE"!
WHAT HAVEN'T I EVER DONE BEFORE?.... HMM!
GIVEN AWAY MONEY!.... THAT'S IT! I'VE NEVER GIVEN AWAY MONEY! THAT'LL MAKE ME LUCKY AGAIN!
WELL, NOW, IF THIS ISN'T DOWNRIGHT HANDY! GLADSTONE GANDER!
GLADDY, OLD BOY, I JUST RESOLVED TO GIVE THIS SACK OF MONEY TO THE FIRST PERSON THAT CAME THROUGH THAT DOOR! HERE, TAKE IT! IT'S YOURS!

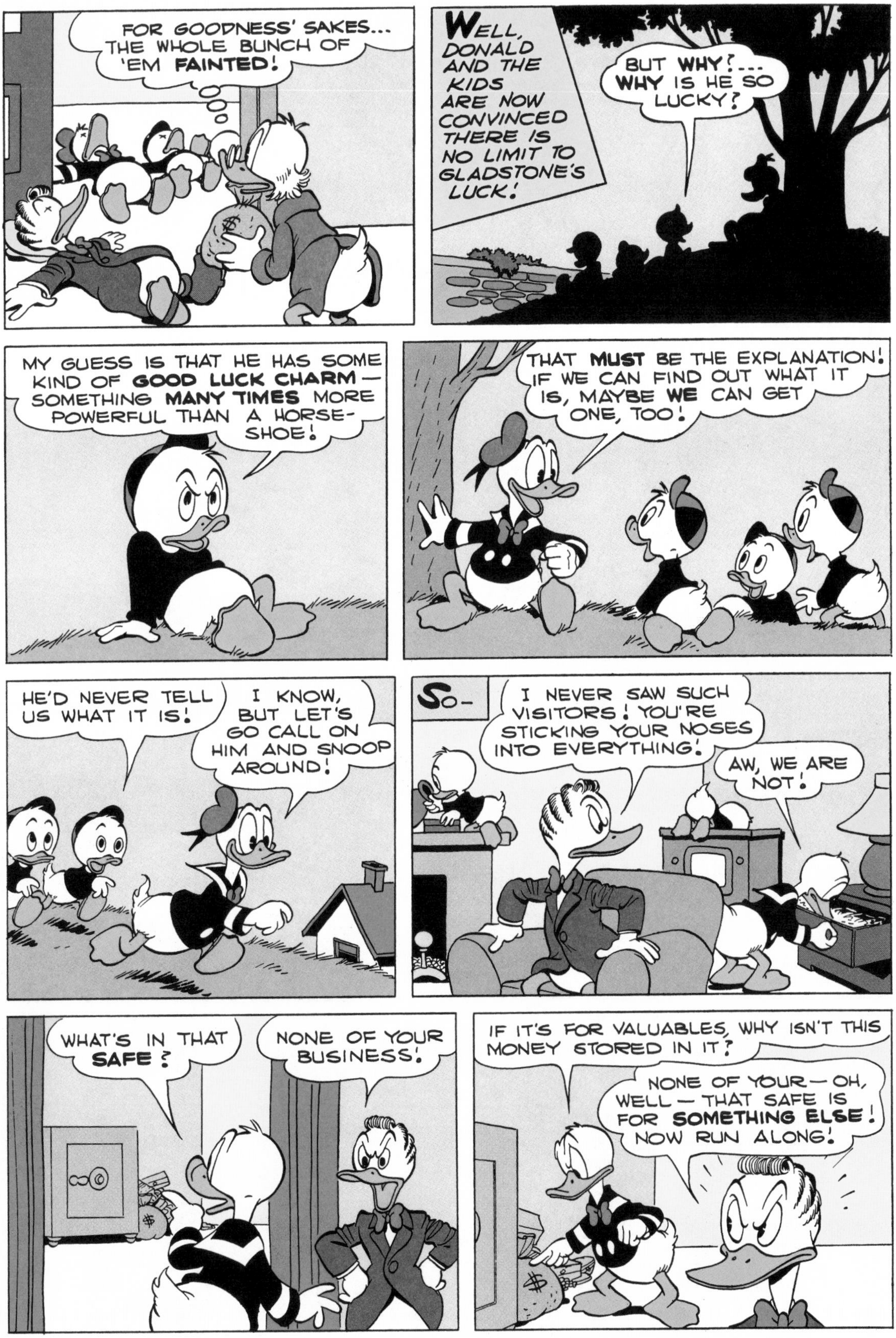
FOR GOODNESS' SAKES... THE WHOLE BUNCH OF 'EM FAINTED!
WELL, DONALD AND THE KIDS ARE NOW CONVINCED THERE IS NO LIMIT TO GLADSTONE'S LUCK!
BUT WHY?... WHY IS HE SO LUCKY?
MY GUESS IS THAT HE HAS SOME KIND OF GOOD LUCK CHARM — SOMETHING MANY TIMES MORE POWERFUL THAN A HORSE-SHOE!
THAT MUST BE THE EXPLANATION! IF WE CAN FIND OUT WHAT IT IS, MAYBE WE CAN GET ONE, TOO!
HE'D NEVER TELL US WHAT IT IS!
I KNOW, BUT LET'S GO CALL ON HIM AND SNOOP AROUND!
SO-
I NEVER SAW SUCH VISITORS! YOU'RE STICKING YOUR NOSES INTO EVERYTHING!
AW, WE ARE NOT!
WHAT'S IN THAT SAFE?
NONE OF YOUR BUSINESS!
IF IT'S FOR VALUABLES, WHY ISN'T THIS MONEY STORED IN IT?
NONE OF YOUR—OH, WELL—THAT SAFE IS FOR SOMETHING ELSE! NOW RUN ALONG!

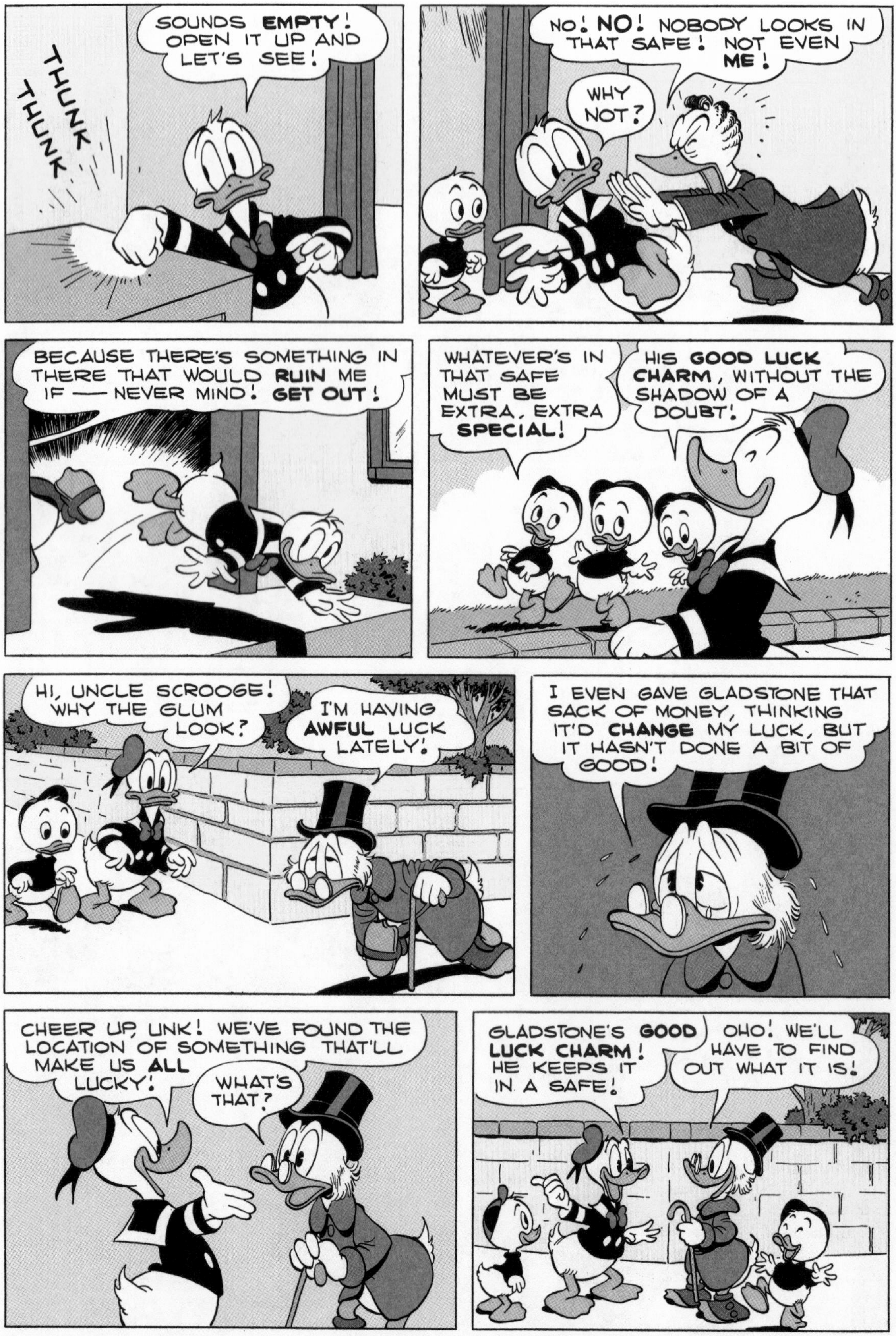
SOUNDS EMPTY! OPEN IT UP AND LET'S SEE!
THUNK THUNK
NO! NO! NOBODY LOOKS IN THAT SAFE! NOT EVEN ME!
WHY NOT?
BECAUSE THERE'S SOMETHING IN THERE THAT WOULD RUIN ME IF — NEVER MIND! GET OUT!
WHATEVER'S IN THAT SAFE MUST BE EXTRA, EXTRA SPECIAL!
HIS GOOD LUCK CHARM, WITHOUT THE SHADOW OF A DOUBT!
HI, UNCLE SCROOGE! WHY THE GLUM LOOK?
I'M HAVING AWFUL LUCK LATELY!
I EVEN GAVE GLADSTONE THAT SACK OF MONEY, THINKING IT'D CHANGE MY LUCK, BUT IT HASN'T DONE A BIT OF GOOD!
CHEER UP, UNK! WE'VE FOUND THE LOCATION OF SOMETHING THAT'LL MAKE US ALL LUCKY!
WHAT'S THAT?
GLADSTONE'S GOOD LUCK CHARM! HE KEEPS IT IN A SAFE!
OHO! WE'LL HAVE TO FIND OUT WHAT IT IS!

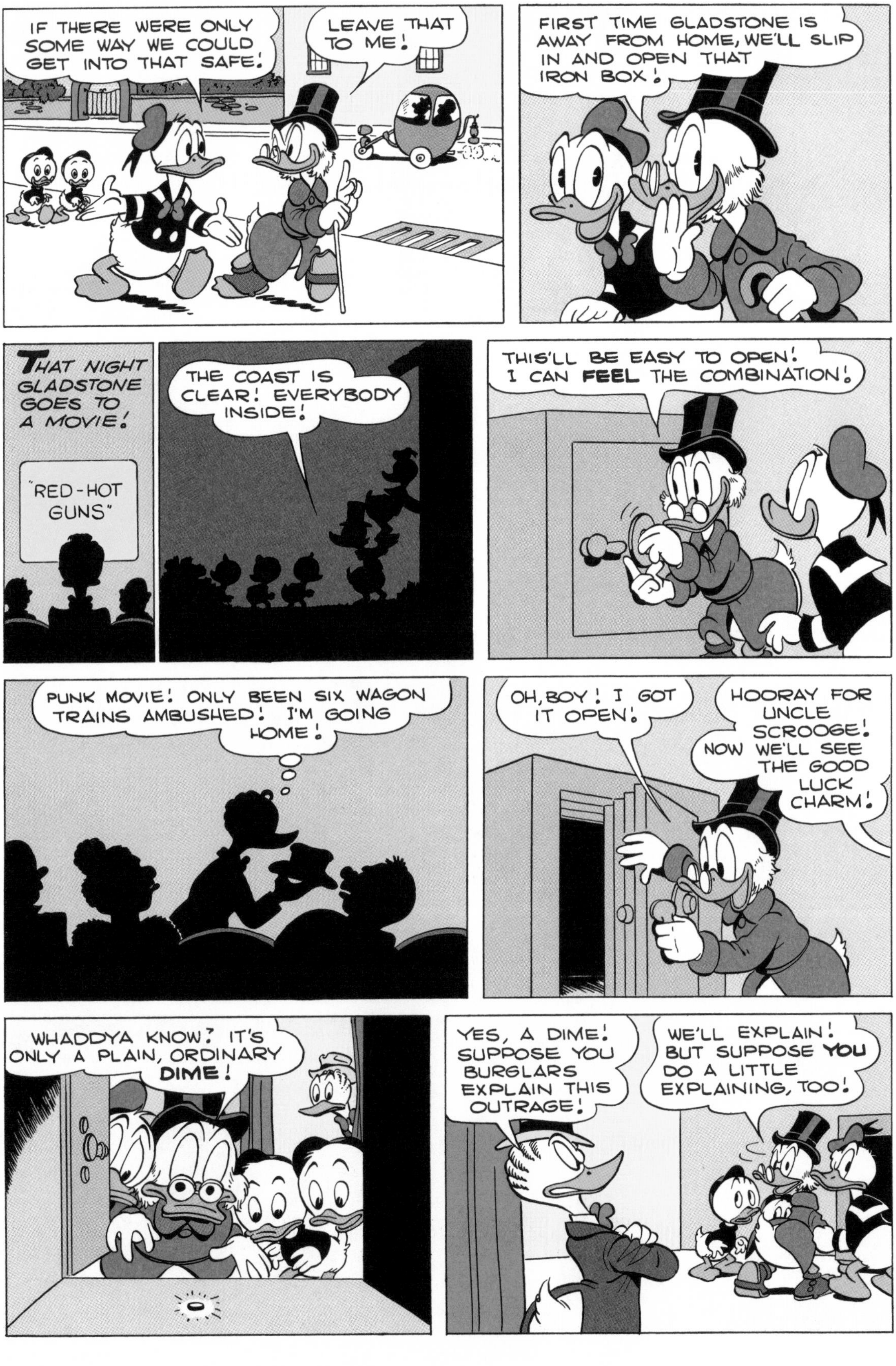
IF THERE WERE ONLY SOME WAY WE COULD GET INTO THAT SAFE!
LEAVE THAT TO ME!
FIRST TIME GLADSTONE IS AWAY FROM HOME, WE'LL SLIP IN AND OPEN THAT IRON BOX!
THAT NIGHT GLADSTONE GOES TO A MOVIE!
"RED-HOT GUNS"
THE COAST IS CLEAR! EVERYBODY INSIDE!
THIS'LL BE EASY TO OPEN! I CAN FEEL THE COMBINATION!
PUNK MOVIE! ONLY BEEN SIX WAGON TRAINS AMBUSHED! I'M GOING HOME!
OH, BOY! I GOT IT OPEN!
HOORAY FOR UNCLE SCROOGE! NOW WE'LL SEE THE GOOD LUCK CHARM!
WHADDYA KNOW? IT'S ONLY A PLAIN, ORDINARY DIME!
YES, A DIME! SUPPOSE YOU BURGLARS EXPLAIN THIS OUTRAGE!
WE'LL EXPLAIN! BUT SUPPOSE YOU DO A LITTLE EXPLAINING, TOO!

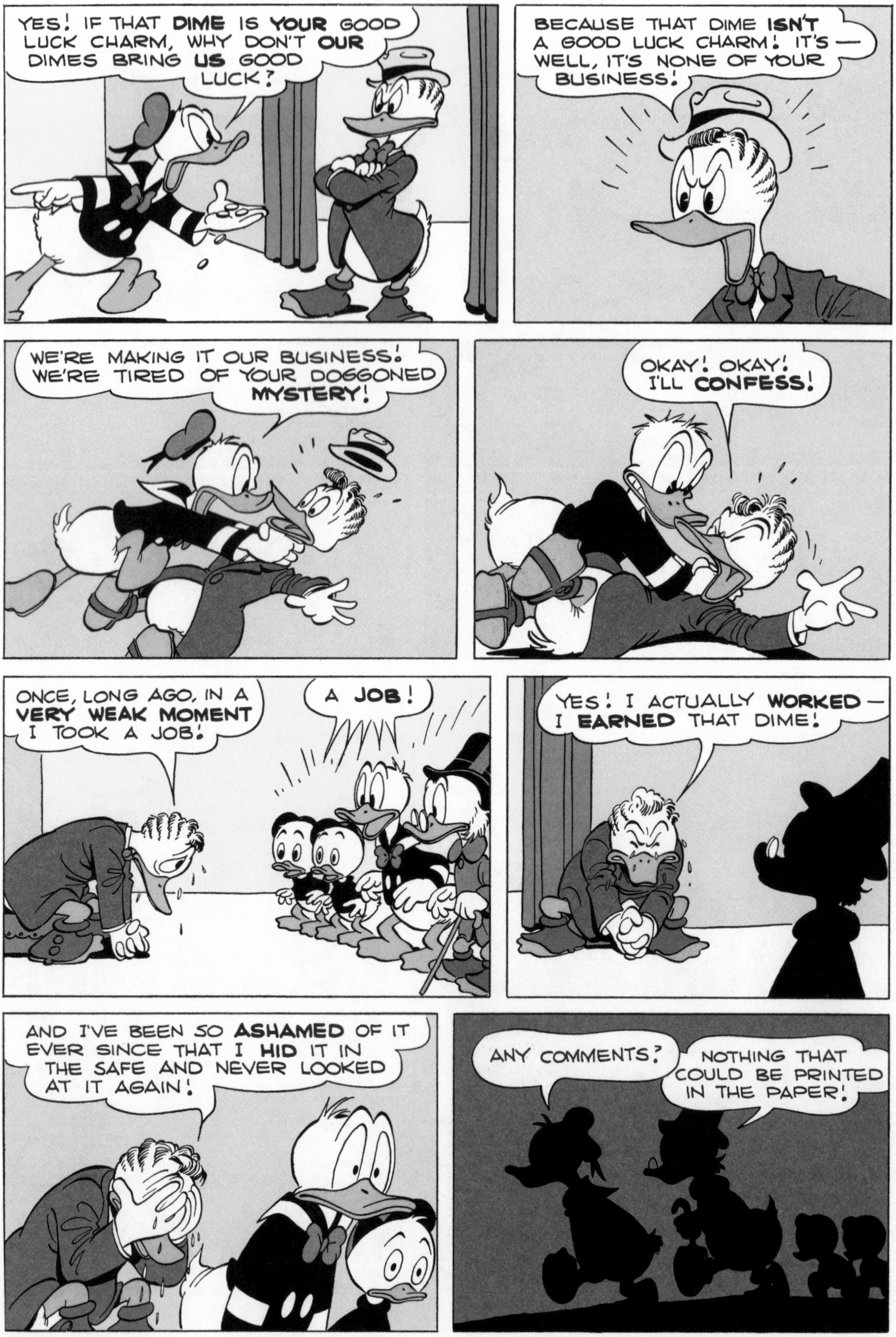
YES! IF THAT DIME IS YOUR GOOD LUCK CHARM, WHY DON'T OUR DIMES BRING US GOOD LUCK?
BECAUSE THAT DIME ISN'T A GOOD LUCK CHARM! IT'S — WELL, IT'S NONE OF YOUR BUSINESS!
WE'RE MAKING IT OUR BUSINESS! WE'RE TIRED OF YOUR DOGGONED MYSTERY!
OKAY! OKAY! I'LL CONFESS!
ONCE, LONG AGO, IN A VERY WEAK MOMENT I TOOK A JOB!
A JOB!
YES! I ACTUALLY WORKED — I EARNED THAT DIME!
AND I'VE BEEN SO ASHAMED OF IT EVER SINCE THAT I HID IT IN THE SAFE AND NEVER LOOKED AT IT AGAIN!
ANY COMMENTS?
NOTHING THAT COULD BE PRINTED IN THE PAPER!

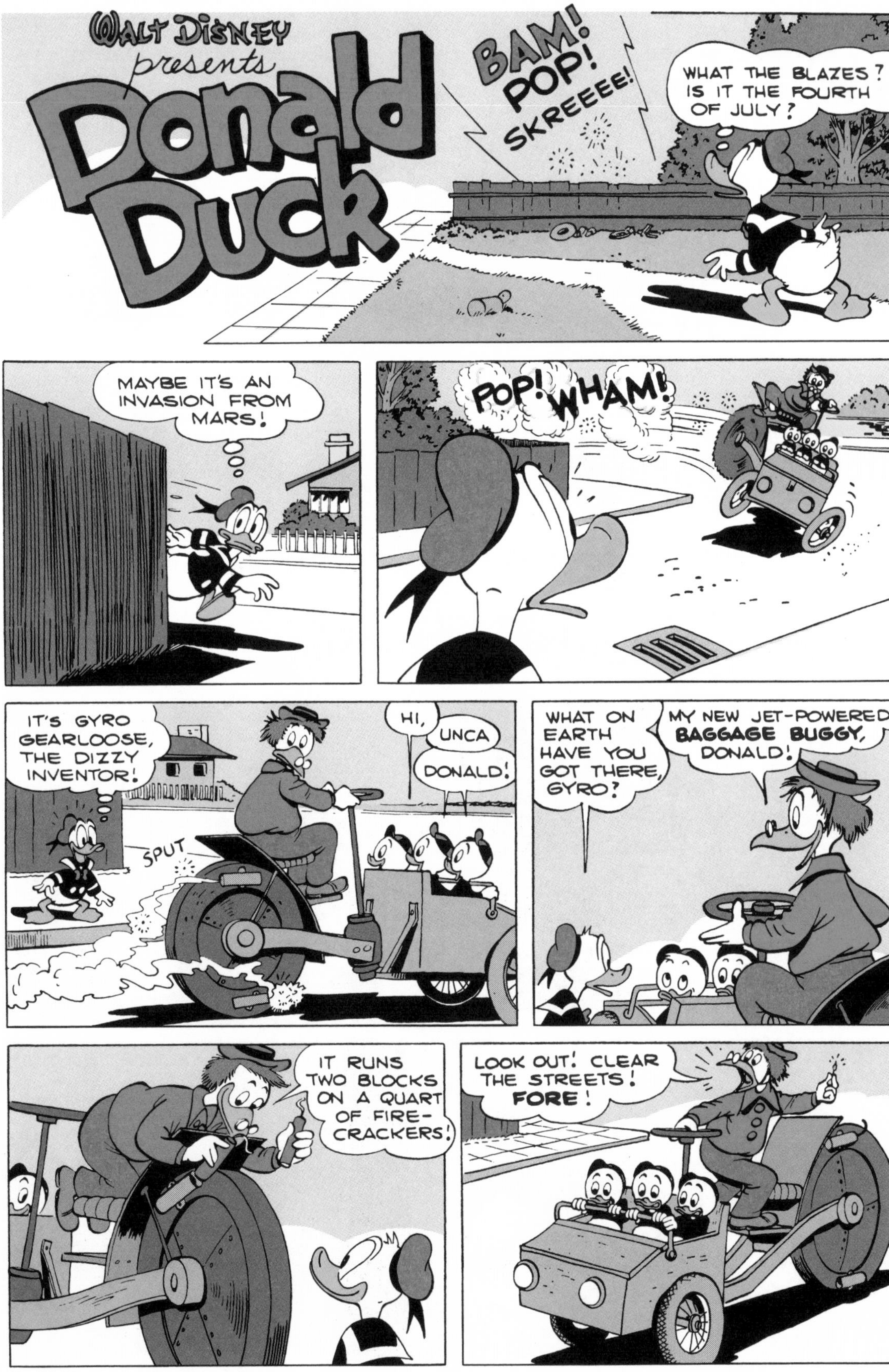
WALT DISNEY
presents
Donald Duck
BAM! POP! SKREEEE!
WHAT THE BLAZES? IS IT THE FOURTH OF JULY?
MAYBE IT'S AN INVASION FROM MARS!
POP! WHAM!
IT'S GYRO GEARLOOSE, THE DIZZY INVENTOR!
HI,
UNCA
DONALD!
SPUT
WHAT ON EARTH HAVE YOU GOT THERE, GYRO?
MY NEW JET-POWERED **BAGGAGE BUGGY**, DONALD!
IT RUNS TWO BLOCKS ON A QUART OF FIRE-CRACKERS!
LOOK OUT! CLEAR THE STREETS! **FORE**!

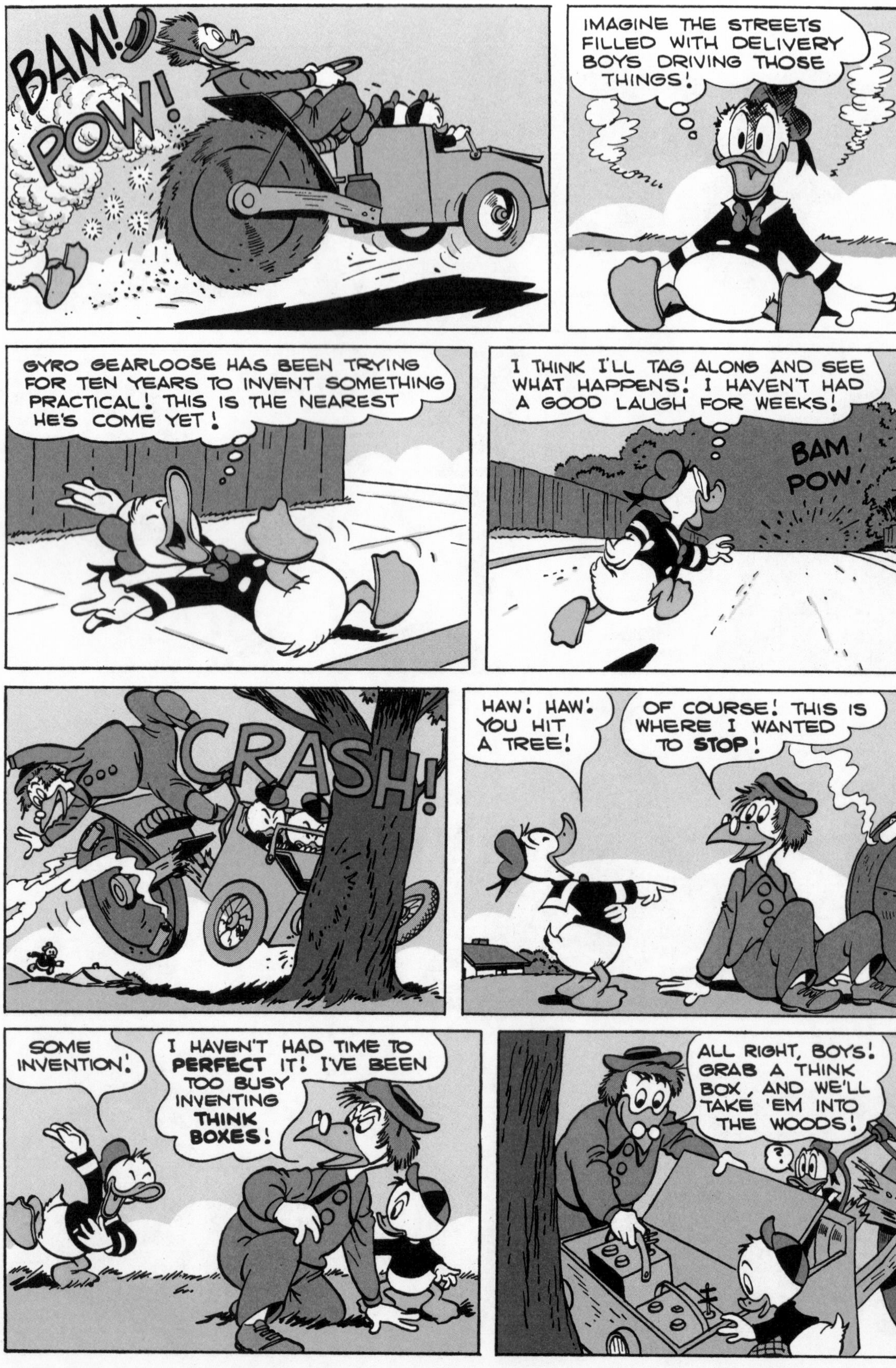
BAM!
POW!
IMAGINE THE STREETS FILLED WITH DELIVERY BOYS DRIVING THOSE THINGS!
GYRO GEARLOOSE HAS BEEN TRYING FOR TEN YEARS TO INVENT SOMETHING PRACTICAL! THIS IS THE NEAREST HE'S COME YET!
I THINK I'LL TAG ALONG AND SEE WHAT HAPPENS! I HAVEN'T HAD A GOOD LAUGH FOR WEEKS!
BAM!
POW!
CRASH!
HAW! HAW! YOU HIT A TREE!
OF COURSE! THIS IS WHERE I WANTED TO STOP!
SOME INVENTION!
I HAVEN'T HAD TIME TO PERFECT IT! I'VE BEEN TOO BUSY INVENTING THINK BOXES!
ALL RIGHT, BOYS! GRAB A THINK BOX, AND WE'LL TAKE 'EM INTO THE WOODS!
?

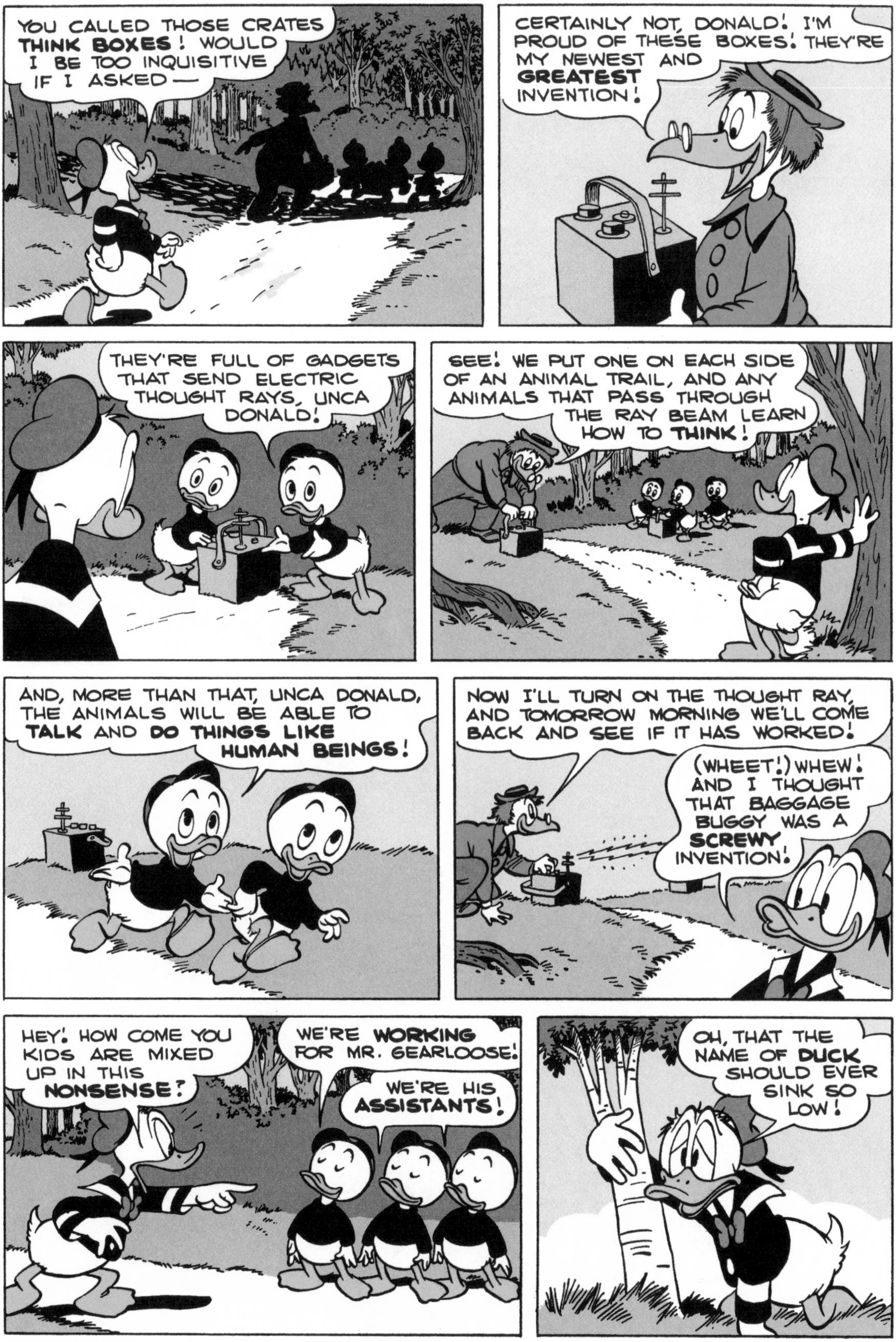
YOU CALLED THOSE CRATES THINK BOXES! WOULD I BE TOO INQUISITIVE IF I ASKED—
CERTAINLY NOT, DONALD! I'M PROUD OF THESE BOXES! THEY'RE MY NEWEST AND GREATEST INVENTION!
THEY'RE FULL OF GADGETS THAT SEND ELECTRIC THOUGHT RAYS, UNCA DONALD!
SEE! WE PUT ONE ON EACH SIDE OF AN ANIMAL TRAIL, AND ANY ANIMALS THAT PASS THROUGH THE RAY BEAM LEARN HOW TO THINK!
AND, MORE THAN THAT, UNCA DONALD, THE ANIMALS WILL BE ABLE TO TALK AND DO THINGS LIKE HUMAN BEINGS!
NOW I'LL TURN ON THE THOUGHT RAY, AND TOMORROW MORNING WE'LL COME BACK AND SEE IF IT HAS WORKED!
(WHEET!) WHEW! AND I THOUGHT THAT BAGGAGE BUGGY WAS A SCREWY INVENTION!
HEY! HOW COME YOU KIDS ARE MIXED UP IN THIS NONSENSE?
WE'RE WORKING FOR MR. GEARLOOSE!
WE'RE HIS ASSISTANTS!
OH, THAT THE NAME OF DUCK SHOULD EVER SINK SO LOW!

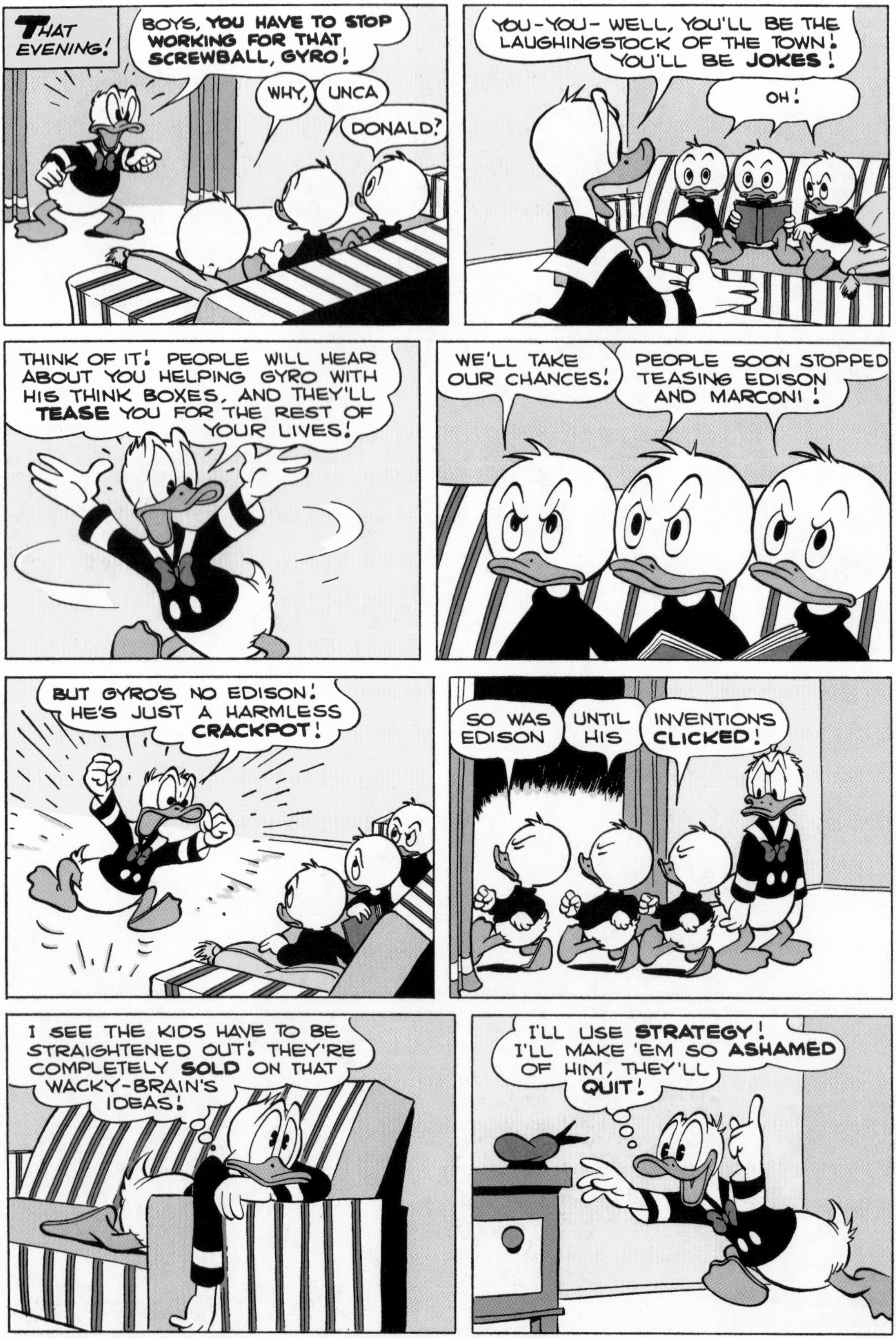
THAT EVENING!
BOYS, YOU HAVE TO STOP WORKING FOR THAT SCREWBALL, GYRO!
WHY,
UNCA
DONALD?
YOU-YOU- WELL, YOU'LL BE THE LAUGHINGSTOCK OF THE TOWN! YOU'LL BE JOKES!
OH!
THINK OF IT! PEOPLE WILL HEAR ABOUT YOU HELPING GYRO WITH HIS THINK BOXES, AND THEY'LL TEASE YOU FOR THE REST OF YOUR LIVES!
WE'LL TAKE OUR CHANCES!
PEOPLE SOON STOPPED TEASING EDISON AND MARCONI!
BUT GYRO'S NO EDISON! HE'S JUST A HARMLESS CRACKPOT!
SO WAS EDISON
UNTIL HIS
INVENTIONS CLICKED!
I SEE THE KIDS HAVE TO BE STRAIGHTENED OUT! THEY'RE COMPLETELY SOLD ON THAT WACKY-BRAIN'S IDEAS!
I'LL USE STRATEGY! I'LL MAKE 'EM SO ASHAMED OF HIM, THEY'LL QUIT!

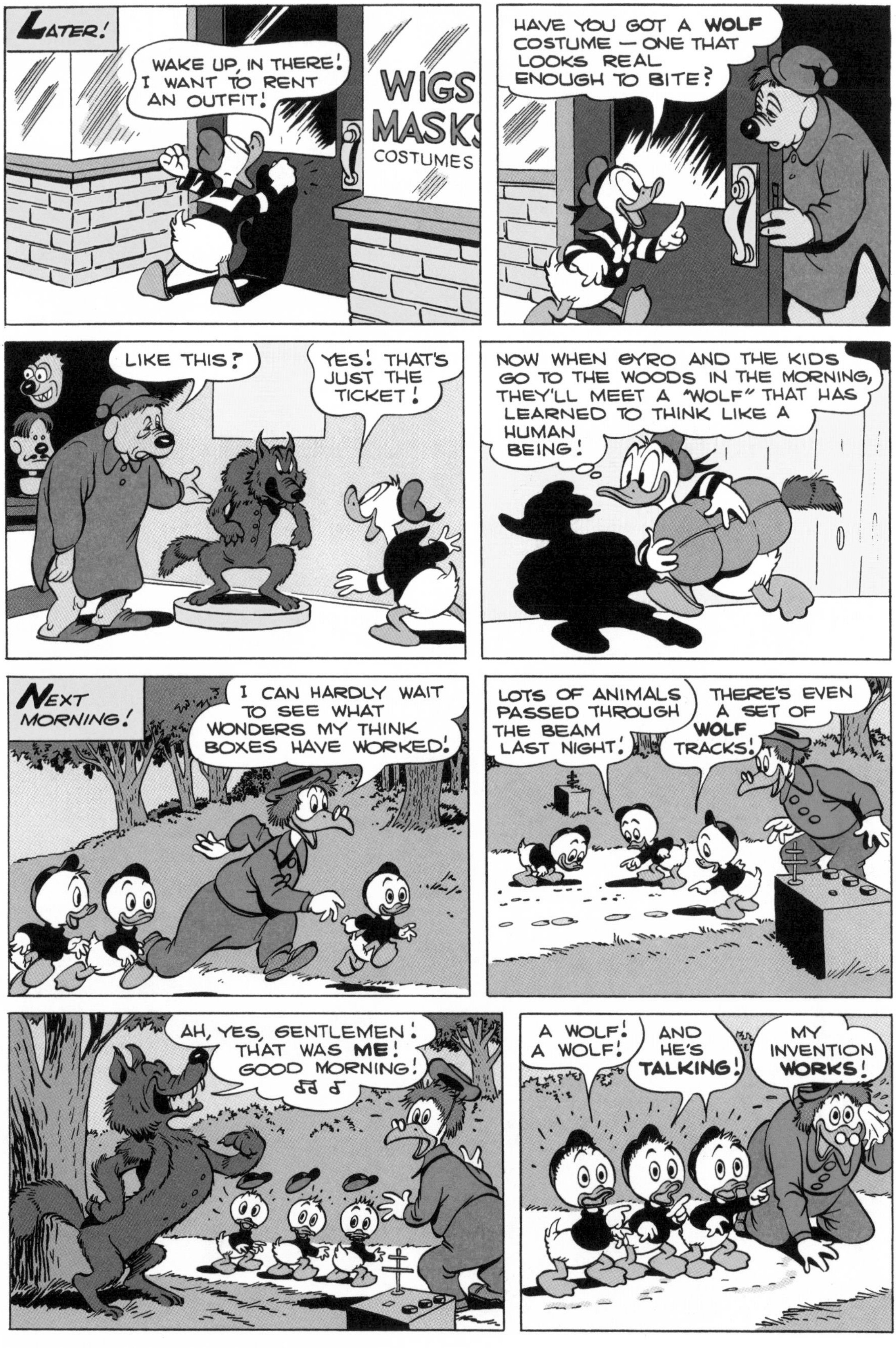
LATER!
WAKE UP, IN THERE! I WANT TO RENT AN OUTFIT!
WIGS MASKS COSTUMES
HAVE YOU GOT A WOLF COSTUME — ONE THAT LOOKS REAL ENOUGH TO BITE?
LIKE THIS?
YES! THAT'S JUST THE TICKET!
NOW WHEN GYRO AND THE KIDS GO TO THE WOODS IN THE MORNING, THEY'LL MEET A "WOLF" THAT HAS LEARNED TO THINK LIKE A HUMAN BEING!
NEXT MORNING!
I CAN HARDLY WAIT TO SEE WHAT WONDERS MY THINK BOXES HAVE WORKED!
LOTS OF ANIMALS PASSED THROUGH THE BEAM LAST NIGHT!
THERE'S EVEN A SET OF WOLF TRACKS!
AH, YES, GENTLEMEN! THAT WAS ME! GOOD MORNING!
A WOLF! A WOLF!
AND HE'S TALKING!
MY INVENTION WORKS!

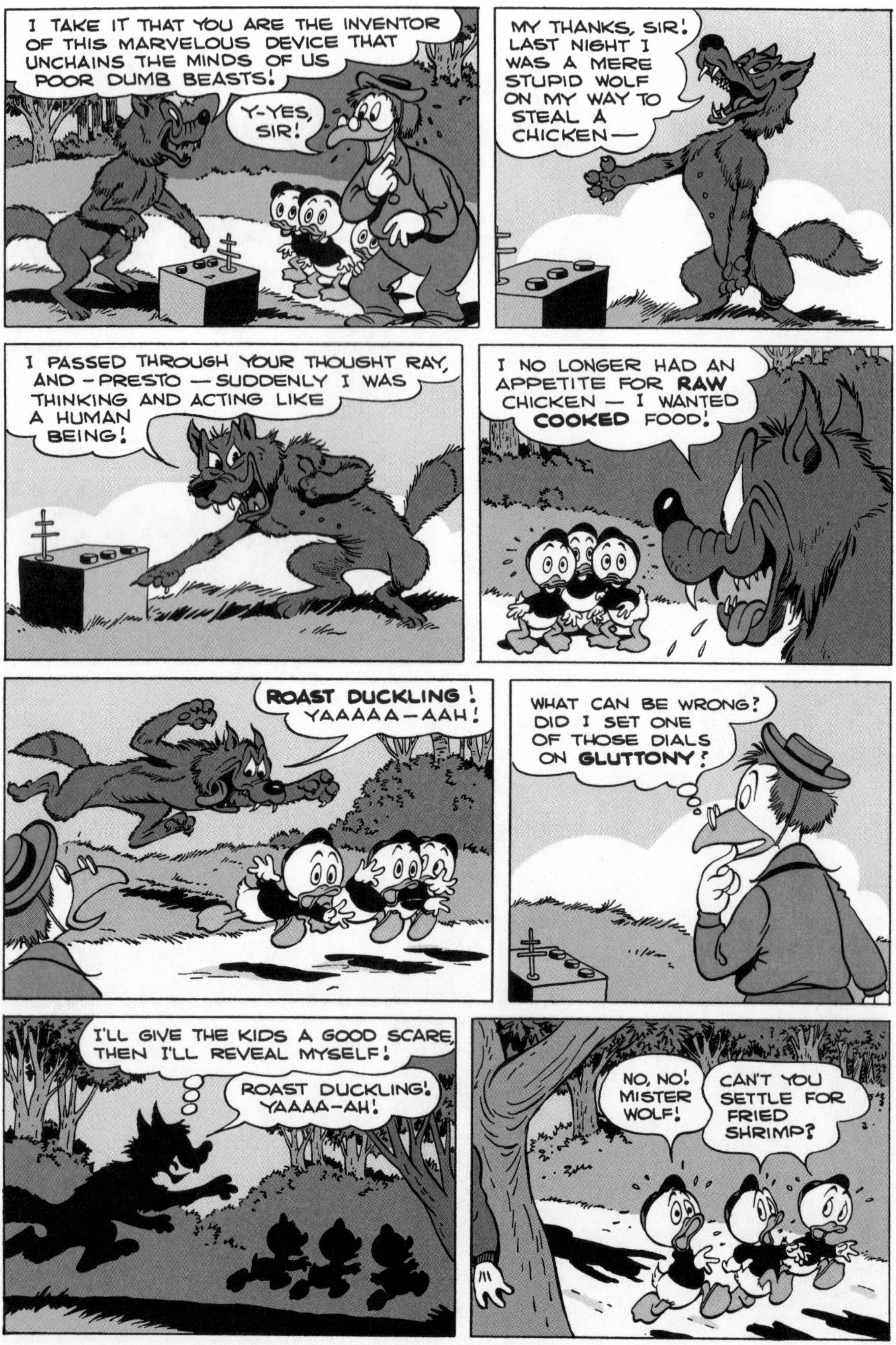
I TAKE IT THAT YOU ARE THE INVENTOR OF THIS MARVELOUS DEVICE THAT UNCHAINS THE MINDS OF US POOR DUMB BEASTS!
Y-YES, SIR!
MY THANKS, SIR! LAST NIGHT I WAS A MERE STUPID WOLF ON MY WAY TO STEAL A CHICKEN—
I PASSED THROUGH YOUR THOUGHT RAY, AND-PRESTO-SUDDENLY I WAS THINKING AND ACTING LIKE A HUMAN BEING!
I NO LONGER HAD AN APPETITE FOR RAW CHICKEN — I WANTED COOKED FOOD!
ROAST DUCKLING! YAAAAA-AAH!
WHAT CAN BE WRONG? DID I SET ONE OF THOSE DIALS ON GLUTTONY?
I'LL GIVE THE KIDS A GOOD SCARE, THEN I'LL REVEAL MYSELF!
ROAST DUCKLING! YAAAA-AH!
NO, NO! MISTER WOLF!
CAN'T YOU SETTLE FOR FRIED SHRIMP?

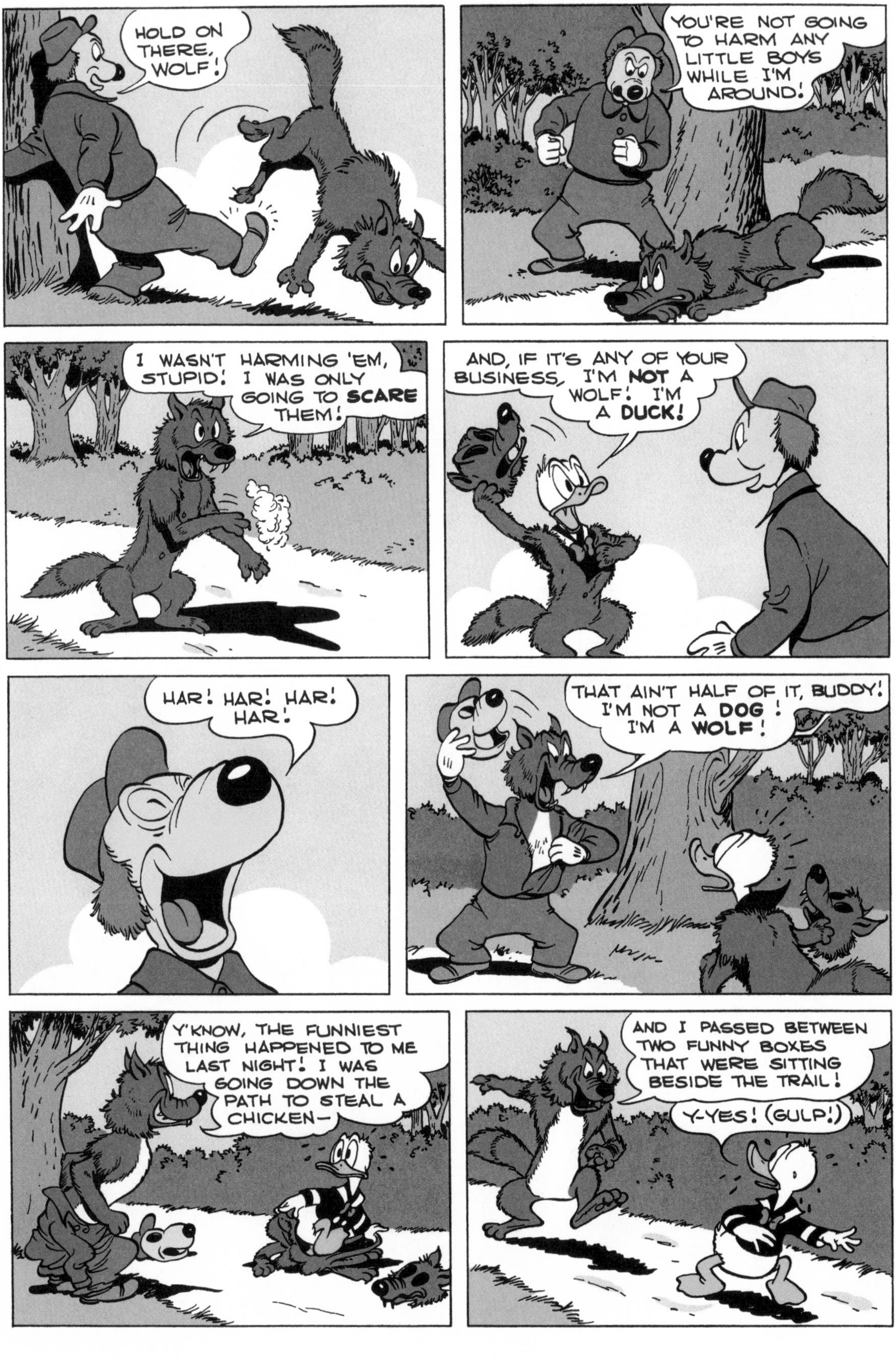
HOLD ON THERE, WOLF!
YOU'RE NOT GOING TO HARM ANY LITTLE BOYS WHILE I'M AROUND!
I WASN'T HARMING 'EM, STUPID! I WAS ONLY GOING TO **SCARE** THEM!
AND, IF IT'S ANY OF YOUR BUSINESS, I'M **NOT** A WOLF! I'M A **DUCK!**
HAR! HAR! HAR! HAR!
THAT AIN'T HALF OF IT, BUDDY! I'M NOT A **DOG**! I'M A **WOLF**!
Y'KNOW, THE FUNNIEST THING HAPPENED TO ME LAST NIGHT! I WAS GOING DOWN THE PATH TO STEAL A CHICKEN—
AND I PASSED BETWEEN TWO FUNNY BOXES THAT WERE SITTING BESIDE THE TRAIL!
Y-YES! (GULP!)

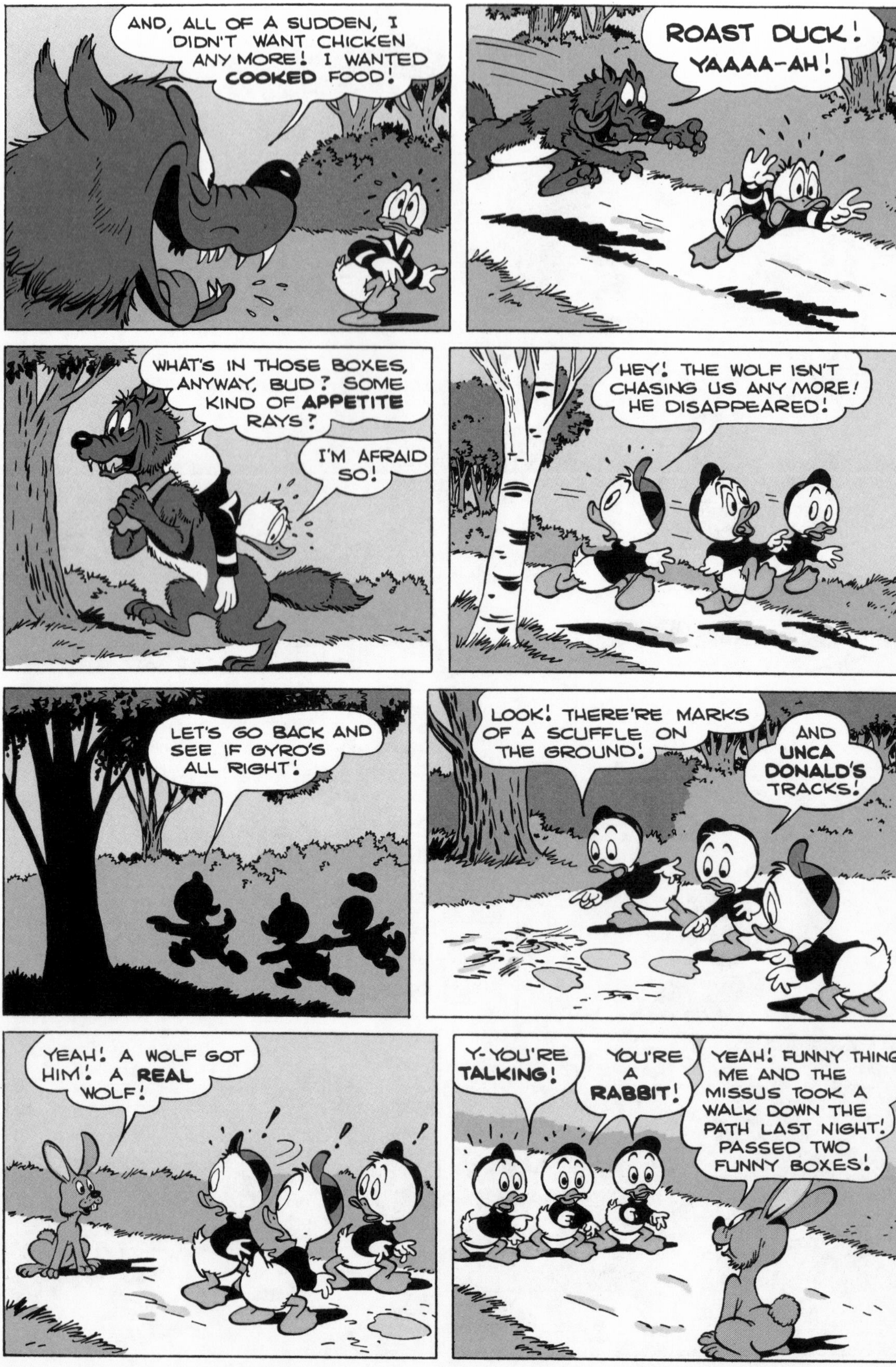
AND, ALL OF A SUDDEN, I DIDN'T WANT CHICKEN ANY MORE! I WANTED COOKED FOOD!
ROAST DUCK! YAAAA-AH!
WHAT'S IN THOSE BOXES, ANYWAY, BUD? SOME KIND OF APPETITE RAYS?
I'M AFRAID SO!
HEY! THE WOLF ISN'T CHASING US ANY MORE! HE DISAPPEARED!
LET'S GO BACK AND SEE IF GYRO'S ALL RIGHT!
LOOK! THERE'RE MARKS OF A SCUFFLE ON THE GROUND!
AND UNCA DONALD'S TRACKS!
YEAH! A WOLF GOT HIM! A REAL WOLF!
Y-YOU'RE TALKING!
YOU'RE A RABBIT!
YEAH! FUNNY THING! ME AND THE MISSUS TOOK A WALK DOWN THE PATH LAST NIGHT! PASSED TWO FUNNY BOXES!

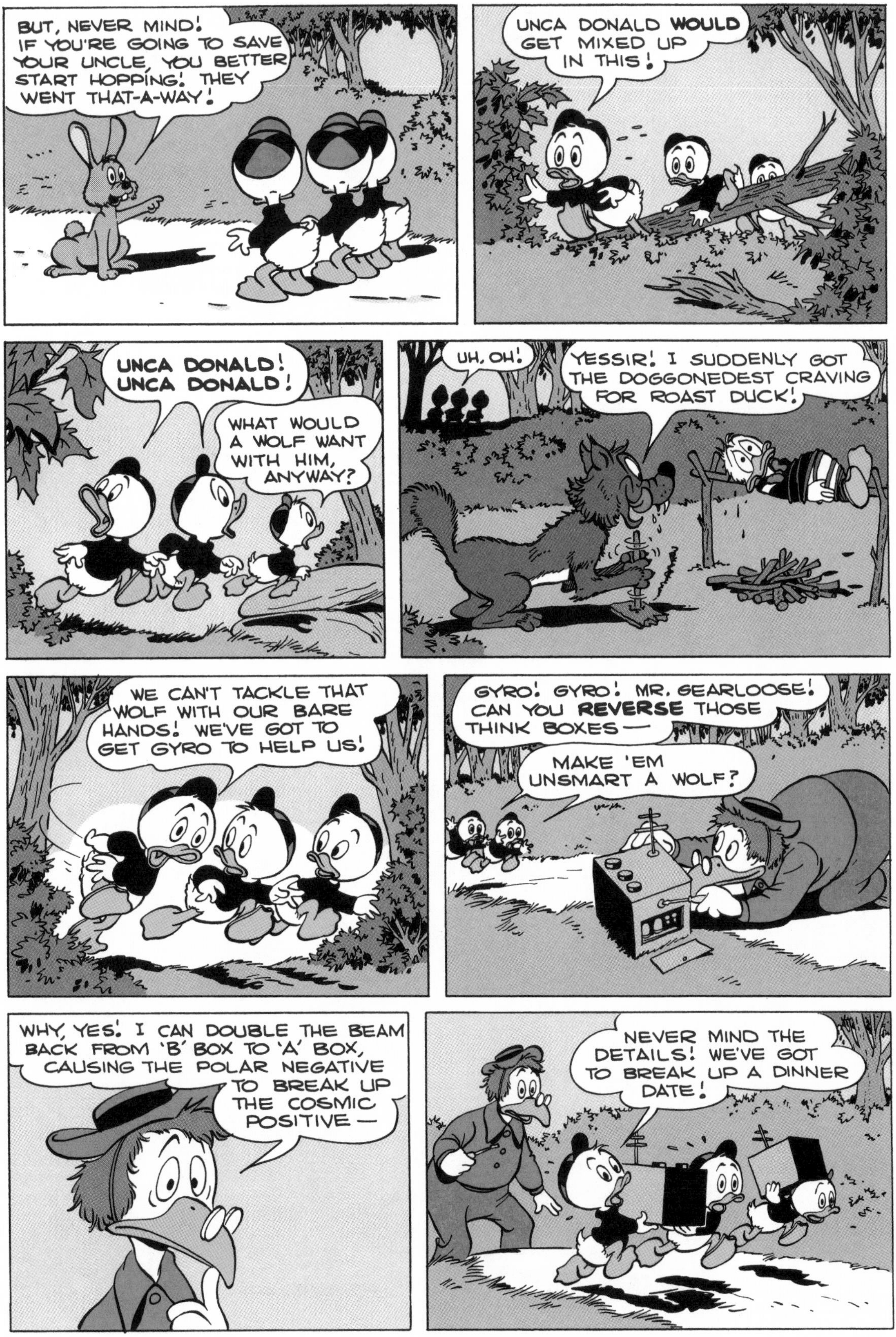
BUT, NEVER MIND! IF YOU'RE GOING TO SAVE YOUR UNCLE, YOU BETTER START HOPPING! THEY WENT THAT-A-WAY!
UNCA DONALD **WOULD** GET MIXED UP IN THIS!
UNCA DONALD! UNCA DONALD!
WHAT WOULD A WOLF WANT WITH HIM, ANYWAY?
UH, OH!
YESSIR! I SUDDENLY GOT THE DOGGONEDEST CRAVING FOR ROAST DUCK!
WE CAN'T TACKLE THAT WOLF WITH OUR BARE HANDS! WE'VE GOT TO GET GYRO TO HELP US!
GYRO! GYRO! MR. GEARLOOSE! CAN YOU **REVERSE** THOSE THINK BOXES—
MAKE 'EM UNSMART A WOLF?
WHY, YES! I CAN DOUBLE THE BEAM BACK FROM 'B' BOX TO 'A' BOX, CAUSING THE POLAR NEGATIVE TO BREAK UP THE COSMIC POSITIVE—
NEVER MIND THE DETAILS! WE'VE GOT TO BREAK UP A DINNER DATE!

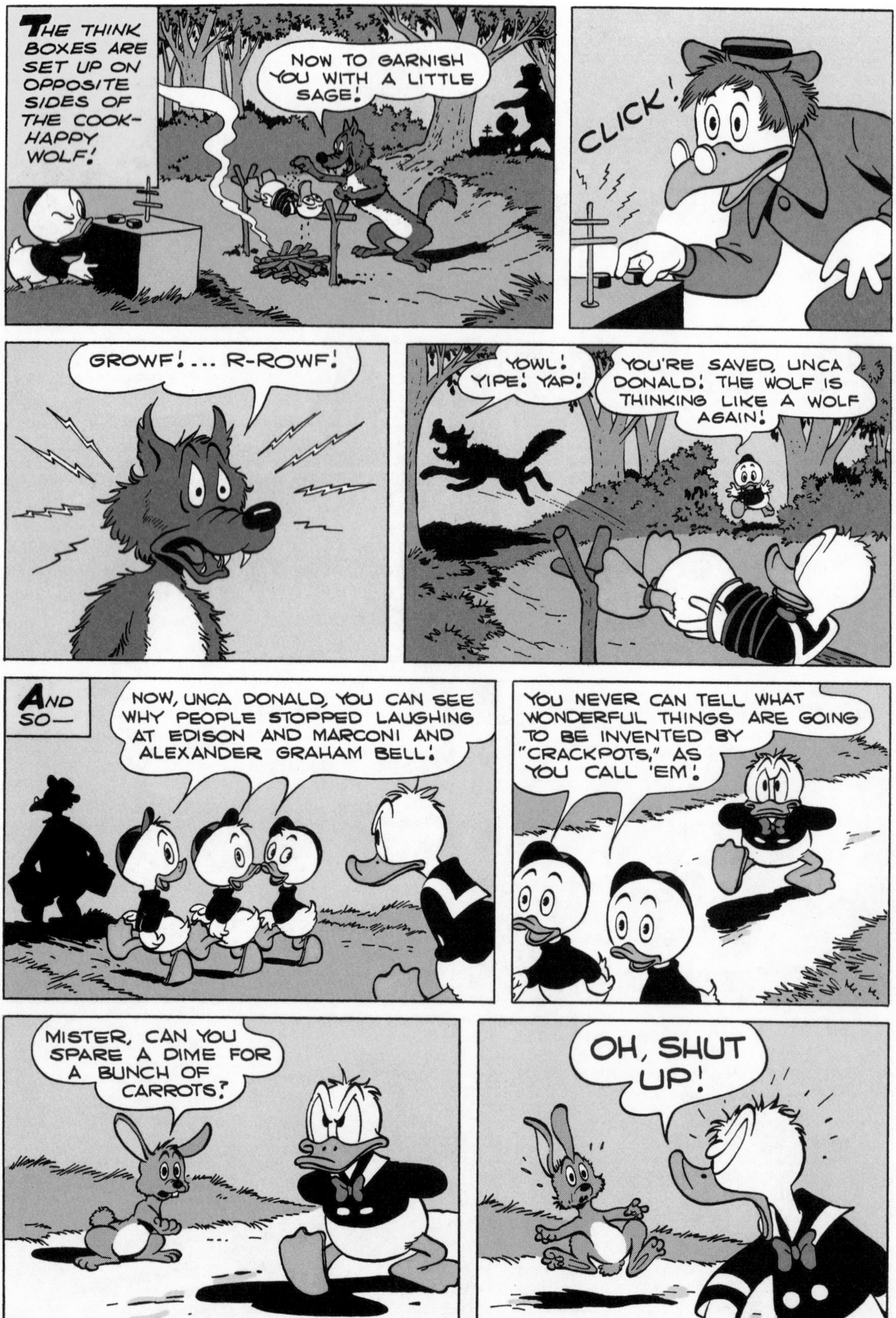
THE THINK BOXES ARE SET UP ON OPPOSITE SIDES OF THE COOK-HAPPY WOLF!
NOW TO GARNISH YOU WITH A LITTLE SAGE!
CLICK!
GROWF!... R-ROWF!
YOWL! YIPE! YAP!
YOU'RE SAVED, UNCA DONALD! THE WOLF IS THINKING LIKE A WOLF AGAIN!
AND SO—
NOW, UNCA DONALD, YOU CAN SEE WHY PEOPLE STOPPED LAUGHING AT EDISON AND MARCONI AND ALEXANDER GRAHAM BELL!
YOU NEVER CAN TELL WHAT WONDERFUL THINGS ARE GOING TO BE INVENTED BY "CRACKPOTS," AS YOU CALL 'EM!
MISTER, CAN YOU SPARE A DIME FOR A BUNCH OF CARROTS?
OH, SHUT UP!

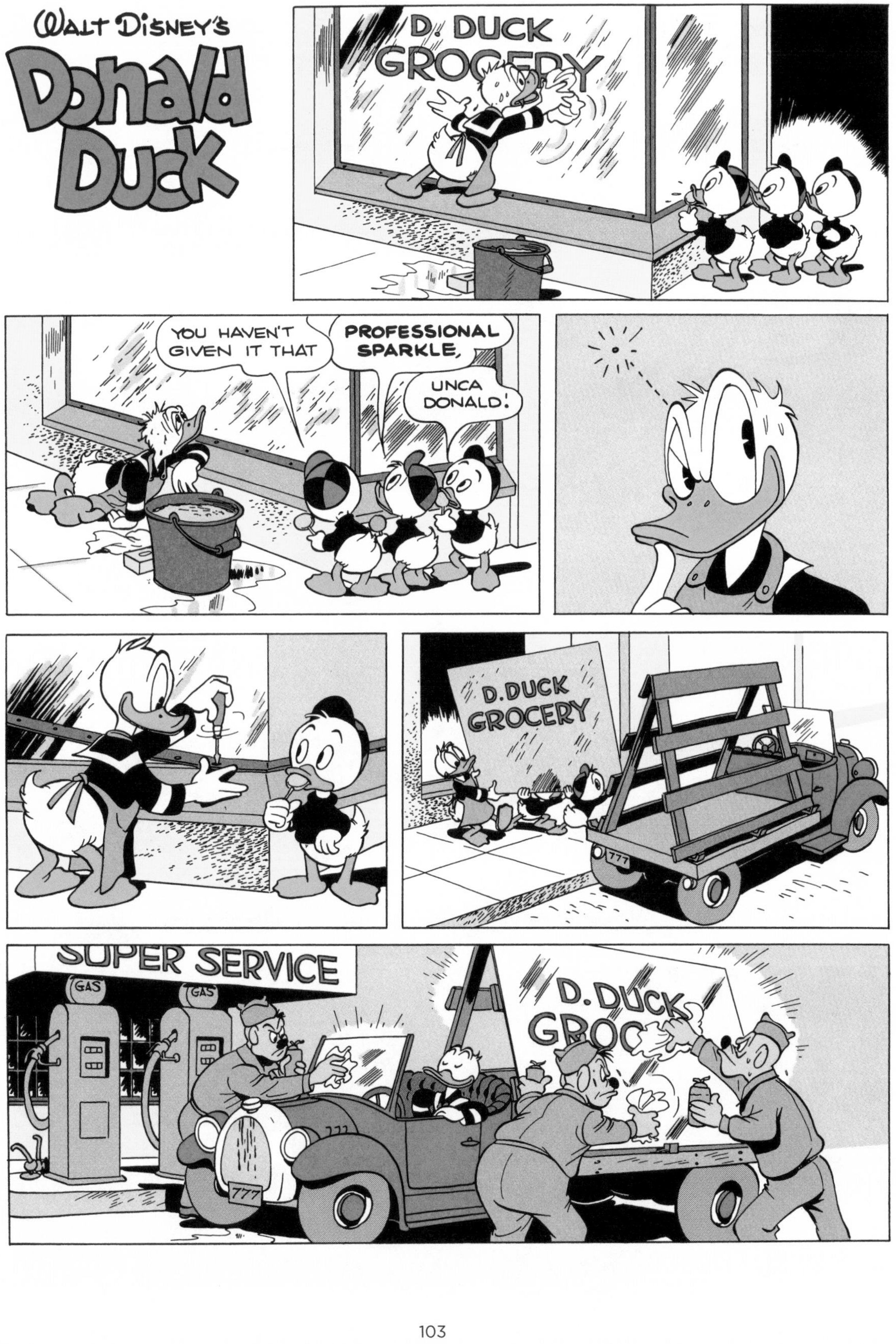
WALT DISNEY'S
Donald Duck
D. DUCK GROCERY
YOU HAVEN'T GIVEN IT THAT
PROFESSIONAL SPARKLE,
UNCA DONALD!
D. DUCK GROCERY
777
SUPER SERVICE
GAS
GAS
D. DUCK GROC
777

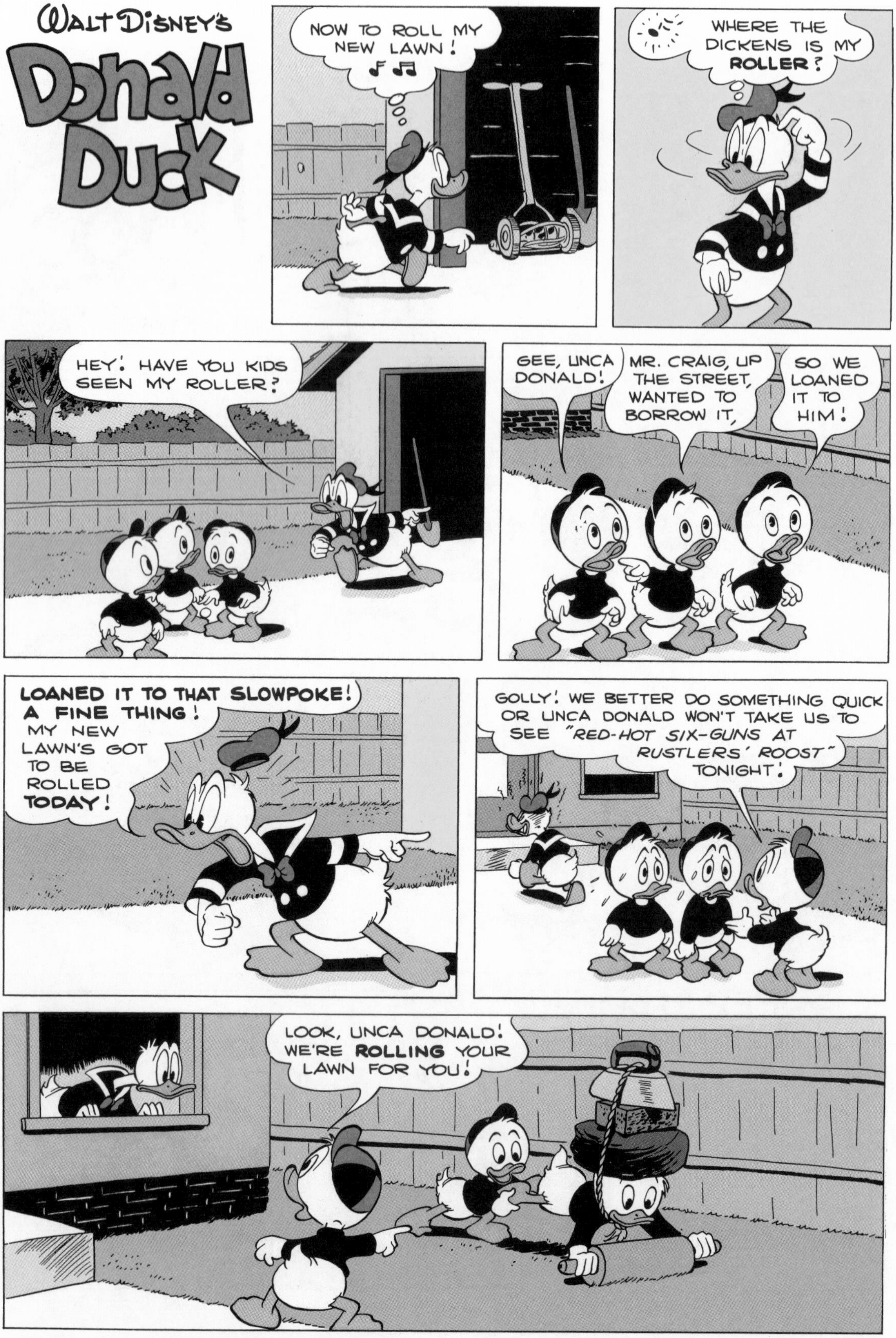
WALT DISNEY'S
Donald Duck
NOW TO ROLL MY NEW LAWN!
WHERE THE DICKENS IS MY ROLLER?
HEY! HAVE YOU KIDS SEEN MY ROLLER?
GEE, UNCA DONALD!
MR. CRAIG, UP THE STREET, WANTED TO BORROW IT,
SO WE LOANED IT TO HIM!
LOANED IT TO THAT SLOWPOKE! A FINE THING! MY NEW LAWN'S GOT TO BE ROLLED TODAY!
GOLLY! WE BETTER DO SOMETHING QUICK OR UNCA DONALD WON'T TAKE US TO SEE "RED-HOT SIX-GUNS AT RUSTLERS' ROOST" TONIGHT!
LOOK, UNCA DONALD! WE'RE ROLLING YOUR LAWN FOR YOU!

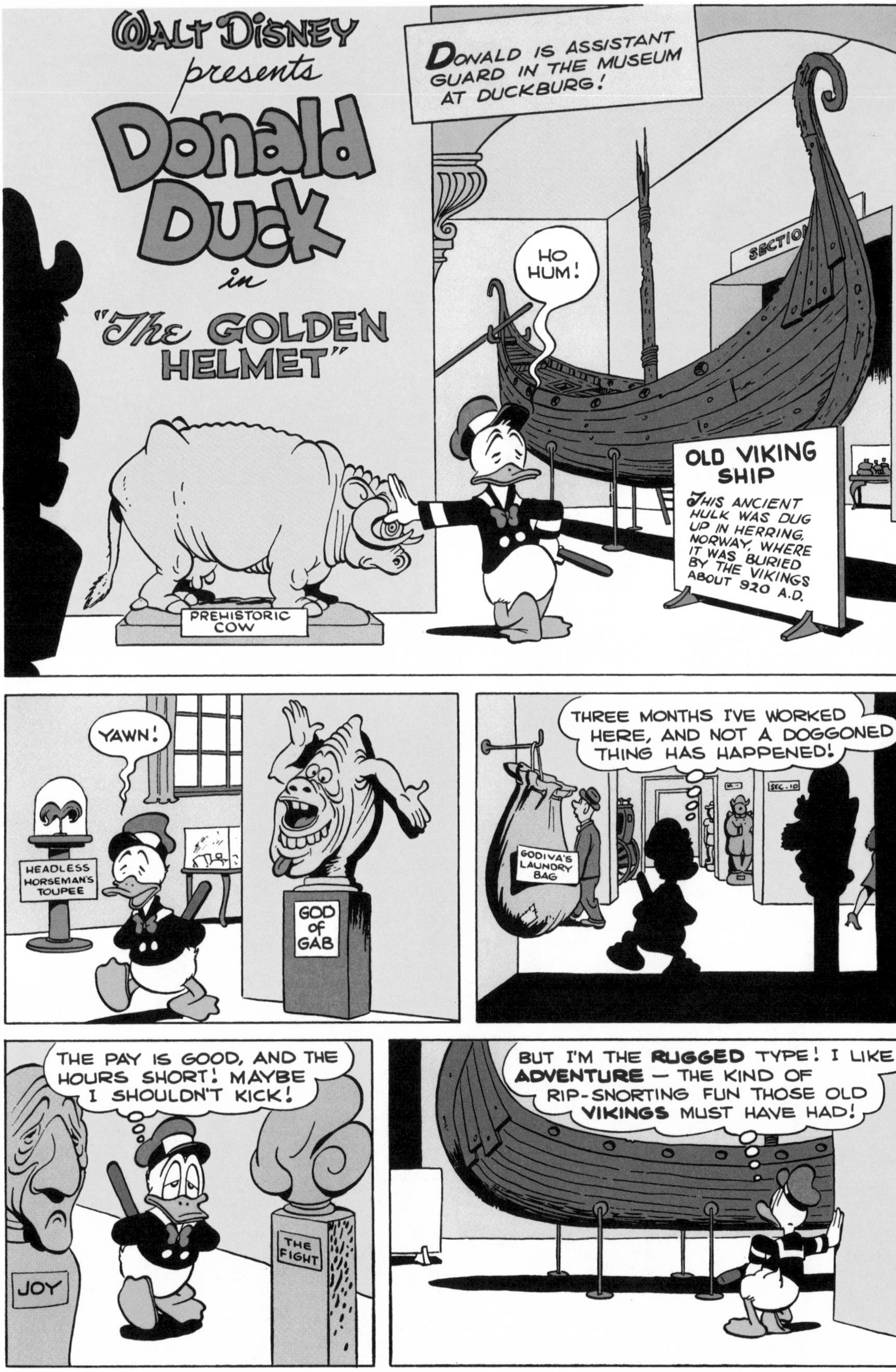
WALT DISNEY
presents
Donald Duck
in
"The GOLDEN HELMET"
DONALD IS ASSISTANT GUARD IN THE MUSEUM AT DUCKBURG!
HO HUM!
SECTION
PREHISTORIC COW
OLD VIKING SHIP
THIS ANCIENT HULK WAS DUG UP IN HERRING, NORWAY, WHERE IT WAS BURIED BY THE VIKINGS ABOUT 920 A.D.
YAWN!
HEADLESS HORSEMAN'S TOUPEE
GOD of GAB
THREE MONTHS I'VE WORKED HERE, AND NOT A DOGGONED THING HAS HAPPENED!
GODIVA'S LAUNDRY BAG
SEC.10
THE PAY IS GOOD, AND THE HOURS SHORT! MAYBE I SHOULDN'T KICK!
JOY
THE FIGHT
BUT I'M THE RUGGED TYPE! I LIKE ADVENTURE — THE KIND OF RIP-SNORTING FUN THOSE OLD VIKINGS MUST HAVE HAD!

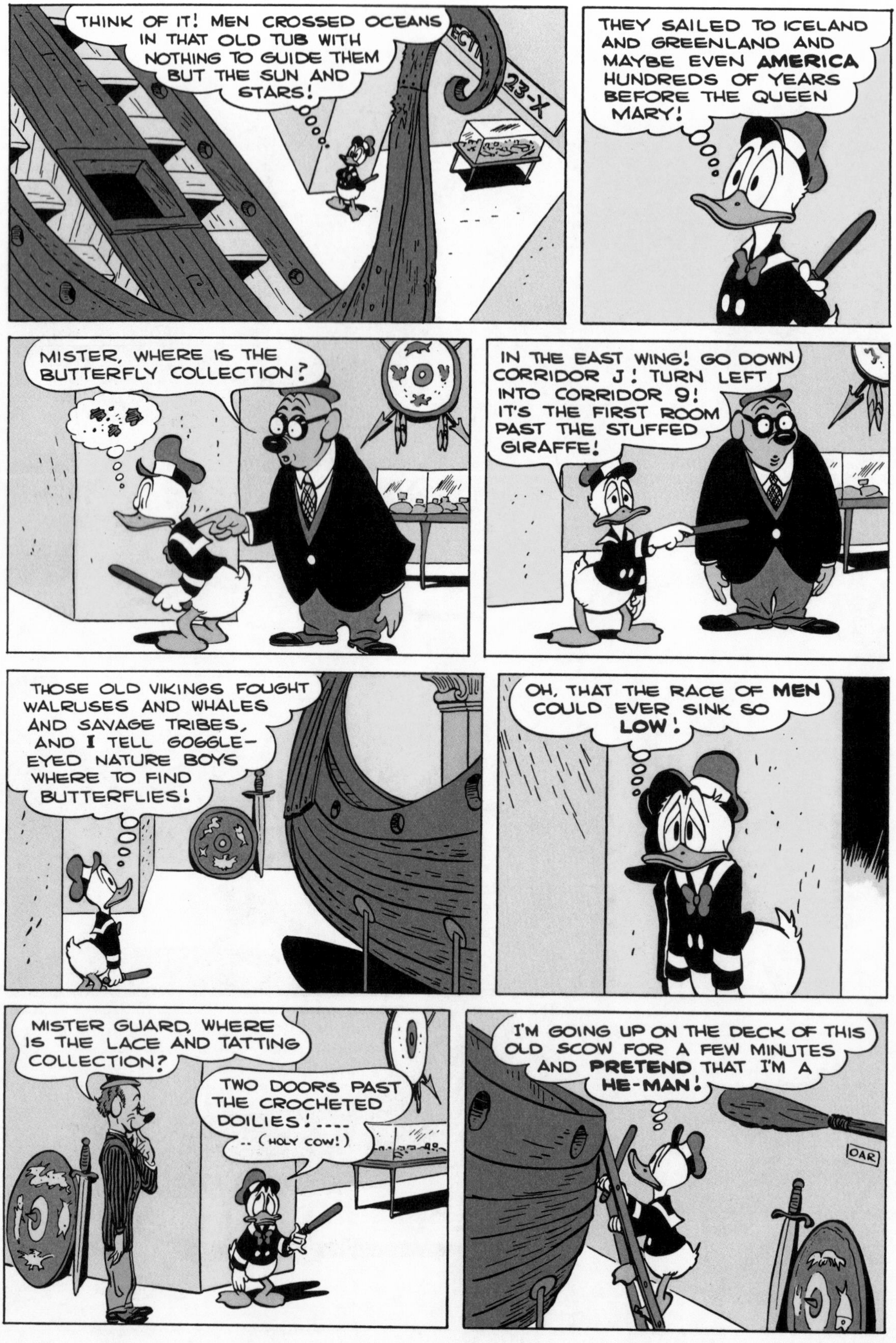
THINK OF IT! MEN CROSSED OCEANS IN THAT OLD TUB WITH NOTHING TO GUIDE THEM BUT THE SUN AND STARS!
23-X
THEY SAILED TO ICELAND AND GREENLAND AND MAYBE EVEN AMERICA HUNDREDS OF YEARS BEFORE THE QUEEN MARY!
MISTER, WHERE IS THE BUTTERFLY COLLECTION?
IN THE EAST WING! GO DOWN CORRIDOR J! TURN LEFT INTO CORRIDOR 9! IT'S THE FIRST ROOM PAST THE STUFFED GIRAFFE!
THOSE OLD VIKINGS FOUGHT WALRUSES AND WHALES AND SAVAGE TRIBES, AND I TELL GOGGLE-EYED NATURE BOYS WHERE TO FIND BUTTERFLIES!
OH, THAT THE RACE OF MEN COULD EVER SINK SO LOW!
MISTER GUARD, WHERE IS THE LACE AND TATTING COLLECTION?
TWO DOORS PAST THE CROCHETED DOILIES! ....
.. (HOLY COW!)
I'M GOING UP ON THE DECK OF THIS OLD SCOW FOR A FEW MINUTES AND PRETEND THAT I'M A HE-MAN!
OAR

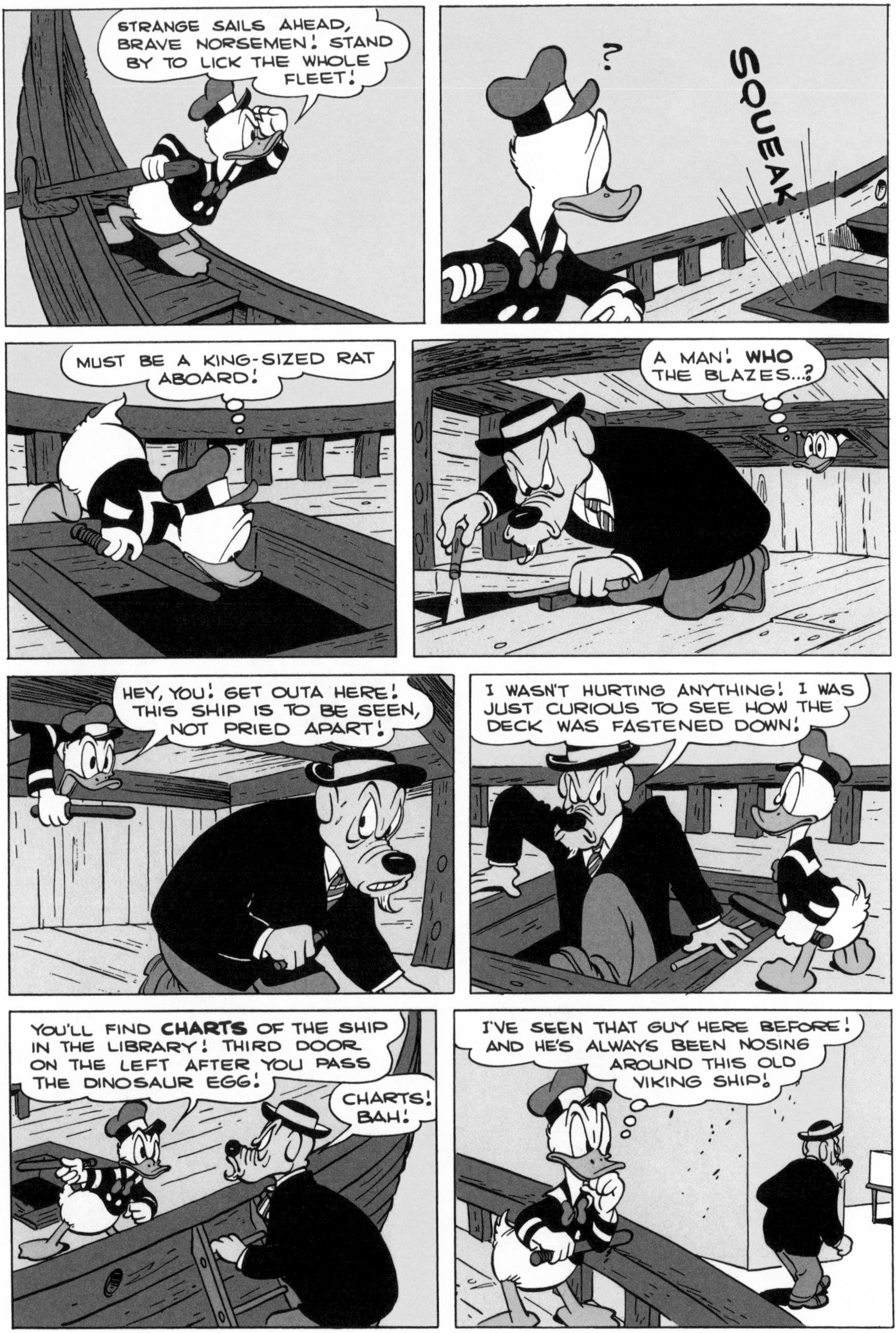
STRANGE SAILS AHEAD, BRAVE NORSEMEN! STAND BY TO LICK THE WHOLE FLEET!
?
SQUEAK
MUST BE A KING-SIZED RAT ABOARD!
A MAN! WHO THE BLAZES...?
HEY, YOU! GET OUTA HERE! THIS SHIP IS TO BE SEEN, NOT PRIED APART!
I WASN'T HURTING ANYTHING! I WAS JUST CURIOUS TO SEE HOW THE DECK WAS FASTENED DOWN!
YOU'LL FIND CHARTS OF THE SHIP IN THE LIBRARY! THIRD DOOR ON THE LEFT AFTER YOU PASS THE DINOSAUR EGG!
CHARTS! BAH!
I'VE SEEN THAT GUY HERE BEFORE! AND HE'S ALWAYS BEEN NOSING AROUND THIS OLD VIKING SHIP!

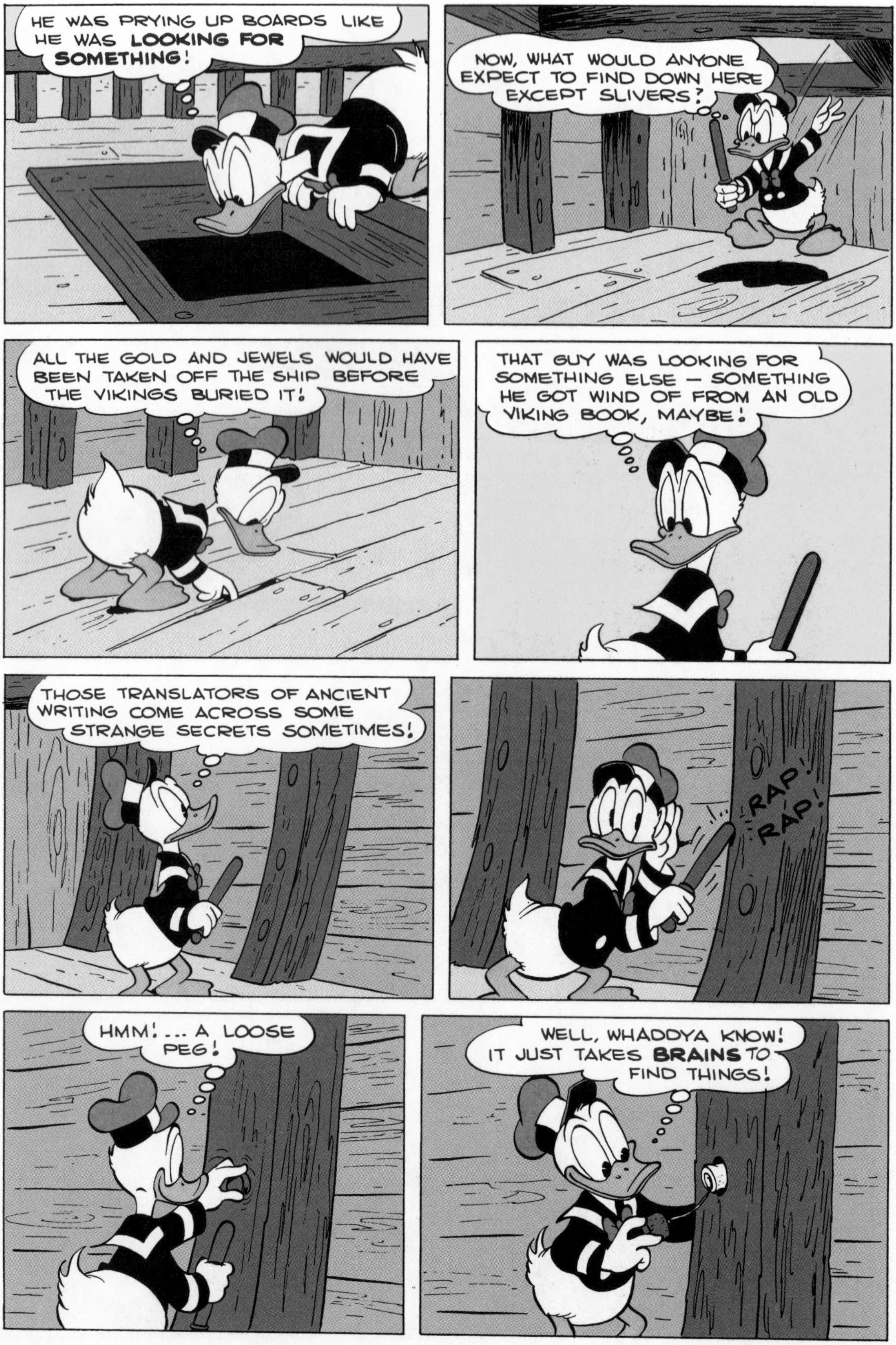
HE WAS PRYING UP BOARDS LIKE HE WAS **LOOKING FOR SOMETHING**!
NOW, WHAT WOULD ANYONE EXPECT TO FIND DOWN HERE EXCEPT SLIVERS?
ALL THE GOLD AND JEWELS WOULD HAVE BEEN TAKEN OFF THE SHIP BEFORE THE VIKINGS BURIED IT!
THAT GUY WAS LOOKING FOR SOMETHING ELSE — SOMETHING HE GOT WIND OF FROM AN OLD VIKING BOOK, MAYBE!
THOSE TRANSLATORS OF ANCIENT WRITING COME ACROSS SOME STRANGE SECRETS SOMETIMES!
RAP! RAP!
HMM! ... A LOOSE PEG!
WELL, WHADDYA KNOW! IT JUST TAKES **BRAINS** TO FIND THINGS!

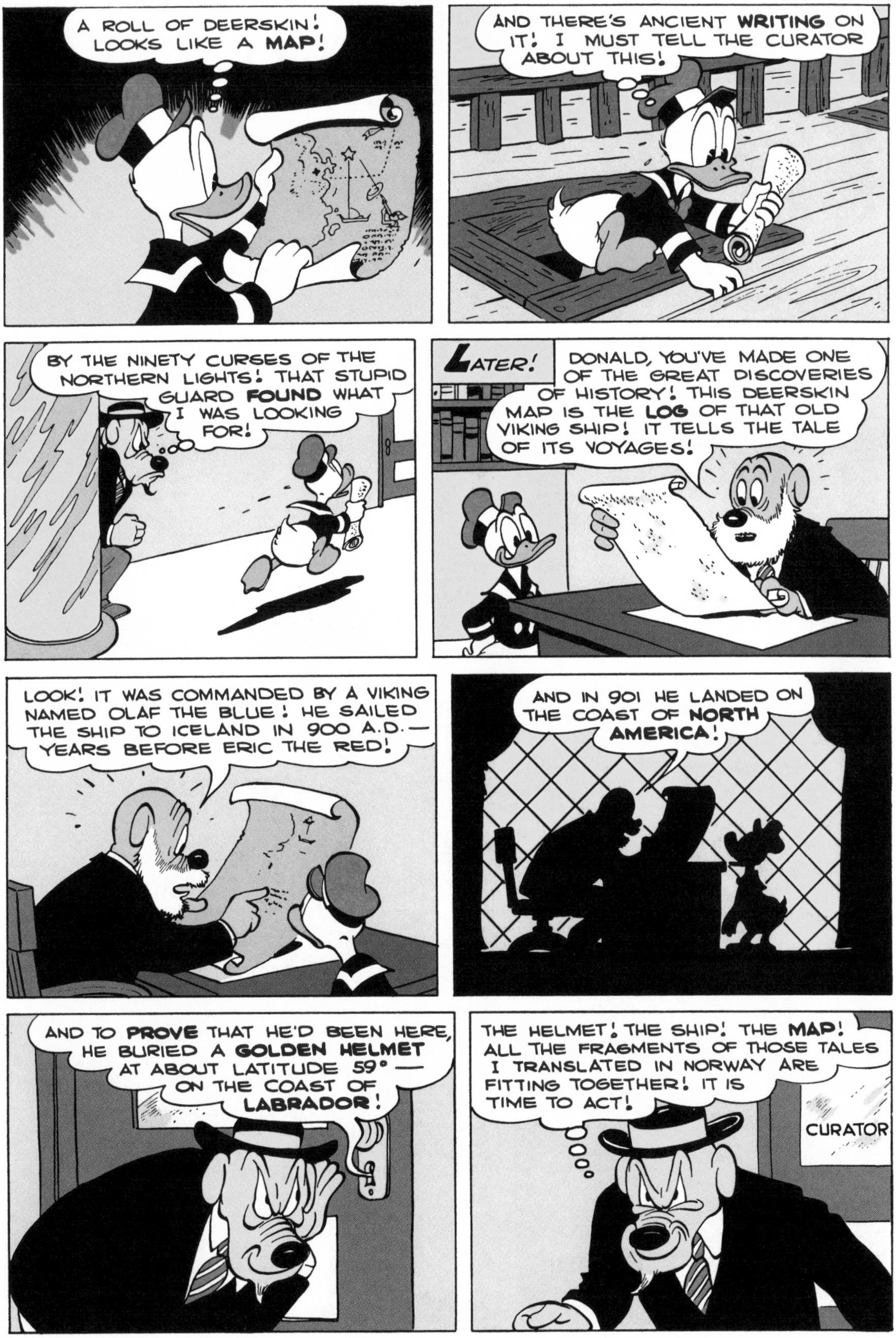
A ROLL OF DEERSKIN! LOOKS LIKE A MAP!
AND THERE'S ANCIENT WRITING ON IT! I MUST TELL THE CURATOR ABOUT THIS!
BY THE NINETY CURSES OF THE NORTHERN LIGHTS! THAT STUPID GUARD FOUND WHAT I WAS LOOKING FOR!
LATER!
DONALD, YOU'VE MADE ONE OF THE GREAT DISCOVERIES OF HISTORY! THIS DEERSKIN MAP IS THE LOG OF THAT OLD VIKING SHIP! IT TELLS THE TALE OF ITS VOYAGES!
LOOK! IT WAS COMMANDED BY A VIKING NAMED OLAF THE BLUE! HE SAILED THE SHIP TO ICELAND IN 900 A.D.— YEARS BEFORE ERIC THE RED!
AND IN 901 HE LANDED ON THE COAST OF NORTH AMERICA!
AND TO PROVE THAT HE'D BEEN HERE, HE BURIED A GOLDEN HELMET AT ABOUT LATITUDE 59° — ON THE COAST OF LABRADOR!
THE HELMET! THE SHIP! THE MAP! ALL THE FRAGMENTS OF THOSE TALES I TRANSLATED IN NORWAY ARE FITTING TOGETHER! IT IS TIME TO ACT!
CURATOR

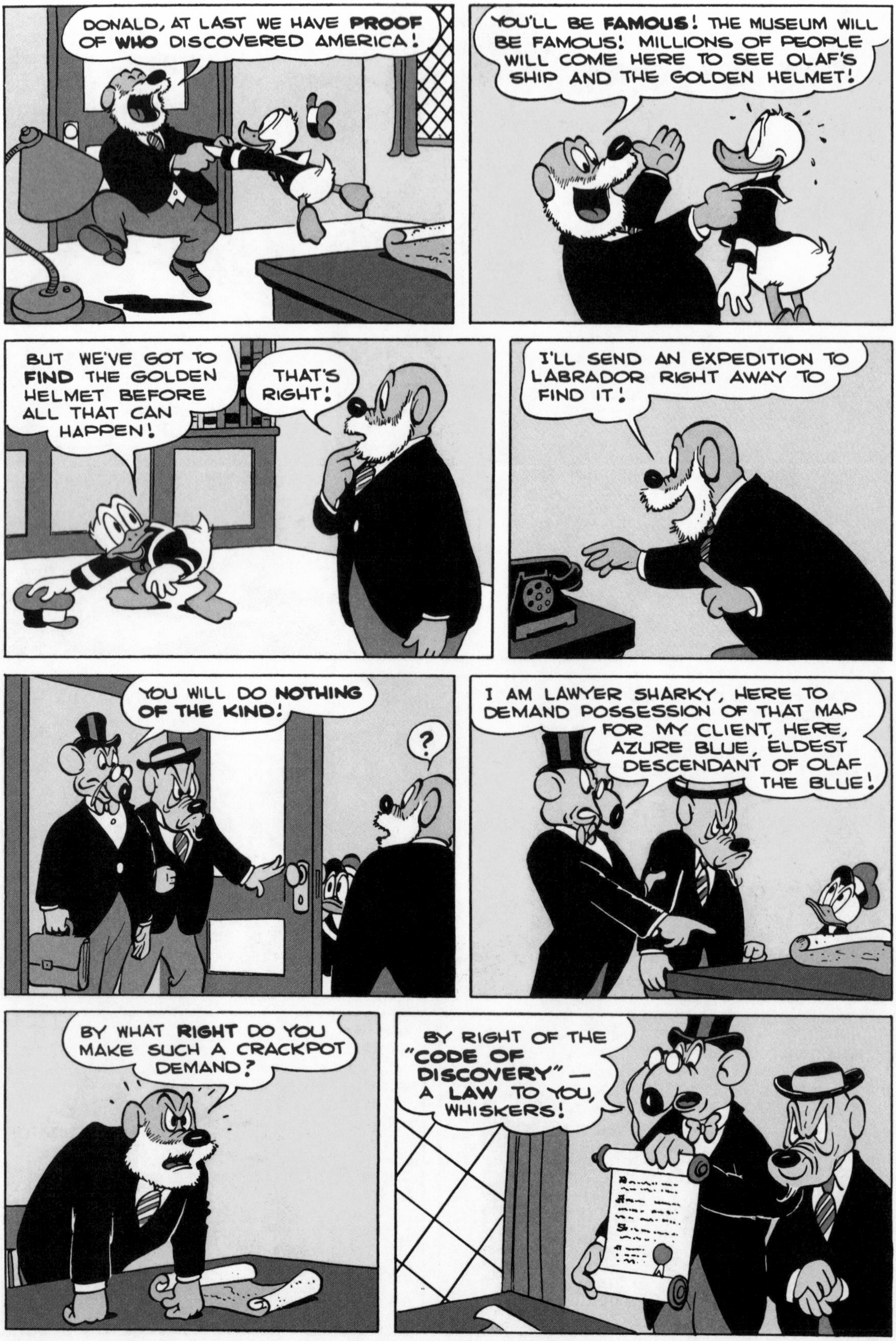
DONALD, AT LAST WE HAVE PROOF OF WHO DISCOVERED AMERICA!
YOU'LL BE FAMOUS! THE MUSEUM WILL BE FAMOUS! MILLIONS OF PEOPLE WILL COME HERE TO SEE OLAF'S SHIP AND THE GOLDEN HELMET!
BUT WE'VE GOT TO FIND THE GOLDEN HELMET BEFORE ALL THAT CAN HAPPEN!
THAT'S RIGHT!
I'LL SEND AN EXPEDITION TO LABRADOR RIGHT AWAY TO FIND IT!
YOU WILL DO NOTHING OF THE KIND!
?
I AM LAWYER SHARKY, HERE TO DEMAND POSSESSION OF THAT MAP FOR MY CLIENT, HERE, AZURE BLUE, ELDEST DESCENDANT OF OLAF THE BLUE!
BY WHAT RIGHT DO YOU MAKE SUCH A CRACKPOT DEMAND?
BY RIGHT OF THE "CODE OF DISCOVERY"— A LAW TO YOU, WHISKERS!

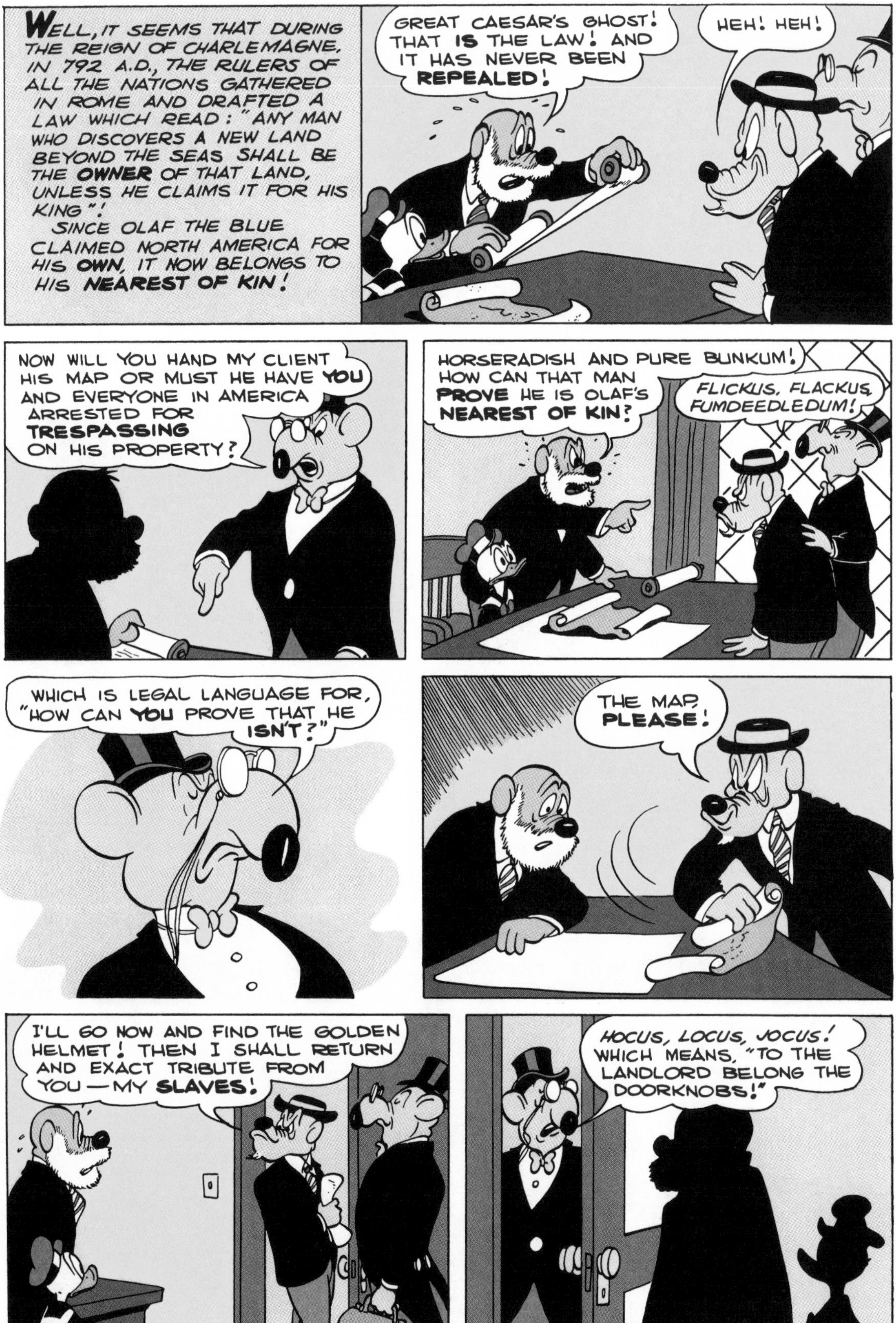
WELL, IT SEEMS THAT DURING THE REIGN OF CHARLEMAGNE, IN 792 A.D., THE RULERS OF ALL THE NATIONS GATHERED IN ROME AND DRAFTED A LAW WHICH READ: "ANY MAN WHO DISCOVERS A NEW LAND BEYOND THE SEAS SHALL BE THE OWNER OF THAT LAND, UNLESS HE CLAIMS IT FOR HIS KING"! SINCE OLAF THE BLUE CLAIMED NORTH AMERICA FOR HIS OWN, IT NOW BELONGS TO HIS NEAREST OF KIN!
GREAT CAESAR'S GHOST! THAT IS THE LAW! AND IT HAS NEVER BEEN REPEALED!
HEH! HEH!
NOW WILL YOU HAND MY CLIENT HIS MAP OR MUST HE HAVE YOU AND EVERYONE IN AMERICA ARRESTED FOR TRESPASSING ON HIS PROPERTY?
HORSERADISH AND PURE BUNKUM! HOW CAN THAT MAN PROVE HE IS OLAF'S NEAREST OF KIN?
FLICKUS, FLACKUS, FUMDEEDLEDUM!
WHICH IS LEGAL LANGUAGE FOR, "HOW CAN YOU PROVE THAT HE ISN'T?"
THE MAP, PLEASE!
I'LL GO NOW AND FIND THE GOLDEN HELMET! THEN I SHALL RETURN AND EXACT TRIBUTE FROM YOU — MY SLAVES!
HOCUS, LOCUS, JOCUS! WHICH MEANS, "TO THE LANDLORD BELONG THE DOORKNOBS!"

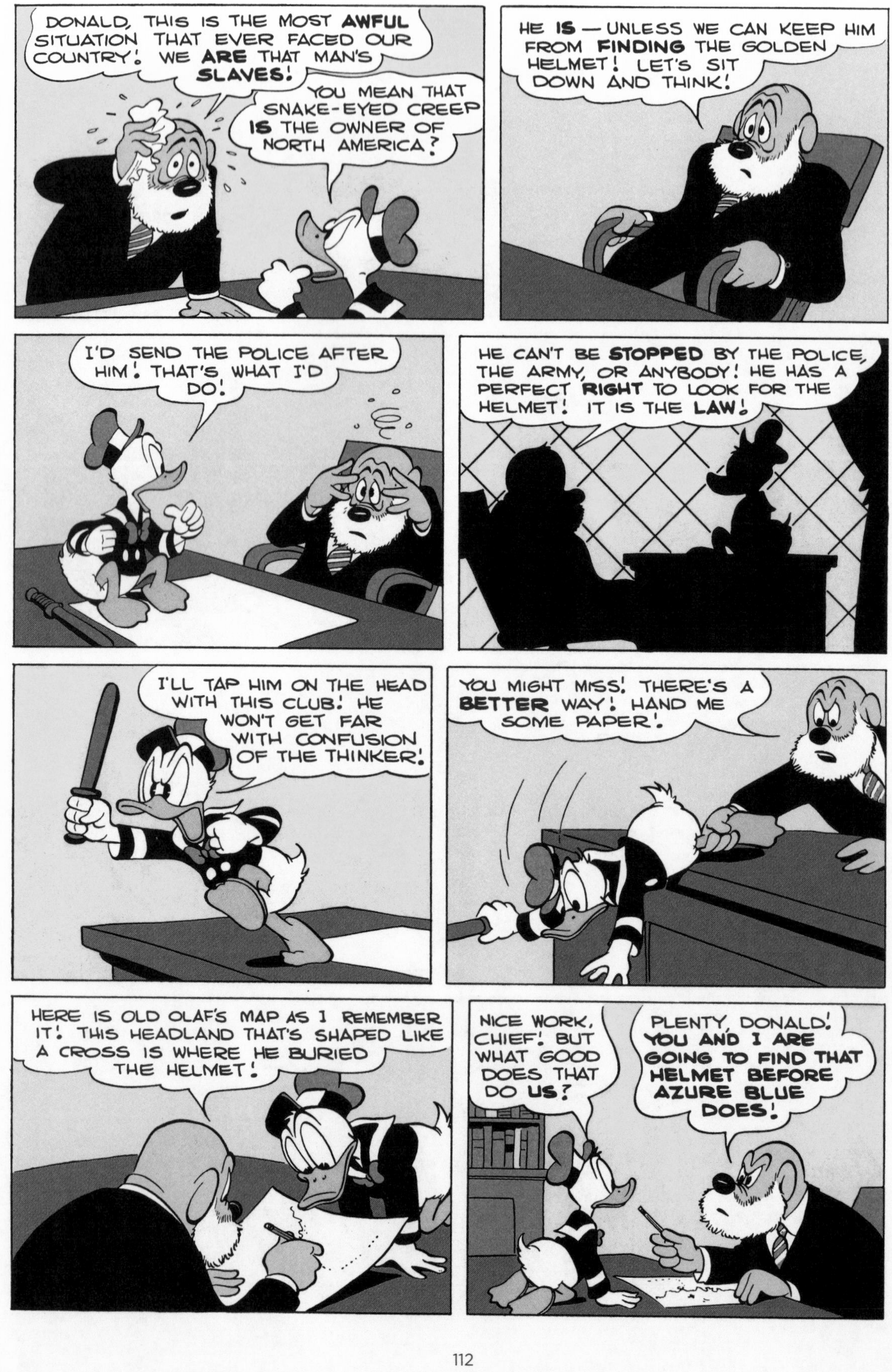
DONALD, THIS IS THE MOST AWFUL SITUATION THAT EVER FACED OUR COUNTRY! WE ARE THAT MAN'S SLAVES!
YOU MEAN THAT SNAKE-EYED CREEP IS THE OWNER OF NORTH AMERICA?
HE IS — UNLESS WE CAN KEEP HIM FROM FINDING THE GOLDEN HELMET! LET'S SIT DOWN AND THINK!
I'D SEND THE POLICE AFTER HIM! THAT'S WHAT I'D DO!
HE CAN'T BE STOPPED BY THE POLICE, THE ARMY, OR ANYBODY! HE HAS A PERFECT RIGHT TO LOOK FOR THE HELMET! IT IS THE LAW!
I'LL TAP HIM ON THE HEAD WITH THIS CLUB! HE WON'T GET FAR WITH CONFUSION OF THE THINKER!
YOU MIGHT MISS! THERE'S A BETTER WAY! HAND ME SOME PAPER!
HERE IS OLD OLAF'S MAP AS I REMEMBER IT! THIS HEADLAND THAT'S SHAPED LIKE A CROSS IS WHERE HE BURIED THE HELMET!
NICE WORK, CHIEF! BUT WHAT GOOD DOES THAT DO US?
PLENTY, DONALD! YOU AND I ARE GOING TO FIND THAT HELMET BEFORE AZURE BLUE DOES!

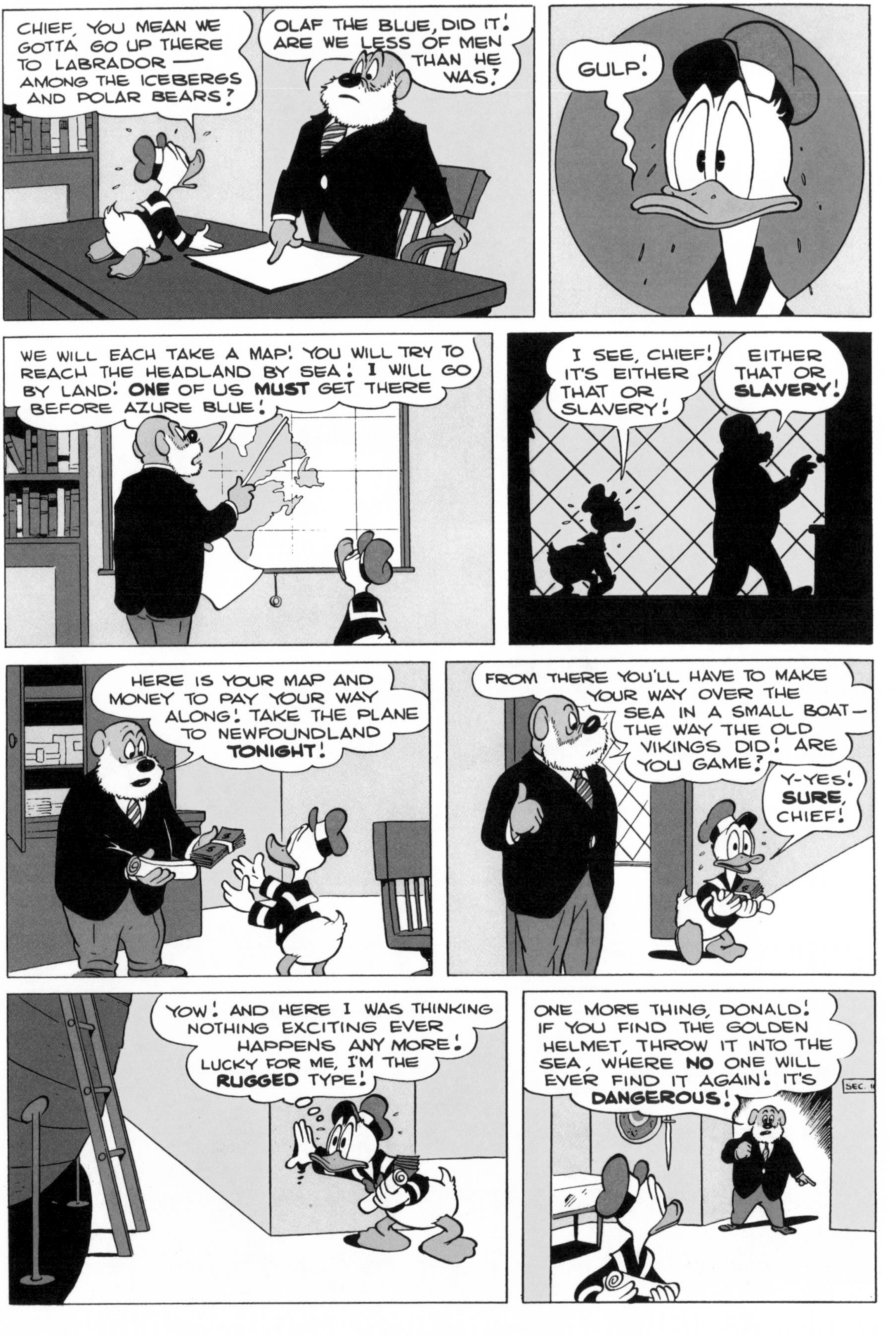
CHIEF, YOU MEAN WE GOTTA GO UP THERE TO LABRADOR — AMONG THE ICEBERGS AND POLAR BEARS?
OLAF THE BLUE, DID IT! ARE WE LESS OF MEN THAN HE WAS?
GULP!
WE WILL EACH TAKE A MAP! YOU WILL TRY TO REACH THE HEADLAND BY SEA! I WILL GO BY LAND! ONE OF US MUST GET THERE BEFORE AZURE BLUE!
I SEE, CHIEF! IT'S EITHER THAT OR SLAVERY!
EITHER THAT OR SLAVERY!
HERE IS YOUR MAP AND MONEY TO PAY YOUR WAY ALONG! TAKE THE PLANE TO NEWFOUNDLAND TONIGHT!
FROM THERE YOU'LL HAVE TO MAKE YOUR WAY OVER THE SEA IN A SMALL BOAT — THE WAY THE OLD VIKINGS DID! ARE YOU GAME?
Y-YES! SURE, CHIEF!
YOW! AND HERE I WAS THINKING NOTHING EXCITING EVER HAPPENS ANY MORE! LUCKY FOR ME, I'M THE RUGGED TYPE!
ONE MORE THING, DONALD! IF YOU FIND THE GOLDEN HELMET, THROW IT INTO THE SEA, WHERE NO ONE WILL EVER FIND IT AGAIN! IT'S DANGEROUS!

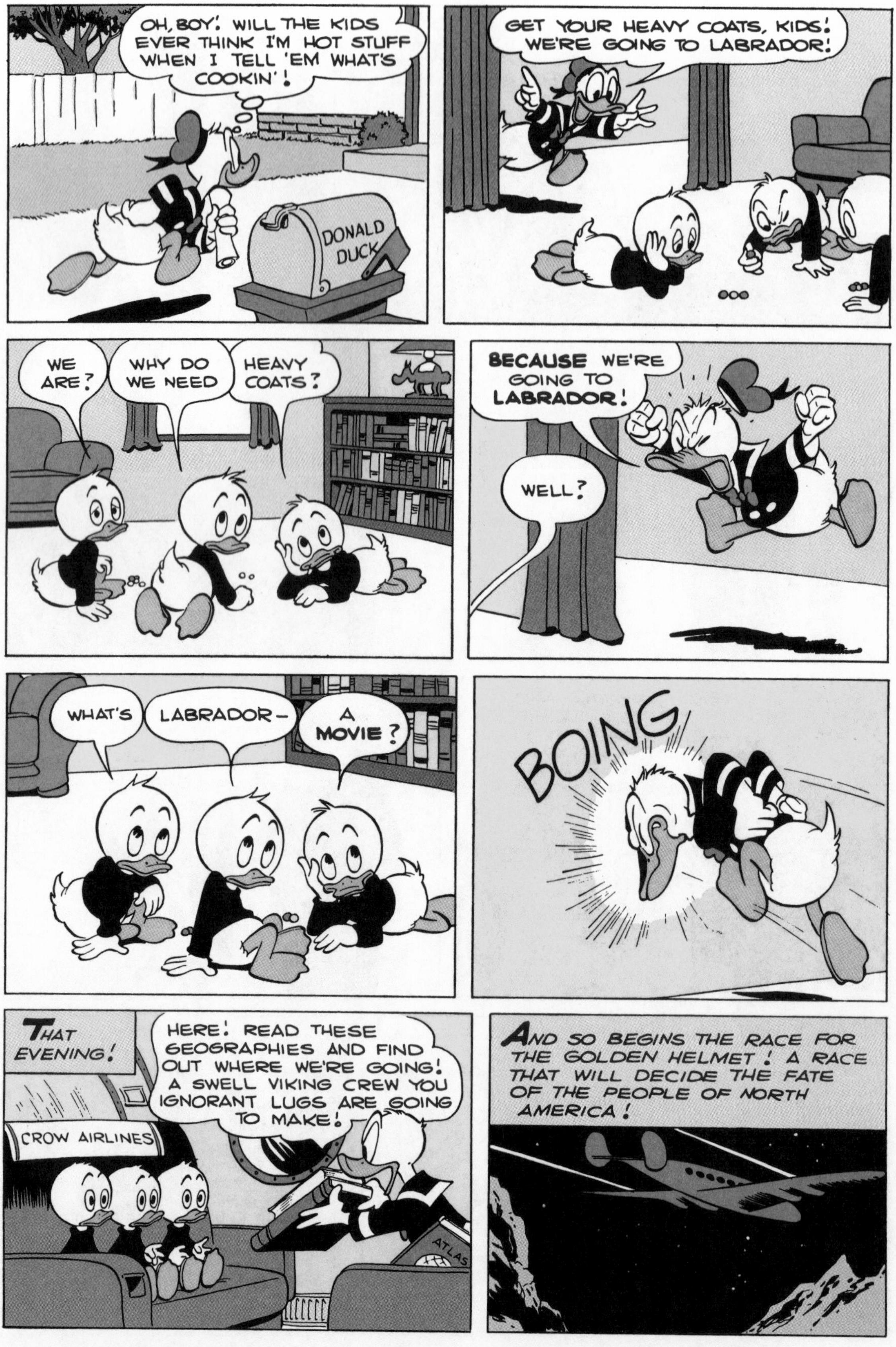
OH, BOY! WILL THE KIDS EVER THINK I'M HOT STUFF WHEN I TELL 'EM WHAT'S COOKIN'!
DONALD DUCK
GET YOUR HEAVY COATS, KIDS! WE'RE GOING TO LABRADOR!
WE ARE?
WHY DO WE NEED
HEAVY COATS?
BECAUSE WE'RE GOING TO LABRADOR!
WELL?
WHAT'S
LABRADOR—
A MOVIE?
BOING
THAT EVENING!
HERE! READ THESE GEOGRAPHIES AND FIND OUT WHERE WE'RE GOING! A SWELL VIKING CREW YOU IGNORANT LUGS ARE GOING TO MAKE!
CROW AIRLINES
ATLAS
AND SO BEGINS THE RACE FOR THE GOLDEN HELMET! A RACE THAT WILL DECIDE THE FATE OF THE PEOPLE OF NORTH AMERICA!

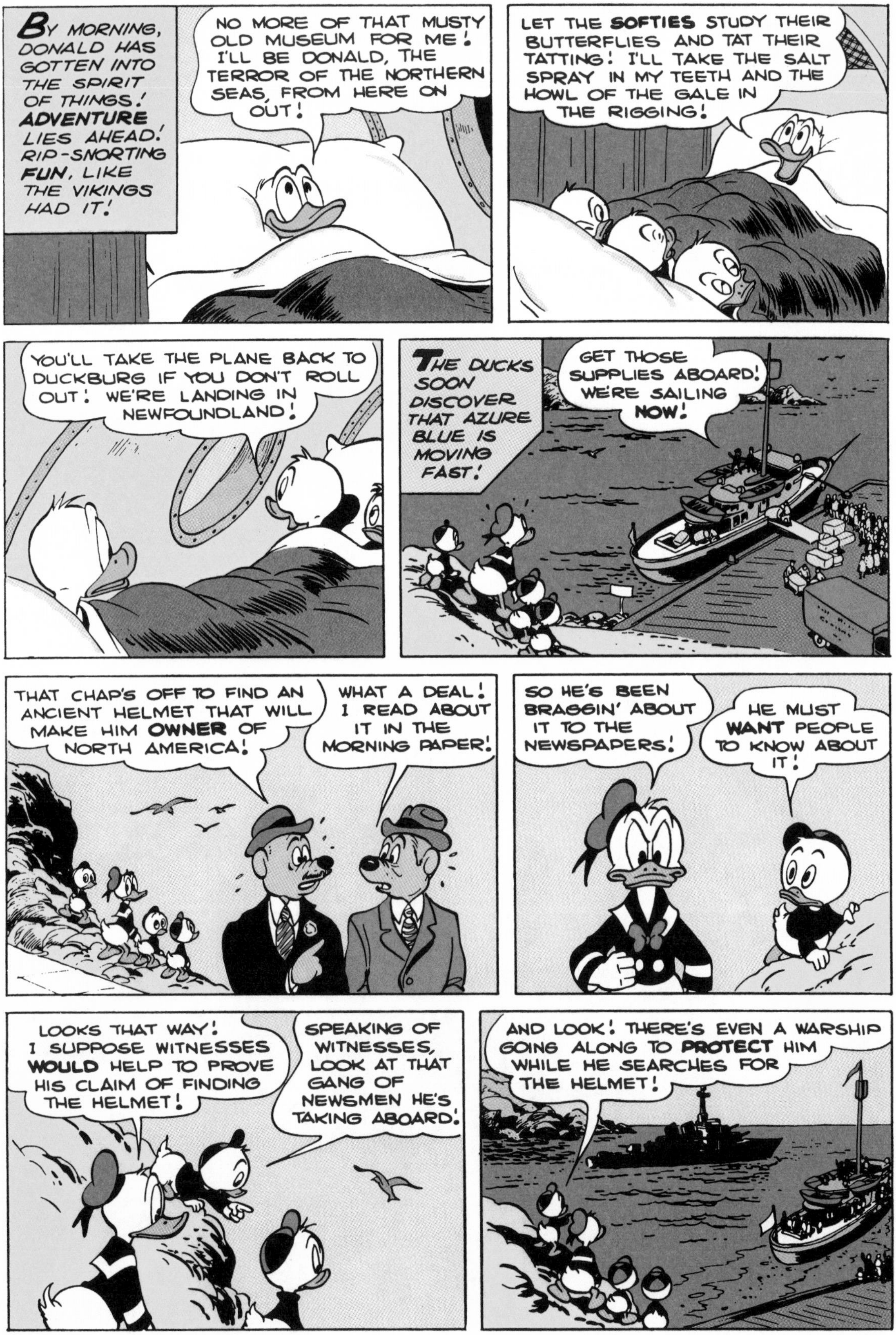
BY MORNING, DONALD HAS GOTTEN INTO THE SPIRIT OF THINGS! ADVENTURE LIES AHEAD! RIP-SNORTING FUN, LIKE THE VIKINGS HAD IT!
NO MORE OF THAT MUSTY OLD MUSEUM FOR ME! I'LL BE DONALD, THE TERROR OF THE NORTHERN SEAS, FROM HERE ON OUT!
LET THE SOFTIES STUDY THEIR BUTTERFLIES AND TAT THEIR TATTING! I'LL TAKE THE SALT SPRAY IN MY TEETH AND THE HOWL OF THE GALE IN THE RIGGING!
YOU'LL TAKE THE PLANE BACK TO DUCKBURG IF YOU DON'T ROLL OUT! WE'RE LANDING IN NEWFOUNDLAND!
THE DUCKS SOON DISCOVER THAT AZURE BLUE IS MOVING FAST!
GET THOSE SUPPLIES ABOARD! WE'RE SAILING NOW!
THAT CHAP'S OFF TO FIND AN ANCIENT HELMET THAT WILL MAKE HIM OWNER OF NORTH AMERICA!
WHAT A DEAL! I READ ABOUT IT IN THE MORNING PAPER!
SO HE'S BEEN BRAGGIN' ABOUT IT TO THE NEWSPAPERS!
HE MUST WANT PEOPLE TO KNOW ABOUT IT!
LOOKS THAT WAY! I SUPPOSE WITNESSES WOULD HELP TO PROVE HIS CLAIM OF FINDING THE HELMET!
SPEAKING OF WITNESSES, LOOK AT THAT GANG OF NEWSMEN HE'S TAKING ABOARD!
AND LOOK! THERE'S EVEN A WARSHIP GOING ALONG TO PROTECT HIM WHILE HE SEARCHES FOR THE HELMET!

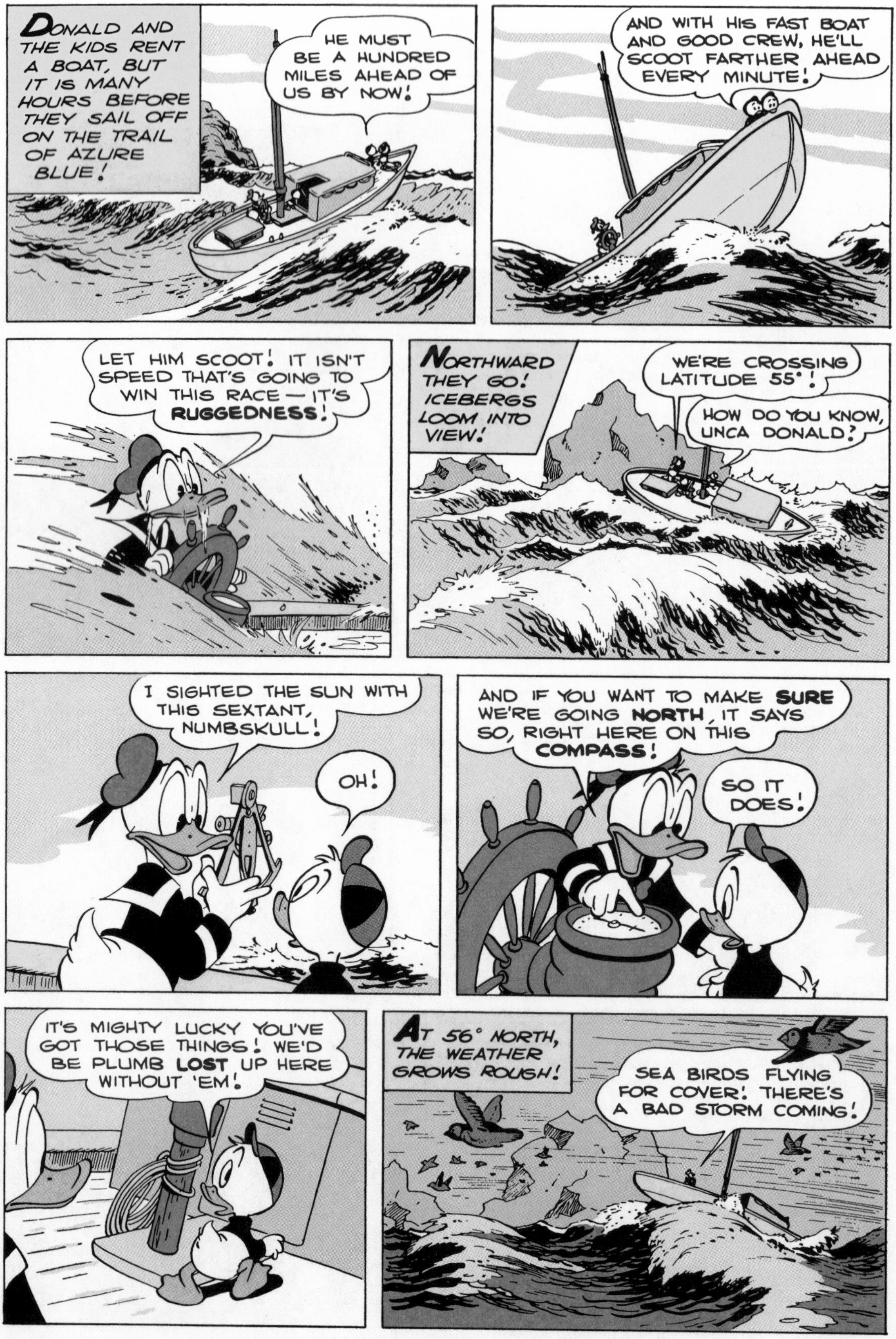
DONALD AND THE KIDS RENT A BOAT, BUT IT IS MANY HOURS BEFORE THEY SAIL OFF ON THE TRAIL OF AZURE BLUE!
HE MUST BE A HUNDRED MILES AHEAD OF US BY NOW!
AND WITH HIS FAST BOAT AND GOOD CREW, HE'LL SCOOT FARTHER AHEAD EVERY MINUTE!
LET HIM SCOOT! IT ISN'T SPEED THAT'S GOING TO WIN THIS RACE—IT'S RUGGEDNESS!
NORTHWARD THEY GO! ICEBERGS LOOM INTO VIEW!
WE'RE CROSSING LATITUDE 55°!
HOW DO YOU KNOW, UNCA DONALD?
I SIGHTED THE SUN WITH THIS SEXTANT, NUMBSKULL!
OH!
AND IF YOU WANT TO MAKE SURE WE'RE GOING NORTH, IT SAYS SO, RIGHT HERE ON THIS COMPASS!
SO IT DOES!
IT'S MIGHTY LUCKY YOU'VE GOT THOSE THINGS! WE'D BE PLUMB LOST UP HERE WITHOUT 'EM!
AT 56° NORTH, THE WEATHER GROWS ROUGH!
SEA BIRDS FLYING FOR COVER! THERE'S A BAD STORM COMING!

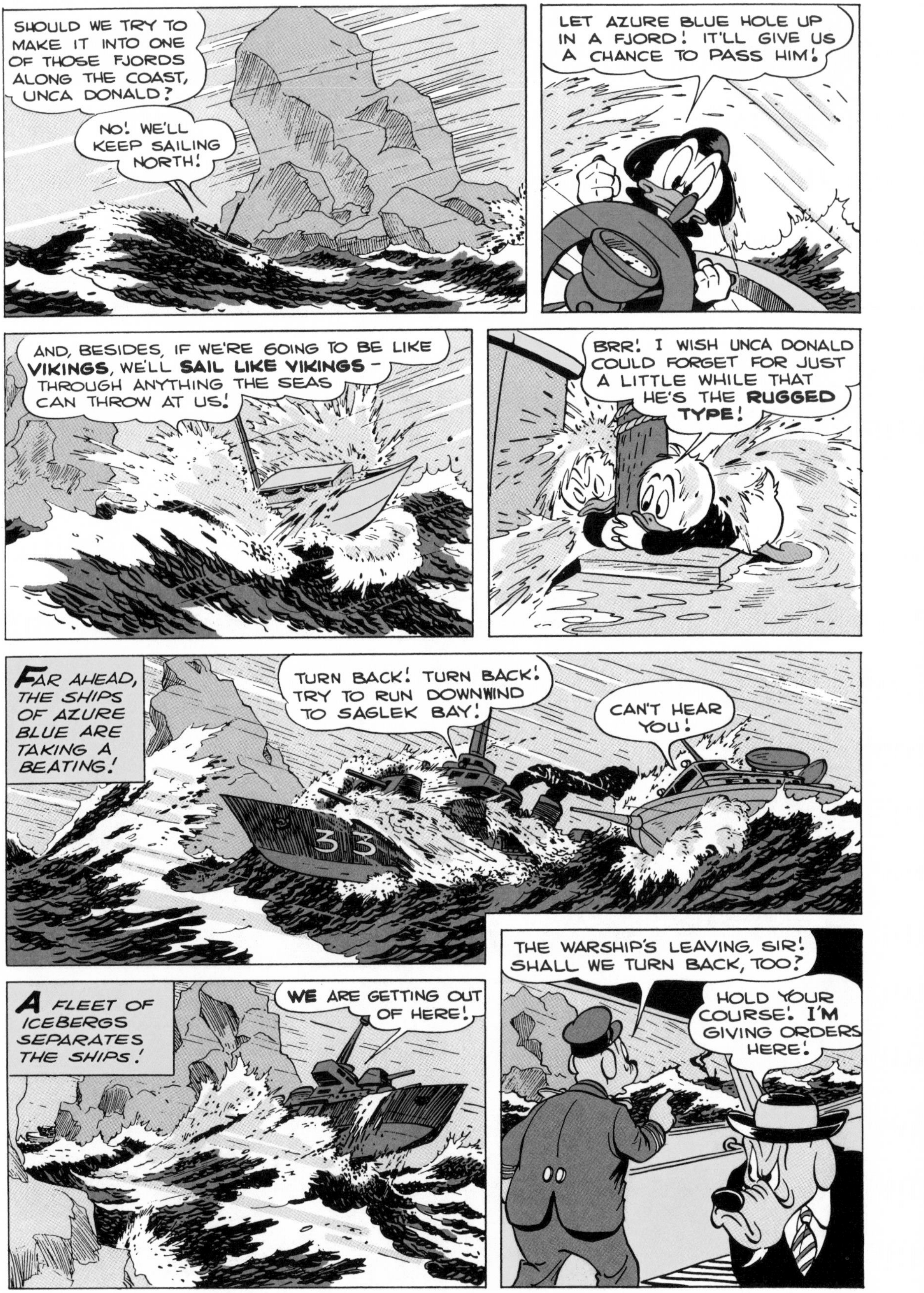
SHOULD WE TRY TO MAKE IT INTO ONE OF THOSE FJORDS ALONG THE COAST, UNCA DONALD?
NO! WE'LL KEEP SAILING NORTH!
LET AZURE BLUE HOLE UP IN A FJORD! IT'LL GIVE US A CHANCE TO PASS HIM!
AND, BESIDES, IF WE'RE GOING TO BE LIKE VIKINGS, WE'LL SAIL LIKE VIKINGS – THROUGH ANYTHING THE SEAS CAN THROW AT US!
BRR! I WISH UNCA DONALD COULD FORGET FOR JUST A LITTLE WHILE THAT HE'S THE RUGGED TYPE!
FAR AHEAD, THE SHIPS OF AZURE BLUE ARE TAKING A BEATING!
TURN BACK! TURN BACK! TRY TO RUN DOWNWIND TO SAGLEK BAY!
CAN'T HEAR YOU!
A FLEET OF ICEBERGS SEPARATES THE SHIPS!
WE ARE GETTING OUT OF HERE!
THE WARSHIP'S LEAVING, SIR! SHALL WE TURN BACK, TOO?
HOLD YOUR COURSE! I'M GIVING ORDERS HERE!

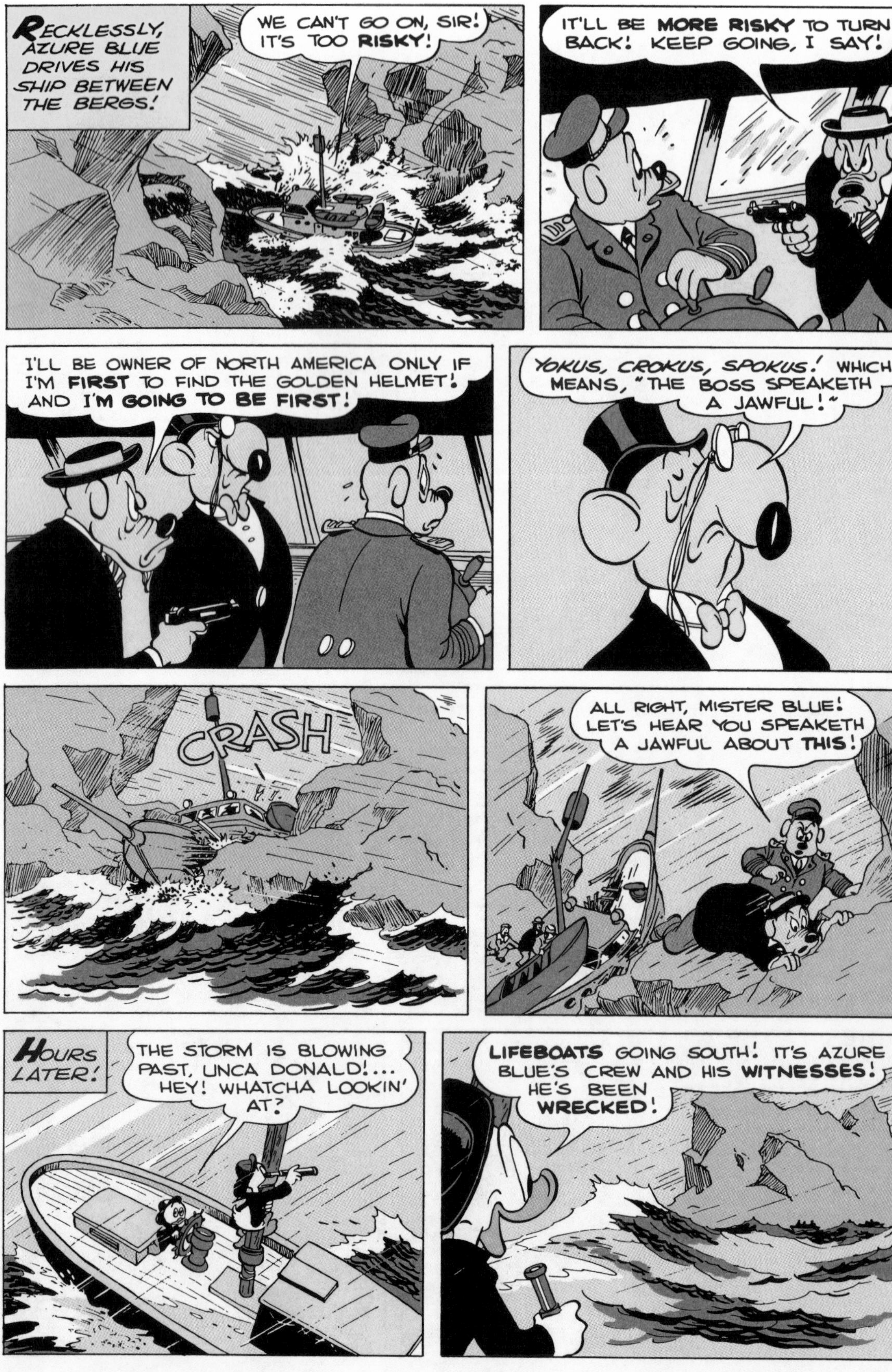
RECKLESSLY, AZURE BLUE DRIVES HIS SHIP BETWEEN THE BERGS!
WE CAN'T GO ON, SIR! IT'S TOO RISKY!
IT'LL BE MORE RISKY TO TURN BACK! KEEP GOING, I SAY!
I'LL BE OWNER OF NORTH AMERICA ONLY IF I'M FIRST TO FIND THE GOLDEN HELMET! AND I'M GOING TO BE FIRST!
YOKUS, CROKUS, SPOKUS! WHICH MEANS, "THE BOSS SPEAKETH A JAWFUL!"
CRASH
ALL RIGHT, MISTER BLUE! LET'S HEAR YOU SPEAKETH A JAWFUL ABOUT THIS!
HOURS LATER!
THE STORM IS BLOWING PAST, UNCA DONALD!... HEY! WHATCHA LOOKIN' AT?
LIFEBOATS GOING SOUTH! IT'S AZURE BLUE'S CREW AND HIS WITNESSES! HE'S BEEN WRECKED!

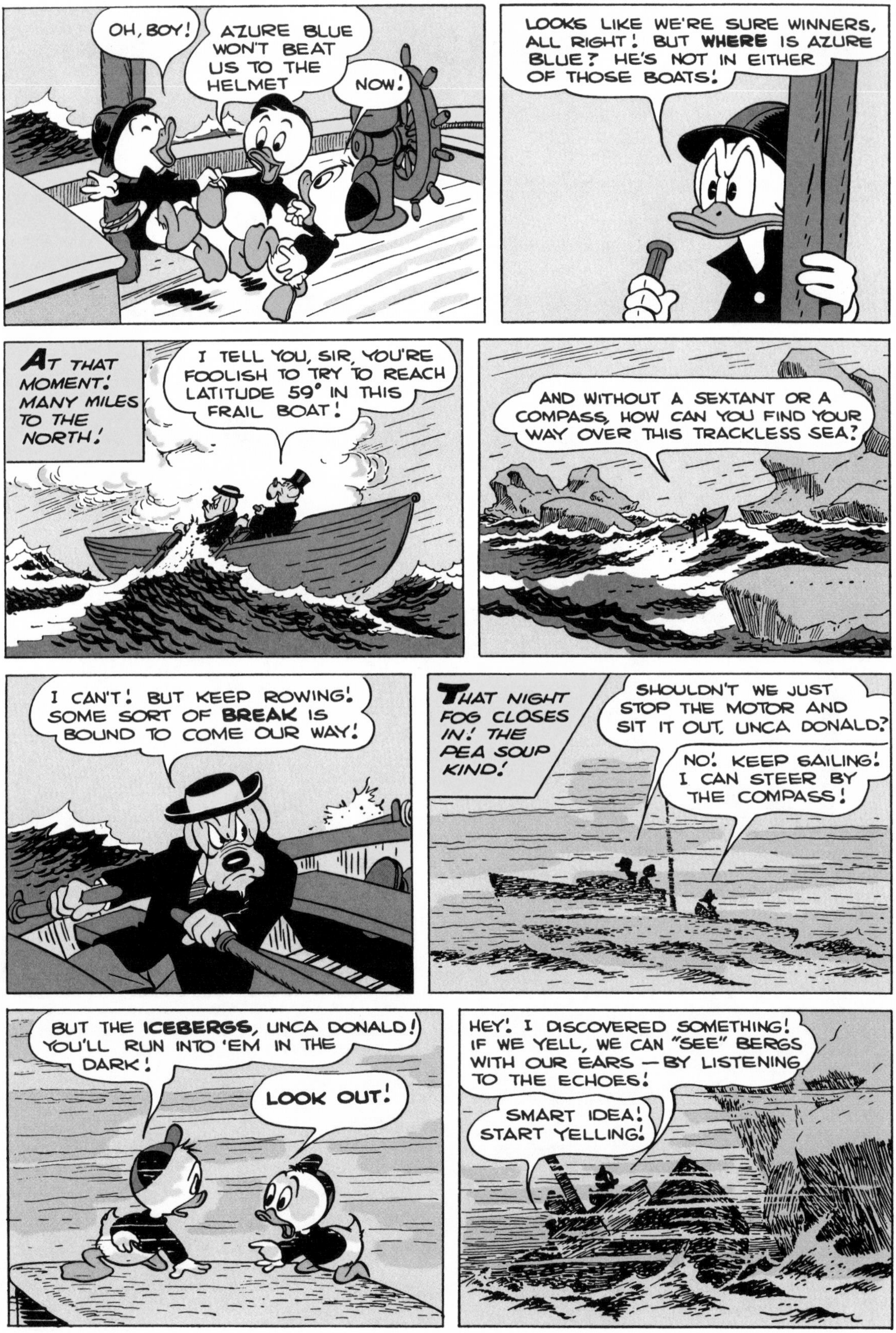
OH, BOY!
AZURE BLUE WON'T BEAT US TO THE HELMET
NOW!
LOOKS LIKE WE'RE SURE WINNERS, ALL RIGHT! BUT WHERE IS AZURE BLUE? HE'S NOT IN EITHER OF THOSE BOATS!
AT THAT MOMENT! MANY MILES TO THE NORTH!
I TELL YOU, SIR, YOU'RE FOOLISH TO TRY TO REACH LATITUDE 59° IN THIS FRAIL BOAT!
AND WITHOUT A SEXTANT OR A COMPASS, HOW CAN YOU FIND YOUR WAY OVER THIS TRACKLESS SEA?
I CAN'T! BUT KEEP ROWING! SOME SORT OF BREAK IS BOUND TO COME OUR WAY!
THAT NIGHT FOG CLOSES IN! THE PEA SOUP KIND!
SHOULDN'T WE JUST STOP THE MOTOR AND SIT IT OUT, UNCA DONALD?
NO! KEEP SAILING! I CAN STEER BY THE COMPASS!
BUT THE ICEBERGS, UNCA DONALD! YOU'LL RUN INTO 'EM IN THE DARK!
LOOK OUT!
HEY! I DISCOVERED SOMETHING! IF WE YELL, WE CAN "SEE" BERGS WITH OUR EARS — BY LISTENING TO THE ECHOES!
SMART IDEA! START YELLING!

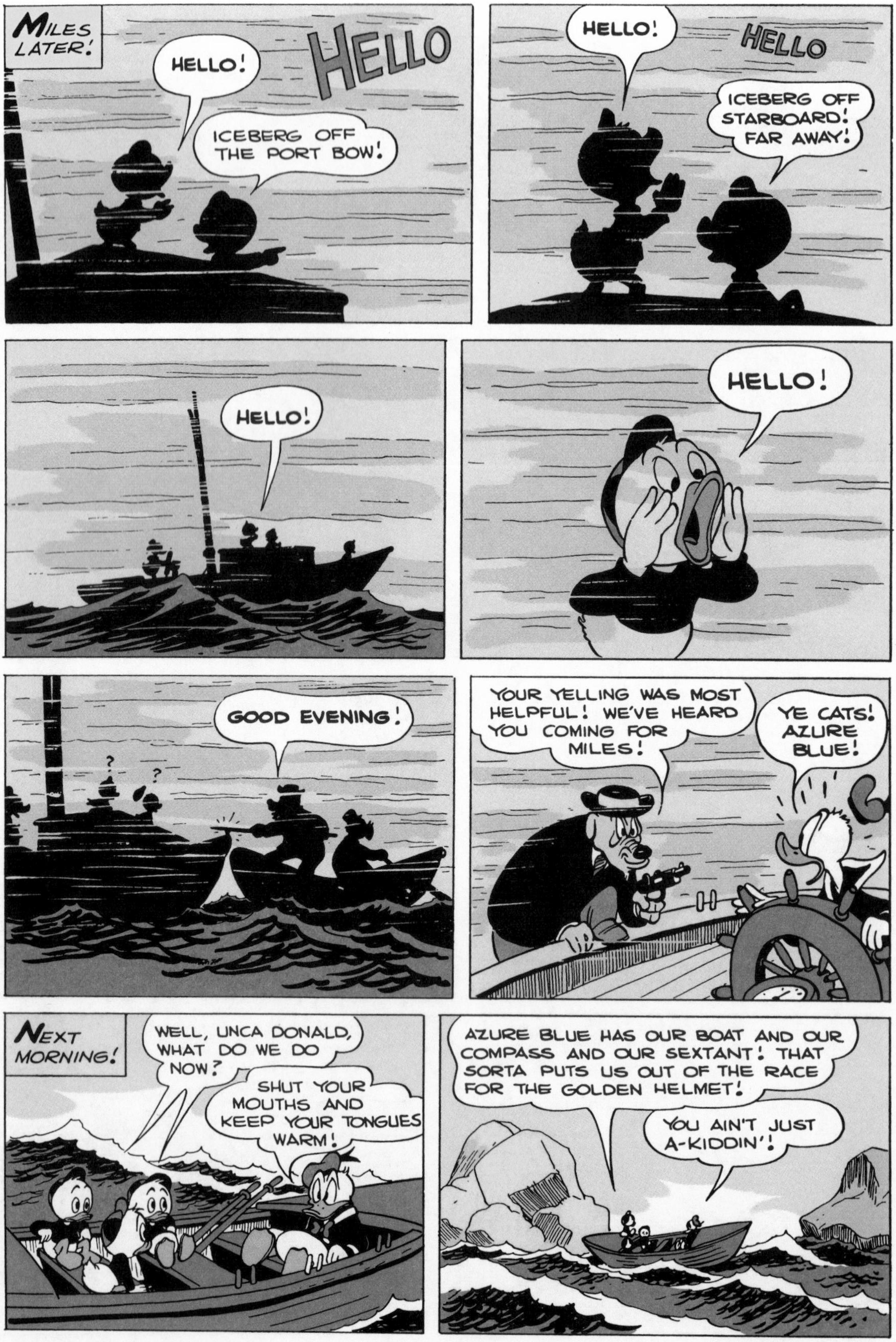
MILES LATER!
HELLO!
HELLO
ICEBERG OFF THE PORT BOW!
HELLO!
HELLO
ICEBERG OFF STARBOARD! FAR AWAY!
HELLO!
HELLO!
GOOD EVENING!
YOUR YELLING WAS MOST HELPFUL! WE'VE HEARD YOU COMING FOR MILES!
YE CATS! AZURE BLUE!
NEXT MORNING!
WELL, UNCA DONALD, WHAT DO WE DO NOW?
SHUT YOUR MOUTHS AND KEEP YOUR TONGUES WARM!
AZURE BLUE HAS OUR BOAT AND OUR COMPASS AND OUR SEXTANT! THAT SORTA PUTS US OUT OF THE RACE FOR THE GOLDEN HELMET!
YOU AIN'T JUST A-KIDDIN'!

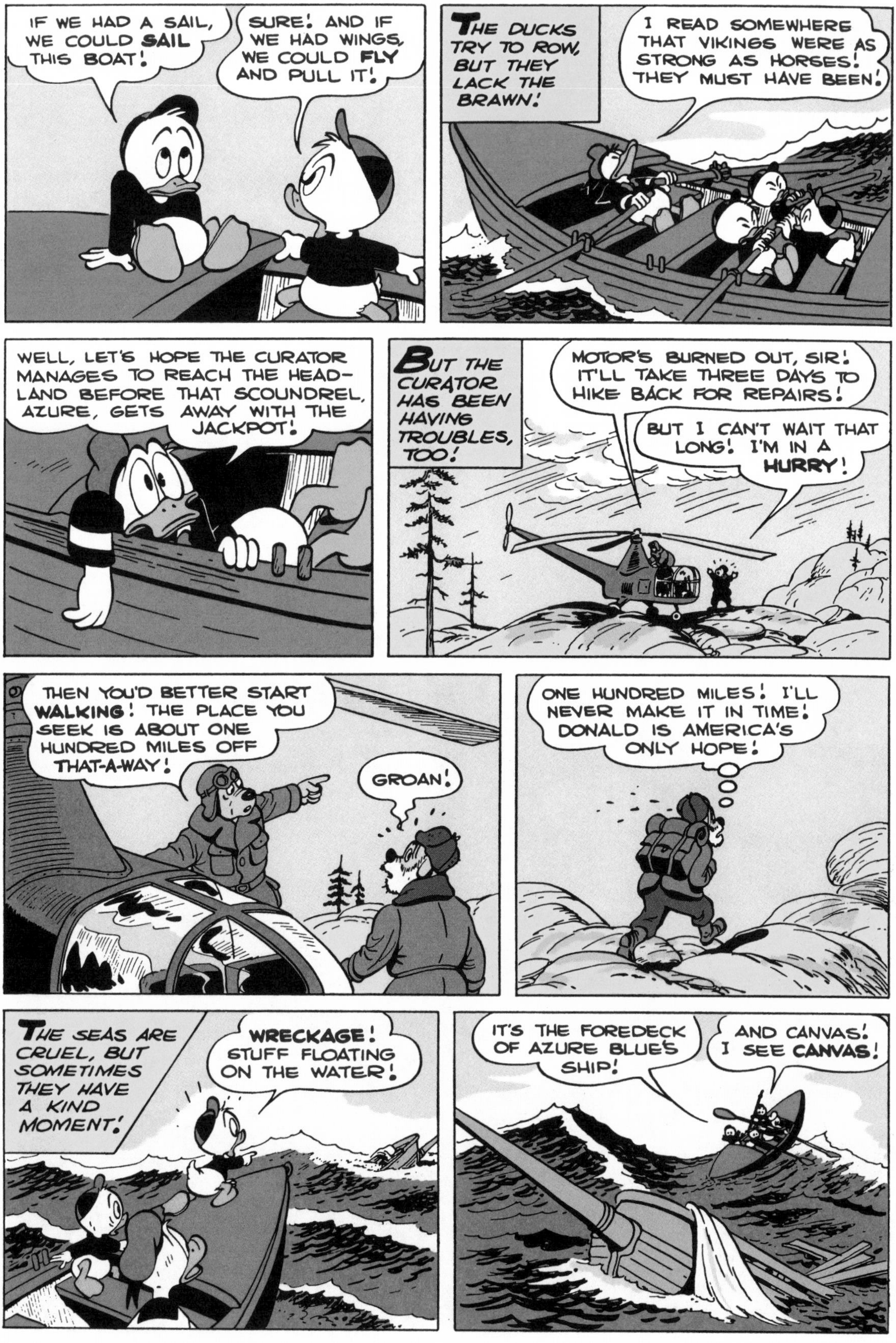

IF WE HAD A SAIL, WE COULD SAIL THIS BOAT!
SURE! AND IF WE HAD WINGS, WE COULD FLY AND PULL IT!
THE DUCKS TRY TO ROW, BUT THEY LACK THE BRAWN!
I READ SOMEWHERE THAT VIKINGS WERE AS STRONG AS HORSES! THEY MUST HAVE BEEN!
WELL, LET'S HOPE THE CURATOR MANAGES TO REACH THE HEAD-LAND BEFORE THAT SCOUNDREL, AZURE, GETS AWAY WITH THE JACKPOT!
BUT THE CURATOR HAS BEEN HAVING TROUBLES, TOO!
MOTOR'S BURNED OUT, SIR! IT'LL TAKE THREE DAYS TO HIKE BACK FOR REPAIRS!
BUT I CAN'T WAIT THAT LONG! I'M IN A HURRY!
THEN YOU'D BETTER START WALKING! THE PLACE YOU SEEK IS ABOUT ONE HUNDRED MILES OFF THAT-A-WAY!
GROAN!
ONE HUNDRED MILES! I'LL NEVER MAKE IT IN TIME! DONALD IS AMERICA'S ONLY HOPE!
THE SEAS ARE CRUEL, BUT SOMETIMES THEY HAVE A KIND MOMENT!
WRECKAGE! STUFF FLOATING ON THE WATER!
IT'S THE FOREDECK OF AZURE BLUE'S SHIP!
AND CANVAS! I SEE CANVAS!

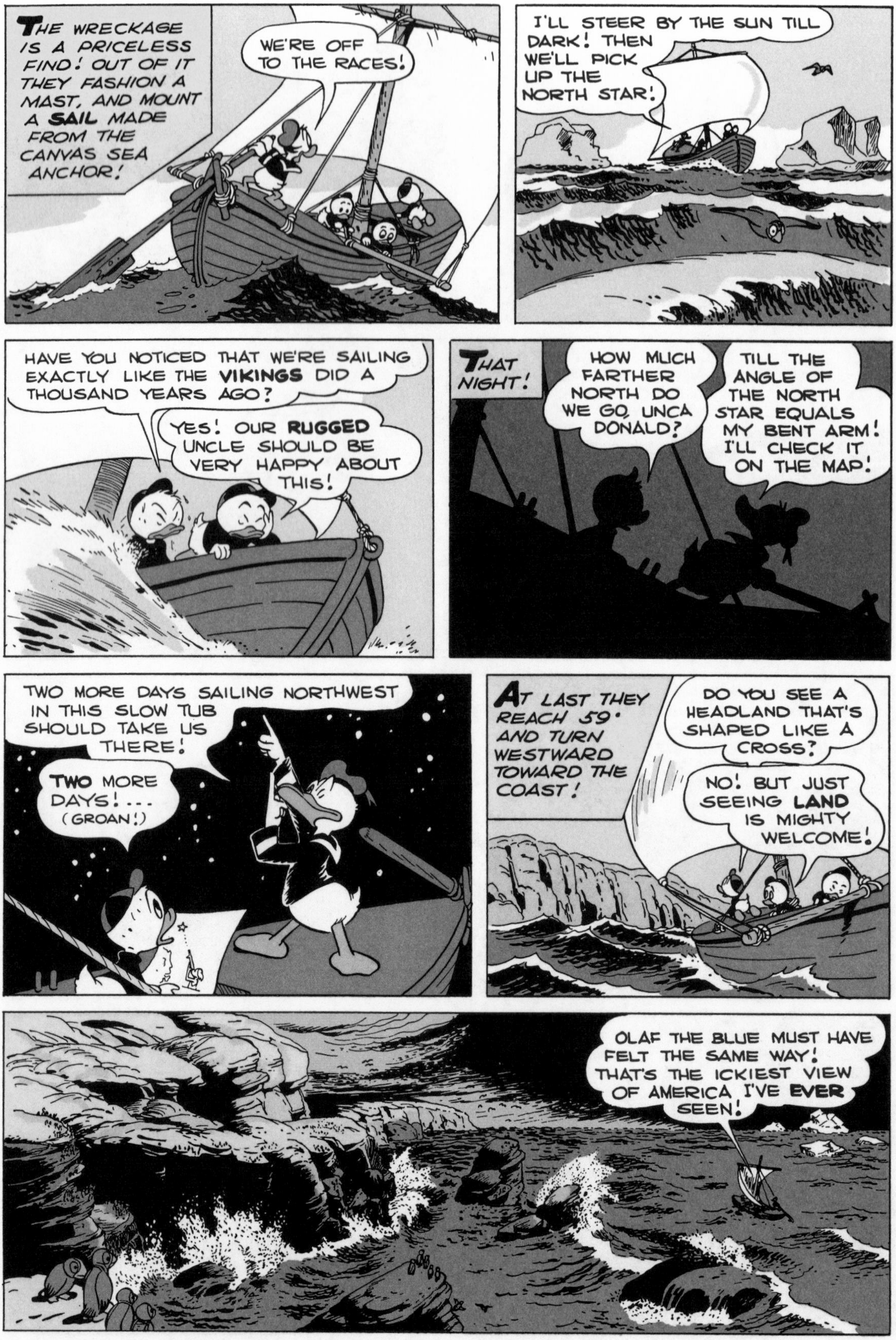
THE WRECKAGE IS A PRICELESS FIND! OUT OF IT THEY FASHION A MAST, AND MOUNT A SAIL MADE FROM THE CANVAS SEA ANCHOR!
WE'RE OFF TO THE RACES!
I'LL STEER BY THE SUN TILL DARK! THEN WE'LL PICK UP THE NORTH STAR!
HAVE YOU NOTICED THAT WE'RE SAILING EXACTLY LIKE THE VIKINGS DID A THOUSAND YEARS AGO?
YES! OUR RUGGED UNCLE SHOULD BE VERY HAPPY ABOUT THIS!
THAT NIGHT!
HOW MUCH FARTHER NORTH DO WE GO, UNCA DONALD?
TILL THE ANGLE OF THE NORTH STAR EQUALS MY BENT ARM! I'LL CHECK IT ON THE MAP!
TWO MORE DAYS SAILING NORTHWEST IN THIS SLOW TUB SHOULD TAKE US THERE!
TWO MORE DAYS! . . . (GROAN!)
AT LAST THEY REACH 59° AND TURN WESTWARD TOWARD THE COAST!
DO YOU SEE A HEADLAND THAT'S SHAPED LIKE A CROSS?
NO! BUT JUST SEEING LAND IS MIGHTY WELCOME!
OLAF THE BLUE MUST HAVE FELT THE SAME WAY! THAT'S THE ICKIEST VIEW OF AMERICA I'VE EVER SEEN!

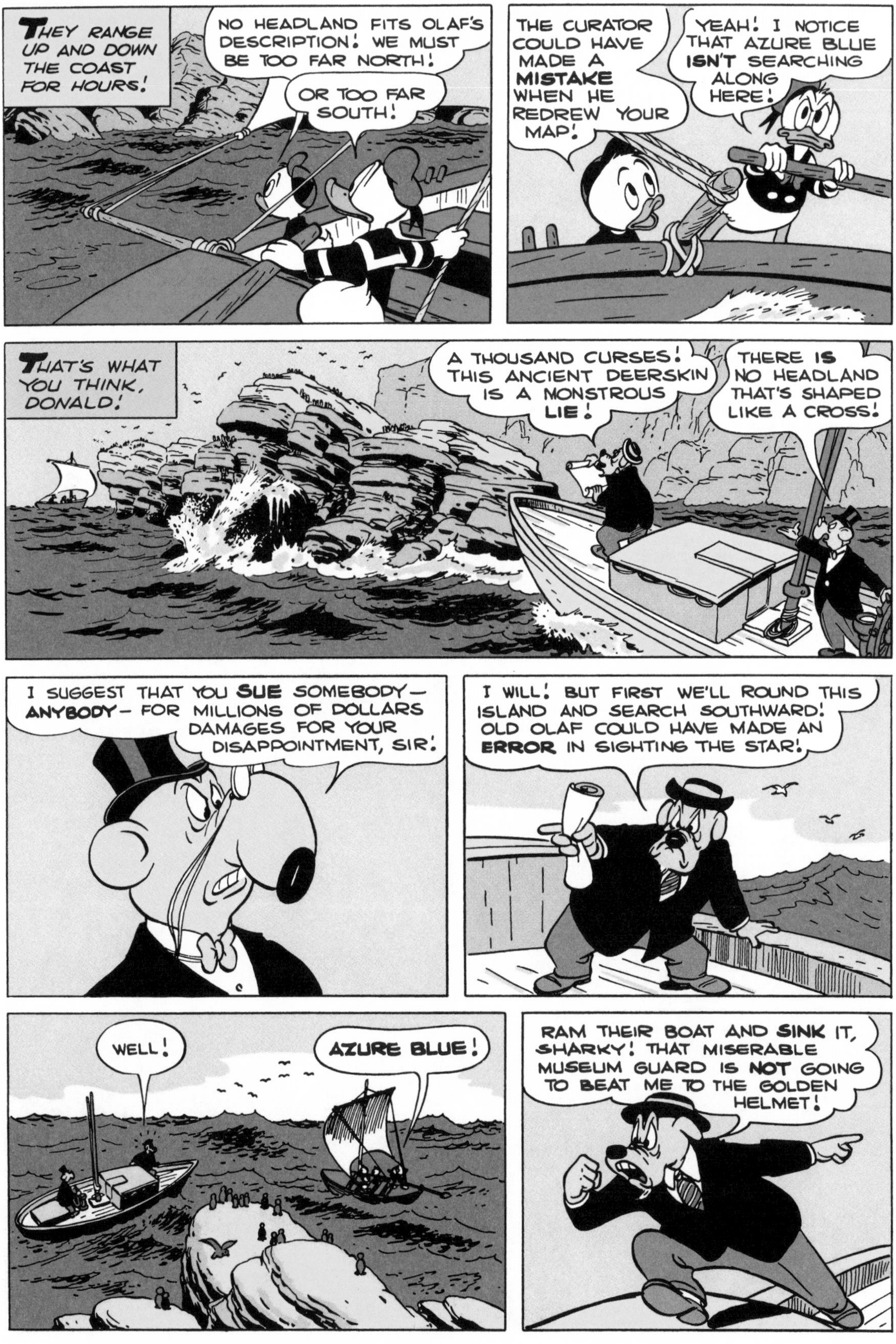
THEY RANGE UP AND DOWN THE COAST FOR HOURS!
NO HEADLAND FITS OLAF'S DESCRIPTION! WE MUST BE TOO FAR NORTH!
OR TOO FAR SOUTH!
THE CURATOR COULD HAVE MADE A **MISTAKE** WHEN HE REDREW YOUR MAP!
YEAH! I NOTICE THAT AZURE BLUE **ISN'T** SEARCHING ALONG HERE!
THAT'S WHAT YOU THINK, DONALD!
A THOUSAND CURSES! THIS ANCIENT DEERSKIN IS A MONSTROUS **LIE**!
THERE **IS** NO HEADLAND THAT'S SHAPED LIKE A CROSS!
I SUGGEST THAT YOU **SUE** SOMEBODY— **ANYBODY**— FOR MILLIONS OF DOLLARS DAMAGES FOR YOUR DISAPPOINTMENT, SIR!
I WILL! BUT FIRST WE'LL ROUND THIS ISLAND AND SEARCH SOUTHWARD! OLD OLAF COULD HAVE MADE AN **ERROR** IN SIGHTING THE STAR!
WELL!
AZURE BLUE!
RAM THEIR BOAT AND **SINK** IT, SHARKY! THAT MISERABLE MUSEUM GUARD IS **NOT** GOING TO **BEAT** ME TO THE GOLDEN HELMET!

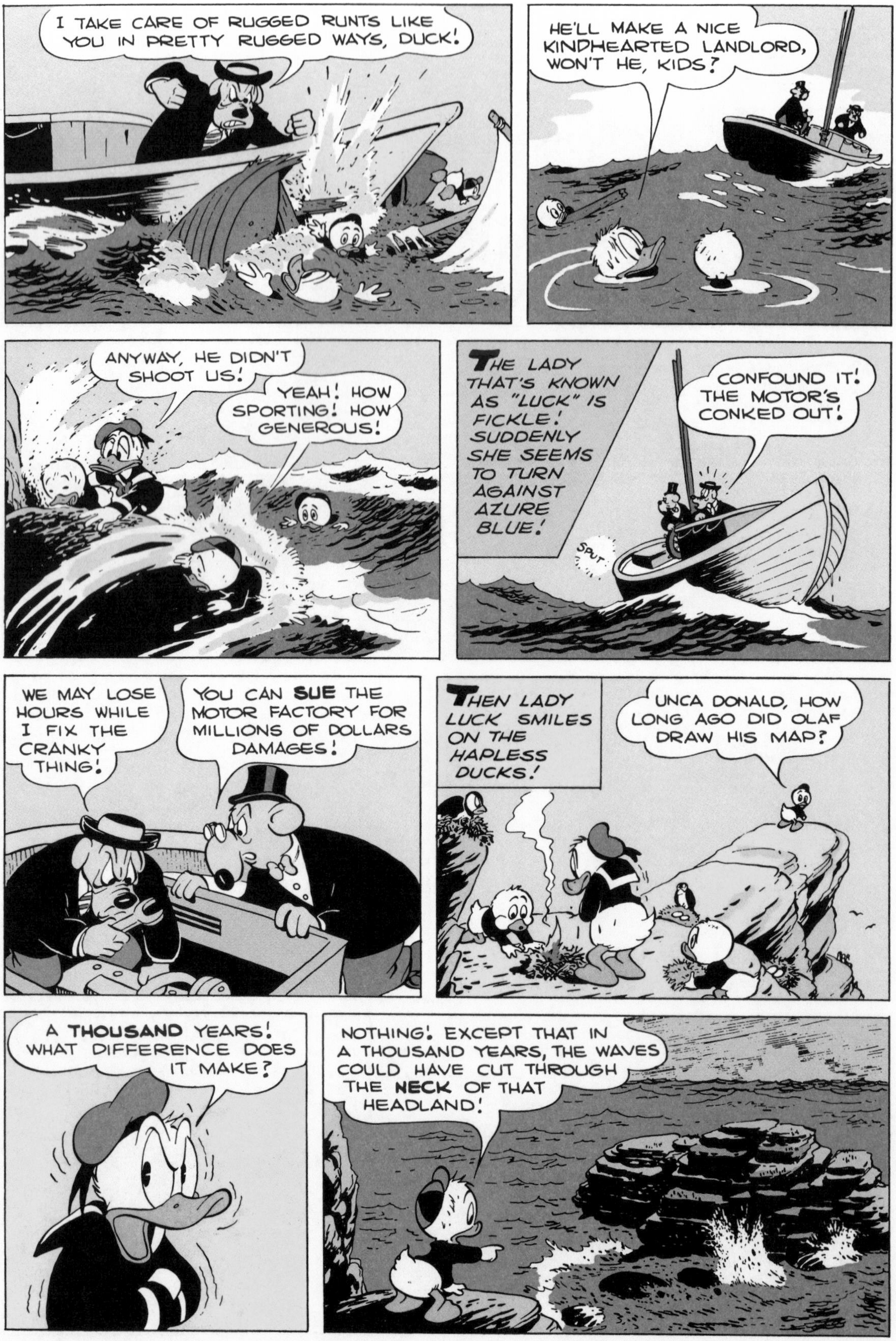
I TAKE CARE OF RUGGED RUNTS LIKE YOU IN PRETTY RUGGED WAYS, DUCK!
HE'LL MAKE A NICE KINDHEARTED LANDLORD, WON'T HE, KIDS?
ANYWAY, HE DIDN'T SHOOT US!
YEAH! HOW SPORTING! HOW GENEROUS!
THE LADY THAT'S KNOWN AS "LUCK" IS FICKLE! SUDDENLY SHE SEEMS TO TURN AGAINST AZURE BLUE!
CONFOUND IT! THE MOTOR'S CONKED OUT!
SPUT
WE MAY LOSE HOURS WHILE I FIX THE CRANKY THING!
YOU CAN SUE THE MOTOR FACTORY FOR MILLIONS OF DOLLARS DAMAGES!
THEN LADY LUCK SMILES ON THE HAPLESS DUCKS!
UNCA DONALD, HOW LONG AGO DID OLAF DRAW HIS MAP?
A THOUSAND YEARS! WHAT DIFFERENCE DOES IT MAKE?
NOTHING! EXCEPT THAT IN A THOUSAND YEARS, THE WAVES COULD HAVE CUT THROUGH THE NECK OF THAT HEADLAND!

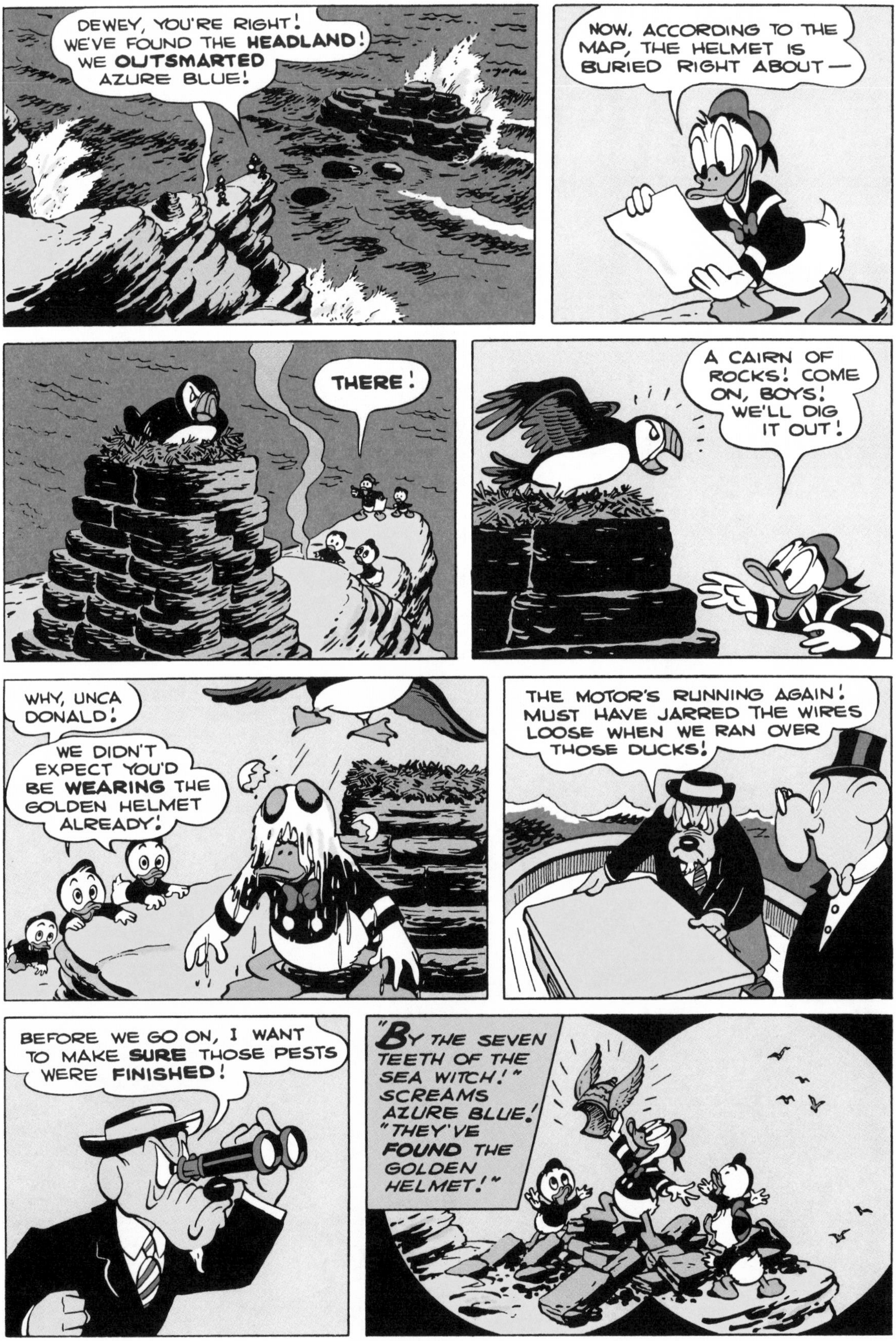
DEWEY, YOU'RE RIGHT! WE'VE FOUND THE HEADLAND! WE OUTSMARTED AZURE BLUE!
NOW, ACCORDING TO THE MAP, THE HELMET IS BURIED RIGHT ABOUT—
THERE!
A CAIRN OF ROCKS! COME ON, BOYS! WE'LL DIG IT OUT!
WHY, UNCA DONALD!
WE DIDN'T EXPECT YOU'D BE WEARING THE GOLDEN HELMET ALREADY!
THE MOTOR'S RUNNING AGAIN! MUST HAVE JARRED THE WIRES LOOSE WHEN WE RAN OVER THOSE DUCKS!
BEFORE WE GO ON, I WANT TO MAKE SURE THOSE PESTS WERE FINISHED!
"BY THE SEVEN TEETH OF THE SEA WITCH!" SCREAMS AZURE BLUE! "THEY'VE FOUND THE GOLDEN HELMET!"

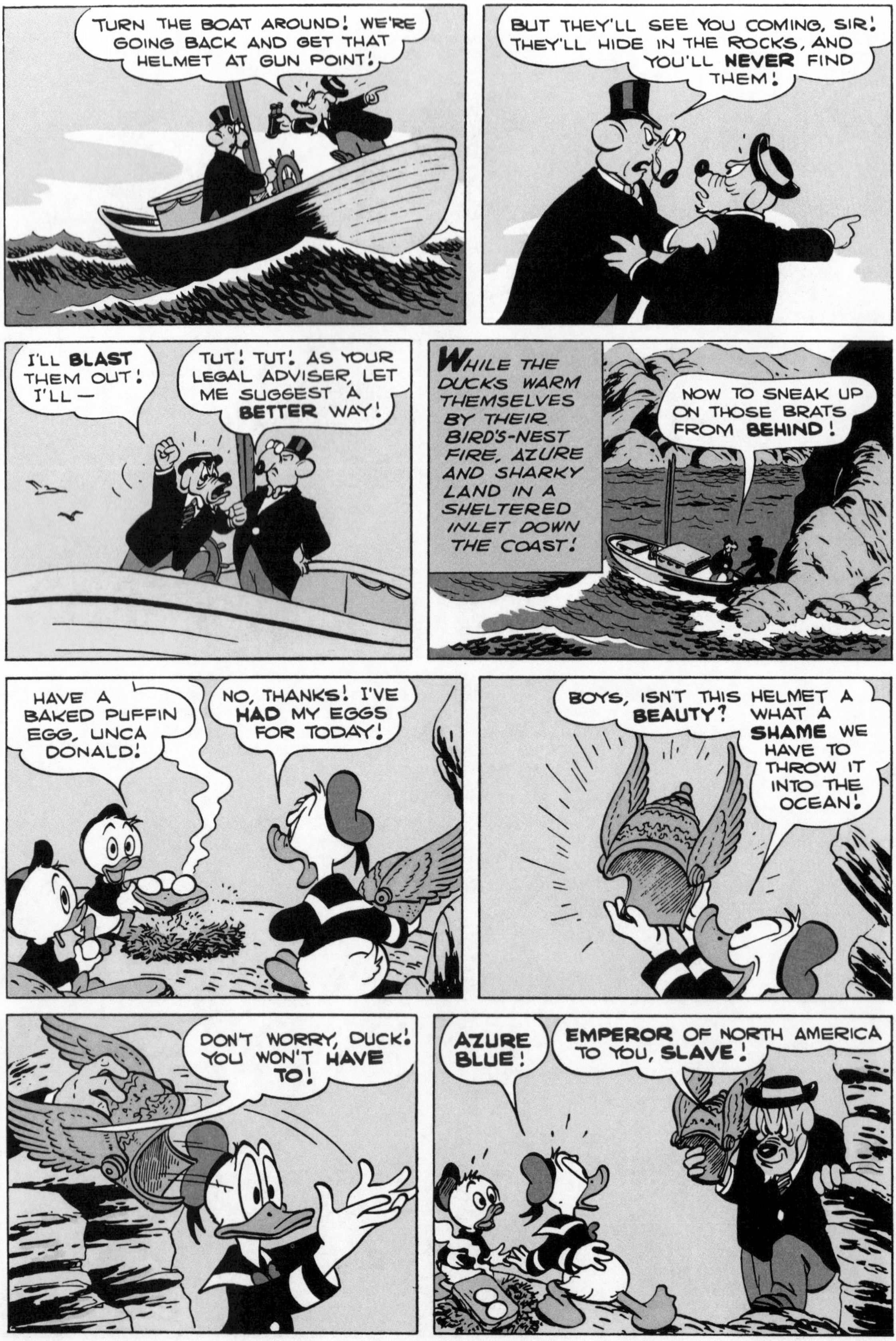
TURN THE BOAT AROUND! WE'RE GOING BACK AND GET THAT HELMET AT GUN POINT!
BUT THEY'LL SEE YOU COMING, SIR! THEY'LL HIDE IN THE ROCKS, AND YOU'LL NEVER FIND THEM!
I'LL BLAST THEM OUT! I'LL —
TUT! TUT! AS YOUR LEGAL ADVISER, LET ME SUGGEST A BETTER WAY!
WHILE THE DUCKS WARM THEMSELVES BY THEIR BIRD'S-NEST FIRE, AZURE AND SHARKY LAND IN A SHELTERED INLET DOWN THE COAST!
NOW TO SNEAK UP ON THOSE BRATS FROM BEHIND!
HAVE A BAKED PUFFIN EGG, UNCA DONALD!
NO, THANKS! I'VE HAD MY EGGS FOR TODAY!
BOYS, ISN'T THIS HELMET A BEAUTY? WHAT A SHAME WE HAVE TO THROW IT INTO THE OCEAN!
DON'T WORRY, DUCK! YOU WON'T HAVE TO!
AZURE BLUE!
EMPEROR OF NORTH AMERICA TO YOU, SLAVE!

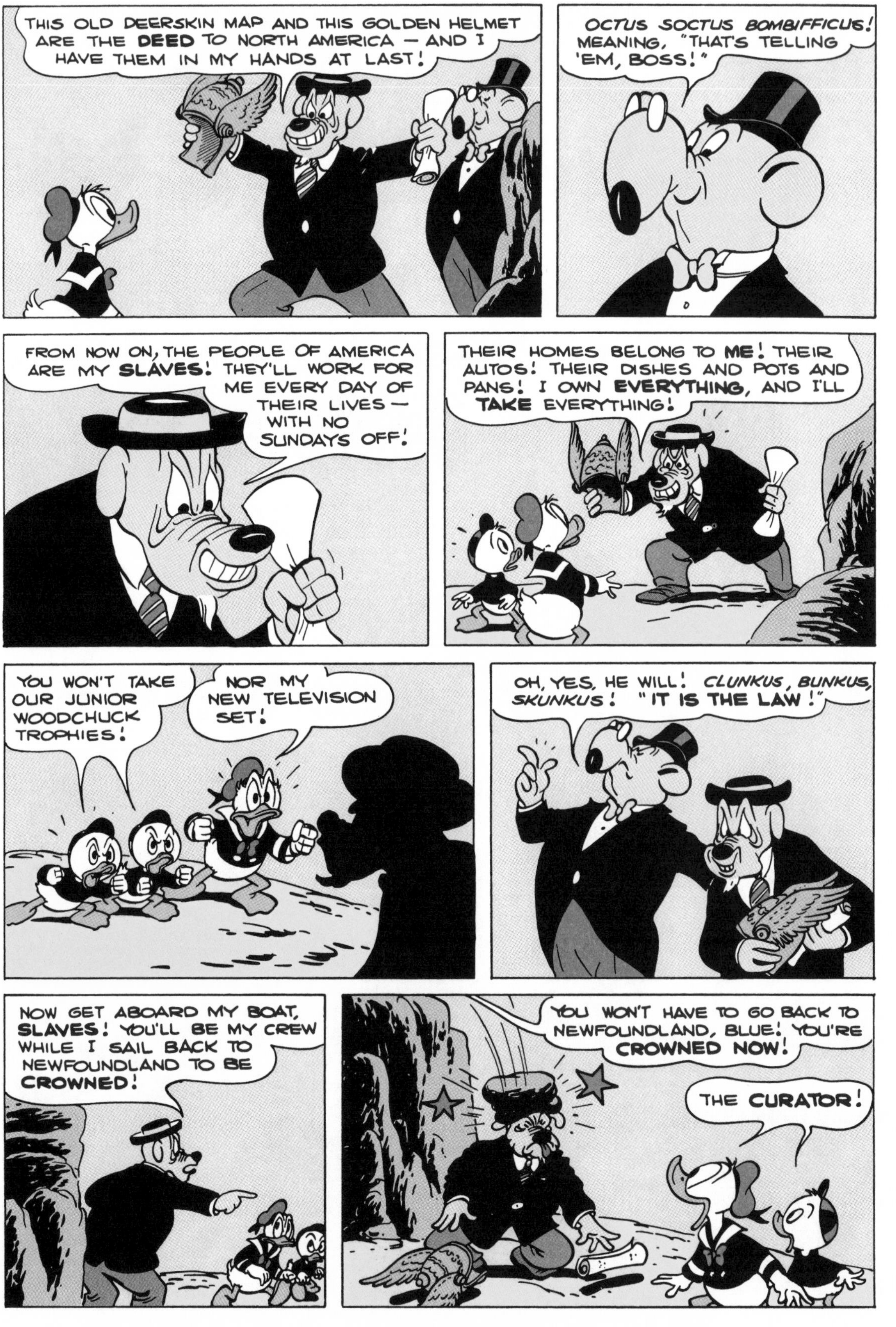
THIS OLD DEERSKIN MAP AND THIS GOLDEN HELMET ARE THE **DEED** TO NORTH AMERICA — AND I HAVE THEM IN MY HANDS AT LAST!
OCTUS SOCTUS BOMBIFFICUS! MEANING, "THAT'S TELLING 'EM, BOSS!"
FROM NOW ON, THE PEOPLE OF AMERICA ARE MY **SLAVES**! THEY'LL WORK FOR ME EVERY DAY OF THEIR LIVES — WITH NO SUNDAYS OFF!
THEIR HOMES BELONG TO **ME**! THEIR AUTOS! THEIR DISHES AND POTS AND PANS! I OWN **EVERYTHING**, AND I'LL **TAKE** EVERYTHING!
YOU WON'T TAKE OUR JUNIOR WOODCHUCK TROPHIES!
NOR MY NEW TELEVISION SET!
OH, YES, HE WILL! *CLUNKUS, BUNKUS, SKUNKUS!* "**IT IS THE LAW!**"
NOW GET ABOARD MY BOAT, **SLAVES**! YOU'LL BE MY CREW WHILE I SAIL BACK TO NEWFOUNDLAND TO BE **CROWNED**!
YOU WON'T HAVE TO GO BACK TO NEWFOUNDLAND, BLUE! YOU'RE **CROWNED NOW**!
THE **CURATOR**!

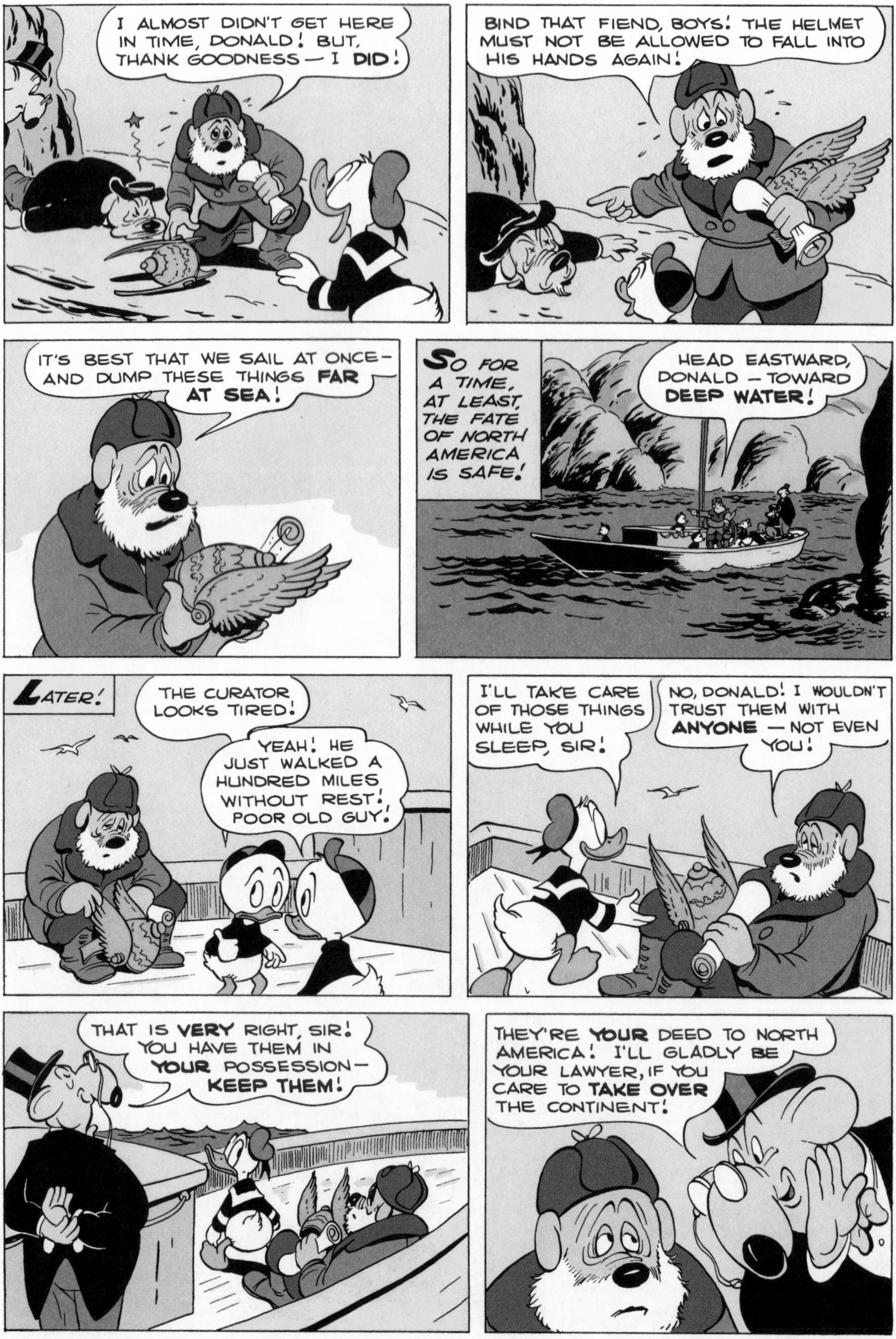
I ALMOST DIDN'T GET HERE IN TIME, DONALD! BUT, THANK GOODNESS — I DID!
BIND THAT FIEND, BOYS! THE HELMET MUST NOT BE ALLOWED TO FALL INTO HIS HANDS AGAIN!
IT'S BEST THAT WE SAIL AT ONCE- AND DUMP THESE THINGS FAR AT SEA!
SO FOR A TIME, AT LEAST, THE FATE OF NORTH AMERICA IS SAFE!
HEAD EASTWARD, DONALD — TOWARD DEEP WATER!
LATER!
THE CURATOR LOOKS TIRED!
YEAH! HE JUST WALKED A HUNDRED MILES WITHOUT REST! POOR OLD GUY!
I'LL TAKE CARE OF THOSE THINGS WHILE YOU SLEEP, SIR!
NO, DONALD! I WOULDN'T TRUST THEM WITH ANYONE — NOT EVEN YOU!
THAT IS VERY RIGHT, SIR! YOU HAVE THEM IN YOUR POSSESSION— KEEP THEM!
THEY'RE YOUR DEED TO NORTH AMERICA! I'LL GLADLY BE YOUR LAWYER, IF YOU CARE TO TAKE OVER THE CONTINENT!

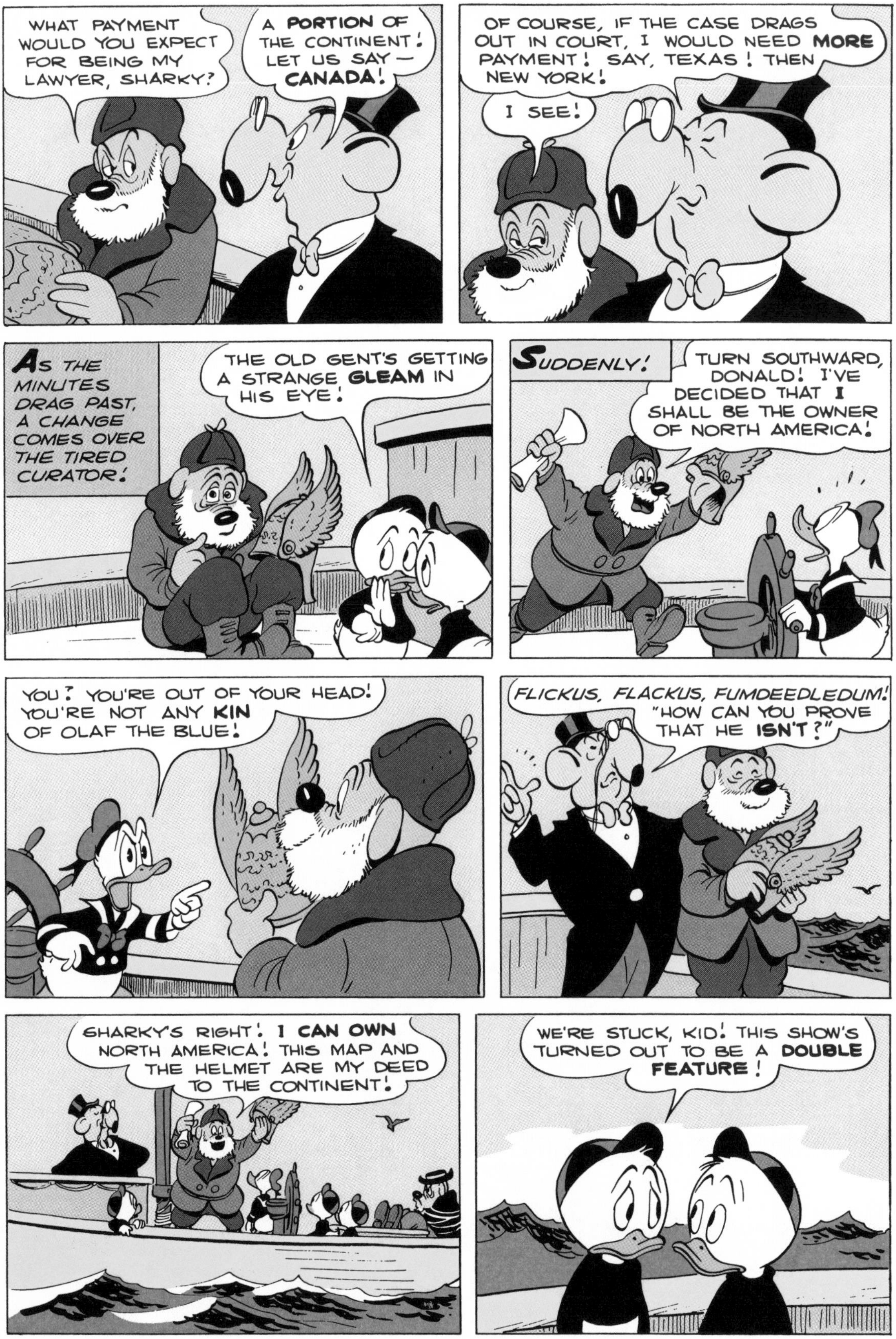
WHAT PAYMENT WOULD YOU EXPECT FOR BEING MY LAWYER, SHARKY?
A PORTION OF THE CONTINENT! LET US SAY — CANADA!
OF COURSE, IF THE CASE DRAGS OUT IN COURT, I WOULD NEED MORE PAYMENT! SAY, TEXAS! THEN NEW YORK!
I SEE!
AS THE MINUTES DRAG PAST, A CHANGE COMES OVER THE TIRED CURATOR!
THE OLD GENT'S GETTING A STRANGE GLEAM IN HIS EYE!
SUDDENLY!
TURN SOUTHWARD, DONALD! I'VE DECIDED THAT I SHALL BE THE OWNER OF NORTH AMERICA!
YOU? YOU'RE OUT OF YOUR HEAD! YOU'RE NOT ANY KIN OF OLAF THE BLUE!
FLICKUS, FLACKUS, FUMDEEDLEDUM! "HOW CAN YOU PROVE THAT HE ISN'T?"
SHARKY'S RIGHT! I CAN OWN NORTH AMERICA! THIS MAP AND THE HELMET ARE MY DEED TO THE CONTINENT!
WE'RE STUCK, KID! THIS SHOW'S TURNED OUT TO BE A DOUBLE FEATURE!

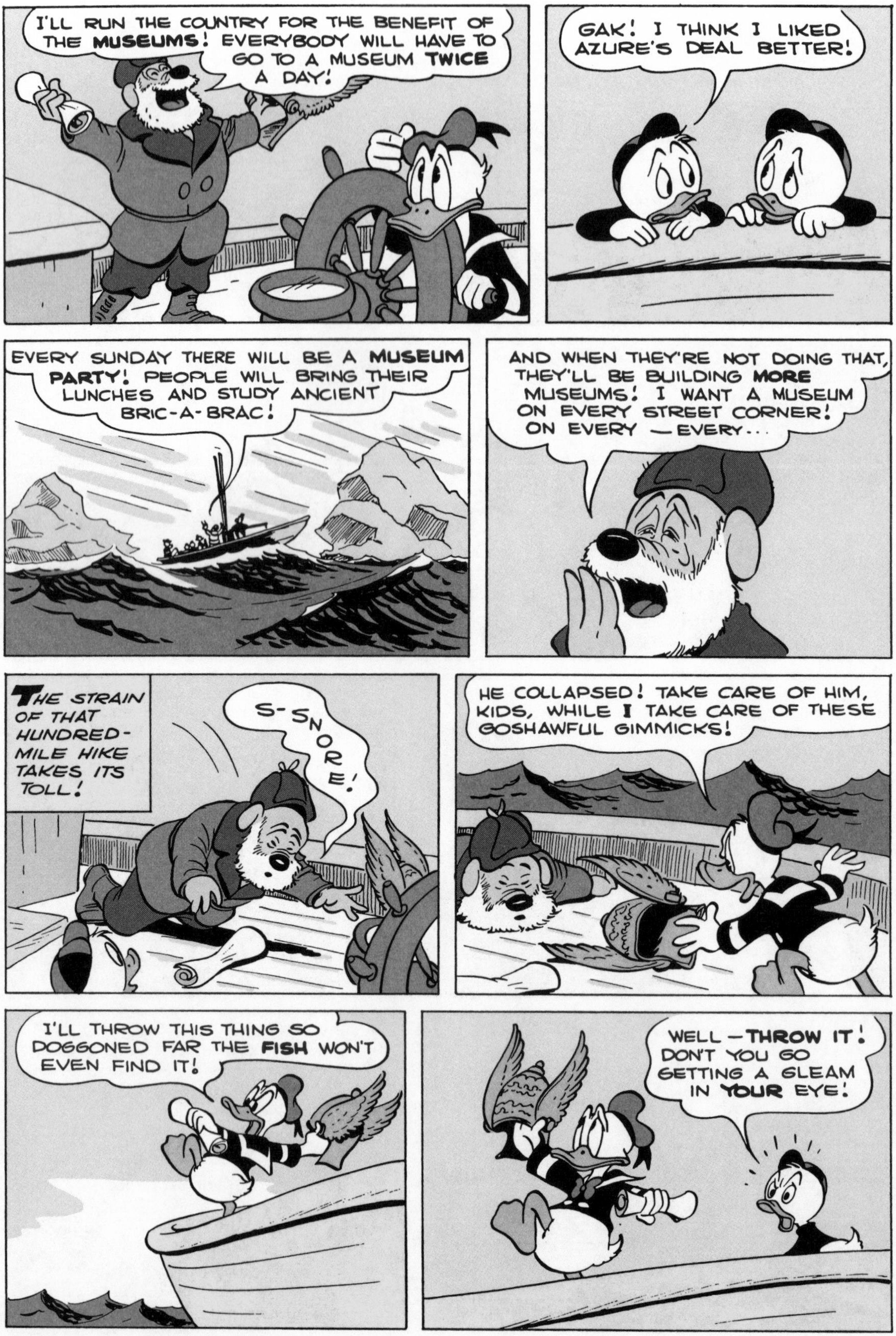
I'LL RUN THE COUNTRY FOR THE BENEFIT OF THE MUSEUMS! EVERYBODY WILL HAVE TO GO TO A MUSEUM TWICE A DAY!
GAK! I THINK I LIKED AZURE'S DEAL BETTER!
EVERY SUNDAY THERE WILL BE A MUSEUM PARTY! PEOPLE WILL BRING THEIR LUNCHES AND STUDY ANCIENT BRIC-A-BRAC!
AND WHEN THEY'RE NOT DOING THAT, THEY'LL BE BUILDING MORE MUSEUMS! I WANT A MUSEUM ON EVERY STREET CORNER! ON EVERY —EVERY...
THE STRAIN OF THAT HUNDRED-MILE HIKE TAKES ITS TOLL!
S-SNORE!
HE COLLAPSED! TAKE CARE OF HIM, KIDS, WHILE I TAKE CARE OF THESE GOSHAWFUL GIMMICKS!
I'LL THROW THIS THING SO DOGGONED FAR THE FISH WON'T EVEN FIND IT!
WELL—THROW IT! DON'T YOU GO GETTING A GLEAM IN YOUR EYE!

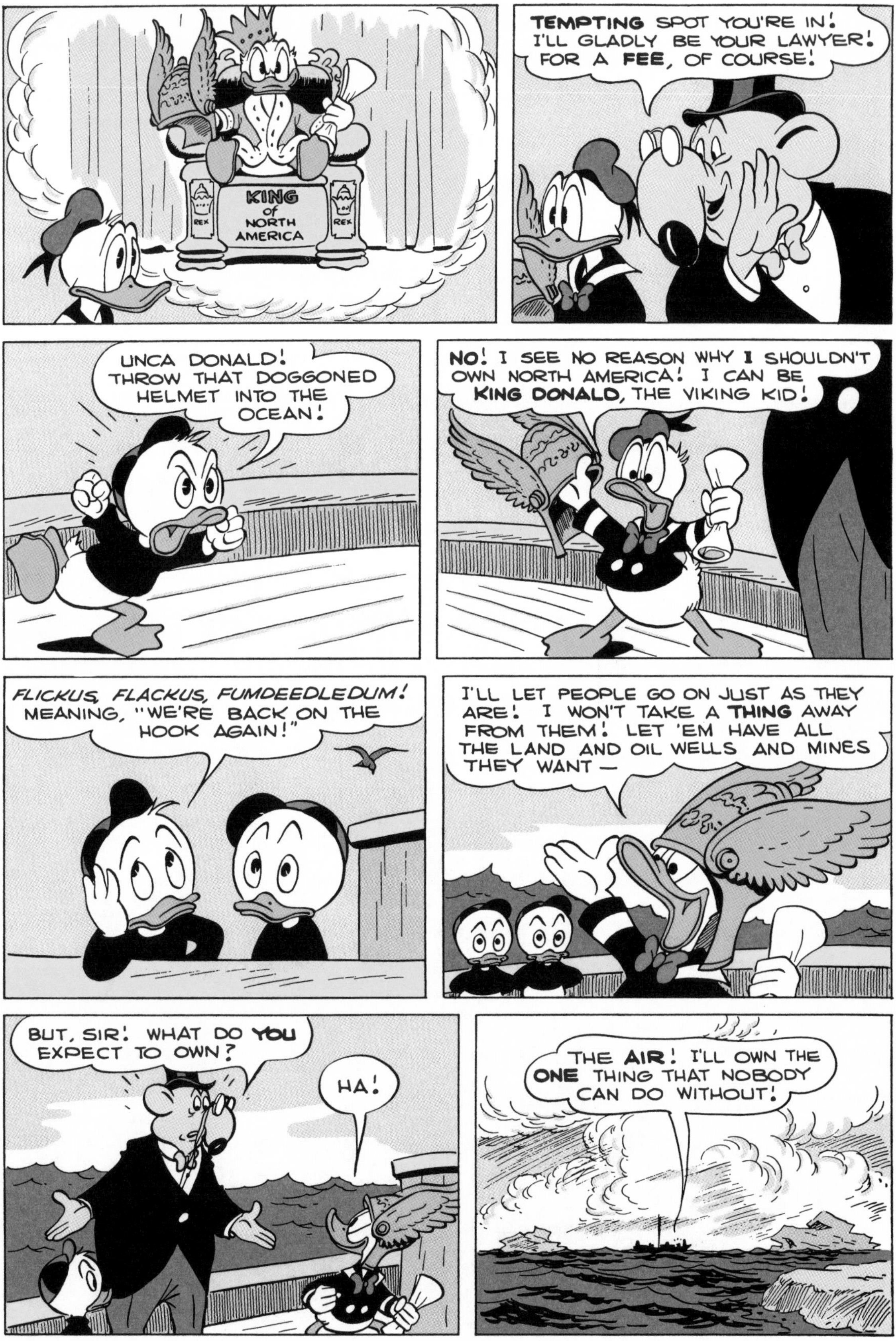
KING of NORTH AMERICA
REX
REX
TEMPTING SPOT YOU'RE IN! I'LL GLADLY BE YOUR LAWYER! FOR A FEE, OF COURSE!
UNCA DONALD! THROW THAT DOGGONED HELMET INTO THE OCEAN!
NO! I SEE NO REASON WHY I SHOULDN'T OWN NORTH AMERICA! I CAN BE KING DONALD, THE VIKING KID!
FLICKUS, FLACKUS, FUMDEEDLEDUM! MEANING, "WE'RE BACK ON THE HOOK AGAIN!"
I'LL LET PEOPLE GO ON JUST AS THEY ARE! I WON'T TAKE A THING AWAY FROM THEM! LET 'EM HAVE ALL THE LAND AND OIL WELLS AND MINES THEY WANT —
BUT, SIR! WHAT DO YOU EXPECT TO OWN?
HA!
THE AIR! I'LL OWN THE ONE THING THAT NOBODY CAN DO WITHOUT!

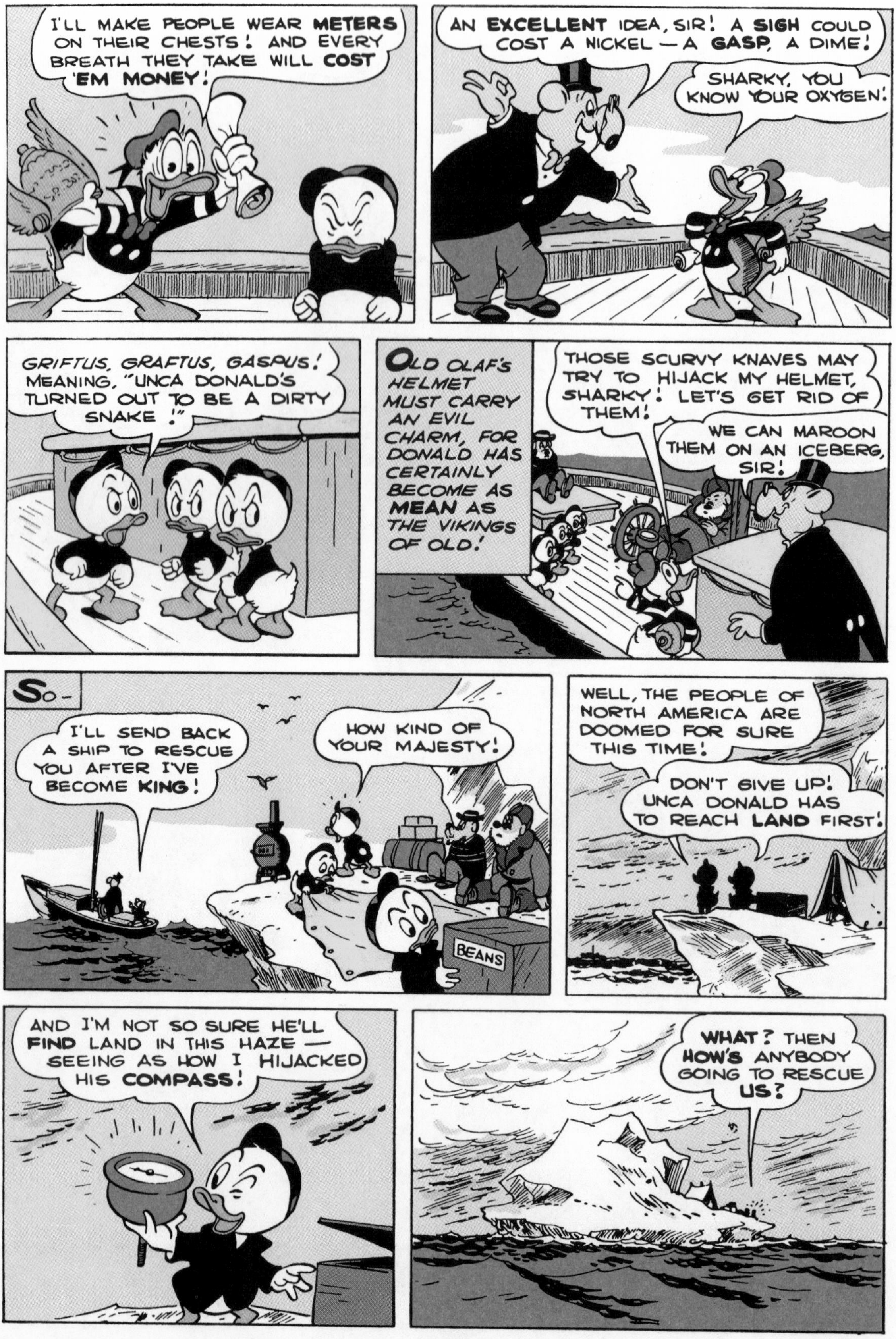
I'LL MAKE PEOPLE WEAR METERS ON THEIR CHESTS! AND EVERY BREATH THEY TAKE WILL COST 'EM MONEY!
AN EXCELLENT IDEA, SIR! A SIGH COULD COST A NICKEL — A GASP, A DIME!
SHARKY, YOU KNOW YOUR OXYGEN!
GRIFTUS, GRAFTUS, GASPUS! MEANING, "UNCA DONALD'S TURNED OUT TO BE A DIRTY SNAKE!"
OLD OLAF'S HELMET MUST CARRY AN EVIL CHARM, FOR DONALD HAS CERTAINLY BECOME AS MEAN AS THE VIKINGS OF OLD!
THOSE SCURVY KNAVES MAY TRY TO HIJACK MY HELMET, SHARKY! LET'S GET RID OF THEM!
WE CAN MAROON THEM ON AN ICEBERG, SIR!
SO-
I'LL SEND BACK A SHIP TO RESCUE YOU AFTER I'VE BECOME KING!
HOW KIND OF YOUR MAJESTY!
BEANS
WELL, THE PEOPLE OF NORTH AMERICA ARE DOOMED FOR SURE THIS TIME!
DON'T GIVE UP! UNCA DONALD HAS TO REACH LAND FIRST!
AND I'M NOT SO SURE HE'LL FIND LAND IN THIS HAZE — SEEING AS HOW I HIJACKED HIS COMPASS!
WHAT? THEN HOW'S ANYBODY GOING TO RESCUE US?

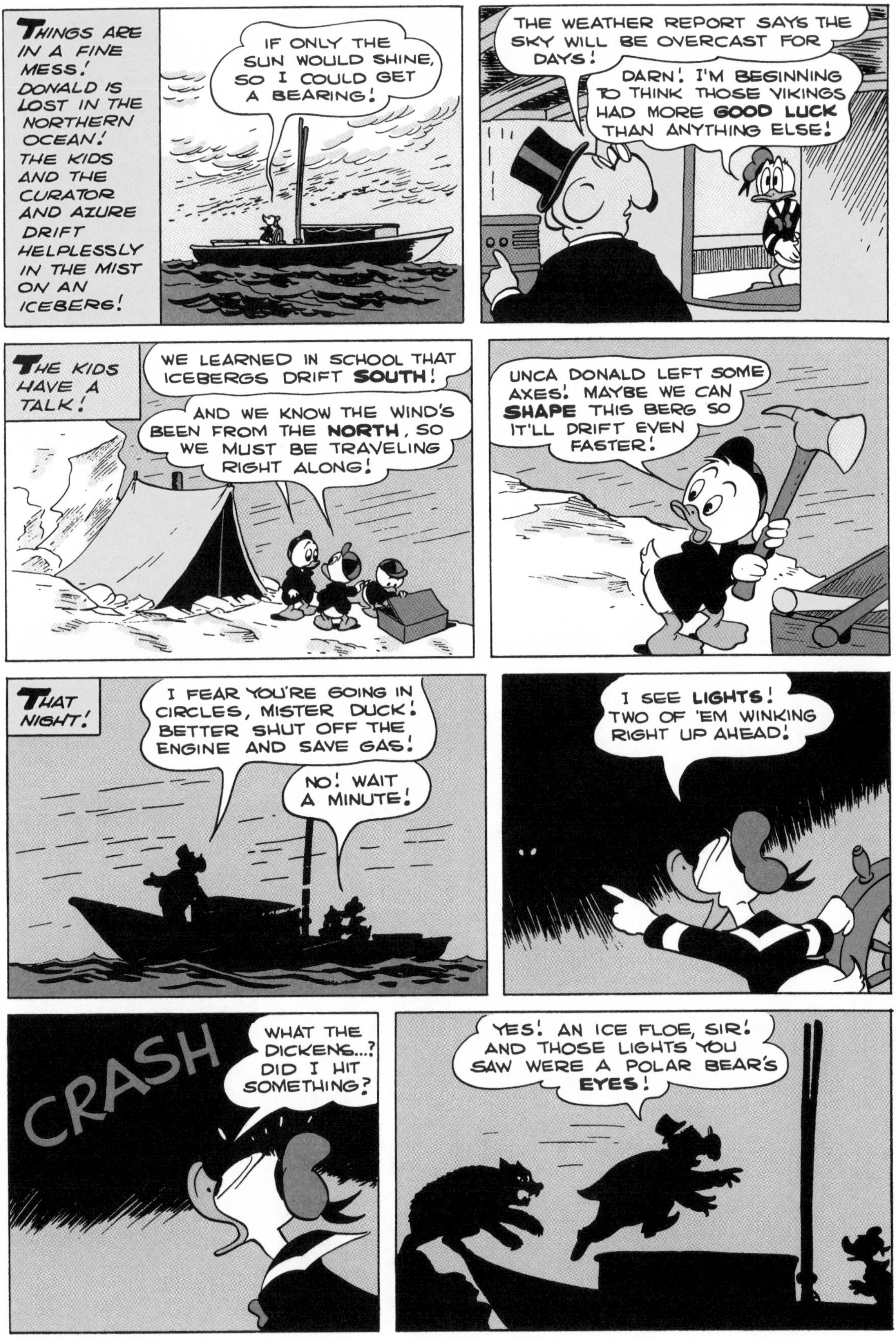
THINGS ARE IN A FINE MESS! DONALD IS LOST IN THE NORTHERN OCEAN! THE KIDS AND THE CURATOR AND AZURE DRIFT HELPLESSLY IN THE MIST ON AN ICEBERG!
IF ONLY THE SUN WOULD SHINE, SO I COULD GET A BEARING!
THE WEATHER REPORT SAYS THE SKY WILL BE OVERCAST FOR DAYS!
DARN! I'M BEGINNING TO THINK THOSE VIKINGS HAD MORE GOOD LUCK THAN ANYTHING ELSE!
THE KIDS HAVE A TALK!
WE LEARNED IN SCHOOL THAT ICEBERGS DRIFT SOUTH!
AND WE KNOW THE WIND'S BEEN FROM THE NORTH, SO WE MUST BE TRAVELING RIGHT ALONG!
UNCA DONALD LEFT SOME AXES! MAYBE WE CAN SHAPE THIS BERG SO IT'LL DRIFT EVEN FASTER!
THAT NIGHT!
I FEAR YOU'RE GOING IN CIRCLES, MISTER DUCK! BETTER SHUT OFF THE ENGINE AND SAVE GAS!
NO! WAIT A MINUTE!
I SEE LIGHTS! TWO OF 'EM WINKING RIGHT UP AHEAD!
CRASH
WHAT THE DICKENS...? DID I HIT SOMETHING?
YES! AN ICE FLOE, SIR! AND THOSE LIGHTS YOU SAW WERE A POLAR BEAR'S EYES!

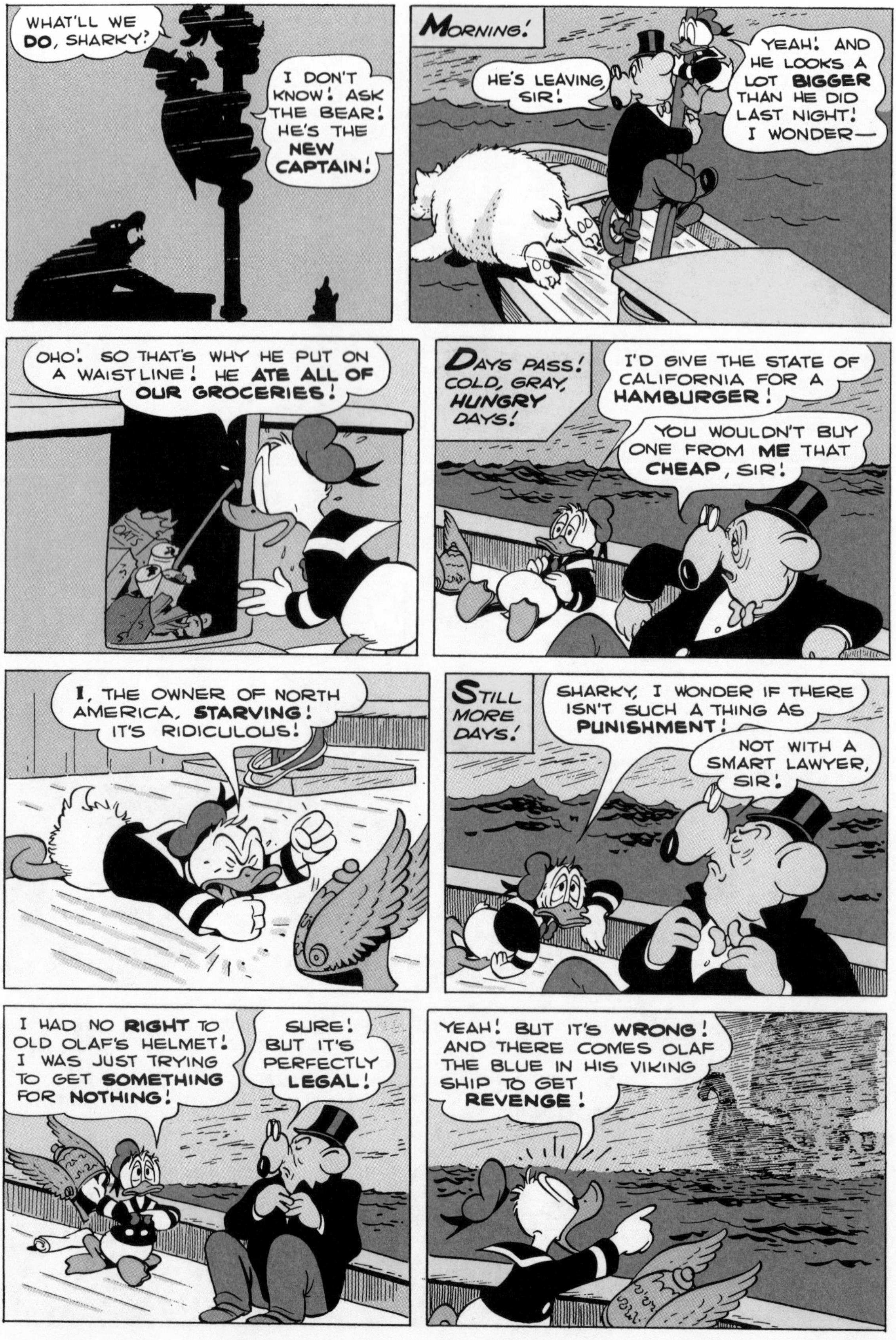
WHAT'LL WE DO, SHARKY?
I DON'T KNOW! ASK THE BEAR! HE'S THE NEW CAPTAIN!
MORNING!
HE'S LEAVING, SIR!
YEAH! AND HE LOOKS A LOT BIGGER THAN HE DID LAST NIGHT! I WONDER—
OHO! SO THAT'S WHY HE PUT ON A WAISTLINE! HE ATE ALL OF OUR GROCERIES!
DAYS PASS! COLD, GRAY, HUNGRY DAYS!
I'D GIVE THE STATE OF CALIFORNIA FOR A HAMBURGER!
YOU WOULDN'T BUY ONE FROM ME THAT CHEAP, SIR!
I, THE OWNER OF NORTH AMERICA, STARVING! IT'S RIDICULOUS!
STILL MORE DAYS!
SHARKY, I WONDER IF THERE ISN'T SUCH A THING AS PUNISHMENT!
NOT WITH A SMART LAWYER, SIR!
I HAD NO RIGHT TO OLD OLAF'S HELMET! I WAS JUST TRYING TO GET SOMETHING FOR NOTHING!
SURE! BUT IT'S PERFECTLY LEGAL!
YEAH! BUT IT'S WRONG! AND THERE COMES OLAF THE BLUE IN HIS VIKING SHIP TO GET REVENGE!

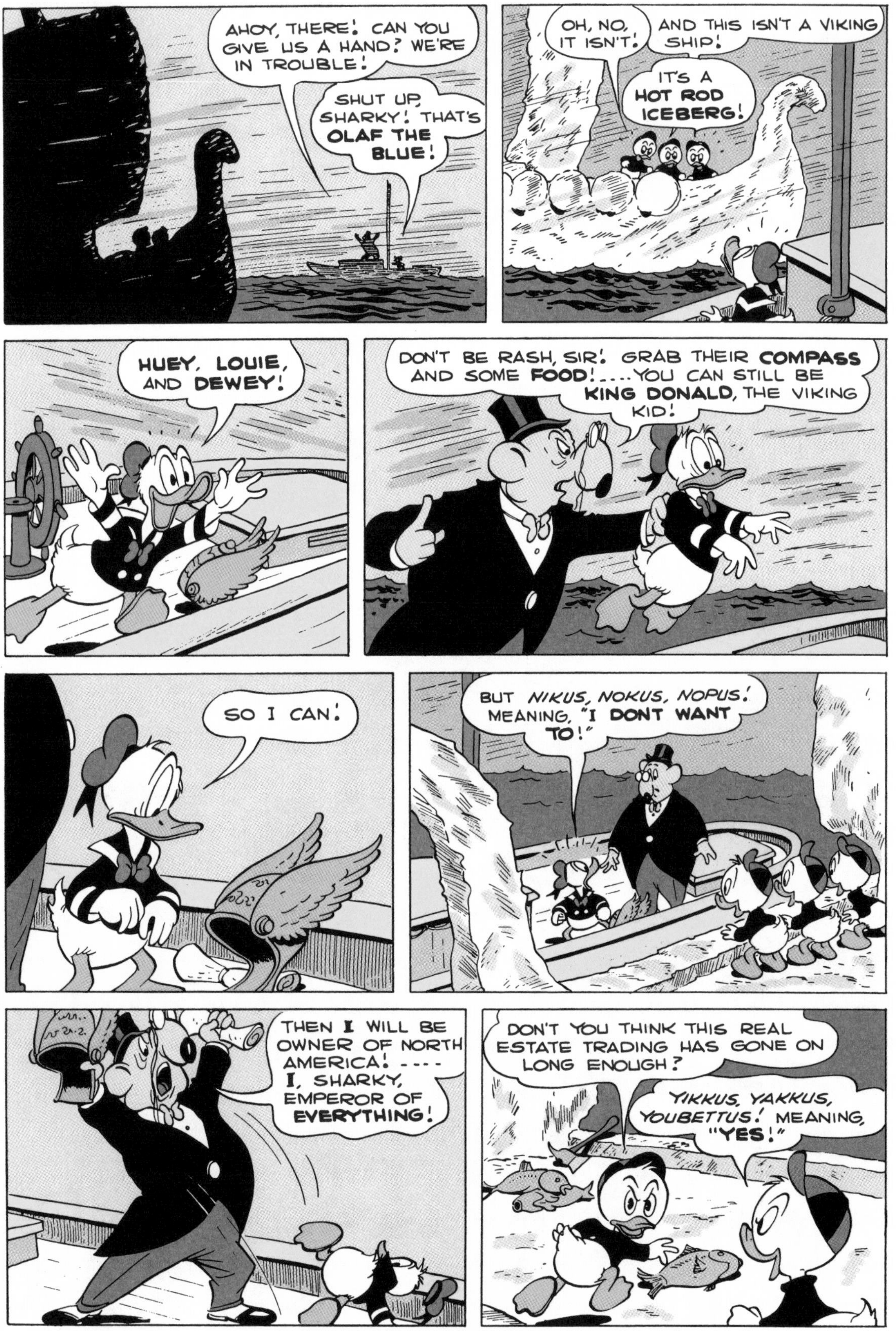
AHOY, THERE! CAN YOU GIVE US A HAND? WE'RE IN TROUBLE!
SHUT UP, SHARKY! THAT'S OLAF THE BLUE!
OH, NO, IT ISN'T!
AND THIS ISN'T A VIKING SHIP!
IT'S A HOT ROD ICEBERG!
HUEY, LOUIE, AND DEWEY!
DON'T BE RASH, SIR! GRAB THEIR COMPASS AND SOME FOOD! ....YOU CAN STILL BE KING DONALD, THE VIKING KID!
SO I CAN!
BUT NIKUS, NOKUS, NOPUS! MEANING, "I DONT WANT TO!"
THEN I WILL BE OWNER OF NORTH AMERICA! ---- I, SHARKY, EMPEROR OF EVERYTHING!
DON'T YOU THINK THIS REAL ESTATE TRADING HAS GONE ON LONG ENOUGH?
YIKKUS, YAKKUS, YOUBETTUS! MEANING, "YES!"

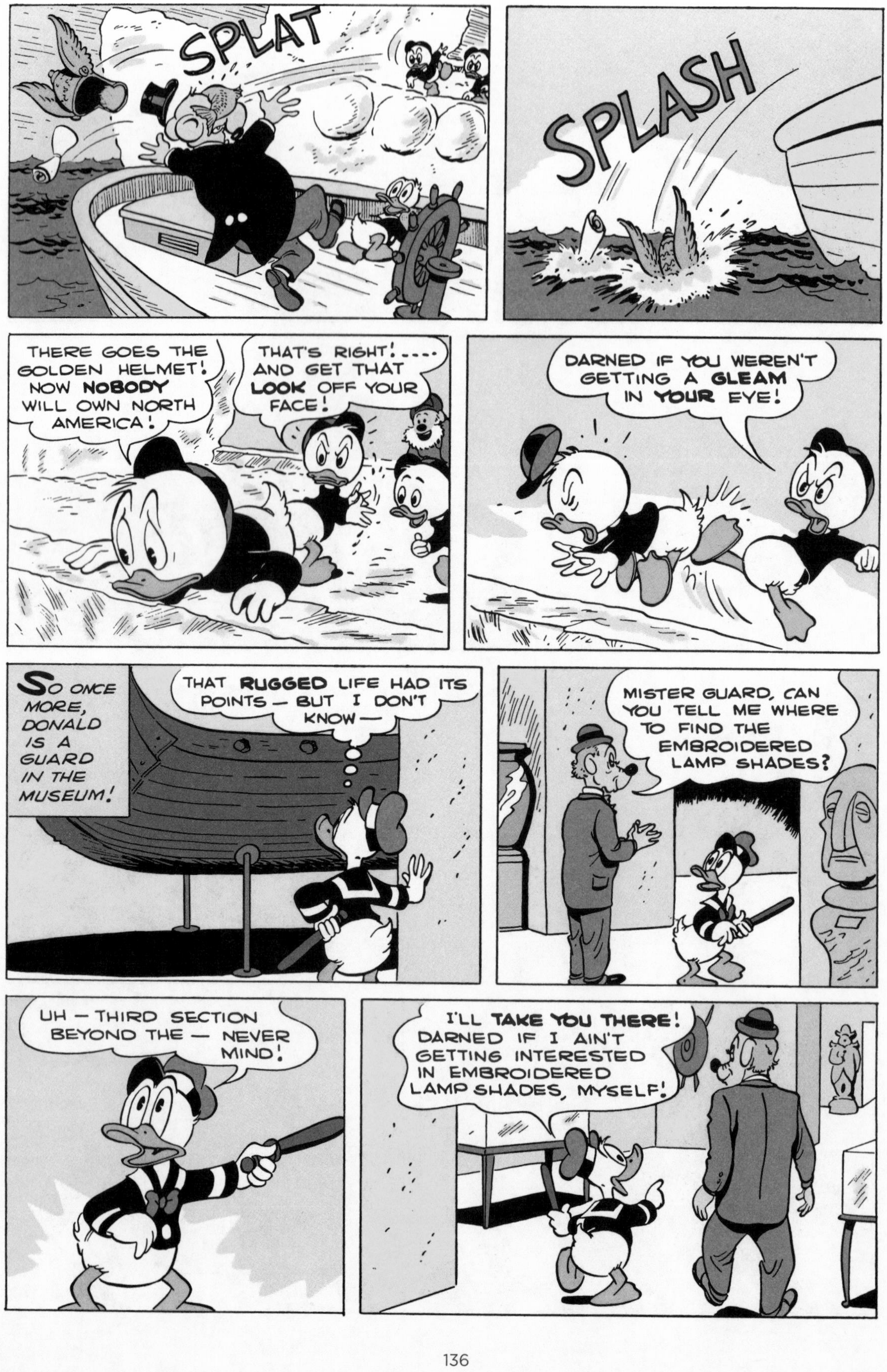
SPLAT
SPLASH
THERE GOES THE GOLDEN HELMET! NOW NOBODY WILL OWN NORTH AMERICA!
THAT'S RIGHT! .... AND GET THAT LOOK OFF YOUR FACE!
DARNED IF YOU WEREN'T GETTING A GLEAM IN YOUR EYE!
SO ONCE MORE, DONALD IS A GUARD IN THE MUSEUM!
THAT RUGGED LIFE HAD ITS POINTS — BUT I DON'T KNOW—
MISTER GUARD, CAN YOU TELL ME WHERE TO FIND THE EMBROIDERED LAMP SHADES?
UH — THIRD SECTION BEYOND THE — NEVER MIND!
I'LL TAKE YOU THERE! DARNED IF I AIN'T GETTING INTERESTED IN EMBROIDERED LAMP SHADES, MYSELF!

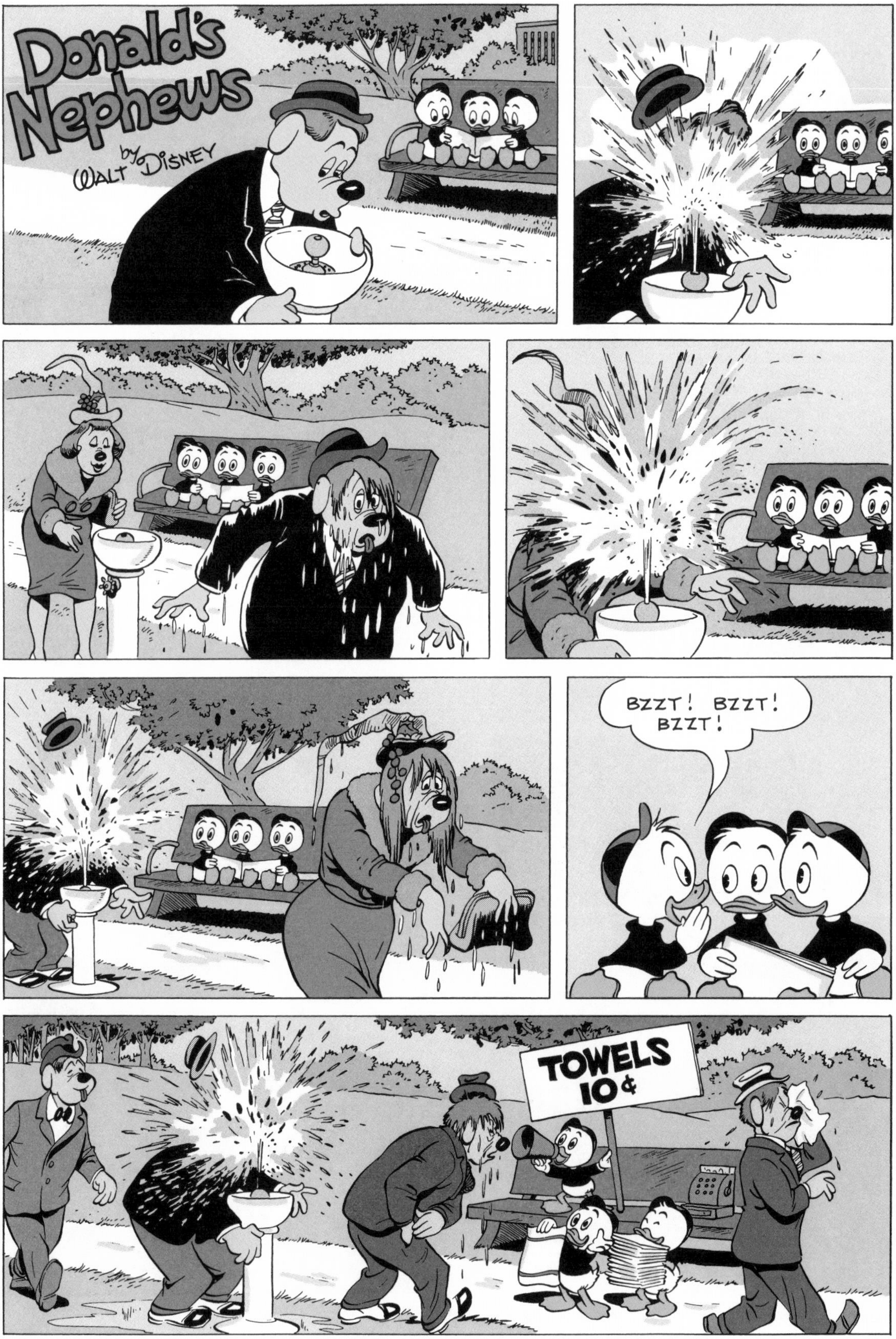
Donald's Nephews
by Walt Disney
BZZT! BZZT! BZZT!
TOWELS 10¢

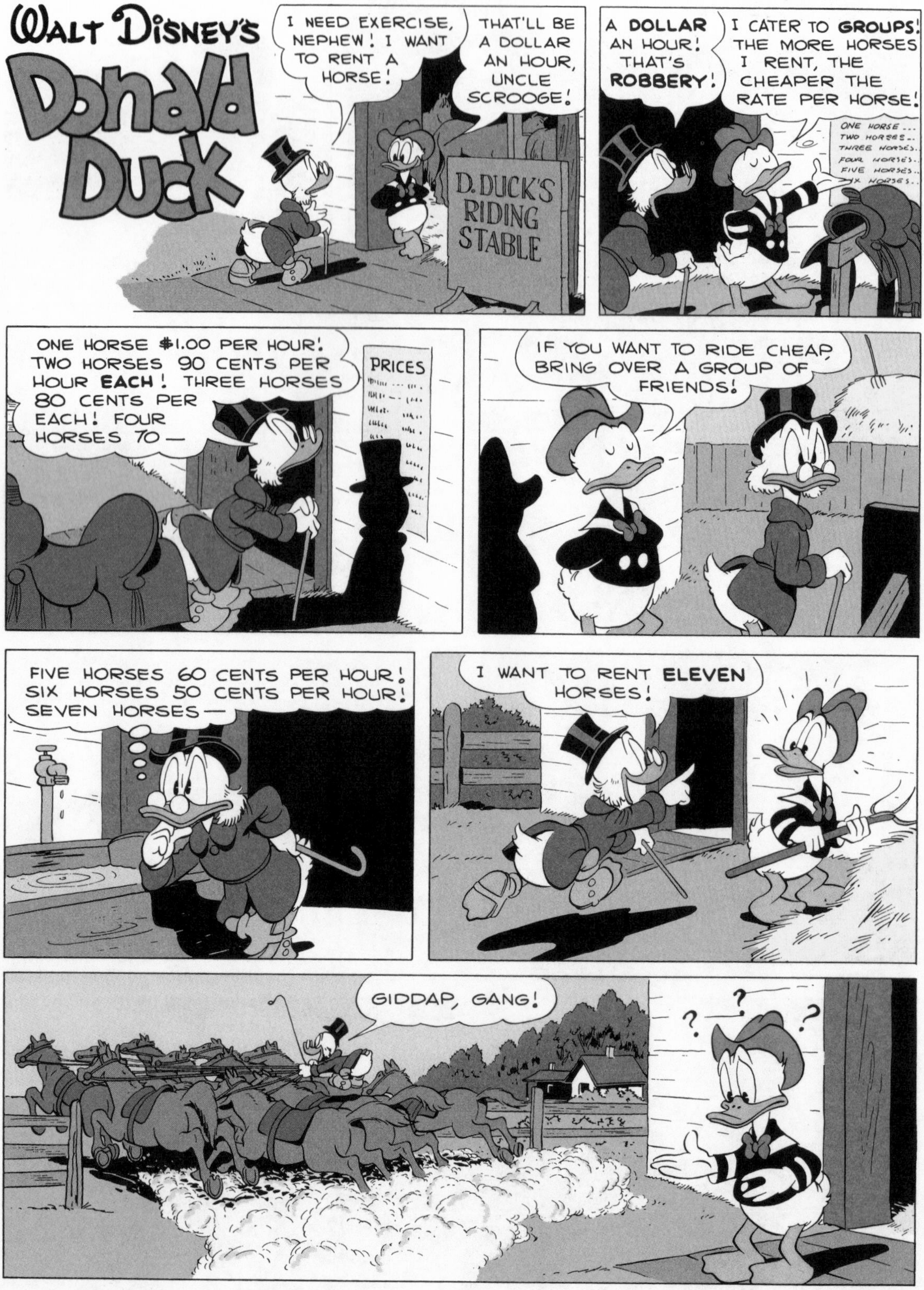
WALT DISNEY'S
Donald Duck
I NEED EXERCISE, NEPHEW! I WANT TO RENT A HORSE!
THAT'LL BE A DOLLAR AN HOUR, UNCLE SCROOGE!
D. DUCK'S RIDING STABLE
A DOLLAR AN HOUR! THAT'S ROBBERY!
I CATER TO GROUPS! THE MORE HORSES I RENT, THE CHEAPER THE RATE PER HORSE!
ONE HORSE...
TWO HORSES..
THREE HORSES..
FOUR HORSES..
FIVE HORSES..
ONE HORSE $1.00 PER HOUR! TWO HORSES 90 CENTS PER HOUR EACH! THREE HORSES 80 CENTS PER EACH! FOUR HORSES 70—
PRICES
IF YOU WANT TO RIDE CHEAP, BRING OVER A GROUP OF FRIENDS!
FIVE HORSES 60 CENTS PER HOUR! SIX HORSES 50 CENTS PER HOUR! SEVEN HORSES—
I WANT TO RENT ELEVEN HORSES!
GIDDAP, GANG!
?
?
?

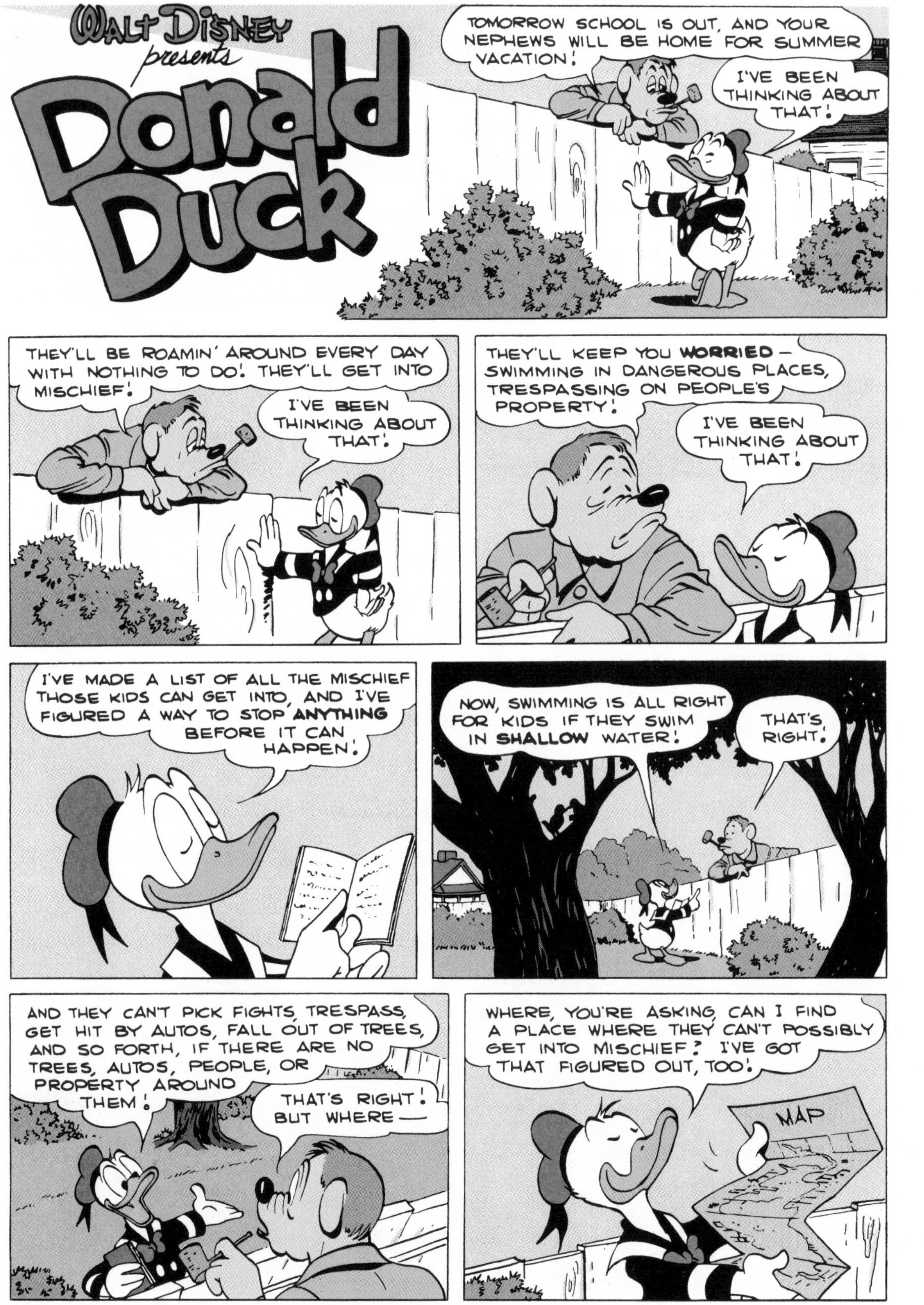
WALT DISNEY
presents
Donald Duck
TOMORROW SCHOOL IS OUT, AND YOUR NEPHEWS WILL BE HOME FOR SUMMER VACATION!
I'VE BEEN THINKING ABOUT THAT!
THEY'LL BE ROAMIN' AROUND EVERY DAY WITH NOTHING TO DO! THEY'LL GET INTO MISCHIEF!
I'VE BEEN THINKING ABOUT THAT!
THEY'LL KEEP YOU WORRIED — SWIMMING IN DANGEROUS PLACES, TRESPASSING ON PEOPLE'S PROPERTY!
I'VE BEEN THINKING ABOUT THAT!
I'VE MADE A LIST OF ALL THE MISCHIEF THOSE KIDS CAN GET INTO, AND I'VE FIGURED A WAY TO STOP ANYTHING BEFORE IT CAN HAPPEN!
NOW, SWIMMING IS ALL RIGHT FOR KIDS IF THEY SWIM IN SHALLOW WATER!
THAT'S RIGHT!
AND THEY CAN'T PICK FIGHTS, TRESPASS, GET HIT BY AUTOS, FALL OUT OF TREES, AND SO FORTH, IF THERE ARE NO TREES, AUTOS, PEOPLE, OR PROPERTY AROUND THEM!
THAT'S RIGHT! BUT WHERE —
WHERE, YOU'RE ASKING, CAN I FIND A PLACE WHERE THEY CAN'T POSSIBLY GET INTO MISCHIEF? I'VE GOT THAT FIGURED OUT, TOO!
MAP

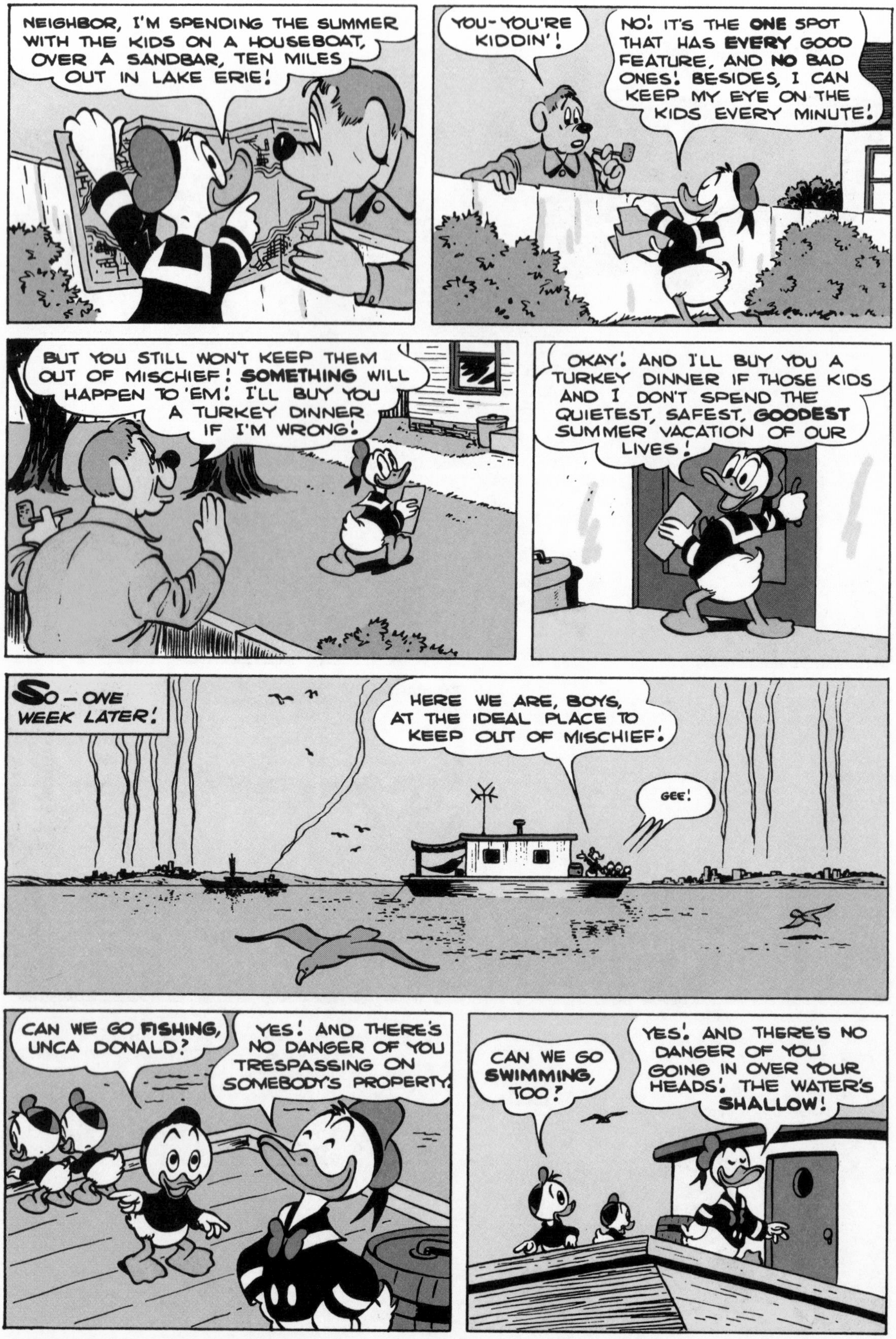
NEIGHBOR, I'M SPENDING THE SUMMER WITH THE KIDS ON A HOUSEBOAT, OVER A SANDBAR, TEN MILES OUT IN LAKE ERIE!
YOU-YOU'RE KIDDIN'!
NO! IT'S THE ONE SPOT THAT HAS EVERY GOOD FEATURE, AND NO BAD ONES! BESIDES, I CAN KEEP MY EYE ON THE KIDS EVERY MINUTE!
BUT YOU STILL WON'T KEEP THEM OUT OF MISCHIEF! SOMETHING WILL HAPPEN TO 'EM! I'LL BUY YOU A TURKEY DINNER IF I'M WRONG!
OKAY! AND I'LL BUY YOU A TURKEY DINNER IF THOSE KIDS AND I DON'T SPEND THE QUIETEST, SAFEST, GOODEST SUMMER VACATION OF OUR LIVES!
SO-ONE WEEK LATER!
HERE WE ARE, BOYS, AT THE IDEAL PLACE TO KEEP OUT OF MISCHIEF!
GEE!
CAN WE GO FISHING, UNCA DONALD?
YES! AND THERE'S NO DANGER OF YOU TRESPASSING ON SOMEBODY'S PROPERTY!
CAN WE GO SWIMMING, TOO?
YES! AND THERE'S NO DANGER OF YOU GOING IN OVER YOUR HEADS! THE WATER'S SHALLOW!

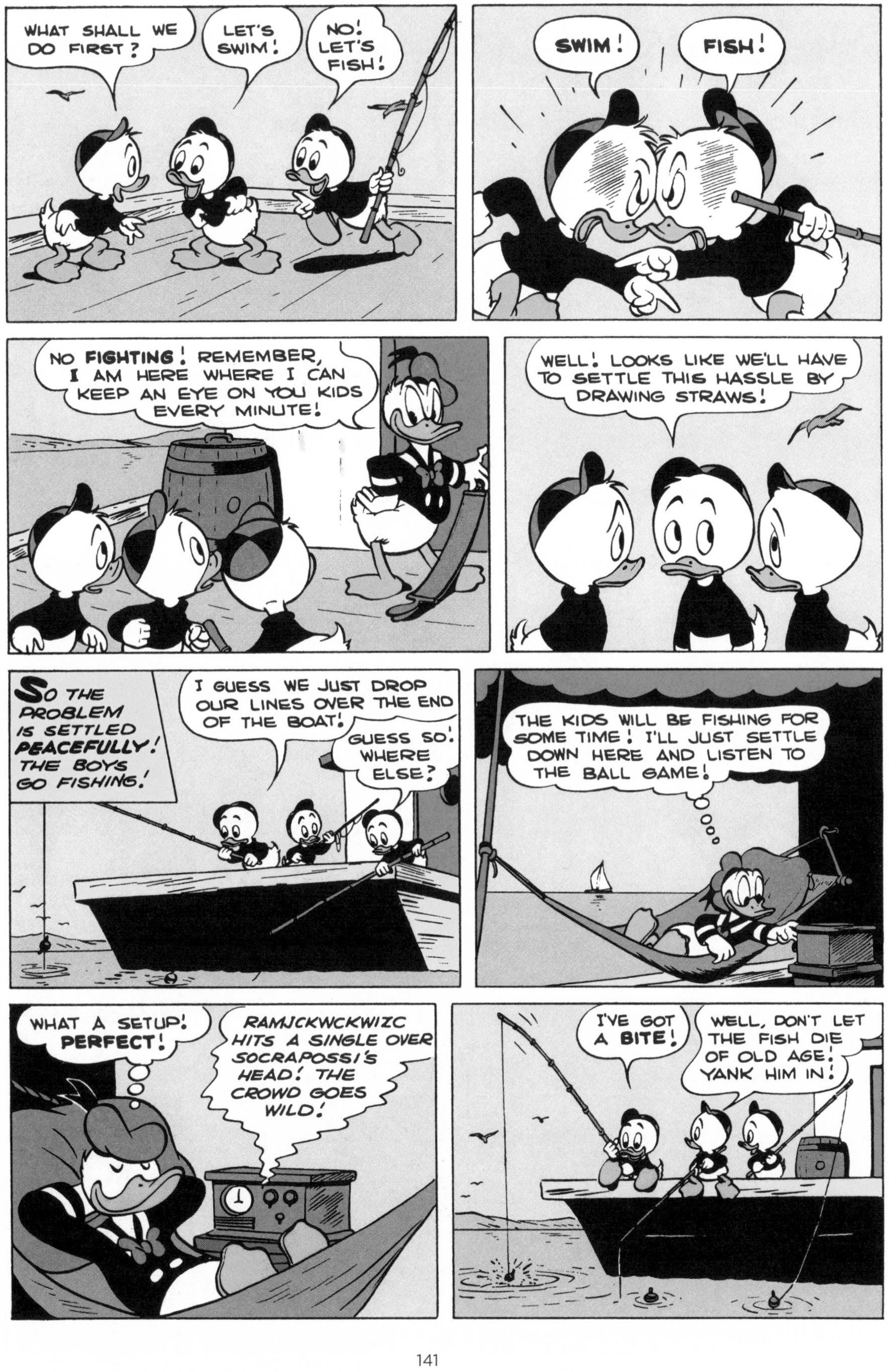
WHAT SHALL WE DO FIRST?
LET'S SWIM!
NO! LET'S FISH!
SWIM!
FISH!
NO FIGHTING! REMEMBER, I AM HERE WHERE I CAN KEEP AN EYE ON YOU KIDS EVERY MINUTE!
WELL! LOOKS LIKE WE'LL HAVE TO SETTLE THIS HASSLE BY DRAWING STRAWS!
SO THE PROBLEM IS SETTLED PEACEFULLY! THE BOYS GO FISHING!
I GUESS WE JUST DROP OUR LINES OVER THE END OF THE BOAT!
GUESS SO! WHERE ELSE?
THE KIDS WILL BE FISHING FOR SOME TIME! I'LL JUST SETTLE DOWN HERE AND LISTEN TO THE BALL GAME!
WHAT A SETUP! PERFECT!
RAMJCKWCKWIZC HITS A SINGLE OVER SOCRAPOSSI'S HEAD! THE CROWD GOES WILD!
I'VE GOT A BITE!
WELL, DON'T LET THE FISH DIE OF OLD AGE! YANK HIM IN!

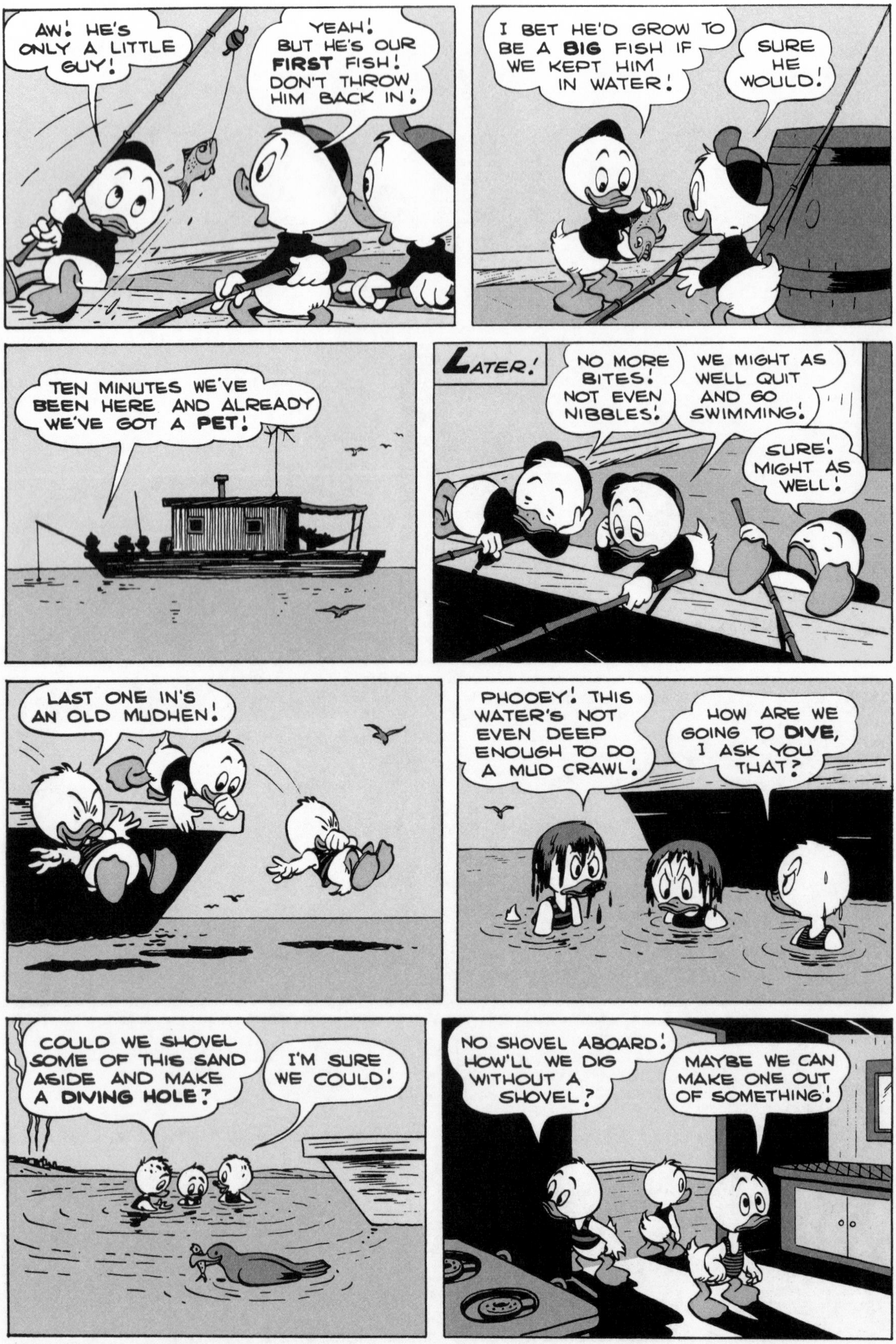
AW! HE'S ONLY A LITTLE GUY!
YEAH! BUT HE'S OUR FIRST FISH! DON'T THROW HIM BACK IN!
I BET HE'D GROW TO BE A BIG FISH IF WE KEPT HIM IN WATER!
SURE HE WOULD!
TEN MINUTES WE'VE BEEN HERE AND ALREADY WE'VE GOT A PET!
LATER!
NO MORE BITES! NOT EVEN NIBBLES!
WE MIGHT AS WELL QUIT AND GO SWIMMING!
SURE! MIGHT AS WELL!
LAST ONE IN'S AN OLD MUDHEN!
PHOOEY! THIS WATER'S NOT EVEN DEEP ENOUGH TO DO A MUD CRAWL!
HOW ARE WE GOING TO DIVE, I ASK YOU THAT?
COULD WE SHOVEL SOME OF THIS SAND ASIDE AND MAKE A DIVING HOLE?
I'M SURE WE COULD!
NO SHOVEL ABOARD! HOW'LL WE DIG WITHOUT A SHOVEL?
MAYBE WE CAN MAKE ONE OUT OF SOMETHING!

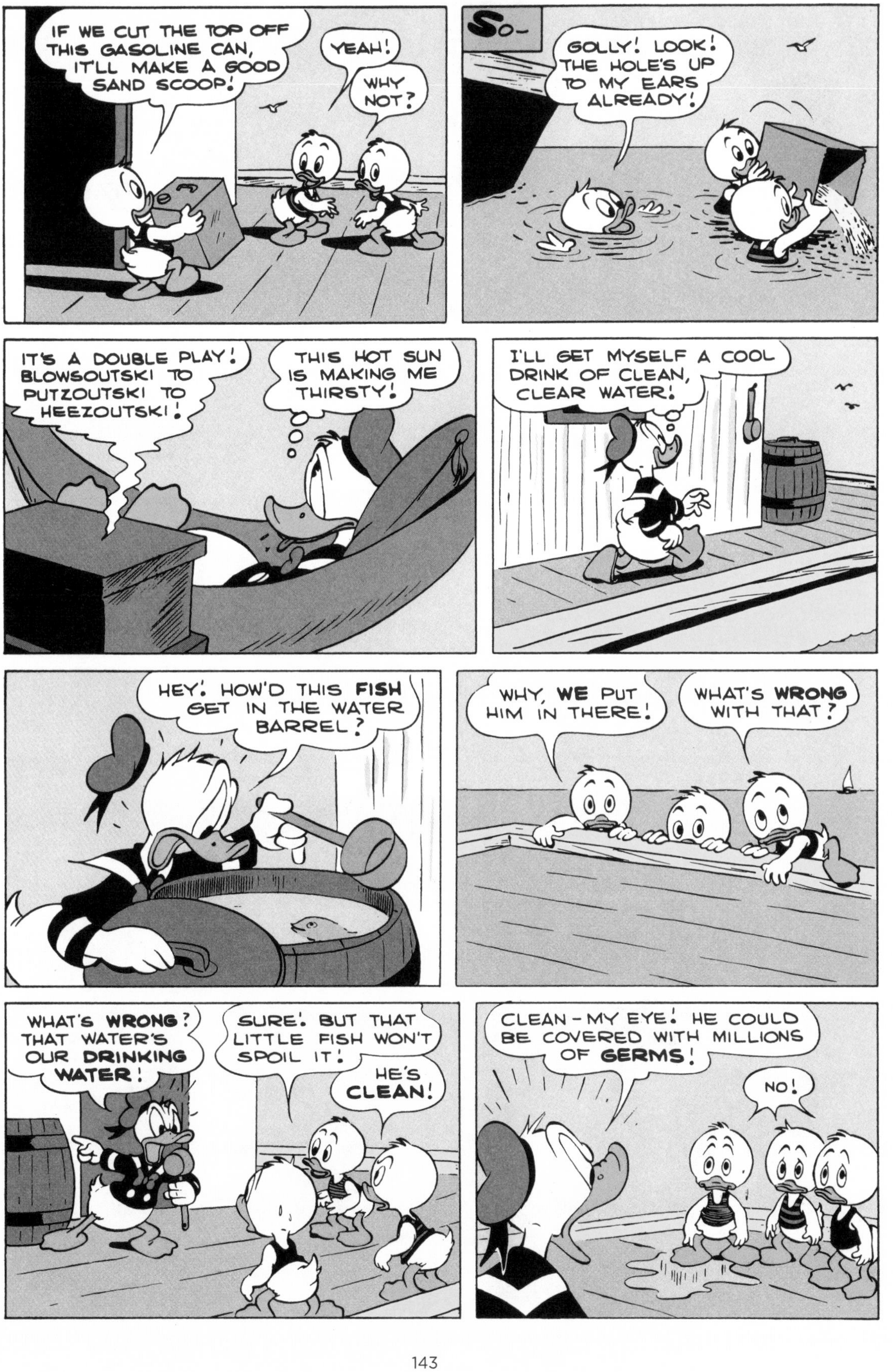
IF WE CUT THE TOP OFF THIS GASOLINE CAN, IT'LL MAKE A GOOD SAND SCOOP!
YEAH!
WHY NOT?
SO-
GOLLY! LOOK! THE HOLE'S UP TO MY EARS ALREADY!
IT'S A DOUBLE PLAY! BLOWSOUTSKI TO PUTZOUTSKI TO HEEZOUTSKI!
THIS HOT SUN IS MAKING ME THIRSTY!
I'LL GET MYSELF A COOL DRINK OF CLEAN, CLEAR WATER!
HEY! HOW'D THIS FISH GET IN THE WATER BARREL?
WHY, WE PUT HIM IN THERE!
WHAT'S WRONG WITH THAT?
WHAT'S WRONG? THAT WATER'S OUR DRINKING WATER!
SURE! BUT THAT LITTLE FISH WON'T SPOIL IT!
HE'S CLEAN!
CLEAN - MY EYE! HE COULD BE COVERED WITH MILLIONS OF GERMS!
NO!

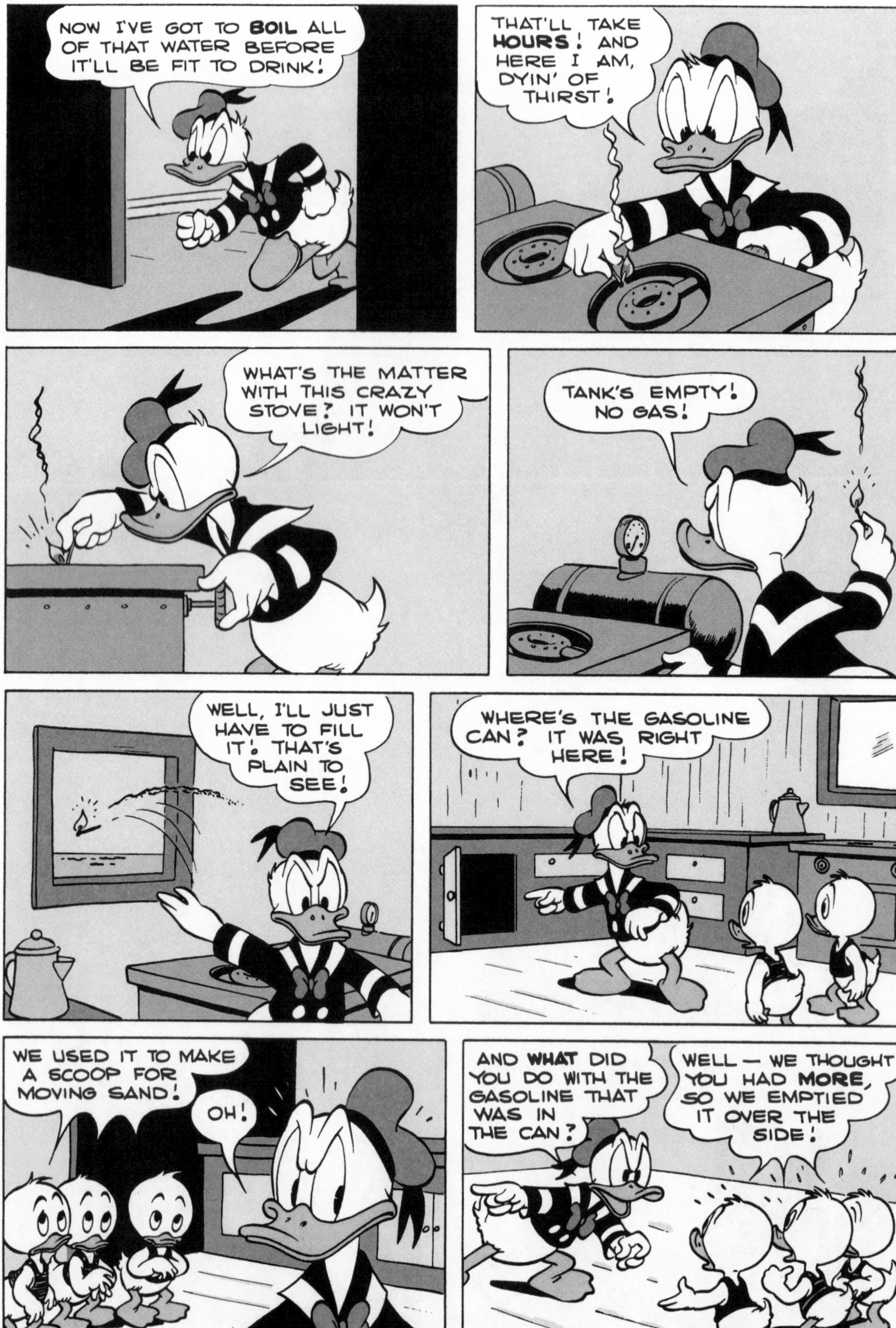

NOW I'VE GOT TO BOIL ALL OF THAT WATER BEFORE IT'LL BE FIT TO DRINK!
THAT'LL TAKE HOURS! AND HERE I AM, DYIN' OF THIRST!
WHAT'S THE MATTER WITH THIS CRAZY STOVE? IT WON'T LIGHT!
TANK'S EMPTY! NO GAS!
WELL, I'LL JUST HAVE TO FILL IT! THAT'S PLAIN TO SEE!
WHERE'S THE GASOLINE CAN? IT WAS RIGHT HERE!
WE USED IT TO MAKE A SCOOP FOR MOVING SAND!
OH!
AND WHAT DID YOU DO WITH THE GASOLINE THAT WAS IN THE CAN?
WELL — WE THOUGHT YOU HAD MORE, SO WE EMPTIED IT OVER THE SIDE!

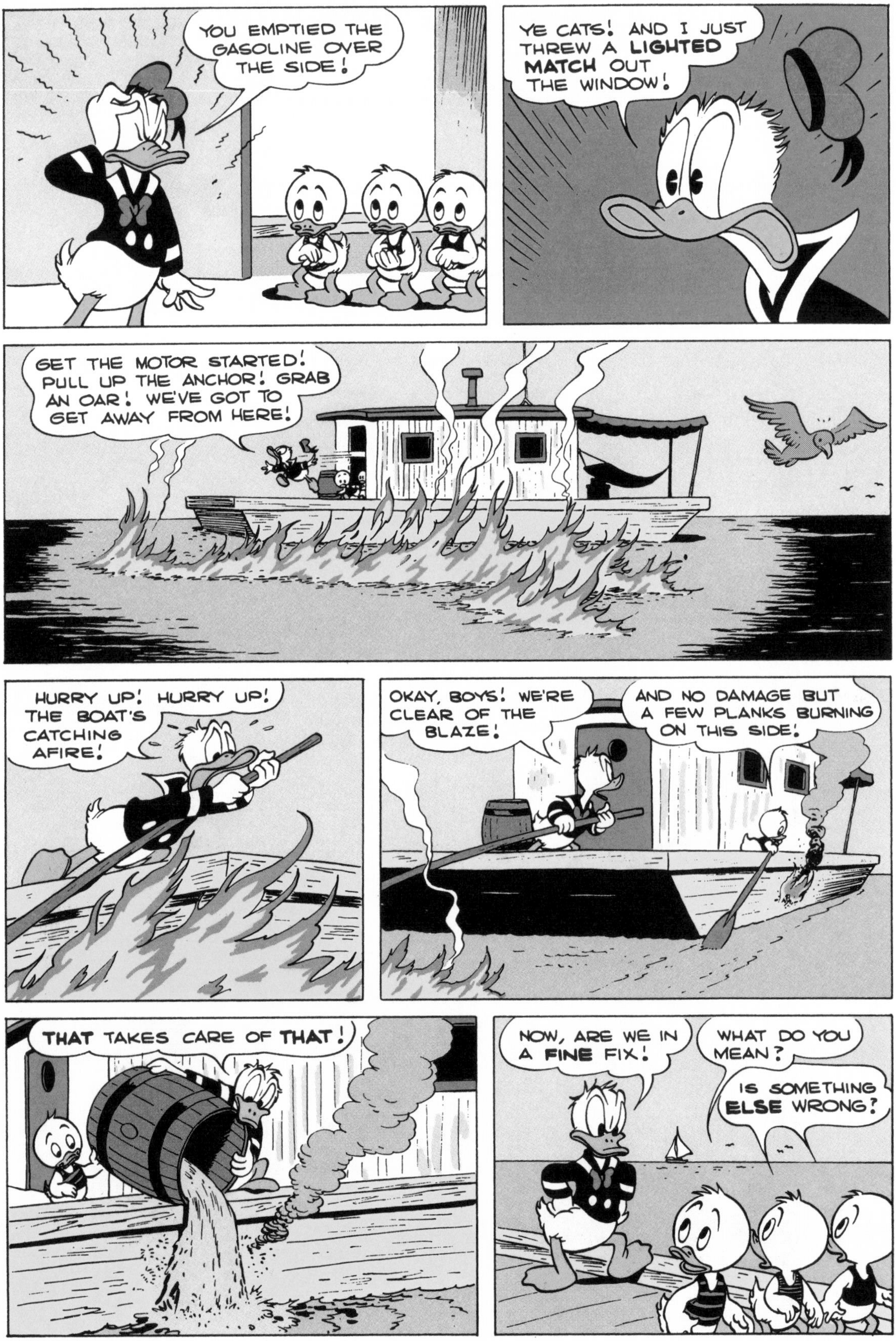
YOU EMPTIED THE GASOLINE OVER THE SIDE!
YE CATS! AND I JUST THREW A **LIGHTED MATCH** OUT THE WINDOW!
GET THE MOTOR STARTED! PULL UP THE ANCHOR! GRAB AN OAR! WE'VE GOT TO GET AWAY FROM HERE!
HURRY UP! HURRY UP! THE BOAT'S CATCHING AFIRE!
OKAY, BOYS! WE'RE CLEAR OF THE BLAZE!
AND NO DAMAGE BUT A FEW PLANKS BURNING ON THIS SIDE!
THAT TAKES CARE OF **THAT**!
NOW, ARE WE IN A **FINE** FIX!
WHAT DO YOU MEAN?
IS SOMETHING **ELSE** WRONG?

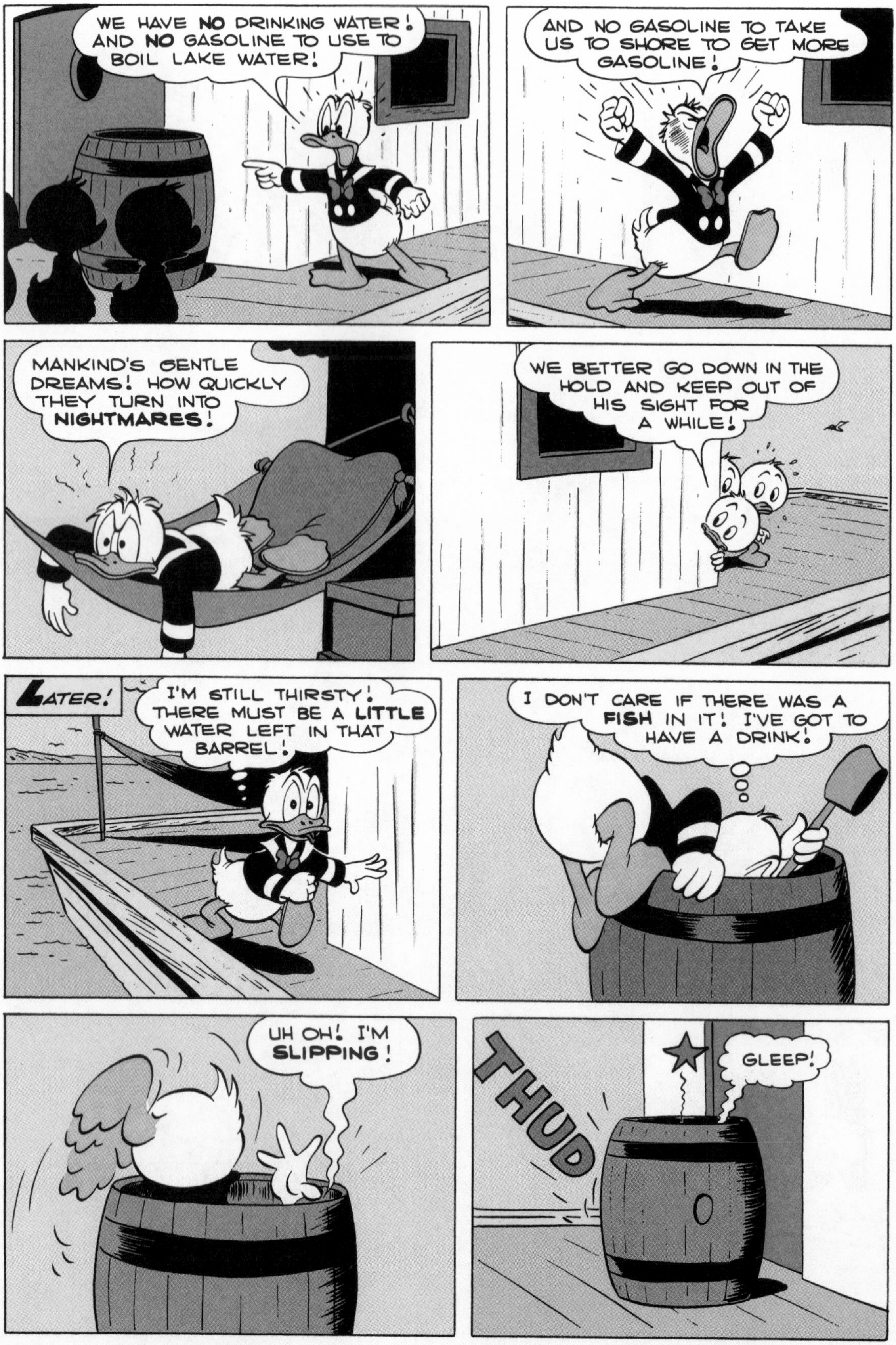
WE HAVE NO DRINKING WATER! AND NO GASOLINE TO USE TO BOIL LAKE WATER!
AND NO GASOLINE TO TAKE US TO SHORE TO GET MORE GASOLINE!
MANKIND'S GENTLE DREAMS! HOW QUICKLY THEY TURN INTO NIGHTMARES!
WE BETTER GO DOWN IN THE HOLD AND KEEP OUT OF HIS SIGHT FOR A WHILE!
LATER!
I'M STILL THIRSTY! THERE MUST BE A LITTLE WATER LEFT IN THAT BARREL!
I DON'T CARE IF THERE WAS A FISH IN IT! I'VE GOT TO HAVE A DRINK!
UH OH! I'M SLIPPING!
THUD
GLEEP!

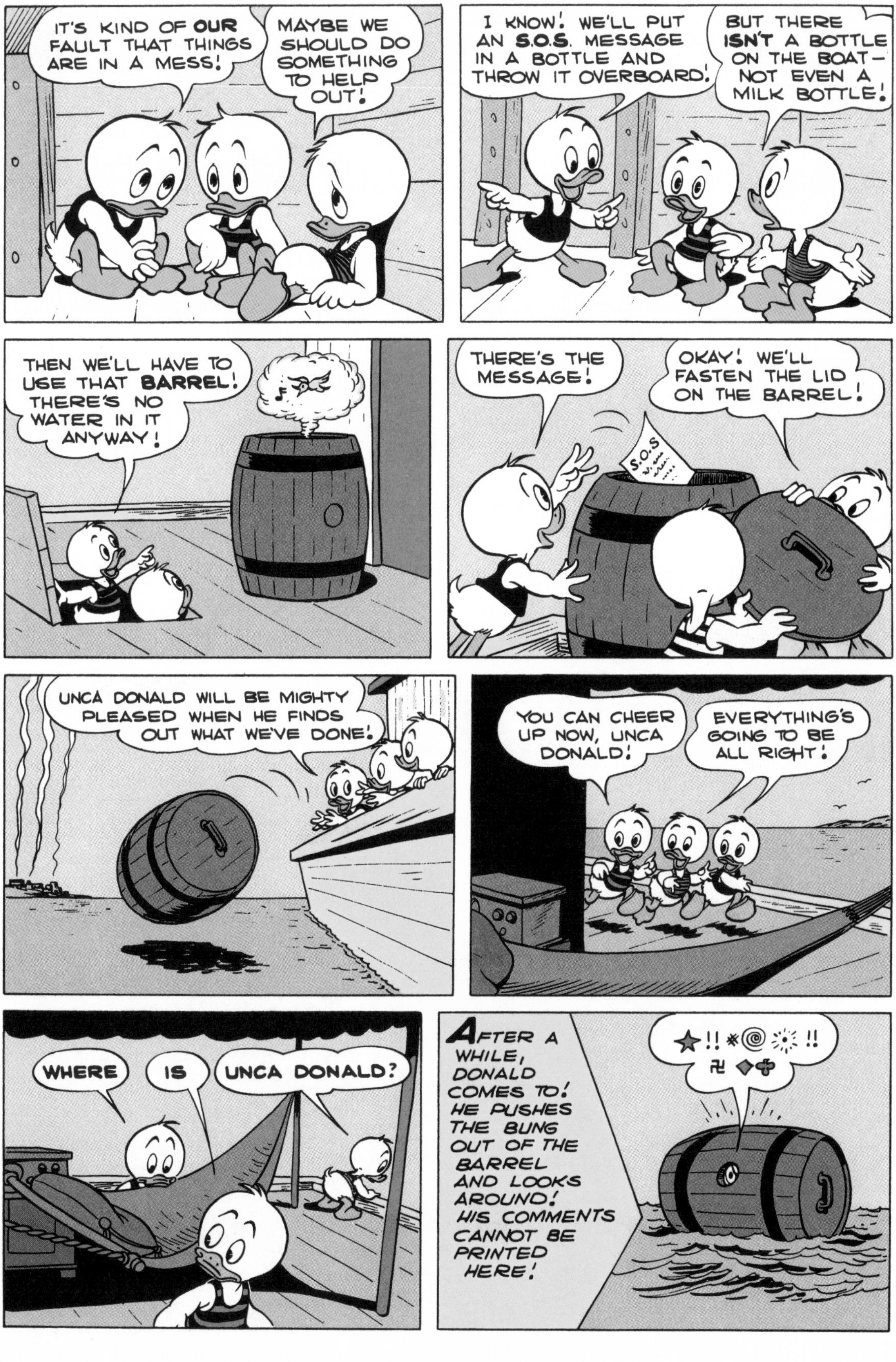
IT'S KIND OF OUR FAULT THAT THINGS ARE IN A MESS!
MAYBE WE SHOULD DO SOMETHING TO HELP OUT!
I KNOW! WE'LL PUT AN S.O.S. MESSAGE IN A BOTTLE AND THROW IT OVERBOARD!
BUT THERE ISN'T A BOTTLE ON THE BOAT— NOT EVEN A MILK BOTTLE!
THEN WE'LL HAVE TO USE THAT BARREL! THERE'S NO WATER IN IT ANYWAY!
THERE'S THE MESSAGE!
OKAY! WE'LL FASTEN THE LID ON THE BARREL!
S.O.S
UNCA DONALD WILL BE MIGHTY PLEASED WHEN HE FINDS OUT WHAT WE'VE DONE!
YOU CAN CHEER UP NOW, UNCA DONALD!
EVERYTHING'S GOING TO BE ALL RIGHT!
WHERE
IS
UNCA DONALD?
AFTER A WHILE, DONALD COMES TO! HE PUSHES THE BUNG OUT OF THE BARREL AND LOOKS AROUND! HIS COMMENTS CANNOT BE PRINTED HERE!

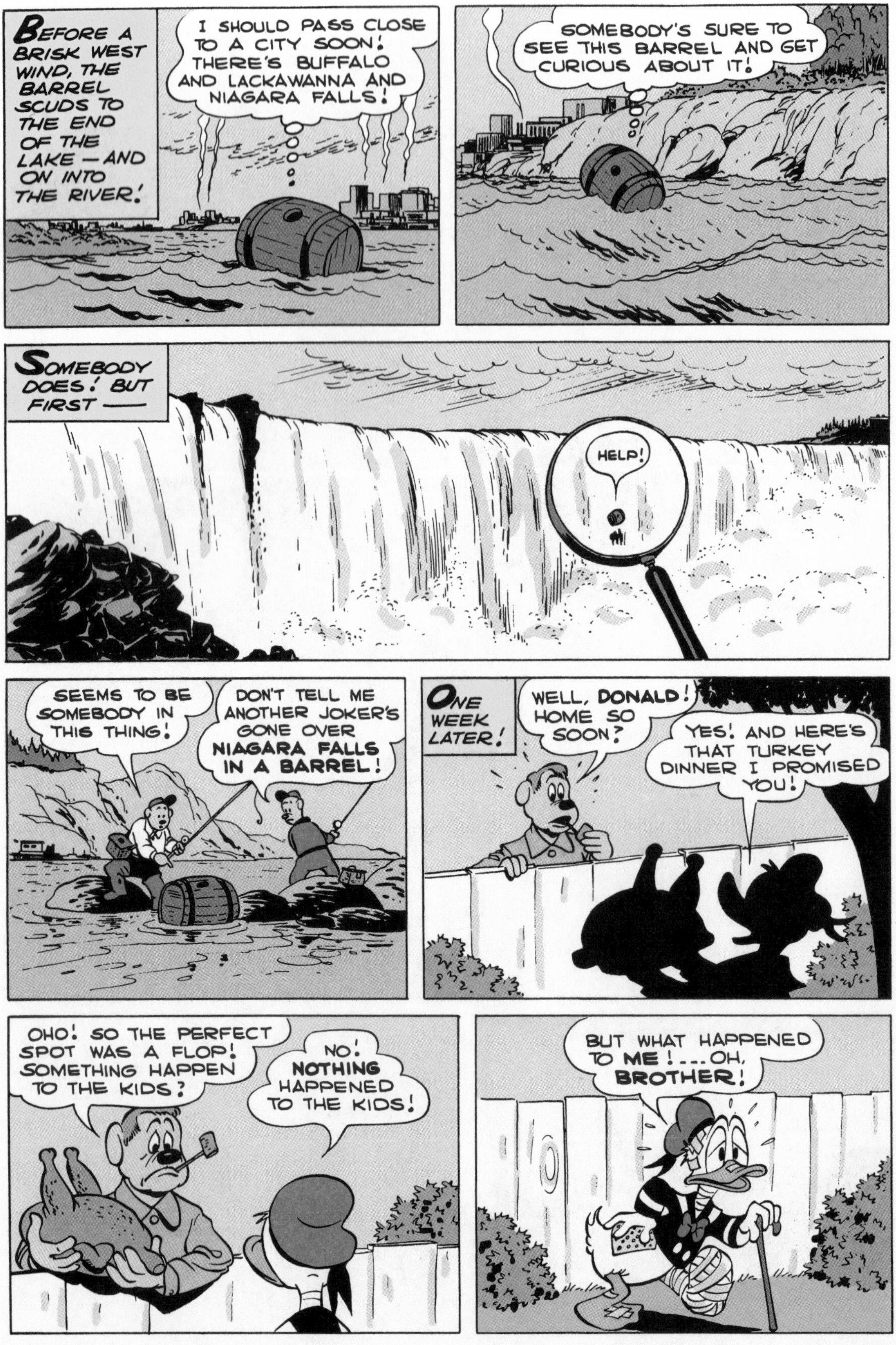
BEFORE A BRISK WEST WIND, THE BARREL SCUDS TO THE END OF THE LAKE—AND ON INTO THE RIVER!
I SHOULD PASS CLOSE TO A CITY SOON! THERE'S BUFFALO AND LACKAWANNA AND NIAGARA FALLS!
SOMEBODY'S SURE TO SEE THIS BARREL AND GET CURIOUS ABOUT IT!
SOMEBODY DOES! BUT FIRST—
HELP!
SEEMS TO BE SOMEBODY IN THIS THING!
DON'T TELL ME ANOTHER JOKER'S GONE OVER NIAGARA FALLS IN A BARREL!
ONE WEEK LATER!
WELL, DONALD! HOME SO SOON?
YES! AND HERE'S THAT TURKEY DINNER I PROMISED YOU!
OHO! SO THE PERFECT SPOT WAS A FLOP! SOMETHING HAPPEN TO THE KIDS?
NO! NOTHING HAPPENED TO THE KIDS!
BUT WHAT HAPPENED TO ME!...OH, BROTHER!

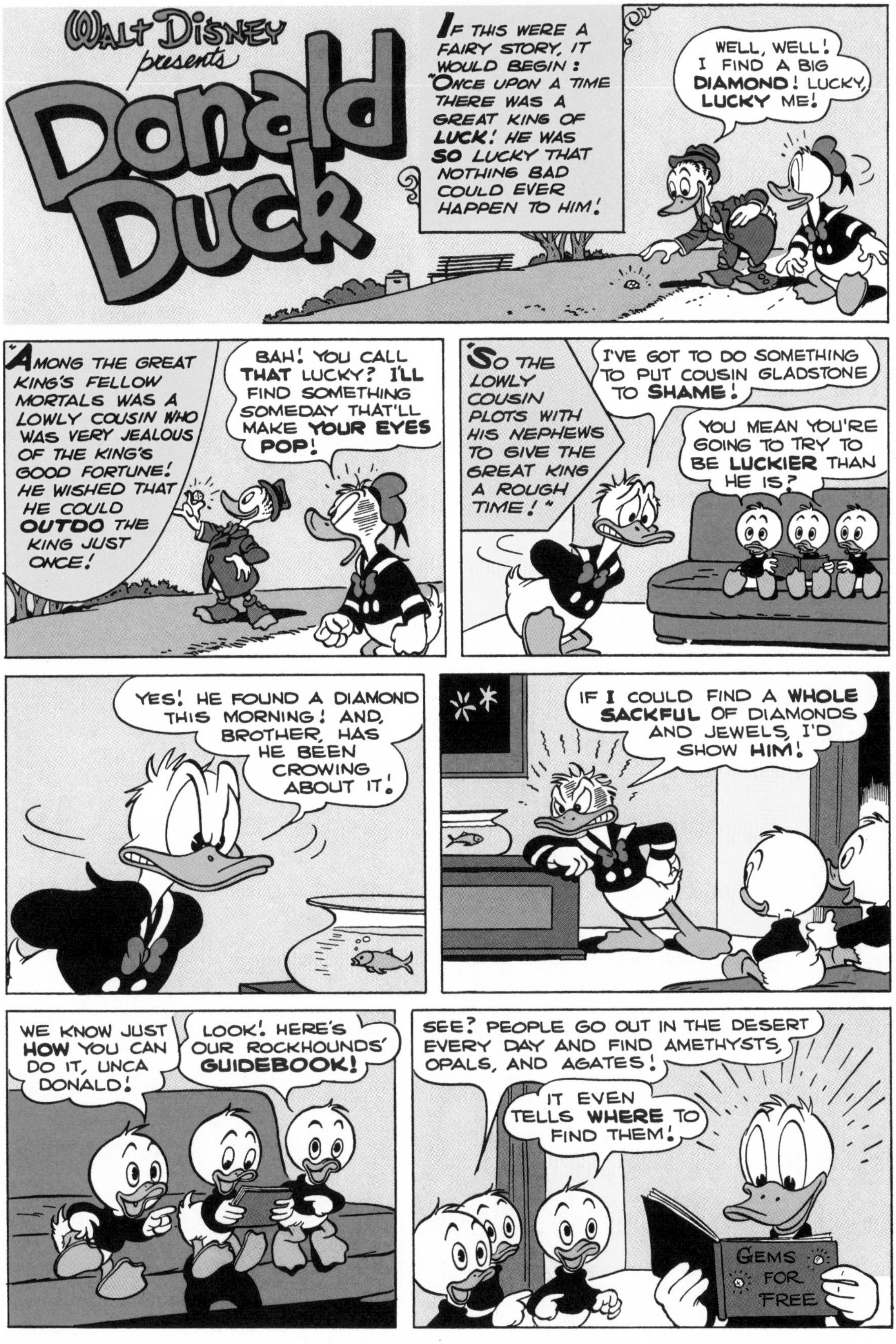
Walt Disney presents
Donald Duck
"If this were a fairy story, it would begin: "Once upon a time there was a great king of LUCK! He was SO lucky that nothing bad could ever happen to him!
WELL, WELL! I FIND A BIG DIAMOND! LUCKY, LUCKY ME!
"Among the great king's fellow mortals was a lowly cousin who was very jealous of the king's good fortune! He wished that he could OUTDO the king just once!
BAH! YOU CALL THAT LUCKY? I'LL FIND SOMETHING SOMEDAY THAT'LL MAKE YOUR EYES POP!
"So the lowly cousin plots with his nephews to give the great king a rough time!"
I'VE GOT TO DO SOMETHING TO PUT COUSIN GLADSTONE TO SHAME!
YOU MEAN YOU'RE GOING TO TRY TO BE LUCKIER THAN HE IS?
YES! HE FOUND A DIAMOND THIS MORNING! AND, BROTHER, HAS HE BEEN CROWING ABOUT IT!
IF I COULD FIND A WHOLE SACKFUL OF DIAMONDS AND JEWELS, I'D SHOW HIM!
WE KNOW JUST HOW YOU CAN DO IT, UNCA DONALD!
LOOK! HERE'S OUR ROCKHOUNDS' GUIDEBOOK!
SEE? PEOPLE GO OUT IN THE DESERT EVERY DAY AND FIND AMETHYSTS, OPALS, AND AGATES!
IT EVEN TELLS WHERE TO FIND THEM!
GEMS FOR FREE

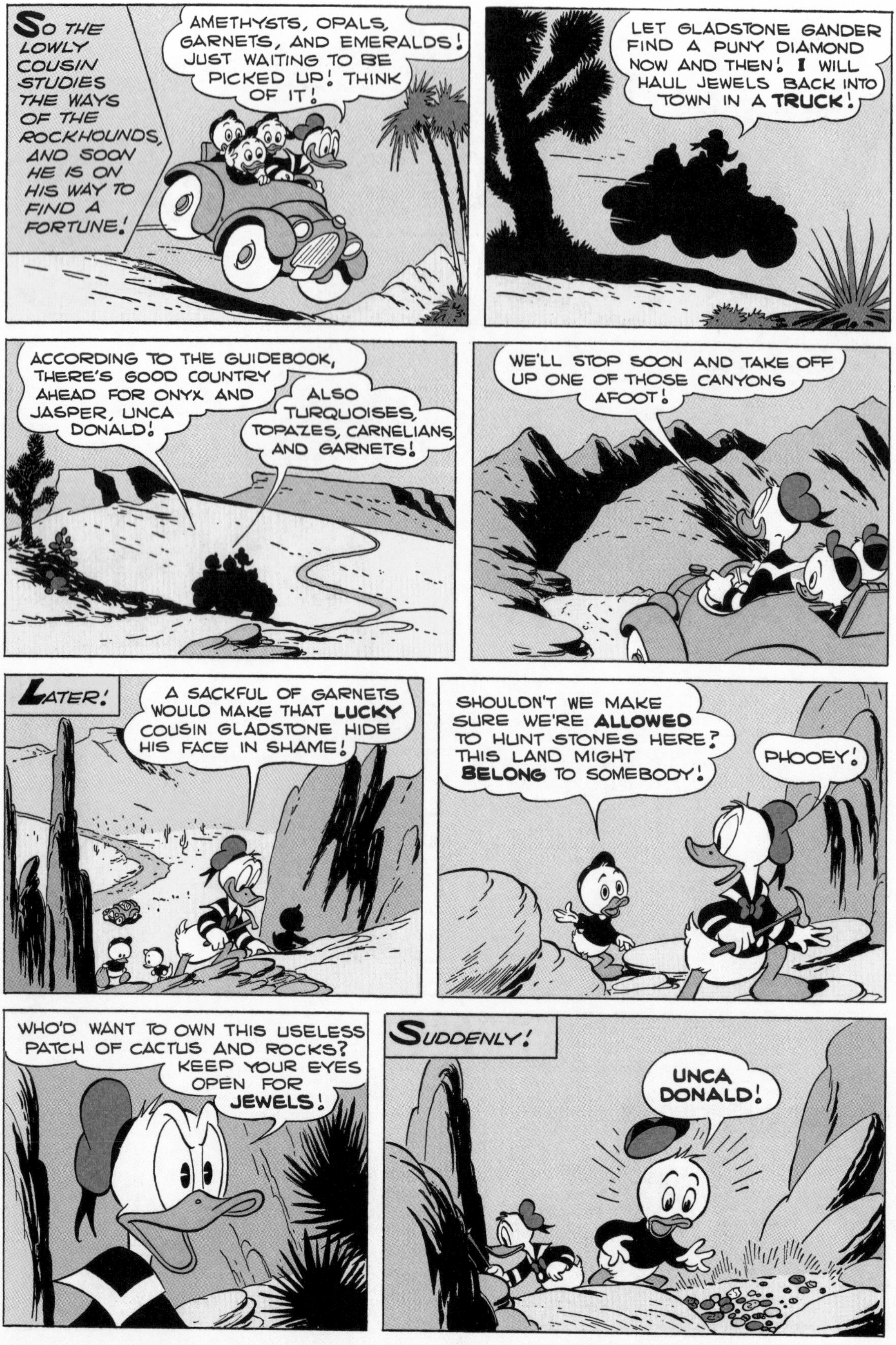
SO THE LOWLY COUSIN STUDIES THE WAYS OF THE ROCKHOUNDS, AND SOON HE IS ON HIS WAY TO FIND A FORTUNE!
AMETHYSTS, OPALS, GARNETS, AND EMERALDS! JUST WAITING TO BE PICKED UP! THINK OF IT!
LET GLADSTONE GANDER FIND A PUNY DIAMOND NOW AND THEN! I WILL HAUL JEWELS BACK INTO TOWN IN A TRUCK!
ACCORDING TO THE GUIDEBOOK, THERE'S GOOD COUNTRY AHEAD FOR ONYX AND JASPER, UNCA DONALD!
ALSO TURQUOISES, TOPAZES, CARNELIANS, AND GARNETS!
WE'LL STOP SOON AND TAKE OFF UP ONE OF THOSE CANYONS AFOOT!
LATER!
A SACKFUL OF GARNETS WOULD MAKE THAT LUCKY COUSIN GLADSTONE HIDE HIS FACE IN SHAME!
SHOULDN'T WE MAKE SURE WE'RE ALLOWED TO HUNT STONES HERE? THIS LAND MIGHT BELONG TO SOMEBODY!
PHOOEY!
WHO'D WANT TO OWN THIS USELESS PATCH OF CACTUS AND ROCKS?
KEEP YOUR EYES OPEN FOR JEWELS!
SUDDENLY!
UNCA DONALD!

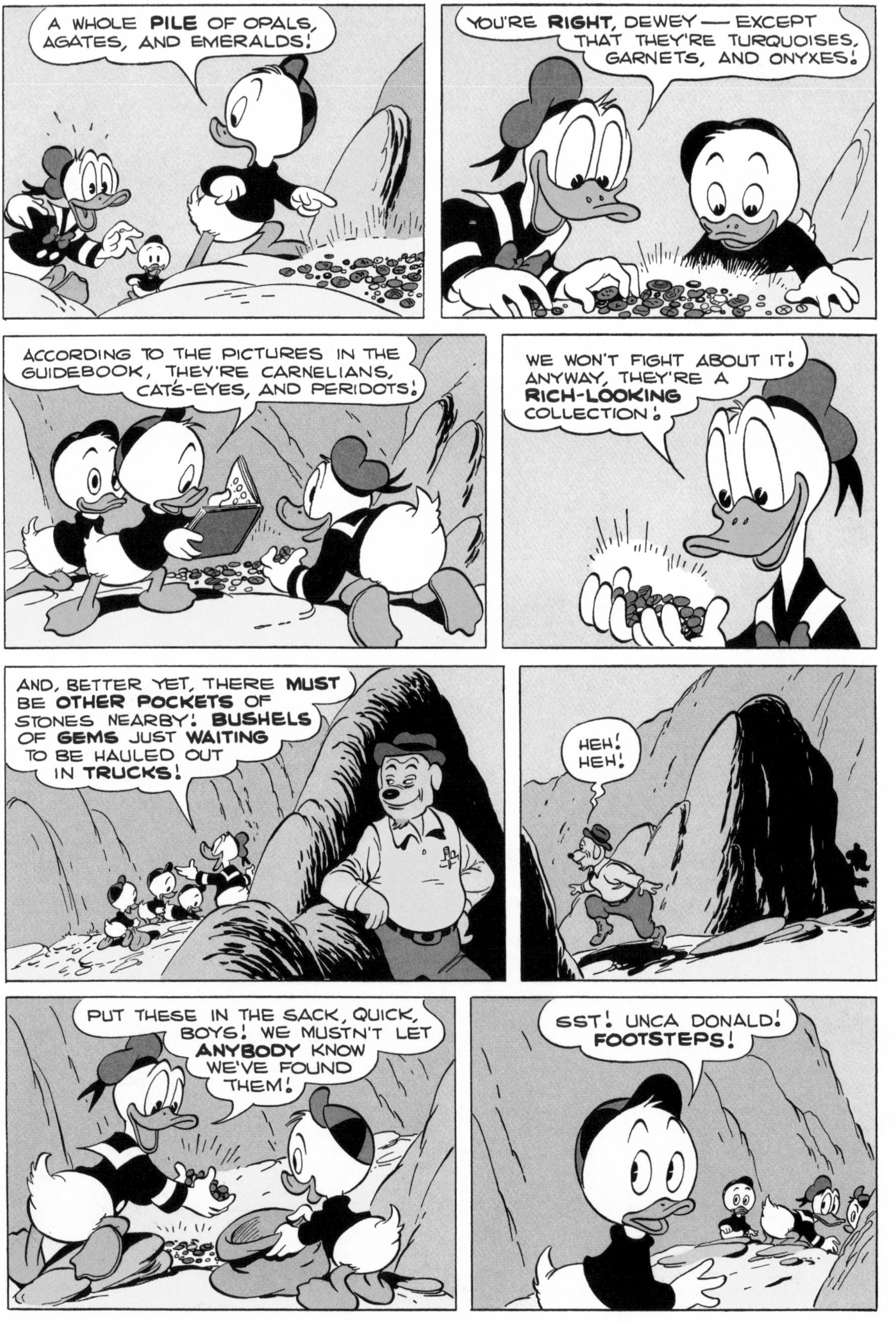

A WHOLE PILE OF OPALS, AGATES, AND EMERALDS!
YOU'RE RIGHT, DEWEY — EXCEPT THAT THEY'RE TURQUOISES, GARNETS, AND ONYXES!
ACCORDING TO THE PICTURES IN THE GUIDEBOOK, THEY'RE CARNELIANS, CAT'S-EYES, AND PERIDOTS!
WE WON'T FIGHT ABOUT IT! ANYWAY, THEY'RE A RICH-LOOKING COLLECTION!
AND, BETTER YET, THERE MUST BE OTHER POCKETS OF STONES NEARBY! BUSHELS OF GEMS JUST WAITING TO BE HAULED OUT IN TRUCKS!
HEH! HEH!
PUT THESE IN THE SACK, QUICK, BOYS! WE MUSTN'T LET ANYBODY KNOW WE'VE FOUND THEM!
SST! UNCA DONALD! FOOTSTEPS!

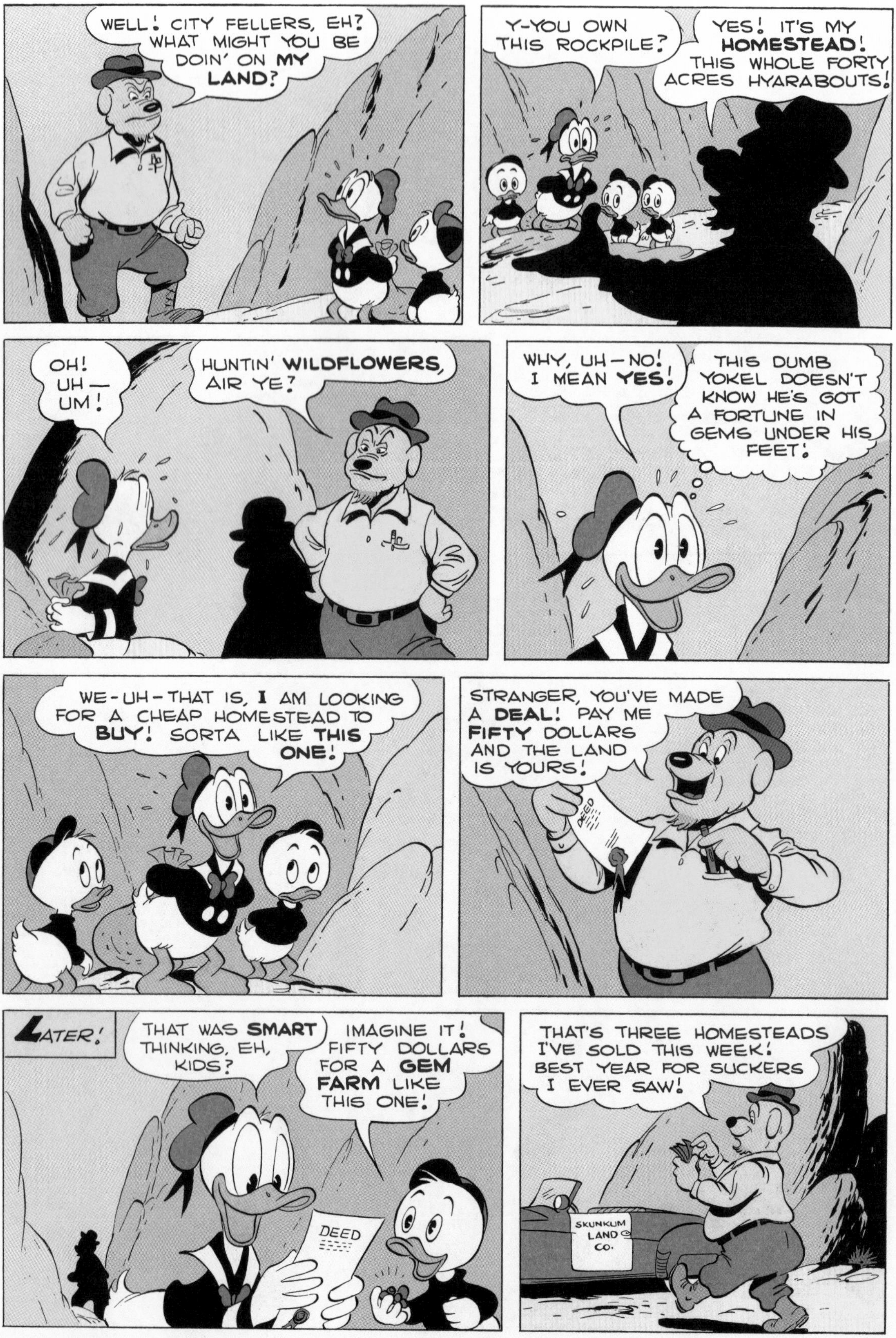

WELL! CITY FELLERS, EH? WHAT MIGHT YOU BE DOIN' ON MY LAND?
Y-YOU OWN THIS ROCKPILE?
YES! IT'S MY HOMESTEAD! THIS WHOLE FORTY ACRES HYARABOUTS!
OH! UH— UM!
HUNTIN' WILDFLOWERS, AIR YE?
WHY, UH—NO! I MEAN YES!
THIS DUMB YOKEL DOESN'T KNOW HE'S GOT A FORTUNE IN GEMS UNDER HIS FEET!
WE-UH-THAT IS, I AM LOOKING FOR A CHEAP HOMESTEAD TO BUY! SORTA LIKE THIS ONE!
STRANGER, YOU'VE MADE A DEAL! PAY ME FIFTY DOLLARS AND THE LAND IS YOURS!
DEED
LATER!
THAT WAS SMART THINKING, EH, KIDS?
IMAGINE IT! FIFTY DOLLARS FOR A GEM FARM LIKE THIS ONE!
DEED
THAT'S THREE HOMESTEADS I'VE SOLD THIS WEEK! BEST YEAR FOR SUCKERS I EVER SAW!
SKUNKUM LAND CO.

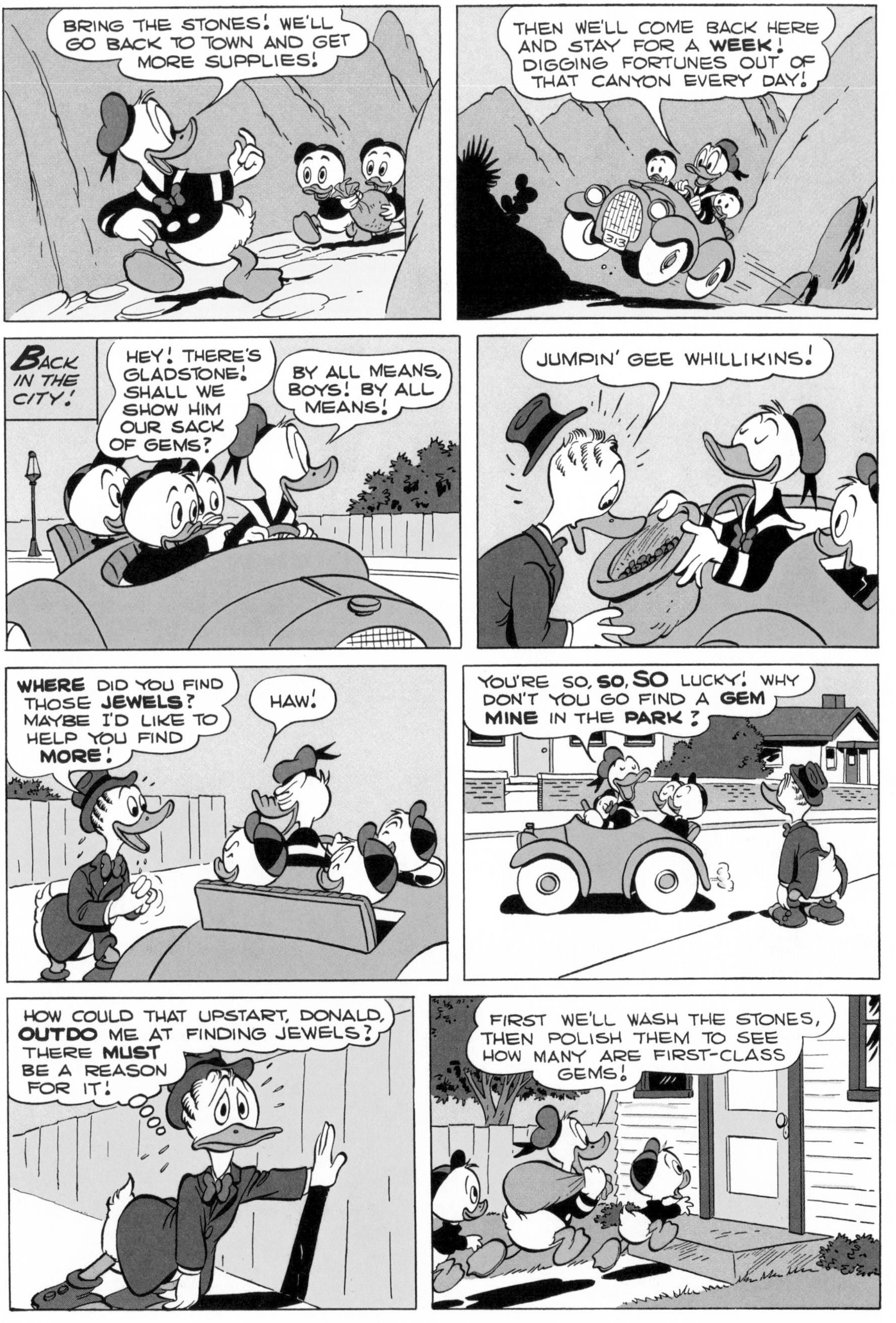
BRING THE STONES! WE'LL GO BACK TO TOWN AND GET MORE SUPPLIES!
THEN WE'LL COME BACK HERE AND STAY FOR A WEEK! DIGGING FORTUNES OUT OF THAT CANYON EVERY DAY!
313
BACK IN THE CITY!
HEY! THERE'S GLADSTONE! SHALL WE SHOW HIM OUR SACK OF GEMS?
BY ALL MEANS, BOYS! BY ALL MEANS!
JUMPIN' GEE WHILLIKINS!
WHERE DID YOU FIND THOSE JEWELS? MAYBE I'D LIKE TO HELP YOU FIND MORE!
HAW!
YOU'RE SO, SO, SO LUCKY! WHY DON'T YOU GO FIND A GEM MINE IN THE PARK?
HOW COULD THAT UPSTART, DONALD, OUTDO ME AT FINDING JEWELS? THERE MUST BE A REASON FOR IT!
FIRST WE'LL WASH THE STONES, THEN POLISH THEM TO SEE HOW MANY ARE FIRST-CLASS GEMS!

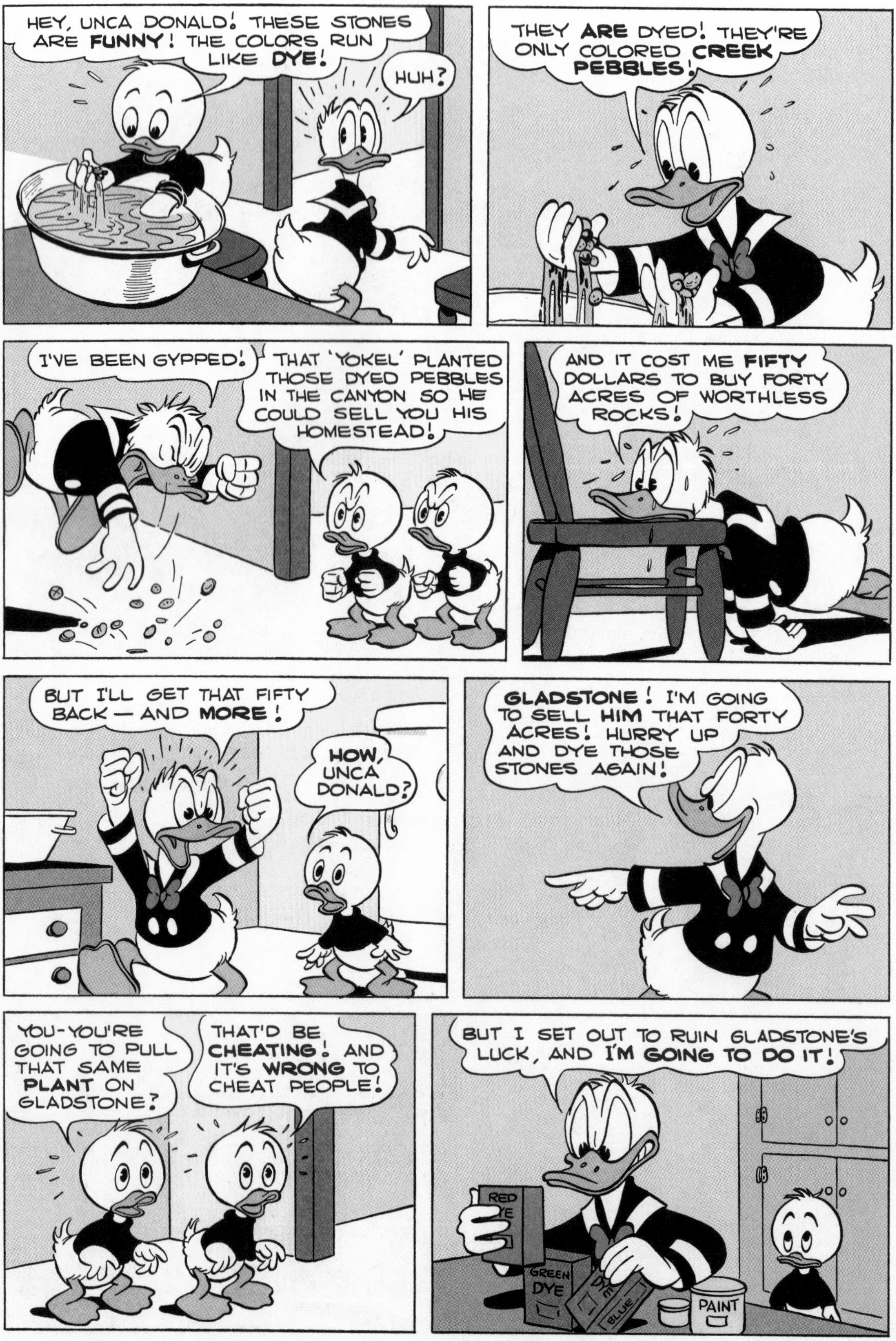
HEY, UNCA DONALD! THESE STONES ARE FUNNY! THE COLORS RUN LIKE DYE!
HUH?
THEY ARE DYED! THEY'RE ONLY COLORED CREEK PEBBLES!
I'VE BEEN GYPPED!
THAT 'YOKEL' PLANTED THOSE DYED PEBBLES IN THE CANYON SO HE COULD SELL YOU HIS HOMESTEAD!
AND IT COST ME FIFTY DOLLARS TO BUY FORTY ACRES OF WORTHLESS ROCKS!
BUT I'LL GET THAT FIFTY BACK — AND MORE!
HOW, UNCA DONALD?
GLADSTONE! I'M GOING TO SELL HIM THAT FORTY ACRES! HURRY UP AND DYE THOSE STONES AGAIN!
YOU-YOU'RE GOING TO PULL THAT SAME PLANT ON GLADSTONE?
THAT'D BE CHEATING! AND IT'S WRONG TO CHEAT PEOPLE!
BUT I SET OUT TO RUIN GLADSTONE'S LUCK, AND I'M GOING TO DO IT!
RED DYE
GREEN DYE
DYE BLUE
PAINT

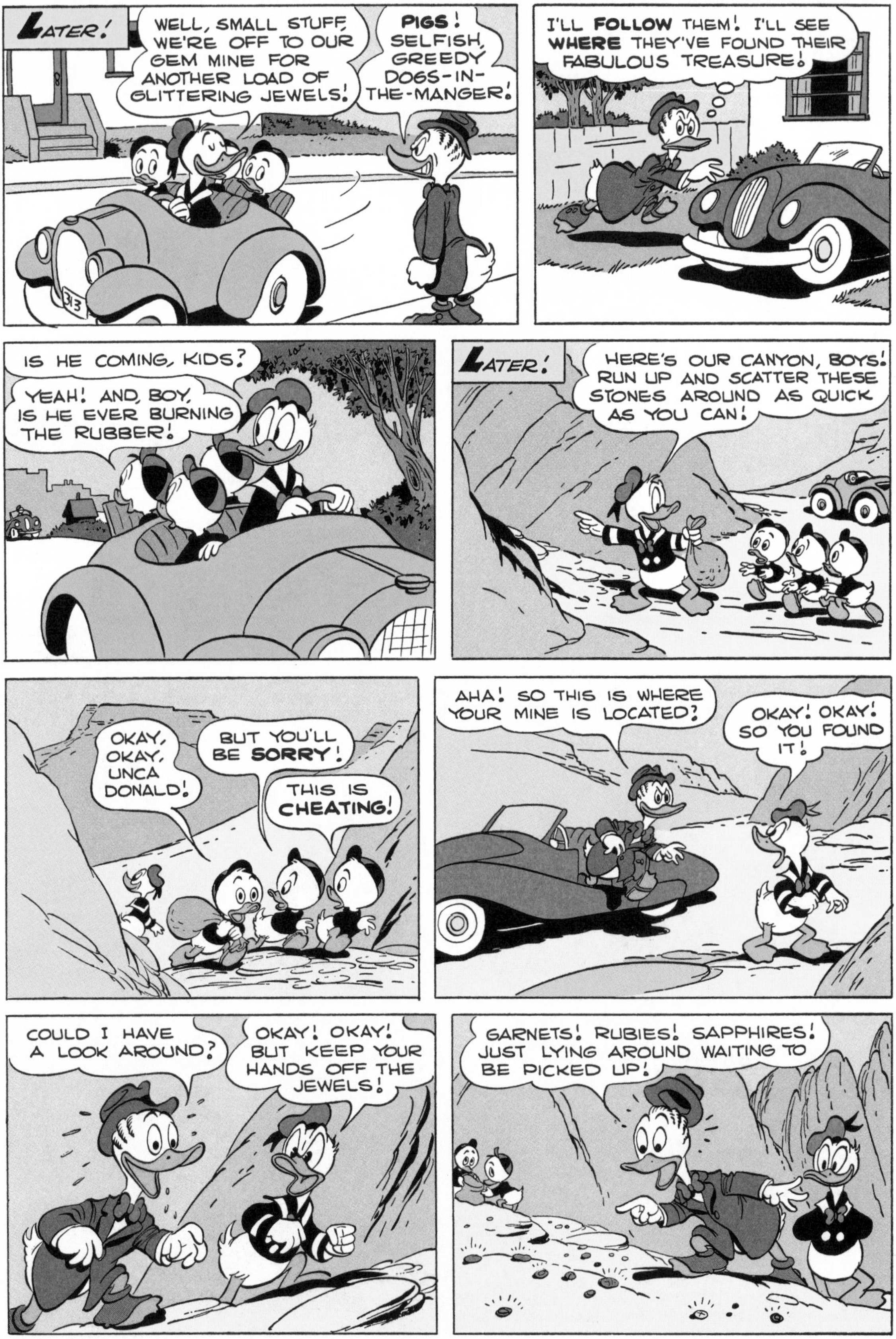
LATER!
WELL, SMALL STUFF, WE'RE OFF TO OUR GEM MINE FOR ANOTHER LOAD OF GLITTERING JEWELS!
PIGS! SELFISH, GREEDY DOGS-IN-THE-MANGER!
I'LL FOLLOW THEM! I'LL SEE WHERE THEY'VE FOUND THEIR FABULOUS TREASURE!
IS HE COMING, KIDS?
YEAH! AND, BOY, IS HE EVER BURNING THE RUBBER!
LATER!
HERE'S OUR CANYON, BOYS! RUN UP AND SCATTER THESE STONES AROUND AS QUICK AS YOU CAN!
OKAY, OKAY, UNCA DONALD!
BUT YOU'LL BE SORRY!
THIS IS CHEATING!
AHA! SO THIS IS WHERE YOUR MINE IS LOCATED?
OKAY! OKAY! SO YOU FOUND IT!
COULD I HAVE A LOOK AROUND?
OKAY! OKAY! BUT KEEP YOUR HANDS OFF THE JEWELS!
GARNETS! RUBIES! SAPPHIRES! JUST LYING AROUND WAITING TO BE PICKED UP!

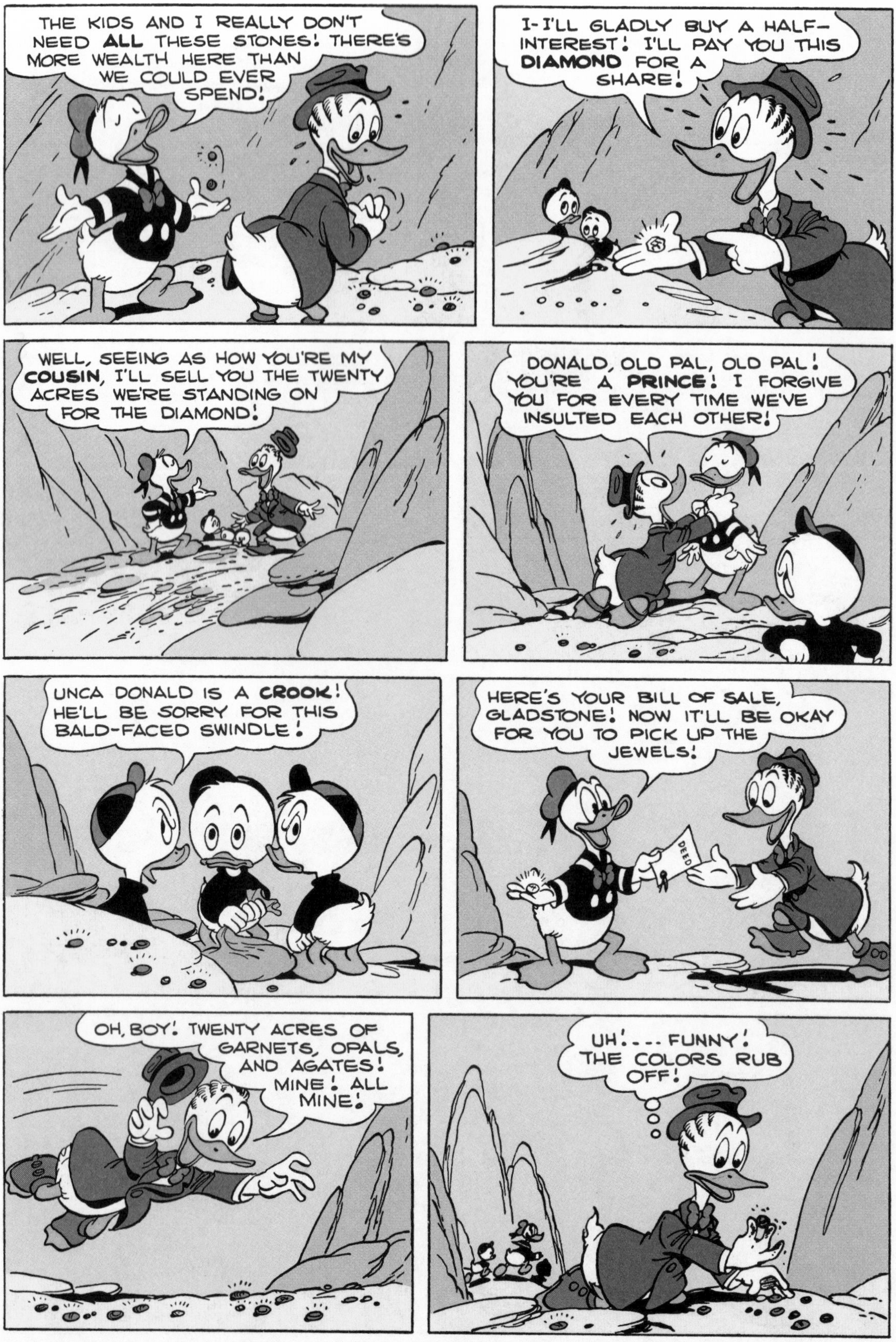
THE KIDS AND I REALLY DON'T NEED ALL THESE STONES! THERE'S MORE WEALTH HERE THAN WE COULD EVER SPEND!
I-I'LL GLADLY BUY A HALF-INTEREST! I'LL PAY YOU THIS DIAMOND FOR A SHARE!
WELL, SEEING AS HOW YOU'RE MY COUSIN, I'LL SELL YOU THE TWENTY ACRES WE'RE STANDING ON FOR THE DIAMOND!
DONALD, OLD PAL, OLD PAL! YOU'RE A PRINCE! I FORGIVE YOU FOR EVERY TIME WE'VE INSULTED EACH OTHER!
UNCA DONALD IS A CROOK! HE'LL BE SORRY FOR THIS BALD-FACED SWINDLE!
HERE'S YOUR BILL OF SALE, GLADSTONE! NOW IT'LL BE OKAY FOR YOU TO PICK UP THE JEWELS!
DEED
OH, BOY! TWENTY ACRES OF GARNETS, OPALS, AND AGATES! MINE! ALL MINE!
UH!... FUNNY! THE COLORS RUB OFF!

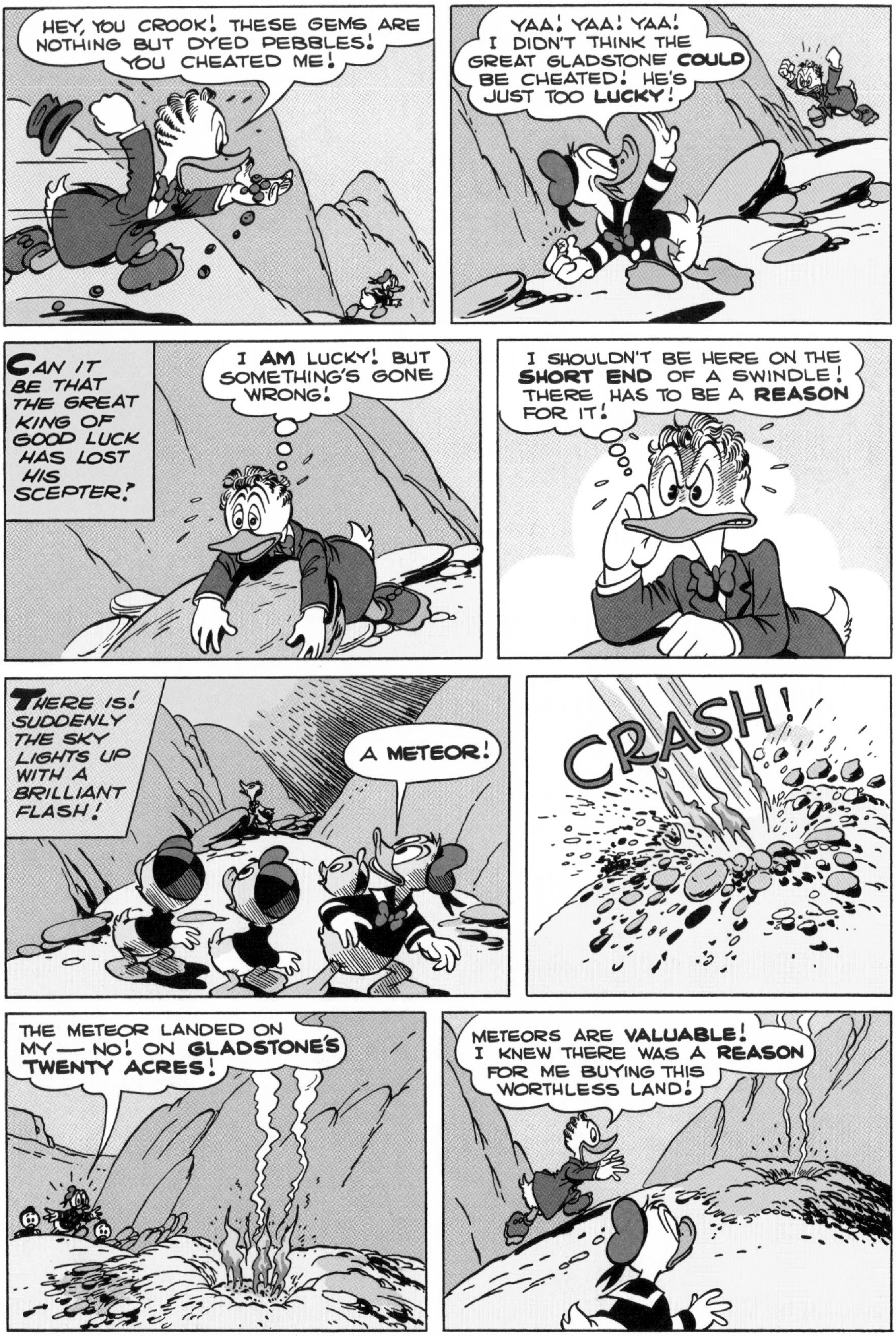
HEY, YOU CROOK! THESE GEMS ARE NOTHING BUT DYED PEBBLES! YOU CHEATED ME!
YAA! YAA! YAA! I DIDN'T THINK THE GREAT GLADSTONE COULD BE CHEATED! HE'S JUST TOO LUCKY!
CAN IT BE THAT THE GREAT KING OF GOOD LUCK HAS LOST HIS SCEPTER?
I AM LUCKY! BUT SOMETHING'S GONE WRONG!
I SHOULDN'T BE HERE ON THE SHORT END OF A SWINDLE! THERE HAS TO BE A REASON FOR IT!
THERE IS! SUDDENLY THE SKY LIGHTS UP WITH A BRILLIANT FLASH!
A METEOR!
CRASH!
THE METEOR LANDED ON MY— NO! ON GLADSTONE'S TWENTY ACRES!
METEORS ARE VALUABLE! I KNEW THERE WAS A REASON FOR ME BUYING THIS WORTHLESS LAND!

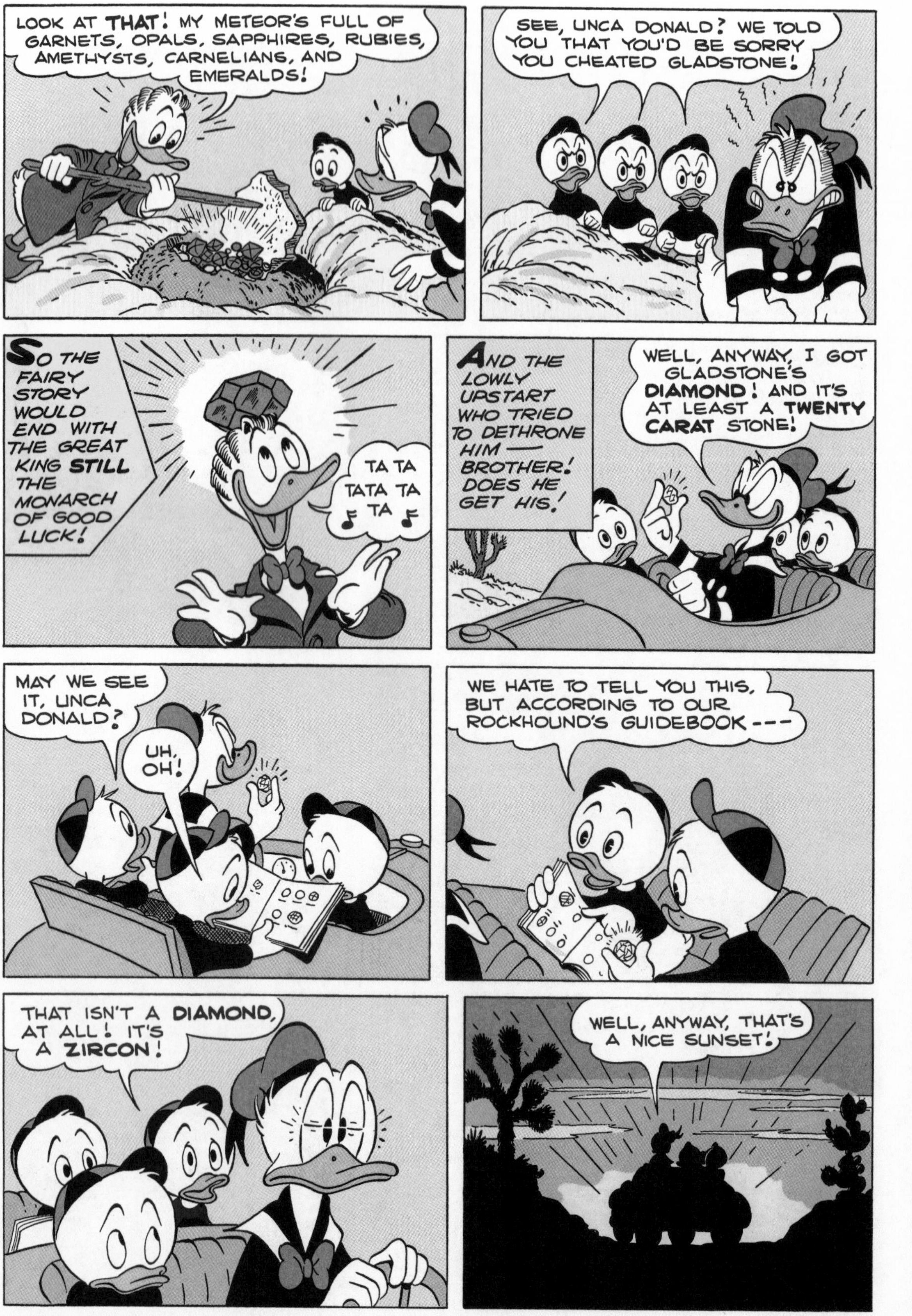
LOOK AT THAT! MY METEOR'S FULL OF GARNETS, OPALS, SAPPHIRES, RUBIES, AMETHYSTS, CARNELIANS, AND EMERALDS!
SEE, UNCA DONALD? WE TOLD YOU THAT YOU'D BE SORRY YOU CHEATED GLADSTONE!
SO THE FAIRY STORY WOULD END WITH THE GREAT KING STILL THE MONARCH OF GOOD LUCK!
TA TA TATA TA TA
AND THE LOWLY UPSTART WHO TRIED TO DETHRONE HIM— BROTHER! DOES HE GET HIS!
WELL, ANYWAY, I GOT GLADSTONE'S DIAMOND! AND IT'S AT LEAST A TWENTY CARAT STONE!
MAY WE SEE IT, UNCA DONALD?
UH, OH!
WE HATE TO TELL YOU THIS, BUT ACCORDING TO OUR ROCKHOUND'S GUIDEBOOK---
THAT ISN'T A DIAMOND, AT ALL! IT'S A ZIRCON!
WELL, ANYWAY, THAT'S A NICE SUNSET!

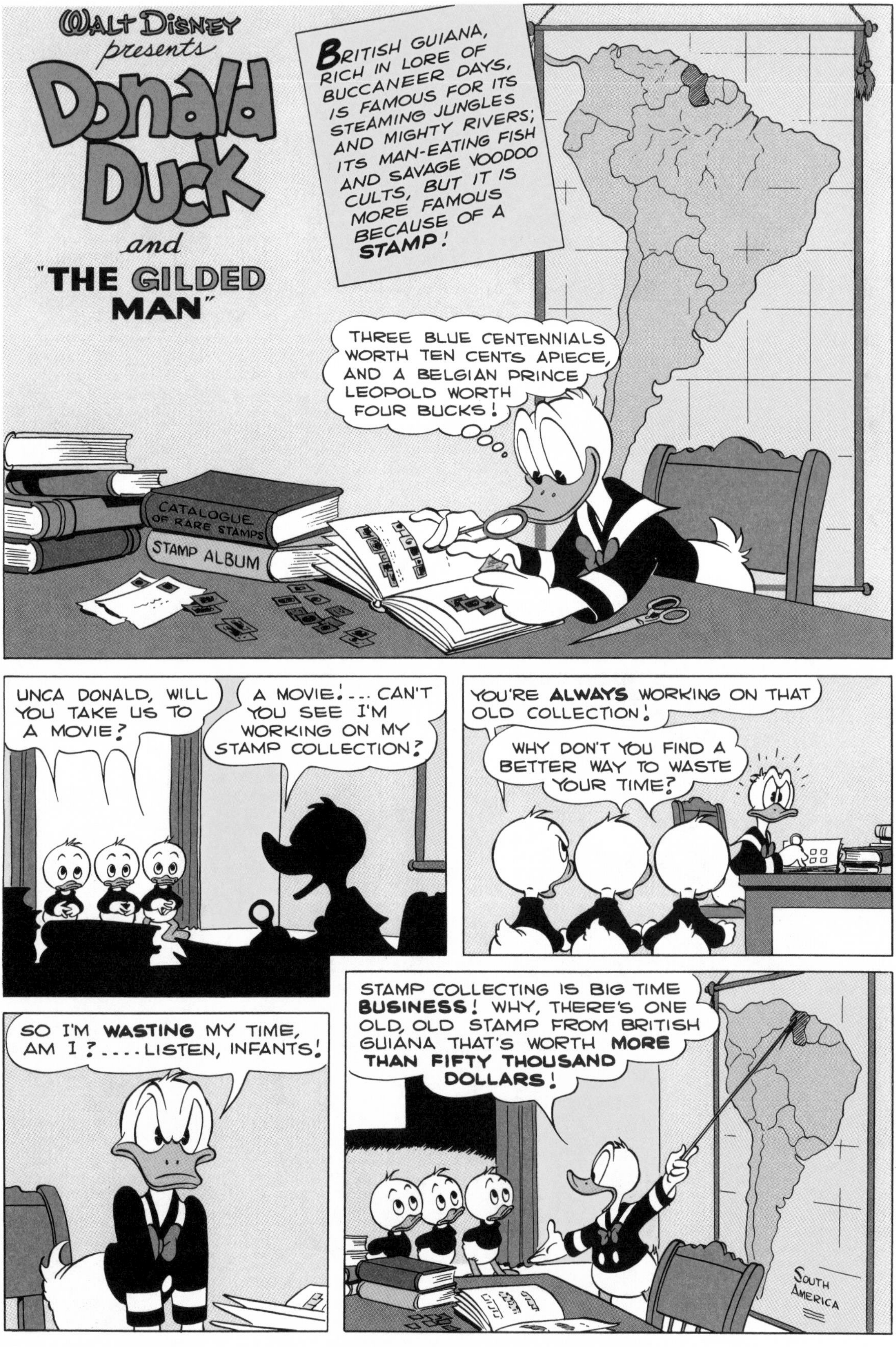
WALT DISNEY presents
Donald Duck
and "THE GILDED MAN"
BRITISH GUIANA, RICH IN LORE OF BUCCANEER DAYS, IS FAMOUS FOR ITS STEAMING JUNGLES AND MIGHTY RIVERS; ITS MAN-EATING FISH AND SAVAGE VOODOO CULTS, BUT IT IS MORE FAMOUS BECAUSE OF A STAMP!
THREE BLUE CENTENNIALS WORTH TEN CENTS APIECE, AND A BELGIAN PRINCE LEOPOLD WORTH FOUR BUCKS!
CATALOGUE OF RARE STAMPS
STAMP ALBUM
UNCA DONALD, WILL YOU TAKE US TO A MOVIE?
A MOVIE!... CAN'T YOU SEE I'M WORKING ON MY STAMP COLLECTION?
YOU'RE ALWAYS WORKING ON THAT OLD COLLECTION!
WHY DON'T YOU FIND A BETTER WAY TO WASTE YOUR TIME?
SO I'M WASTING MY TIME, AM I?.... LISTEN, INFANTS!
STAMP COLLECTING IS BIG TIME BUSINESS! WHY, THERE'S ONE OLD, OLD STAMP FROM BRITISH GUIANA THAT'S WORTH MORE THAN FIFTY THOUSAND DOLLARS!
SOUTH AMERICA

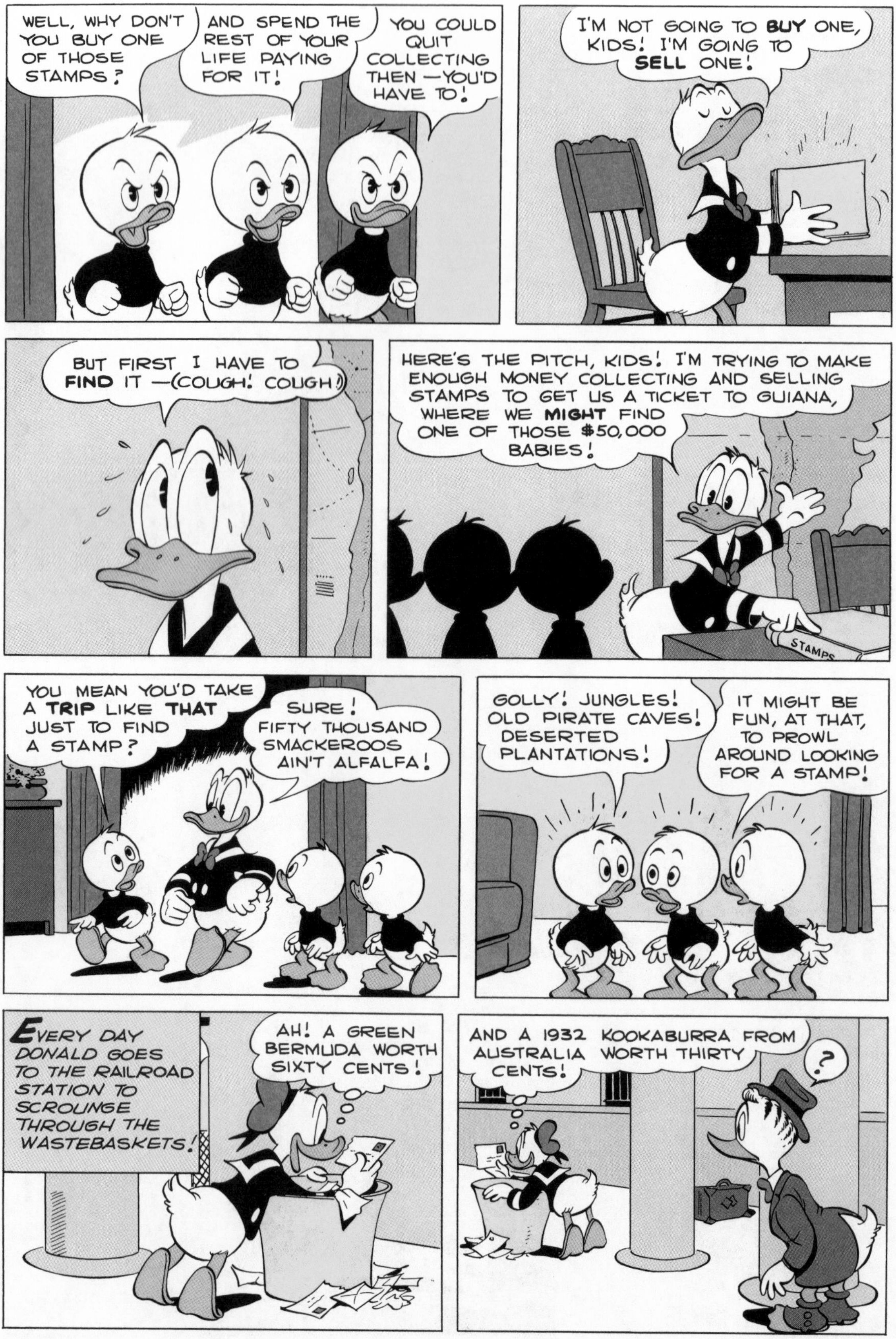
WELL, WHY DON'T YOU BUY ONE OF THOSE STAMPS?
AND SPEND THE REST OF YOUR LIFE PAYING FOR IT!
YOU COULD QUIT COLLECTING THEN —YOU'D HAVE TO!
I'M NOT GOING TO **BUY** ONE, KIDS! I'M GOING TO **SELL** ONE!
BUT FIRST I HAVE TO **FIND** IT —(COUGH! COUGH!)
HERE'S THE PITCH, KIDS! I'M TRYING TO MAKE ENOUGH MONEY COLLECTING AND SELLING STAMPS TO GET US A TICKET TO GUIANA, WHERE WE **MIGHT** FIND ONE OF THOSE $50,000 BABIES!
STAMPS
YOU MEAN YOU'D TAKE A **TRIP** LIKE **THAT** JUST TO FIND A STAMP?
SURE! FIFTY THOUSAND SMACKEROOS AIN'T ALFALFA!
GOLLY! JUNGLES! OLD PIRATE CAVES! DESERTED PLANTATIONS!
IT MIGHT BE FUN, AT THAT, TO PROWL AROUND LOOKING FOR A STAMP!
EVERY DAY DONALD GOES TO THE RAILROAD STATION TO SCROUNGE THROUGH THE WASTEBASKETS!
AH! A GREEN BERMUDA WORTH SIXTY CENTS!
AND A 1932 KOOKABURRA FROM AUSTRALIA WORTH THIRTY CENTS!
?

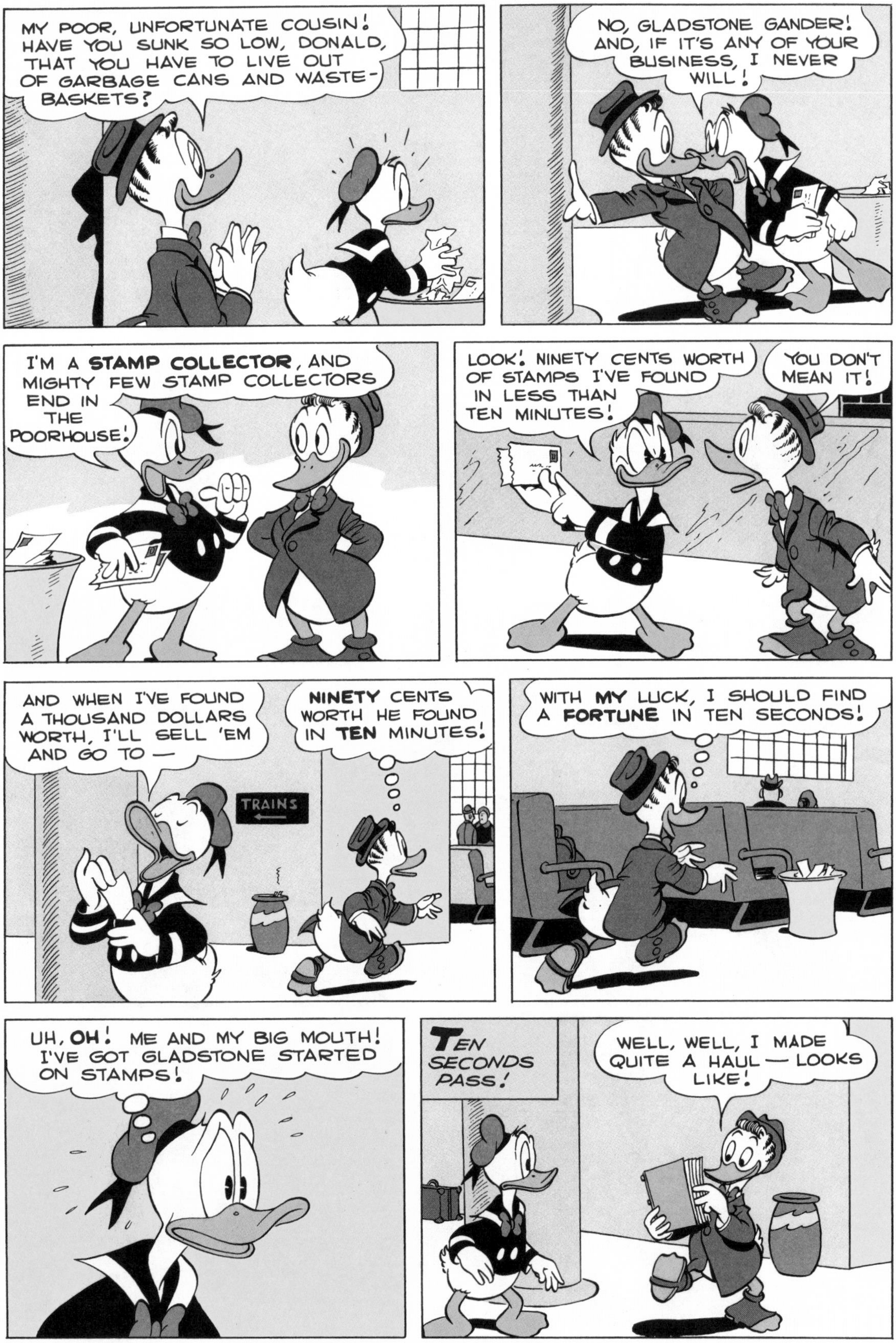

MY POOR, UNFORTUNATE COUSIN! HAVE YOU SUNK SO LOW, DONALD, THAT YOU HAVE TO LIVE OUT OF GARBAGE CANS AND WASTE-BASKETS?
NO, GLADSTONE GANDER! AND, IF IT'S ANY OF YOUR BUSINESS, I NEVER WILL!
I'M A STAMP COLLECTOR, AND MIGHTY FEW STAMP COLLECTORS END IN THE POORHOUSE!
LOOK! NINETY CENTS WORTH OF STAMPS I'VE FOUND IN LESS THAN TEN MINUTES!
YOU DON'T MEAN IT!
AND WHEN I'VE FOUND A THOUSAND DOLLARS WORTH, I'LL SELL 'EM AND GO TO —
NINETY CENTS WORTH HE FOUND IN TEN MINUTES!
TRAINS
WITH MY LUCK, I SHOULD FIND A FORTUNE IN TEN SECONDS!
UH, OH! ME AND MY BIG MOUTH! I'VE GOT GLADSTONE STARTED ON STAMPS!
TEN SECONDS PASS!
WELL, WELL, I MADE QUITE A HAUL — LOOKS LIKE!

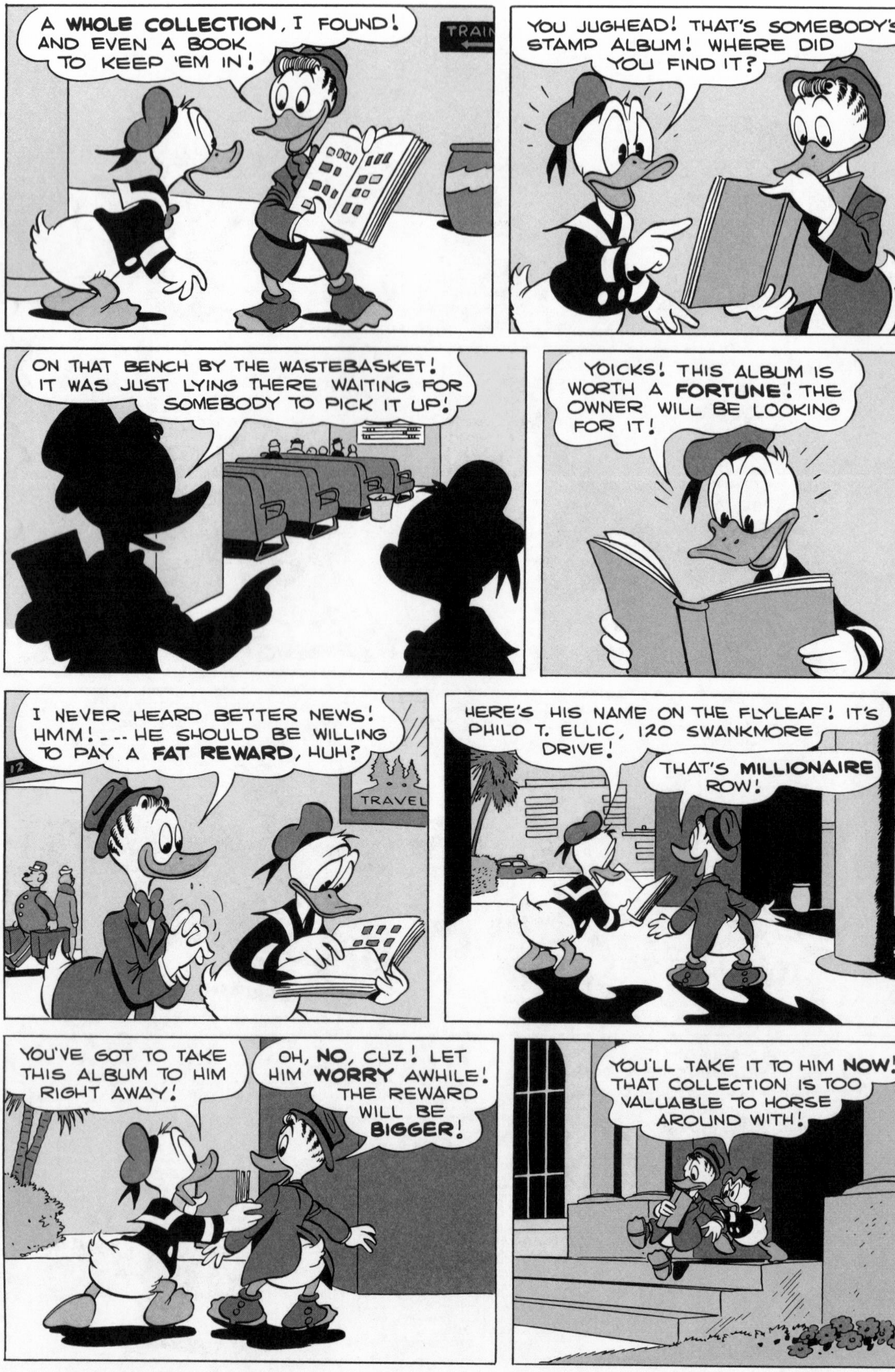
A WHOLE COLLECTION, I FOUND! AND EVEN A BOOK TO KEEP 'EM IN!
TRAIN
YOU JUGHEAD! THAT'S SOMEBODY'S STAMP ALBUM! WHERE DID YOU FIND IT?
ON THAT BENCH BY THE WASTEBASKET! IT WAS JUST LYING THERE WAITING FOR SOMEBODY TO PICK IT UP!
YOICKS! THIS ALBUM IS WORTH A FORTUNE! THE OWNER WILL BE LOOKING FOR IT!
I NEVER HEARD BETTER NEWS! HMM! --- HE SHOULD BE WILLING TO PAY A FAT REWARD, HUH?
TRAVEL
HERE'S HIS NAME ON THE FLYLEAF! IT'S PHILO T. ELLIC, 120 SWANKMORE DRIVE!
THAT'S MILLIONAIRE ROW!
YOU'VE GOT TO TAKE THIS ALBUM TO HIM RIGHT AWAY!
OH, NO, CUZ! LET HIM WORRY AWHILE! THE REWARD WILL BE BIGGER!
YOU'LL TAKE IT TO HIM NOW! THAT COLLECTION IS TOO VALUABLE TO HORSE AROUND WITH!

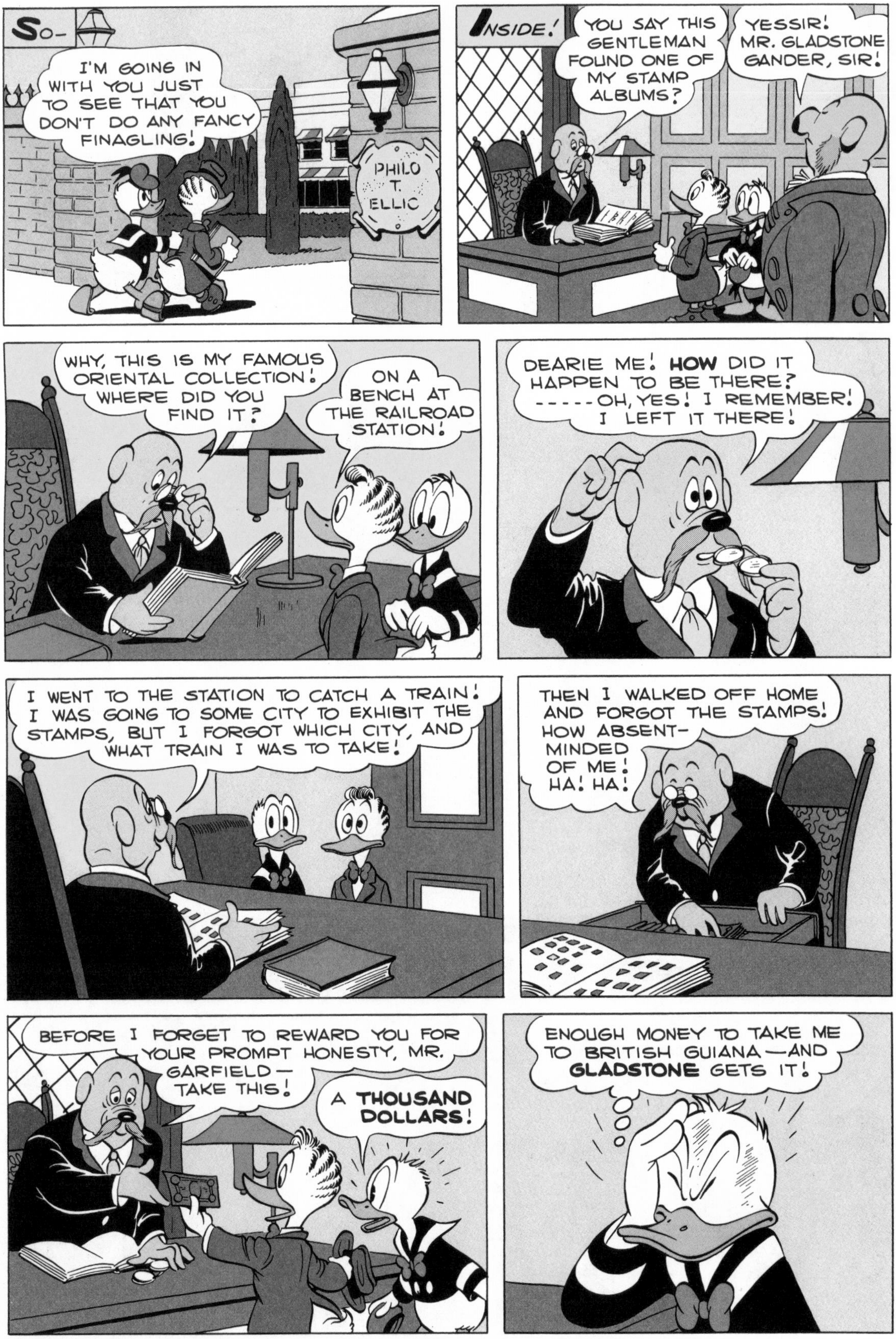
SO-
I'M GOING IN WITH YOU JUST TO SEE THAT YOU DON'T DO ANY FANCY FINAGLING!
PHILO T. ELLIC
INSIDE!
YOU SAY THIS GENTLEMAN FOUND ONE OF MY STAMP ALBUMS?
YESSIR! MR. GLADSTONE GANDER, SIR!
WHY, THIS IS MY FAMOUS ORIENTAL COLLECTION! WHERE DID YOU FIND IT?
ON A BENCH AT THE RAILROAD STATION!
DEARIE ME! **HOW** DID IT HAPPEN TO BE THERE? -----OH, YES! I REMEMBER! I LEFT IT THERE!
I WENT TO THE STATION TO CATCH A TRAIN! I WAS GOING TO SOME CITY TO EXHIBIT THE STAMPS, BUT I FORGOT WHICH CITY, AND WHAT TRAIN I WAS TO TAKE!
THEN I WALKED OFF HOME AND FORGOT THE STAMPS! HOW ABSENT-MINDED OF ME! HA! HA!
BEFORE I FORGET TO REWARD YOU FOR YOUR PROMPT HONESTY, MR. GARFIELD— TAKE THIS!
A **THOUSAND DOLLARS**!
ENOUGH MONEY TO TAKE ME TO BRITISH GUIANA—AND **GLADSTONE** GETS IT!

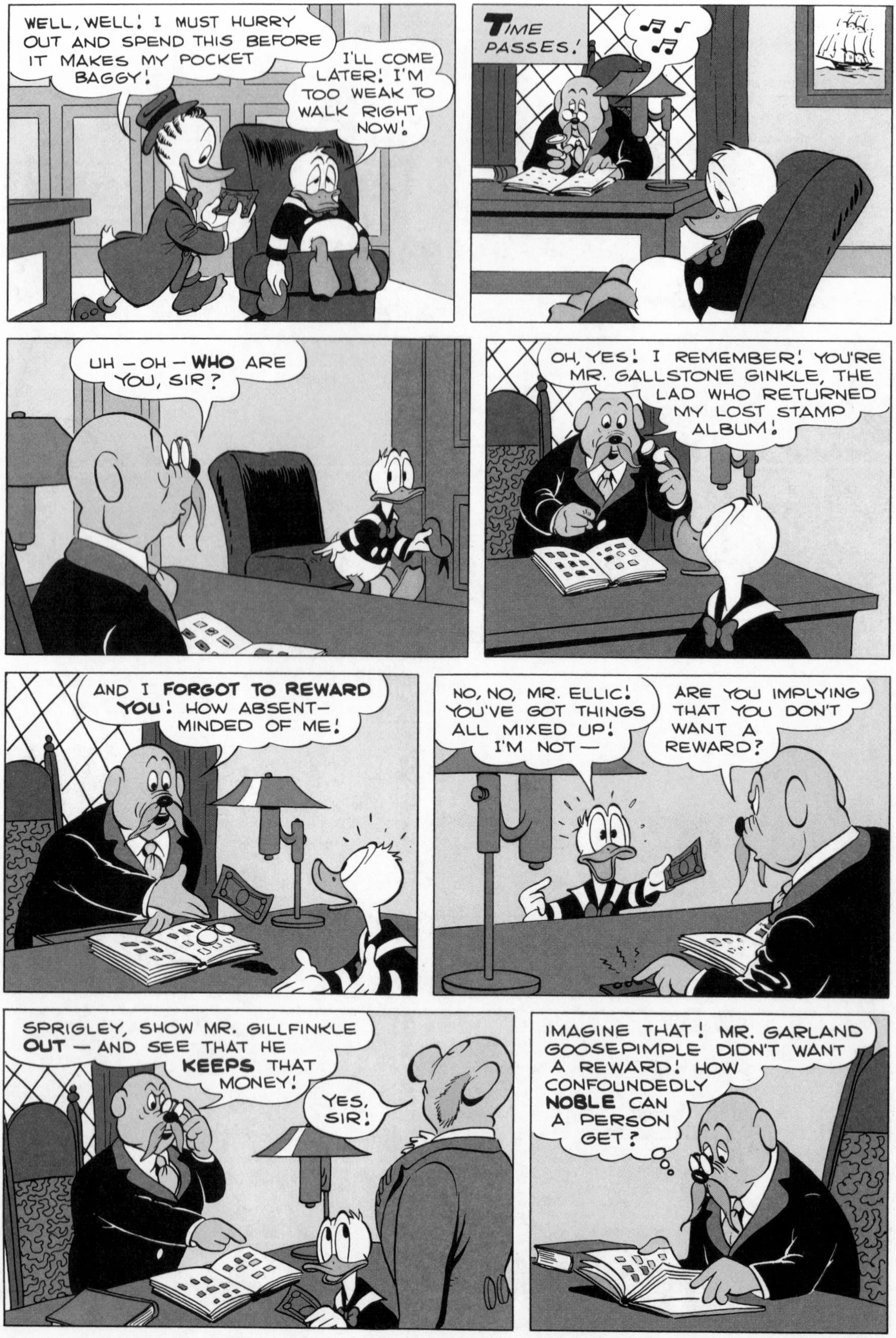
WELL, WELL! I MUST HURRY OUT AND SPEND THIS BEFORE IT MAKES MY POCKET BAGGY!
I'LL COME LATER! I'M TOO WEAK TO WALK RIGHT NOW!
TIME PASSES!
UH — OH — WHO ARE YOU, SIR?
OH, YES! I REMEMBER! YOU'RE MR. GALLSTONE GINKLE, THE LAD WHO RETURNED MY LOST STAMP ALBUM!
AND I FORGOT TO REWARD YOU! HOW ABSENT-MINDED OF ME!
NO, NO, MR. ELLIC! YOU'VE GOT THINGS ALL MIXED UP! I'M NOT —
ARE YOU IMPLYING THAT YOU DON'T WANT A REWARD?
SPRIGLEY, SHOW MR. GILLFINKLE OUT — AND SEE THAT HE KEEPS THAT MONEY!
YES, SIR!
IMAGINE THAT! MR. GARLAND GOOSEPIMPLE DIDN'T WANT A REWARD! HOW CONFOUNDEDLY NOBLE CAN A PERSON GET?

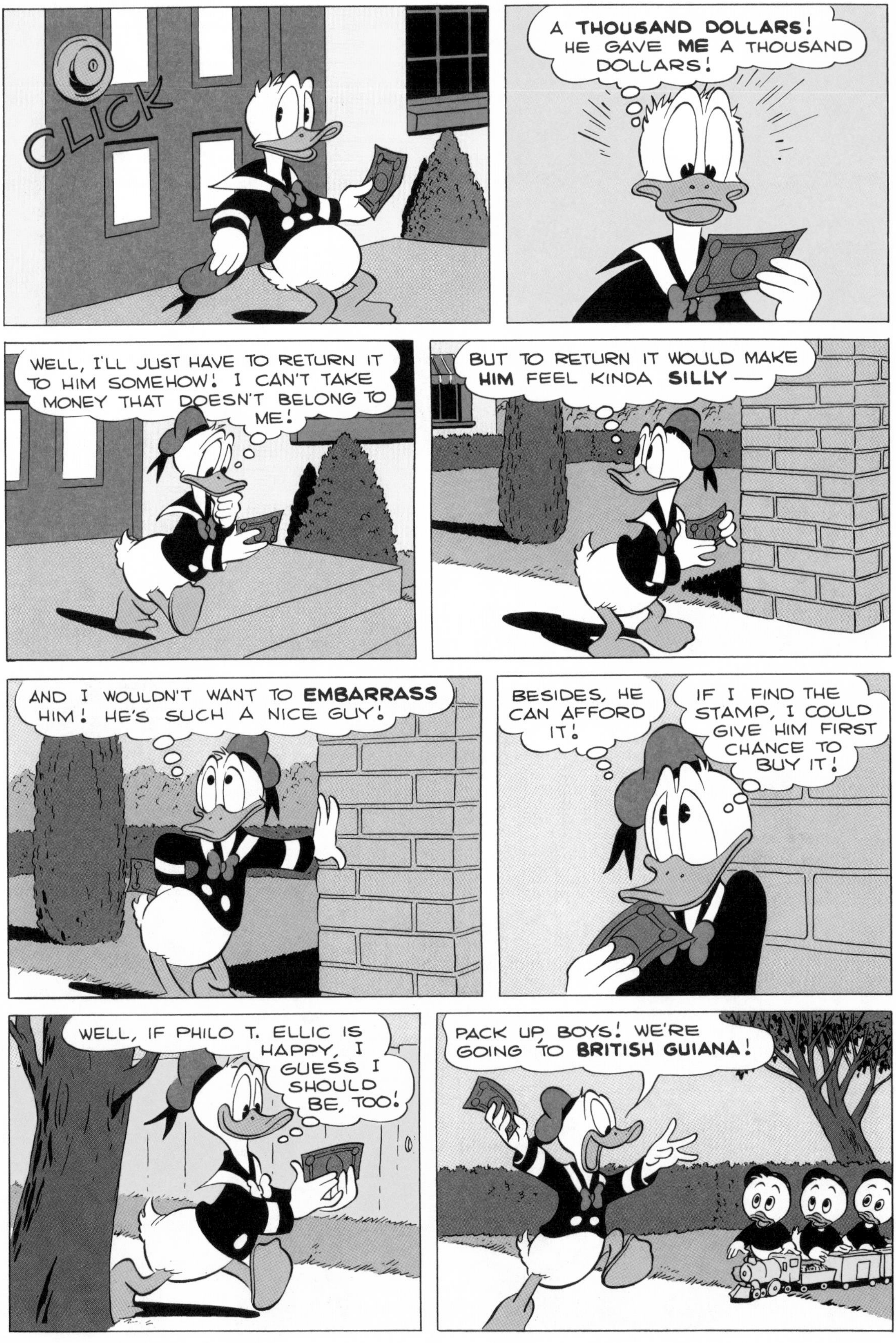
CLICK
A THOUSAND DOLLARS! HE GAVE ME A THOUSAND DOLLARS!
WELL, I'LL JUST HAVE TO RETURN IT TO HIM SOMEHOW! I CAN'T TAKE MONEY THAT DOESN'T BELONG TO ME!
BUT TO RETURN IT WOULD MAKE HIM FEEL KINDA SILLY —
AND I WOULDN'T WANT TO EMBARRASS HIM! HE'S SUCH A NICE GUY!
BESIDES, HE CAN AFFORD IT!
IF I FIND THE STAMP, I COULD GIVE HIM FIRST CHANCE TO BUY IT!
WELL, IF PHILO T. ELLIC IS HAPPY, I GUESS I SHOULD BE, TOO!
PACK UP, BOYS! WE'RE GOING TO BRITISH GUIANA!

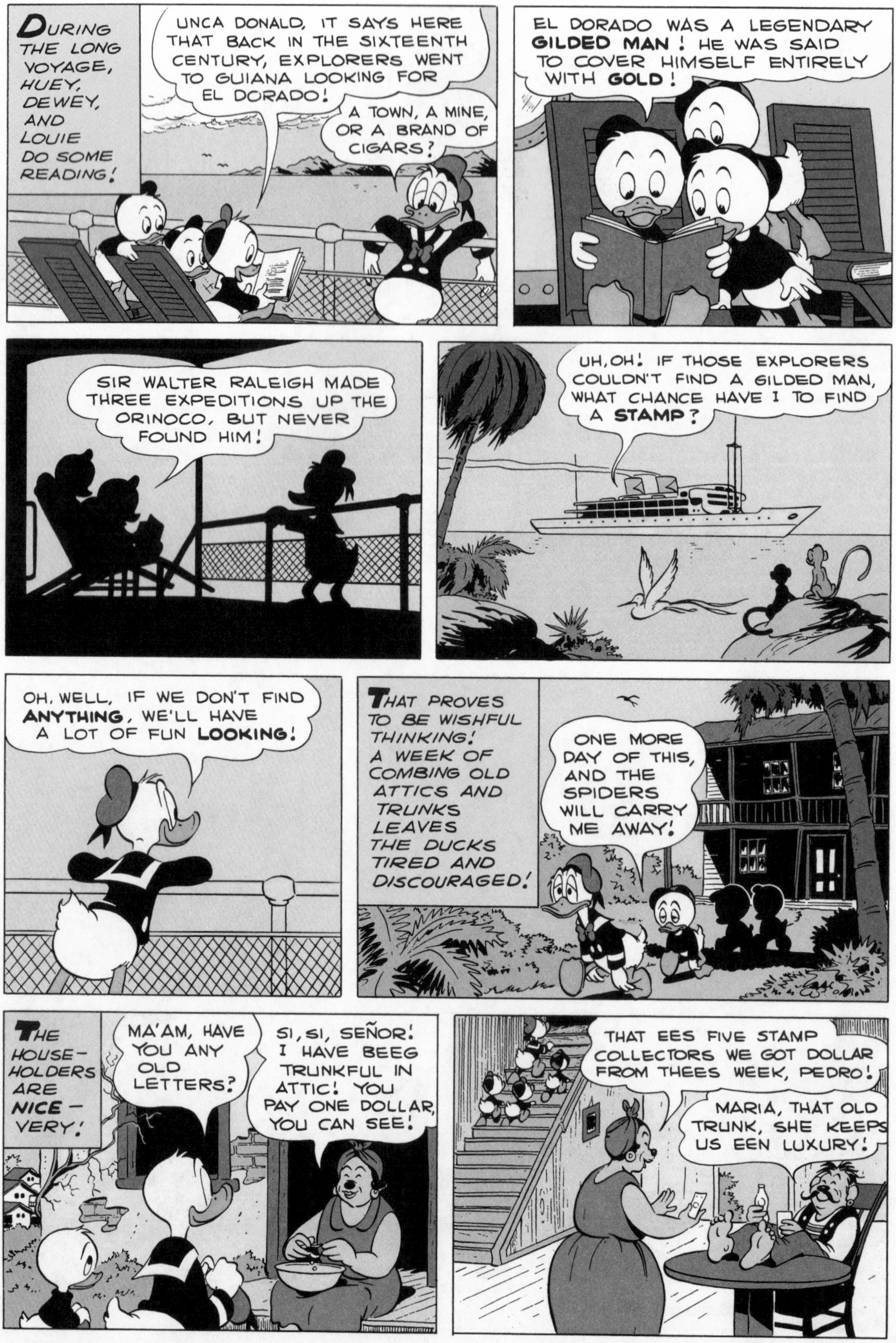
DURING THE LONG VOYAGE, HUEY, DEWEY, AND LOUIE DO SOME READING!
UNCA DONALD, IT SAYS HERE THAT BACK IN THE SIXTEENTH CENTURY, EXPLORERS WENT TO GUIANA LOOKING FOR EL DORADO!
A TOWN, A MINE, OR A BRAND OF CIGARS?
EL DORADO WAS A LEGENDARY GILDED MAN! HE WAS SAID TO COVER HIMSELF ENTIRELY WITH GOLD!
SIR WALTER RALEIGH MADE THREE EXPEDITIONS UP THE ORINOCO, BUT NEVER FOUND HIM!
UH, OH! IF THOSE EXPLORERS COULDN'T FIND A GILDED MAN, WHAT CHANCE HAVE I TO FIND A STAMP?
OH, WELL, IF WE DON'T FIND ANYTHING, WE'LL HAVE A LOT OF FUN LOOKING!
THAT PROVES TO BE WISHFUL THINKING! A WEEK OF COMBING OLD ATTICS AND TRUNKS LEAVES THE DUCKS TIRED AND DISCOURAGED!
ONE MORE DAY OF THIS, AND THE SPIDERS WILL CARRY ME AWAY!
THE HOUSE-HOLDERS ARE NICE—VERY!
MA'AM, HAVE YOU ANY OLD LETTERS?
SI, SI, SEÑOR! I HAVE BEEG TRUNKFUL IN ATTIC! YOU PAY ONE DOLLAR, YOU CAN SEE!
THAT EES FIVE STAMP COLLECTORS WE GOT DOLLAR FROM THEES WEEK, PEDRO!
MARIA, THAT OLD TRUNK, SHE KEEPS US EEN LUXURY!

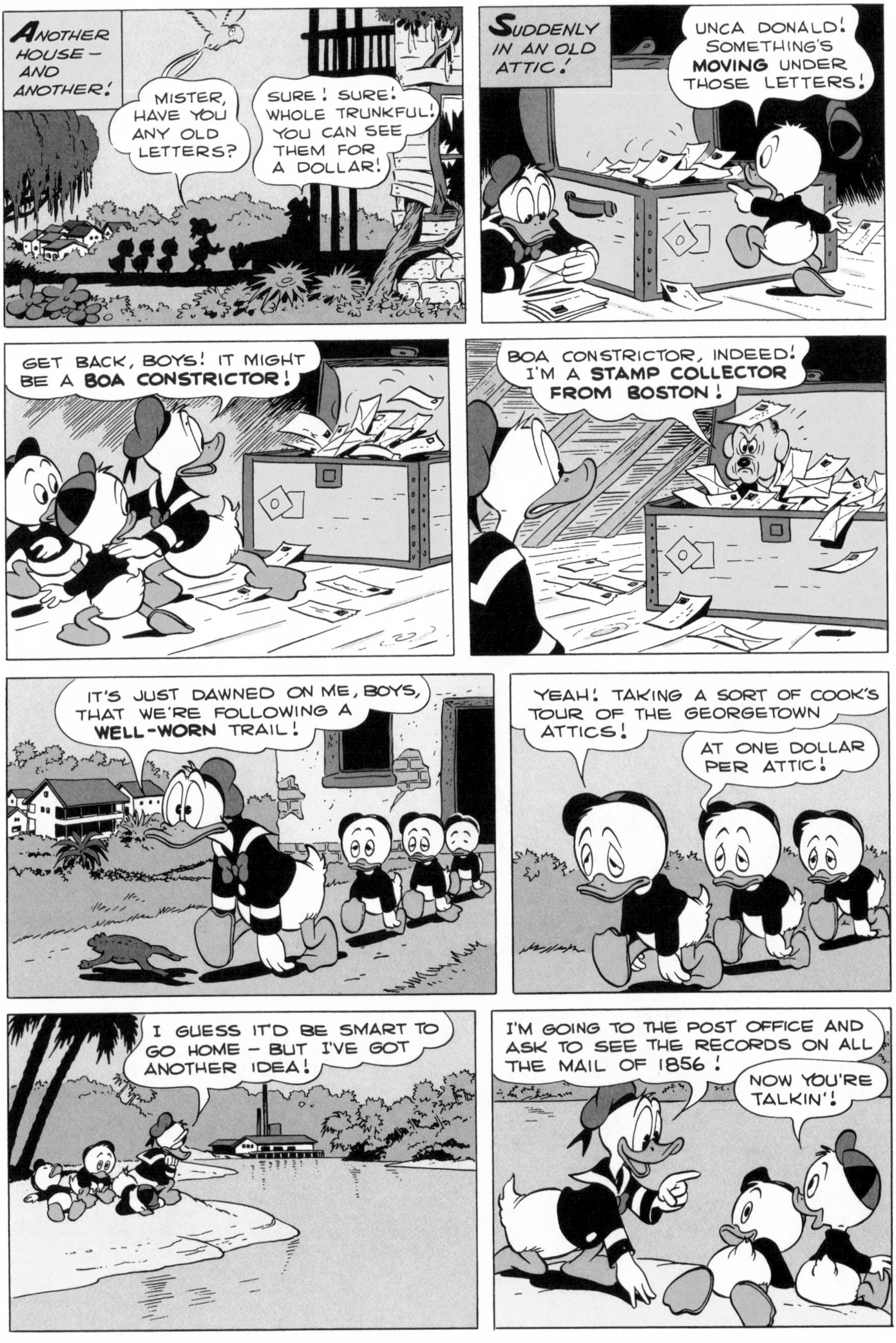
ANOTHER HOUSE — AND ANOTHER!
MISTER, HAVE YOU ANY OLD LETTERS?
SURE! SURE! WHOLE TRUNKFUL! YOU CAN SEE THEM FOR A DOLLAR!
SUDDENLY IN AN OLD ATTIC!
UNCA DONALD! SOMETHING'S MOVING UNDER THOSE LETTERS!
GET BACK, BOYS! IT MIGHT BE A BOA CONSTRICTOR!
BOA CONSTRICTOR, INDEED! I'M A STAMP COLLECTOR FROM BOSTON!
IT'S JUST DAWNED ON ME, BOYS, THAT WE'RE FOLLOWING A WELL-WORN TRAIL!
YEAH! TAKING A SORT OF COOK'S TOUR OF THE GEORGETOWN ATTICS!
AT ONE DOLLAR PER ATTIC!
I GUESS IT'D BE SMART TO GO HOME — BUT I'VE GOT ANOTHER IDEA!
I'M GOING TO THE POST OFFICE AND ASK TO SEE THE RECORDS ON ALL THE MAIL OF 1856!
NOW YOU'RE TALKIN'!

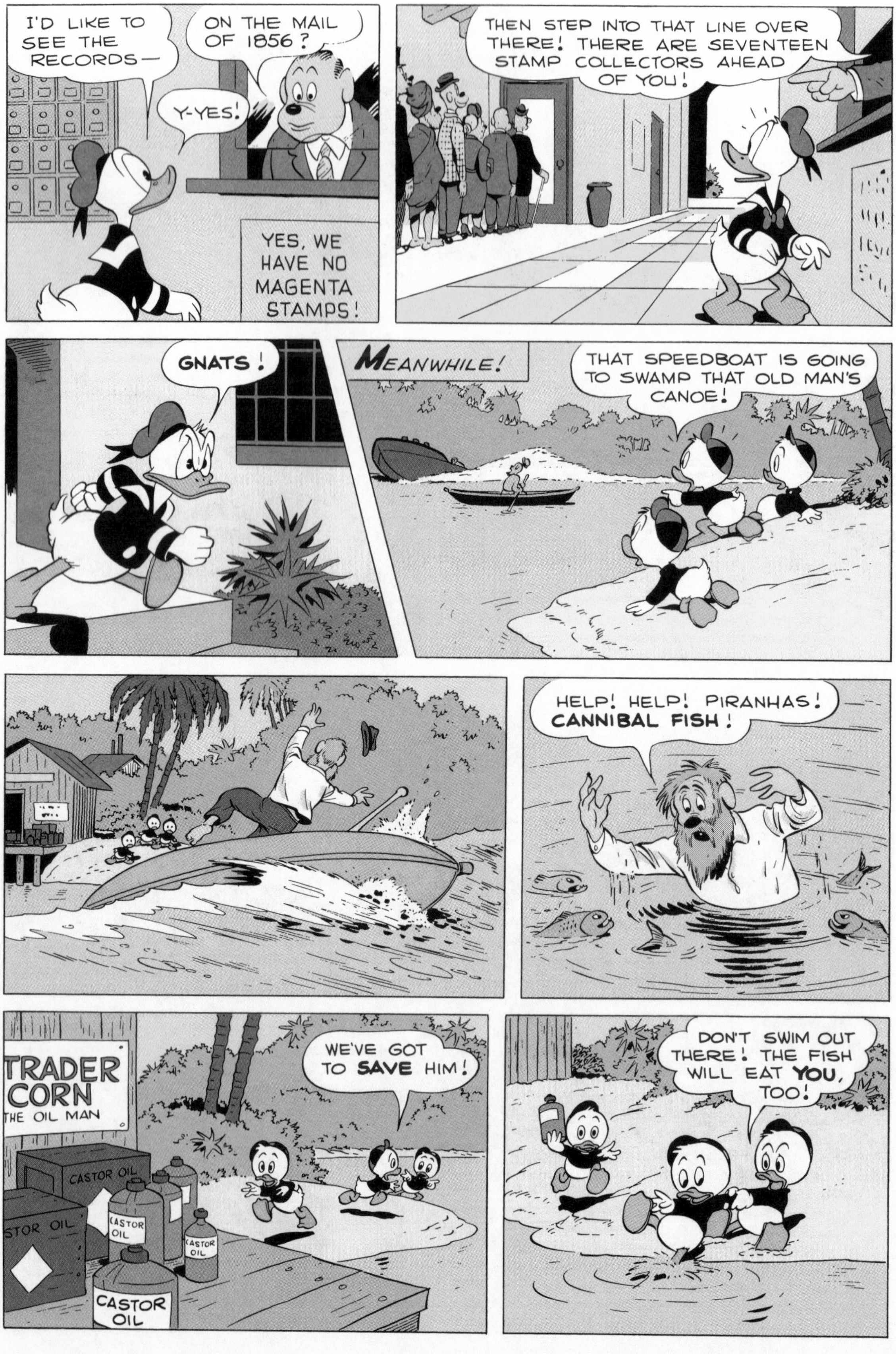
I'D LIKE TO SEE THE RECORDS—
ON THE MAIL OF 1856?
Y-YES!
YES, WE HAVE NO MAGENTA STAMPS!
THEN STEP INTO THAT LINE OVER THERE! THERE ARE SEVENTEEN STAMP COLLECTORS AHEAD OF YOU!
GNATS!
MEANWHILE!
THAT SPEEDBOAT IS GOING TO SWAMP THAT OLD MAN'S CANOE!
HELP! HELP! PIRANHAS! CANNIBAL FISH!
TRADER CORN
THE OIL MAN
CASTOR OIL
STOR OIL
CASTOR OIL
CASTOR OIL
CASTOR OIL
WE'VE GOT TO SAVE HIM!
DON'T SWIM OUT THERE! THE FISH WILL EAT YOU, TOO!

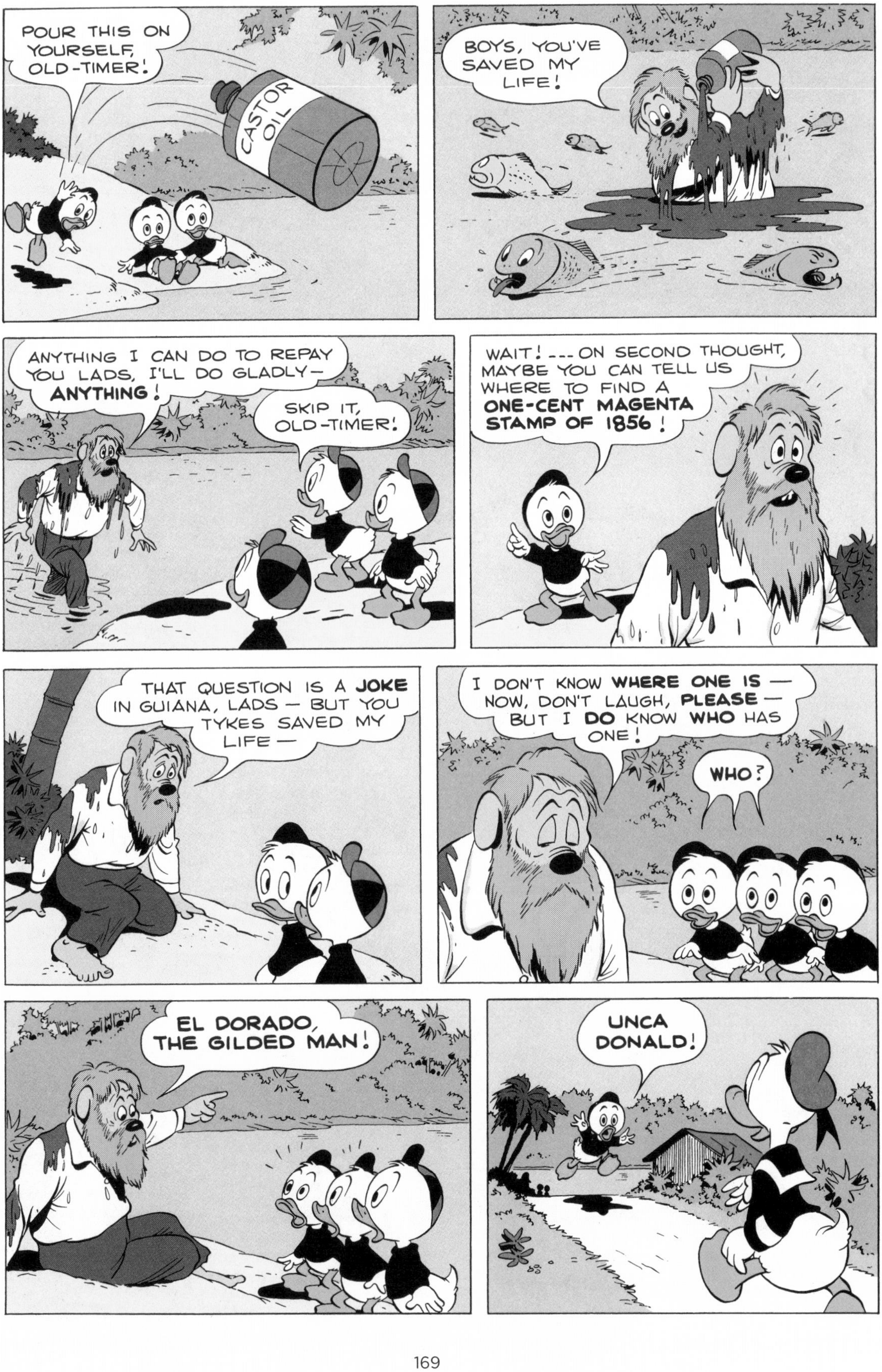
POUR THIS ON YOURSELF, OLD-TIMER!
CASTOR OIL
BOYS, YOU'VE SAVED MY LIFE!
ANYTHING I CAN DO TO REPAY YOU LADS, I'LL DO GLADLY— ANYTHING!
SKIP IT, OLD-TIMER!
WAIT! --- ON SECOND THOUGHT, MAYBE YOU CAN TELL US WHERE TO FIND A ONE-CENT MAGENTA STAMP OF 1856!
THAT QUESTION IS A JOKE IN GUIANA, LADS — BUT YOU TYKES SAVED MY LIFE —
I DON'T KNOW WHERE ONE IS — NOW, DON'T LAUGH, PLEASE — BUT I DO KNOW WHO HAS ONE!
WHO?
EL DORADO, THE GILDED MAN!
UNCA DONALD!

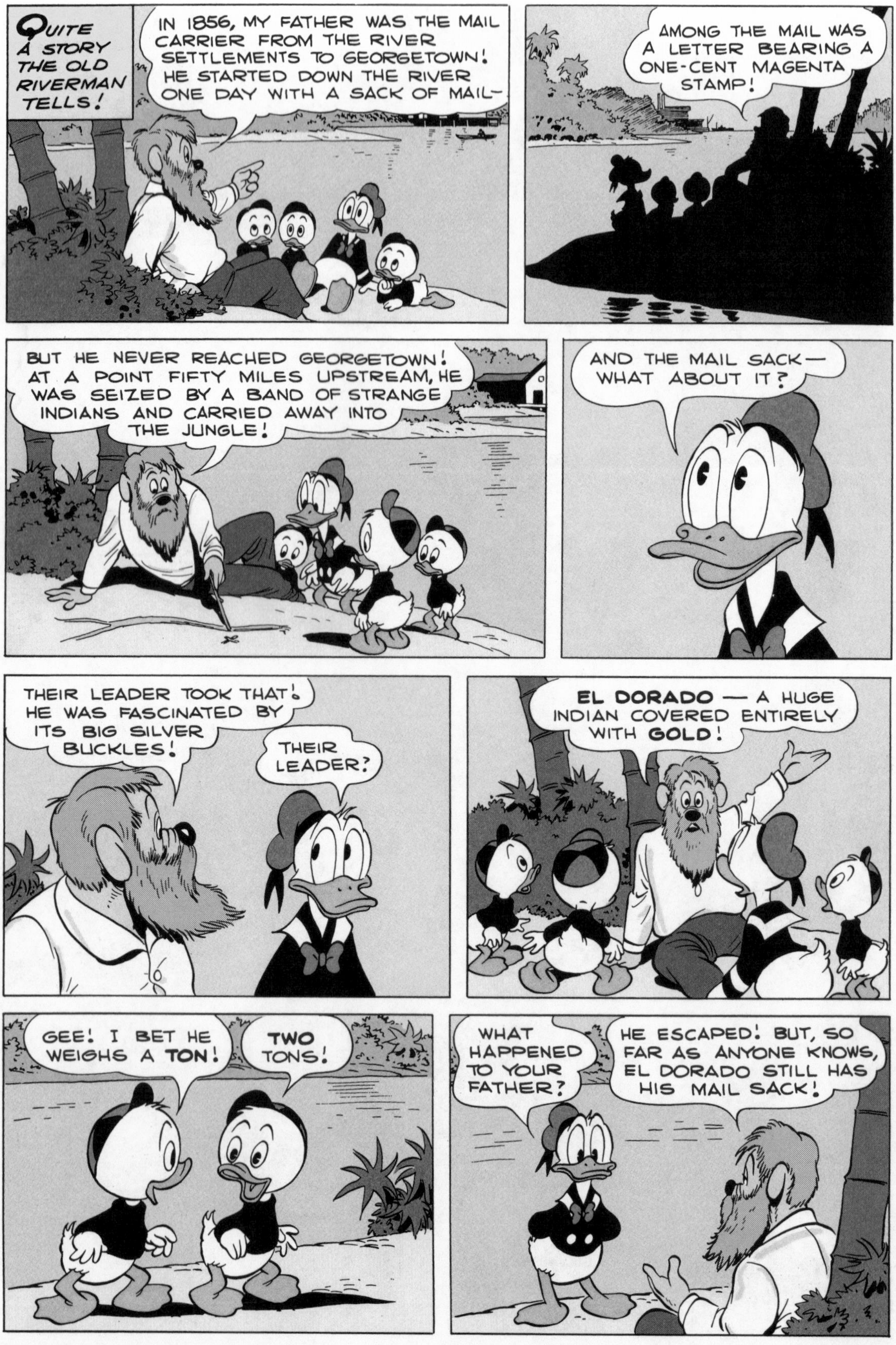
QUITE A STORY THE OLD RIVERMAN TELLS!
IN 1856, MY FATHER WAS THE MAIL CARRIER FROM THE RIVER SETTLEMENTS TO GEORGETOWN! HE STARTED DOWN THE RIVER ONE DAY WITH A SACK OF MAIL—
AMONG THE MAIL WAS A LETTER BEARING A ONE-CENT MAGENTA STAMP!
BUT HE NEVER REACHED GEORGETOWN! AT A POINT FIFTY MILES UPSTREAM, HE WAS SEIZED BY A BAND OF STRANGE INDIANS AND CARRIED AWAY INTO THE JUNGLE!
AND THE MAIL SACK— WHAT ABOUT IT?
THEIR LEADER TOOK THAT! HE WAS FASCINATED BY ITS BIG SILVER BUCKLES!
THEIR LEADER?
EL DORADO — A HUGE INDIAN COVERED ENTIRELY WITH GOLD!
GEE! I BET HE WEIGHS A TON!
TWO TONS!
WHAT HAPPENED TO YOUR FATHER?
HE ESCAPED! BUT, SO FAR AS ANYONE KNOWS, EL DORADO STILL HAS HIS MAIL SACK!

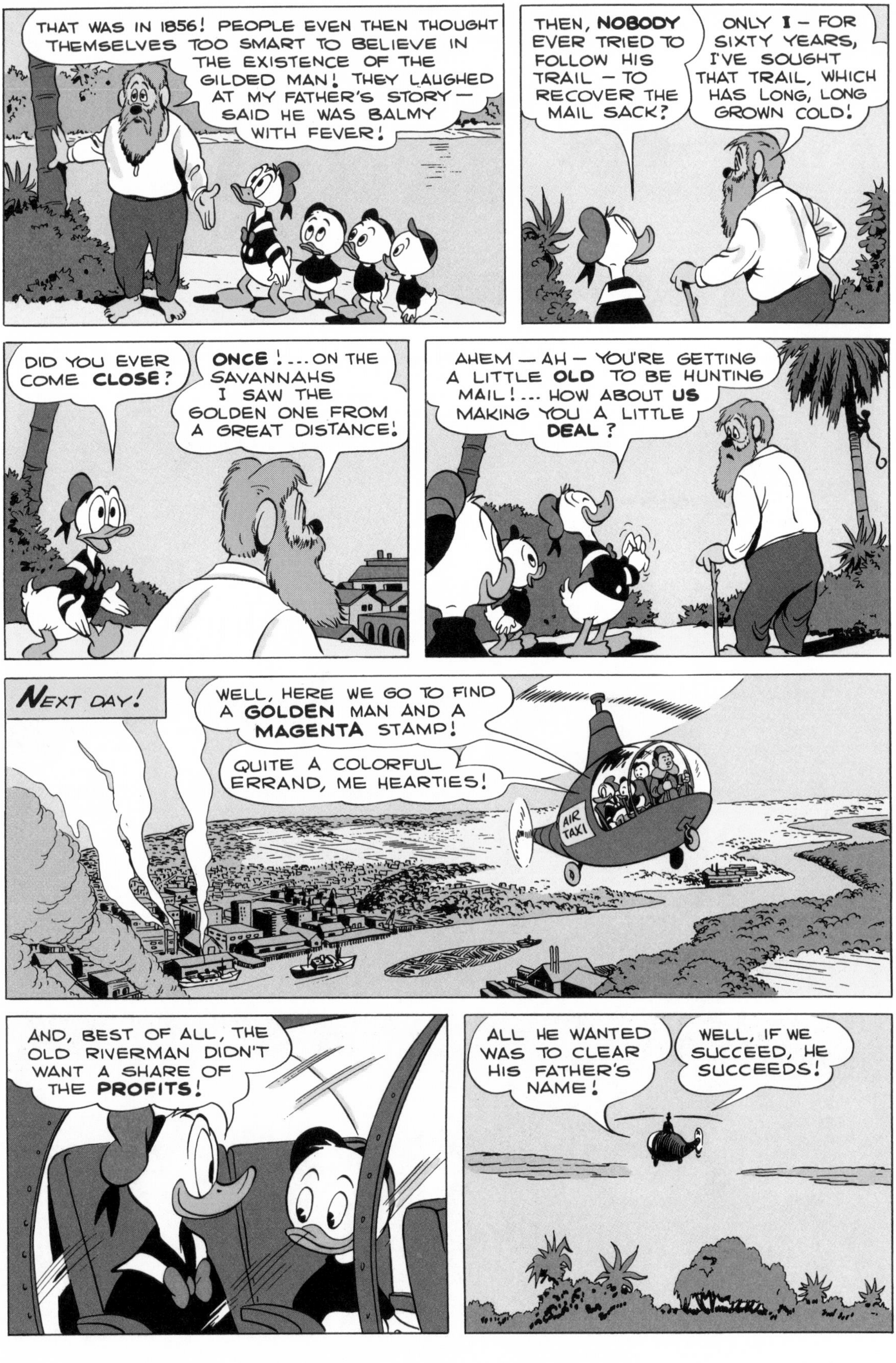
THAT WAS IN 1856! PEOPLE EVEN THEN THOUGHT THEMSELVES TOO SMART TO BELIEVE IN THE EXISTENCE OF THE GILDED MAN! THEY LAUGHED AT MY FATHER'S STORY — SAID HE WAS BALMY WITH FEVER!
THEN, NOBODY EVER TRIED TO FOLLOW HIS TRAIL — TO RECOVER THE MAIL SACK?
ONLY I — FOR SIXTY YEARS, I'VE SOUGHT THAT TRAIL, WHICH HAS LONG, LONG GROWN COLD!
DID YOU EVER COME CLOSE?
ONCE!... ON THE SAVANNAHS I SAW THE GOLDEN ONE FROM A GREAT DISTANCE!
AHEM — AH — YOU'RE GETTING A LITTLE OLD TO BE HUNTING MAIL!... HOW ABOUT US MAKING YOU A LITTLE DEAL?
NEXT DAY!
WELL, HERE WE GO TO FIND A GOLDEN MAN AND A MAGENTA STAMP!
QUITE A COLORFUL ERRAND, ME HEARTIES!
AIR TAXI
AND, BEST OF ALL, THE OLD RIVERMAN DIDN'T WANT A SHARE OF THE PROFITS!
ALL HE WANTED WAS TO CLEAR HIS FATHER'S NAME!
WELL, IF WE SUCCEED, HE SUCCEEDS!

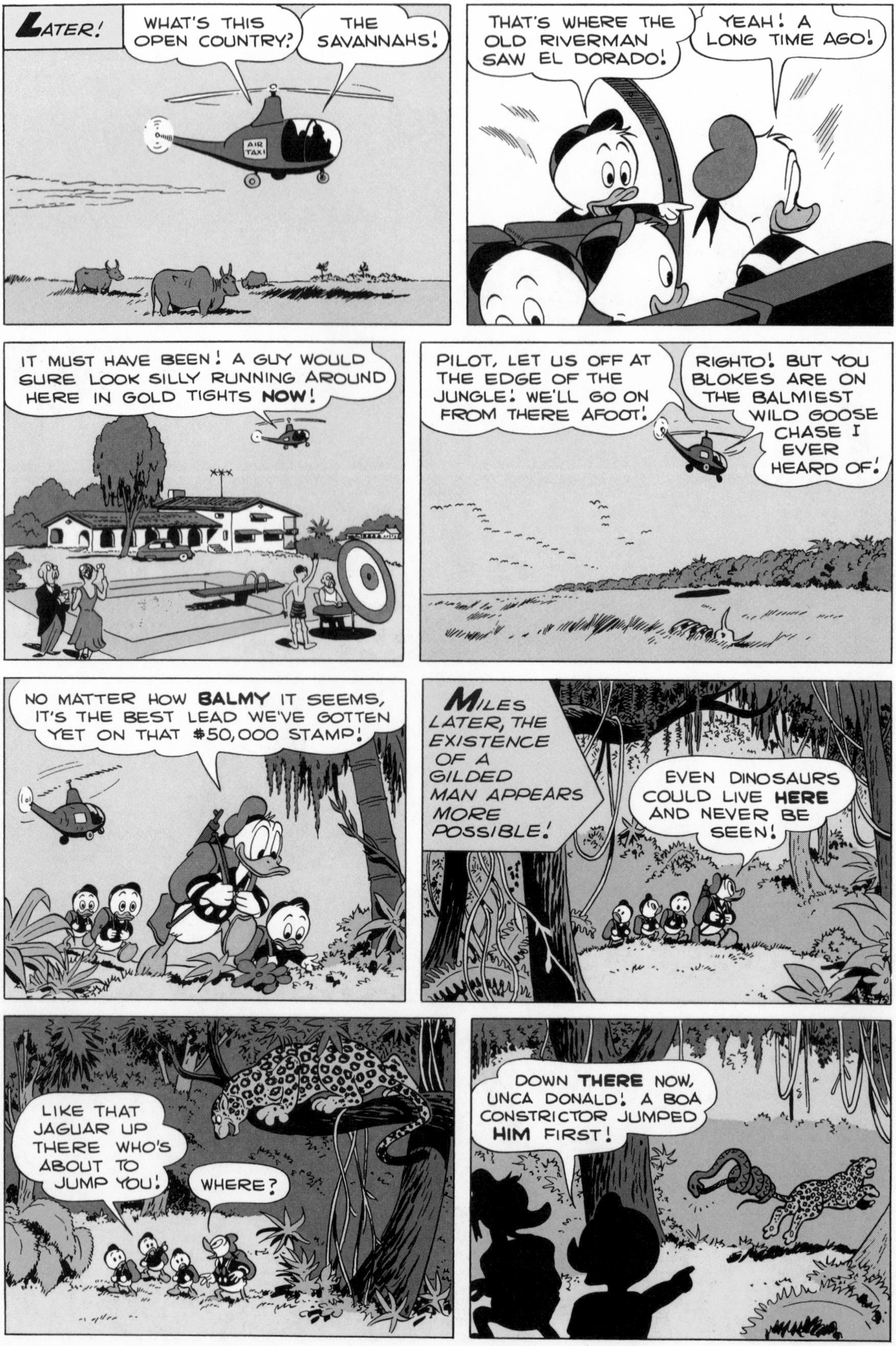
LATER!
WHAT'S THIS OPEN COUNTRY?
THE SAVANNAHS!
AIR TAXI
THAT'S WHERE THE OLD RIVERMAN SAW EL DORADO!
YEAH! A LONG TIME AGO!
IT MUST HAVE BEEN! A GUY WOULD SURE LOOK SILLY RUNNING AROUND HERE IN GOLD TIGHTS NOW!
PILOT, LET US OFF AT THE EDGE OF THE JUNGLE! WE'LL GO ON FROM THERE AFOOT!
RIGHTO! BUT YOU BLOKES ARE ON THE BALMIEST WILD GOOSE CHASE I EVER HEARD OF!
NO MATTER HOW BALMY IT SEEMS, IT'S THE BEST LEAD WE'VE GOTTEN YET ON THAT $50,000 STAMP!
MILES LATER, THE EXISTENCE OF A GILDED MAN APPEARS MORE POSSIBLE!
EVEN DINOSAURS COULD LIVE HERE AND NEVER BE SEEN!
LIKE THAT JAGUAR UP THERE WHO'S ABOUT TO JUMP YOU!
WHERE?
DOWN THERE NOW, UNCA DONALD! A BOA CONSTRICTOR JUMPED HIM FIRST!

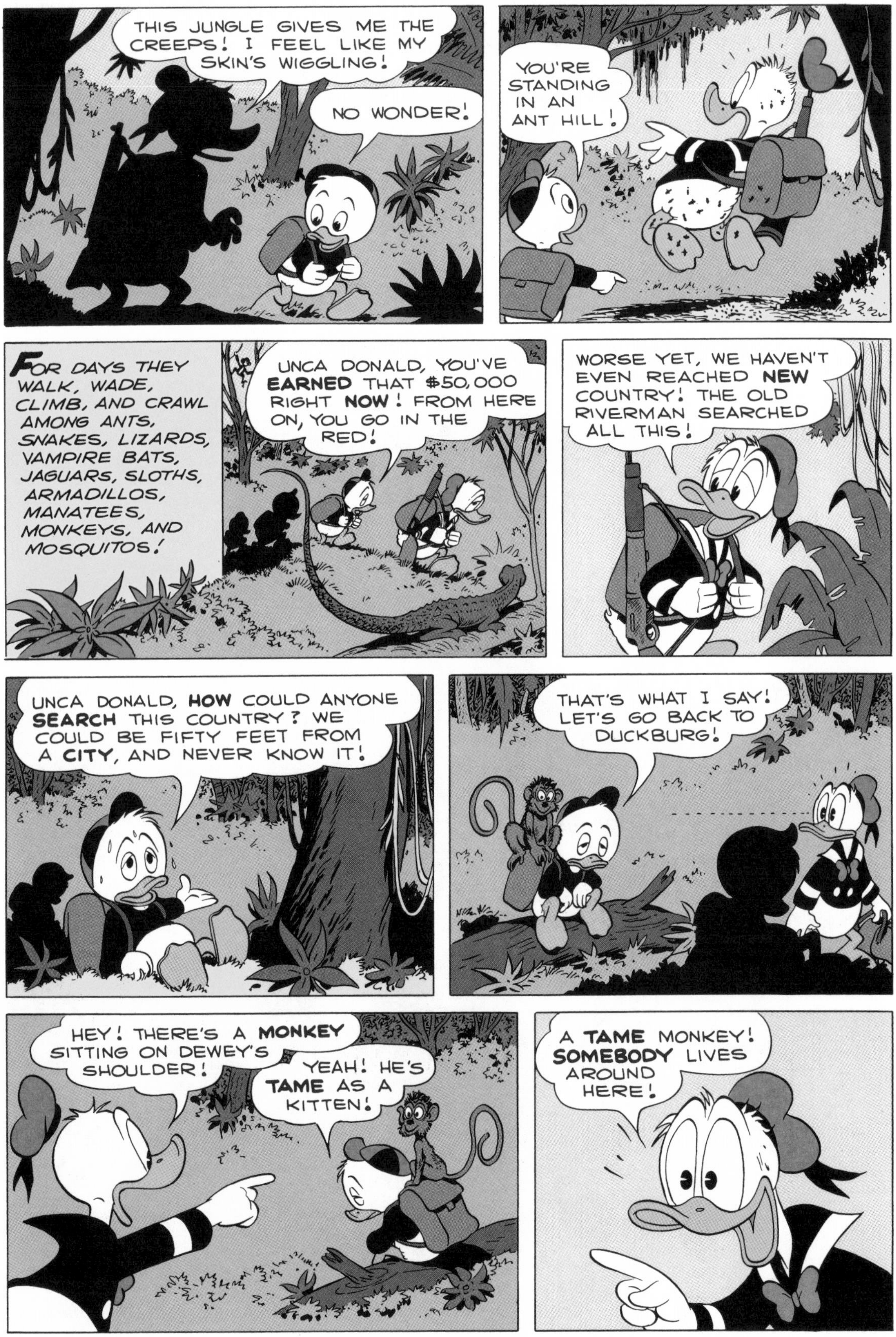
THIS JUNGLE GIVES ME THE CREEPS! I FEEL LIKE MY SKIN'S WIGGLING!
NO WONDER!
YOU'RE STANDING IN AN ANT HILL!
FOR DAYS THEY WALK, WADE, CLIMB, AND CRAWL AMONG ANTS, SNAKES, LIZARDS, VAMPIRE BATS, JAGUARS, SLOTHS, ARMADILLOS, MANATEES, MONKEYS, AND MOSQUITOS!
UNCA DONALD, YOU'VE **EARNED** THAT $50,000 RIGHT **NOW**! FROM HERE ON, YOU GO IN THE RED!
WORSE YET, WE HAVEN'T EVEN REACHED **NEW** COUNTRY! THE OLD RIVERMAN SEARCHED ALL THIS!
UNCA DONALD, **HOW** COULD ANYONE **SEARCH** THIS COUNTRY? WE COULD BE FIFTY FEET FROM A **CITY**, AND NEVER KNOW IT!
THAT'S WHAT I SAY! LET'S GO BACK TO DUCKBURG!
HEY! THERE'S A **MONKEY** SITTING ON DEWEY'S SHOULDER!
YEAH! HE'S **TAME** AS A KITTEN!
A **TAME** MONKEY! **SOMEBODY** LIVES AROUND HERE!

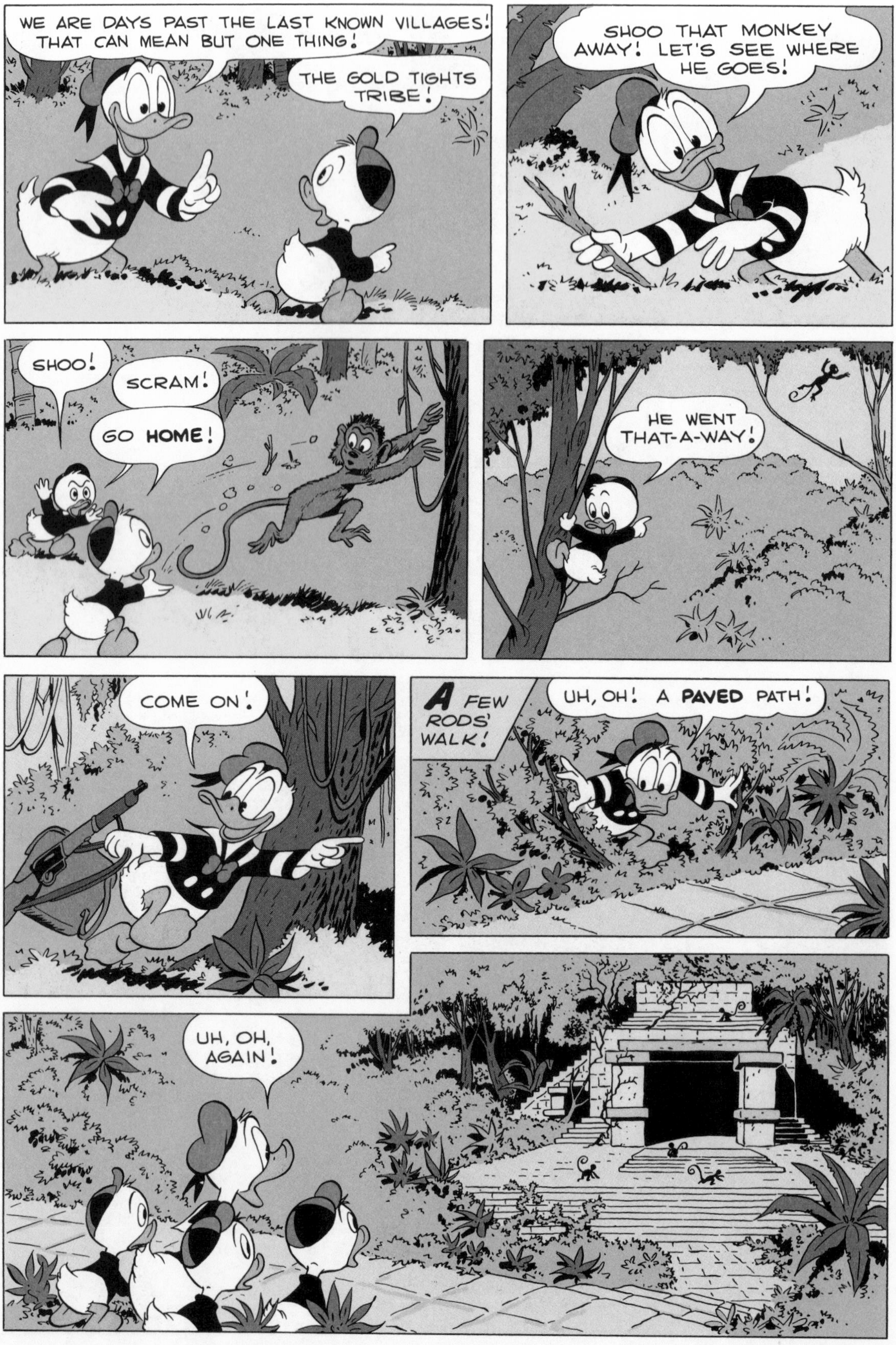
WE ARE DAYS PAST THE LAST KNOWN VILLAGES! THAT CAN MEAN BUT ONE THING!
THE GOLD TIGHTS TRIBE!
SHOO THAT MONKEY AWAY! LET'S SEE WHERE HE GOES!
SHOO!
SCRAM!
GO HOME!
HE WENT THAT-A-WAY!
COME ON!
A FEW RODS' WALK!
UH, OH! A PAVED PATH!
UH, OH, AGAIN!

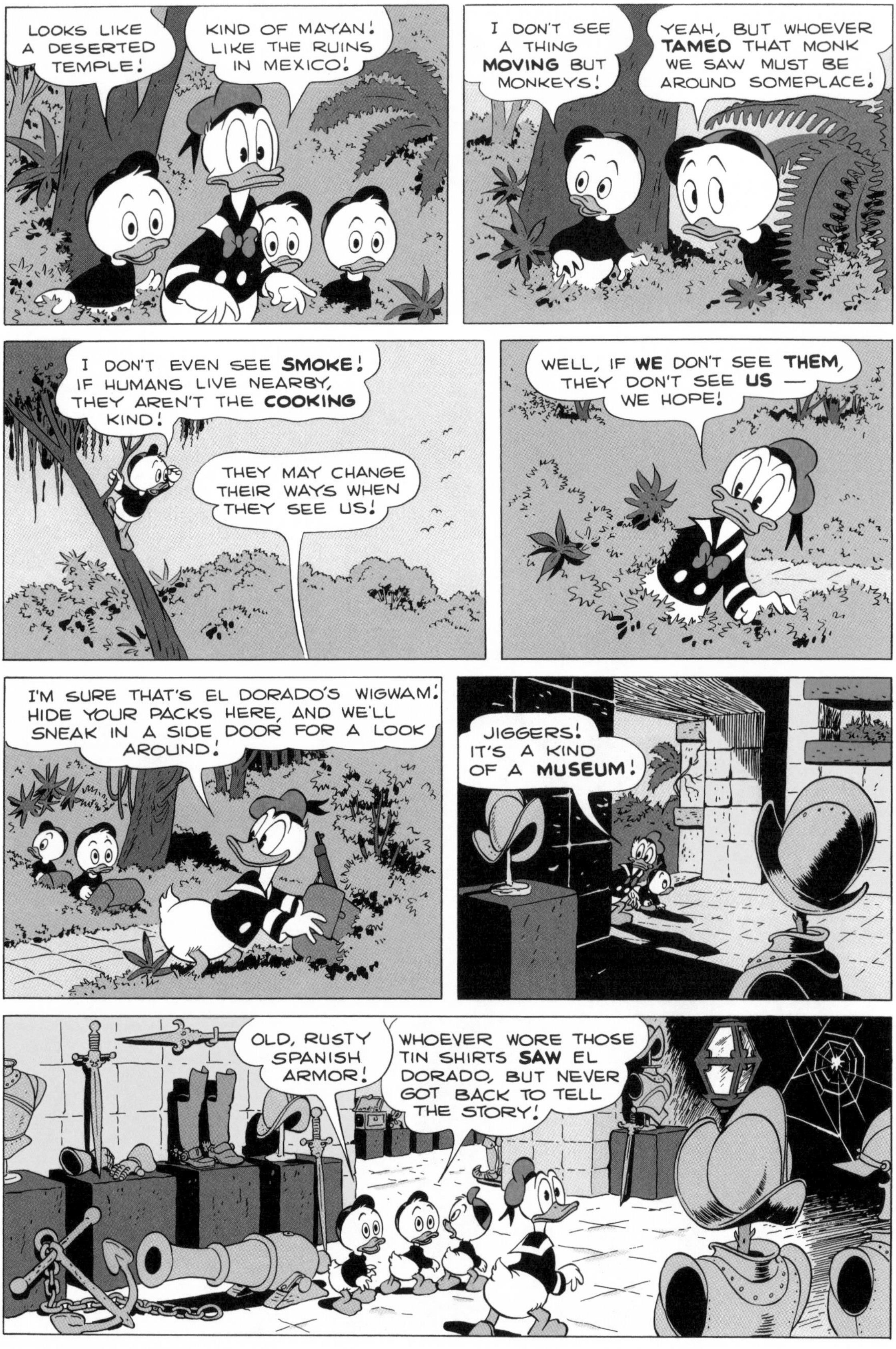
LOOKS LIKE A DESERTED TEMPLE!
KIND OF MAYAN! LIKE THE RUINS IN MEXICO!
I DON'T SEE A THING MOVING BUT MONKEYS!
YEAH, BUT WHOEVER TAMED THAT MONK WE SAW MUST BE AROUND SOMEPLACE!
I DON'T EVEN SEE SMOKE! IF HUMANS LIVE NEARBY, THEY AREN'T THE COOKING KIND!
THEY MAY CHANGE THEIR WAYS WHEN THEY SEE US!
WELL, IF WE DON'T SEE THEM, THEY DON'T SEE US — WE HOPE!
I'M SURE THAT'S EL DORADO'S WIGWAM! HIDE YOUR PACKS HERE, AND WE'LL SNEAK IN A SIDE DOOR FOR A LOOK AROUND!
JIGGERS! IT'S A KIND OF A MUSEUM!
OLD, RUSTY SPANISH ARMOR!
WHOEVER WORE THOSE TIN SHIRTS SAW EL DORADO, BUT NEVER GOT BACK TO TELL THE STORY!

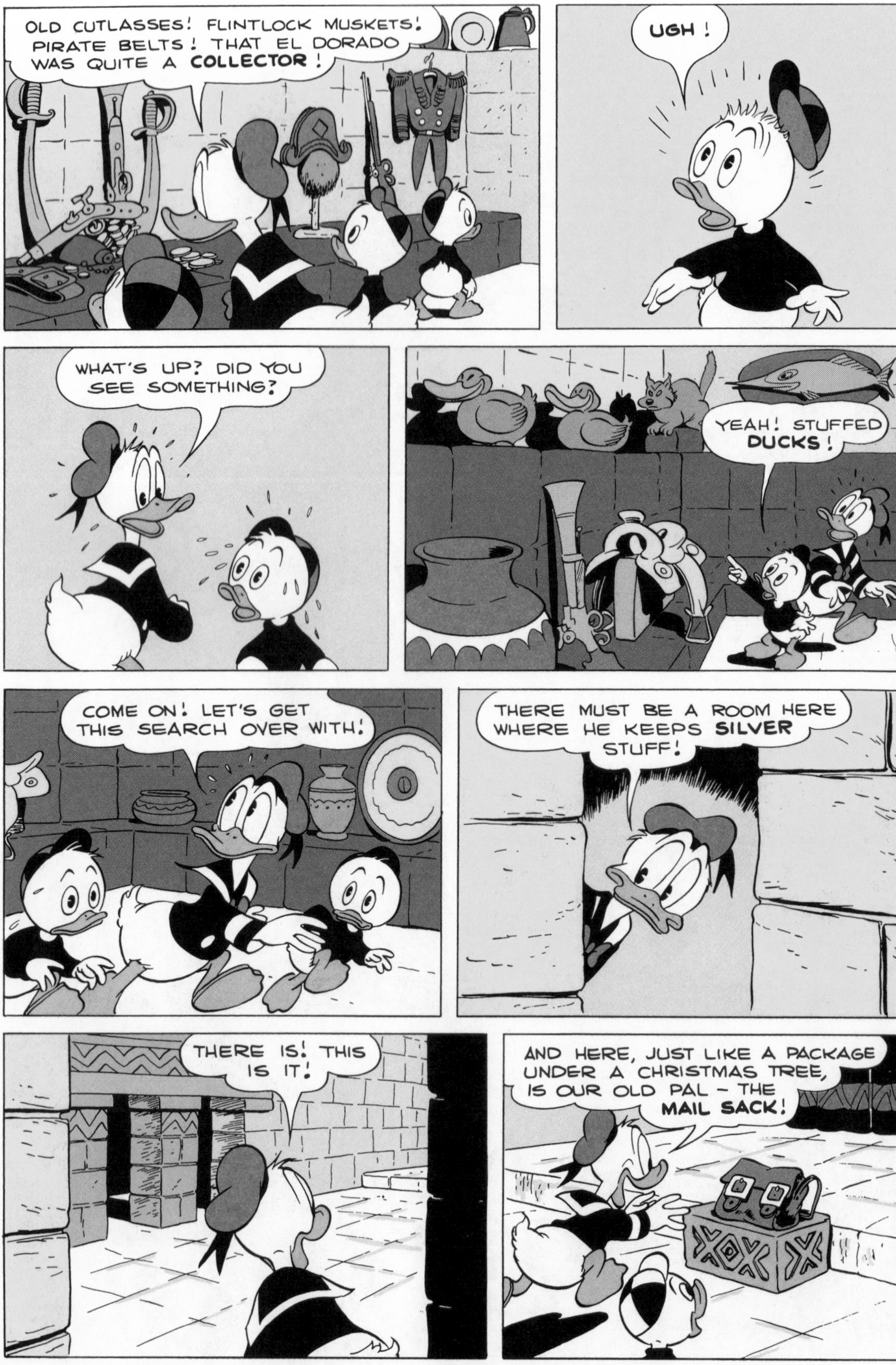
OLD CUTLASSES! FLINTLOCK MUSKETS! PIRATE BELTS! THAT EL DORADO WAS QUITE A **COLLECTOR**!
UGH!
WHAT'S UP? DID YOU SEE SOMETHING?
YEAH! STUFFED **DUCKS**!
COME ON! LET'S GET THIS SEARCH OVER WITH!
THERE MUST BE A ROOM HERE WHERE HE KEEPS **SILVER** STUFF!
THERE IS! THIS IS IT!
AND HERE, JUST LIKE A PACKAGE UNDER A CHRISTMAS TREE, IS OUR OLD PAL – THE **MAIL SACK**!

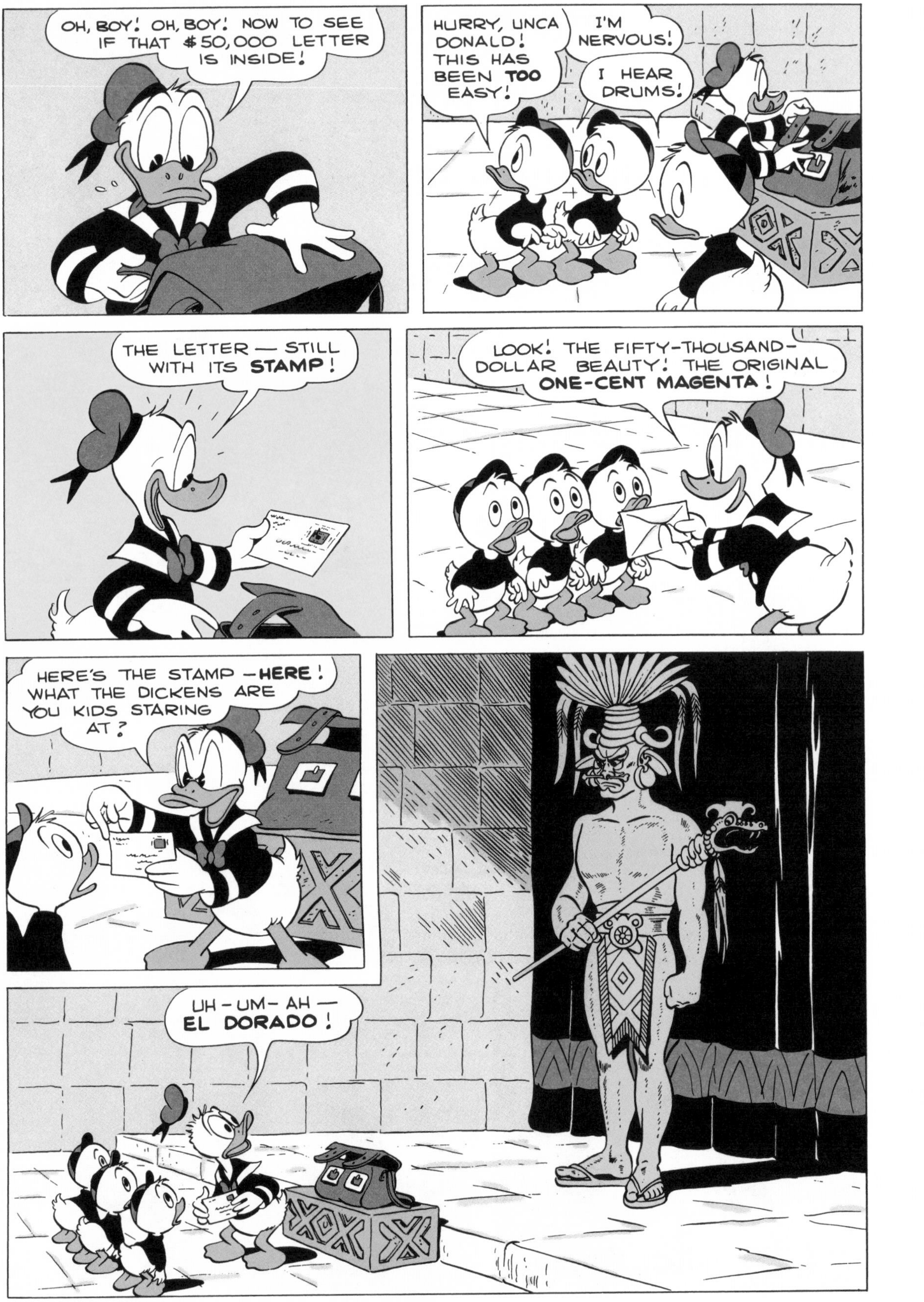
OH, BOY! OH, BOY! NOW TO SEE IF THAT $50,000 LETTER IS INSIDE!
HURRY, UNCA DONALD! THIS HAS BEEN TOO EASY!
I'M NERVOUS!
I HEAR DRUMS!
THE LETTER — STILL WITH ITS STAMP!
LOOK! THE FIFTY-THOUSAND-DOLLAR BEAUTY! THE ORIGINAL ONE-CENT MAGENTA!
HERE'S THE STAMP — HERE! WHAT THE DICKENS ARE YOU KIDS STARING AT?
UH-UM-AH — EL DORADO!

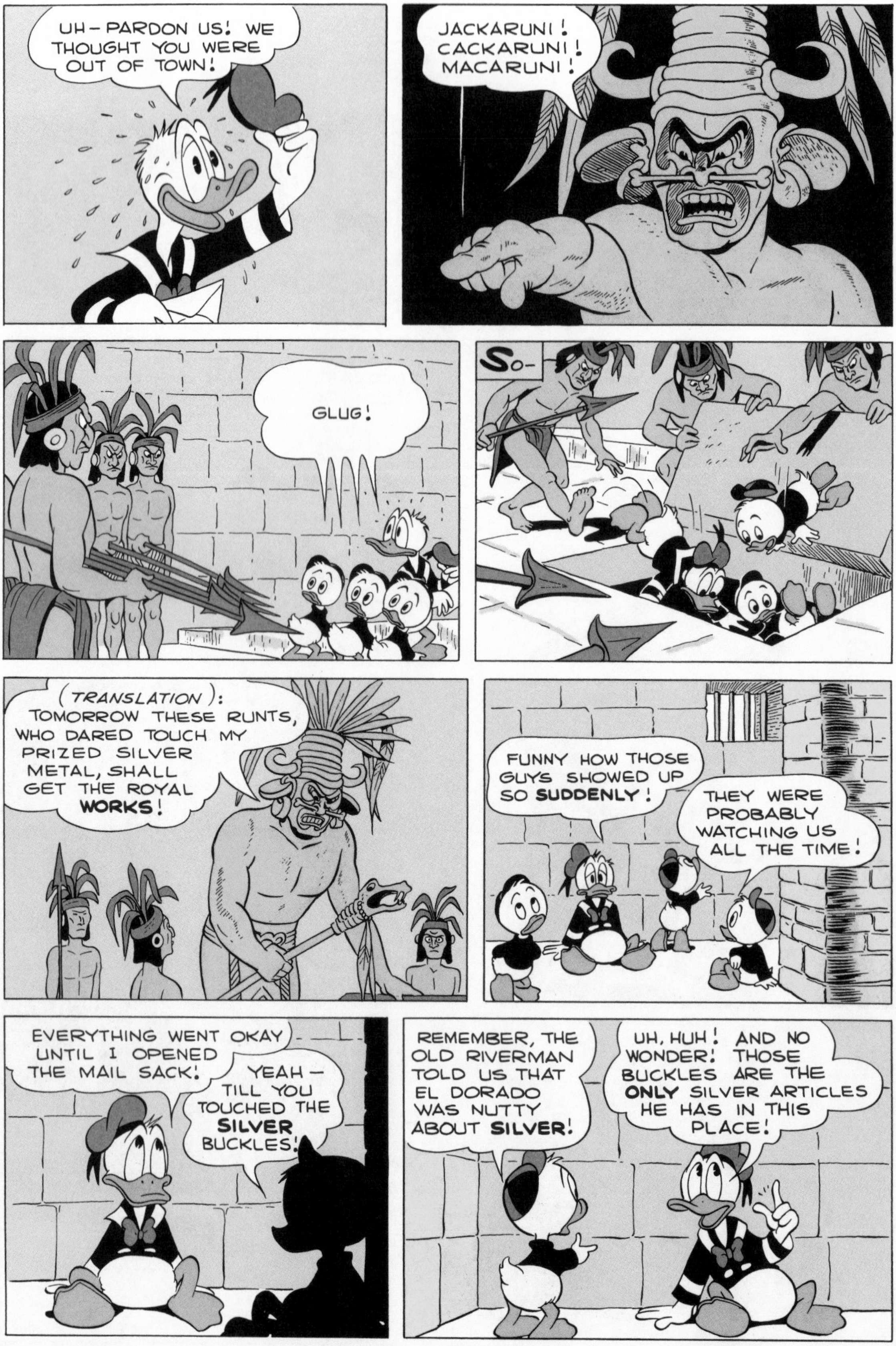
UH-PARDON US! WE THOUGHT YOU WERE OUT OF TOWN!
JACKARUNI! CACKARUNI! MACARUNI!
GLUG!
SO-
(TRANSLATION): TOMORROW THESE RUNTS, WHO DARED TOUCH MY PRIZED SILVER METAL, SHALL GET THE ROYAL WORKS!
FUNNY HOW THOSE GUYS SHOWED UP SO SUDDENLY!
THEY WERE PROBABLY WATCHING US ALL THE TIME!
EVERYTHING WENT OKAY UNTIL I OPENED THE MAIL SACK!
YEAH-TILL YOU TOUCHED THE SILVER BUCKLES!
REMEMBER, THE OLD RIVERMAN TOLD US THAT EL DORADO WAS NUTTY ABOUT SILVER!
UH, HUH! AND NO WONDER! THOSE BUCKLES ARE THE ONLY SILVER ARTICLES HE HAS IN THIS PLACE!

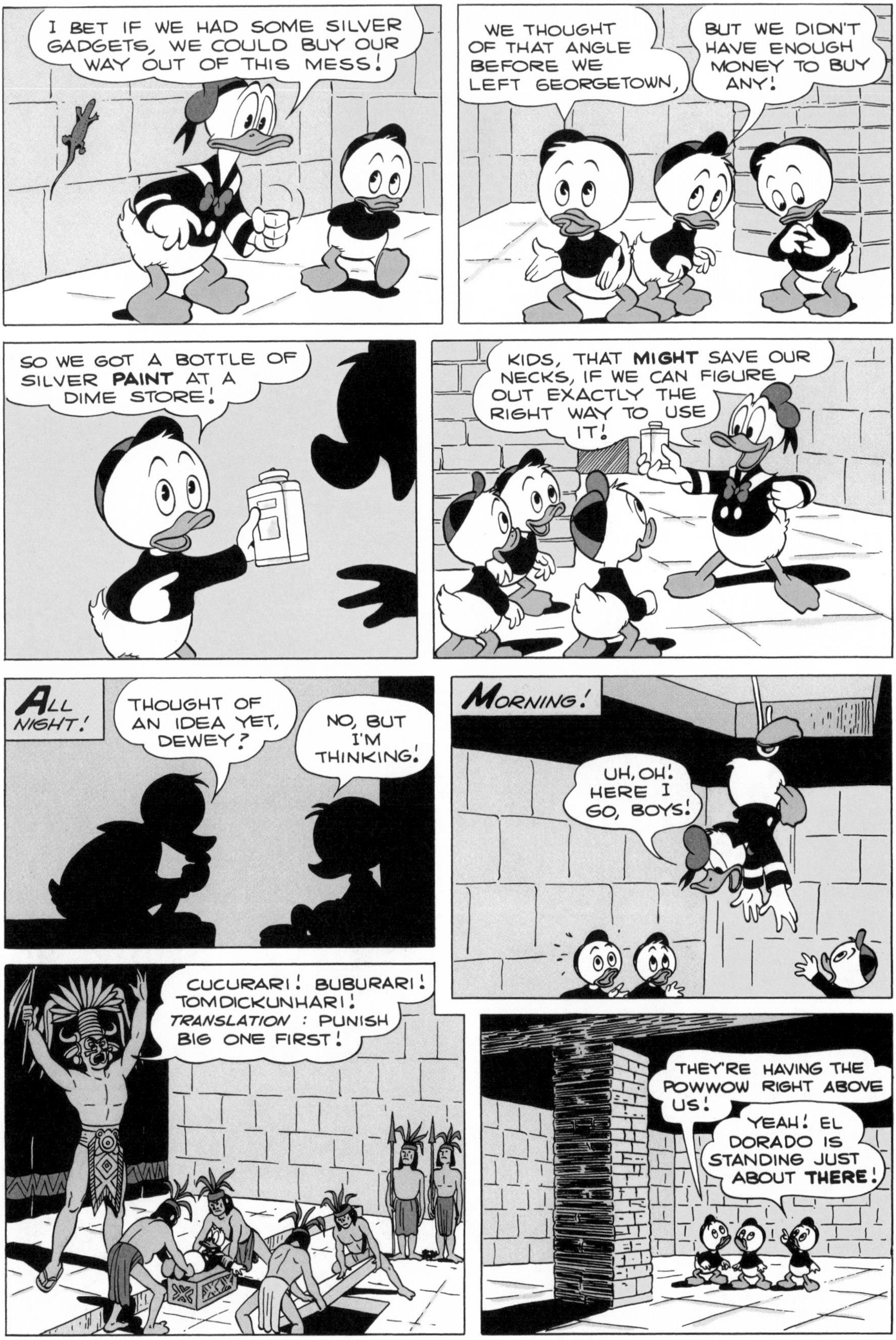
I BET IF WE HAD SOME SILVER GADGETS, WE COULD BUY OUR WAY OUT OF THIS MESS!
WE THOUGHT OF THAT ANGLE BEFORE WE LEFT GEORGETOWN,
BUT WE DIDN'T HAVE ENOUGH MONEY TO BUY ANY!
SO WE GOT A BOTTLE OF SILVER PAINT AT A DIME STORE!
KIDS, THAT MIGHT SAVE OUR NECKS, IF WE CAN FIGURE OUT EXACTLY THE RIGHT WAY TO USE IT!
ALL NIGHT!
THOUGHT OF AN IDEA YET, DEWEY?
NO, BUT I'M THINKING!
MORNING!
UH, OH! HERE I GO, BOYS!
CUCURARI! BUBURARI! TOMDICKUNHARI! TRANSLATION : PUNISH BIG ONE FIRST!
THEY'RE HAVING THE POWWOW RIGHT ABOVE US!
YEAH! EL DORADO IS STANDING JUST ABOUT THERE!

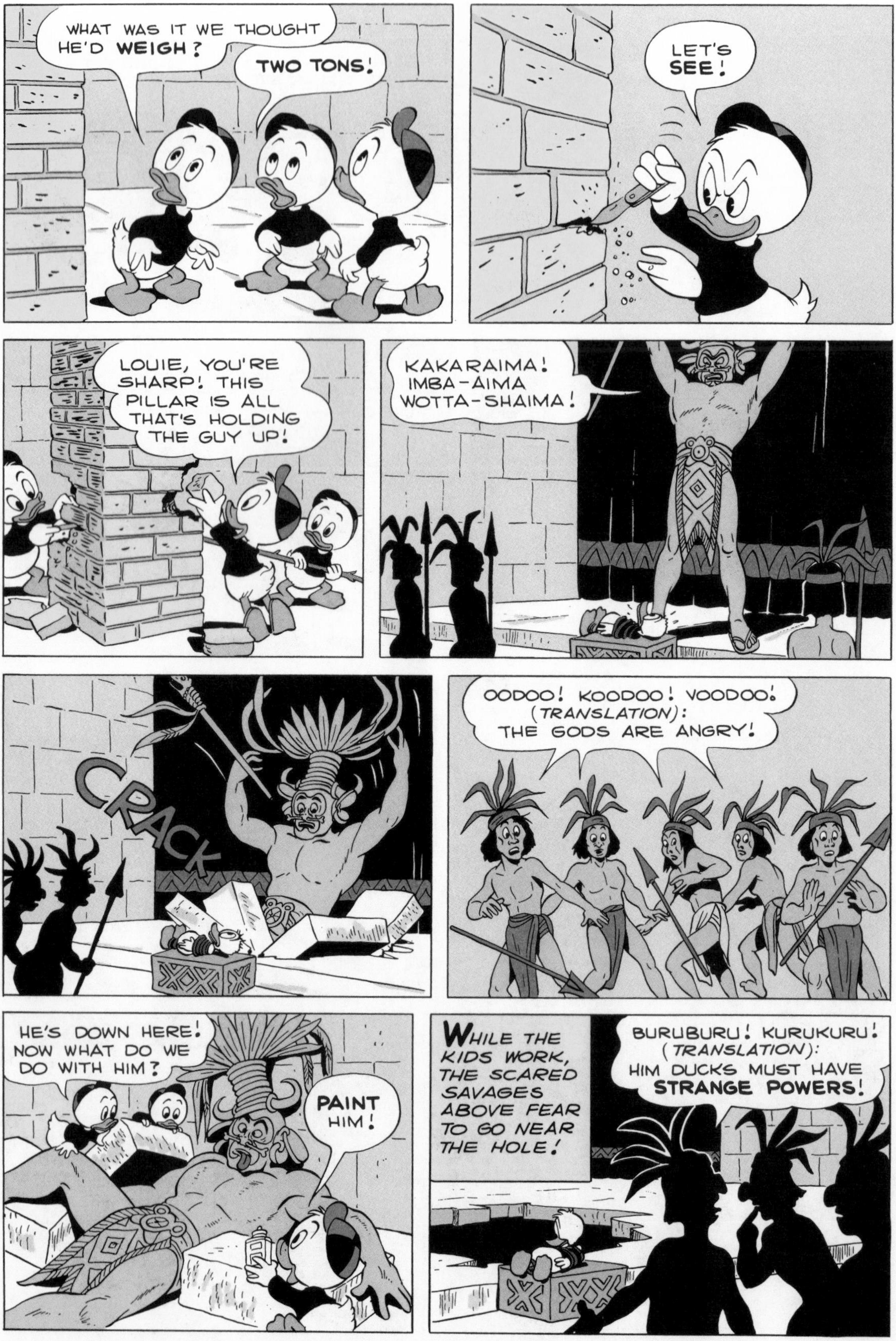
WHAT WAS IT WE THOUGHT HE'D WEIGH?
TWO TONS!
LET'S SEE!
LOUIE, YOU'RE SHARP! THIS PILLAR IS ALL THAT'S HOLDING THE GUY UP!
KAKARAIMA! IMBA-AIMA WOTTA-SHAIMA!
CRACK
OODOO! KOODOO! VOODOO! (TRANSLATION): THE GODS ARE ANGRY!
HE'S DOWN HERE! NOW WHAT DO WE DO WITH HIM?
PAINT HIM!
WHILE THE KIDS WORK, THE SCARED SAVAGES ABOVE FEAR TO GO NEAR THE HOLE!
BURUBURU! KURUKURU! (TRANSLATION): HIM DUCKS MUST HAVE STRANGE POWERS!

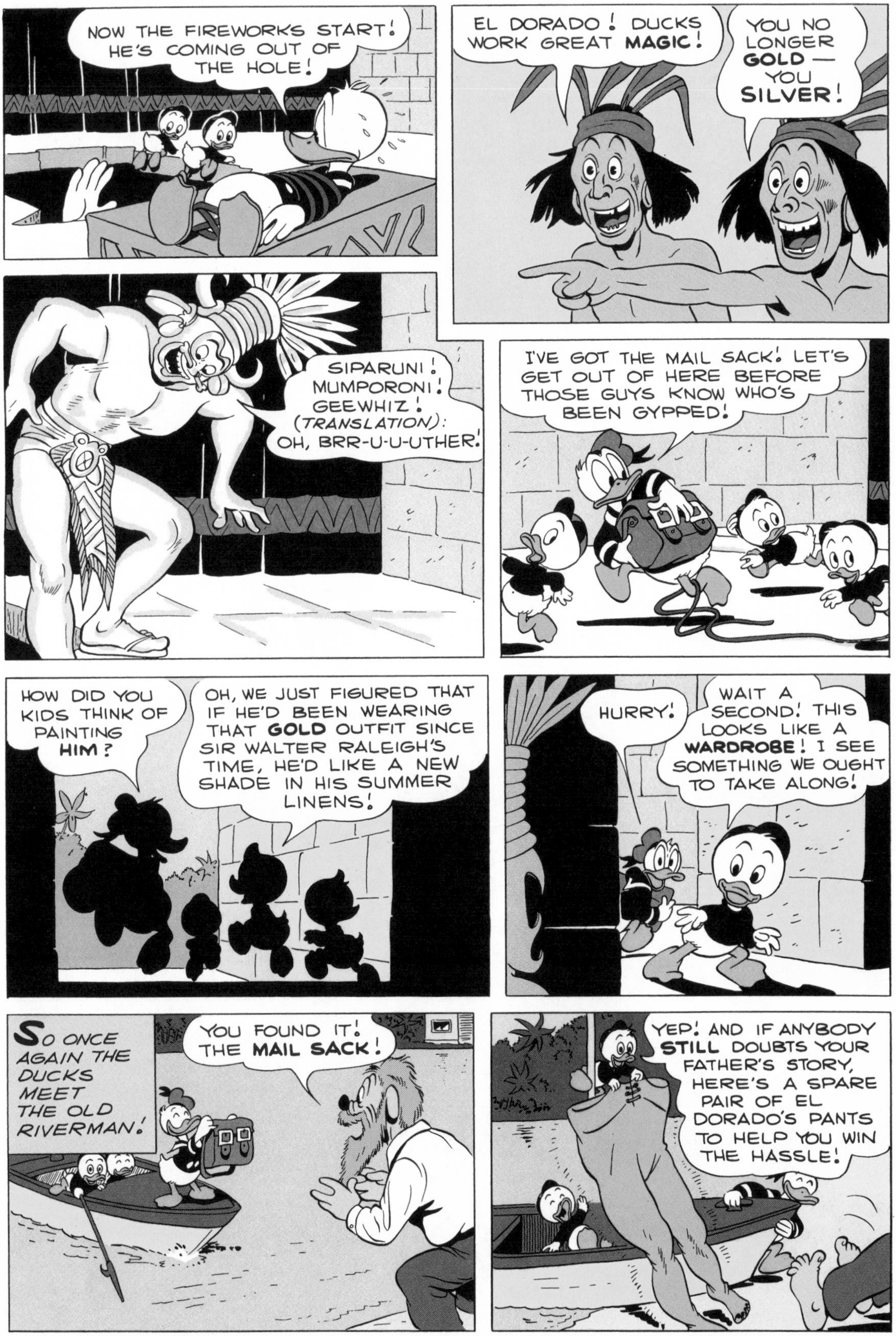
NOW THE FIREWORKS START! HE'S COMING OUT OF THE HOLE!
EL DORADO! DUCKS WORK GREAT MAGIC!
YOU NO LONGER GOLD — YOU SILVER!
SIPARUNI! MUMPORONI! GEEWHIZ! (TRANSLATION): OH, BRR-U-U-UTHER!
I'VE GOT THE MAIL SACK! LET'S GET OUT OF HERE BEFORE THOSE GUYS KNOW WHO'S BEEN GYPPED!
HOW DID YOU KIDS THINK OF PAINTING HIM?
OH, WE JUST FIGURED THAT IF HE'D BEEN WEARING THAT GOLD OUTFIT SINCE SIR WALTER RALEIGH'S TIME, HE'D LIKE A NEW SHADE IN HIS SUMMER LINENS!
HURRY!
WAIT A SECOND! THIS LOOKS LIKE A WARDROBE! I SEE SOMETHING WE OUGHT TO TAKE ALONG!
SO ONCE AGAIN THE DUCKS MEET THE OLD RIVERMAN!
YOU FOUND IT! THE MAIL SACK!
YEP! AND IF ANYBODY STILL DOUBTS YOUR FATHER'S STORY, HERE'S A SPARE PAIR OF EL DORADO'S PANTS TO HELP YOU WIN THE HASSLE!

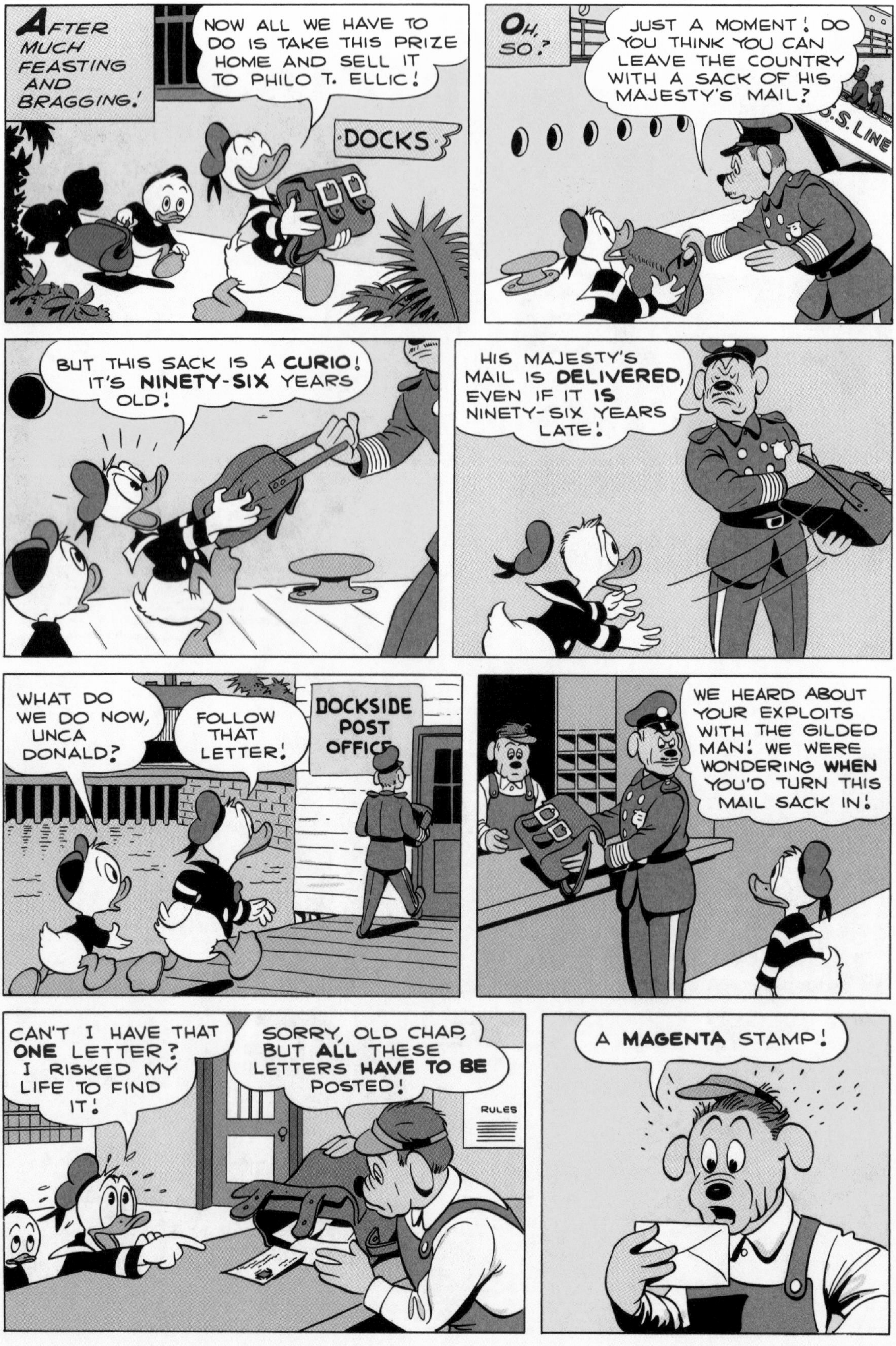

AFTER MUCH FEASTING AND BRAGGING!
NOW ALL WE HAVE TO DO IS TAKE THIS PRIZE HOME AND SELL IT TO PHILO T. ELLIC!
DOCKS
OH, SO?
JUST A MOMENT! DO YOU THINK YOU CAN LEAVE THE COUNTRY WITH A SACK OF HIS MAJESTY'S MAIL?
S.S. LINE
BUT THIS SACK IS A **CURIO**! IT'S **NINETY-SIX** YEARS OLD!
HIS MAJESTY'S MAIL IS **DELIVERED**, EVEN IF IT **IS** NINETY-SIX YEARS LATE!
WHAT DO WE DO NOW, UNCA DONALD?
FOLLOW THAT LETTER!
DOCKSIDE POST OFFICE
WE HEARD ABOUT YOUR EXPLOITS WITH THE GILDED MAN! WE WERE WONDERING **WHEN** YOU'D TURN THIS MAIL SACK IN!
CAN'T I HAVE THAT **ONE** LETTER? I RISKED MY LIFE TO FIND IT!
SORRY, OLD CHAP, BUT **ALL** THESE LETTERS **HAVE TO BE** POSTED!
RULES
A **MAGENTA** STAMP!

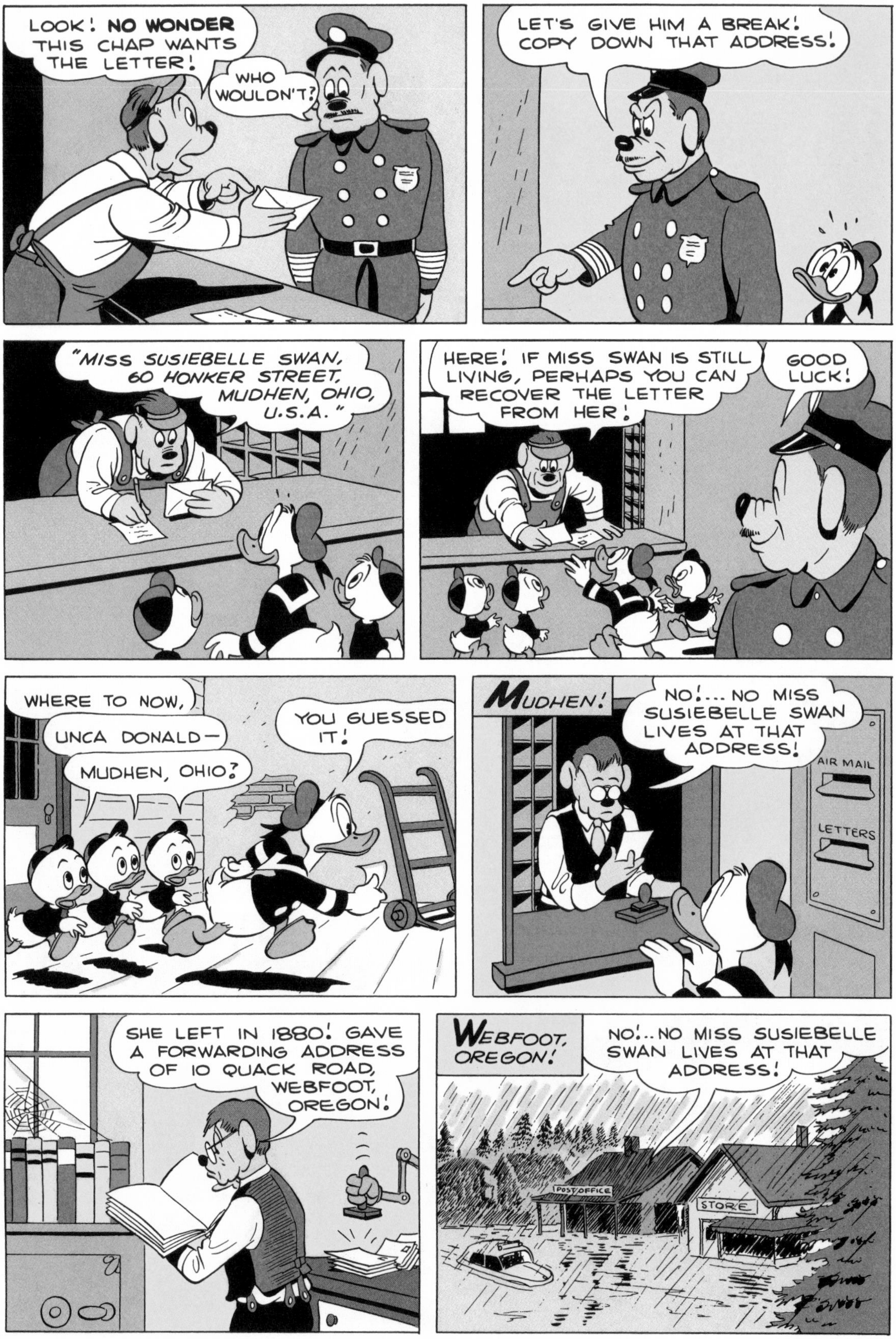
LOOK! NO WONDER THIS CHAP WANTS THE LETTER!
WHO WOULDN'T?
LET'S GIVE HIM A BREAK! COPY DOWN THAT ADDRESS!
"MISS SUSIEBELLE SWAN, 60 HONKER STREET, MUDHEN, OHIO, U.S.A."
HERE! IF MISS SWAN IS STILL LIVING, PERHAPS YOU CAN RECOVER THE LETTER FROM HER!
GOOD LUCK!
WHERE TO NOW,
UNCA DONALD—
MUDHEN, OHIO?
YOU GUESSED IT!
MUDHEN!
NO!... NO MISS SUSIEBELLE SWAN LIVES AT THAT ADDRESS!
AIR MAIL
LETTERS
SHE LEFT IN 1880! GAVE A FORWARDING ADDRESS OF 10 QUACK ROAD, WEBFOOT, OREGON!
WEBFOOT, OREGON!
NO!...NO MISS SUSIEBELLE SWAN LIVES AT THAT ADDRESS!
POST OFFICE
STORE

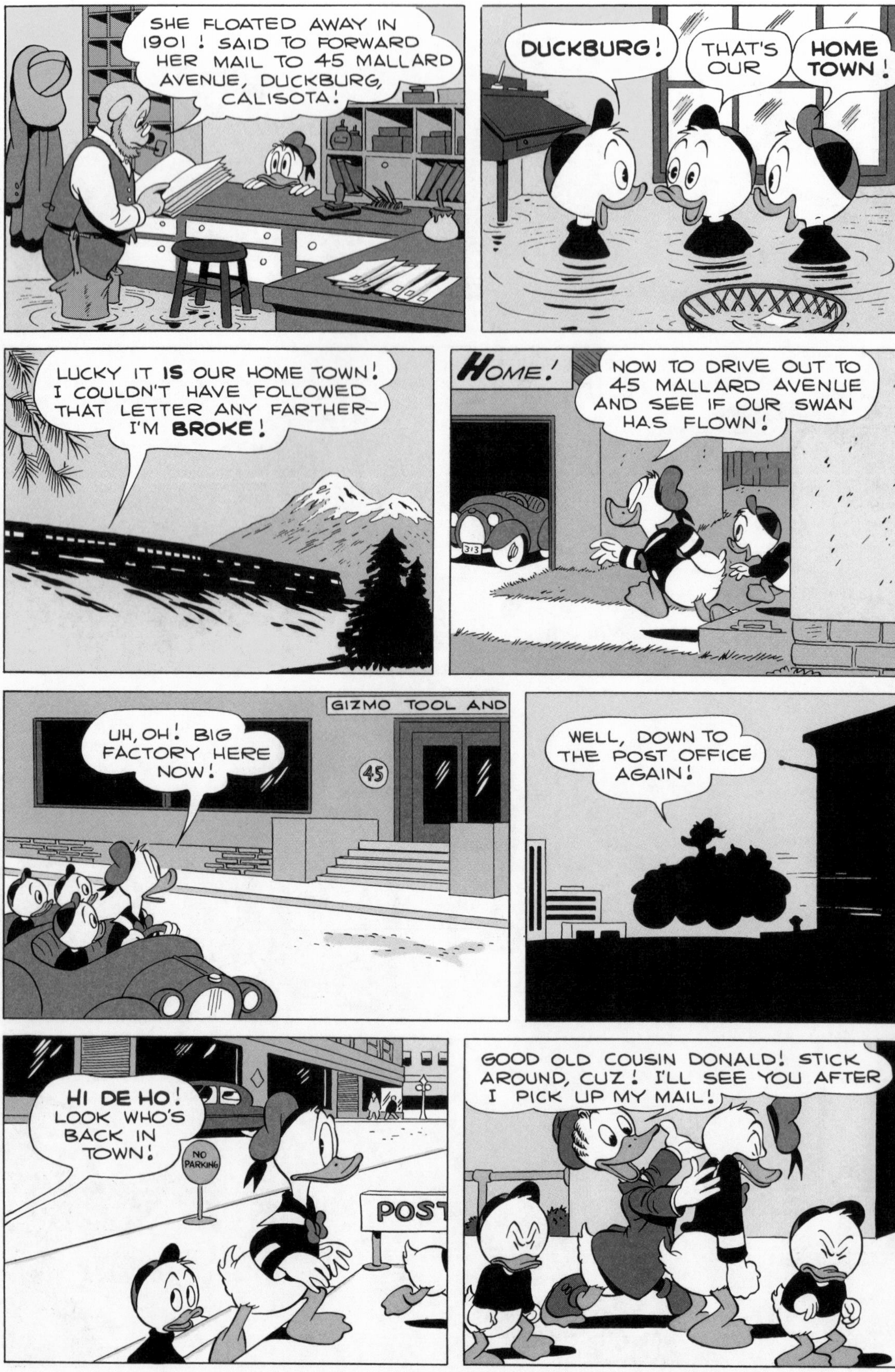
SHE FLOATED AWAY IN 1901! SAID TO FORWARD HER MAIL TO 45 MALLARD AVENUE, DUCKBURG, CALISOTA!
DUCKBURG!
THAT'S OUR
HOME TOWN!
LUCKY IT IS OUR HOME TOWN! I COULDN'T HAVE FOLLOWED THAT LETTER ANY FARTHER— I'M BROKE!
HOME!
NOW TO DRIVE OUT TO 45 MALLARD AVENUE AND SEE IF OUR SWAN HAS FLOWN!
313
GIZMO TOOL AND
45
UH, OH! BIG FACTORY HERE NOW!
WELL, DOWN TO THE POST OFFICE AGAIN!
HI DE HO! LOOK WHO'S BACK IN TOWN!
NO PARKING
POST
GOOD OLD COUSIN DONALD! STICK AROUND, CUZ! I'LL SEE YOU AFTER I PICK UP MY MAIL!

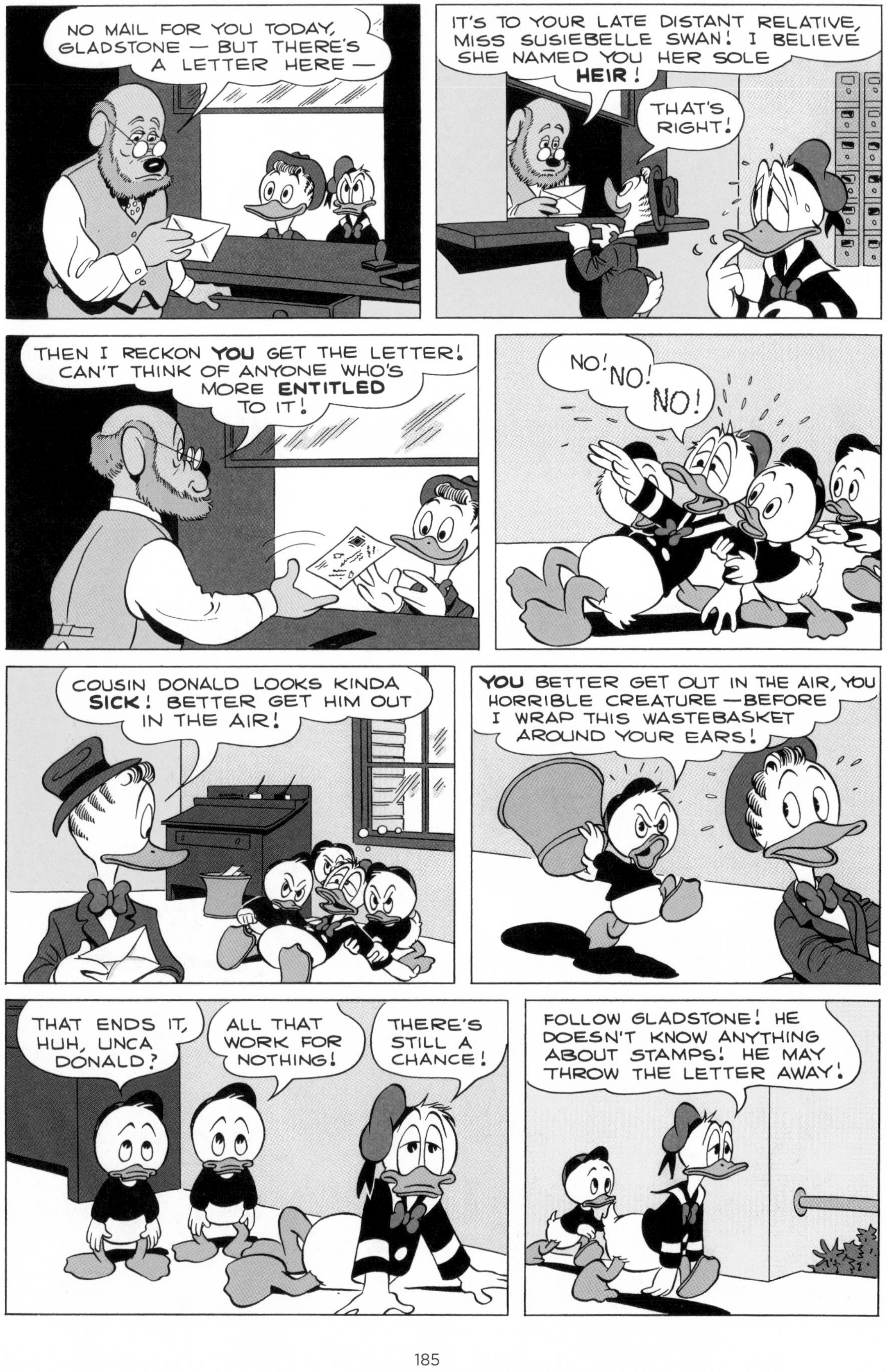

NO MAIL FOR YOU TODAY, GLADSTONE — BUT THERE'S A LETTER HERE —
IT'S TO YOUR LATE DISTANT RELATIVE, MISS SUSIEBELLE SWAN! I BELIEVE SHE NAMED YOU HER SOLE **HEIR**!
THAT'S RIGHT!
THEN I RECKON **YOU** GET THE LETTER! CAN'T THINK OF ANYONE WHO'S MORE **ENTITLED** TO IT!
NO! NO! NO!
COUSIN DONALD LOOKS KINDA **SICK**! BETTER GET HIM OUT IN THE AIR!
YOU BETTER GET OUT IN THE AIR, YOU HORRIBLE CREATURE—BEFORE I WRAP THIS WASTEBASKET AROUND YOUR EARS!
THAT ENDS IT, HUH, UNCA DONALD?
ALL THAT WORK FOR NOTHING!
THERE'S STILL A CHANCE!
FOLLOW GLADSTONE! HE DOESN'T KNOW ANYTHING ABOUT STAMPS! HE MAY THROW THE LETTER AWAY!

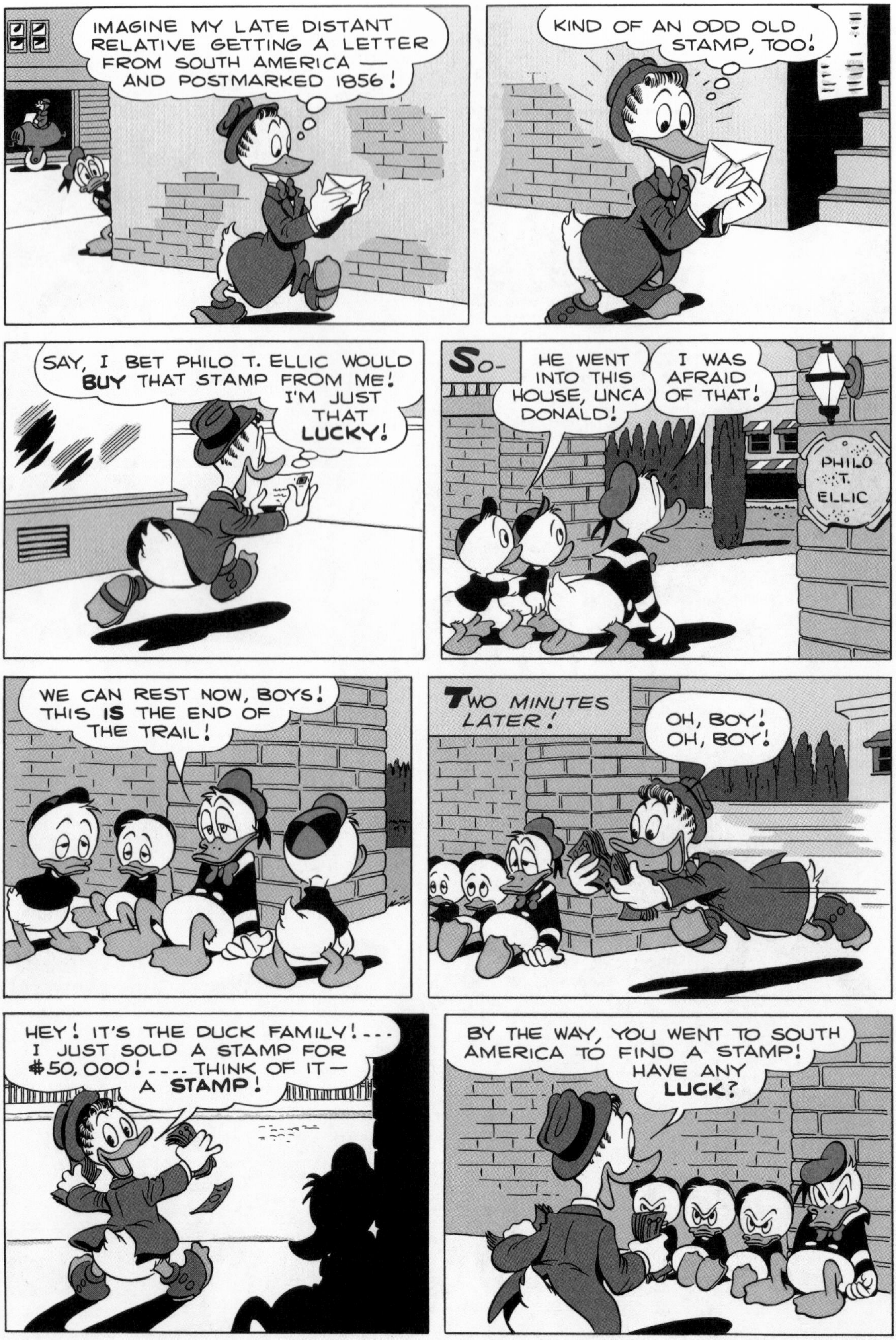
IMAGINE MY LATE DISTANT RELATIVE GETTING A LETTER FROM SOUTH AMERICA — AND POSTMARKED 1856!
KIND OF AN ODD OLD STAMP, TOO!
SAY, I BET PHILO T. ELLIC WOULD BUY THAT STAMP FROM ME! I'M JUST THAT LUCKY!
SO-
HE WENT INTO THIS HOUSE, UNCA DONALD!
I WAS AFRAID OF THAT!
PHILO T. ELLIC
WE CAN REST NOW, BOYS! THIS IS THE END OF THE TRAIL!
TWO MINUTES LATER!
OH, BOY! OH, BOY!
HEY! IT'S THE DUCK FAMILY! --- I JUST SOLD A STAMP FOR $50,000! ---- THINK OF IT — A STAMP!
BY THE WAY, YOU WENT TO SOUTH AMERICA TO FIND A STAMP! HAVE ANY LUCK?

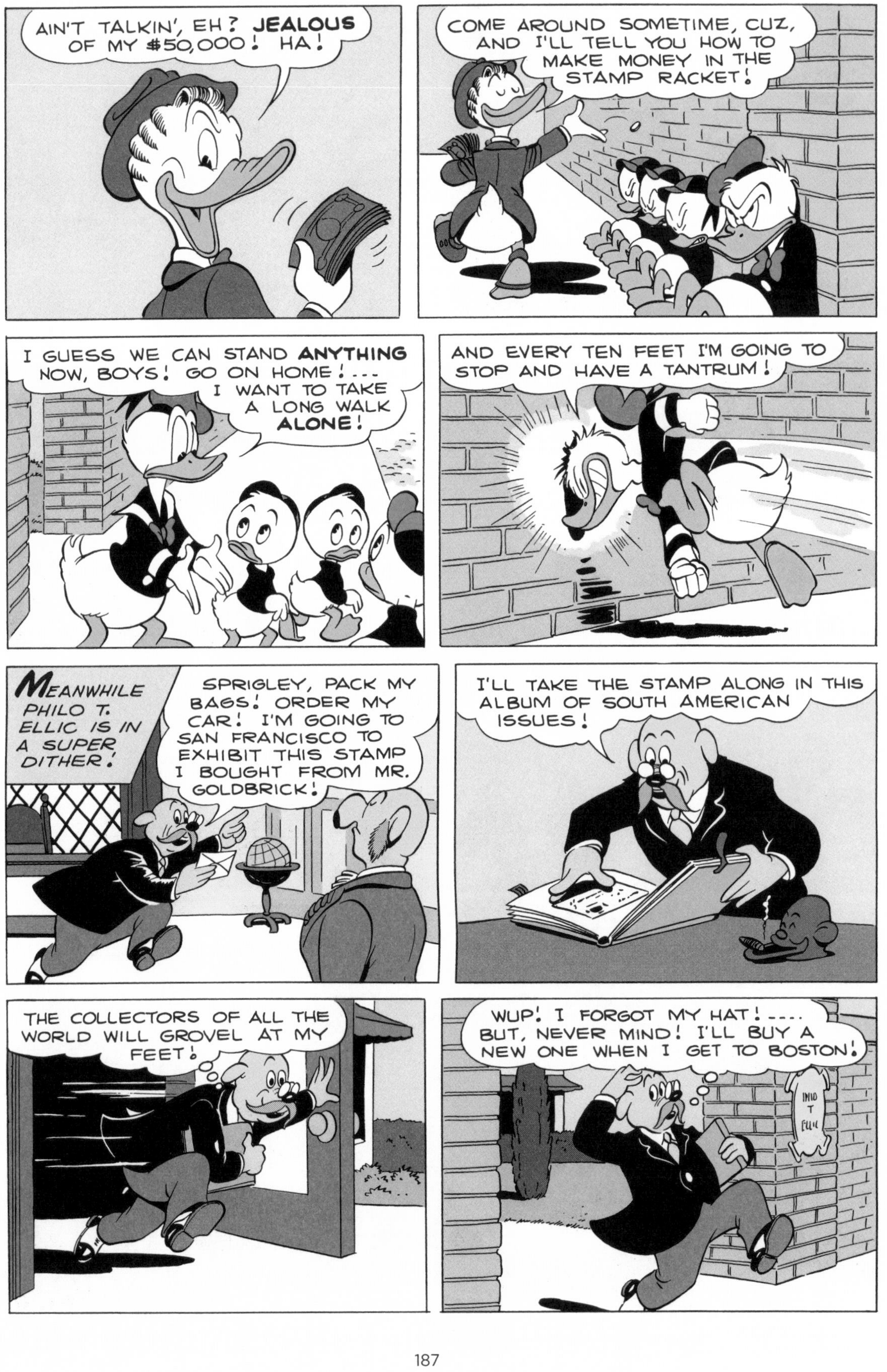
AIN'T TALKIN', EH? **JEALOUS** OF MY $50,000! HA!
COME AROUND SOMETIME, CUZ, AND I'LL TELL YOU HOW TO MAKE MONEY IN THE STAMP RACKET!
I GUESS WE CAN STAND **ANYTHING** NOW, BOYS! GO ON HOME! ... I WANT TO TAKE A LONG WALK **ALONE**!
AND EVERY TEN FEET I'M GOING TO STOP AND HAVE A TANTRUM!
MEANWHILE PHILO T. ELLIC IS IN A SUPER DITHER!
SPRIGLEY, PACK MY BAGS! ORDER MY CAR! I'M GOING TO SAN FRANCISCO TO EXHIBIT THIS STAMP I BOUGHT FROM MR. GOLDBRICK!
I'LL TAKE THE STAMP ALONG IN THIS ALBUM OF SOUTH AMERICAN ISSUES!
THE COLLECTORS OF ALL THE WORLD WILL GROVEL AT MY FEET!
WUP! I FORGOT MY HAT! .... BUT, NEVER MIND! I'LL BUY A NEW ONE WHEN I GET TO BOSTON!

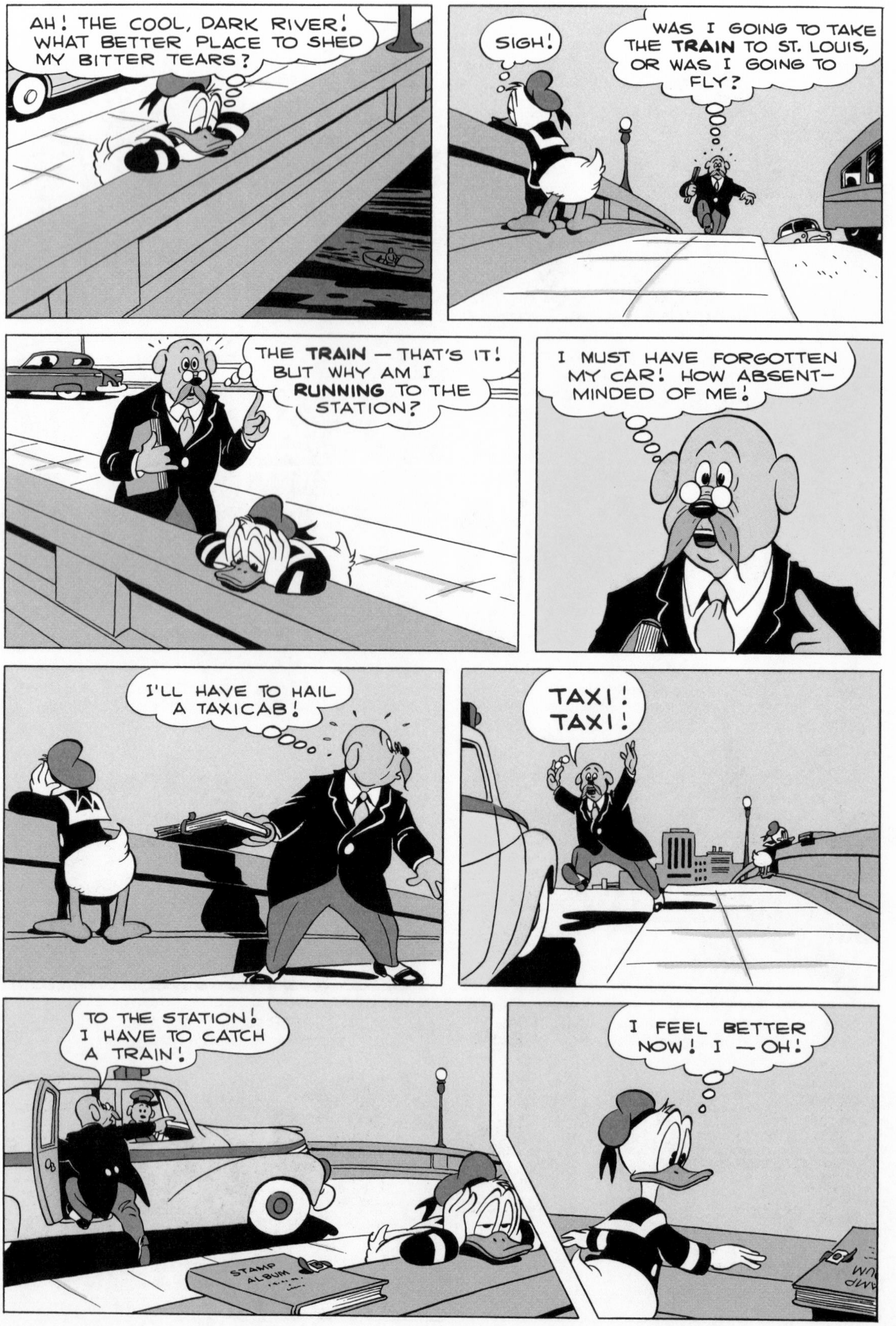
AH! THE COOL, DARK RIVER! WHAT BETTER PLACE TO SHED MY BITTER TEARS?
SIGH!
WAS I GOING TO TAKE THE TRAIN TO ST. LOUIS, OR WAS I GOING TO FLY?
THE TRAIN — THAT'S IT! BUT WHY AM I RUNNING TO THE STATION?
I MUST HAVE FORGOTTEN MY CAR! HOW ABSENT-MINDED OF ME!
I'LL HAVE TO HAIL A TAXICAB!
TAXI! TAXI!
TO THE STATION! I HAVE TO CATCH A TRAIN!
STAMP ALBUM
I FEEL BETTER NOW! I — OH!

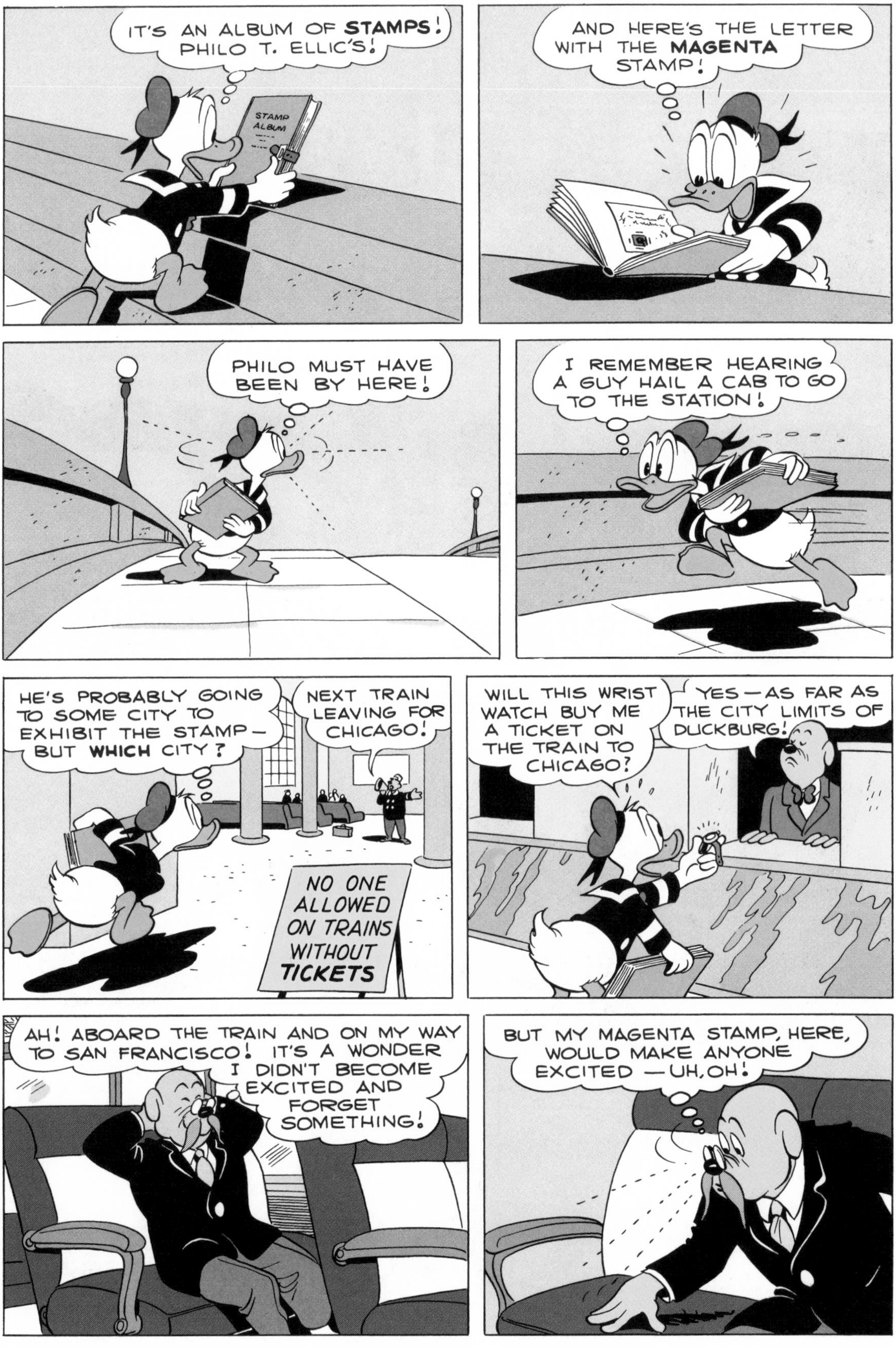

IT'S AN ALBUM OF STAMPS! PHILO T. ELLIC'S!
STAMP ALBUM
AND HERE'S THE LETTER WITH THE MAGENTA STAMP!
PHILO MUST HAVE BEEN BY HERE!
I REMEMBER HEARING A GUY HAIL A CAB TO GO TO THE STATION!
HE'S PROBABLY GOING TO SOME CITY TO EXHIBIT THE STAMP— BUT WHICH CITY?
NEXT TRAIN LEAVING FOR CHICAGO!
NO ONE ALLOWED ON TRAINS WITHOUT TICKETS
WILL THIS WRIST WATCH BUY ME A TICKET ON THE TRAIN TO CHICAGO?
YES—AS FAR AS THE CITY LIMITS OF DUCKBURG!
AH! ABOARD THE TRAIN AND ON MY WAY TO SAN FRANCISCO! IT'S A WONDER I DIDN'T BECOME EXCITED AND FORGET SOMETHING!
BUT MY MAGENTA STAMP, HERE, WOULD MAKE ANYONE EXCITED —UH, OH!

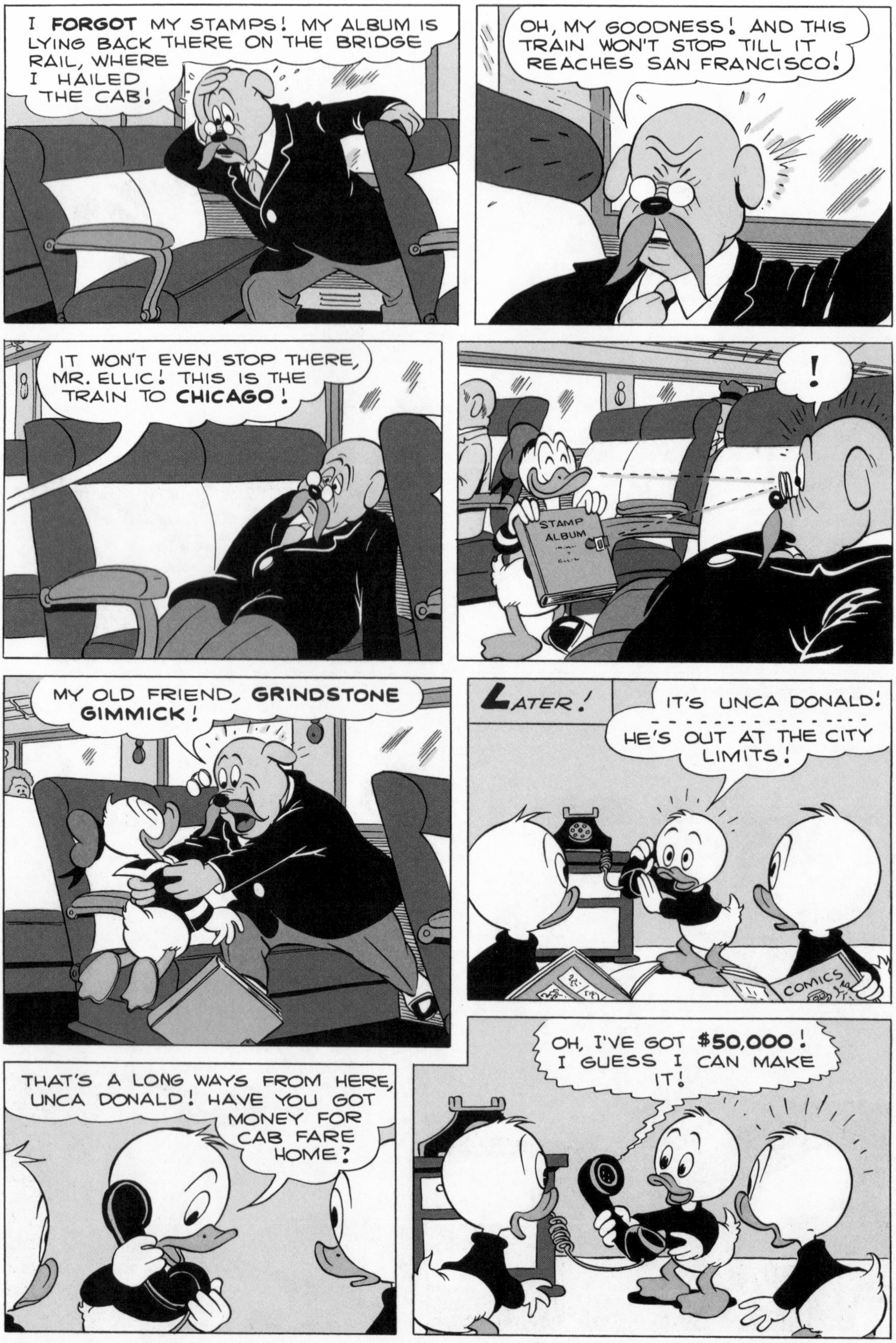
I FORGOT MY STAMPS! MY ALBUM IS LYING BACK THERE ON THE BRIDGE RAIL, WHERE I HAILED THE CAB!
OH, MY GOODNESS! AND THIS TRAIN WON'T STOP TILL IT REACHES SAN FRANCISCO!
IT WON'T EVEN STOP THERE, MR. ELLIC! THIS IS THE TRAIN TO CHICAGO!
!
STAMP ALBUM
MY OLD FRIEND, GRINDSTONE GIMMICK!
LATER!
IT'S UNCA DONALD!
HE'S OUT AT THE CITY LIMITS!
COMICS
THAT'S A LONG WAYS FROM HERE, UNCA DONALD! HAVE YOU GOT MONEY FOR CAB FARE HOME?
OH, I'VE GOT $50,000! I GUESS I CAN MAKE IT!

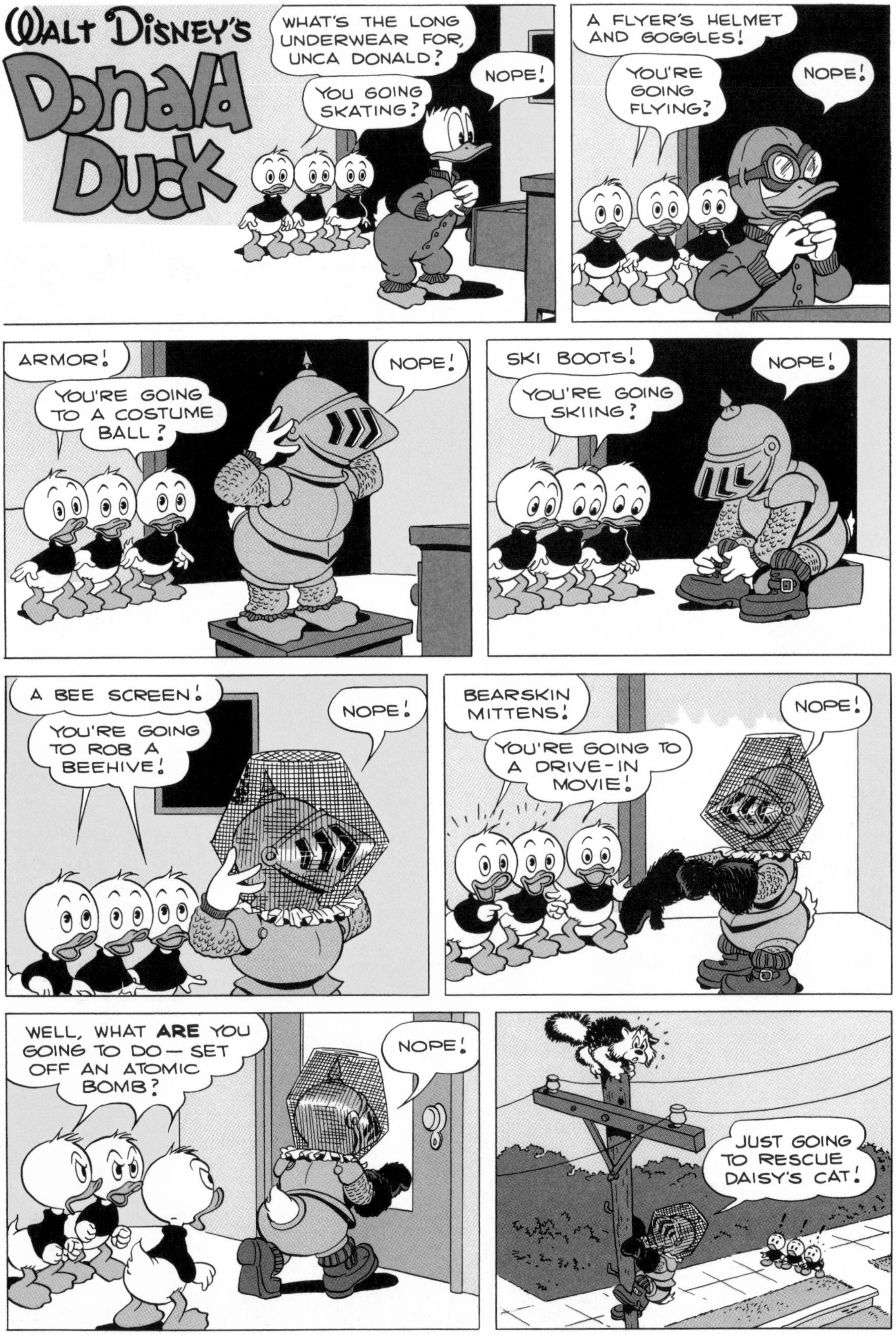
WALT DISNEY'S
DONALD DUCK
WHAT'S THE LONG UNDERWEAR FOR, UNCA DONALD?
YOU GOING SKATING?
NOPE!
A FLYER'S HELMET AND GOGGLES!
YOU'RE GOING FLYING?
NOPE!
ARMOR!
YOU'RE GOING TO A COSTUME BALL?
NOPE!
SKI BOOTS!
YOU'RE GOING SKIING?
NOPE!
A BEE SCREEN!
YOU'RE GOING TO ROB A BEEHIVE!
NOPE!
BEARSKIN MITTENS!
YOU'RE GOING TO A DRIVE-IN MOVIE!
NOPE!
WELL, WHAT **ARE** YOU GOING TO DO— SET OFF AN ATOMIC BOMB?
NOPE!
JUST GOING TO RESCUE DAISY'S CAT!

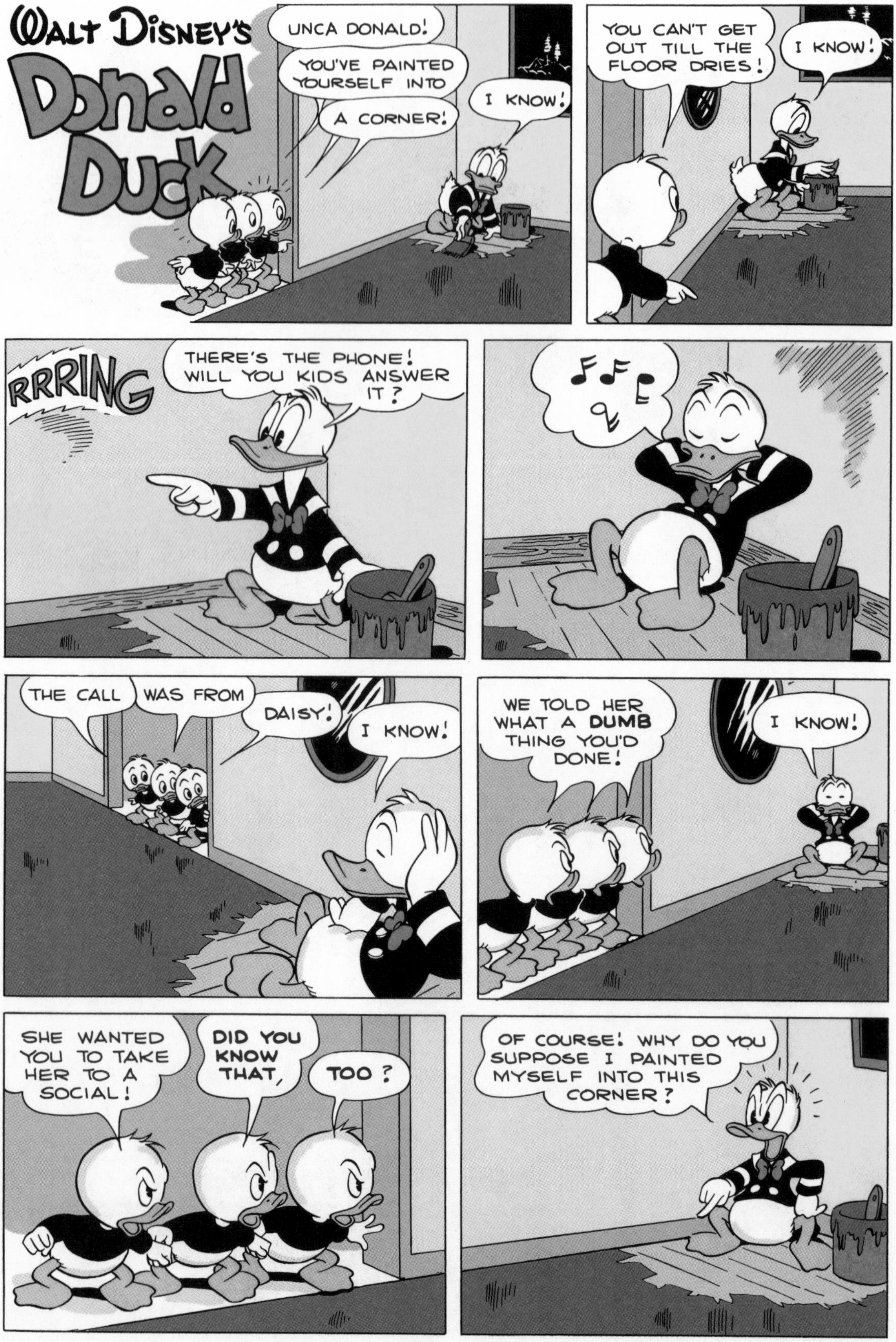
WALT DISNEY'S
Donald Duck
UNCA DONALD!
YOU'VE PAINTED YOURSELF INTO
A CORNER!
I KNOW!
YOU CAN'T GET OUT TILL THE FLOOR DRIES!
I KNOW!
RRRING
THERE'S THE PHONE! WILL YOU KIDS ANSWER IT?
THE CALL
WAS FROM
DAISY!
I KNOW!
WE TOLD HER WHAT A DUMB THING YOU'D DONE!
I KNOW!
SHE WANTED YOU TO TAKE HER TO A SOCIAL!
DID YOU KNOW THAT,
TOO?
OF COURSE! WHY DO YOU SUPPOSE I PAINTED MYSELF INTO THIS CORNER?

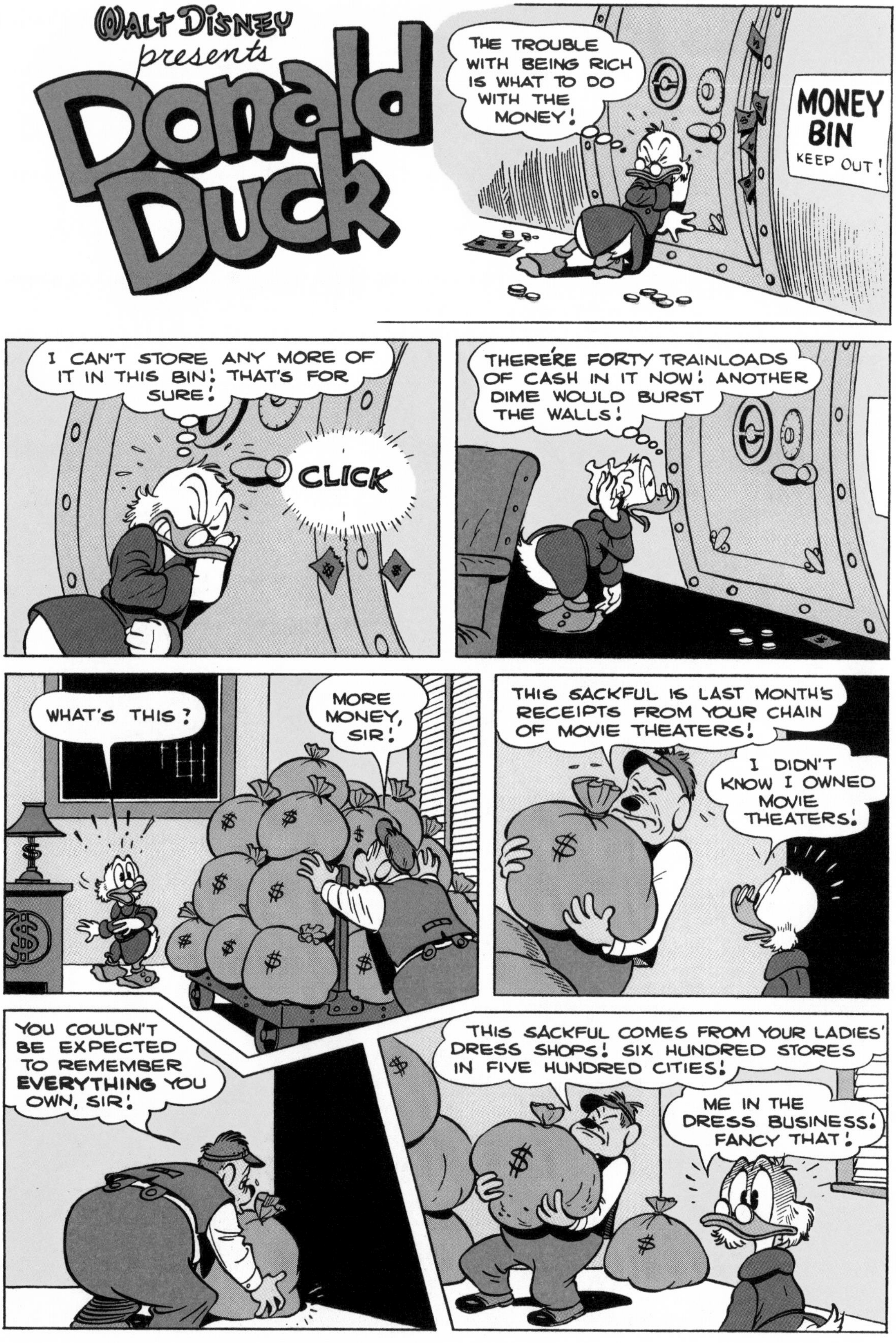
WALT DISNEY
presents
Donald Duck
THE TROUBLE WITH BEING RICH IS WHAT TO DO WITH THE MONEY!
MONEY BIN
KEEP OUT!
I CAN'T STORE ANY MORE OF IT IN THIS BIN! THAT'S FOR SURE!
CLICK
THERE'RE FORTY TRAINLOADS OF CASH IN IT NOW! ANOTHER DIME WOULD BURST THE WALLS!
WHAT'S THIS?
MORE MONEY, SIR!
THIS SACKFUL IS LAST MONTH'S RECEIPTS FROM YOUR CHAIN OF MOVIE THEATERS!
I DIDN'T KNOW I OWNED MOVIE THEATERS!
YOU COULDN'T BE EXPECTED TO REMEMBER EVERYTHING YOU OWN, SIR!
THIS SACKFUL COMES FROM YOUR LADIES' DRESS SHOPS! SIX HUNDRED STORES IN FIVE HUNDRED CITIES!
ME IN THE DRESS BUSINESS! FANCY THAT!

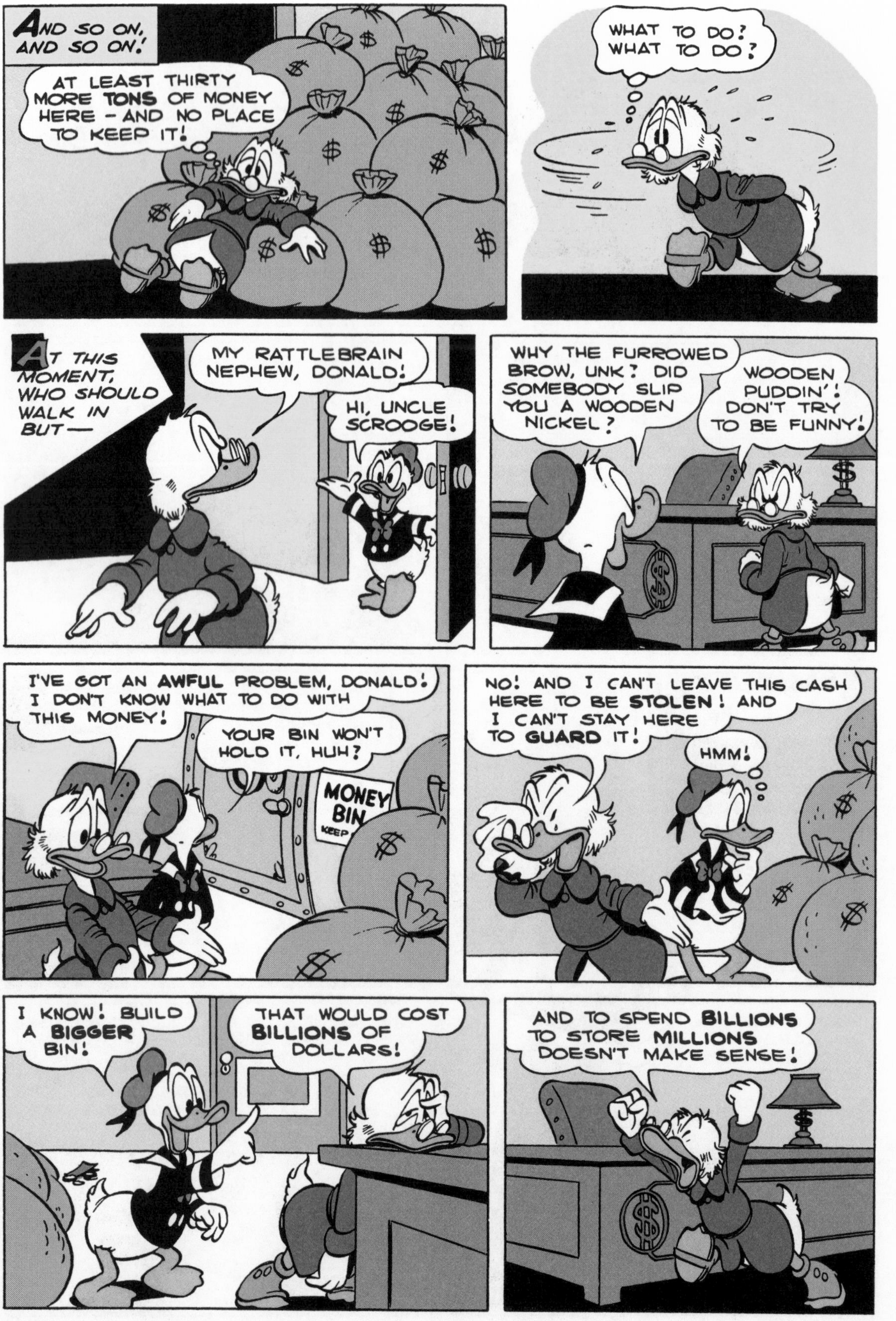
AND SO ON, AND SO ON!
AT LEAST THIRTY MORE TONS OF MONEY HERE – AND NO PLACE TO KEEP IT!
WHAT TO DO? WHAT TO DO?
AT THIS MOMENT, WHO SHOULD WALK IN BUT—
MY RATTLEBRAIN NEPHEW, DONALD!
HI, UNCLE SCROOGE!
WHY THE FURROWED BROW, UNK? DID SOMEBODY SLIP YOU A WOODEN NICKEL?
WOODEN PUDDIN'! DON'T TRY TO BE FUNNY!
I'VE GOT AN AWFUL PROBLEM, DONALD! I DON'T KNOW WHAT TO DO WITH THIS MONEY!
YOUR BIN WON'T HOLD IT, HUH?
MONEY BIN
KEEP
NO! AND I CAN'T LEAVE THIS CASH HERE TO BE STOLEN! AND I CAN'T STAY HERE TO GUARD IT!
HMM!
I KNOW! BUILD A BIGGER BIN!
THAT WOULD COST BILLIONS OF DOLLARS!
AND TO SPEND BILLIONS TO STORE MILLIONS DOESN'T MAKE SENSE!

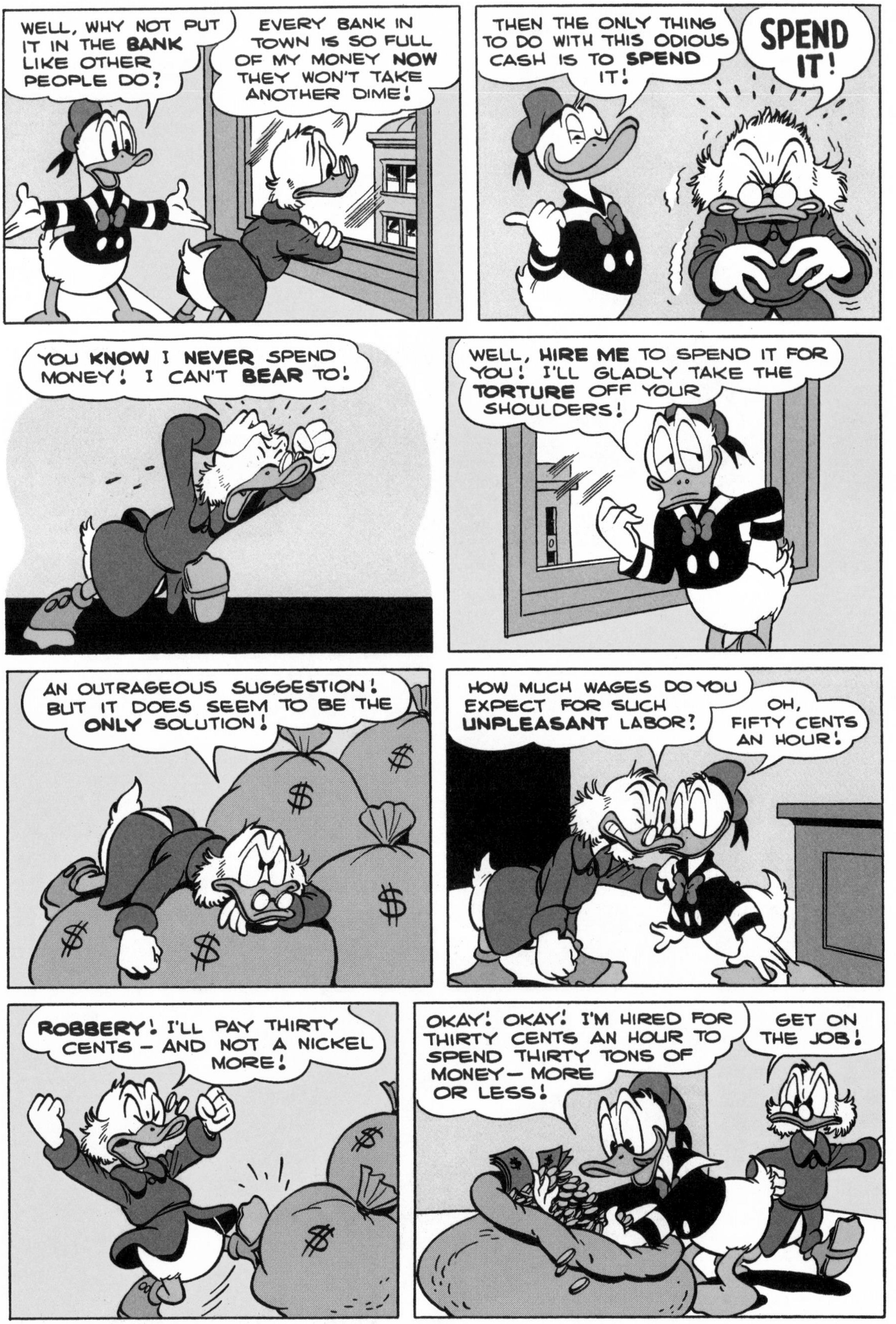
WELL, WHY NOT PUT IT IN THE BANK LIKE OTHER PEOPLE DO?
EVERY BANK IN TOWN IS SO FULL OF MY MONEY NOW THEY WON'T TAKE ANOTHER DIME!
THEN THE ONLY THING TO DO WITH THIS ODIOUS CASH IS TO SPEND IT!
SPEND IT!
YOU KNOW I NEVER SPEND MONEY! I CAN'T BEAR TO!
WELL, HIRE ME TO SPEND IT FOR YOU! I'LL GLADLY TAKE THE TORTURE OFF YOUR SHOULDERS!
AN OUTRAGEOUS SUGGESTION! BUT IT DOES SEEM TO BE THE ONLY SOLUTION!
HOW MUCH WAGES DO YOU EXPECT FOR SUCH UNPLEASANT LABOR?
OH, FIFTY CENTS AN HOUR!
ROBBERY! I'LL PAY THIRTY CENTS – AND NOT A NICKEL MORE!
OKAY! OKAY! I'M HIRED FOR THIRTY CENTS AN HOUR TO SPEND THIRTY TONS OF MONEY – MORE OR LESS!
GET ON THE JOB!

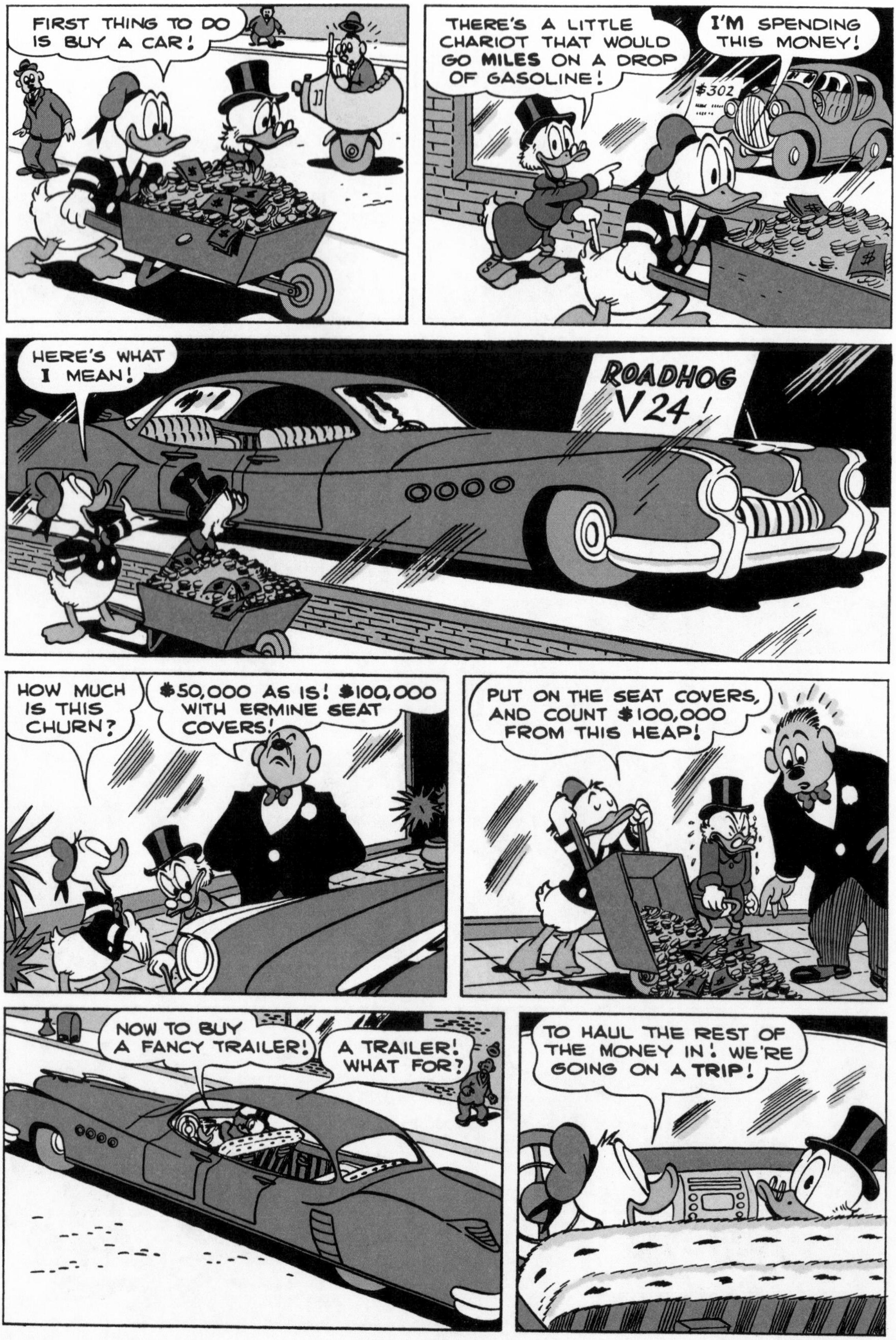
FIRST THING TO DO IS BUY A CAR!
THERE'S A LITTLE CHARIOT THAT WOULD GO MILES ON A DROP OF GASOLINE!
I'M SPENDING THIS MONEY!
$302
HERE'S WHAT I MEAN!
ROADHOG V24!
HOW MUCH IS THIS CHURN?
$50,000 AS IS! $100,000 WITH ERMINE SEAT COVERS!
PUT ON THE SEAT COVERS, AND COUNT $100,000 FROM THIS HEAP!
NOW TO BUY A FANCY TRAILER!
A TRAILER! WHAT FOR?
TO HAUL THE REST OF THE MONEY IN! WE'RE GOING ON A TRIP!

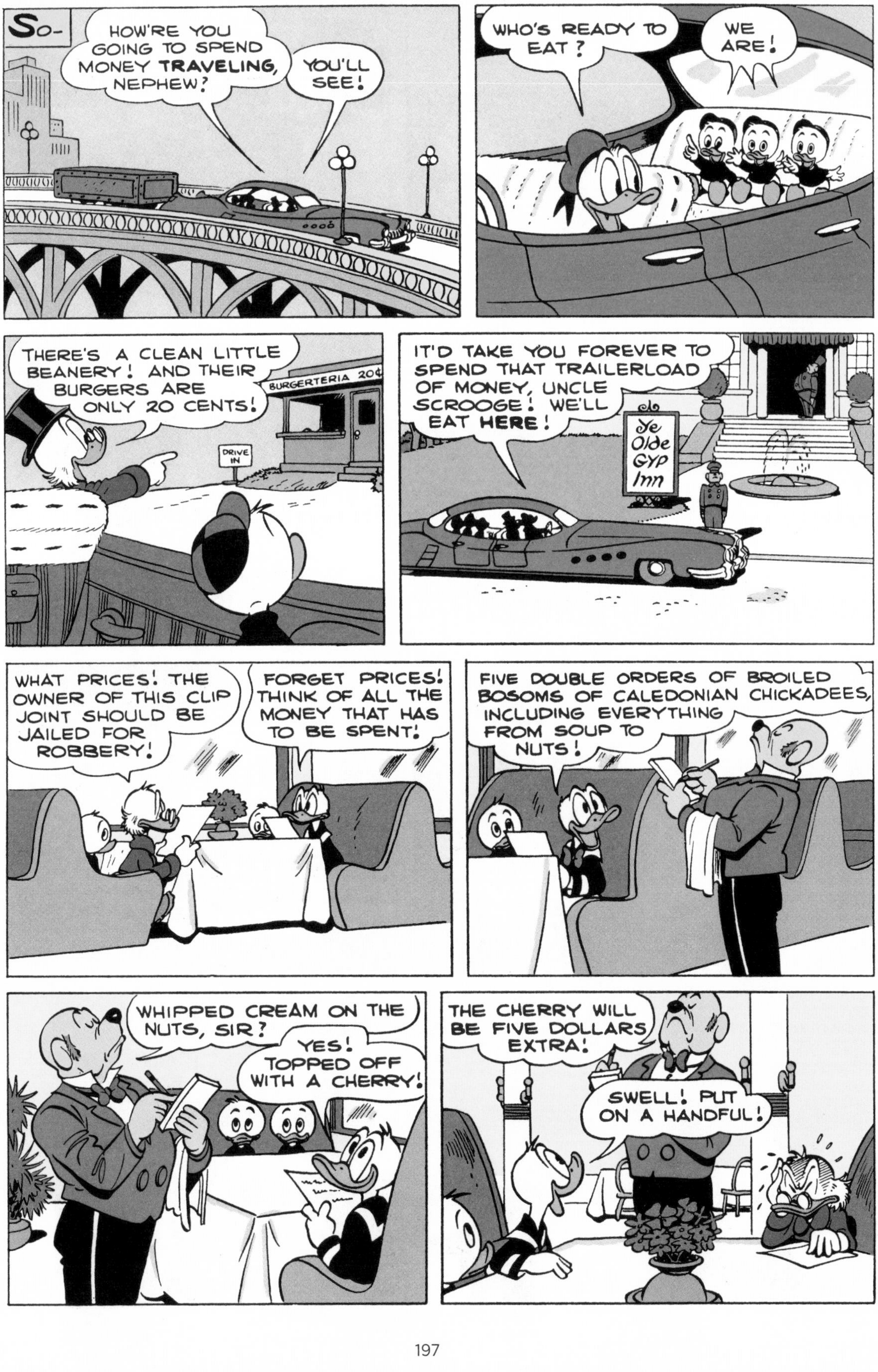
SO-
HOW'RE YOU GOING TO SPEND MONEY TRAVELING, NEPHEW?
YOU'LL SEE!
WHO'S READY TO EAT?
WE ARE!
THERE'S A CLEAN LITTLE BEANERY! AND THEIR BURGERS ARE ONLY 20 CENTS!
BURGERTERIA 20¢
DRIVE IN
IT'D TAKE YOU FOREVER TO SPEND THAT TRAILERLOAD OF MONEY, UNCLE SCROOGE! WE'LL EAT HERE!
Ye Olde GYP Inn
WHAT PRICES! THE OWNER OF THIS CLIP JOINT SHOULD BE JAILED FOR ROBBERY!
FORGET PRICES! THINK OF ALL THE MONEY THAT HAS TO BE SPENT!
FIVE DOUBLE ORDERS OF BROILED BOSOMS OF CALEDONIAN CHICKADEES, INCLUDING EVERYTHING FROM SOUP TO NUTS!
WHIPPED CREAM ON THE NUTS, SIR?
YES! TOPPED OFF WITH A CHERRY!
THE CHERRY WILL BE FIVE DOLLARS EXTRA!
SWELL! PUT ON A HANDFUL!

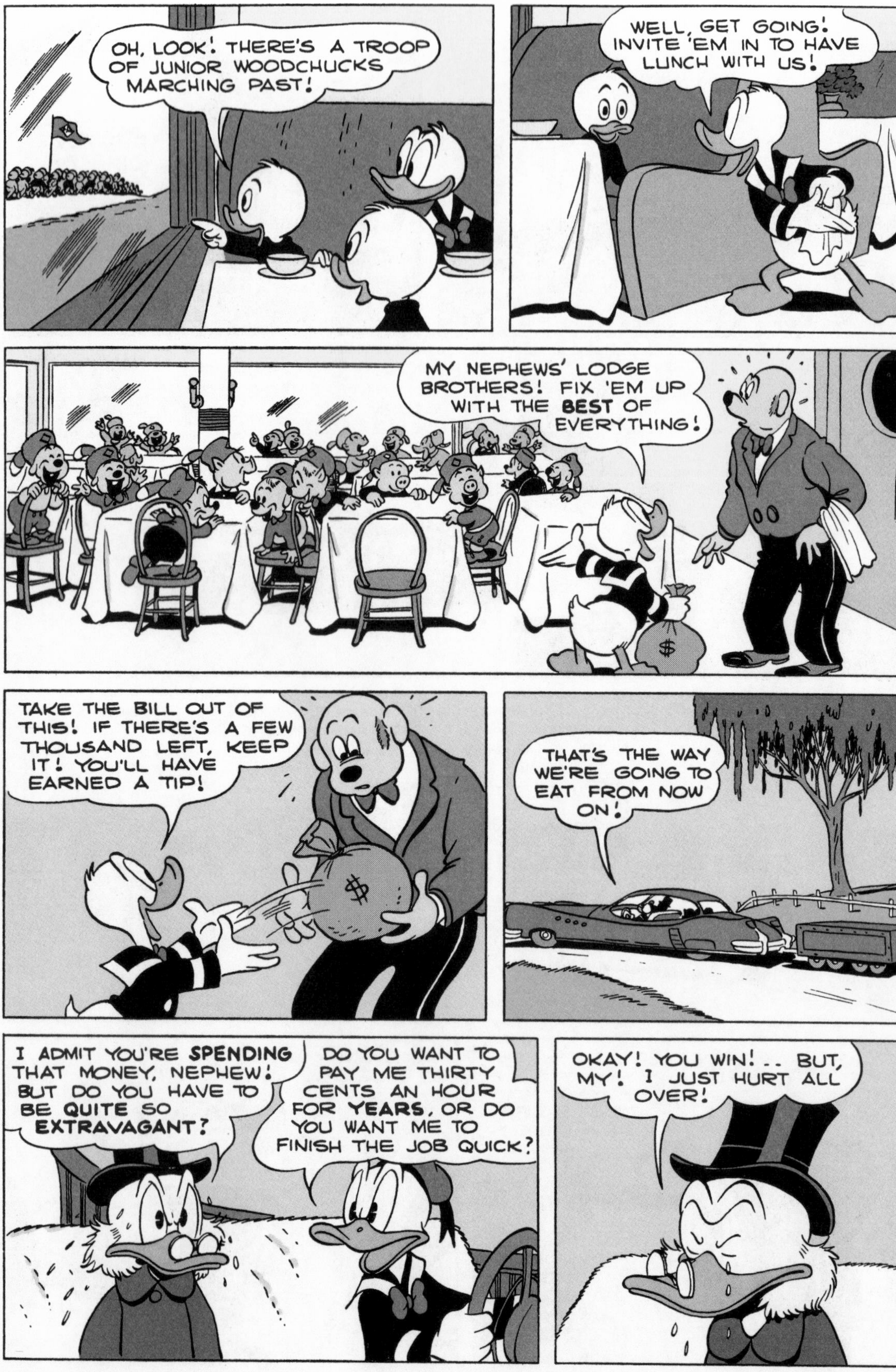
OH, LOOK! THERE'S A TROOP OF JUNIOR WOODCHUCKS MARCHING PAST!
WELL, GET GOING! INVITE 'EM IN TO HAVE LUNCH WITH US!
MY NEPHEWS' LODGE BROTHERS! FIX 'EM UP WITH THE BEST OF EVERYTHING!
TAKE THE BILL OUT OF THIS! IF THERE'S A FEW THOUSAND LEFT, KEEP IT! YOU'LL HAVE EARNED A TIP!
THAT'S THE WAY WE'RE GOING TO EAT FROM NOW ON!
I ADMIT YOU'RE SPENDING THAT MONEY, NEPHEW! BUT DO YOU HAVE TO BE QUITE SO EXTRAVAGANT?
DO YOU WANT TO PAY ME THIRTY CENTS AN HOUR FOR YEARS, OR DO YOU WANT ME TO FINISH THE JOB QUICK?
OKAY! YOU WIN! .. BUT, MY! I JUST HURT ALL OVER!

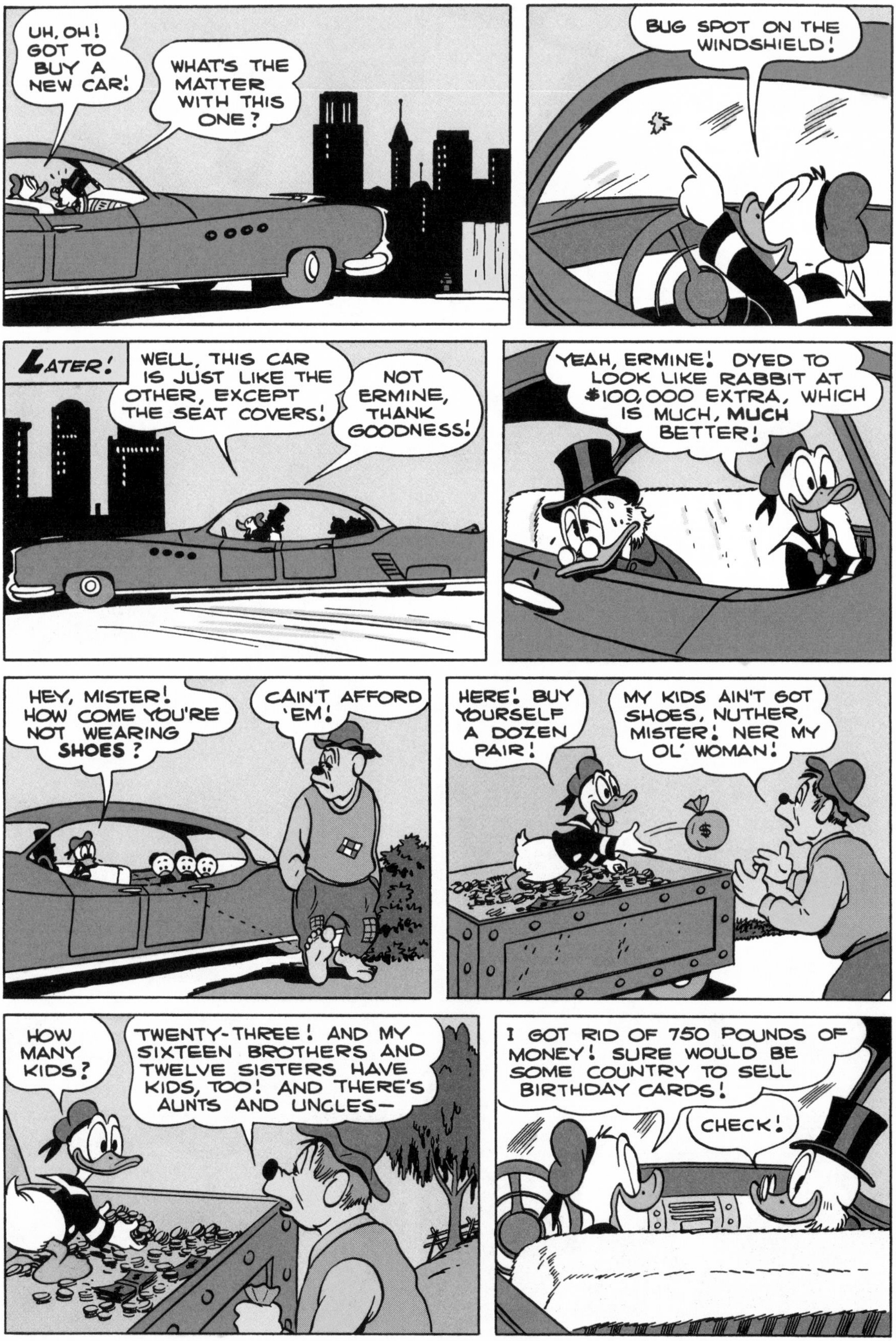
UH, OH! GOT TO BUY A NEW CAR!
WHAT'S THE MATTER WITH THIS ONE?
BUG SPOT ON THE WINDSHIELD!
LATER!
WELL, THIS CAR IS JUST LIKE THE OTHER, EXCEPT THE SEAT COVERS!
NOT ERMINE, THANK GOODNESS!
YEAH, ERMINE! DYED TO LOOK LIKE RABBIT AT $100,000 EXTRA, WHICH IS MUCH, **MUCH** BETTER!
HEY, MISTER! HOW COME YOU'RE NOT WEARING **SHOES**?
CAIN'T AFFORD 'EM!
HERE! BUY YOURSELF A DOZEN PAIR!
MY KIDS AIN'T GOT SHOES, NUTHER, MISTER! NER MY OL' WOMAN!
HOW MANY KIDS?
TWENTY-THREE! AND MY SIXTEEN BROTHERS AND TWELVE SISTERS HAVE KIDS, TOO! AND THERE'S AUNTS AND UNCLES—
I GOT RID OF 750 POUNDS OF MONEY! SURE WOULD BE SOME COUNTRY TO SELL BIRTHDAY CARDS!
CHECK!

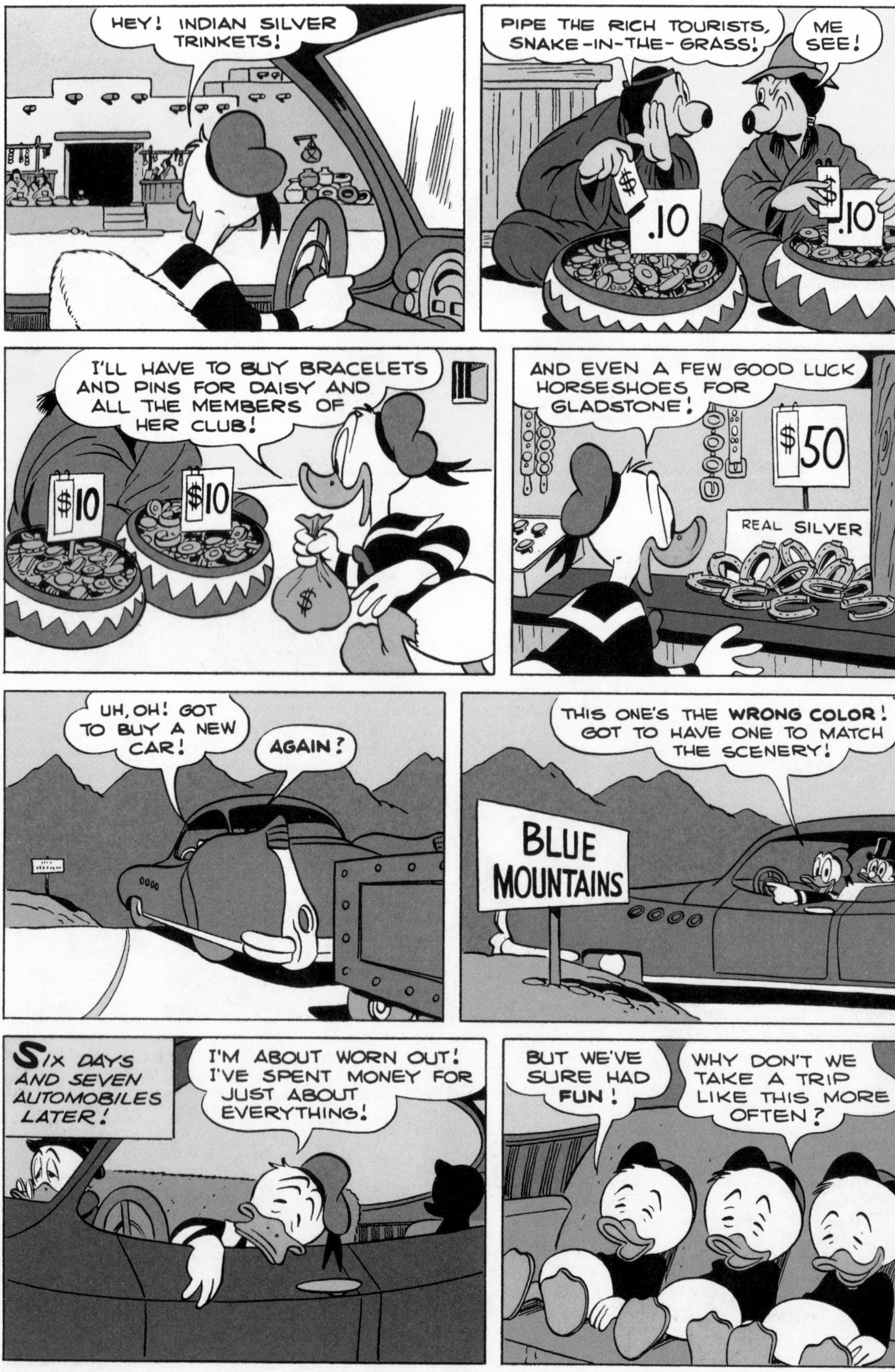
HEY! INDIAN SILVER TRINKETS!
PIPE THE RICH TOURISTS, SNAKE-IN-THE-GRASS!
ME SEE!
$
.10
$
.10
I'LL HAVE TO BUY BRACELETS AND PINS FOR DAISY AND ALL THE MEMBERS OF HER CLUB!
$10
$10
$
AND EVEN A FEW GOOD LUCK HORSESHOES FOR GLADSTONE!
$50
REAL SILVER
UH, OH! GOT TO BUY A NEW CAR!
AGAIN?
THIS ONE'S THE WRONG COLOR! GOT TO HAVE ONE TO MATCH THE SCENERY!
BLUE MOUNTAINS
SIX DAYS AND SEVEN AUTOMOBILES LATER!
I'M ABOUT WORN OUT! I'VE SPENT MONEY FOR JUST ABOUT EVERYTHING!
BUT WE'VE SURE HAD FUN!
WHY DON'T WE TAKE A TRIP LIKE THIS MORE OFTEN?

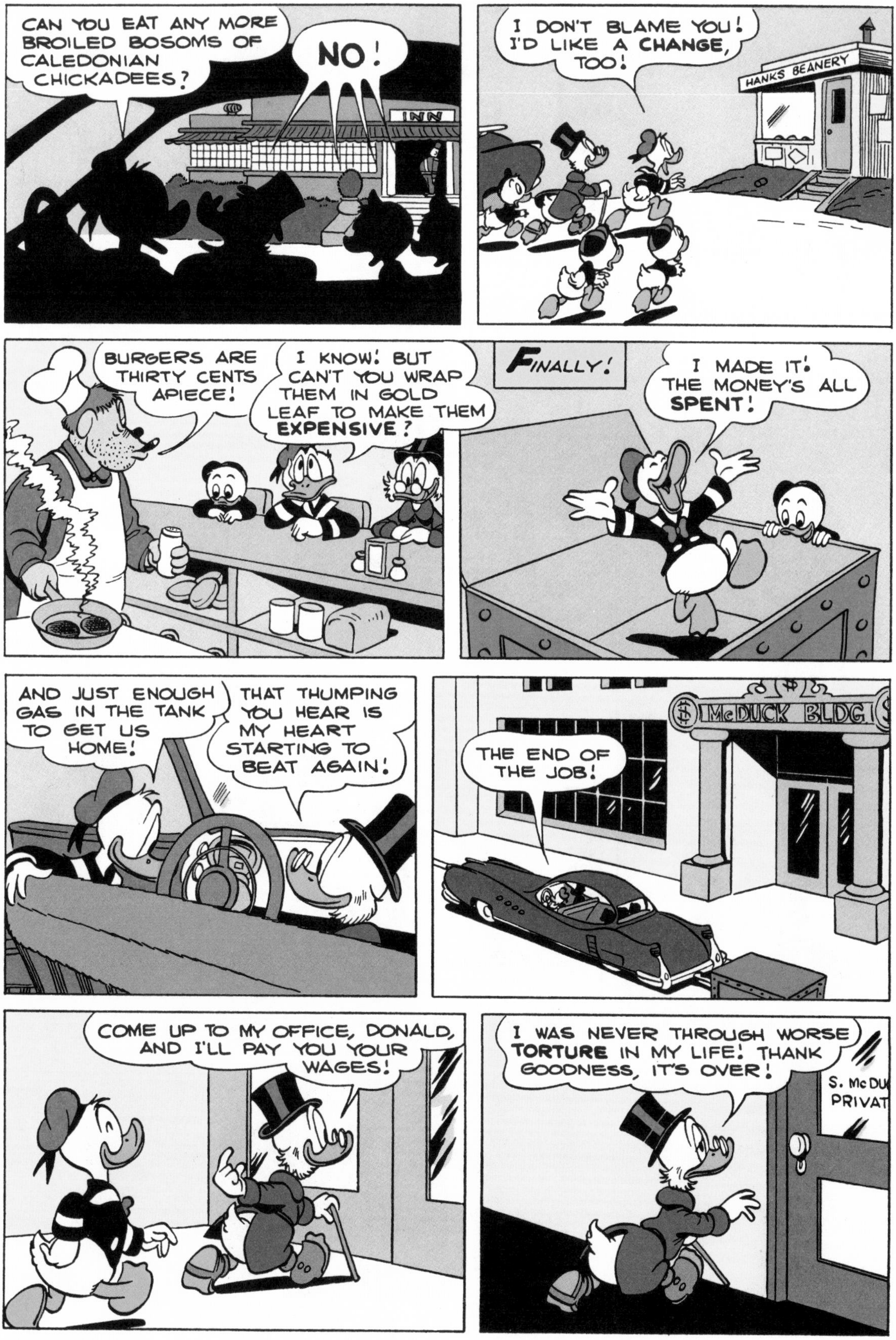
CAN YOU EAT ANY MORE BROILED BOSOMS OF CALEDONIAN CHICKADEES?
NO!
INN
I DON'T BLAME YOU! I'D LIKE A CHANGE, TOO!
HANKS BEANERY
BURGERS ARE THIRTY CENTS APIECE!
I KNOW! BUT CAN'T YOU WRAP THEM IN GOLD LEAF TO MAKE THEM EXPENSIVE?
FINALLY!
I MADE IT! THE MONEY'S ALL SPENT!
AND JUST ENOUGH GAS IN THE TANK TO GET US HOME!
THAT THUMPING YOU HEAR IS MY HEART STARTING TO BEAT AGAIN!
McDUCK BLDG
THE END OF THE JOB!
COME UP TO MY OFFICE, DONALD, AND I'LL PAY YOU YOUR WAGES!
I WAS NEVER THROUGH WORSE TORTURE IN MY LIFE! THANK GOODNESS, IT'S OVER!
S. McDU
PRIVAT

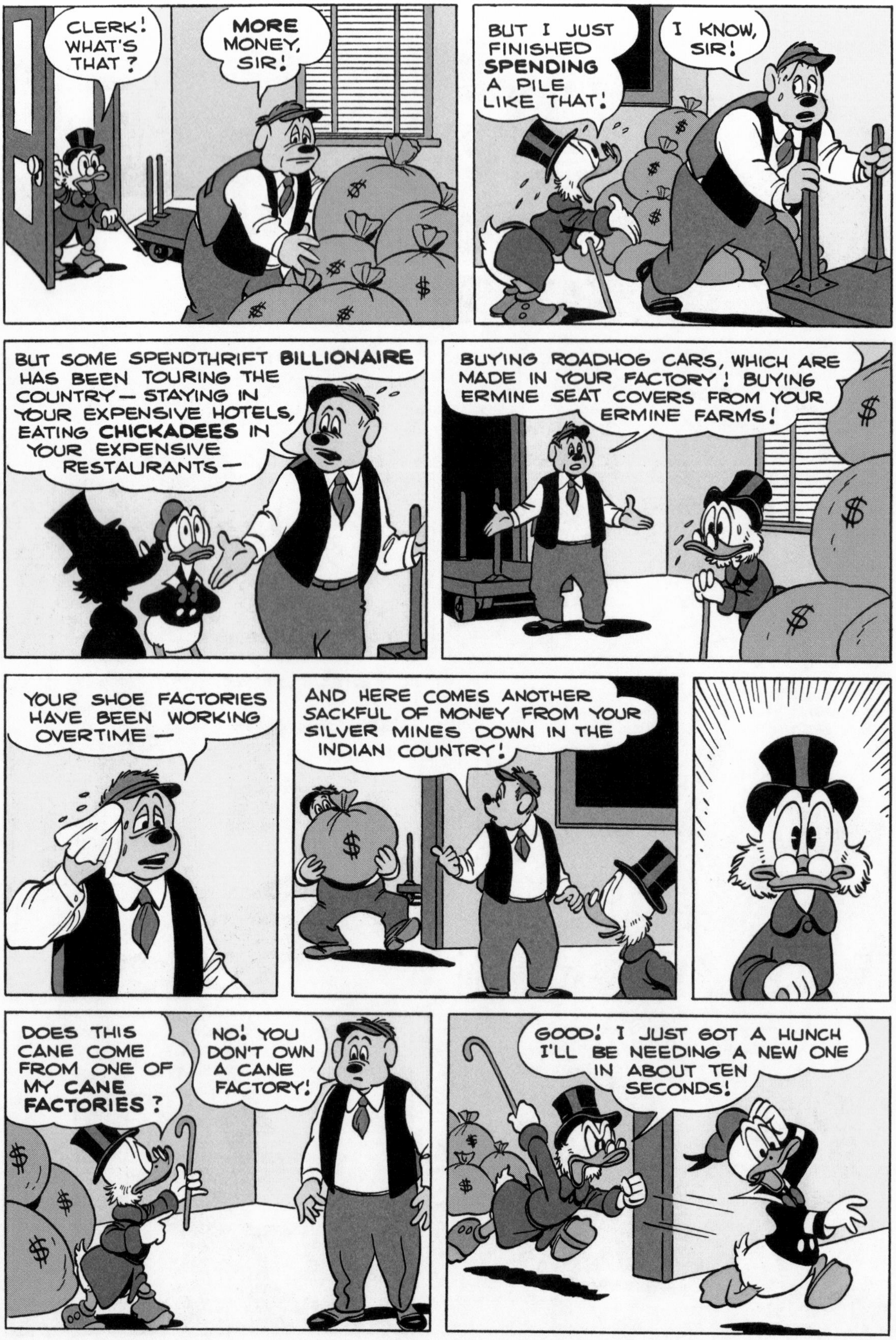

CLERK! WHAT'S THAT?
MORE MONEY, SIR!
BUT I JUST FINISHED SPENDING A PILE LIKE THAT!
I KNOW, SIR!
BUT SOME SPENDTHRIFT BILLIONAIRE HAS BEEN TOURING THE COUNTRY — STAYING IN YOUR EXPENSIVE HOTELS, EATING CHICKADEES IN YOUR EXPENSIVE RESTAURANTS —
BUYING ROADHOG CARS, WHICH ARE MADE IN YOUR FACTORY! BUYING ERMINE SEAT COVERS FROM YOUR ERMINE FARMS!
YOUR SHOE FACTORIES HAVE BEEN WORKING OVERTIME —
AND HERE COMES ANOTHER SACKFUL OF MONEY FROM YOUR SILVER MINES DOWN IN THE INDIAN COUNTRY!
DOES THIS CANE COME FROM ONE OF MY CANE FACTORIES?
NO! YOU DON'T OWN A CANE FACTORY!
GOOD! I JUST GOT A HUNCH I'LL BE NEEDING A NEW ONE IN ABOUT TEN SECONDS!

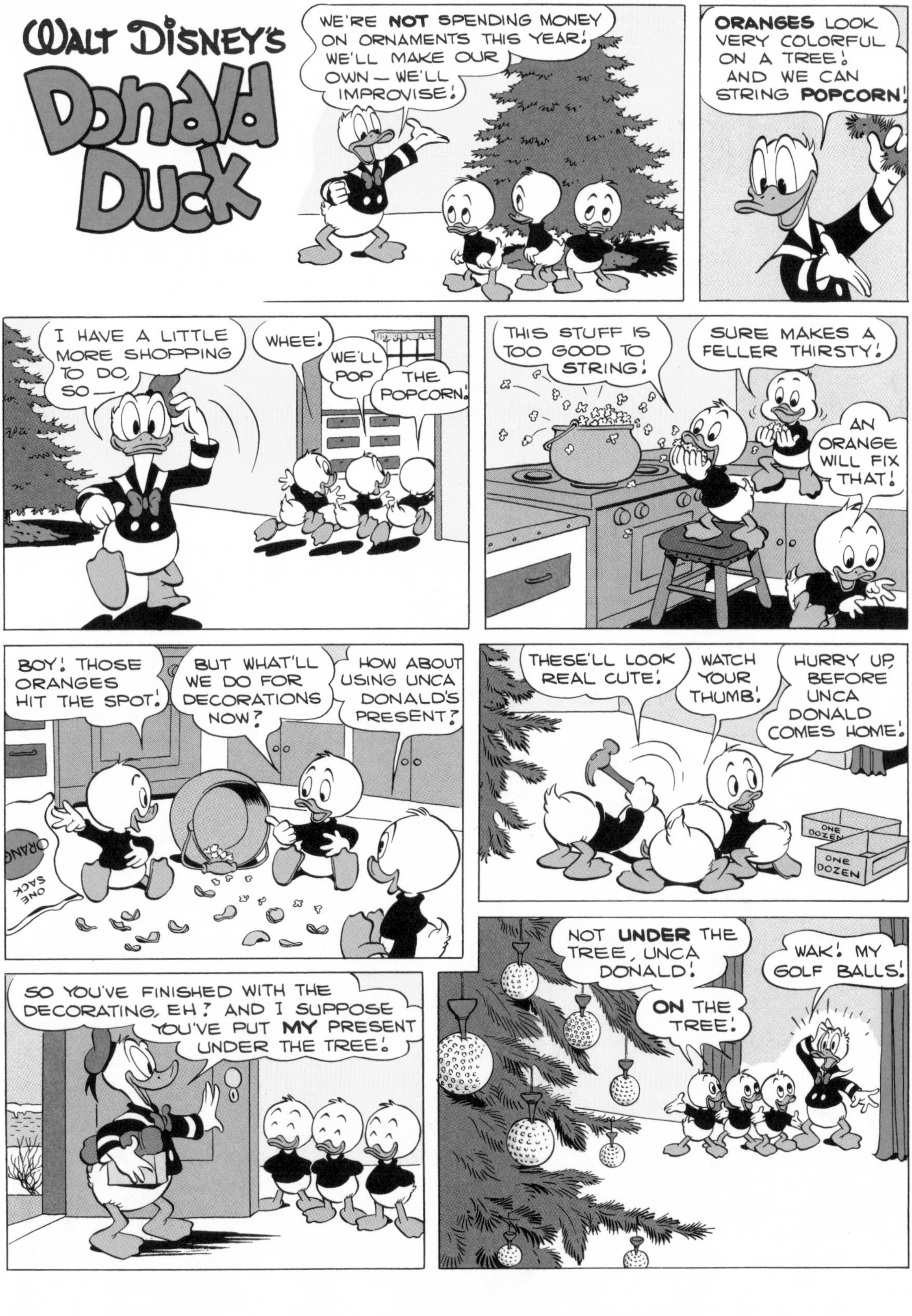
WALT DISNEY'S
Donald Duck
WE'RE NOT SPENDING MONEY ON ORNAMENTS THIS YEAR! WE'LL MAKE OUR OWN — WE'LL IMPROVISE!
ORANGES LOOK VERY COLORFUL ON A TREE! AND WE CAN STRING POPCORN!
I HAVE A LITTLE MORE SHOPPING TO DO, SO —
WHEE!
WE'LL POP
THE POPCORN!
THIS STUFF IS TOO GOOD TO STRING!
SURE MAKES A FELLER THIRSTY!
AN ORANGE WILL FIX THAT!
BOY! THOSE ORANGES HIT THE SPOT!
BUT WHAT'LL WE DO FOR DECORATIONS NOW?
HOW ABOUT USING UNCA DONALD'S PRESENT?
ONE SACK
THESE'LL LOOK REAL CUTE!
WATCH YOUR THUMB!
HURRY UP, BEFORE UNCA DONALD COMES HOME!
ONE DOZEN
ONE DOZEN
SO YOU'VE FINISHED WITH THE DECORATING, EH? AND I SUPPOSE YOU'VE PUT MY PRESENT UNDER THE TREE!
NOT UNDER THE TREE, UNCA DONALD!
ON THE TREE!
WAK! MY GOLF BALLS!

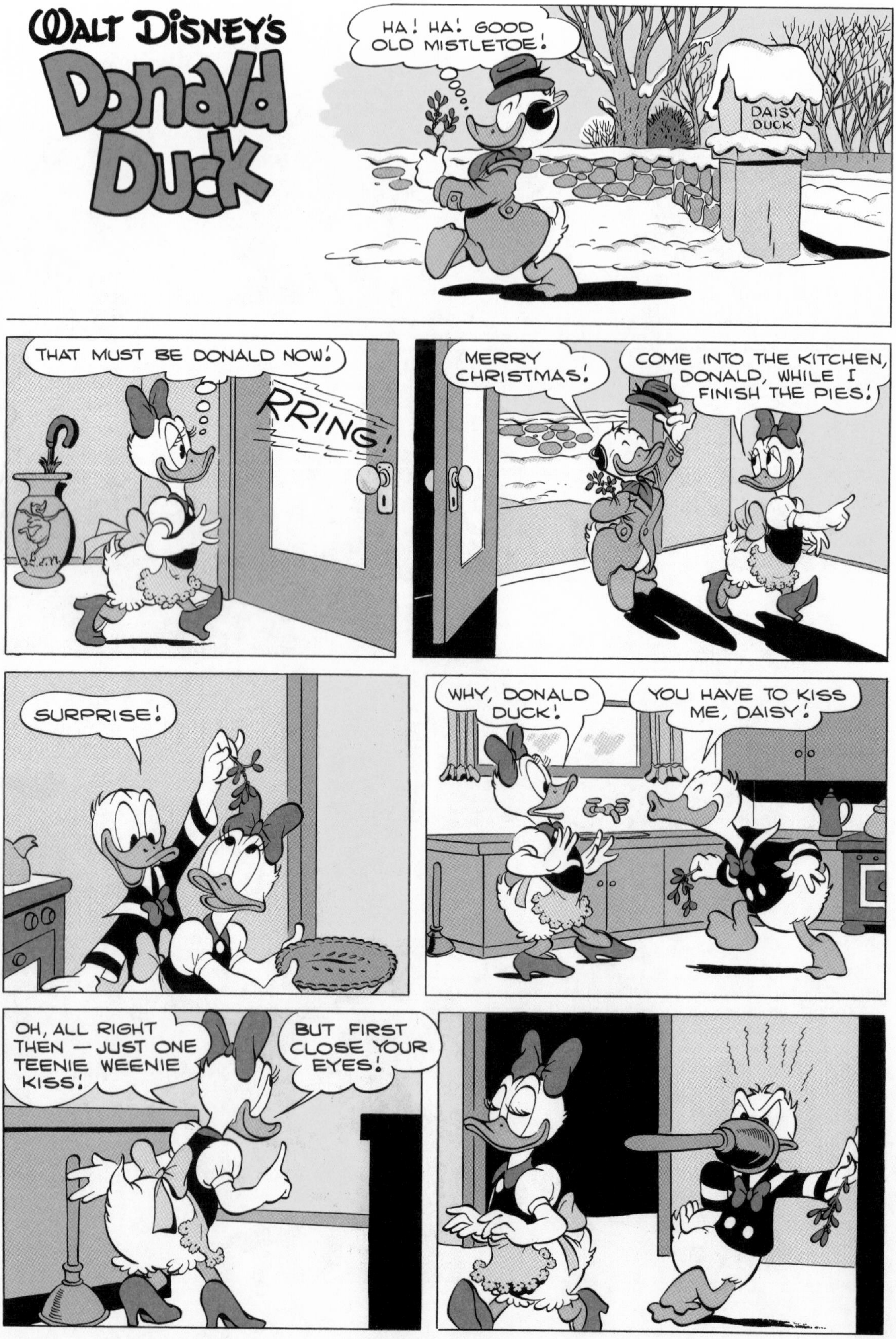
WALT DISNEY'S
Donald Duck
HA! HA! GOOD OLD MISTLETOE!
DAISY DUCK
THAT MUST BE DONALD NOW!
RRING!
MERRY CHRISTMAS!
COME INTO THE KITCHEN, DONALD, WHILE I FINISH THE PIES!
SURPRISE!
WHY, DONALD DUCK!
YOU HAVE TO KISS ME, DAISY!
OH, ALL RIGHT THEN — JUST ONE TEENIE WEENIE KISS!
BUT FIRST CLOSE YOUR EYES!

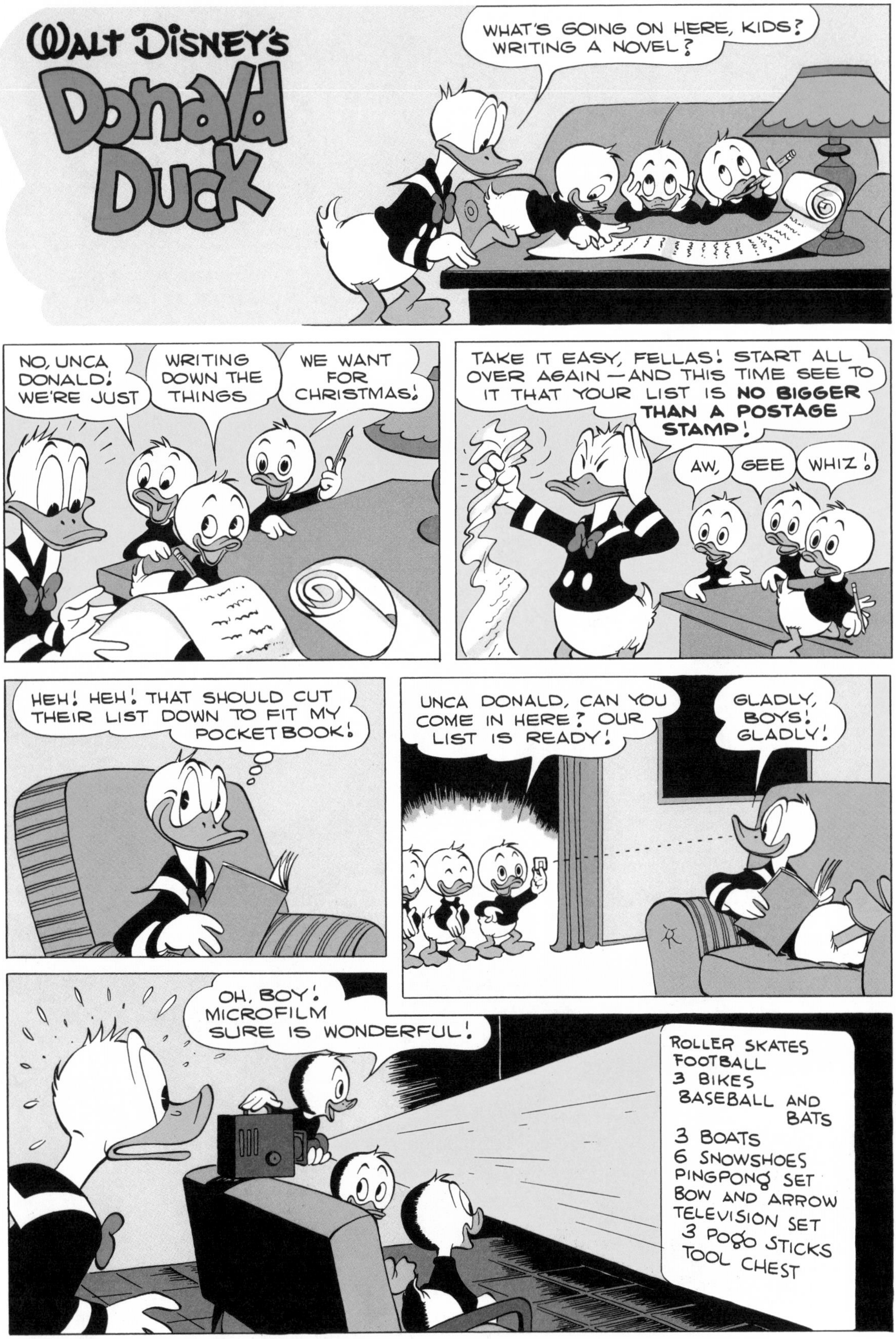
WALT DISNEY'S
Donald Duck
WHAT'S GOING ON HERE, KIDS? WRITING A NOVEL?
NO, UNCA DONALD! WE'RE JUST
WRITING DOWN THE THINGS
WE WANT FOR CHRISTMAS!
TAKE IT EASY, FELLAS! START ALL OVER AGAIN — AND THIS TIME SEE TO IT THAT YOUR LIST IS NO BIGGER THAN A POSTAGE STAMP!
AW,
GEE
WHIZ!
HEH! HEH! THAT SHOULD CUT THEIR LIST DOWN TO FIT MY POCKETBOOK!
UNCA DONALD, CAN YOU COME IN HERE? OUR LIST IS READY!
GLADLY, BOYS! GLADLY!
OH, BOY! MICROFILM SURE IS WONDERFUL!
ROLLER SKATES
FOOTBALL
3 BIKES
BASEBALL AND BATS
3 BOATS
6 SNOWSHOES
PINGPONG SET
BOW AND ARROW
TELEVISION SET
3 POGO STICKS
TOOL CHEST

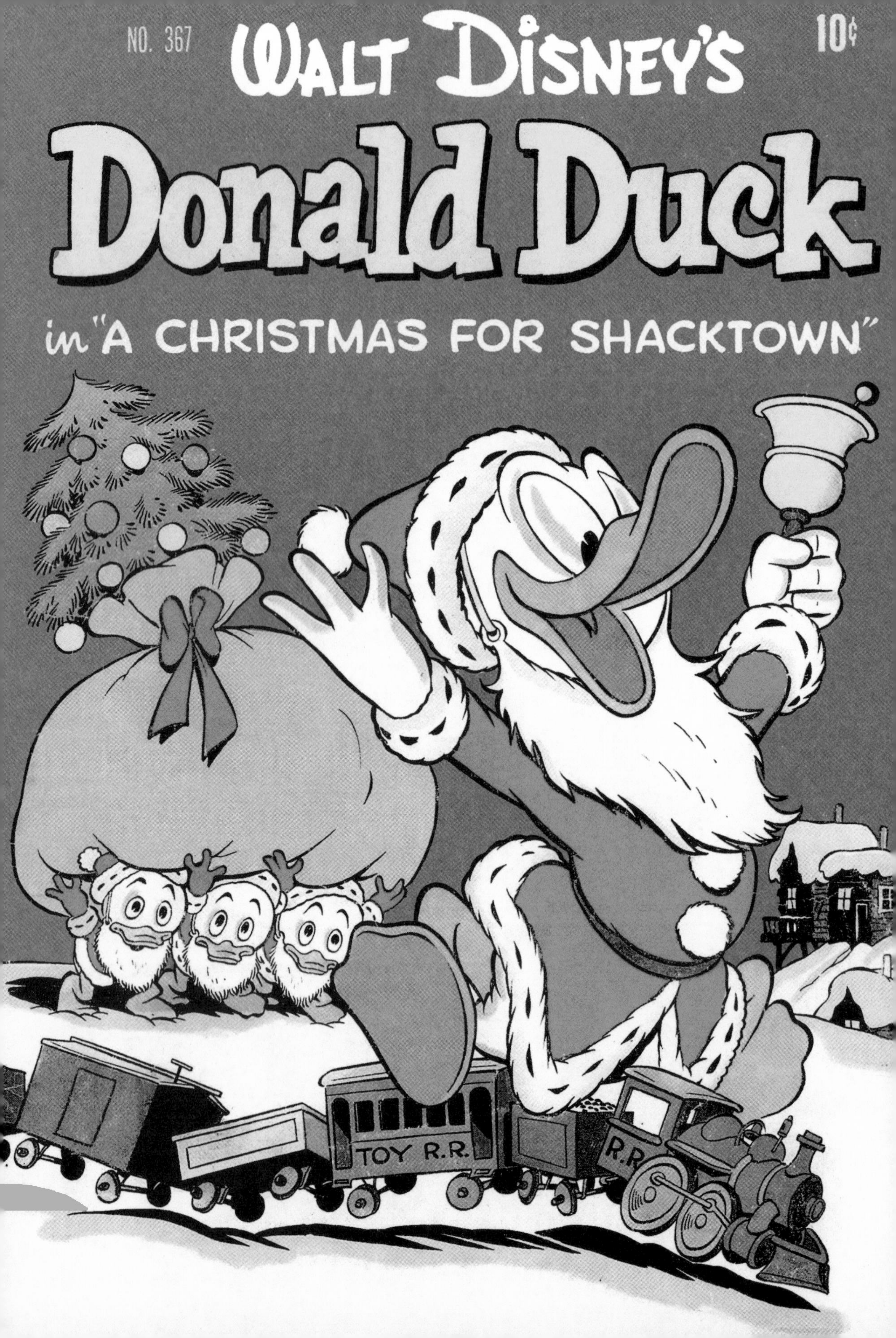

NO. 367
WALT DISNEY'S
10¢
Donald Duck
in "A CHRISTMAS FOR SHACKTOWN"
TOY R.R.
R.R.

Story Notes

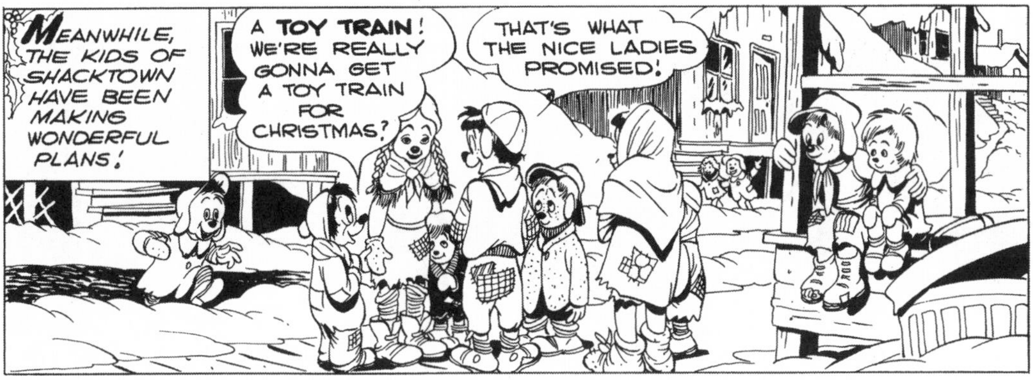

MEANWHILE, THE KIDS OF SHACKTOWN HAVE BEEN MAKING WONDERFUL PLANS!
A TOY TRAIN! WE'RE REALLY GONNA GET A TOY TRAIN FOR CHRISTMAS?
THAT'S WHAT THE NICE LADIES PROMISED!

A CHRISTMAS FOR SHACKTOWN *p. 1*

While Carl Barks was no rebel, his one great dissent with his society was in the matter of Christmas. That holiday, which all of mass entertainment thinks of as Payday, was to Barks just another day when men are wicked in their hearts.

"A Christmas For Shacktown" was perhaps his most significant concession to the season that he viewed with distaste as a festival of greed, materialism, and false sentiment. Huey, Dewey, and Louie have their visions of sugar plums curdled when they take a shortcut through Shacktown, a scene of impoverishment that would have sent Jacob Riis running for the Super Technika.

Clearly, no feast will survive the presence of these specters. The three bodhisattvas determine to sacrifice their own holiday and recruit the fortunate of Duckburg to bring Christmas to the children of Shacktown. Donald is naturally happy to back the play with the last dollar of his Uncle Scrooge's money.

Where Donald is sure Scrooge has enough money to make any wish of his come true, Scrooge considers "enough" to be a concept that doesn't apply to money, even as his hoard attains a mass that can no longer be supported by the Earth's crust.

Like the scene in *Guys and Dolls* where Nathan Detroit tries to lure Sky Masterson into a rigged proposition bet, then Sky turns the tables with an impromptu proposition bet to his own advantage, Scrooge, in his Caledonian savvy, makes his contribution dependent on Donald matching it. (I never approved of the TV cartoon's depiction of Scrooge with a Scottish accent, as to me he is as American as cold beer, but here we have an infant Scrooge dandled on a Scottish knee in Scotland, so there you go.) Nevertheless, Scrooge winds up keeping Christmas in a way that all the ghosts in the Haunted Mansion couldn't scare out of him.

Barks's "A Christmas For Shacktown" would provide the setting for the very first comic strip ever drawn by a budding young cartoonist named Robert Crumb.

— R. Fiore

THE BIG BIN ON KILLMOTOR HILL *p. 33*

Finally the king has his castle. "The Big Bin On Killmotor Hill" sees the debut of a central icon in Scrooge McDuck's mythology: the Money Bin. Tall, huge, positioned on a hilltop — Killmotor Hill — overlooking Duckburg, the Bin is at once a castle and a prison. Here is the fortress in which Scrooge keeps all his money — or at

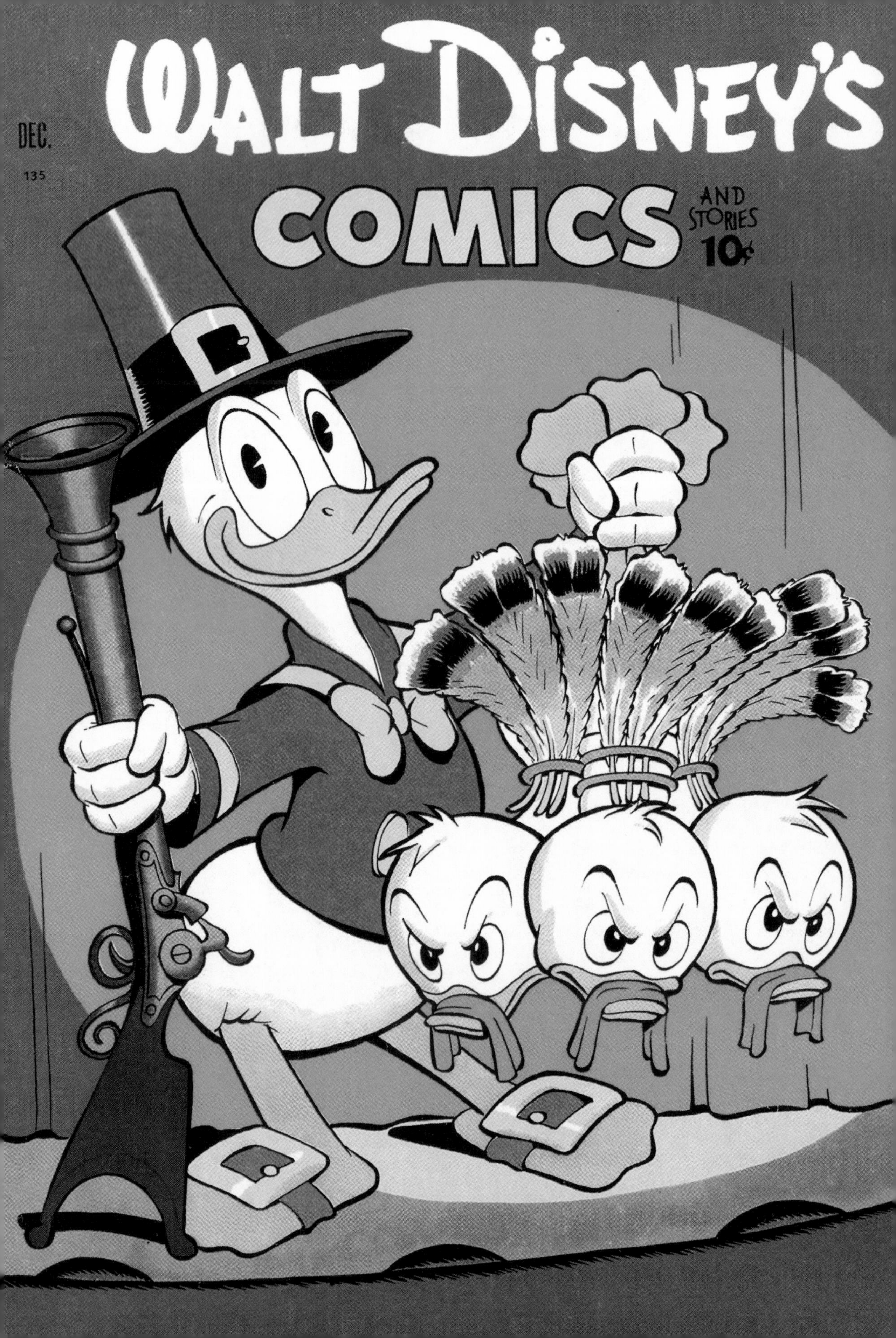
WALT DISNEY'S
DEC.
135
COMICS
AND STORIES
10¢

AND I LIKE TO RUN AROUND IN IT IN MY BARE FEET AND FEEL THOUSAND-DOLLAR BILLS CRACKLING BETWEEN MY TOES!

least the money he loves most. Here he has fun touching it, looking at it, swimming in it (perhaps substituting "him" or "her" for "it," since money is effectively Scrooge's favorite person). But then comes the prison factor. Protected by boobytraps and radar, the Bin seems impossible for a burglar to get into — but, as we see in this story, it's also very difficult to get *out* of.

As cartoonist Don Rosa wrote in the notes to his "Life And Times Of Scrooge McDuck" series, "The Big Bin On Killmotor Hill" "was simply when Barks first came up with the classic idea of a Money Bin, but thereafter he treated the Bin as though it had *always* been around." Today it is almost inconceivable that a reader could think of Scrooge without picturing his Money Bin as well. This is why, in Rosa's own version of Duck continuity, he establishes that a young Scrooge built the Bin as soon as he arrived in Duckburg.

The Money Bin's real-life story began with a huge water reservoir constructed by multi-millionaire William F. Whittier. Founder of the town of Hemet, California — Barks's home for

many years — Whittier pumped water from the reservoir to a huge treatment plant on Hemet's Park Hill. The iconic building on a hill inspired the home of Scrooge's fortune.

And with the Bin came the Beagle Boys. This gang of robbers had just been created in *Walt Disney's Comics And Stories* the previous month — and they would become permanently linked with the Bin. The Beagle Boys' only goal seems to be robbing Scrooge by draining the Bin. Sometimes it is Scrooge himself, constantly worrying about a Beagle heist, who unwittingly makes the task easier for the Beagles, as we see in this tale.

With the creation of the Money Bin and the introduction of the Beagle Boys, Carl Barks has almost refined Scrooge into the classic character we all know today. Barks has yet to make him more sympathetic and adventurous but this would occur in the classic "Only A Poor Old Man," published just three months after "The Big Bin On Killmotor Hill" (See *Walt Disney's Uncle Scrooge: "Only A Poor Old Man"* in this series).

— Stefano Priarone

GLADSTONE'S USUAL GOOD YEAR *p. 43*

If there were a *Baseball Abstract* for comic books, the box score for another pitcher's duel between Donald Duck and Gladstone Gander in "Gladstone's Usual Good Year" would look something like this:

Goal: Donald wants to win a raffle for a turkey, so he buys every ticket — except the one bought by Gladstone.

Total number of Donald's attempts: Three.

Means by which Donald will cheat: In the

NOW, PUT YOUR TICKET IN *THERE*!

WHAT ON EARTH ARE *THOSE*?

MY TICKETS!

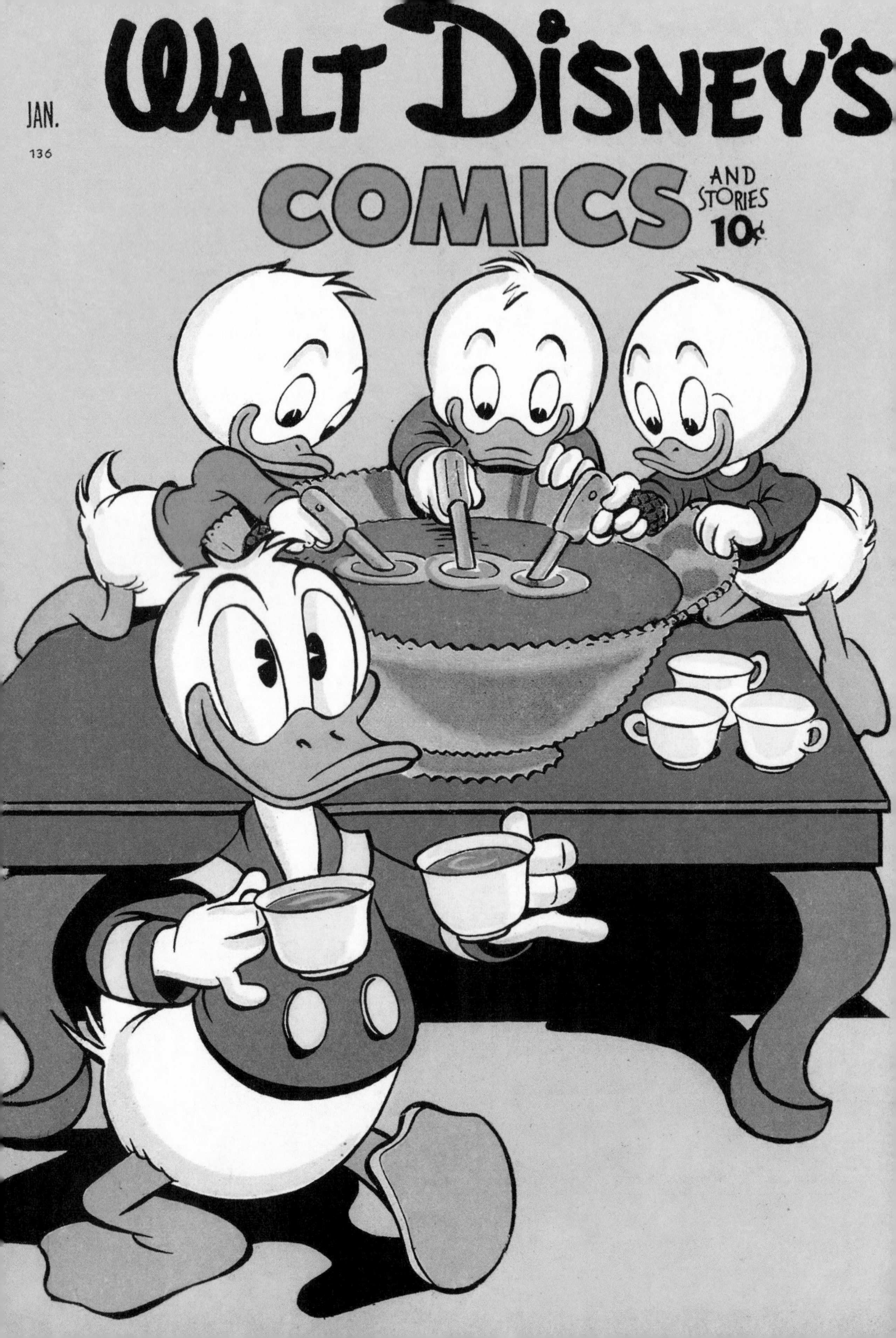
WALT DISNEY'S
JAN.
136
COMICS
AND STORIES
10¢

OH, MY STARS! HERE COMES THAT SCREAMING COWBOY!
OH, BURY ME THAR—
ROAR
AND THERE GOES ANOTHER AVALANCHE!

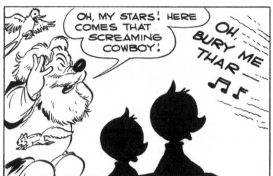

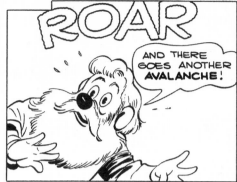

first raffle, he roughens his tickets with pinholes so they'll be more likely to be picked; in the second raffle, he impregnates his tickets with steel so they can be picked out with a magnet; in the third, he organizes his own raffle and buries Gladstone's single ticket underneath a mountain of his own tickets.

Means by which Gladstone's luck foils Donald anyway: In the first raffle, Gladstone's ticket is more thoroughly roughened by a porcupine; in the second, the attempt Donald's nephews make to cheat on his behalf negates his own plan; in the third, an earthquake upends the mountain of tickets.

Quality of Donald's rage: Impotent.

— R. Fiore

THE SCREAMING COWBOY *p. 53*

The 8-year-old Carl Barks was fascinated by the cowboys he met while shoveling hay on an Oregon ranch. He respected their simplicity and toughness — day after day they accomplished demanding tasks with only the most basic supplies. The adult Barks admired popular "singing cowboys" of the 1930s and '40s — stars like Gene Autry and Roy Rogers, who sang of cattle drives and the American West. With "Screaming Cowboy," Barks gently parodies Autry and his contemporaries, while creating a double of the self-centered duck, who's known to engage in a little yelling.

It would be easy to see this as just another funny story in which Donald's selfishness leads to a series of disasters — in this case, a chain of avalanches initiated by his song. Barks often said that one of his great themes was "pride goeth before a fall" (or an avalanche), and the prideful Donald, it seems, wants to hear his tune over and over simply because he wrote it. But reading it that way sells Donald short. He longs to hear the music performed on the record, the kind of homespun sounds Barks loved and saw as an antidote to popular music's excesses: "Ah! ♥ that jug band!" (Donald's love is so deep that words can't express it). Just as he appreciated the simplicity of the cowboy ethic, Barks cherished the old-timey character of jug bands.

Barks once described his taste in music as "straight hillbilly." For all its elegance and inventiveness, his cartooning aesthetic is "straight hillbilly" too. Like "the old turkey-in-the-straw type of music" he preferred, his stories, especially 10-pagers like "The Screaming Cowboy," were rigorously formulaic: they opened with the introduction of a theme/problem (such as a yelling cowboy), featured a series of gags based on that problem (with each iteration offering a variation), and ended with a solution already present in the theme. In this story, the song's opening lyric "Oh, bury me thar with my battered git-tar" resolves once Donald is happily buried in an avalanche with a battered jukebox that plays his beloved jug band.

While we admire the ease and clarity of stories like "The Screaming Cowboy," Barks would likely remind us of how much careful planning and, at times, painful effort his comics required. Like the cowboys of his youth, he dedicated himself to his work. With only the most basic supplies — pencil, ink, and paper — Barks accomplished demanding artistic tasks, day after day.

— Ken Parille

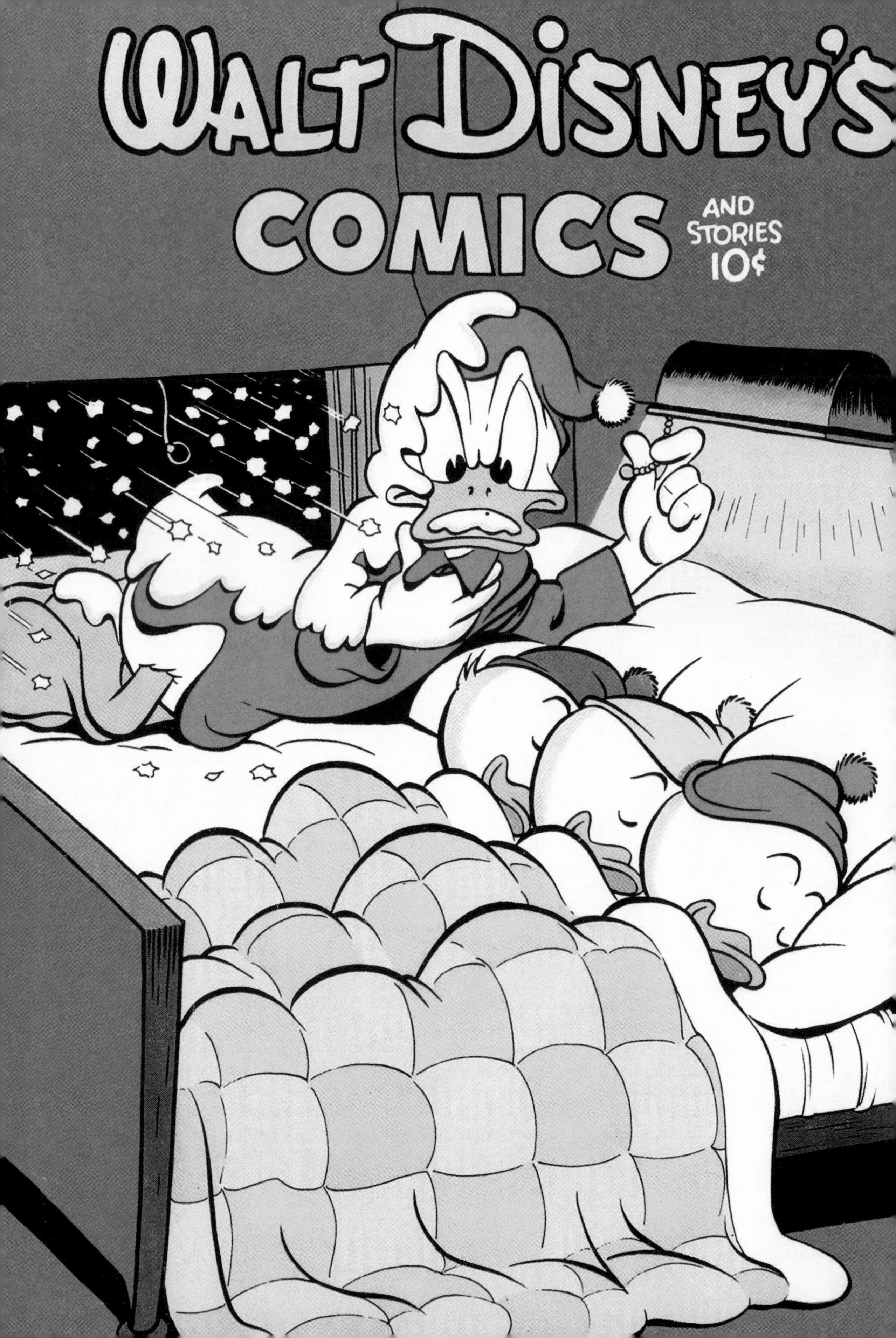
WALT DISNEY'S
COMICS
AND STORIES
10¢

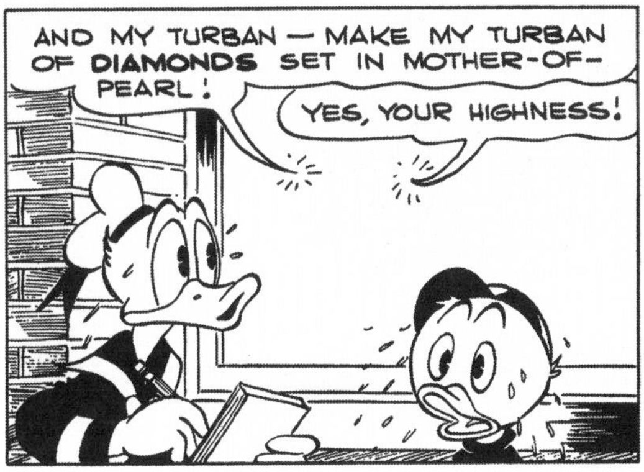
AND MY TURBAN — MAKE MY TURBAN OF DIAMONDS SET IN MOTHER-OF-PEARL!
YES, YOUR HIGHNESS!

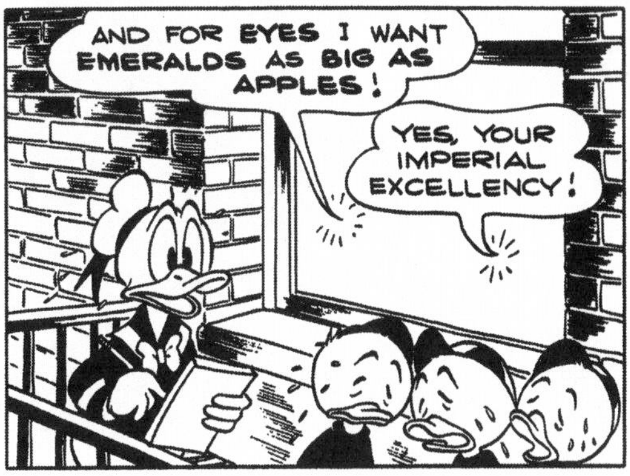
AND FOR EYES I WANT EMERALDS AS BIG AS APPLES!
YES, YOUR IMPERIAL EXCELLENCY!

STATUESQUE SPENDTHRIFTS *p. 63*

More than 20 years after the publication of some of his stories, Carl Barks confessed to a certain amazement over what he'd been able to include: "I thought, how in the hell did I get away with that?" he told interviewer Donald Ault. About "Statuesque Spendthrifts" specifically, he remarked: "Oh man, that was full of cynicism."

The story's black humor is rooted in its broad satiric swipes, while antic pantomimes invite the immediate laughs. Character motivation and internal states are clearly established by look alone. Poses and faces are as directly and easily read as an articulate silent movie comedy. This is not to say expressions lack all subtlety — see, for instance, the range captured in Donald's eyes when he visits Scrooge in the Money Bin to provoke the old tycoon.

The plot develops along ordered steps at breakneck speed. Just as quickly, the increasingly outrageous and unsettling statuary comes to overwhelm the scales of man and nature, towering over the cityscape and frightening the beasts of the field. No one intervenes in the runaway competition — not the diverted citizenry, not its opportunistic public servants, and certainly not Donald, initially the provocateur and, eventually, a co-conspirator. The unchecked crescendo portends farcical grief.

Given Barks's reading habits, it seems quite possible he was familiar with potlatch ceremonies of Native Americans in the Pacific Northwest. Potlatches were gift-giving occasions such as weddings or social celebrations. In troubled times, they also functioned as a means of conflict resolution — as a pointed display of their material might, rival chieftains would ostentatiously bestow more and more extravagant gifts to demonstrate the depth and breadth of their resources and their willingness to lavish available treasure. This would go on until the more profligate side was driven toward — and sometimes into — destitution and ruination, much like the maharajah here.

Barks scrupulously avoided controversial issues in his comics, but it's hard to overlook a parallel to the nuclear arms race of the period, particularly the intimidating test detonations of bigger and ever-bigger bombs conducted by the United States and the Soviet Union. In this light, the aghast, woeful expression of the Ducks on the bottom of page 69 and the panicked looks of the politicians as they realize the dimensions of the forces they have unleashed suggests additional meaning.

That the era's atomic weapons and Duckburg's colossi stand alike as monuments to inutility offers both historical insight and enduring implications.

— Rich Kreiner

ROCKET WING SAVES THE DAY *p. 73*

Carl Barks opens "Rocket Wing Saves the Day" with a famous phrase from the work of Alfred, Lord Tennyson, the 19th century poet celebrated for his musicality and metrical precision: "In the Spring, a young man's fancy lightly turns to thoughts of — "

Barks cuts Tennyson's quote off before the final word ("love") and hands the reins to Donald, who literally woos Daisy with a series of "woos." To emphasize how unmusically Donald sings, Barks draws an eavesdropping seagull with an agitated expression.

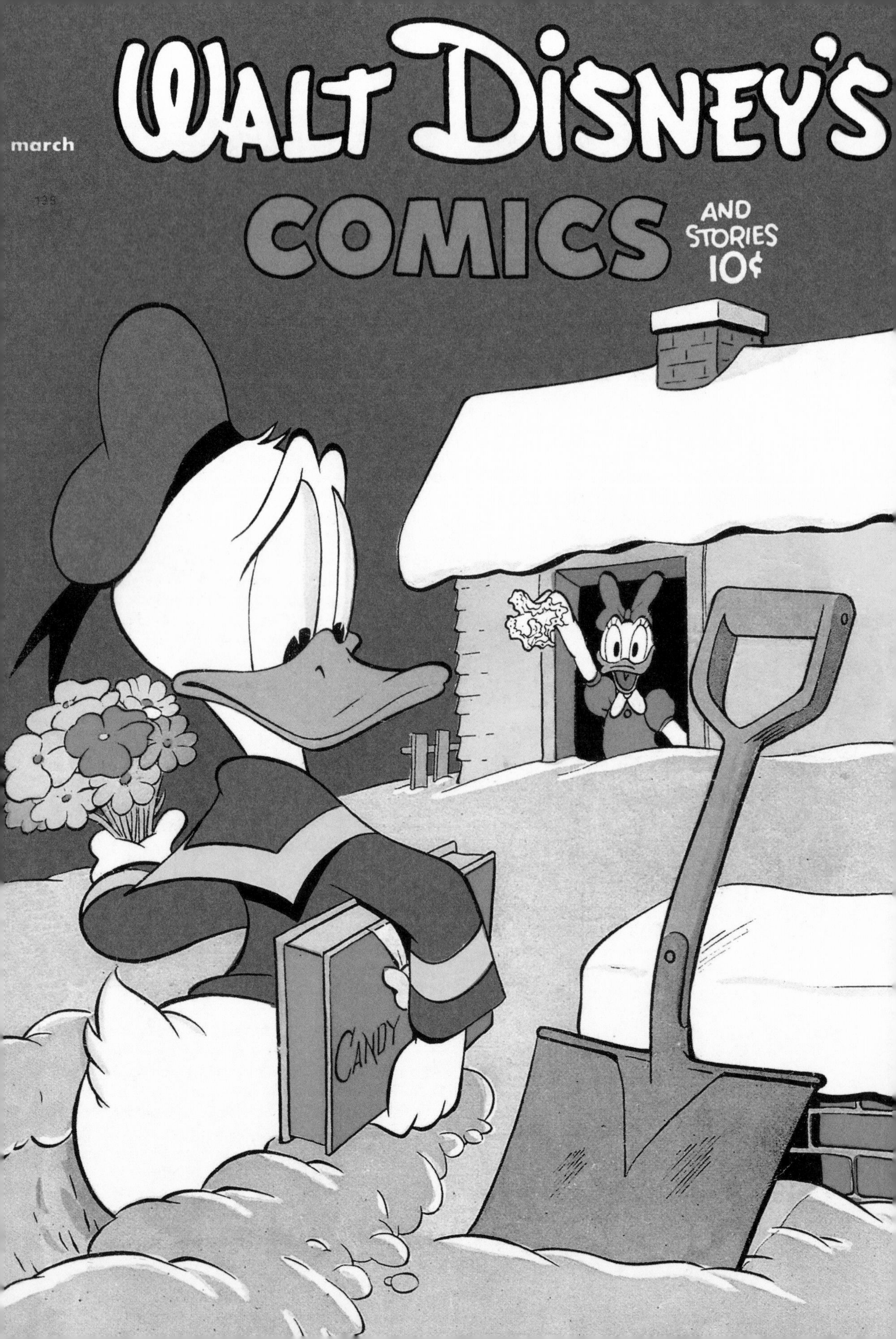
WALT DISNEY'S
march
COMICS
AND STORIES
10¢
CANDY

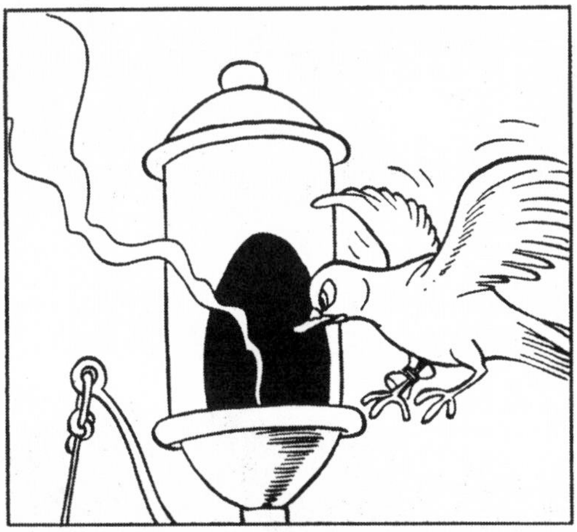

For Barks, the "sound" of his text matters as much as the believability of his characters and the timing of his gags. Like a poet, he pays careful attention to meter, even counting syllables to ensure that a line has just the right rhythm. This practice, Barks noted, helps to "create an even flow, so that it was almost like prose poetry the way the ducks' voices would come in."

Barks believed that a good comic book story is, by definition, one that can be read effortlessly. Its language must be minimal and musical. Even during a moment of sea-borne distress, Donald finds just the right rhyme: "My good luck's played out! That's a waterspout!"

Barks also wants his characters' names to be aurally interesting, like the alliterative Daisy Duck or the rhyming Huey, Dewey, and Louie. The pigeons' names are inspired by a contemporary technology known for its powerful sonic qualities: World War II-era military rocket and jet engines. The homing pigeon, Rocket Wing, takes his name from America's first rocket-powered plane, the Northrop MX-324 Rocket Wing. Donald gives Rocket Wing the mean-spirited alliterative and onomatopoeic epithet of Buzzbomb, nickname of the German V-1 missile infamous for its buzzing sound. One of Rocket Wing's opponents is Sabrejet, a name based on the American F-86 Sabre, a transonic jet fighter in wide use when this story was first published.

The story's intrigue revolves around flight and sound: a series of whistles sidetracks Rocket Wing from his mission. Just as the seagull is disturbed by Donald's "woos," Rocket Wing is distracted by the nephews' "tooos" and "toots," as well as the many whistles that "toot," "tweet," "fweet," and "twoot." Always interested in thematic (and aural) closure, Barks neatly wraps up the story's "zooming" and whistling in the last two panels — for the first time, a bell rings, then the story ends with an image of technologically produced silence: Rocket Wing has won the race because the nephews have cleverly equipped him with a set of sound-blocking earmuffs.

— Ken Parille

GLADSTONE'S TERRIBLE SECRET *p. 83*

If there was one character in his universe that Carl Barks genuinely found distasteful it was Gladstone Gander. Uncle Scrooge might be a miser and a bully, but he'd earned his fortune through work and personal sacrifice. Even the criminal Beagle Boys are often brilliantly creative in their efforts to part Scrooge from his gold, and their unscrupulousness was always entertaining — often even for Scrooge himself, who considered them to be his worthiest adversaries.

But Gladstone inspires only negative emotions from Barks and his creations — outrage, envy, bewilderment, and despair. All of these emotions are on display in "Gladstone's Terrible Secret," as Donald and his nephews swing from the pits of their despair — Gladstone makes "the rest of us feel so futile!" a defeated Donald moans — to (in the very next panel) determined outrage: "There *must* be a *limit* to his luck! There must be *something* he can't get for nothing!"

Of course, there is no limit. But neither is there any secret that can be stolen, copied, or patented. Unlike Scrooge's fortune, which

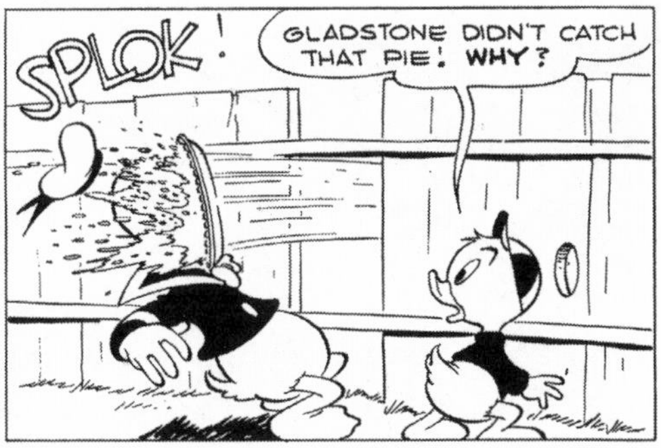
SPLOK!
GLADSTONE DIDN'T CATCH THAT PIE! WHY?

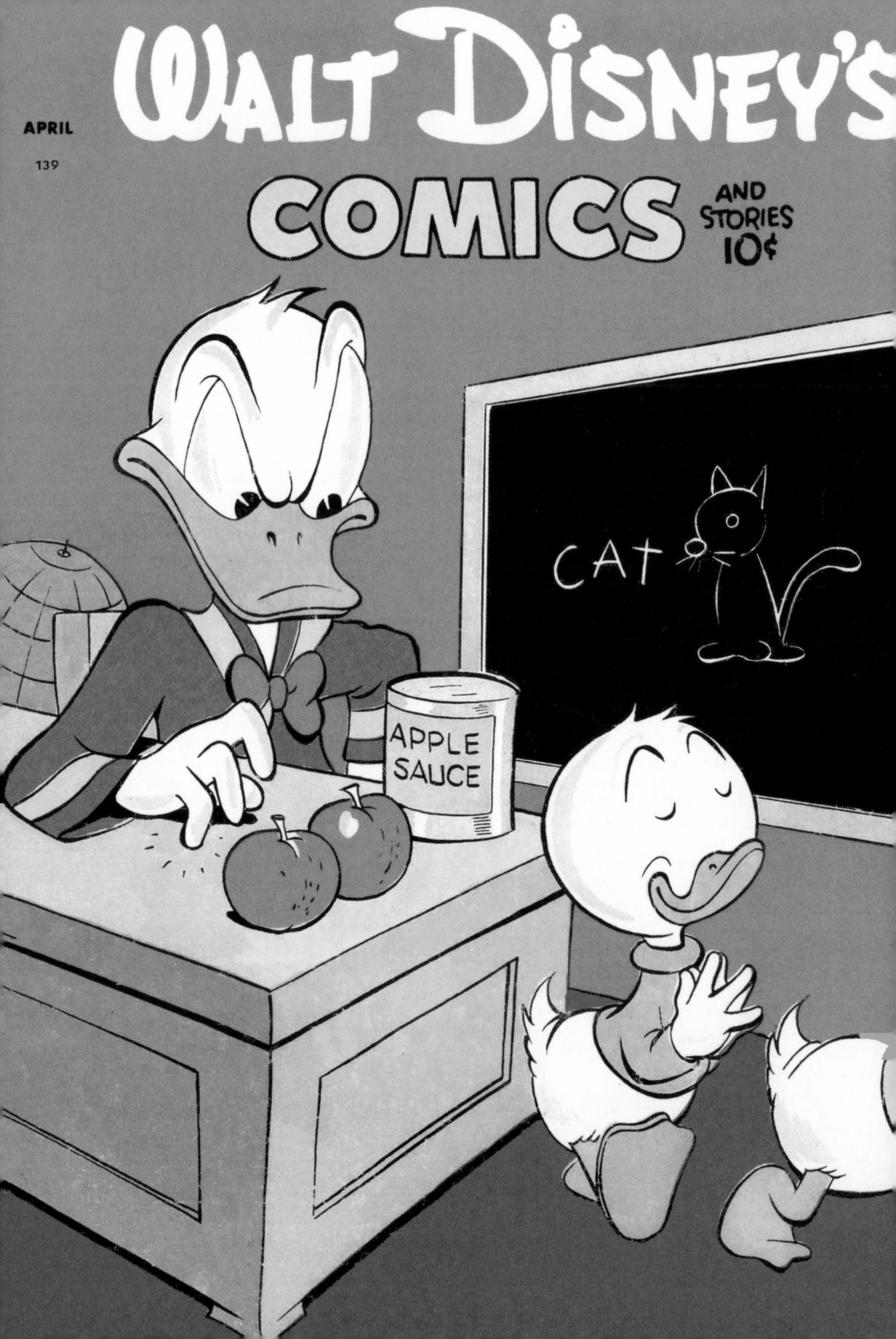
WALT DISNEY'S
APRIL
139
COMICS
AND STORIES
10¢
CAT
APPLE SAUCE

always remains vulnerable to theft, market forces, or natural disaster, Gladstone's good fortune is unassailable and non-transferable.

In their attempts to unlock Gladstone's secret, Donald, Scrooge, and the nephews discover, not the talisman they hope for, but a souvenir from Gladstone's most shameful day when, in a fit of weakness, he once labored for money. "That dime isn't a good luck charm!" Gladstone shouts to the safecrackers. "It's — well, it's none of your business!"

Indeed, the dime is none of anyone's business, and Gladstone intends to keep it that way — locked away, forever out of circulation, breaking (or at least burying) the transaction that almost connected Gladstone irrevocably to a market economy and to everyone else's business.

The dime Gladstone has buried in his safe, untouched since the day it was earned, is liable to "ruin" him — and not just because he worries about his reputation in the eyes of Donald and Scrooge. Perhaps even more urgently, Gladstone has come to believe that only his fanatical rejection of all labor and market exchange has allowed him to continue to live in the effortless style to which he has become accustomed.

Even taking on a "really tough" test to prove the extent of his luck smacks too much of "work" for Gladstone. The secret to his success, at least so far as Gladstone understands it, is never doubting his ability to get something — everything — for nothing. The dime represents his one moment of doubt and the one potential link to his "ruin."

But all of this is what Gladstone experiences at the sight of his dime. What Donald, Scrooge, and the nephews experience is another thing entirely, and something that cannot be printed in the paper. In fact, so horrified are they by what they have heard that Donald and the rest are rendered mute — and in silhouette — as if, after the wide range of negative emotions their faces have conveyed throughout the story, there is no image, no expression left to convey the depths of their disgust for Gladstone at this moment. Or that of Barks himself.

— Jared Gardner

THE THINK BOX BOLLIX *p. 93*

There was never really any doubt that Barks was writing about human beings that just happened to look like ducks. In this story he clearly

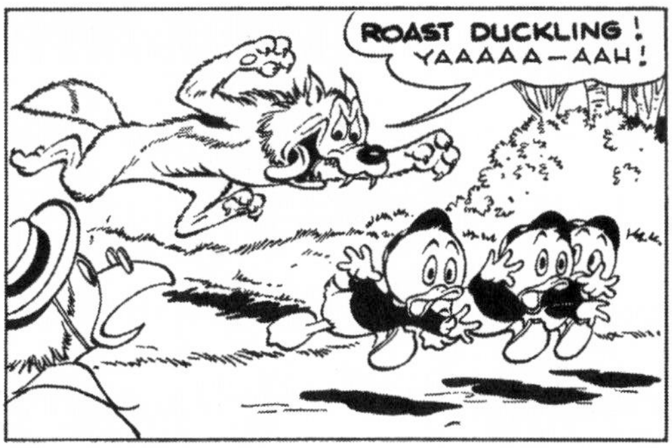
ROAST DUCKLING!
YAAAAA—AAH!

decided to have some fun with this conceit, and in the process created one of his most disturbing, as well as hilarious, tales of funny animals "talking and doing things like human beings."

Barks uses commonplace cartoon metaphor to blur the distinctions by which we define natural order. The ducks describe themselves as "human beings" as they set up the Think Boxes that will unsettle their identities and set in motion a series of events in which the actions of man and beast are mirrored.

When Donald dresses up as a wolf to teach Gyro and the kids a lesson, he could almost pass as the real thing were it not for the row of buttons down his chest (noticed only by the reader). To the kids, his mock voracity for "roast duckling" is truly terrifying, making them forget their self-described "humanity" and identify as feathered prey.

Typical of Barks's ironic approach to causality, the subsequent reversal seems the direct result of Donald's arrogant intervention. The real wolf is disguised as the kind of snout-faced everyman Barks routinely employs to suggest transparently a human being, but jarringly reminds us that its prototype is a dog.

Barks here merges comedy and terror with great acuity. The image of duck and wolf shedding their disguises, masks falling, carries a surrealist tinge, while Donald's creeping realization that he is suddenly "roast duck" to his aggressor is conveyed with distinct menace recognizable to any kid who has experienced a playful situation turn ugly.

On one level, the story can be read as a self-reflexive allegory of the cartoonist's trade: making animals talk and act like humans. But the parallels drawn between Donald and the wolf, panel-to-panel, are telling on a more profound level. Donald is only out to create fun, yet there is something bestial in his

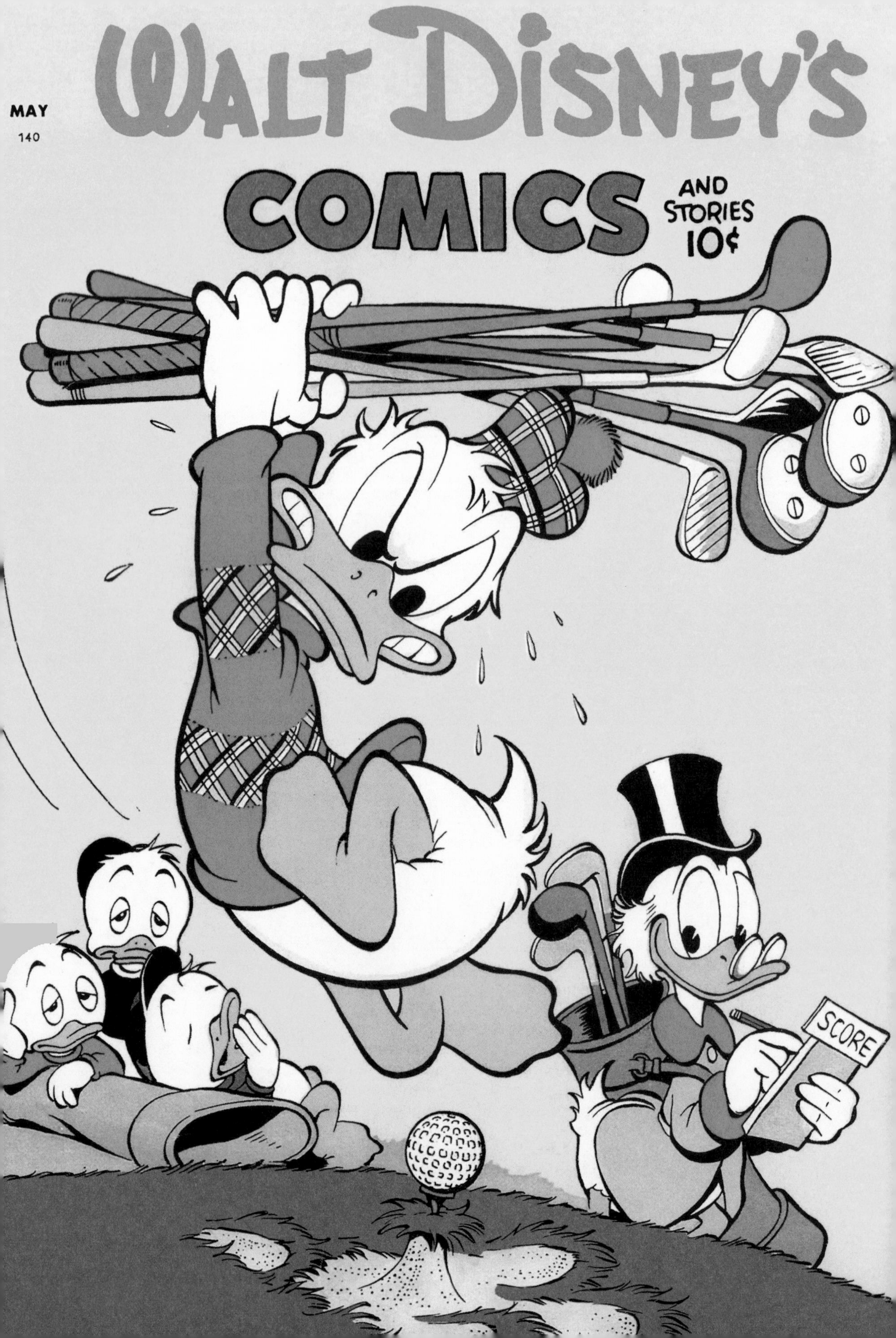
MAY
140
WALT DISNEY'S
COMICS
AND STORIES
10¢
SCORE

"transformation." And the wolf only becomes a real threat once its sentience is heightened to human levels. This is a story about how we define our humanity as something beyond our natural proclivities and how we mask the latter, socially and subconsciously.

Gyro Gearloose, whom Barks had just introduced as a bit player the previous month, appears in the first of several stories focusing on the perils and promise of science. His invention works, but to terrible effect, and, disconcertingly, his approach to the situation remains detachedly intellectual throughout.

Yet it does not seem wrong when the kids tip him as the next Edison. Although they have just been down the rabbit hole, scrambling to undo the consequences of their experiment, they walk away wide-eyed at its possibilities. Made painfully aware that he is unable to affect the situation either way, Donald tells the pesky rabbit reminding him about it to shut up.

— Matthias Wivel

THE GOLDEN HELMET *p. 105*

"The Golden Helmet" is a veritable symphony of the themes and elements that fired Carl Barks's imagination throughout his career.

As a rip-roaring adventure, it's a quest for an object of great value and power involving a race over treacherous territory to an exotic, unforgiving locale.

The ordeal is complicated by twists, turns, and calamitous reversals of fortune. Betrayals and shifting alliances within a (relatively) broadened cast roil the plot and confound anticipation. Unlike heroic contests of myth and legend, incredulity makes a shambles of any question about who might actually be a worthy claimant of the prize.

Humor and hazard travel beak-by-jowl. Comedic caricatures oppose scowls of sour and oily villainy. Eyes are expressive, animated; grotesqueries kept to a minimum. With Sharky, Barks created his paragon of shysters, an unscrupulous for-hire mouthpiece spouting Latinate gibberish on behalf of whoever enjoys, momentarily, the upper hand. Plus there are puffins!

Even heaped this high, two additional features stand out. One is the dynamic rhythm sustained throughout the epic. Each scene is fully fleshed out, every break neatly timed. Tension never slackens as the discrete parts of the lively tale are kept in smooth working order. It is high praise to say a comic book story has no throwaway panels, but this yarn illustrates that compliment. Every picture tells a story.

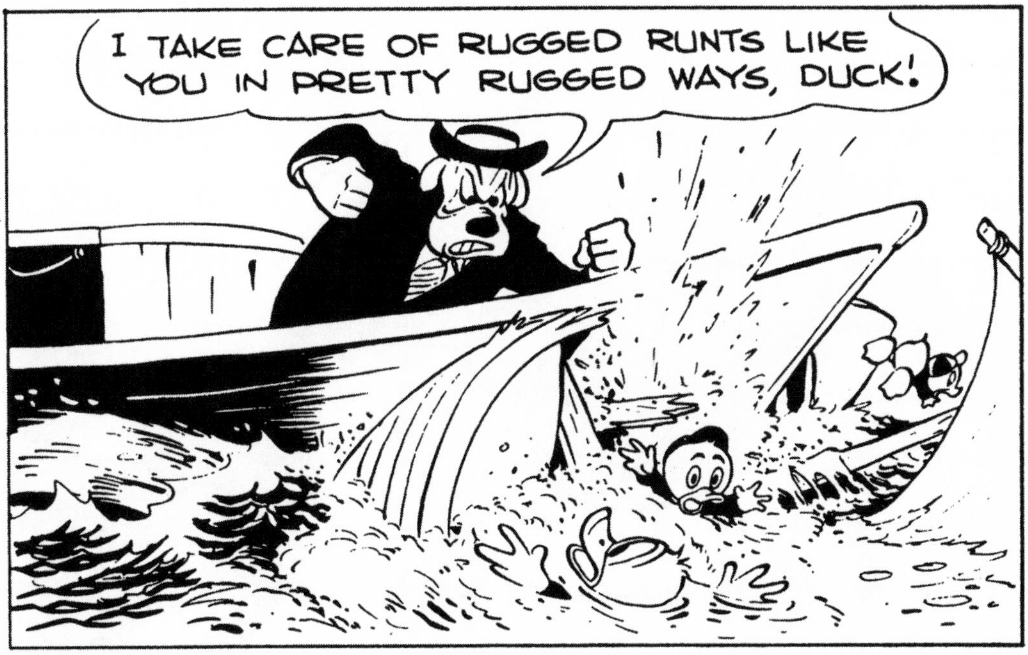
I TAKE CARE OF RUGGED RUNTS LIKE YOU IN PRETTY RUGGED WAYS, DUCK!

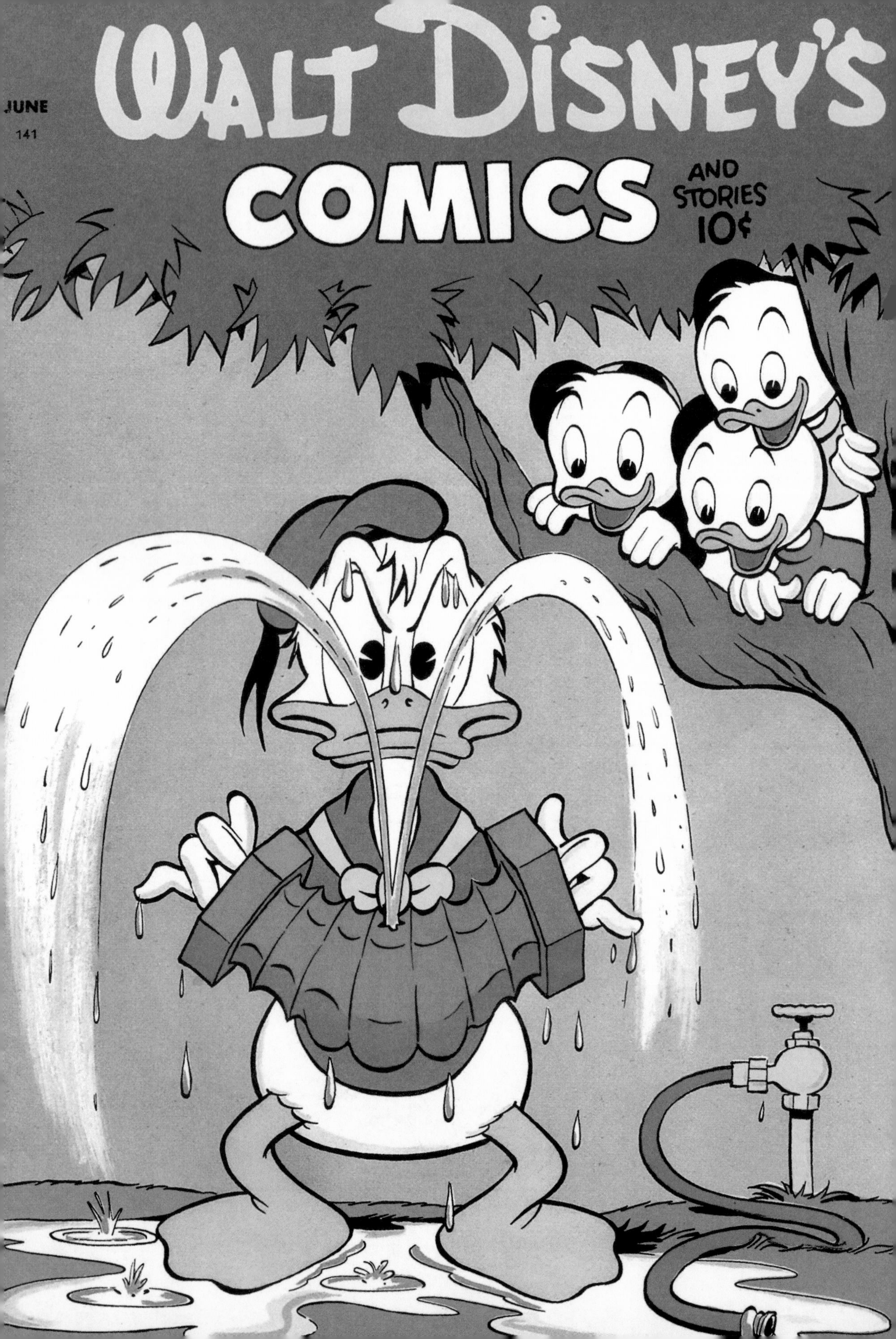

WALT DISNEY'S
JUNE
141
COMICS
AND STORIES
10¢

And what pictures! In the opening splash panel, the ennui-debilitated Donald graphically establishes the spiritual malaise that makes a tonic of the exertions to follow. In the second page's first panel, we look down — as would the sun and stars that Donald evokes — upon the recovered ship, its oar holes now more prominent, demonstrating Barks's regard for accuracy and fidelity: these holes appear only where they should, placed proximately to the planks that were once the seats of rowers.

Elsewhere, on a different emotional plane entirely, the sight of *Azure Blue* ramming the Ducks amidships, splintering their boat and plowing them under, remains a genuinely frightening image.

A second noteworthy feature is Barks's tacit recognition of the commonality, the underlying universals of all humanity, as exemplified by his players. The dream of grandeur that successively overpowers cast members virtually (or venally) defines what it is to be human. All will be tempted. All will stray, or at least precariously flirt. In particular, the exhausted curator's fantasy, that of museum proliferation and mandatory attendance, is heartbreakingly laughable with its crimped horizon and pathetic lack of vision — so much like the foolish longings that agitate everybody other than us.

— Rich Kreiner

HOUSEBOAT HOLIDAY *p. 139*

Comedians call it the "rule of three" or the "comic triple," the feeling that repeating an element three times over the course of a story or joke is sweeter, funnier, and more complete than repetitions based on any other number. That's why the three bears have three objects (bowls of porridge, chairs, beds) for Goldilocks to ruin, why a trio of clergy (a priest, a rabbi, and a minister) always walks into a bar together, and why Carl Barks, stellar artist and comedian, built "Houseboat Holiday" around so many comic triads.

The story follows a three-part structure: Donald makes a bet with his neighbor, suffers mishaps on the boat, then returns and delivers the turkey dinner to the neighbor. In the first three panels of "Houseboat Holiday," the neighbor describes a hypothetical (and soon to be true) scenario of ever-escalating summer vacation mischief, to which Donald repeats the same confident reply three times: "I've been thinking about that."

Not deeply enough, of course, since all goes comically awry.

On the third page of the story, Donald lounges in his hammock — we see him three times in this hammock, in increasingly successive states of agitation — and gloats over his plan to keep his nephews out of trouble. "What a setup! Perfect!" thinks Donald.

And a perfect setup it is — from Barks — for the story he wants to tell.

In the story's extended middle, Huey, Dewey, and Louie drop a fish into the water barrel, pour gasoline into the lake, and pitch the water barrel overboard with an S.O.S. message inside. Those three actions lead to three comic consequences: the ruined drinking water, the fire surrounding the houseboat, and Donald's ride over Niagara Falls. (Note Donald's comic

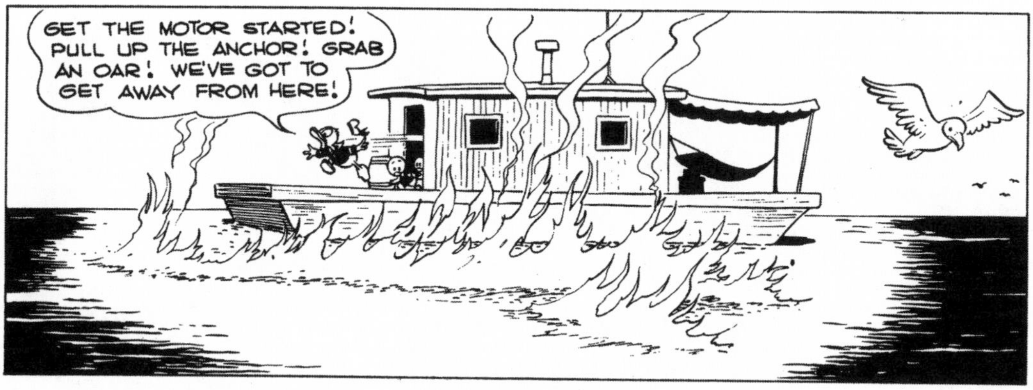
GET THE MOTOR STARTED! PULL UP THE ANCHOR! GRAB AN OAR! WE'VE GOT TO GET AWAY FROM HERE!

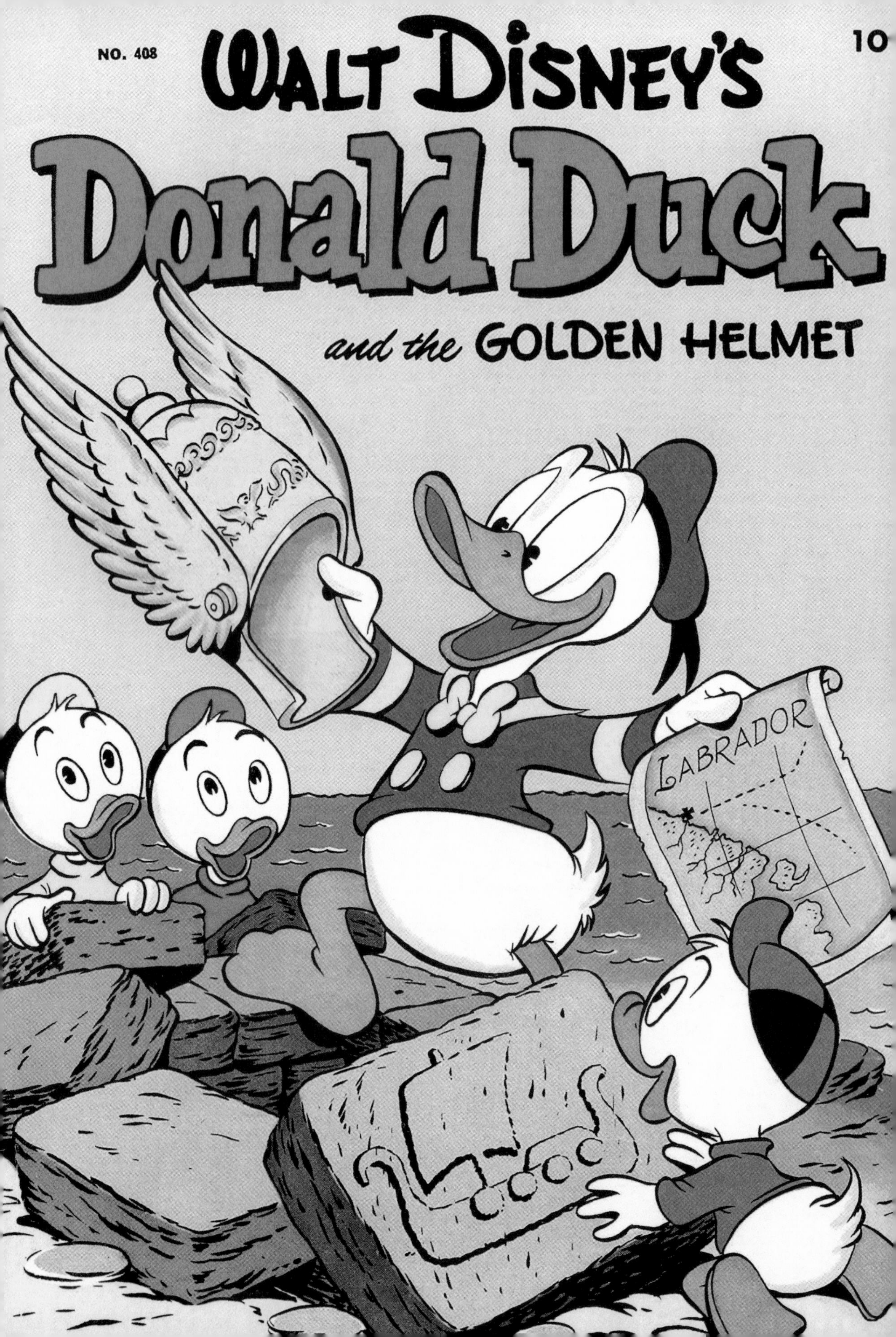
NO. 408
10
WALT DISNEY'S
Donald Duck
and the GOLDEN HELMET
LABRADOR

sing-song triple chant — "There's Buffalo and Lackawanna and Niagara Falls!" — as his barrel inexorably floats down the Niagara River toward the falls.)

"Houseboat Holiday" isn't Barks at his deepest or most inventive, but it's a lovely joke machine, a toy wound up by three turns of the key that delivers big laughs.

— Craig Fischer

GEMSTONE HUNTERS *p. 149*

At the climax of "Gemstone Hunters," "the sky lights up with a brilliant flash" and a gem-laden meteor crashes into the earth on the land of the "great king of luck," Gladstone Gander. It seems miraculous, like something in a fairy tale, but the words in the very first panel, "If this were a fairy story," suggest otherwise.

In a bid to outdo Gladstone on a quest for precious stones, Donald buys 40 acres of apparently gem-strewn land that has been salted with fake jewels. Discovering he's been swindled, Donald immediately tries to pull the same scam on Gladstone. It works, and Gladstone is at last humiliated — until a jewel-laden meteor crashes into Gladstone's land. The primary story ends with the narration, just as at the outset, both affirming and denying its fable-like qualities ("the fairy story would end...").

Visually, Barks depicts the ironic fairy tale atmosphere in the halo of lines of differing lengths above jewels of differing values and around characters' heads, to indicate surprise, anger, or frustration. The second longest expressive lines are around Gladstone as he gloats over still being "monarch of good luck," and the shortest are in Donald's eyes when he learns the "diamond" Gladstone used to buy Donald's land is a relatively worthless zircon.

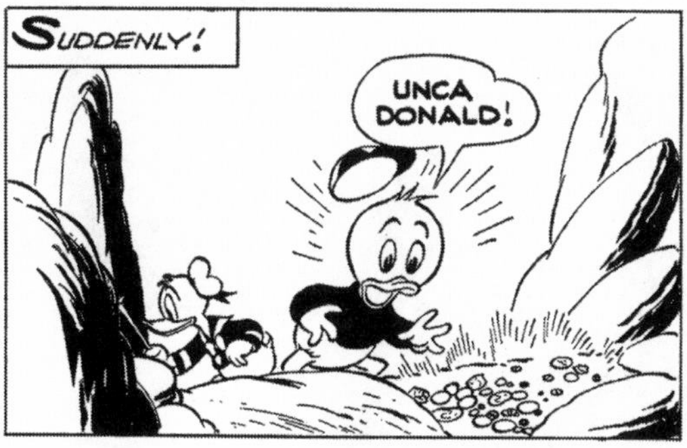
SUDDENLY!
UNCA DONALD!

The minuscule lines in Donald's eyes are juxtaposed in the next panel with the longest halo lines in the story — emanating from the sun — as the Ducks ride off in silhouette, basking in the incandescence of the heavenly body that sustains all life on earth, a reminder of the relative insignificance of earthbound riches.

— Donald Ault

THE GILDED MAN *p. 159*

"The Gilded Man" elegantly brings together several of Barks's key concerns as an artist. It is a nimbly paced, lushly staged yarn, spun over the vagaries of fortune and the question of the moral imperative, leavened by colonialist tension.

The story's exotic draw is a Pre-Columbian city based on the conquistador's legend of El Dorado, populated by superstitious throwbacks from central casting and presided over by the outsize gilded man of the title. But Barks actually, and somewhat unusually, divides the action fairly evenly between home and away. In doing so, he not only contrasts the trimmed hedges of Millionaire Row with the sandy banks of the Essequibo Delta, but illustrates the transplanting of the former to the latter in the form of plush bungalows dotting the savannahs, while old colonial houses decay next to the rising Georgetown smokestacks.

(British) Guyana appealed because of its enduring interest to philatelists. The one-cent magenta is no legend, and it provided Barks with his absurd premise — the hunt for a piece of erstwhile ephemera made priceless by the logic of capitalism. It is the same logic that motivates the story's emblematic antagonists — on the home front, Philo T. Ellic, the kindly but clueless billionaire with the punned-out name; in South America, El Dorado, the angry golden giant. Both are collectors of perceived symbolic capital, whether in the form of magenta stamps or silvered armor, implicated equally (if largely obliviously) in the same materialist order.

As he often does, Gladstone Gander personifies the arbitrariness of this system, idly reaping the benefits of Donald's ever-honest efforts, snatching success from him time and again. The story thus integrates Barks's paramount concern with moral action in an absurd world into an explicitly materialist framework, anticipating the thematic structure of many a great Scrooge tale to come.

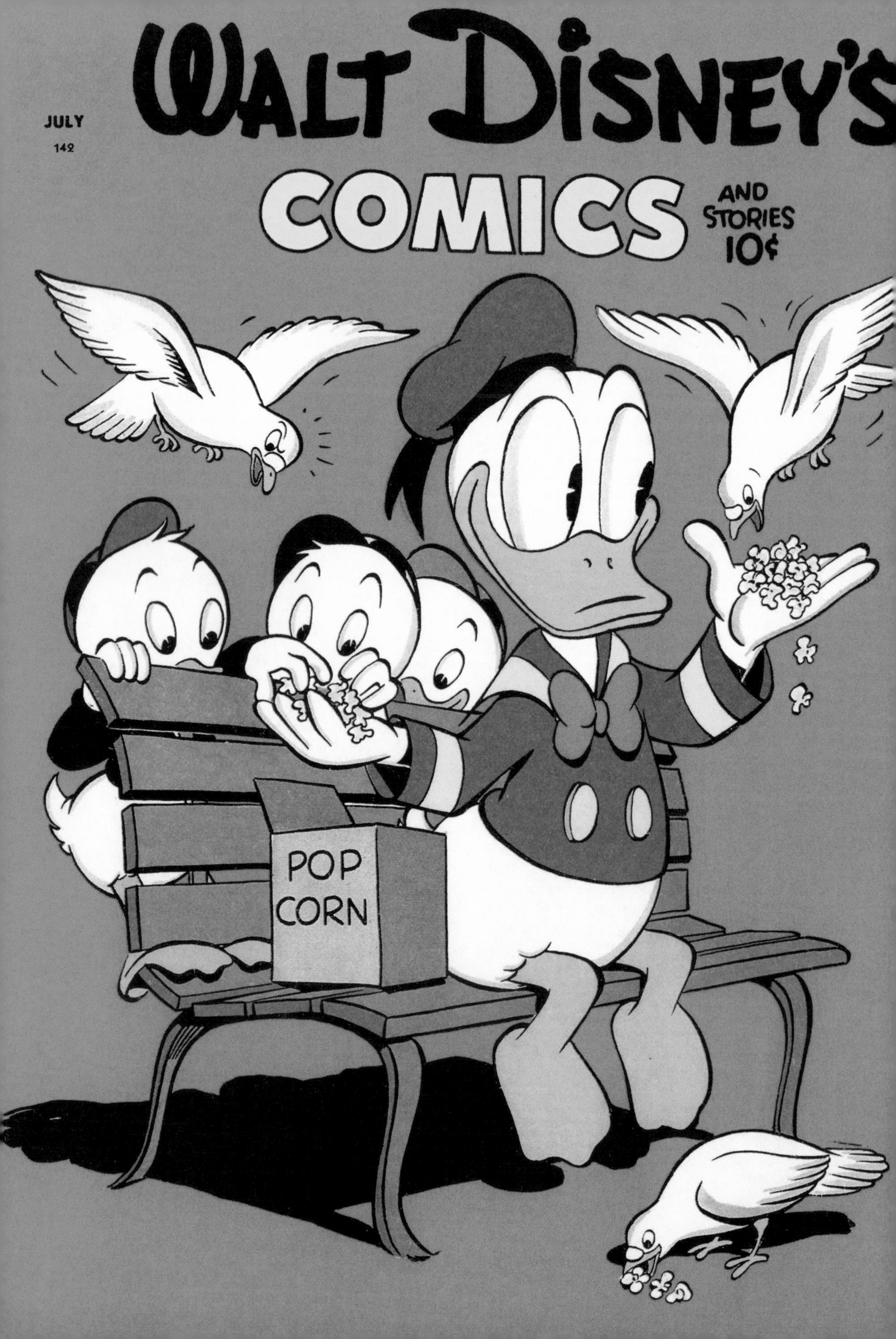
Walt Disney's
JULY
142
COMICS
AND
STORIES
10¢
POP
CORN

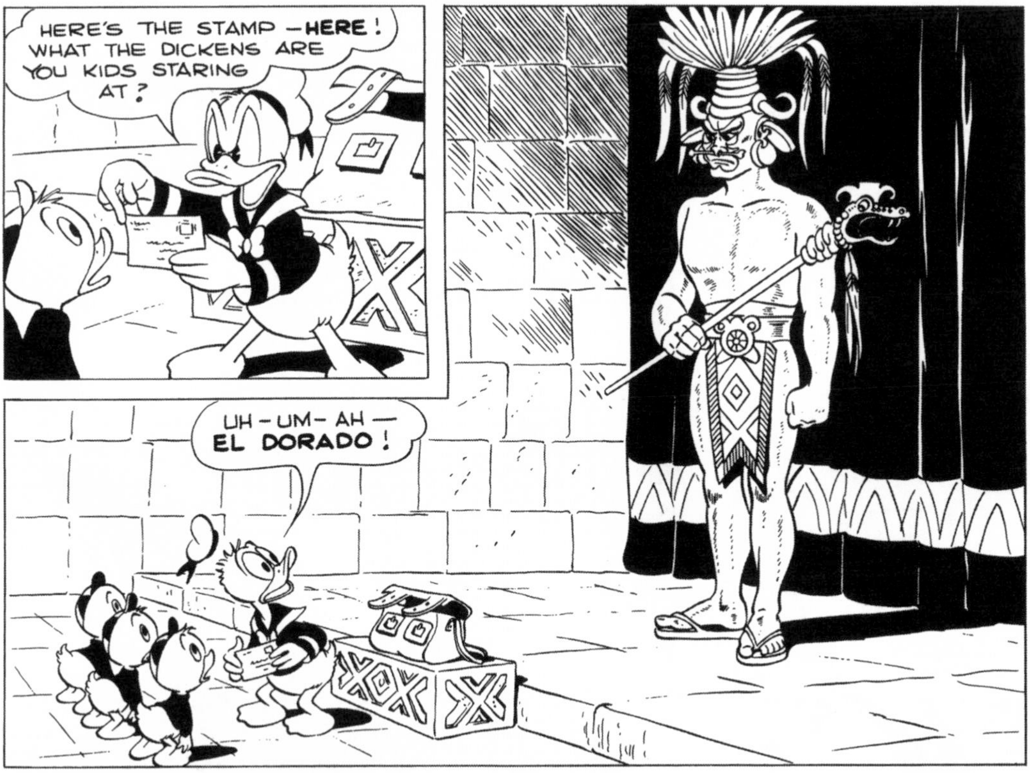
HERE'S THE STAMP — HERE! WHAT THE DICKENS ARE YOU KIDS STARING AT?
UH - UM - AH — EL DORADO!

Characteristically for Barks, Donald achieves the happy end we feel he deserves only via the kind of fortuitous happening that hitherto has worked against him. The one-cent magenta, pursued so assiduously yet lost at every turn, drops suddenly into Donald's possession, prompting a selfless act that luckily nets him the cash prize he had sought from the outset. This is among Barks's most ironic and most hopeful moments.

— Matthias Wivel

SPENDING MONEY *p. 193*

Gladstone's crisis in "Gladstone's Terrible Secret" is the fear that he would be forced to circulate his earnings and thereby lose his power to remain blissfully outside of the market economy. Scrooge's dilemma in "Spending Money" is similar in certain respects — both Gladstone and Scrooge have a constitutional allergy to the circulation of money — but where they diverge makes all the difference in the world.

For Scrooge, there are only two things to do with money: You use it to buy new businesses, thereby guaranteeing still more money to come or, as he demonstrated in "Only a Poor Old Man," (see *Walt Disney's Uncle Scrooge: "Only A Poor Old Man"* in this series), you literally "pool" it — fill a swimming pool with it, each coin in the ocean of money representing a cherished memory of an experience, a triumph, a risk that paid off.

But what happens when you finally own all the businesses and there is literally no more room in the Money Bin? This is the dilemma that confronts Scrooge in "Spending Money." It is time to do what he could never bring himself to do before. It is time to spend money, not on businesses, but on himself — to engage in the consumer culture that has always, for Scrooge, been a most outrageous sucker's bet.

Fortunately, Donald is there to help. For a mere 30 cents an hour, Donald offers to take Scrooge on a whirlwind cross-country tour to dispose of his thirty tons of surplus money. For the first time in his billionaire life, Scrooge is

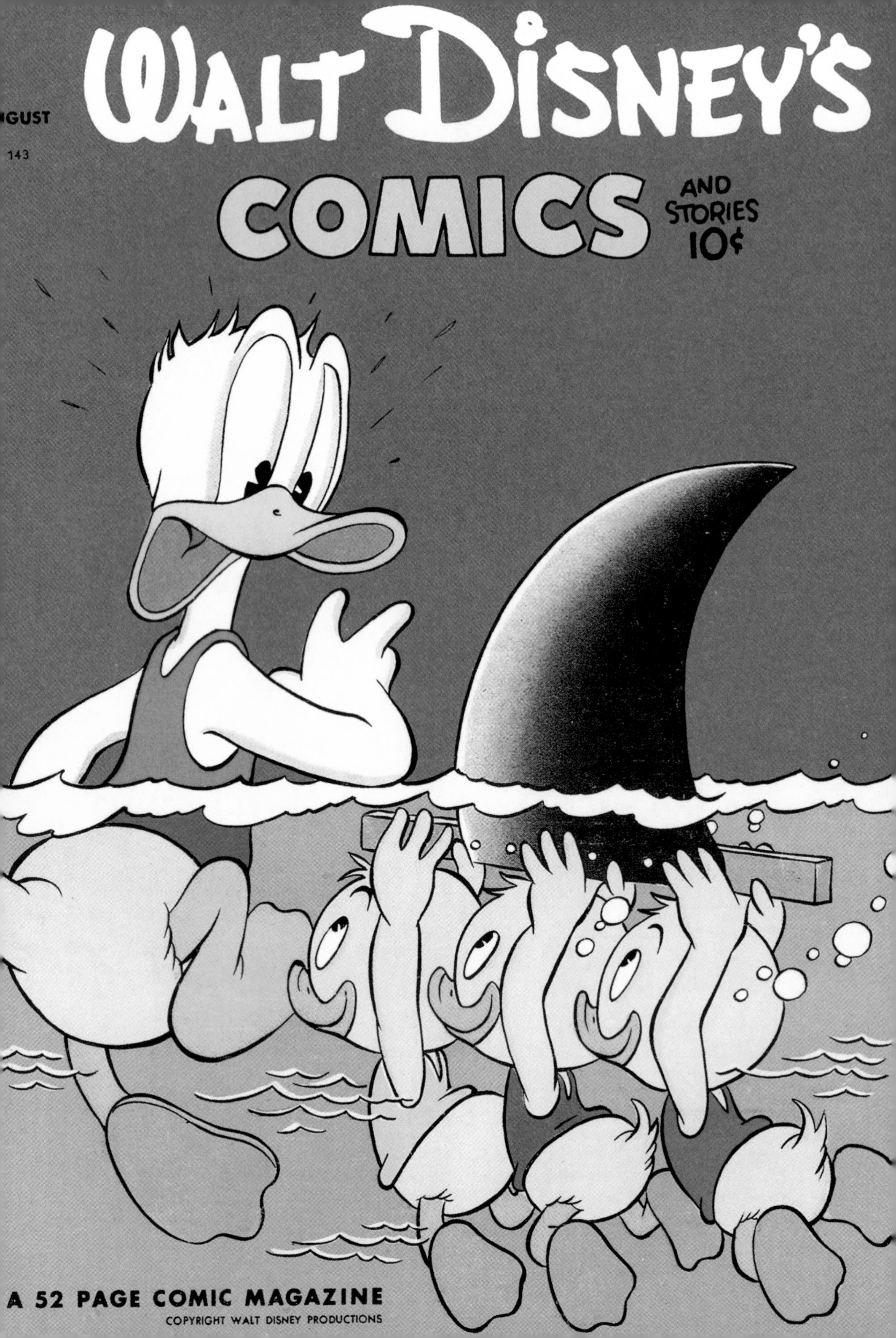

WALT DISNEY'S
GUST
143
COMICS
AND STORIES
10¢
A 52 PAGE COMIC MAGAZINE
COPYRIGHT WALT DISNEY PRODUCTIONS

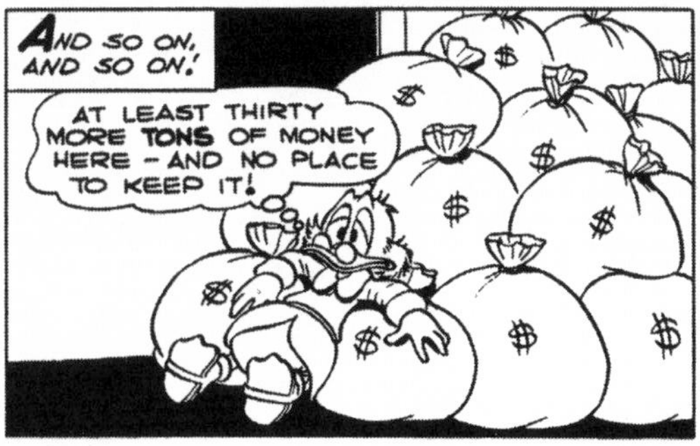
AND SO ON, AND SO ON!
AT LEAST THIRTY MORE TONS OF MONEY HERE – AND NO PLACE TO KEEP IT!

introduced to a world of luxury goods: stretch limousines with ermine seat covers and broiled bosoms of Caledonian chickadees. He discovers the tourist traps in Indian country that his skinflint nature would have instinctively avoided. And — in what is perhaps the only episode in his adventure in which he seems to take any pleasure — he performs charity for one barefoot yokel's seemingly endless roster of shoeless family members.

But a happy ending is not in the cards for our poor rich man. For Scrooge now lives in an economy in which he can never play the role of consumer — all money spent circulates only back to him. Spending money anywhere, on anything, only serves to bring in still more money to Scrooge, who now *is* the economy — all of it. The prospect of drowning in a sea of money for Scrooge is now a very real, very horrible, possibility.

— Jared Gardner

THE DONALD DUCK ONE-PAGERS

This volume's collection of one-page strips offers a unique contrast.

Having proven himself a masterful cartoonist adept at every aspect of his craft, Carl Barks was generally left to his own devices by his publisher. But archivists report that fully six of the nine gags included here originated as scripts from editors passed along to Barks to be reworked and committed to paper.

The single-page joke is a straightforward if rigorous form, a wedded two-step of setup and payoff. Successful examples need to be both economical in generating interest early and generous in repaying attention late.

This group offers several tactics for building the narrative. One involves the diversionary puzzlement of Donald removing his plate glass storefront to achieve his goal in "Full Service Windows" *(p. 103).* A readily believable sequence of boys being boys delays the novel resolution of their inedible decorations in "Treeing Off" *(p. 203).* Its last panel has been enlarged and shaped uniquely to provide ample

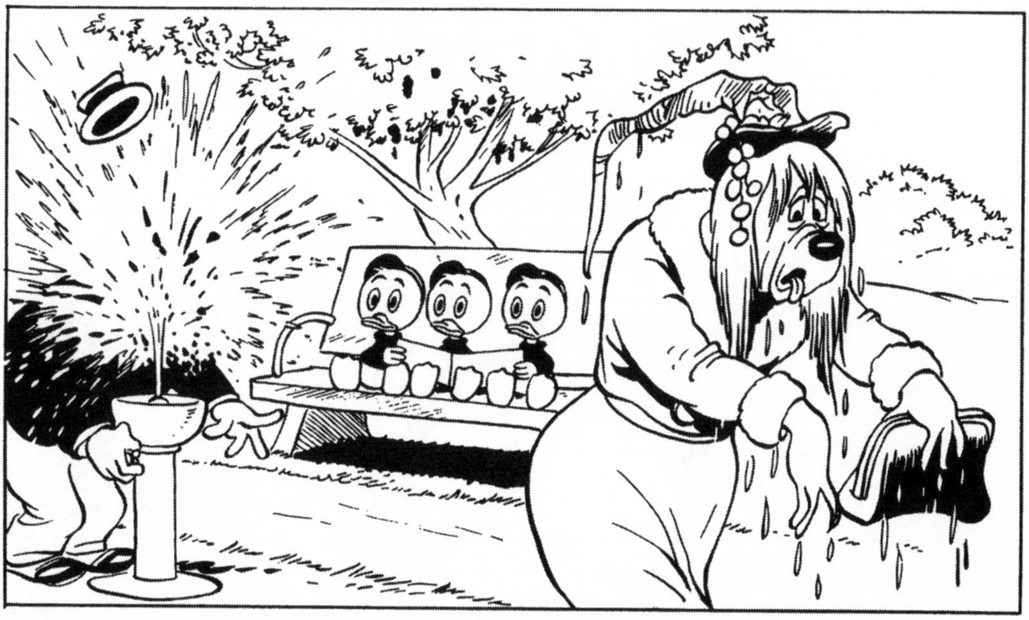

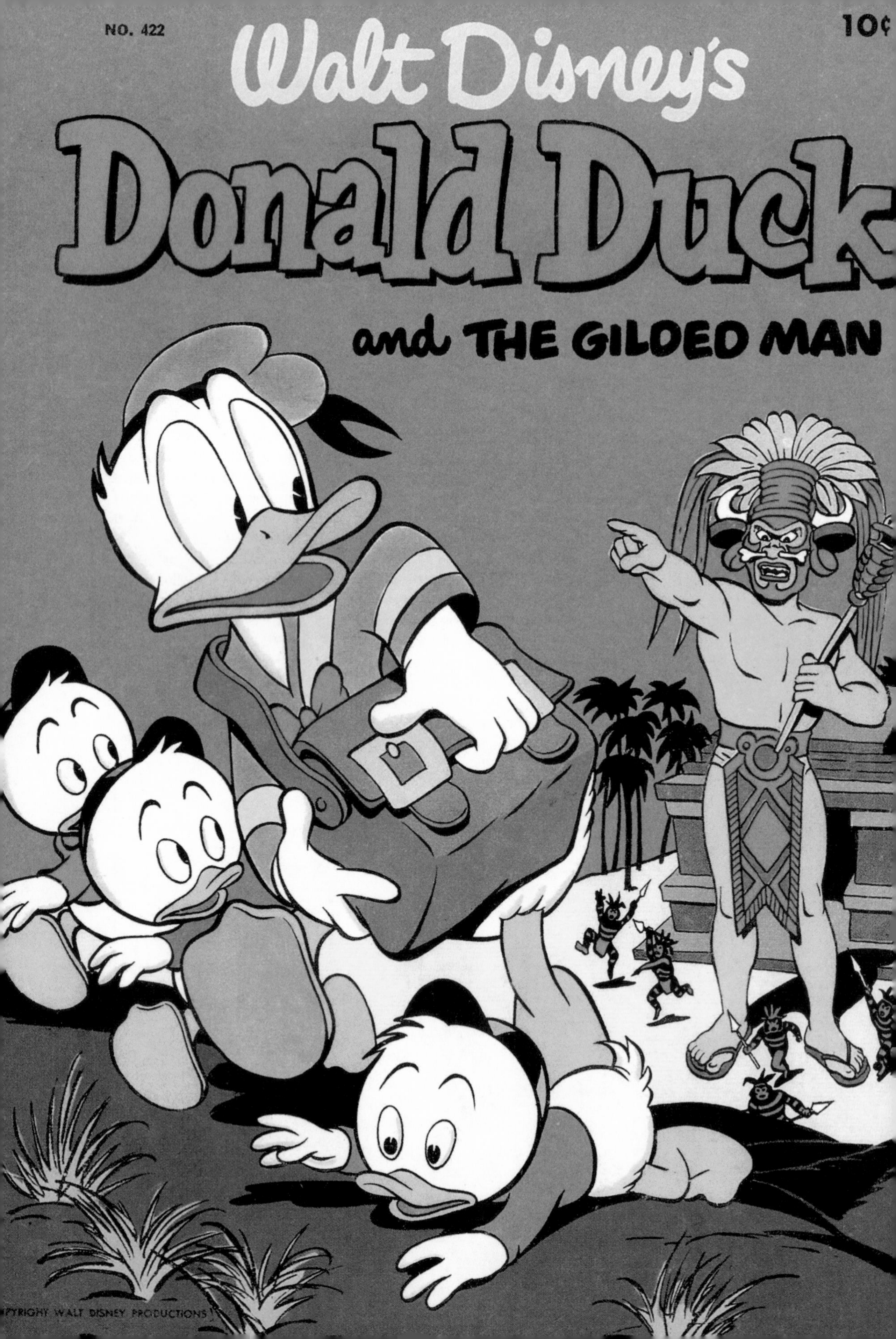
NO. 422
10¢
Walt Disney's
Donald Duck
and THE GILDED MAN
PYRIGHT WALT DISNEY PRODUCTIONS

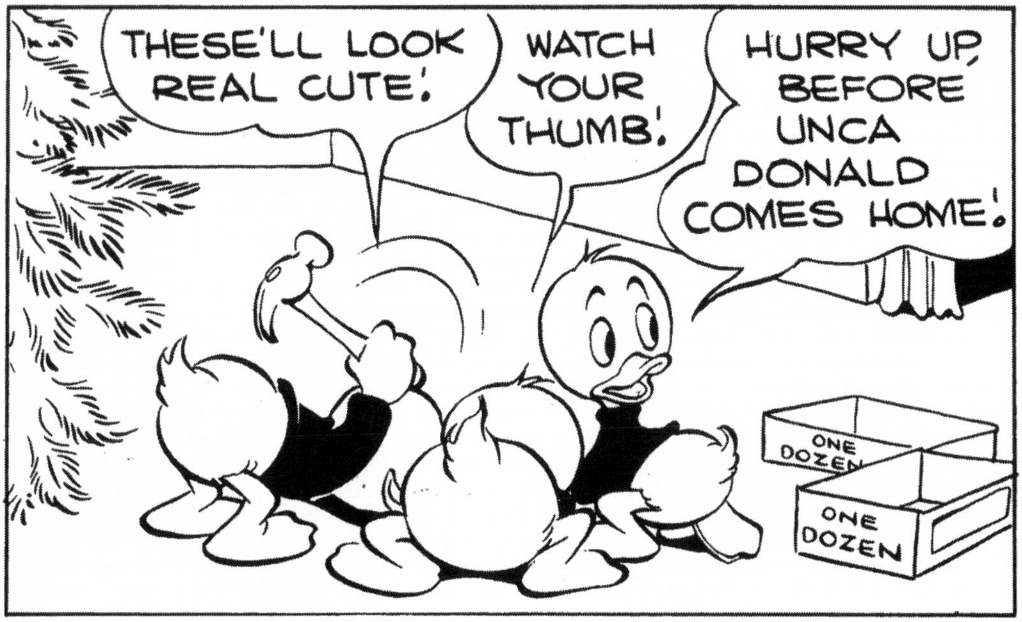
THESE'LL LOOK REAL CUTE!
WATCH YOUR THUMB!
HURRY UP BEFORE UNCA DONALD COMES HOME!
ONE DOZEN
ONE DOZEN

room and maximum impact for the concluding surprise, itself impossible to miss along the left-most margin. Another tack is framing an impossible task, the likes of which Donald presents to his nephews in "Projecting Desires" *(p. 205).*

Obviously there's genuine skill involved in constructing such a final panel, one that really "sells" the joke. In this Barks is especially accomplished. He makes it easy to overlook everything but the laugh. Given the inventive and visually striking remedy to the family plight in "Rigged-Up Roller" *(p. 104),* we don't react to the anatomical torture involved in the ducklings' makeshift solution. Thanks to the graphic arrangement of the nephew's profiteering at the climax of "Awash in Success" *(p. 137),* we don't notice that successive drinkers stubbornly refuse to be forewarned by prior soakees. By the end of "Christmas Kiss" *(p. 204),* we have been primed by Donald's comically puckered and sucker-like lips not to wonder about the plunger's dubious fit over his formidable beak.

Less successful single-page strips betray their bare bones structure. They skimp on either preparation or reward to the point where gags don't resemble anecdotes but one-panel punch lines afforded a bit of lead-in. Barks, in distinction, staged his pages like micro-dramas. The three strips that he originated exclusively — "Stable Prices," "Armored Rescue," and "Crafty Corner" — benefit from a more seamless conjunction of set-up and pay-off. Beginnings do not so much run up to as sensibly usher in their climaxes. Intrigue and comic tension are established at first and resolved at last.

In "Stable Prices" *(p. 138),* patient narrative development is critical (especially for us slow in ciphering) to clearly establish a mathematical progression. In "Armored Rescue" *(p. 191),* a measured, coherent sequence makes odd behavior palatable: note how Donald is introduced in skivvies and ends fully clad and in action. Why, when the scene opens in "Crafty Corner" *(p. 192),* has Donald knowingly painted himself into a predicament? We await the unforeseeable yet cartoon-plausible explanation. Each brief story is a practical demonstration of the difference between selling a joke and providing the opportunity to wholeheartedly buy in.

— Rich Kreiner

Carl Barks

LIFE AMONG THE DUCKS

by DONALD AULT

ABOVE: *Carl Barks at the 1982 San Diego Comic-Con. Photo by Alan Light.*

"I was a real misfit," Carl Barks said, thinking back over an early life of hard labor — as a farmer, a logger, a mule-skinner, a rivet heater, and a printing press feeder — before he was hired as a full-time cartoonist for an obscure risqué magazine in 1931.

Barks was born in 1901 and (mostly) raised in Merrill, Oregon. He had always wanted to be a cartoonist but everything that happened to him in his early years seemed to stand in his way. He suffered a significant hearing loss after a bout with the measles. His mother died. He had to leave school after the eighth grade. His

father suffered a mental breakdown. His older brother was whisked off to World War I.

His first marriage, in 1921, was to a woman who was unsympathetic to his dreams and who ultimately bore two children "by accident," as Barks phrased it. The two divorced in 1930.

In 1931, he pulled up stakes from Merrill and headed to Minnesota, leaving his mother-in-law, whom he trusted more than his wife, in charge of his children.

Arriving in Minneapolis, he went to work for the *Calgary Eye-Opener*, that risqué magazine. He thought he would finally be drawing cartoons full time but the editor and most of the staff were alcoholics, so Barks ended up running the whole show.

In 1935 he took "a great gamble" and, on the strength of some cartoons he'd submitted in response to an advertisement from the Disney Studio, he moved to California and entered an animation trial period. He was soon promoted to "story man" in Disney's Donald Duck animation unit, where he made significant contributions to 36 Donald cartoon shorts between 1936 and 1942, including helping to create Huey, Dewey, and Louie for "Donald's Nephews" in 1938. Ultimately, though, he grew dissatisfied. The production of animated cartoons "by committee," as he described it, stifled his imagination.

For that and other reasons, in 1942 he left Disney to run a chicken farm. But when he was offered a chance by Western Publishing to write and illustrate a new series of Donald Duck comic book stories, he jumped at it. The comic book format suited him and the quality of his work persuaded the editors to grant him a freedom and autonomy he'd never known and that few others were ever granted. He would go on to write and draw more than 6,000 pages in over 500 stories and uncounted hundreds of covers between 1942 and 1966 for Western's Dell and Gold Key imprints.

Barks had almost no formal art training. He had taught himself how to draw by imitating his early favorite artists — Winsor McCay (*Little Nemo*), Frederick Opper (*Happy Hooligan*), Elzie Segar (*Popeye*), and Floyd Gottfredson (*Mickey Mouse*).

He taught himself how to write well by going back to the grammar books he had shunned in school, making up jingles and rhymes, and inventing other linguistic exercises to get a natural feel for the rhythm and dialogue of sequential narrative.

Barks married again in 1938 but that union ended disastrously in divorce in 1951. In 1954, Barks married Margaret Wynnfred Williams, known as Garé, who soon began assisting him by lettering and inking backgrounds on his comic book work. They remained happily together until her death in 1993.

He did his work in the California desert and often mailed his stories into the office. He worked his stories over and over "backward and forward." Barks was not a vain man but he had confidence in his talent. He knew what

hard work was, and he knew that he'd put his best efforts into every story he produced.

On those occasions when he did go into Western's offices he would "just dare anybody to see if they could improve on it." His confidence was justified. His work was largely responsible for some of the best-selling comic books in the world — *Walt Disney's Comics And Stories* and *Uncle Scrooge*.

Because Western's policy was to keep their writers and artists anonymous, readers never knew the name of the "good duck artist" — but they could spot the superiority of his work. When fans determined to solve the mystery of his anonymity finally tracked him down (not unlike an adventure Huey, Dewey, and Louie might embark upon), Barks was quite happy to correspond and otherwise communicate with his legion of aficionados.

Given all the obstacles of his early years and the dark days that haunted him off and on for the rest of his life, it's remarkable that he laughed so easily and loved to make others laugh.

In the process of expanding Donald Duck's character far beyond the hot-tempered Donald of animation, Barks created a moveable locale (Duckburg) and a cast of dynamic characters: Scrooge McDuck, the Beagle Boys, Gladstone Gander, Gyro Gearloose, the Junior Woodchucks. And there were hundreds of others who made only one memorable appearance in the engaging, imaginative, and unpredictable comedy-adventures that he wrote and drew from scratch for nearly a quarter of a century.

Among many other honors, Carl Barks was one of the three initial inductees into the Will Eisner Comic Awards Hall of Fame for comic book creators in 1987. (The other two were Jack Kirby and Will Eisner.) In 1991, Barks became the only Disney comic book artist to be recognized as a "Disney Legend," a special award created by Disney "to acknowledge and honor the many individuals whose imagination, talents, and dreams have created the Disney magic."

As Roy Disney said on Barks's passing in 2000 at age 99, "He challenged our imaginations and took us on some of the greatest adventures we have ever known. His prolific comic book creations entertained many generations of devoted fans and influenced countless artists over the years.... His timeless tales will stand as a legacy to his originality and brilliant artistic vision."

Biographies

Donald Ault is Professor of English at the University of Florida; founder and editor of *ImageTexT: Interdisciplinary Comics Studies*; author of two books on William Blake (*Visionary Physics* and *Narrative Unbound*); editor of *Carl Barks: Conversations*; and executive producer of *The Duck Man: An Interview with Carl Barks* (video).

R. Fiore, he explains, makes his way in life working Square John jobs, when they let him, not far from Historic Duckburg. This marginal existence has even from time to time led onto the grounds of the Walt Disney Company, which is an interesting place. In his spare time he's been writing about comic strips and animation longer than you've been alive, my child.

Craig Fischer is Associate Professor of English at Appalachian State University. His 'Monsters Eat Critics' column, about comics' multifarious genres, runs at *The Comics Journal* website (tcj.com).

Jared Gardner studies and teaches comics at the Ohio State University, home of the Billy Ireland Cartoon Library & Museum. He is the author of three books, including *Projections: Comics and the History of 21st-Century Storytelling* (Stanford University Press, 2011). He is a contributing writer to *The Comics Journal*.

Rich Kreiner is a longtime writer for *The Comics Journal* and a longertime reader of Carl Barks. He lives with wife and cat in Maine.

Ken Parille is the author of *The Daniel Clowes Reader* (Fantagraphics, 2012) and has published essays on Louisa May Alcott and boyhood, the mother-son relationship in antebellum America, TV bandleader Lawrence Welk, and, of course, comics. His writing has appeared in *The Nathaniel Hawthorne Review, The Journal of Popular Culture, The Boston Review, The Believer,* and *The Comics Journal*. He teaches literature at East Carolina University.

Stefano Priarone was born in Northwestern Italy about the time when a retired Carl Barks was storyboarding his last Junior Woodchucks stories. He writes about popular culture in many Italian newspapers and magazines, was a contributor to the Italian complete Carl Barks collection, and wrote his thesis in economics about Uncle Scrooge as an entrepreneur (for which he blames his aunt, who read him Barks Scrooge stories when he was 3 years old).

Matthias Wivel is an art historian specializing in Italian Renaissance art. He has been active as a comics critic, editor, and activist for a decade-and-a-half.

Where did these duck stories first appear?

EDITOR'S NOTE: "The Complete Carl Barks Disney Library" collects Donald Duck and Uncle Scrooge stories originally published in the traditional American four-color comic book format. Barks's first Duck story appeared in October 1942. The volumes in this project are numbered chronologically but are being released in a different order. This is volume 11.

Stories within a volume may or may not follow the exact original publication sequence of the original comic books. We may take the liberty of re-arranging the sequence of the stories within a volume for editorial or presentation purposes.

The original comic books were published under the "Dell" logo and some appeared in the so-called "Four Color" series — a name that appeared nowhere inside the comic book itself, but is generally agreed upon by historians to refer to the series of "one-shot" comic books published by Dell that have sequential numbering. The *Four Color* issues are also sometimes referred to as "One Shots."

Most of the stories in this volume were originally published without a title. Some stories were retroactively assigned a title when they were reprinted in later years. Some stories were given titles by Barks in correspondence or interviews. (Sometimes Barks referred to the same story with different titles.) Some stories were never given an official title but have been informally assigned one by fans and indexers. For the untitled stories in this volume, we have used the title that seems most appropriate. The unofficial titles appear below with an asterisk enclosed in parentheses (*).

The following is the order in which the stories in this volume were originally published.

Walt Disney's Comics and Stories #135
(December 1951)
Cover
The Big Bin On Killmotor Hill (*)

Four Color #367 (January 1952)
Cover
Treeing Off (*)
A Christmas For Shacktown
Christmas Kiss (*)
Projecting Desires (*) [aka Stamp-Sized Christmas List (*)]

Walt Disney's Comics and Stories #136
(January 1952)
Cover
Gladstone's Usual Good Year (*)

Walt Disney's Comics and Stories #137
(February 1952)
Cover
The Screaming Cowboy (*)

Walt Disney's Comics and Stories #138
(March 1952)
Cover
Statuesque Spendthrifts (*)

Walt Disney's Comics and Stories #139
(April 1952)
Cover
Rocket Wing Saves The Day (*)

Walt Disney's Comics and Stories #140
(May 1952)
Cover
Gladstone's Terrible Secret (*)

Walt Disney's Comics and Stories #141
(June 1952)
Cover
The Think Box Bollix (*)

Four Color #408 (July-August 1952)
Cover
Full-Service Windows (*)
The Golden Helmet
Rigged-Up Roller (*) [aka Rigged-Up Lawn Roller]
Awash In Success (*)

Walt Disney's Comics and Stories #142
(July 1952)
Cover
Houseboat Holiday (*)

Walt Disney's Comics and Stories #143
(August 1952)
Cover
Gemstone Hunters (*)

Four Color #422 (September-October 1952)
Cover
Stable Prices (*)
The Gilded Man
Armored Rescue (*) [aka Armored Cat Rescue]
Crafty Corner (*)

Walt Disney's Comics and Stories #144
(September 1952)
Cover
Spending Money (*)